To Reid Lineberger —

A fine soldier and officer who served his country well during the European Theater campaigns in World War II. No officer was admired more within the confines of the 126th Ordnance as this book will so indicate. Trusted judgement, patience and courage is a tribute to his good leadership.

A fine American whom it is my pleasure to call my life-long friend.

Warmest personal regards,
Mendith L. Butterton
March 3 - 1973

METRIC 16

MEREDITH L. BUTTERTON

Moore Publishing Company
Durham, North Carolina

Copyright 1972 by Moore Publishing Company, Durham, North Carolina. All rights reserved. Printed in the United States of America.
Library of Congress Catalog Card Number: 72-90711
ISBN 0-87716-038-4

Dedicated to Jenny and Larry and David, who because of countless hours of research and writing were deprived of that many hours of companionship.

The author reminisces with General Omar Bradley.

FOREWORD

I have always considered the work of our Ordnance troops as one of the greatest contributions to the success of any operation. I never issued any attack order in combat until I had carefully checked the number of rounds of ammunition per gun that were available to the units committed. In addition, the maintenance of all of our equipment was in the hands of our Ordnance troops. Any unit which lacks the facilities for maintaining its equipment has limited combat value. In the early days of organization the maintenance of equipment . . . particularly of motor vehicles . . . was one of our greatest problems.

In general, it can be properly stated that no combat unit could be wholly efficient unless it was supported by a well-trained Ordnance unit.

Omar N Bradley

Omar N. Bradley
General Of The Army

COMMENDATION

During the drive across Europe the Americans demonstrated a swiftness of movement that amazed not only the Germans but our European Allies. Aside from the fighting qualities of our men, our rapid drive would not have been possible without the expert use of armored vehicles and motor transportation. The latter was dependent on the Ordnance troops that served the Corps and its divisions.

The ordnance motor maintenance companies, including your 126th Ordnance (Medium Maintenance) Company, attached to the 9th Infantry Division, did a splendid job and made a major contribution to the success of the VII Corps which led the First Army from Normandy to the Elbe.

J Lawton Collins

J. Lawton Collins
General, U. S. Army (Ret.)

★★★★

CONTENTS

I	A Sound Beginning	3
II	Tennessee Maneuvers	16
III	Final Preparations	33
IV	Crossing In Style	48
V	England – Courage Personified	57
VI	Invasion!	81
VII	Battle For Normandy	102
VIII	Driving For St. Lo	139
IX	Chase Across France	163
X	Belgium – Land Of Enchantment	229
XI	Germany – The Third Reich	247
XII	For Better or Worse	278
XIII	Surprise In The Ardennes	302
XIV	Destruction In The Rhineland	332
XV	Collapse In The East	372
XVI	The Road Back	423
XVII	l'affair de St. Quentin	437
XVIII	The Last Convoy	448

". . . The function of Ordnance in World War II was to help provide firepower and mobility. Both are essential elements of combat efficiency. The tactical commander relies on firepower for strength; and for the ability to apply his strength at the most effective time and place, he relies on mobility. In the European campaign, Ordnance kept the guns firing and the vehicles moving. Close support of the combat forces in fast-moving situations was made possible by a flexible Ordnance field organization evolved early in the war. Throughout the campaign unpredictable problems were posed by enemy reaction, difficult terrain, and inherent shortages in certain types of material. These problems were solved time and again by Ordnance ingenuity and devotion to duty."

> General William C. Westmoreland
> Chief of Staff
> United States Army

". . . The Ordnance effort in World War II was tremendous, responsible, efficient, and effective. The efficiency and responsibility of Ordnance troops, especially those units that were detailed with the various armies, corps and divisions were of the highest order. They maintained the Ordnance equipment in the battle with hard work, long hours, and great imagination. They kept supplies, particularly parts and ammunition, flowing to the front. They made good use of materials captured from the enemy with dispatch and intelligence.

The Ordnance personnel from the top to the bottom showed extraordinary capability, and made themselves an integral part of the great team, cooperating to the fullest extent at all levels."

> General Jacob L. Devers (Ret.)
> Commanding, Sixth Army Group
> European Theater of Operations
> 1944-45

". . . Mr. Butterton's tribute to the Ordnance company of the Ninth Infantry Division would be echoed by every division commander speaking for his Ordnance unit. Fire and movement are the prime means of victory in combat and the division ordnance company maintains the weapons and transport essential to both."

> General Maxwell D. Taylor (Ret.)
> Commanding, 101ST AIRBORNE DIVISION
> European Theater of Operations
> 1944-45

". . . The FIRST U. S. ARMY'S long and meritorious record from the beaches of Normandy through the Battle of The Bulge to the surrender by the German Army, leaves no doubt as to the quality of its' leadership or the outstanding ability of the fighting personnel down through the ranks. However; too often in writing or studying military campaigns, one is prone to forget the support units without which the combat troops could not have carried out their missions.

The FIRST ARMY was blessed with magnificent service troops and it is most difficult for me to commend one service more than the others. I must state though, that our Ordnance troops performed superbly and without such support we never could have achieved our mission of defeating the German Army."

Lt. Gen. William B. Kean (Ret.)
Chief of Staff, FIRST U. S. ARMY
European Theater of Operations
Nov. 1943 – Oct. 1947

". . . In the European Theater during World War II no attack plan could have been successful and no victory achieved without the backup support of Ordnance."

Lt. Gen. Troy H. Middleton (Ret.)
Commanding, VIII CORPS
European Theater of Operations
1944-45

". . . An army cannot operate in combat without good Ordnance troops and the commander who neglects them does so at the risk of being defeated on the battlefield.

I was very proud of the Ordnance men of the 9TH DIVISION and V Corps and did not hesitate to give them combat missions when needed. They always performed like the good soldiers they were. They could shoot straight as many of the enemy, much to their sorrow found out."

Lt. Gen. Clarence R. Huebner (Ret.)
Commanding, V CORPS
European Theater of Operations
February – July, 1945

". . . The performance of Ordnance troops within the NINTH ARMY during the ETO campaigns was outstanding and unquestionably the same can be said of the Ordnance troops of FIRST ARMY during the same period.

Our Ordnance troops certainly played an important part in crushing the enemy in the field by effectively supplying and maintaining the vast quantities of weapons, ammunition and other ordnance material used by the combat troops.

I cannot speak too highly of the efficiency, flexibility, ingenuity and dedicated overall performance of all Ordnance troops during the entire existence of the campaign. They certainly played an important part in smashing the enemy forces in the field."

> General William H. Simpson (Ret.)
> Commanding, NINTH U. S. ARMY
> European Theater of Operations
> 1944-45

". . . During the Ardennes Campaign the dedication to duty and support of the combat troops displayed by the Ordnance personnel of FIRST ARMY drew their warm praise and contributed tremendously to their success."

> General Matthew B. Ridgway (Ret.)
> Commanding, XVIII AIRBORNE CORPS
> European Theater of Operations
> 1944-45

". . . There is no doubt that the 9th Infantry Division as well as all other combat machinery could not have kept the dynamic pace set during 1944-45 in pursuit of the German armies without vital Ordnance support. As a backup unit to our own Division Ordnance the Ninth is grateful for the fine work your own 126th Ordnance Medium Maintenance Company performed in helping achieve victory."

> Maj. Gen. Louis A. Craig (Ret.)
> Commanding 9TH INFANTRY DIVISION
> European Theater of Operations
> August 1944 — May, 1945

". . . The achievements of the 9th Division would not have been possible without Ordnance support of the highest caliber. The 126th has reason to be proud of its record. Without such support the whole free world could have been left in chaos and defeat."

> Maj. Gen. John B. Medaris (Ret.)
> Ordnance Officer, FIRST U. S. ARMY
> European Theater of Operations
> 1944-45

". . . It generally is recognized by everyone who was involved with the 9th Infantry Division during the European operations in World War II, that Ordnance support was complete and adequate. This includes support for between thirty and forty thousand combat troops when you consider the Division with its attached troops.

It follows that this tremendously successful combat support job was due largely to the 126th Ordnance Company, which joined the Division in Winchester, England in April, 1944, several months before the invasion of Europe, and remained with it until May, 1945."

> Lt. Col. William H. Waikart (Ret.)
> Division Ordnance Officer
> 9th Infantry Division
> European Theater of Operations
> May, 1945 — February, 1946

". . . There is no question in my mind but that the Ordnance, as a whole and all the individuals and units thereof, more than contributed their share, both in supply, repairs, etc., toward the ultimate defeat of the German army and the unparalleled success of the allied armies."

> Col. Arthur H. Luse (Ret.)
> VII CORPS Ordnance Officer
> European Theater of Operations
> 1944-45

". . . From early July, 1944 through May of 1945 it was my assigned duty to command the 184th Ordnance Battalion and at its peak strength this Battalion consisted of 1,289 men. Typical of this courageous group of American combat support troops was the 126th Ordnance Medium Maintenance Company. From April, 1944 until May, 1945 this technically competent unit provided skilled third echelon maintenance support of the 9th Infantry Division. Each and every member of the 126th is to be commended for their part in making an outstanding performance of Ordnance service and we are proud to have had the 126th Ordnance as one of the companies in the 184th Ordnance Battalion."

                        Robert A. Hudson, Lt. Col.
                        Commanding, 184th Ordnance Battalion
                        European Theater of Operations
                        July, 1944 — May, 1945

PREFACE

An offensive can progress no faster than its rifleman, and by the same token the rifleman can advance no farther than his weapon will allow. If that rifle is not in top working order; if it fails him . . . then ineffectiveness will follow and his progress will be for naught. That his equipment is in top condition becomes first the responsibility of the Army Ordnance Department. The fighting man will be the first to admit that without these preparatory and backup forces there would be little effective fighting.

To the troops in this highly adaptive department falls the task of research, provision, testing, proving and keeping in operation "everything that rolls, shoots, is shot, or is dropped from the air." In the European Theater of Operations during World War II the inventiveness and ingenuity of Ordnance figured prominently in the pattern of combat successes which was repeated thousands of times all the way from Normandy to the Red Army juncture on the Elbe River. At the cessation of hostilities in May of 1945 over 150,000 Ordnance troops were active in this Theater and far in excess of one half of them were, or had been in the combat zone.

During this same period this Department was faced with responsibility of 1,200 major items and its complete catalogue contained over 350,000 separate items, ranging from watch springs and firing pins to 20-ton howitzers and 45-ton tanks. Moreover, Ordnance spare parts and supplies, the life-blood of maintenance, reached a total of 500,000 tons in the European Theater by the end of April, 1945. In a single month . . . February, 1945, Ordnance men of the **FIRST UNITED STATES ARMY** repaired and returned to service more than 9,000 general purpose vehicles, 2,500 combat vehicles, 20,000 small arms, 1,800 artillery pieces and 4,000 Ordnance instruments.

Thus did the American Army in Europe enjoy a combination of

fire power, mobility and armored might never before seen in warfare.

More than half a million vehicles were on hand to transport men and supplies; 80,000 tanks, tank destroyers, armored cars and half-tracks were available to provide the spearhead power for five United States armies; 3,750,000 hand-weilded small arms and automatic weapons; 50,000 pieces of artillery; and millions of rounds of ammunition.

Did Ordnance have a responsibility?

"Metric 16" is the story of a small energetic forward mobile Ordnance company assigned the specific task of performing maintenance in a medium capacity.

Activated the last day of January, 1943 . . . its life span lasted three years, and while engrossing some 12,000 miles beginning in North Carolina, embracing the breadth of England and shuttling over much of the European continent and back to New York, its experiences are recorded in depth to give a candid insight of the daily routine employed by most Ordnance troops in the field. Come and join the rolling convoys and share in its interesting travels . . . all the while noting its accomplishments and many disappointments against the backdrop of the war's progress. Note too, the valued and interesting comments of many top military leaders interviewed by the author, recalling their decisions and evaluations as they look back on this massive and historical European conflict.

Come and have an intimate part of the varied expressions of personalities and feel the anxieties that throbbed within this restless unit as it moved with a great Army and walked a sort of "tight rope" behind, alongside . . . and at times, together with a fine combat Division.

Meredith R. Rutherford

METRIC 16

I

A SOUND BEGINNING

The busy bristling induction center at Fort Custer, Michigan was only a few hours behind and the heavily-laden troop train now moved along at regulated speeds, well on its way southeast. It was 1943 and that it was well into the month of February, notably the 19th., appeared inconsequential for it had already become obvious by mid-day that this had blossomed into one of the hottest and most surly days any midwinter month could ever produce.

On the other hand, possibly the extreme warmth of the day and unregulated heat of the Chesapeake & Ohio Railway's several fully packed coaches and pullman cars would have made little difference had it not been for the heavy woolen clothing or the uncomfortable scratchy underwear that showed those with tender perspiring skins no mercy, or the ill-fitting shoes to which no one was accustomed and definitely the shifting of the overstuffed duffle bag issued previously to each man at Fort Custer. There would be frequent stops, innumerable inspections and untold anxieties but by early afternoon the next day it would roll deep into North

Carolina and there discharge its passengers in a military camp not yet two years old and which no one aboard except perhaps the train crew had ever heard of.

Perhaps under ordinary circumstances this trip could very well have developed into one of more pleasant anticipations, but this was the beginning of an absolute new experience to each of these men who only a short time before were civilians ready to embark into whatever the business, professional or industrial world held in store. Within the span of a few days, and though inevitable; all former aspirations and plans had been sidetracked as they found themselves complete raw recruits bound by an oath taken when first entering the United States Army. This, then . . . would represent the first journey toward a new life to which each would be subjected for the war's duration . . . a war that America had feebly attempted to avoid but was forced to enter some fourteen months previous.

From all sections of Detroit, particularly the Polish neighborhoods of Hamtramck many had been plucked, while others came from the further central and northern cities of Saginaw, Flint, Port Huron and a few scattered cities in mid-Michigan. The preponderance of ages ranged from nineteen to twenty-four years. A few were twenty-five or so and even less were in their early thirties. To many; particularly those older, the prospect of this new life was viewed with much reluctance and a strong tinge of pessimism for it meant unlimited separation from established families and loved ones. To most of the younger; especially those not yet having planned their life it would present a tremendous challenge, producing perhaps unusual experiences that ordinarily would not be found in the normal pattern of life, and whether for better or worse it would surely ring with an ever-changing graph of excitement. Present feelings notwithstanding and the immediate future somewhat nebulous the fact remained that each man, the same as many thousands; like it or not, were sworn soldiers in the Army of the United States . . . dedicated solely to erasing the prevailing tyranny and restoring an atmosphere of peace throughout the world.

On over the broad plains and well-cultivated farms of Ohio the train rolled, across the patchwork of Kentucky's blue-grass country, now turned a wintry brown, on through the rugged twisting mountains of West Virginia and the painted hills and valleys of Virginia and into North Carolina. Through it all many of these young men looked out on a world they knew existed but had never seen.

The daylong and overnight experience . . . extended into early afternoon of Friday, the 20th for something like one hundred and forty wilted and weary enlisted men as the train backed into a Southern Railway siding leading into Camp Butner just north of Durham, North Carolina.

At about the same time, over the tracks of the Milwaukee Railroad a similar southbound troop train pulled out from the induction center of Camp Grant, Illinois . . . heavily-laden with perhaps as many recruits as the train from Fort Custer. From an interchange point at Evanston, Illinois the Louisville & Nashville Railroad would carry the train through Kentucky, Tennessee and into Atlanta, Georgia. Though all on board were scheduled for assignments all over the south, east and southwest, less than twenty that had come from areas in southern and mid-Illinois as well as the great city of Chicago would ultimately find their way to Camp Butner and there eventually swell the ranks of a newly-activated Ordnance Company to one hundred sixty three men.

A pre-arranged assembly area awaited the first train where crisp greetings were sternly voiced by a sharp stocky individual with a firm jaw whose rigid expression did not exude one of immediate warmth. Dressed immaculately in olive drab he sported on either upper sleeve three stripes up and three stripes down with a 'diamond insignia' of the same color clearly visible in the center of those chevrons. The identity and full significance of those stripes came early for this soldier was the new "Top Kick" . . . and he was but literally . . . the new boss! Carrying the highest rank attainable in non-commissioned officer ranks First Sergeant Manley Botting was keen in judgment; he possessed much prudence in army procedure and was endowed with exceptional powers of persuasion.

Botting had worked at a number of jobs after finishing high school in Birmingham, Michigan. Before being called in the army's first draft in 1940 the sturdily-built ruddy complexioned sergeant, while working during the day at Chrysler Corporation, sought a degree in metallurgy in evening classes at Wayne University. Though he was the "mouthpiece" of the commanding officer he would in the months ahead, demonstrate leadership to each of us. He would lend a sympathetic ear when problems became compounded . . . but if on the other hand one did not "snap to" when ordered, "he can," as was so aptly put, "expect a bite in the tail!"

A snappy throaty authoritative voice thundered:

"F-A-L-L IN!!!"

We did! . . . for this guy sounded like he meant business!

With no difficulty and little persuasion all recruits quickly "tuned in on the message" and congregating into groups immediately set out on a march that would span but a few blocks. A 2½-ton 6 x 6 truck was dispatched thereby sparing each the ordeal of lugging heavy duffle bags. In a few minutes we stood before the new quarters . . . a forlorn-looking collection of frame weather-board-constructed barracks a block long on "D" Street. Remaining "at ease" for a short time in front of the barracks, a soon-to-be familiar order . . . "T-e-n-n-hut!" . . . quickly deciphered as "A-tten-tion!!" rang out and its' tone brought each man to attention in an explicit orderly fashion! Introduction of the new company officers and training sergeants followed, the latter to bear a technical reference as "cadre."

Though all officers were extracted from various military posts some of the cadre had come from Headquarters XIII CORPS, Providence, Rhode Island but most from Fort Devens, Massachusetts on January 30. Summarily then, the 126th Ordnance Medium Maintenance Company was officially activated as a unit at Camp Butner, North Carolina on January 30, 1943 almost three weeks prior to arrival of its initial troop complement.

Immediate evaluation would confirm that everyone could by and large be considered as being virtually "in the same boat," for not only were the "rookies" from Fort Custer new to this company, but *all* officers and cadre as well.

Situated in Granville County and surrounded by counties contiguous to the rich tobacco growing industry, colorful Camp Butner, then still in its infancy . . . activated in fact in June of the previous year, was located thirteen miles north of the cigarette.

manufacturing city of Durham, where also is situated famed Duke University. Fifteen miles to the north is the small tobacco marketing town of Oxford and five miles to the east where highways No. 15, 56 and 50 intersect lay the little-known farm community of Creedmoor. Approximately forty-five thousand soldiers were stationed here in 1943. Red Cross service clubs or USO equivalent were established in many of the not too distant towns of Roxboro, Hillsboro, Oxford, Henderson, Louisburg, Burlington and the great University center at Chapel Hill. Transportation, erractically scheduled ran to each point. Because of its' close proximity moderately scheduled bus service was extended from camp into Durham. With a population however, exceeding little more than the camp many considered it nothing less than a chore to venture into town on a Saturday afternoon or night, and because of the excessive crowds this trip soon was viewed as a strenuous experience, producing no rewards, and only added credence to an oft repeated statement that "one almost has to stand in line to walk down the street!" Perhaps the most active center was Raleigh; North Carolina's capital city, located some thirty miles southeast.

Camp Butner was established as a training center for Army Ground Forces redeployment troops. In the regional vicinity of the 4th Military Service Command and under immediate supervision of the XIII CORPS, the camp came under full jurisdiction of the SECOND UNITED STATES ARMY. Spread out over some 40,000 acres and saturated with tall long-needle pines amid undeveloped scrub oaks most of its asphalt-paved streets ran in number sequence as well as letters of the alphabet and are so named. The camp at the time was laid off beautifully . . . reminding one in retrospect of a typical old-time Army camp. Within this reservation sixteen Post Exchanges (PX) operated along with four service clubs, and a well-staffed post office that soon found itself doing a brisk business. Several well-equipped guest houses were prominent for the purpose of providing temporary quarters for families visiting from long distances when lodging was not available in nearby towns.

The camp station hospital fast grew to prominence and soon acquired status as an United States Army General Hospital for casuals and general therapy. Extremely active and boasting the most modern facilities this busy center soon after the war would for a time continue to serve as one of the nation's leading military convalescent installations.

Further out on the camp's red clay-banked western fringes was located a vast and expansive rifle range where during the still dying gasps of winter many cold days were endured by our complement and where was endlessly sought increased weapons marksmanship ability. We would return to this range again in late fall to further test our competency.

The camp served as a prisoner-of-war compound and its nearly one thousand German and Italian prisoners were utilized in labor battalions for North Carolina state highway and road work as well as assisting in farm production in several locations throughout the state.

The 126th considered itself fortunate in locating in one of the choice sections of the camp, in that because of elevated terrain . . . roughly five feet above street level, there never existed the danger of inundation as were some locations where following heavy extensive rains, a drainage problem existed. Approximately fifty feet separated the barracks from the street, and beginning east from "C" Street to "D" Street stood a two-story barracks containing the Automotive section. Next to that the single-story household equipment and utility storage building with a kitchen-mess hall complex adjacent thereto. The Orderly room came next, and with adjoining rooms also housed the supply room, (clothing, bedding and toiletries) mail room and recreation room; each in separate distinct compartments. Two additional double-story barracks were situated on the extreme western end of the block containing the Artillery and Instrument groups, also the Recovery, Headquarters and Small Arms sections.

Arranged in competitive fashion directly behind the barracks lay the training grounds used jointly by ours and some surrounding companies. Most assemblies and formations were held in the street, always with troops facing the barracks. Some fifty yards to the extreme west on "D" Street stood PX No. Six and directly behind was the much-used post office. At that same intersection was located Guest House No. One (assigned our area) and directly across the street from the main Guest House was found busy

Service club No. One.

On "B" Street, to the company's extreme east was situated the wire-enclosed redoubtable stockade . . . less fashionably known as the "Pokey." Staffed with a nucleus of extremely harsh supervisors whose methods and disciplinary tactics some inmates claimed to have bordered on sheer brutality, all doubts are dispelled that some in our unit will remember it with somber recollections.

Webster defines brutal as being "harsh, severe, and grossly ruthless." Brutality is defined as "the state of being brutal." It has been said that some, unable to cope with the prison's regulations were placed in dark solitary confinement for three days with only bread and water. This, for little more than the slightest infraction. Is this brutality? Was flogging of incorrigibles considered brutality? Would it make a mockery of Webster's definition to be forced to walk a post for fifteen hours with no break, carrying a full field pack, helmet and greatcoat at times in the broiling summer heat; or in the winter with full field pack, uniform and only long underwear? How about being forced to dig a hole six feet deep, six feet wide and six feet long with a long-handled shovel under a building whose flooring is elevated little more than three feet from the ground. These were among the rumors of "goings on" that wafted from some of those released from the "Pokey." Some of this could have been true for this facility bore a strange reputation, but if these alleged acts were ever truly confirmed by authoritative investigators it never became our lot to learn. Only those that "did their time" know that.

Between the stockade and the barracks, separated by several yards from either facility, a motor pool was arranged with sufficient garage space to house and maintain vehicles for several companies.

Stationed in Camp Butner all of 1943 with exception of summer maneuvers employed in Tennessee, the 126th Ordnance Company's specific assignment became one of application of technical maintenance assistance to the also Butner-based 78TH INFANTRY DIVISION. Through this assistance close harmony existed between our company and the 778th Ordnance Light Maintenance Company of that DIVISION. Maj. Gen. Edwin Parker was Commanding General of the 78TH and would continue in that capacity throughout its many heroic operations to the end of the war in Europe.

We were not denied topflight entertainment here and it became our pleasure to sponsor a couple of company dances while in this location. Always held in Service Club No. One, the 78TH DIVISION dance band never disappointed anyone while furnishing music for each. Several celebrities visited from time to time; motion picture stars John Garfield and Anne Gwynn, the zany Ritz Brothers from Hollywood, the celebrated strip-tease artist; Gypsy Rose Lee, and Joe Louis, heavy-weight boxing champion of the world engaged in a brief exhibition near the end of our tenure.

As acting Company Commander, Ist. Lt. Sumner Kallet, a snappily-dressed 29-year old from Newark, N. J. would find this responsibility one of short duration. Already slated, along with several other young officers to attend the now thriving Army War College, he would on February 14 be alleviated of that responsibility by Captain Glenn H. Collins. Not too long out of Camp Breckenridge, Kentucky Collins became the first full-time company commander of the 126th. Lt. Kallet served as executive officer for ten days, moving out on the 24th. 2nd. Lts. O. Reid Lineberger of Hickory, N. C., Norman Grove from Baltimore, Maryland, Robert Banov, Shelbyville, Tenn., Milton White, Austin, Texas and Robert Sheahan from Cleveland, Ohio were during this early period subordinate company officers.

The remaining days of February went fast and swiftly faded in reissuance of clothing and rifles. The M-I and '03 rifles were about equally distributed and a very small few were allocated the Thompson '45-caliber submachine gun. Miscellaneous equipment was distributed and an abundance of orientation was given . . . designed to familiarize everyone with rules and regulations of the new and modern army.

The first of March found the company ready to embark into eight weeks of harsh basic training.

Basic training opened with no great shock and little delight, but it became something to cope with . . . for although envisioned as a course that would strengthen the muscles and build the body, most had not contemplated the intensity of its demands and each day found the pace accelerated with much vigor. As one commented; "not a bit as easy as the movies!" The days and weeks passed and with youth and anxiety in our favor and long before the first phase had reached its "high water mark" the crunching obstacle course and close order drill and the long hikes and guard responsibility, and even kitchen duty (K.P.) fell into simply a matter of daily well-paced performance. Moreover, ridiculous as it sounds . . . it actually became fun.

Captain Collins; a bouncy energetic 33-year old outdoor enthusiast from Cincinnati and on active duty since May of 1941, delighted in demanding extensive and unrelenting "bone breaking" hikes and it would not be remiss to confirm that just when it seemed the weary muscles would respond no more he would take great joy in shouting . . . "Double Time! . . . MARCH!" Who had ever heard of "Double Time . . . March?" Strapped with full field pack and heavy training rifle this "atrocious" order meant no less than to increase a steady marching gait to a slow trot, the rate of movement determined only by the commander. The Captain was proud of his unusual command, but before basic training faded to a close the boys were near beating the "Old Man" at his own game and it was *he* that did the puffing and it was *he* that was yielding plenty of ground! "The Old Man" . . . as he was called, was quick to admit that the new recruits, most eight to ten years his junior and whom while reviewing when first stepping from the train he had compassionately described as "looking like they had been on a three-day diet of hamburgers and coke," now were really beginning to "shape up."

There was a method behind his insistence of maintaining a rapid and strenuous pace however, and an article appearing in the Sunday morning edition of The News & Observer at Raleigh, N. C., dated May 9, 1943, corroborated his actions:

"Captain Glenn H. Collins, the company commander, is principally concerned with creation of a highly skilled ordnance organization capable of performing its combat responsibilities without a hitch. Too, he is a keen student of physical training and he is putting his men through a rugged program to condition them for the fight to come."

The order of the day soon became a fixed routine and everything fell into a pattern with exception of a small few uncompromising misfits. The inability to accept responsibility as civilians doubtless was imbedded in the character of these so deep and because of this lack of stability it became apparent that even the army would have trouble changing this unfortunate failing. This then, led to inevitable personality clashes! Good-natured, yes; but endowed with a combination of stubbornness and self-pity they drifted into the category of "losers." Rather than adhere to the army's outlined regimentation it became obvious that the stockade was preferable.

Saturday morning was a time of brisk activity and testing of muscles of the occupants as all floors and windows became targets of reluctant scrubbing. Foot lockers and clothes neatly arranged and lined up for early morning inspection was a must and it was viewed as a standing order for the drainage ditch in front of the barracks to be completely freed of all debris that had accumulated following a heavy rain. Rotating orderlies were posted as company "fire guards" with principal assignment to keep the fires in the boiler room functioning at a moderate level. Because of the "excellence of performance" in this assignment a couple of the personnel were eventually appointed that unenviable task for extensive periods. Bill Hunkins, a loud and good-natured lad from Flint, Michigan who spent so much time in this capacity that he unwittingly earned the title . . . "Demon of the Boiler Room," declared:

"If John L. Lewis knew how much coal I'd crammed in that damn furnace, he'd have me paying union dues!"

In the latter days of preliminary training Lieutenants White and Banov left the company when both drew overseas assignments. Dispatched to the camp hospital, Lieutenant Sheahan, an original officer, shortly thereafter was awarded a medical separation from the army.

With eight weeks of running, falling, jumping, crawling and squirming behind we were to become part of Colonel Sidney S. Eberle's vital SECOND ARMY Special troops at Camp Butner and a rigorous period of specialized technical training would begin. Because most were talented with a background of technical skill or possessed an aptitude for it they were selected for Ordnance in the first place. Yet; though many were already well-versed in specific mechanics they would still find it necessary to learn from "the ground up" for the army would have it no other way.

The same feature article in The News & Observer of May 9, 1943 emphasized in part, that point:

"Captain Collins pointed out that the majority of young soldiers in his organization were inducted into the service before becoming trained for civilian careers. Because of the training they will receive in the 126th, they will be developing skills that will prove useful after they return to civilian life. And because most of them have expressed a liking for technical work, they will be preparing for future careers rather than just "marking time" until the end of the war."

Some would be dispatched to schools of specialization in several parts of the country; the heavy artillery course at Aberdeen, Maryland or an extended tank and general tractor course at the same school. Extensive schooling at the Automotive school in Fort Crook, Nebraska; the basic machinist course in Springfield, Illinois, the light artillery school at Fort Ord, California and the Track Vehicle Chassis school in Centerline, Michigan awaited some.

The company was then broken down into specialty sections and the likely choices and aptitudes of the men were taken into consideration for section placement. Each soldier would concentrate on his particular field and become thoroughly familiar with it. He further was expected to familiarize himself with other phases of Ordnance work so as to fit in and insure continuity of service in emergent times. Colonel Eberle expected his troops to be nothing less than the "Jacks of all mechanical trades;" but there could be rewards in this, for many could in essence be preparing for future careers.

Related sections of the company would be patterned along the following lines:

Artillery: This unit to concentrate on repair and maintenance of all artillery weapons handled by the company.

Instrument: To repair and maintain all instruments used by a combat division. This would include gun sites, compasses, prisms and even watches.

Automotive: Each to be trained to repair all army vehicles. Third echelon motor maintenance would be learned and, having done so, one should be able to go into motors and remedy most of the elementary automotive ailments that may develop.

Recovery: To operate heavy vehicular equipment and be in position to remove damaged tanks and other salvageable equipment and if repairable, do one's best to repair it. Overseas, this function could be expected to progress at times under fire.

Small Arms: To repair and maintain all weapons up to the 20mm cannon. This unit to be equipped with a small arms truck that can operate in the field.

Service: The highly flexible workshop; welding, cutting, spot repair to all vehicles as the need be.

Headquarters and Supply: Specifically administrative. Each section to operate on its' own merits as the situation warrants. Supply especially concerned with maintaining inventory for company personnel capacity.

Consummation of this hard training found a few voluntarily taking examinations, and passing with exceptionally high marks were allowed to enter the Army War College which at this time was seeking to enroll those quickly adaptable to specialized training. Though referred to in GI terms as ASTP the army spelled it out for what it was, Army Specialized Training Program.

Restless and reckless, some went AWOL . . . and though the army termed it Absent Without Official Leave, everyone else looked upon it as . . . "Over The Hill." Although this unquestionably was viewed with some dismay it was an age-old course to the Army as rarely would any unit escape this irregularity during its' course of activity. Dee McCalmont, an overgrown husky Private from Michigan and Richard Kowalczeski, an uncompromising chap with the same rating, and one who never did appear to be "quite with it" went "Over the Hill" so many times that they were generally referred to as our "AWOL buddies" . . . finally in a *permanent* status.

While awaiting orders for the maneuver period a considerable bit of restless time was consumed observing war training films and absorbing maneuver orientation. During this uneasy period and as an escape from the boredom of these facets not a few of the men religiously "rode the sick book," so often in fact that eventually for some a medical discharge resulted.

II

TENNESSEE MANEUVERS

Hardly had the thirteen weeks of basic and specialized training concluded when orders were received from Headquarters, Army Ground Forces, Washington, D. C. directing the 126th Ordnance to the vast Tennessee maneuver area and to prepare to engage by June 26 in the second phase of maneuvers. The first phase was still in progress and would be until that date. The SECOND UNITED STATES ARMY, with headquarters in Memphis, Tennessee at this period maintained jurisdiction over all eastern maneuvers, not only that presently conducted in Tennessee but to include those held in North and South Carolina, Louisiana and later West Virginia. Consequently, following a tremendous exertion of hard work . . . heavily exemplified by the mobilizing, assembling, categorizing and inspection of equipment, we were then ready for the journey by rail to the maneuver area.

Methodically chaining the vehicles taut and shackling them down on flat cars and working late into the night, we rolled out of Camp Butner aboard the Southern Railway early morning of June 15.

Crossing the western and northwestern portions of North Carolina, skirting eastern Tennessee and on up into lower Kentucky we arrived at Franklin, Kentucky late the following day. Engaged the entire first night unloading vehicles and enjoying far less sleep than was wished for the complement pulled out the following morning by truck convoy . . . bound for Scottsville, Kentucky . . . 26 hilly and winding miles slightly to the northeast.

Remaining but three days . . . engaging in orientation, inventory checks, and spot inspections we moved early morning of the 20th down across the Tennessee state line into Westmoreland, some 23 miles distant. Here an additional three days was consumed. Morning of June 24 we arrived in Gallatin to align ourselves with instructions pertinent to the maneuver plan of the Ordnance department. This would give us ample time, too, to recheck supplies . . . for each Ordnance maintenance unit was instructed to bring along a load of spare parts in relation to its field operations . . . supposedly a normal thirty-day maintenance supply. This would prove inconclusive, for who could tell what a thirty-day supply would mean, what with losses, accidents and unforeseeable damage? It would however, allow a little time to locate supply points, for at the moment the only big depot that we could properly identify was the Ordnance Base General Depot at Camp Forrest, Tennessee; some one hundred miles south in the vicinity of Tullahoma. Two field depots were soon located at Portland, near Gallatin (inventoried to support the north force) and at Manchester, near Camp Forrest (inventoried to support the south force). We would learn, as maneuvers progressed, that Ordnance maintenance units would be distributed throughout the maneuver area in accordance with the requirements existing upon the development of each situation.

Embracing hundreds of miles and thousands upon thousands of acres the maneuver boundary paralleled the Kentucky-Tennessee border east to west for some seventy-five miles. Beginning at Mitchellville, Tennessee right at the Kentucky border, extending due south along state highway No. 41 approximately five miles east of Nashville all the way down to Farmington the obvious crooked boundary suddenly swings eastward to Shelbyville, thence south again to Winchester, an approximate distance of some one

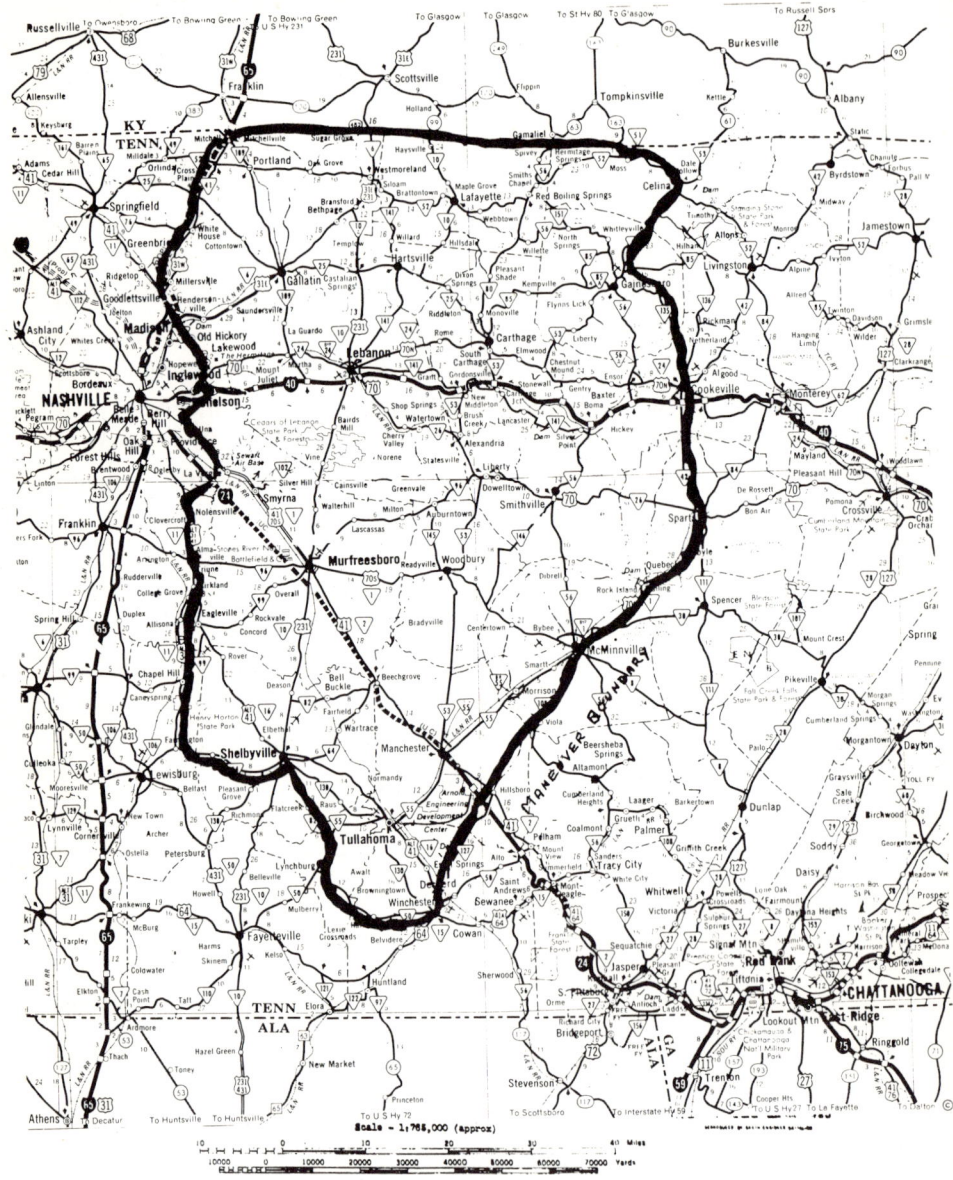

**BOUNDARY MAP
TENNESSEE MANEUVER AREA
1943**

Annex No. 8 to M.M. No. 4.
THE FOLLOWING PLACES ARE OFF LIMITS AT ALL TIMES:

A. All locks and dams on the Cumberland River.
B. Smyrna Airbase, for participating ground troops.
C. Director headquarters, Observer's Camp, and Second Army Installations, in the vicinity of Lebanon, for all participating ground troops.
D. Camp Forrest for all participating ground troops.
E. Property or localities posted with "OFF LIMIT" signs.

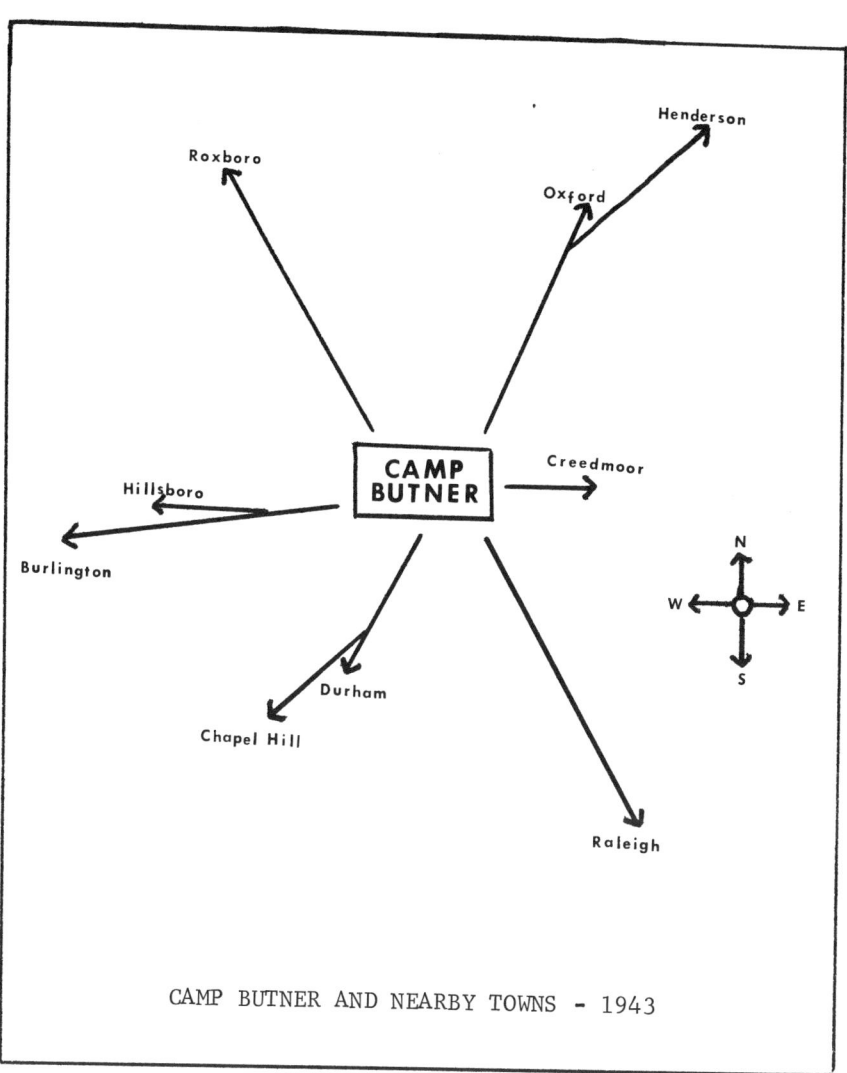

CAMP BUTNER AND NEARBY TOWNS - 1943

hundred miles. The boundary then juts up in a rather northeastward arc, (and can be marked approximately one hundred fifty miles) embracing Hillsboro, Viola and McMinnville to follow state highway No. 55 all the way into Sparta. Marked from here almost due north paralleling state highway No. 42 to Cookeville, picking up the twisting Cumberland River a few miles north to follow that flow through Celina, the maneuver boundary meets itself to complete a cycle at Moss on the Tennessee-Kentucky border.

Embracing most of the northern area within these boundaries is known generally as the Cumberland River Valley; thousands of acres of gently rolling farmland interspersed with groves of trees and frequent small streams. The entire area is latticed with a very closely spaced roadnet with many small dirt roads, others surfaced with crushed rock and several hard-surfaced state and national routes. The soil is very thin in many places, except in the bottom lands along the river. The maneuver area is bounded on the north of the Cumberland River by a range of hills having very heavy cover and steep sides.

Within the area to the south and east to west, where nearly eighty years previous, forces of the Confederate Army of Tennessee commanded by Maj. Gen. Braxton Bragg swirled in battle for three days against Union forces of General William Rosecrans, that saw nearly 20,000 killed and the entire western wing of the Union Army scattered and threatened until withdrawal became necessary; the land topography is found much the same as in the north. With all operations conducted under actual field conditions SECOND ARMY maneuvers primarily was based upon operations of two armies, which theoretically opposing each other in mock battles were designated RED and BLUE. BLUE assumed the role of aggressor and RED was assigned defense, occupation and further charged with establishing delaying action. To distinguish between the two a small colored strip of cloth was worn on the shoulder of each soldier; the color indicative of its respective army. During our entire participation our unit was assigned Army RED. Each week both armies operating within established maneuver boundaries were assigned specific "problems" geared to seizure, occupation of or defense of a town. This would include fording rivers under heavy fire . . . either by assault boats or ponton bridges, mining principal bridge approaches when retreating and evacuation under fire. On the other hand, learning the practical defense of strategic bridges, setting up roadblocks, securing vital hills, and the application of priceless reconnaissance into "enemy" territory was vital to both armies. Although explosive charges were placed in strategic locations for effect only, dummy ammunition was used in actual firing.

Service and supply troops did not escape a multitude of problems either. They must learn to establish railheads, cover evacuation of supplies and move (oftimes under fire) Base Depots. Setting up camouflage and obtaining replacement parts would become feverish tasks! Camouflage was a strong word! No vehicle lights would shine at night and no objects, including vehicles to protrude from camouflage in the open field, or from trees, or anything detectable. Perfection of field sanitation was a *must*, and *all* foxholes and latrines *must be* refilled before evacuation! Field hospitals and ambulances had to be clearly marked! Special Army ground forces observation and spot check teams were many . . . oftimes appearing suddenly. They were exacting and they were *tough*!

The SECOND U. S. ARMY, with headquarters at Memphis, Tennessee was commanded by Lt. Gen. Ben H. Lear although actual direction of Tennessee maneuvers was the responsibility of Lt. Gen. Lloyd R. Fredendall, who earlier had commanded II CORPS forces in North Africa. Under jurisdiction of III CORPS, commanded by Maj. Gen. Harold R. Bull, dawn of July 5 saw the second phase of maneuvers begin as Army BLUE, armed with might of the 80TH INFANTRY and 10TH ARMORED DIVISIONS commanded by Maj. Gens. Horace L. McBride and Paul W. Newgarden, respectively; and supported by the 71st. Field Artillery Brigade, two anti-aircraft (automatic weapons) Groups, one combat engineer Group, a Tank Destroyer Battalion and sufficient air support, moved into contact against Army RED engaging in immediate aggressive action. Army RED, composed of the 83RD INFANTRY DIVISION, commanded by Maj. Gen. Frank W. Milburn, a combat team of the 101ST AIRBORNE DIVISION, (this unit operating as an Infantry Division would cease maneuver participation July 16) the 16th. Mechanized Cavalry, two Tank

Destroyer Groups, one Anti-aircraft (Automatic weapons) Group, one Combat Engineer Group and sufficient air support drew a defensive line while engaging the attacking force with orders to hold fast.

The pattern for the month of July was set with specific "problems" assigned both armies. July 11-17 would see Army BLUE pressing aggressive action against a covering force to force withdrawal of the "enemy" across a named obstacle. Army RED initiating a delaying action would hold an orderly line while crossing of major troop elements while Army RED sets up a strong defense of a specific river line. Army BLUE in final week (July 25-31) to engage in fierce combat and initiate aggressive action to force withdrawal of Army RED while latter Army will meet this engagement and set up a delaying action.

Throughout August, and in fact until conclusion of the second phase Army BLUE would continue its' aggressive role. A difference however, would occur in role of the participants. The 83RD INFANTRY would team up with 10TH ARMORED . . . and with its' supporting units would now make up Army BLUE; thereby gaining experience of attack. The 80TH INFANTRY DIVISION would join Army RED, and with its' supporting units would find out what it means to be on the defensive!

Time was running out! Final assignments were definite! From August 1 through the 28th under assimilated battle conditions the two armies would follow set patterns of objectives, or for a more technical field term, its' "problem." Heavy stress was put on reconnaisance, establishing bridgeheads and railheads, and again . . . evacuation of supplies. In this instance army truck companies would become "live wires" and the now heavily burdened railroads would be put to the evacuation test! The Louisville & Nashville, the Tennessee Central and the Nashville Chattanooga & St. Louis Railroads, operating within the maneuver region would play a major part. Army BLUE to immediately pursue a coordinated attack of prepared positions. Army RED to seize an objective, assume its occupation and prepare for defense! Army BLUE: Pursue attack of an assigned river line to allow for crossing of major elements. Army RED: Defense of that river line. August 22-28 (final week). BLUE: Advance to contact and take aggressive action. RED: Establish a delaying action of a considerable distance. BLUE: Initiate persistence that would lead to a breakthrough of a position. RED: Set up a defense of a new position . . . ending with "problem" drawn up so loosely and overextended that collapse is inevitable!

From these excruciating mock battles thousands of troops (some 80,000 at the peak of maneuvers) would learn new methods of attack, they would increase knowledge in the art of defense and in general not only exchanging but testing and proving the foremost modern knowledge known to the field soldier which would become relevant to his conduct in battle.

The 126th gained too, a vast knowledge of responsibility. A responsibility that made it indelibly aware that Ordnance is "the man behind the man behind the gun" . . . as numerous disabled guns, artillery pieces, mortars, tanks and lighter vehicles poured into its field workshops. Evacuation of disabled vehicles became an extremely attentive matter. There was no letup during maneuver hours as the 126th found itself performing all types of maintenance; repairing or replacing piston rings, water pumps, transmissions, clutches, grease seals, carburetors, axel bearings, steering mechanisms, wheel bearings, shock absorbers, and even finishing off with lubrication. All of this to be done without interfering with the actual tactical maneuver exercise. Our job: "Get them back into action with the utmost dispatch!"

Passes to nearby towns were issued about twice a week, though only after the "problem" had been completed. When visits were made to local bars other "problems" arose between members of the RED and BLUE Armies, both adamantly insisting that *theirs* was the "best damn army in Tennessee!" But following a bit of bare-knuckled teeth-rattling, jaw-smashing and chair throwing it was usually unanimously agreed that the *real* "problem" still remained out in the field rather than on the local bar-room floor. In the meantime though, a lot of steam had been released, the taut muscles had been limbered . . . and, "what the heck?" agreed everyone, "tomorrow is another day!" Occasional passes to nearby towns gave some an opportunity to engage when possible in indiscriminate flirtation with any local "farmer's daughter."

There were other restrictions too. All vehicles must observe speed limits, maximum personnel vehicle loading was enforced and orders were firmly noted on every bulletin board:

"No driver will proceed to operate a vehicle within the maneuver area without a trip ticket."

From SECOND ARMY headquarters in Memphis, Circular No. 44 dated 8 June, 1943 states:

"Off Limits areas so designated will not be entered at any time. Barns, sheds, other farm buildings and dwellings will not be entered during tactical operations. Crop lands will not be used as bivouac sites. When necessary to remove fences to permit access to certain areas, it will be done with a minimum of damage. Unnecessary cutting or removing of fences is prohibited."

> By order of:
> L. R. Fredendall, Lt. Gen.
> Commanding,
> Maneuver Army Ground Forces

The above applied at all times and many such circulars were distributed. "Off Limits" particularly applied to all locks and dams on the Cumberland River.

A lot of "hell" was raised especially by property owners with regard to destruction of personal property, and the United States Government would be the target of much criticism and numerous claims. Much correspondence would be exchanged between such owners, congressmen, senators, military officers and the War Department . . . some so strong as to suggest that action be taken to remove the United States Army from the State of Tennessee! A case in point is illustrated in interesting excerpts of documented correspondence exchanged between one Mr. H. E. Alexander, President, Bank of Hartsville, Hartsville, Tennessee; Tom Stewart, U. S. Senator from that state, and Lt. Gen. Lesley J. McNair, Chief Army Ground Forces, Washington, D. C., each demonstrative of such feeling:

June 28, 1943

'Dear Sen. Stewart:

"Please take necessary measures with War Dept. in Washington to have U. S. troops refrain from unnecessary destruction of crops, buildings, wells, fences, etc., and if possible to avoid using Trousdale County for maneuver exercises."

Truly yours,

H. E. Alexander'

Senator Stewart forwards message to War Department in Washington and General McNair replied:

July 8, 1943

'Dear Sen. Stewart:

"I should be only too glad if the maneuvers now in progress could avoid using Trousdale County in order that the country might be spared all inconveniences in connection with this phase of the war effort. Unfortunately, however, three occasions of such use are in prospect now, . . . 11-17 July, 18-24 July and 8-14 August 1943."

Very truly yours,

L. J. McNair, Lt. Gen.
Chief, Army Ground Forces
Washington, D. C.'

August 23, 1943

'Dear Sen. Stewart:

"Since the last phase August 8-14, almost ruined my farm almost adjoining Hartsville, having cut new and heavy wire fences, which are not now replaceable, crops destroyed and other needless damage done, etc., etc., I am wondering whether more similar maneuvers will be inflicted on Trousdale County or us? I am sure you have this information or can readily get it. In the NEW YORK TIMES of August 15, General McNair mentions only "Tennessee,

Louisiana, West Virginia and the California-Arizona desert" as maneuver territory, whereas, in all fairness, we feel this destruction should be spread, if necessary, and Trousdale County be relieved of what might be almost complete destruction if things are to go on as in the past maneuvers."

Truly yours,

H. E. Alexander'

The Senator again writes:

September 1, 1943

'Dear General McNair:

"This will acknowledge receipt of your letter of August 31 concerning Mr. H. E. Alexander of Hartsville, Tennessee.

I certainly do not intend to become any party to force the Army out of Trousdale County, or to be a bearer of false or trivial complaints.

I am enclosing copy of letter which is going forward to Mr. Alexander today and upon receipt of further information from him concerning the matter I shall advise you."

Sincerely yours,

Tom Stewart'

The flow of correspondence continued, but in the end no claim would be sufficiently satisfied until the war's end.

Without question these new living conditions, insofar as we were concerned, were something of a rarity. It required sleeping out in the open, or if preferred . . . in puptents and it took *some* getting accustomed to.

We had already become acquainted with obligations that are demanded of a soldier, but on the other hand we had become a bit spoiled by comfortable quarters and accorded excellent "chow" in the North Carolina garrison. Decidedly during this outdoor living the food was found to be quite the contrary! Too, it was quickly learned that if a messkit was not washed with explicit thoroughness one's regularity routine would quickly become upset. Moreover, one did not have to gaze into a crystal ball to learn why cheese was so frequently mixed into the diet!

Dysentery ran riot! It was dysentery in technical terms but to the soldiers of the entire United States Army it was a "bug" uncomfortably known as the "GIs" . . . and while on maneuvers many involuntarily became a real authority on it, and before the war's end thousands would come to grips with it! We were fortunate however, that from the endless "chigger" bites nothing serious resulted. A slight wave of tick-borne Tularemia and Rocky Mountain Spotted Fever had flared up briefly in late May but was put down in early June prior to our arrival.

During these convoys our company traveled through and camped on scores of farms, dug in on rock-studded slopes and slashed our way through brush-covered and scrub and tree-infested areas. Extremely hilly terrain often made the going slow and rough and as most of the farm backroads were unpaved and dusty our march usually ended with the entire convoy covered with a thick coat of dust. Moreover, if rain prevailed, as often it did, the mud-spattered vehicles needed little camouflage.

Additional towns were learned. Well-balanced towns of Lafayette, Baxter, Murfreesboro, Lebanon, Gallatin, Donelson and Shelbyville were but a few. On the other hand, there was an abundance of villages and communities whose identity was forgotten as soon as they were cleared. There is little question that a good portion of eastern Tennessee saw at one time or another either the entire 126th convoy movements or some vehicle or vehicles on specific assignment. From the border of Kentucky south almost to the border of Alabama; a shade east of Nashville . . . and back across through the Tennessee-North Carolina boundary.

In the latter days of August after the second phase of maneuvers was declared officially ended it was noted that we had been engaged in this historical activity for some two months. Upon receipt of orders to return to the company's home base in Camp

Butner an area was designated on the immediate southern outskirts of Gallatin in which to form a "company street." In this colorful setting pup-tents were assembled with two men sharing each. This sprawling area surrounding a perimeter south of Gallatin was occupied not only by the 126th but other units as well who now had become veterans of the great Tennessee summer maneuvers. Thus from our hilly position one could view for acres and acres the almost continuous neat row after row of pup-tents and subsequent formations of perhaps two thousand soldiers occupying the vast rolling area. Daily assemblies were held without fail and specific duties continued to be assigned. Passes were issued freely in the evening to anyone desiring to visit neighboring towns.

Gallatin was less than a mile north of this location, but with an excessive number of soldiers already there and coming in from other directions, the desire to visit the town was harbored only by those who wished to enjoy a shower, take in an always overcrowded movie, or perhaps on Sunday, attend church. There was however, some diversion in the capital city of Nashville, some 30 miles to the southwest. Trips to this interesting and hospitable city were made with more frequency as "pass trucks" shuttled out every day and returned every night.

In late June . . . in fact three days after becoming embroiled in this summer engagement, two new company officers were received as replacements for those lost in Camp Butner. 2nd. Lt. Harry G. Able of Philadelphia, a big husky recent graduate of Officer Candidate School in Aberdeen Proving Ground, Maryland exuded much savvy and personality for a young officer and would prove as "able" as his name implied. Newton Frielich came from Detroit and had been a 2nd. Lt. a little longer than Able, and though somewhat older displayed quite noticeably a tendency of less confidence and by exercising quite a different temperament made it obvious. Seventeen new enlisted personnel replacements joined our ranks in early August, each having had training at Fort Crook, Nebraska and Aberdeen Proving Ground in Maryland to supplement those having been released to ASTP colleges during the early summer.

***

Bugles blew all down the line early morning of September 2, alerting many units with orders to move out. Unit by unit the tent city began breaking up and by mid-morning we were leaving Gallatin behind and turning east. Some forty miles beyond we moved through the larger town of Carthage. A wet and misty atmosphere prevailed all morning causing frequent delays and slowing our timetable considerably. Several times cloaked in tight heavy fog, we pulled to the side of the road, shut off motors and patiently waited for sufficient visibility. By noon the clouds opened up and revealed sunny skies, and except for occasional light precipitation the atmosphere remained clear all afternoon. More than appreciated the good weather came too late . . . for as a result of the morning's hampered visibility we were able to reach only as far as Cookeville . . . considerably less than one hundred miles from point of origin.

Because of torrential downpours during this approximate 15-hour encampment, outside operations were greatly curtailed and little if any work was done. Spending the night the entire company was obliged to sleep and accept the staid comfort of Tennessee Polytechnical Institute's spacious gymnasium floor located just beyond the town's eastern outskirts.

An early and leisurely breakfast next morning was some consolation for the supposedly "free" evening which because of rain we had been deprived. Following rebriefing of all sections leaders convoy protocol began to take shape lest we become separated . . . and we moved out. East from Cookeville the movement would consume the entire day, and by late afternoon Knoxville's city limits were reached. One did not have to glance at his watch to know that it was a little past five PM because the sidewalks and streets suddenly began to take on an air of hurried activity as people filed out of shops, stores and office buildings to begin their homeward trek.

Though traffic gradually increased the convoy was not unduly violated with civilian vehicles, and unobstructed we continued to wind through the city, moving across the high and wide overpass that spans the sprawling Louisville & Nashville rail yards to reach Highway No. 70-East. Though the sun was fast diminishing plenty of daylight was still with us and slightly more than a mile east of the city a signal was given to slowly veer from the highway to the right . . . where an open grassy sloping field was waiting. A study of the mileage gauge indicated Cookeville to be 108 miles behind.

Because of its almost unlimited space this spot had been obviously selected by a liason team prior to arrival of the company's main body. Within fifty yards north across the road was popular Chilhowie Amusement Park and it was pleasing to note that activities appeared to be in "full swing!" Though we would spend but a night it could not have been operating at a more welcomed time and would serve as a medium of relaxation and entertainment to offset the grueling monotony of a ten-week maneuver period.

An unscheduled assembly quickly followed evening "chow" and a brief but exacting summary was administered by the "Old Man" . . . pointedly suggesting the jeopardy in which the questionable trip passes could be placed. Strutting up and down in front of the formation, his eyes through steel-rimmed glasses shifting from ground to sky, and then in reverse pattern, Captain Collins spoke broadly:

"We've had a good trip so far, men; let's keep it up all the way to Camp Butner. I don't want any trouble in town and especially with other troops that may be camped around here." He eased a final warning;

"I know all of you are keyed up after the long period and grind these several weeks . . . and I know it won't take much to 'set you off'. But be on your best behavior . . . or you're going to be in trouble.!"

Before dismissal Sgt. Botting added:

"Go into town if you like, but the company *will*; repeat, *WILL* move out at four AM!" His voice trailing off; "If you happen to miss the convoy . . . well, that is going to be nobody's problem but yours!"

Anxieties began to assemble long before midnight which made it appear as though the "pep talk" had not been heard! Though the Captain meant every word of it there were growing hints that the talk would fail in its' purpose.

The 131st Ordnance (MAM) Company of some 150 men and

officers, had for two months been participants in summer maneuvers too, and when beginning an encampment in an adjoining field shortly after our arrival little time elapsed before unfriendly barbs between personnel of both companies became sharp insults. Somehow a superficial notion was expressed that a far greater contribution to the vast Tennessee engagement had been applied by their unit than had ours. Stubbornly and imaginatively we too harbored that same vain notion and by late evening, fatigued and keyed up as both companies were, sarcastic remarks had reached a sharp edge; none of which at this point could easily be retracted.

An express smirk smacking of deviousness came from the other side of the hedges which though supposedly in disguise, was nothing less than a challenge.

"How the hell did you guys get in the army . . . buy your way in?"

The response could not be avoided . . . and it came fast!

"Look who's talking . . . what kind of outfit is this? You guys a bunch of 'pill rollers' or something? Understand you just parked and watched the maneuvers. Surely they didn't let you participate!"

"Participate?" came a quick retort; "Are you kidding? We just cleaned up the Tennessee maneuvers while you guys must have been digging latrines the whole time. This is bound to be a latrine digging outfit, isn't it?" Someone added; "Sure smells like it!"

The tempo increased:

"There's one thing for damn sure . . . we ain't 4-Fs, but you guys sure as hell look like 'em!"

Harsh feelings grew intense! And so it went with the crux of the discussion narrowing down to just "who was tougher than who!" It was too late now . . . it was coming too close and the night could not pass until that was settled, nonetheless, physically!

The heated name-calling did in no way diminish. It did in fact roll on! Someone got too close to someone else and gave a shove! A fist lashed out and made contact with flesh! A sharp smack! That did it! A spontaneous clash and then many got into it! Action could not be contained! Fists and insults flew to and from all directions! Blood was spattered, teeth loosened and heads banged . . . but again nothing had been settled! Nothing settled in that direction of course, but something was settled very early next morning by the company commander. A toned-down reprimand came early from the C.O. That the "Old Man" was upset . . . there was little question, but he did not fly into a rage. He was cool and did not even raise his voice. In his rebuke however, one clearly understood the words . . . "no passes," a penalty far more punitive than the extracurricular physical encounter suffered the night before. Passes *were* cancelled for the remainder of the journey, which completion was not expected for another two days.

Collins, long retired as a full Colonel and living in Cincinnati, recalls:

"Yes, I remember clearly making the talk at Knoxville. I remember too, that all the while I was talking I could see signs of trouble brewing, and while I knew how restless the men were after the lengthy weeks of hard work I didn't expect them to get into such a big "hassle" as developed! I remember telling somebody; "Boy! if this gets out they'll kick us *all* out of the army!"

The former C.O. remembered his restrictive measures imposed as a result:

"Pass restrictions? Had to do it. But you've got to admit it made good soldiers out of all of you."

Though the rigid four o'clock evacuation order was meant to be definite it would not be easy to adhere to and a little additional time was allowed to gather personal items that were misplaced during the night's melee. Fortunate indeed was this delay for those that somehow had managed to spend the night, or the best part of it deep in the city otherwise surely would have been left behind.

Convoying through the eastern Appalachian ranges we wound snakelike and made our way through the deep gorges and tall pines streaking the rugged and rocky slopes of Tennessee and into the scenic Great Smoky Mountains. The North Carolina boundary line at Hot Springs was crossed around 1:30 PM. Some forty twisting miles east and two hours later we were in Asheville. Far to the east lay our next encampment; Hickory, but almost two more hours on the road would be expended before we would enter that furniture manufacturing city approximately 60 miles away. Though mileage keepers advised of a movement of 186 miles since Knoxville one normally would assume that after wrestling with those big GMC trucks and other vehicles through the twisting mountains every man would be at the point of exhaustion. Not so! *Tired*, yes; but there were still active signs of enthusiasm. That enthusaism would have to be contained . . . for still viewing with dismay the Knoxville incident the Captain had no intention of relenting and all were restricted to the camp grounds.

The sun broke through early on the morning of September 5 and we prepared to evacuate the campus grounds of Hickory's Lenoir-Rhyne College where camp had been made. Before this day would end the trip would be over. Blue skies with spotty white clouds and enough breeze to diminish the humidity it would be a move that would carry us through some of western and central Carolina's industrious cities; Statesville, Salisbury, Lexington, High Point, Greensboro and several smaller thriving communities. As the last half of the afternoon drew nigh this group of road-weary GIs rolled through Burlington . . . and 20 miles beyond, into Durham. After 171 miles the convoy entered Camp Butner's eastern gates somewhere around five-thirty. It was "home" again as we moved right back into the same barracks on 20th and "D" Streets that were ours prior to maneuvers.

The scene remained generally as was left although Mother Nature would find it hard to be denied and inattention to the grounds had allowed weeds and grass to get out of hand. Some building maintenance would be required and as a few replacements were picked up during maneuvers living quarters would be rearranged for accommodation.

Since departure in mid-June a detachment of Military Police (MPs) had moved in to occupy barracks within close proximity of our area. Here again, youthful egotism replaced reasoning . . . for from the start it was obvious that compatibility would not be attained by either unit . . . at least for the time being. Popularity-wise, military police rated a poor percentage compared to troops having less authority.

In the spacious table and chair-clustered lounge of PX No. Six the same evening of our return this ill feeling was further substantiated. Sharp glances, smirking stares, snappy orders:

"Straighten that tie, soldier! Button that collar! Fix that cap!"

They were orders with which we had been unaccustomed during the fast action-packed weeks in Tennessee. They were hard to take, and a bevy of uncomplimentary stinging words exchanged between the maneuver hardened 126th and the unpopular authority-weilding MPs quickly reflected a mutual feeling of disrespect. A grab of a shirt . . . a shove here, a swing there and two or three little scuffles quickly developed. They were *indeed* good ones, one or two bordering on a major fight. The remainder of the evening found the PX closed. Morning came and with it came disciplinary measures that had to be administered. Those involved bore the responsibility that followed and it was the same old story. Reduction in rank for some, "KP" for many, and the entire company suffering extended pass restrictions. It didn't seem fair but that's the way it works; and from the top . . . it was obvious that some time yet would be required before release of all the "steam" from the maneuver-oriented 126th would reach full measure!

The camp in the meantime was to acquire a new Post Commander. Colonel Herbert M. Poole would in a few days replace Colonel Harold W. Huntley who had commanded the post since the camp's activation in June of 1942.

III

FINAL PREPARATIONS

Swiftly moving into early October the 126th., now attached to Headquarters & Headquarters Detachment of the 66th Ordnance Battalion would enter a final phase of training that was to be well-paced and highly concentrated in Camp Butner.

Clyde L. Miller of Pattersonville, New York, who in mid-summer joined the unit as a Second Lieutenant, received the silver bars of First Lieutenant when in late September he succeeded Captain Collins as Commanding Officer. Although *not* his first assignment, the husky 27-year-old Lieutenant, a bit shy and a trifle uncertain in the beginning was a product of OCS at Aberdeen, Maryland would experience his *first* unit command.

Mr. Anton Rueth, a big reticent "do-it-by-the-book" regular army soldier carrying the rank of a Junior Grade (JG) Warrant Officer, having acquired much military "savvy" during his 16 years service and reportedly serving some years in the German army in the "old country" prior to that came in from Camp Breckinridge,

Kentucky to join the company on September 29. His was the Army's only rank whose grade was preceeded by the title, "Mister."

Engrossing a multitude of activities this final phase of training placed heavy importance on increased orientation in relation to the enemy. Stepped up physical activity that stressed extensive hikes, immediate identification of both enemy and friendly aircraft, higher qualification on the rifle range; and to test the *real* reflexes and physical endurance there was no escaping the infiltration course. Some called this latter process an "ordeal" . . . and unquestionably it was grueling, for one is required with rifle in hand to crawl and squirm forward on his belly . . . using only his elbows for forward traction over some 250 feet of terrain . . . often through mud and clay. As one progresses explosives spasmodically are detonated in selected spots and accompanied by *live* machine gun ammunition fired intermittently in violent spurts directly overhead. It was a touchy test . . . where one must keep his wits about him. Replying to one young rookie when asked, "What would happen if I raise to my knees to adjust my rifle," a supervisor answered; "Soldier, if you have the misfortune to raise your head even as much as six inches then more than likely a ventilated head would be the result!" This, in substance was a trial run equivalent to that under battle conditions.

Innumerable movies, some tinged with propaganda . . . strongly dealt with advance preparations, the awareness of many pitfalls to confront the soldier overseas, and once committed to battle the viciousness with which the enemy could adapt himself was stressed. We were strongly reminded of the rights entitled a soldier as provided by the Geneva Convention should one have the misfortune to be captured. Basically, in the end one would have to be keen in his own judgement in most situations similar to these specifically pointed out. Particular attention was focused on definite company assignments of each man; that is . . . the specific responsibility with which each individual would be charged while serving in the company, and this primarily to be geared for the war's duration. Some of these responsibilities would of a necessity be altered or even completely changed from time to time but for the moment everybody would know specifically just what was expected of him.

That this last training period was exacting was unquestionable but it did not exclude the regularity of scouring and scrubbing the barracks on Friday nights. Accentuation was always prominent on window cleaning, spotless floors and prompt Saturday morning inspections, which by this time little excuse was found for anyone not being diligently prepared.

A camp precedent would be established when a two-day "boycott" was staged against the company mess-hall in sort of retaliation for what was considered unnecessary belligerency from the Chief cook and some of his kitchen personnel. Sergeant Earle Jackson, a beefy behemoth from Dawson Springs, Kentucky, an extremely friendly person when out of the kitchen though on the job demanding discipline and perfection bordering almost on silence during the three daily meals. When displeased he expressed it stronger by prancing through the dining hall shouting "AT EASE!!" at the top of his lungs . . . followed often with a blast of words uncomplimentary to those at the tables. Due respect was paid him until one day during a noon meal we were flayed with a tongue-lashing followed with a stinging ultimatum:

"I don't want to hear another word from nobody!

I said 'AT EASE' and I mean '*AT EASE*'!" Then he added, "and if you don't like it, don't let the doorknob hit you in the tail on the way out!"

Slightly stunned, the obvious thought struck everyone . . . "Whoa, wait just a minute! Who the hell does he think he is?"

That did it . . . and someone spoke up:

"I've had enough of this crap . . . and damned if I think we should take anymore of it!"

Orderly and with deliberate intent one by one the men left the tables and silently filed out the screen door. In a short time the only thing left in the hall was the kitchen personnel, a couple of slightly appalled officers and empty tables bedecked with hot food!

The afternoon passed quickly and at 5:00 PM a routine formation was held in the "company street" with everyone present. The bugler sounded "To The Colors." Attentively the colors were honored and saluted. At 5:05 the traditional "Retreat" was sounded. Everyone stood "At Ease." The men broke ranks and at 5:30 the bugler sounded "Assembly" and again the men formed a "company street." The bugler sounded "Chow call;" the men broke ranks . . . but for "chow" there were few takers as only a handful filed into the mess hall. Breakfast, lunch and dinner the following day saw *no one* enter the hall except the kitchen personnel and company officers. The "boycott" was on! No breakfast the next morning. No lunch. How long this unprecedented move would last was anyone's guess because *nobody* was leading it, but unquestionably it was getting a little ridiculous, and not fully realizing it . . . a little reckless. Word by now had drifted to Battalion headquarters. The next "Retreat" formation found the 66th Ordnance Headquarters Battalion Commander, Lt. Col. H. L. Wells; a sharp career officer meticulously neat and whose every command was expressed with much gusto, delivering a poignant warning that was tantamount to a good "chewing out," and one that would affect the continuation of the "boycott."

His address was not lengthy, but we were particularly impressed with the stern rebuke, as he said:

"You men better get one thing straight right now! You're not boys anymore, you're men! You're not civilians anymore, you're soldiers! The sooner you recognize that the better the Army will function!"

The Colonel ended it with a dramatic challenge:

"Now you men have presented your gripes and you've had your fun. You are hereby ordered to get back to your duties immediately or, and I want you to hear this clearly; I will instruct your C.O. to start court martial processes without delay. And while you're thinking about it you can chew that along with your bitching!"

No question that a strong point had been made, and by the same token a lesson was learned . . . one, that had the issue *really* been pressed could well have ended in unpleasantries for the entire company. Was the walkout justified? To some degree we would say yes, in light of the fact that it brought this particular problem to the attention of the Battalion commander (which by no means was intended). We were however, glad to drop it as no one clamored a confrontation with . . . or felt disposed to tangle with the Colonel. As one put it; "With this experience and style he would *eat* you alive!" Yet, from this encounter due respect for all concerned did prevail henceforth.

The hard crust of instructional preparation began to taper off the latter part of 1943 though an important stage of training had yet to be accomplished. The four week field operation bivouac that was scheduled for the woods surrounding Camp Butner had yet to be dealt with. In the second week in December . . . remembered dismally as many had all but discounted any illusion of getting home for Christmas; our field packs were made up and we began the march to this area, a location some two miles northeast of the barracks and just short of the camp's entrance from that direction. Accordingly, this assignment meant that there would be no return to the barracks until after the New Year.

On the day of our march into those woods it could not easily be denied that winter was fast reaching its' coldest peak and it appeared to settle momentarily in the Raleigh-Durham area. Moreover; recollections are not so dimmed and records will reveal that on the same evening weather readings reflected the thermometer dropping several degrees below twenty and we experienced one of the most frigid and uncomfortable nights ever in North Carolina. A dismaying factor . . . and those in charge should have insisted, was lack of full camping preparation as most of us brought only light blankets, light clothing and the like, not at all conducive to winter camping. We were as sheep for no announcement was made as to the bivouac extension and little if any thought was given to anticipations of such excruciating weather as this. That one would give thought of exchanging the warmth of comfortable barracks in the dead of winter for an arrangement so distressing as this was absolutely unimaginable! By the second night, however, under a cloak of supposed "secrecy" this situation was corrected insofar as many were concerned, for a good portion of the men were in possession of their respective bedrolls and additional blankets.

"What the hell," commented one; "if we're going to spend a week out here 'roughing it' we might as well do it in comfort!"

From whence did this assistance come? With authorization to

return to quarters issued to practically no one, how were they retrieved? Considering the matter trivial the officers would only "second guess" but looking in the opposite direction they really could care less. They already had theirs!

The small few designated to return and pick up rations; mail, parts and miscellaneous items, etc., capitalized handsomely on requests and bribes packaged in the promised form of anything from KP alleviation and guard duty, exchanges of weekend passes, to the almighty dollar. Load after load of personal individual sleeping equipment "secretly" rolled in under cover of the tarpaulin-covered vehicles!

The 14th and 15th of December brought two full days of snows that at times appeared to reach blizzard dimensions, and engulfing this region weather readings hovered between twelve and fourteen degrees! Food froze and hands became numb and compliance to field training could not effectively be met. Sensing no apparent let-up and fully cognizant of the weather's continued rule the Battalion commander forwarded a message to Lt. Miller. Summoning all section leaders the Lieutenant relayed the communication, and in effect issued an order:

"Tell your men to break camp . . . we're going back in," adding, "Colonel Wells has 'humanely' relieved us of the bivouac commitment."

By two PM of the sixth day we were on our way back to the barracks. Inasmuch as this was only a field training operation, was this the right thing to do? Maybe yes and maybe no . . . but without reservation it was welcomed! The next year we would not be so fortunate . . . for in a war zone there is no ordering in out of the weather!

Originally scheduled for four weeks in the wooded encampment we were hard put to complete six days, and with realistic irony . . . not a single complaint was uttered by anyone regarding the two mile trek back to the heated barracks.

From time to time a man was lost. Not literally, though several factors compelled the company to drop some familiar names and add new ones to the roster. The camp hospital continued to thrive and on occasion one found it necessary to enter that facility . . . either for observation, therapy, or perhaps to actually mend some fracture. Some were singled out to fill ranks of another undermanned company designated by Battalion headquarters. Familiar names like Hogan, Chapman, Withrow, Smith, Zinn, Kruschel, Butzin, Cole; each having been with us several months would soon be gone. But in a few days from different parts of the country new names would become familiar; Runyon, DePrey, Dale, Chrest, Belyk, Mico, Bonnell, Twiss, and up from Fort Bragg came Private Elias Howe, a 33-year-old New Englander who, while bearing a name of historical repute was found nevertheless to be endowed with unusual humility. Each would find his place and remain an integral part of the unit during the war's entirety.

There existed at this time a crusade for enlistments in the Army Air Corps, and possibly to associate themselves with the glamour that this "new" branch apparently offered, a small few were accepted . . . though not without first completing rigid mental and physical examinations. With complete confidence in the future and with unbounded eagerness Privates Bruce Evans and James Graves of the "Wolverine" and "Buckeye" states, respectively; along with Hriar Boshnakian, a short chunky lad of Armenian extraction whose boundless energetic personality we would miss, were the first to go.

Privates Joe Schfranack, Joe Moore, John Andrushko and Pfc. John Gorniak, each from Detroit received medical discharges. Some two weeks later Pfc's Roy Tew, a former silverware plater from Meridan, Conn., Chicagoan Lawrence Kilgallon, T/5 George Osterman of Detroit; and an old dispirited buddy, Private C. B. White; the slow-moving "don't-give-a-damn" character from Shreveport, La. were awarded discharges for various medical reasons. Too old . . . too tired . . . irregular heartbeat . . . tricky knee . . . hernia . . . perforated eardrum . . . flat feet; it didn't matter. They could not under present conditions do the job assigned. So, for them . . . their military obligations were now completed.

Lanky and personable 2nd. Lt. Lester Ryals of Florida joined us in the latter days of November. Before he could get his "feet wet" both he and congenial 2nd. Lt. Harry Able received quick orders and shipped out simultaneously . . . a day or so prior to Christmas. The slim curly-haired Lieutenant from Florida wasn't around long enough to establish too close an acquaintance, though we were some dismayed to see Lt. Able leave. A year later in Europe an opportunity to again see them both did come to us . . . Lt. Ryals as Maintenance Officer in the 28TH INFANTRY DIVISION'S Light Maintenance Company and Lt. Able in FIRST ARMY's 84th. Chemical Battalion.

A week before Christmas, *surprisingly* a number of furloughs were allotted. Restricted to five days only those living within a reasonable mileage radius would benefit, for since at this time saddled with an unoffical alert for possible overseas movement many denied themselves this opportunity. There was little cause for dismay however, for during the previous September and October *most* everyone had enjoyed a 15-day leave anyway.

The new year of 1944 found the company restless but still at Camp Butner.

In early January four new officers were received. 2nd. Lts. James G. Black, a slim gravel-voiced young man from Brownwood, Texas and James D. Prendergast, a keen motorcycle enthusiast from La Moille, Illinois . . . equally as young and equally as slim were first to arrive. Snappily dressed and in top condition both were ready to tackle their respective responsibilities immediately. Both could in fact, because of their extreme youthful appearance almost pass for high school students. Appearance could not belie age however, for having recently graduated from O.C.S. each had been "through the mill." Two days later they were joined by Ist. Lts. William Nye of Washington, D. C. and Daniel Oxman from New York City, and though already having experienced assignment in other units, both were older and appeared somewhat less imaginative.

Now under heavy alert, by the 4th of February all vehicles were turned into the camp's motor pool complex and preparations to leave were fast nearing completion. The company was under orders to "be prepared to evacuate Camp Butner at a moment's notice . . . destination to be specified later." Late Tuesday afternoon of the 5th with full field pack and duffle bag we boarded assigned coaches, and as darkness approached we moved out . . . taking with us unparalleled memories and experiences of basic and technical training. Long would be the thoughts of final visits from or to families, some of whom had shared in those specially prepared palatable Thanksgiving and Christmas dinners in our own dining hall. We were leaving behind, and not reluctantly, exciting episodes of PX No. Six and the indomitable "Pokey" and all the dramatic events that pervaded its compound. One did not find it easy to say goodbye to all of the newly-made friends both within the camp and surrounding communities, most especially since it was highly unlikely that they would ever be seen again.

From North Carolina a five to seven hour ride aboard the Southern Railway carried the train through Virginia and into the District of Columbia where on a siding in the gargantuan Potomac Yards we would park for several hours, not to move in fact until late morning. Locomotives of the Pennsylvania Railroad backed into the siding to make contact with our awaiting troop caravan. Following the abominal routine jerking and shifting not until noon did we begin the final leg of the trip that would carry us through Maryland, Delaware and into New Jersey. Combating the rigors of boredom while enroute KP assignments were meted out while others were appointed general "policing up" details.

Camp Kilmer, New Jersey was under dominance of a grey overcast sky on the extremely frigid afternoon of the 6th as we debarked from the train at the same time as did our Camp Butner associates, the 66th Ordnance Battalion, with whom we had shared the approximate 24-hour ride.

"Damn, can't we ever shake those guys," commented one. A section leader replied: "Take a good look at 'em because as of this moment our association with them is over." True; for today there would be reassignments for both units.

In this great sprawling area filled with overseas-bound troops we would in a short time be caught up in the obvious air of hustle and haste that constantly pervades this military post. Activated in May, 1942 and embracing over 1,824 acres of New Jersey rolling hills and wooded land that included even at this period forty one miles of paved well-marked roads, Camp Kilmer was actually an installation of the New York Port of Embarkation, having been named for New Jersey's famed World War I soldier-poet, Alfred Joyce Kilmer. It was the first army camp constructed exclusively for staging of troops and its purpose was to receive, assemble, feed, house, inspect and properly equip troops destined for foreign duty *before* actual embarkation through the Port of New York. The camp would before the war's end process more than one-third of the total number of troops serving in overseas theaters of war.

Its' 1,800-bed hospital, which was the only military hospital on the east coast to receive sick and wounded returning from overseas theaters was to be, throughout the war, the recipient of all military veterans and hospital patients from the European Theater, Mediterranean, Atlantic and Caribbean Commands.

Located near the community of Stelton, New Jersey the camp is situated three miles east of New Brunswick; thirty miles south of New York City and fifty five miles north of Philadelphia.

A complete physical inspection awaited each soldier within twenty four hours of his arrival in camp and again within forty eight hours of his departure from the United States.

For days there had been no letup in the severe cold weather all along the eastern region and Atlantic seaboard and here in early February just above freezing temperatures lay dormant over the camp.

In very short order we occupied specially assigned barracks. Appearing to be excessively larger the maximum billiting capacity of each dwelling far exceeded that in the North Carolina camp . . . to such a degree, in fact, that a single building could almost house the entire company. It was noted however, that perhaps the basic reason for its vast housing capacity lay in the use of double-deck bunks whereas in Camp Butner each man was assigned a single cot.

One feature, conspicuously prominent and puzzling, raised immediate concern and precipitated open comment. Inasmuch as strict training had taught us to leave an area cleaner than had been found, it was assumed without question that other troops followed the same rule. One look and one began to wonder if all other troops were exempt from that rule as these barracks lay in an absolute state of disorder, obviously by those occupying a few days before! Disheveled newspapers, magazines and tissue paper was scattered from one end of the building to the other. Tooth brushes, shoe polish, shoe strings, shaving equipment, broken rolls of toilet paper, excess clothing and other discarded personal items lay scattered everywhere. Unsightly gobs of muddy clay in various clumps disfigured the floors . . . up and downstairs. Clay from the camp's cold damp grounds had been tracked for several days from boots of departed soldiers who during that time apparently *had not once* cleaned the building. Maybe we had been spoiled . . . for nowise was it in keeping with army procedure . . . to which we had become accustomed. How could a unit remain here a full week without working the place over at least a couple times? "Whose responsibility is this?" asked one of the non-coms. "Who the heck is supposed to clean up this mess?"

"Maybe they have permanent camp orderlies to take care of this," someone suggested.

We should have known . . . for ten minutes had barely passed when the answer came. Somebody yelled, "AT EASE!" Standing at the head of the steps, trying to conceal a mischevious grin Sgt. Botting thundered an order:

"Don't any of you guys break an arm grabbing a scrub brush and a bucket . . . and enough water and soap . . . and . . . oh yeah, . . . there are plenty brooms over here!" Gradually and reluctantly and accompanied by a vocabulary of words and phrases found only in the military, buckets, brooms, soap and brushes were put to action.

Someone quipped: "Hey Sarge; you're going to give us a hand, aren't you!"

Botting quickly replied: "You're not out of your mind, are you! . . . keep scrubbing!"

We didn't like it a bit! . . . but in the days ahead a lot of tasks would be performed that we wouldn't like!

Instructions issued by the camp commander were still in effect and would continue, stating that newly arriving troops automatically inherited the task of again establishing a state of cleanliness and order to the barracks even though its' disorder was caused by departing troops. We could look forward to some respite however, for those succeeding us would fall heir to that same privilege upon our departure.

There was on the other hand a brighter side of Camp Kilmer. The food, insofar as army food goes was far more selective than any yet experienced and each meal appeared to be more palatable than the day before. Armed with this incentive, whenever a volunteer assignment arose or choice of detail was necessitated, KP unanimously became that favorite detail. Activities in the day-room and post theaters presented some means of relaxation and recreation. Extensive passes were issued those wishing to visit the great metropolis of New York City, roughly a fifty minute ride by train to the north. Moreover, those whose homes were in the New York-Pennsylvania-New Jersey region received leaves of absence, each not to exceed twelve hours.

This five day period was by no means all pleasure for we received briefings as to proper seating positions on the train when enroute to Brooklyn harbor, the art of embarking and debarking from a vessel, and in event of emergency . . . abandonment of ship. The weapons course was visited and combat training films were viewed. We learned with some misapprehension, to operate the new type of gas mask. Additional troop formation programs were studied and digested and there appeared to be endless orientation on the soldier as an individual. The manner of one's conduct while among foreigners was of primary importance and many suggestions relative to use of currency when overseas was important. (Many learned the latter the hard way while crossing the ocean . . . in emotion-packed games where phrases such as "Snake eyes!" . . . "Come to me baby!" "Come on seven . . . I need you *now*!" . . . and long-familiar uncomplimentary remarks when manipulating those "square ivories" were uttered in short bursts of frustration!)

A day prior to departure new clothing was issued. *New indeed* was an additional set of fatigues bearing an extremely sensitive odor that was classified as impregnated clothing, a garment heavily treated chemically as a preventive against possible use of enemy poison gases. Considerably stiffer than the normal garment it exuded an oily, almost nauseous odor.

Recurrence of a foot injury put Private James Privoznik in the camp hospital. (Several months later in Germany he was to lose his life in action against the enemy.) Seven new replacements were received that would raise company strength to its normal level. Privates John Emerick from Canton, Illinois; Rufus Strickland and Holman Cheek, both from South Carolina; and Werner Lasch, a 33-year-old portly second-generation German from Philadelphia who in time would render invaluable service as an interpreter. Privates Tony Hizon, a slender young Filipino-American, Denver Waggoner, who because of immediate hospitalization upon reaching England we would never really get to know, and 22-year-old Arthur Richardson, a stocky thick-shouldered Nebraskan with a flair for roughness though ironically answering to the name of "Junior" became the last to report for duty.

Though kept under sealed orders one would have little difficulty, what with the open blatant preparations in almost pin-pointing the overseas destination. Only on the last day was notice received, even then unofficially, that it was the European Theater. Not a single note of dissent was uttered for preference to Europe far exceeded that of the Pacific Theater.

We had been ready for several hours when the "word" finally came a little after ten o'clock Tuesday night of the 10th. To dress in full class-A (O.D.) uniform required no real effort but saddled with the accompanying paraphanalia would be considered something slightly less than a mean task. Across the cold camp grounds to the railroad station we marched . . . laden with leggings, helmet, overcoats, full field pack, canteen with cartridge belt, a couple of compact K-rations, rifle that for want of dexterity grew heavier with every step, and shouldering the heavy dark green duffle bag . . . clumsy and clearly marked with indentification and so fully packed that seemingly had reached a bursting point we again boarded special Pennsylvania Railroad day coaches. On through north central Jersey we would by midnight steam into the highly active Port of Embarkation in Brooklyn.

A brief ferry shuttle from the Army terminals followed. Accompanied by a slight windy drizzle intermingled with a lingering fog . . . so dense in fact that even the thousands of harbor lights were barely penetrable, and amidst heavy swells thrashing against the craft's bow we were within twenty minutes pulling up beside the vast embarkation dock.

Only those in authority in possession of secret MOVEMENT ORDER documents knew the exact procedure ordered beyond this point. "Secret Document CKH 370.5 (No. 41) dated 8 February, 1944 to North River, Staten Island and Brooklyn Army Base Terminals, New York, thence to an overseas destination aboard

SHIPS No. 102 and 125."

Certain restrictions contained in this MOVEMENT ORDER proved reasonable and would be adhered to, and though we were not to know the full contents then, we were earlier orally instructed thusly:

"Canteens will be filled with water prior to departure from this station, and contents *WILL NOT BE* touched prior to boarding ship."

"Smoking aboard ship *after* embarkation will be limited to areas designated in ship's regulations."

Item Number 5 was particularly interesting:

"Pets *WILL NOT* accompany troops. Quarantine regulations prohibit their being taken into foreign countries, and any animals smuggled aboard ship will be destroyed prior to debarkation."

Greeted by a small all-Negro group of musicians selected from an army band detachment one would find it hard to forget the selection they were playing; one of the current popular "hits of the day . . . "Pistol Packing Mama!" It is highly unlikely too, to forget the pleasantries of Red Cross canteen service units on the job tirelessly distributing hot coffee and doughnuts that were so warmly appreciated on that cold and lacklustre February night.

Now for final details, each of which must be checked with minute accuracy. All flaws or misinterpretations must be corrected here! A final double check . . . and there would be no more, for any item unchecked would have to remain that way until overseas destination was reached. Private Bob DePrey, a recent company addition from the "Hoosier" state while viewing each army order with skepticism and who in the past had found it rather difficult to make precise assemblies, experienced no problem making this one!

Ship boarding commenced around 1:30 AM and as each man shuffled up the gangplank a port official drawing from an alphabetically arranged roster methodically called each last name loud and clear. It was a simple procedure and with no horseplay each responded in the same manner with his first name and middle initial.

Now at this last hour while filing up that gangplank there was little doubt that most hearts were beginning to fill with a depressive feeling of melancholia. Faces showed it! Thoughts of most everyone became full blown with a mixture of doubt, patriotism and a wish to be home. Certainly it seemed that way to those leaving their wives and children. Perhaps not necessarily so much a feeling of dread but rather one that bore a solemn sense of obligation. Private Joe Puklus, then a 24-year old father of two tried to recall:

"I'm not sure whether I was proud, scared or what. I did suddenly realize though that this was *it* and I couldn't turn around and say . . . 'Wait a minute, I want out!' It reminded me of a sort of 'last roll call' or perhaps the way a condemned prisoner must feel when his last reprieve has been turned down and he must now 'face the music'!" He added, "Frankly, I was damn glad to get on with it."

Perhaps this mood was expressive of each of us and perhaps in all of us there was a little pride mixed with responsibility, and as we moved on the sober reality hit us all . . . one hundred fifty nine enlisted men and seven officers! One fact was conclusive; we were now actually on board and harboring any thoughts of turning back would be completely out of the question! We could at this point all have well said unanimously:

"Let's go!! . . . Let's get it over with!!" "We've come this far . . . let's see what's up ahead!"

IV

CROSSING IN STYLE

Although soldiers continued to file into the ship the last man of the 126th had long since come aboard and by 3:30 AM everyone had been assigned areas, compartments and respective bunks. Our billits, down several winding flights from the main deck were located on "E" deck just above the ship's waterline and not until we were well-situated was it learned . . . a little to our astonishment, that actually we were aboard the great passenger liner, Queen Mary.

Converted into a troopship in 1941 the ship began military transport service that year when transporting British troops to areas in the Pacific. In mid-1942 she began carrying American soldiers in unscheduled crossings to Europe. In June, 1943 this former British luxury liner; 1,000 feet in length, measuring a breadth of 118 feet and 124 feet. from the keel to top of its structure, and weighing 81,250 tons, then the world's second largest ocean-going vessel; second only to her sistership . . . Queen

Elizabeth, began on-schedule "ferry" service across the Atlantic, transporting U. S. servicemen to the United Kingdom.

A wartime agreement, a sort of lend-lease in reverse between Great Britain and the United States put the monster ship in "ferry" service transporting American troops to the British Isles although continuing to be operated and maintained by an English crew. Completed in May of 1936 in the great shipyards at Clydebank, Scotland the Queen Mary held a peacetime capacity of 3,000 persons including an 1,000-man crew. On this particular trip there was reported on board somewhere near 14,000 troops. On her many crossings as a troopship she carried between 11,000 and 15,000 troops on each trip.

Remaining in port the entire day and night of the 11th, the "Queen" in early morning of February 12 steamed out of the harbor before many were aware. With weather worsening and snow falling heavy, a clinging mist accompanying the snow shrouded the entire harbor and visibility could not have been more than 1500 yards. Some managed to glimpse the majestic Statue of Liberty as the ship glided nearby, and later . . . despite a prolonged fog that reduced our view from the deck to obscurity our first day at sea began relatively calm.

The day passed quickly and night found us far at sea. On the second day we were told that it was natural to expect many to become victims of seasickness. Because a great majority had never even boarded a ship before this had been envisioned and was taken well in stride as these effects in a short time would be shaken off.

A fierce storm lashed the high seas on the third day with heavy winds beginning very early in the morning, increasing with intensity and lasting out the full day to continue throughout the entire night. Mountainous waves estimated from forty to fifty feet high crashed and swept the bow and forward decks and assaulted the ship throughout most of this period . . . but failed to deter the "Queen's" powerful persistence and she maintained her normal speeds as would a real champion. By noon of the fourth day the seas had rescinded to normalcy.

It was especially interesting to note during the night when the storm reached its greatest pitch and we had settled in our respective bunks below decks (for actually they were set in four and six tier bunk formation) just how little the storm seemed to disturb anyone below. The great ship seemed to roll only enough to keep our prostrate forms in a slow steady swaying motion . . . and with that the rhythmic sway of creaking canvas bunks could be heard throughout the night.

Because of the tremendous complement of troops on board the galley personnel were in continuous operation twenty-four hours around the clock and troops had to settle for a diet consistency of two meals per day. Although the first serving began at 6:30 AM and the second at 3:30 PM it was close to 10:00 AM and 5:30 PM respectively, before our unit, along with hundreds of others entered the mammoth dining hall or the former first class salon; now stripped of its magnificence . . . to take our places at the enormous wooden tables and benches. The food, as unpalatable as any we could ever hope to encounter became at times even more difficult to digest because of the ship's great prolonged, sometimes 18-degree roll in the ocean's turbulent waters that often sent food trays, tableware and assorted table condiments sliding and skimmering down and across the long tables.

Menus rotated with the days and though this was considered a GI menu; powdered eggs, (boiled if preferred) coffee that stayed chilled longer than warm, hard bread with marmalade and occasionally bacon hardly filled the bill. We felt without question that the men served two and three hours earlier fared better but for us each day meant relatively the same. Little improvement was found in the evening meal; stewed salmon a couple evenings and English-style stew or spam the rest of the time. How this hash was prepared was anybody's guess but it was by no means appetizing and could not be considered of the best digestive quality. Cheese, chilled coffee and bread that some swore was "mixed with cement" accompanied the evening meal. There was occasionally, fruit and ice cream.

Under the circumstances this may have been the best that could be done, for feeding some 11,000 to 15,000 troops developed into a monumental task and feeding each to his satisfaction was an impossible task. Viewing with apprehension, however, an unusual diet to which we were not yet accustomed it was found one could not easily adapt himself in so short a period of time. Irrespective of its' lack of appeal and despite the tremendous quantity loaded aboard the ship at New York prior to each sailing; 400 tons of food that included 155,000 pounds of meat, 21,400 pounds of bacon and ham, 8,000 jars of jam, 31,400 pounds of canned fruit, 53,600 pounds of butter and powdered eggs and milk, 29,000 pounds of fresh fruit, 200,000 eggs (30,000 boiled daily) and 60,000 cartons of ice cream; there appeared hardly enough food to sufficiently quench the appetites of all troops aboard.

The "chow" lines were tremendous! Though the first meal began at six thirty in the morning three lines abreast were already extended nearly three decks and by time serving was well under-way these lines had extended through the halls, down the winding stairs to several decks below. This feeding operation took an incredible amount of time and for an absolute fact by time the last troops were served breakfast, hardly more than an hour elapsed before serving of the next meal commenced in late afternoon! The lines were orderly and one did not stop to quibble with kitchen personnel because he thought he had not been served sufficiently for a hard-eyed MP stood nearby and kept the lines moving at a registered pace.

There was, fortunately, eight army PXs and canteens aboard, each doing a thriving business, particularly serving those who simply could not endure the "chow." Even with this addition there were several occasions where many were positive that "starvation pangs" had already set in! Moreover; the limited assortment of edible commodities distributed by the canteens were not of quality to relieve those prolonged "pangs." The food perhaps was the principal disappointment of the entire trip. It did not help moral and further; in no way did it alleviate the agony of a growing list of seasick victims.

Standing Orders were posted in every unit compartment. One, clear to all was specific:

"All orders will be issued in the spirit that this ship is engaged in a combined operation of war, requiring a full loyalty, obedience and co-operation from all personnel on board."

Another regulation spelled it out plainly and succinctly:

"Enlisted men will wear fatigues unless specifically stated otherwise; officers will wear shirts and ties (and) blouses, if available, during the evening meal."

That this ship was *overcrowded* is a gross understatement! Actually there was not adequate bunk space to fill the needs of all aboard and many slept on sections of the ship's 750-foot promenade deck, though that deck portion was enclosed for this purpose. An estimated one-third of the troops slept on decks. Many enlisted personnel and officers of the Women's Army Corps (WAC) were aboard and though GIs were allowed to speak to them they earlier were instructed to be discreet in "keeping your distance." It was not unusual to note in the milling crowd a one or two-star general . . . or naval commanders and captains, but with extreme crowded conditions saluting was neither necessary nor mandatory. Lieutenant Colonels, full Colonels and Lieutenant Commanders appeared to be almost as freely distributed as Corporals and Sergeants and this became understandable when it was learned that a great protion of the 4TH INFANTRY DIVISION was aboard. Rank and position mattered little at this time for each would have a part to play in the mighty drama that was to begin in a few months. At the moment, "getting there" was the uppermost thought of all.

During daylight hours almost everyone kept moving to prevent the spread of boredom and this was good. Because of the tremendous number of troops the ship was sectioned off into three areas and each man was given a small metal identification tag when first boarding, denoting his respective area. No one was admitted to the mess hall without his proper color tag and he was not supposed to enter areas that did not correspond with his color. MPs checked continually to see that "wrong colors" did not get into improper sections. Ours was the RED area, *supposedly* restricting us from the bows aft to the main stairway. Many somehow, despite the "off limits" classification of some areas wandered aimlessly and curiously about most of the ship's twelve decks . . . inspecting its fascinating depth, and many hundreds of names and initials were added to the thousands already carved into the wooden deck and railings.

Small booklets entitled "Short Guide to Great Britain", issued by the army's Special Services Division were given each of us . . . designed to stipulate the inherent differences of opinions and customs and "do's and don'ts" that would confront everyone when in England. One item of specific interest in the booklet was pointed out and suggested definite adherence:

"You are higher paid than the British "Tommy." Don't rub it in. Play fair with him. He can be a pal in need.

If you are invited to eat with a family don't eat too much. Otherwise you may eat up their weekly rations."

Lifebelts were to be worn at all times when leaving respective compartments and *no one* was allowed on deck without one. One of the ship's regulations pointedly made this clear:

"Personnel will not climb in the ship's rigging, sit on the railings, life rafts, or climb into the lifeboats. With both feet on the deck you cannot fall overboard. If anyone falls overboard IT WILL BE IMPOSSIBLE TO STOP THE SHIP FOR RECOVERY PURPOSES."

In the beginning a good look at the monstrous white-capped waves breaking as far as the eye could see and no one wanted this to happen. Very few would fail to carry his lifepreserver. To quell growing anxieties movies were shown daily and evenings, and live concerts were given in one of the great halls. These normally relaxing features as well as the abandon ship drills, sometimes twice daily, only relieved temporarily the restlessness of the men.

As on all previous Atlantic trips the Queen Mary traveled the North Atlantic charting a distinct "zig-zag" course purposely to avoid contact with enemy ships or submarines . . . though it was claimed with her tremendous speed as an ocean-going vessel, boasting a full speed of nearly thirty-three knots per hour, she could outrun any submarine in the enemy undersea fleet. Alarm and anxieties were not paramount however, for it was general knowledge that U-Boat threats in the Atlantic had long been on the wane.

Fully radar-equipped and armed with a number of anti-aircraft and rocket-firing weapons as well as two 4-inch guns she was fairly-well prepared to do battle if the occasion arose. The "Queen" made twenty eight round trips during the war and that occasion never arose! In all her many crossings as a troopship the Queen Mary had never been hit or disabled by enemy fire and only once had met with possible serious disaster.

In midafternoon on the second day of October, 1942 just six days out of New York, and transporting a great portion of the U.S. 29TH INFANTRY DIVISION to Europe . . . some 10,000 American troops, the "Queen," just off the coast of Donegal, Northern Ireland and cruising at a normal speed of 28.5 knots (30mph) amidst extremely heavy swells, was to experience an incredible act of gross negligence on the part of one of her escort ships, the 4200-ton British cruiser H.M.S. Curacao.

Failing in attentiveness to adhere to restricted distances to the starboard side of the great troopship the Curacao gradually . . . then suddenly found itself steaming dangerously alongside the liner, too late it would seem to alter her course! A collision was inevitable! A mighty swipe of the "Queen's" bow against the Curacao's stern spun the smaller ship into a 90-degree angle and broadside into the "Queen's" path! Like the thud of a great meataxe the "Queen" plowed right through the middle of the cruiser . . . splitting her in half, sending both sections within minutes to the bottom! 338 officers and men of the stricken vessel were trapped, crushed and chopped to pieces by the threshing of the great liner's four 35-ton propellers! Like a monstrous juggernaut the "Queen," under orders, continued on her course . . . leaving rescue operations to other ships of the convoy! Only the Captain, one other officer and 99 seamen from the destroyed cruiser were saved.

No one aboard the "Queen" was injured but it can be attested that many prayers and vows became succinct in their renewal. The waterline bow of the big ocean liner did very well suffer some serious and extensive damage though repairs did not commence until all troops were unloaded the following day.

On the sixth day our ship sailed distantly past the rocky northern tip of the mainland of Northern Ireland, perhaps fifteen miles distant, though clearly visible to all. Up the Firth of Clyde the "Queen" steamed, very close and then past the age-old summer resort island of Arran, whose snow covered peaks and rolling landscape at this moment proved an etching of beauty jutting out of Scotch waters. Somewhere around four in the afternoon of the 18th, less than a mile offshore between the harbors of Gourock and Greenock, Scotland the ship's three 16-ton anchors were lowered.

The day was clear, the water placidly calm; seemingly without a ripple, and with exception of an occasional blast from any one of the local commercial harbor craft . . . from our standing position on the ship's lower deck the harbor commanded a view as breath-taking and enchanting as any picture postal card could possibly indicate, despite waters in this entire region thickly infested with allied naval and armed merchant ships of war, and shorelines bristling with anti-aircraft defenses. The magnificent port of Greenock seemed almost to be set apart from the rest of the world. Almost completely surrounded by a backdrop of endless rows of green mountains . . . from this ship it appeared the only outlet would be via the rocky palisades rising some four to five hundred feet to overlook the relatively narrow passageway through which we had entered and where effectively strung and submerged were established anti-submarine nets.

Irrespective of the natural beauty and enchantment completely encompassing . . . such as is rarely seen especially under the circumstances, it was impossible to disregard for one moment the lingering gnawing of hunger gripping many, which discomfort was brought on by unpalatable and limited rations on board during the past six days. We looked forward anxiously to getting ashore but remained aboard ship during the entire night of the 18th. and most of the 19th. Around noon we were commanded to "check all gear and be prepared to leave the ship by 3:00 PM." We were prepared by three but did not take our position to debark until approximately 5:00 PM. Down the ramp through the great ship's side we stepped down into government-contracted civilian tug boats and fishing launches to be transported ashore.

Ironically in the galley of the smaller craft seasoned cooks were preparing the crew's evening meal during our approximate thirty minute trip to shore and the penetrable tantalizing aroma of french fried potatoes and ham proved too much for many of we "underfed" GIs.

"Boy! Does that *ever* smell good!" quipped someone.

"Wow! I can't take much more of this!" called out another.

"Hey, Mac! How much for some of them potatoes!"

Bargaining immediately got under way and by time the launches and tugs reached shore it was accepted that supper would be extremely light for the crews that evening . . . but on the other hand, now there would be a lot more extra money to spend than there would have been had not the hungry Americans boarded the boats. No one had to take a vote to conclude that this was unquestionably the only *real* decent food enjoyed since leaving the United States.

Landing with dispatch and quickly assembling on Greenock's age-worn docks we began a march set in cadence through ancient cobblestoned streets for several hundred yards to the railroad station, warmly viewed all the way with intent eyes of local folk from every street corner and sidewalk and most doorways and windows as though we were the only GIs ever to pass this way. There greeted at the station by a Scotch military band in full dress, one would liken it to a page from National Geographic Magazine when beholding the multi-colored plaid costumes complete with kilts, tams, knee-stockings and flowing shawl accompanied by the hideous bleating and shrieking noises that only bagpipes can produce.

No more than half an hour later we were shuffling into chilly and drab compartments of a British Railways passenger train which would transport us to a destination further south . . . a destination under sealed orders and known only to the company commander at this time. Before pulling out of the station the Red Cross Canteen personnel again were there on the job and this time their services were more than ever appreciated; gifting each man with candy, cigarettes, hot coffee and doughnuts, along with many other small items that would greatly insure additional comfort on the journey about to be undertaken.

V

ENGLAND – COURAGE PERSONIFIED!

Aboard dimly lit coaches of the London Midland & Scottish Railways Limited we moved out of Greenock around seven o'clock which meant that approximately some two hours had elapsed since leaving the great ship. In no time the train gained an even rhythmic momentum and now was clipping along at an advanced pace. By this time a light mist now engulfed the entire region and we suddenly became keenly aware that the atmospheric picture beauty of the afternoon had quickly transformed into a greying evening. Moving on, the Scottish countryside came to us just as had been envisioned. Quaint cottages with thatched roofs, winding roads and picket fences, and distantly from our window on occasion we saw gathered flocks of sheep accompanied by shepherd and dogs; . . . truly symbolic of this spacious green country. Now and then a crumpled skeletal wall that obviously had once been a mansion in the midst of a lordly estate standing way off alone; a mute reminder perhaps, of great landowners of another era. Placid lakes, perpetually ringed by a never-ending wave of green hills revealed to us fully a vivid picture of ancient and rustic Scotland.

Steaming into the busy commercial center and great seaport of Glasgow on the Clyde River . . . a metropolis second to none in the shipbuilding industry and reportedly second largest city in the entire British Isles, a halt was called for only a brief period. Several miles due south we moved through the large rail center of Carstairs. During the next three hours our train passed through the great sprawling farmlands and many smaller industrious textile centers that make up part of the Scottish Lowlands and long before midnight the English border was crossed and we moved rapidly on down into the shoe manufacturing city of Carlisle. Swaying and clickity-clacking through and across the now darkened peaks and valleys of Cumberland and Westmorland Counties the blacked-out troop train streaked into Huddersfield . . . and then Sheffield.

"We're making jolly well good time, we could hardly do better," commented one of the conductors. "You Yanks will be there in no time a'tall." That sounded reasonable to us but it did not answer the question; "Be *where* in no time?" A precise schedule obviously was being followed, however; for it was close to two AM when the train rolled into Derby to creep along and halt on a siding near the busy railyards. We got out, and though the chilled English air was refreshing we were yet obliged to line up to partake of hot coffee and sandwiches from a British mobile canteen manned by British women volunteers. Though under the auspices of the United States army these women exuded extreme warmth at a time when it was much appreciated. No more than thirty to forty minutes elapsed before two shrill blasts of the engine's whistle signaled an order to get moving and in short order we assumed our respective places on board. Though still under cover of darkness the GI-laden transport, perhaps ten cars in length and carrying many troops in addition to our own was once more rolling through the heart of "merry old England."

The early dawning hours of the 20th found those of us awake lifting the shades a little and peeping through semi-greying darkness over and beyond the spacious rail yards at the great industrial center of Birmingham as the train braked to move very slowly into the well-lighted terminal station that in a couple hours would start humming with activity. The stop would be brief . . . long enough only to get track clearance and move on out beyond the city. The sun was coming up and began sifting through the forests and hilly countryside, and some forty to fifty miles south the train began braking speed preparatory to crossing an extensive rail bridge spanning the Avon River at Stratford . . . a picturesque town whose legend long has been indelible in English literary classics. The full flower of daylight embraced the country as the charcoal-grey troop train skirted slowly through the cathedral city of Gloucester. Some forty miles south and a little more than a hour later we were in and through Bristol. Somewhere around ten o'clock a few station hands gave courteous nods as we hauled our bags from the train at a quaint community called Temple Meads Station, six miles south of Bristol on Bridgewater Road.

Six canvas covered army 6 x 6 2½-ton trucks loaded with one hundred fifty nine weary officers and men appeared to be recklessly tearing through the otherwise peaceful English countryside . . . emphasizing every bump, every sharp turn and abrupt stop. Local topography as seen from the back of a truck was beautiful but with those "wild bucks" at the wheel carrying out their "no stop" orders it was far from enjoyable. It was very cold, it was uncomfortable and it was spoiling a 24-hour trip that most everyone otherwise had considered pleasant.

Some twenty minutes had passed since boarding and now the trucks had stopped. Down went the tailgates and we were greatly relieved and elated to find ourselves stepping out into the center of a lovely village named Blagdon.

Situated at the northern base of the vast rolling Mindip Hills in County Somerset, and 12 miles south of Bristol the little town of Blagdon (actually incorporated as a Parish) prior to outbreak of war in 1939 engrossed a population of approximately eight hundred to one thousand persons. At the time of our location this figure had exceeded many more than that due to the many evacuees that sought refuge from Bristol during the days when the German Luftwaffe was saturating that city with its aerial "blitzkrieg." The community is built on and around a high sloping hill overlooking a broad two-mile body of water widely known as the Yeo lake-reservoir (Lake Blagdon), long famed for its trout fishing. Not unlike other communities of similar topography the town's central makeup pattern begins at the foot of this hill and extends all the way to the top to continue its descent down the other side. Extremely narrow streets wind throughout the closely-knit shops and private dwellings embracing these streets, so close in fact that because of sudden abrupt turns of the streets the widely-built American vehicles in their characteristic haste often left deep scrape marks on some dwellings when passing through. This; much to the consternation of the occupants!

Private homes on streets leading out from the center of the village were more fortunate in that many nestled comfortably above street level with individual yards backed up against rock walls as a buffer protection.

Commencing from center of the village one would have to travel uphill at an almost 45-degree angle through the more densely settled residential area to reach the hill's crest, approximating a distance of something less than half a mile. This route frequently was used later for one of the company's more vigorous hikes which unquestionably entailed dynamic effort . . . most especially when the challenging "double time" command was ordered! The *return* trip was a different story.

From the summit one of the most magnificent views of all Somerset's rolling countryside could be enjoyed, and with the prominence of many picturesque hills in this region many "unbiased" Englishmen boast Somerset to be the "most beautiful county in all of southern England." They were not far from wrong.

An atmosphere of tranquility interwoven into natural beauty would well-describe this entire territory and all over the countryside even the grass appeared to remain green all year around. Most of the property within a good radius of miles was controlled by the industrious Wills family, whose name was borne on one of England's most popular manufactured tobaccos . . . the Wills Player cigarettes. Occupation of the town citizens varied. Though commuting to and from Bristol many were engaged in some type of defense or Government specialty while others maintained private and commercial work. Some were natural tillers of the soil . . . and many willingly became gentleman farmers basically to help with the war effort and to some degree finding it advantageous to their own personal sustenance. Within the village itself were established garage owners and mechanics, shopkeepers, a few pub operators, commercial traders and sufficient miscellaneous employment . . . including a small fibre-bag factory that kept Blagdon's daily routine thriving.

Overlooking the broad expanse of the lake and lower countryside . . . and across the spacious ravine directly southeast of our headquarters majestically stood Blagdon's Parish church . . . St. Andrews; one of the oldest Anglican churches in southeastern England. Displaying the architectural fascination that is characteristic of all English churches dating from the mediaeval period, this edifice with its' ancient crawling moss and ivy-infested graveyard soon became an extremely popular target of everyone possessing a camera in the company.

The 126th. Ordnance became the first American troop unit to be stationed here and as a consequence the reception and courtesy afforded by the local populace reached proportions that are usually reserved for returning "home-town heroes." Years will pass of course but only the most pessimistic could ever believe that the kindness, friendship and personal affection of the people of Blagdon will ever be forgotten. For our entertainment these people sponsored dances most every Saturday night. They opened a canteen for our disposal (with their rations) and escorted on sight-seeing tours all who desired . . . this on their own time and with whatever transportation they could muster. Eager to have us attend church services on Sunday morning, it was not uncommon at all to be invited to share meager family rations for Sunday dinners. Their homes became no less our homes if we so desired. Most of those who experienced sentry duty at headquarters entrance guardpost in the center of town will well-remember the elderly couple living in the apartments across the street bringing hot tea in the middle of those chilly nights. It was most comforting too, to engage in conversation with tall and erect Constable Small as he made his rounds through the pitch dark streets at intervals of the night. It was amusing in the daytime to see him, with his unusually long legs pedaling his bicycle on duty.

Lieutenant Miller had insisted on nothing less than full cooperation with the local people, saying:

"We have every reason to believe that if you treat these people as you treated your folks at home you can expect the same courtesy in return."

The days that followed would give credence to the truth in those words!

The British had been engaged in over four years of war prior to arrival of the 126th. Consequently by the time we arrived in England resources of these people had become seriously depleted; to say the least, life's more luxurious items had long-vanished, especially so with the civilians. Sugar and quality meats were a thing of the past and gasoline for private autos went primarily to those connected in some way with Government functions. Clothing of superior quality long was depleted during the early days of the war and none of the department stores or restaurants could boast of anything worth buying. There were many, many children who had never even seen any type of outside lights at night, perceiving nothing but darkness when leaving the dwelling. Taking all of this in consideration one would not find it hard to reason why the present and possible immediate future life of England had definitely descended beyond normalcy and only time would tell just when the progressive trend would begin again.

Bicycles conspicuously replaced the automobile as one of the chief modes of private conveyance. Buses of the most out-dated type were in use for commuters so desiring, and in some areas even the horse and wagon was once again brought to the public as a positive means of transportation. Deprived of the many conveniences, weighted down with personal and economic burdens and mindful of the fact that having already been engaged in total war for over four years, the people continued their everyday affairs with such nonchalance that it appeared as though there had never been any other way. They would not dwell on the war's depravity unless you spoke of it first. Pride perhaps was the answer . . . and the British were second to none when it came to exhibiting and harboring tremendous pride!

A highly conservative people . . . not given to excessive outward emotion caused us in our youthful judgment to label the British early as subdued and unfriendly, particularly those in the larger cities. Traditionally reserved, yes . . . and infinitely hard to understand at first. We couldn't fathom the necessity for placing so much importance on royalty; we thought it a little ridiculous to hold the King and Queen in such high veneration; or why they insisted on breaking for tea at ten in the morning and four in the afternoon. The time comes of course when perhaps everyone learns that everyone else is entitled to his way of life and on our part it took very little reasoning and time to get acclimated to the British "oddities."

Their "pubs" were our taverns, their "chemist shops" our drugstores, "stout" became our beer, "lorries" . . . our trucks; "wireless" for radio, "bobbies" for policemen, their custom of driving on the left hand side of the road, and none the least their humorless jokes which were always dry but nevertheless enjoyable.

Little effort was required to note that their ways were basically the same as ours; only the identity needed clarifying. We learned early that when standing in line we were simply "queueing up" to attend movies, which were their "cinemas" . . . or "flicks." We had however, a devil of a time distinguishing between their currency and our own. Twopence, (pronounced "tupence") halfpenny, ("hapennie") half-a-crown, ("Haalf crown," emphasizing the broad "a") the shilling, bob, guinea, etc. When making a local purchase and the monetary identification became too complicated one simply reached in his pocket, pulled out a handful of English coins and said; "You figure it out, take what you need!"

These were some of the things with which we soon became well-acquainted, even as they adjusted themselves to some of the contrasting American actions. Quickly adopted were two outstanding and traditional past-times. The omnipresent game of "darts" . . . played in every "pub," and their extremely appetizing "fish and chips" which was welcomed with great enthusiasm by most every GI in the British Isles. Many hours of pleasure were taken in the town's popular "pubs" . . . The Queen Adelaide, The Seymour Arms and the George Inn, where until eleven o'clock each evening (except Sunday) one could fill up on all the ale and stout available and engage in conversation with the local folk that never ceased to be interesting.

Somerset and surrounding counties possessed an aura rich with ancient, mediaeval and legendary history and from the onset many took rapid strides to share its' interests. Blagdon itself dated back beyond the ninth century . . . and that would mean even before the Norman conquest. Passes were issued almost at will on weekends to any and all of the interesting locales. The oft-bombed city of Bristol . . . twelve miles to the north, and one of the largest and most industrious in England, became a chief weekend attraction.

Located in the West Midlands just six miles east of where the Bristol Channel flows into the River Severn in the northwest corner of Somerset County, Bristol then was a great city of some 435,000 (1940) people. Noted for its' massive docks sprawling on both sides of the River Avon, its' flourishing shipbuilding and aircraft industries, production of manufactured tobacco and leather goods this city dates back to Anglo-Saxon times when William the Conqueror abounded within its' confines.

Hit by seventy-six German air raids in the six years of war Bristol suffered the complete destruction of over 3,000 dwellings; and saddest of all . . . some 1,300 of its' inhabitants . . . men, women and children, lost their lives during these raids.

Especially known for famed Clifton University, which housed for several months headquarters of the United States FIRST ARMY; its' magnificent cathedrals and the well-traversed Suspension Bridge suspended two hundred and forty five breathtaking feet above the majestic Avon River and Gorge, these attractions drew the attention of most everyone in the company at some time during our sojourn.

Visiting the not too distant storybook town of Wells some twelve miles southwest of our location, and its' world-renown cathedral or Cheddar Gorge with its' many mysterious and interesting caves was always an enjoyable afternoon well-spent. The smaller towns of Chewton Mindip, Chew Magna, Burrington Coombe, Axbridge and Wrington were within easy bicycling distance, and of a certainty the most popular spot focused on Weston Super-Mare, an exciting resort town on the River Severn. An approximate ten-mile run by bus due west from Blagdon, Weston Super-Mare offered a little more active entertainment than did any of the other surrounding locations. Amusement rides out on the Grand Pier; the invigorating medicinal baths; the many curio shops and the relaxing dances held nightly at the Winter Gardens Pavilion . . . to the music of many of England's best dance orchestras made the resort a favorite.

The big cities were interesting but more endearing was the friendship and homespun antiquity of the little villages of Churchill, East Harptree and West Harptree; each, when one was up to it . . . within one-and-a-half to two miles walking distance from Blagdon where warm welcomes were always extended either in the individual homes, at community dances or the local "pubs."

On Blagdon's northside on the rambling Wills estate at the foot of the hill . . . and but a few yards from the magnificent Wills mansion were housed the Automotive and Recovery sections in recently constructed barracks. Approximately one-quarter of a mile up and beyond the hill just off the center of town the balance of the company occupied a stately though somewhat "run down" old mansion with attached quarters. Known as Blagdon Court and situated on three rolling acres closed in by hewn stone walls with huge iron gates marking the entrance, history had long pervaded this many-roomed edifice which dated beyond the eighteenth century. During that period this structure had replaced a manor once owned by the Duke of Somerset which since mediaeval times had been an estate of magnificent splendor.

"Hut-two-three-four! Hut-two-three-four! Hut-two-three-four!" This rhythmic cadence became a daily familiar sound in early morning to those living in or near the center of town.

"In cadence, count!" shouted a sergeant in charge. Then 50-odd voices picked up the count: "Hut-two-three-four! Hut-two-three-four!" A rhythmic ditty followed: "She-left! She-left! I-had-a-pretty-girl-but-she-left!" to match the cadence count. This daily ritual reverberated down the hillsides and through the streets to reach the ears of all who would be about their business so early in the morning. To the townspeople it was colorful and they surveyed it with interest. To get to and from "chow" which was served in an adjoining structure in the headquarters area complex it became necessary for personnel of the two sections located at the bottom of the hill to make their way on foot. It seldom failed to be amusing to the residents located on the main road to watch them employ these daily marches in cadence through the narrow streets and past the little shops. Especially was it delightful to the children who not infrequently found it amusing to run gaily along beside or behind this group.

If it was amusing to the local folk there were occasions when it became something less than hilarious to the boys for often the early morning atmosphere was rumpled when with messkits in hand, they would at a given signal shake these instruments *in unison* for a period of perhaps half a minute! One can imagine what this did to the early morning silence in extremely narrow streets hemmed in by closely-knit shops and apartments! The abrupt rattling and clanking of some fifty-odd messkits together was likened to about ten thousand discarded tin cans thrown down a lengthy coal chute! There was little wonder why whispers were made, without malice, regarding "those Yanks with their devilish tins!" But it was all in fun!

Only on rainy days were the residents spared this ordeal as trucks were employed to transport the troops to and from. Trucks were also dispatched for special assemblies.

Almost two weeks passed before we first heard German aircraft motors. Though doubtless targeted for defense facilities south of Bristol the Luftwaffe was considerably off course and enough to give us much alarm. Fortunately, far from being direct recipients the bombs fell quite some distance from our area but the silent streaks from searchlights scanning the skies and the steady unfamiliar drone of enemy planes together with the dramatic explosions and hideous flashes rumbling throughout the still countryside breaking the inky blackness of night left a sober and uneasy feeling that remained throughout the night.

At Blagdon the 126th. Ordnance was assigned to the 86th Ordnance Battalion with that Battalion and all of its's subordinates under jurisdiction of 52nd. Ordnance Group and attached to the prominently emerging United States FIRST ARMY. Having left its' home base at Governor's Island, New York in October, 1943 the FIRST ARMY had since its' arrival in England been methodically undergoing a gigantic expansion program and rapid build-up in strength, material and trained personnel. Few could foretell the tremendously important and spectacular role it was yet to play in the approaching months across the English Channel and on the European Continent.

By the end of March preparations were in motion to move from this lovable village to another location further southeast in England. We were not at all reluctant to pay ourselves a broad compliment with respect to personal behavior . . . for never at any time prior to or after occupation of this community was our disciplinary mark any higher. We enhanced a reputation for cooperation and exuded full respect to the townspeople which they perhaps for a long time were not likely to forget. Lieutenant Miller commented on it; Sgt. Botting commented on it; and as the Lord Mayor of Blagdon in so many words so tactfully put it one night during our big company farewell party at The Seymour Arms . . .

> "You 'chaps' must be proud of the heritage that you bring from America. For we in Blagdon are extremely pleased at the friendliness and excellent conduct displayed by each of you, and we will not forget it."

He obviously was not aware of the "hell" that we were *capable* of raising but it sounded good anyway and summarily; in Blagdon the 126th Ordnance was at its finest!

***

Little enthusiasm was noted and none was felt as we left Blagdon early morning of March 31. East through the broad expanse of Somerset over narrow winding roads that for miles were dotted on either side with stout cedars we charted an unusual route, one that was designated for long American convoys such as ours, which at the same time would reduce obstruction to civilian traffic using the more narrow roads that wind through the Mindip area. We swung northeast away from the Mindip Hills and a *long* twenty miles found the convoy skirting the majestic old city of Bath whose ancient spas and medicinal baths established by the Romans remain the most celebrated in England. Now utilizing a more broad main road, all the while rolling southeast, and following closely the flow of the brownish waters of the River Avon we were twenty miles later rolling into the approaches of the age-old city of Warminster . . . now a great American supply depot; and ringed with high brick walls since Anglo-Saxon times remained even now in an impressively remarkable state. Almost the same distance was required before pressing within close proximity of the inexplicable and legendary Stonehenge . . . and then straight into the cathedral city of Salisbury.

From the city's heart . . . turning slightly east a route was followed for ten miles in a straight line that took us across the vast windy Salisbury Plains into a compound of well-used Nisson huts known as Lopcombe's Camp. Arriving just before noon a mileage check showed a distance of seventy-one miles. That it required almost three hours to get here seemed questionable for it would appear that the mileage should amount to much more. When one considers, however; the circuitous route employed and the winding extremely narrow roads that rise and fall with the many hills and known better by civilian drivers who by our standards cannot be classified as the best in the world, plus our many stops . . . perhaps we actually did well.

Situated in southern England in the extreme western corner of County Hampshire, less than a mile in fact from County Wiltshire's eastern boundary and embracing the region of the British Southern Military Command, Lopcombe's Camp had long been utilized as a training installation for British troops prior to and during the early war days. Some recent rehabilitation had been administered the camp to house the overflow of American troops. Encompassing roughly four square miles the view in either direction from the camp was dominated by miles of slightly rolling hills and spacious farmland broken only by an occasional grove of trees. With an historic ring this land is geographically known as the Salisbury Plains and is sectioned off in many areas into individual farms. Moreover, because of the unprocessed deposits of crude limestone and chalk vegetation abounded freely.

Steel corrugated oval-shaped Nisson huts constituted all living quarters. Although new to us at the moment this type of quarters had long established its' identity in most United States Army camps throughout all of England. Especially prevalent at airbases they were also utilized in field hospital areas and practically every base located outside of metropolitan boundaries. We occupied the extreme northeast corner of the camp and of the eleven huts assigned the company an average of twenty men were allotted each; perhaps a little less to some huts or a little more to others. Four of these housed the company headquarters and Orderly Room, vehicle parts supply, company and motor pool office . . . and one alone was shared by the company's seven officers.

During this two-month occupation many different units would be quartered here . . . some permanent, some transient; but the largest single group during this particular period was the 7TH MECHANIZED CAVALRY REGIMENT, a highly trained and highly active unit that would distinguish itself on the continent in later months.

Five and a half feet deep, surrounding each dwelling (excepting the front and rear exits) a trench remarkably paralleling the type utilized by American doughboys in World War I represented primary protection against possible enemy air action that at this stage was not ruled out. Operating less than three miles due east across the plains from our quarters a military airfield maintained cooperatively by the U. S. 9TH AIR FORCE and British Royal Air Force Command serviced with brisk regularity warplanes of both Commands. Constantly taking off and returning when completing respective missions over enemy targets on the German-occupied continent the drone of light and medium fighter-bombers during all hours of the night was taken in stride. With frequent Luftwaffe retaliatory raids against the many military installations in the Southern Base Command region, this airfield no exception; it was always reasoned that a chance attack on Lopcombe could be within the realm of a possibility . . . though to date nothing like that had happened. To us it was the Luftwaffe, though the British had long ago named them "Jerry."

Although spared any direct attack we did with considerable frequency spring from our bunks at night, rush outside and watch in wonder an unfortunate "Jerry" aircraft inextricably entangled in the giant web of Allied searchlights. With dynamic consistency their destruction was administered by ground-based anti-aircraft fire and in some areas by Allied interceptor night fighters.

Camp activities was in no-wise on a par with the multi-freedom of Blagdon. If one could in his mind, compare ice cream to medicine or a massive riot to a Sunday School picnic the resemblance between Blagdon and this camp would be that far removed. In spite of a post theater, a recreation room and assorted sports equipment to be put in action the nonchalant "free wheeling", the general mixing with townspeople, the beauty of springtime in a lovely English village that had been ours daily would sorely be missed. With time running out it was highly unlikely that we would ever embrace again a similar experience. A strong concentration toward a new adjustment must be initiated ... and soon such an adjustment began to take shape!

This installation, centered almost evenly between the two nearest towns; Andover in County Hampshire to the east, only nine miles distant and reached by local bus in approximately twenty minutes; and in the opposite direction the larger and more favorable town of Salisbury, some ten miles west of the camp, reached in twenty to thirty minutes. Because of more widespread activities visitation to Salisbury far exceeded the other.

Its' dwellings perpetually fashioned in typical English antiquity this city of some 34,000 situated along the lazy-flowing River Avon into which empties three considerably smaller streams ... the Nadder, the Wylye and the Bourne, would represent a cameraman's paradise. One cannot forget the many friendly "pubs" both within the city and in the suburban areas. One cannot overlook the assorted articulate gift shops and the quaint setting and low lights of the eating houses; most fashionable among them ... The King's Arms Inn, Red Lion Hotel and the Victorian Restaurant ... each prominently styled in the Tudor design with furnishings vicariously reminiscent of the Queen Anne period. As an historical interest we were much impressed with the city's many meticulously preserved landmarks and well-cared-for structures; chief among them the active multi-steepled and imposing mammoth Salisbury cathedral. Completed back in the twelfth century this magnificent cathedral with its' main spire rising over four hundred feet represented the tallest in England.

Salisbury and Andover, the most prominent two cities in these two counties were not at all the only places visited. Those obtaining transportation, and this was freely furnished; wandered into many of the smaller communities and villages that made up Counties Wiltshire and Hampshire. Amesbury . . . Stockbridge . . . Barton Stacey . . . Wilton . . . Middle Wallop . . . Basingstoke . . . Shrewton . . . Romsey; all became familiar names. Prearranged trips carried many out to the ancient and mysterious Stonehenge on the Salisbury plains. Nor were passes restricted to the Wiltshire-Hampshire area as many reveled in the opportunity to visit some of southern England's more prominent cities. Who did not visit the great metropolis of London . . . and get caught up in the perpetual human "merry-go-round" of Piccadilly Circus? To strike a historical note many traveled to the industrious seaport of Southampton and the busy naval base and port of Portsmouth where commanding the attention of all visitors still was majestically berthed British Admiral Horatio Nelson's nineteenth century flagship . . . the "H.M.S. Victory."

Some fifteen miles to the southeast was a "must" on any tourist's agenda . . . Winchester. Famed for its' mighty cathedral and university this lovely city continues to be a prominent religious and educational center; and as history records, boasts not only of dating back to the days of the Anglo-Saxons; but under Alfred The Great, Canute and William The Conqueror was for a long time the capital of mediaeval England.

Lying west on the English Channel were celebrated seaside resorts of Bournemouth, Weymouth, Exmouth and Torquay . . . and pleasurable visits were made to each.

Though each trip rang with an air of enthusiasm, both as an historic interest and simply to have some place to go there still remained one spot that overshadowed them all. Blagdon! The number of trips made back to Blagdon; legal or otherwise, were not likely to be recorded. Piecemeal, by bus and train and by military vehicle some returned. Because a "little bit of home" dwelt within the village the desire to return became so insatiable and the unauthorized visits so numerous it gradually would mark the end of a "good thing." On more than one occasion a sort of "dodging game" was played as some of the men and officers took care to avoid being seen by the others in the community.

It soon would end indeed . . . for one morning at group formation during the first week in May the order came.

"Blagdon declared Off Limits for all personnel of the 126th. Ordnance (MM) Company"

> by order of Lieutenant Clyde L. Miller
> Commanding Officer

A circular posted on the bulletin board, which no one had excuse to escape further substantiated the order.

"Who wants to go to Salisbury?" was freely asked.

"Yes, who *does* want to go to Salisbury . . . or Andover for that matter? It ain't worth it!" a reply came from those that had frequently made the trip to both places. Too many nightly visits to Salisbury ceased to be amusing; it was exhaustive and actually grew to be something less than an ordeal to make the trip. Because Salisbury was not an overly large city it was obvious that the few spots of entertainment were no match for the tremendous ratio of soldiers visiting nightly. Consequently, whatever thrill there might have been was never fully enjoyed. Every "pub" and even the Red Cross service club was packed and jammed every night and the density of cigarette smoke dominated the atmosphere. Roaming the dark streets at night without any form of light no longer was fun. The Regal and The Odeon, both downtown leading cinemas were always unduly overcrowded and if the movie was slightly less than interesting those attending showed signs of gross restlessness. It was concluded then, that unless one had a specific place to go in any one of the towns, rather than accept the liberty of going and perhaps risk a possibility of missing transportation back to the installation most resigned themselves simply to spend an evening within the camp's immediate vicinity. Activities now confined basically to camp most were willing to settle down evenings and enjoy the radio, or "rigged" speaker, with which almost every hut soon boasted.

That after-hours passed with interest was without question for we welcomed whatever entertainment to come our way. The load was lightened too, by reading all material available. Scanning pages of assorted items from the armed forces newspaper, Stars and Stripes, whose contents though often smacking with a tinge of inaccuracy nevertheless kept interest on a high level. A morale boost came to every GI too, when receiving his copy of the popular Yank magazine that did in a lighter vein keep one informed of armed forces activities all over the globe. Cards remained a primary pastime and almost everyone got the opportunity to recall family anecdotes and exchange positive opinions as to how the war should be fought. The dice were tossed a time or two and rare was the person who did not religiously keep up with the Armed Forces Radio Network beamed in from London.

Camp confinement, notably evenings, became devoid of boredom when one could look forward to a hard-to-get snack. Hardly anyone at this time was not familiar with the appetizing English "fish and chips" combination, which by and large had no equal insofar as availability was measured. With camp location ten miles from nowhere, as it were; procurement became the primary problem. Two "pass trucks" were authorized to leave camp each evening; one for Salisbury and one, in the opposite direction, to Andover . . . transporting only those wishing to spend an evening in town. Because, however of the late hour scheduled return, appetites would have diminished and desires deflated. Only in emergencies would authorization be given for other vehicles to depart, and without a "trip ticket" no one could pass the sentry at the gate. A means therefore, had to be devised to fetch these refreshments.

"Borrowing" a jeep from the motor pool was a risky thing to do, particularly at night, but it had to be done, and almost each evening one or two men "volunteered" this compliment. A jeep *was* "borrowed" and the sentry *was* persuaded to "shut his eyes." Persuaded? How? When promised an order of this delectable potion, overlooking a "trip ticket" would by no means be the hardest thing in the world for any sentry to do, particularly in late evening when mouths could easily water, and especially in so isolated a place as Lopcombe's Camp!

In the beginning only two men were required to fulfill this task. Because however, of the growing quantity of orders a third man would be added. Salisbury was the point of acquisition and in that city two ventured inside a shop to place their order, often standing uneasily in line with nervous apprehension, while the other remained in the vehicle parked outside with motor running; and often because of a suspicious glance from a roving MP found it necessary to circle the block. For . . . caught in town or on the road without a "trip ticket" could mean trouble that nobody wanted! In the late days of May when restrictions were applicable to most everything this became part of a nightly program, and "fish and chips" orders soon escalated to near forty or fifty per evening. Further; as a note of supposed "secrecy," even some officers, keenly aware of these unauthorized trips . . . but pretending not to be; eventually submitted similar requests. After all, *they* got hungry too!

Training grew in intensity . . . to become keenly pronounced as the days passed and air of seriousness settled over the company. Morning calisthenics began early and became the first major routine of the day. Close order drill followed that made breakfast heartily welcome. Strenuous long hikes through the vast rolling countryside kept our bodies physically able and our minds sharp. That the men of the 126th were perhaps more physically fit during the latter days at Lopcombe than at any other time during their army careers could hardly be questioned.

Not only the 126th but all units on this tightly packed island were undergoing training of similar severity. One could visit the Ordnance Southern Base Section up at Tidworth some forty miles north and see an area thickly infested with heavy concentrations of armor, most in use by the "keyed up" 2ND and 3RD ARMORED DIVISIONS stationed in that vicinity. The many forests in southern England were teeming with paratroopers, highly seasoned infantry and the fearsome hard-hitting U. S. Rangers whose constant assimilated drilling would have them well-prepared for the "real thing" when it came. Returning from a parts depot near Newbury, some thirty miles northeast of Lopcombe, lanky and personable Sergeant Al Rapin from Saginaw, Michigan and assistant chief of the small arms section was quick to give his impressions:

"The woods around that town are just crawling with paratroopers . . . and boy! are they *ever* mean-looking bastards!

Heads shaved, *man* they've got machine guns, knives and everything else! They're ready! When the 'Krauts' tangle with them they're gonna' have problems!"

Field artillery and tank destroyer howitzer units constantly accelerated meaningful "dry run" tests, and strongly impressive was the strength and accuracy displayed by the airborne glider troops whose CG4 gliders towed by attached cables to C-47 cargo planes in the late days soared silently but fearlessly over this region several times. Fast appearing on the scene these gliders would represent the Western Allies' "one-two punch," that landing en masse behind enemy lines would gain an early surprise foothold advantage on the continent.

Now openly active and no longer "under wraps" no GI in the United Kingdom could believe anything less than the accelerated pressure now being applied would soon have to be put to reality! A continuous flow of troops and supplies arrived daily from the United States. All who were aware of the extensive concentrations of Allied troops in the British Isles, the innumerable caches of ammunition and explosives deposited all over southern and central England, the millions of tons of supplies and a tremendous amount of military equipment and weaponry already here had no recourse other than to know that another gigantic "front" somewhere on the European continent was inevitable! To date this "somewhere" continued to remain top secret! Discussions regarding a proposed "front" became widespread.

"Would it be up from the Mediterranean . . . against the coast of northern Italy?" That certainly would relieve the pressure on the Allied forces in the south and central areas of that torn country who to date had not even reached Rome.

"What about the Balkans? That looks like a logical invasion route," expressed one. "Coming in from the Adriatic or Ionian Sea say, into Greece, Yugoslavia or Albania . . . wouldn't we be highly welcomed by the people in that area?"

Someone answered; "Logical for attack, yes; but illogical from a supply back-up operation inasmuch as 1,000 dangerous sea miles lay between that area and the British Isles."

"Perhaps a thrust across the North Sea along the coast of Holland! How about that!"

One presented a thought that even Norway was vulnerable. One said a direct thrust on Germany itself may be in the works!

There were many thoughts until one of the more practical minded laid out a map and reasoned:

"Take a good look across the English Channel. What do you see? France! Hundreds of miles of coastline just waiting!" He continued; "Obvious, yes; but that just may be the point. Less than a hundred miles across at any point, and this island loaded to the gills with GIs? . . . Couldn't say exactly where, but, man . . . it's gotta be France, it can't be anywhere else!"

An attentive look at the map and it could not belie with its' natural geographical location of the two countries, these suggestions.

Further down on the Channel coast the ports were jammed with thousands of amphibious vehicles, and ponton and Bailey Bridge equipment were laid out row upon row. Concentrations of light and heavy artillery pieces, thousands of steel perforated landing mat sections, hundreds of ambulances . . . bright Red Cross markings conspicuously painted on each, thousands of huge coils of Signal Corps telephone wire, and many military items though camouflaged as best as could be done, were on immediate alert . . . ready to move at a given signal! At the Ordnance General Base Depots near Taunton and Hilsea and at Ashchurch . . . for miles, almost as far as the human eye could see stretched endless rows of tanks, armored vehicles, tank destroyers and half-tracks, amassed ready for distribution at a moment's notice. Further up at Cheltenham, the Allies' mightiest supply base in southern England; supplies for individual units were being drawn at a much more rapid rate than previously.

The 126th Ordnance in the first week of May was assigned, though unattached, to serve the veteran 9TH INFANTRY DIVISION, a much-decorated battle-tested participant of the North African-Sicilian campaigns.

First activated in 1919 the 9TH INFANTRY DIVISION has served as a regular army unit since that time. It was reactivated at Fort Bragg, North Carolina in the late summer of 1940. Experiencing short-lived commands of temporary commanding generals at this reservation in the DIVISION's build-up, its morale and efficiency can in large measure be credited to the dynamic and far-sighted leadership of then Maj. Gen. Jacob L. Devers, who at that time headed not only the DIVISION but was post commander of Fort Bragg as well. General Devers, later to wear four stars and command the SIXTH ARMY GROUP in Europe, expressed his recollections to the author years later:

> "During the early days at Fort Bragg we were only about 10,000 strong. Made up predominantly of recruits from New York and Tennessee it was amazing, despite the unusual contrasting backgrounds; that is to say, the city boys from New York knowing nothing about those from the hills of Tennessee, and vice-versa; to note the strong compatibility that grew in such a short time. All of us lived in tents out on the reservation grounds then; in fact we built all those roads out there, and though tempers flared from time to time, due to a great extent the oppressive heat; I never saw such garrison soldiery. Their cooperation and pride never faltered. Proud? Although I had this command for only a short period, I kept up with them throughout the war . . . and I was never more proud of any Division."

Scoring the initial landings in North Africa and serving throughout that entire campaign, engaging in the important battles of El Guettar, Casablanca and Oran, mopping up in Tunisia and invading and fighting all the way through Sicily, the DIVISION since July, 1942 had as its' commander, Maj. Gen. Manton S. Eddy. The Sicilian operation completed, the DIVISION was shipped to England. Its' forces scattered throughout the Hampshire and Wiltshire County areas, many in close proximity of Lopcombe's Camp, 9TH headquarters was deeply imbedded in the age-old town of Winchester.

The 9TH INFANTRY DIVISION consisted of three infantry regiments; the 39th, 47th, and 60th . . . four artillery battalions; the 26th, 34th, 60th and 84th. Also the 15th. Engineer Battalion, the 9th. Medical Battalion, 9th. Signal Company, 9th. Quartermaster Company, 9th. Reconnaissance Mechanized Cavalry,

709th. Ordnance Light Maintenance Company, plus a Military Police platoon, a DIVISION Band and an administrative Headquarters Company. Within Headquarters structure were four sections that handled all military functions of the DIVISION, designated; G-I (personnel), G-2 (intelligence), G-3 (plans and training), and G-4 (supply and transportation). These sections in actuality were its' eyes and ears.

The 746th Tank Battalion, 899th Tank Destroyer and the 376th Anti-Aircraft Automatic Weapons Battalions while not incorporated within the organic structure of the 9TH was attached to and supported this fighting machine during the entire European campaign.

A heavy personal blow was dealt Lieutenant Miller during the late days of May when he was transferred from command. We were going to miss the Lieutenant for he had been with us since Tennessee maneuvers. Though some may have thought him to be a little aloof at times he really wasn't. He could be an extremely interesting person and always had the company at heart, seemingly wanting to be on the same level as the enlisted men and at the same time remain an officer. Because of the thin line separating this status it could not easily be done.

In front of the CP during his last moments of command he addressed the Ist. Sergeant;

"Sergeant Botting, you've been with these boys a long time . . . since the beginning." The words didn't come easy. "I love this company so you be sure to take good care of it."

A driver awaiting, he climbed into his jeep . . . and eyes fast welling with tears he exchanged salutes with his attentive staff and drove away. Subsequently appointed Commanding officer of the 974th. Ordnance Evacuation Company he was promoted to Captain shortly after his new company's departure from England.

Ist. Lt. Alfred Orsenigo, a tall balding mustachioed easy-going soldier of Italian extraction from Mt. Vernon, New York moved in as Commanding Officer. Lately of the 6th. Ordnance Battalion and appearing a little older than his thirty-six years he would bring with him ample administrative experience and competent leadership.

Ist. Lt. Jack D. Palmer, a twenty-nine year old husky adventurer in his own right from Pasadena, California . . . usually sporting a well-worn cigar stub, and whose insistence of wearing his helmet at a conspicuously cocked angle soon bore him an individualist trademark; and Ist. Lt. John Wallace, a rancher turned mechanic from Idaho, replaced Ist. Lts. William Nye and Daniel Oxman.

All necessary invasion equipment and rations drawn and having turned in all excess or superflous clothing, along with unnecessary personal items, the last week in May and first of June found the 126th. in feverish preparation of camouflage nets, industriously applying waterproofing compound and painting and repairing all vehicles. Careful attention was applied to testing and cleaning all pieces of artillery and each weapon. There could be no doubt of it now; the long awaited "invasion fever" was in the air and the "real thing" could come any day! We knew it and the Germans knew it as brought out in nightly propaganda programs so amusingly broadcast by "Axis Sally" and "Midge" . . . the self-styled "GI Sweetheart," whose programs that included latest American song hits were beamed through the BBC by shortwave from Germany . . .coming through to us at several intervals.

One of the most popular ballads of enemy and Allied forces alike during this period had long been introduced by these two professionals. "Lili Marlene," a German composition written to elevate morale of German troops was first brought to fore during the North African campaign but its' melancholic phrases and catchy tune became so pleasing that it made a big hit with American and British troops . . . to make a lasting impression.

The first week in June was rapidly drawing to a close and now the overall picture was coming in focus for all to see! In actuality the "great stage" was set; all rehearsals were complete; the stage hands had everything in readiness and the entire show was awaiting "the opening word" from the director for the "curtain" to rise! That director was General Dwight D. Eisenhower, Supreme Commander-Allied Forces in Europe. The hours fast diminishing, the minutes were clicking by . . . and now it was only a question of when!!

It was a warm Monday evening . . . June 5th, and with midnight hastily approaching most everyone with exception of those patrolling the camp were turned in for the night. Only minutes after midnight an increasing drone of planes began gradually to unfold from the north and as the minutes ticked off the roar mounted to almost deafening proportions and tiny blinking lights were spread all across the English sky. Reasoning this great flight to be one of unusual dimensions one of the guards, short stocky Jim Locke, began to tremble excitedly and moments later in anxiety burst into the hut where most of headquarters and some supply personnel were sleeping, shouting:

"Hey, you guys! Come out here! Come out here quick!"

By this time the drone had reached its full power and practically every one was fully aroused to find themselves outside gazing in great wonder at the nonending stream of planes streaking steadfast in the direction of the English Channel.

"Hot dog! . . . man, just look at that!" said one.

"Boy! We're gonna' get their tails now!" joined another.

"Fantastic!" exclaimed one, and summoning his imagination when noting the hundreds of tiny lights flickering under the wings; "Looks like a million stars blinking up there!"

Speculation circulated as to their destination. It was only normal to reason it to be just another bomber formation directed for Germany or some other strategic target. Some opinioned that perhaps this was one of those frequent night plane maneuvers. Some expressed no impression at all. With wave after wave of the powerful armada roaring over for almost two hours there could be little doubt now that *this was it!!*

From nine military airbases in England 822 transport planes had become airborne before midnight to strike out in the same ultimate direction . . . France! The invasion of the continent of Europe was now in progress . . . for in the hundreds of gliders towed by those very planes were some 17,000 airborne troops . . . poised and eager . . . to parachute, drop and land in the blackness and uncertainty of an unfamiliar territory called Normandy . . . the northernmost sector of Nazi-occupied France! This was what the enemy had *long* feared and the free world had *long* awaited. This was the prelude to "D-DAY!!"

VI

INVASION!!

A cloudy dawn of Tuesday, June 6 found a portion of the English Channel whose waters, contained in an inverted arc of receding shoreline . . . forming the Bay of Seine, the focal point of the eyes of all the world along a coastline of some fifty miles. The long-planned and unquestionably most powerfully conceived amphibious invasion the world had ever known was now under way!! Eagerly and almost passionately awaited by most military planners and dubiously opposed by others! This was "D–DAY!!!"

An early edition of the Norfolk Virginian Pilot on the same morning streamed bold headlines:

"INVASION IS UNDER WAY!
Americans, British and Canadians Pour Into France With Eisenhower Directing!"

In a one-sentence communique from Supreme Headquarters,

Allied Expeditionary Forces came an early announcement:

"Under the command of General Eisenhower, Allied naval forces supported by strong air forces began landing Allied armies this morning on the northern coast of France."

From several highly active ports in southern England and moving in a pattern stretching wide for twenty miles steamed an Allied flotilla comprising some 4,000 ships and smaller boats in support of this mammoth assault that included an assortment of landing and supply boats and warships. Within the few miles radius of specifically assigned invasion routes the larger vessels . . . battleships, cruisers and destroyers strategically spaced were already in action as salvo after salvo roared from gun mounts on decks directed to the now alert and well-concealed enemy on shore! American and British destroyers maneuvered in and out of positions and with savage violence exchanged barrages with German shore batteries . . . each seeking the other's vulnerable spot! The 14-inch guns of the battleships U.S.S. "Nevada," the "Arkansas," and "Texas" and 16-inch guns of the British battlewagons H.M.S. "Warspite," "Ramillies" and "Nelson" backed by Allied naval power to include the American cruisers U.S.S. "Augusta," "Tuscaloosa" and "Quincy" thundering with 8-inch guns boomed their authority in a determined effort to silence the highly-aroused positions of the Wermacht's mighty shore batteries deployed within the confines of two strategic beaches!

LST's, LCT's, LCI's, LCVP's and the many amphibious landing craft transporting men and equipment through windblown choppy waters of the Bay of The Seine moved in ever closer to shore, and with the breaking of early morning . . . grey and dim though it was, became subsequent targets for murderous fire coming from now highly alarmed defenses. Their surprise now diminished the Germans had brought up deadly 75's, 105's and 88-milimeter guns and other high-velocity weapons and quickly positioned them in and around the rocky cliffs and grounds beyond the shore. The air sang with streams of shells and flak, and explosions and confusion reverberated throughout the attack basin! Not infrequently a craft was hit and shattered . . . blowing many into the water or spilling them out from all angles. An impenetrable smokescreen laid down by support planes gave brief protection to landing craft, but many before reaching shallow landing areas were hit and a number of GIs weighted down with heavy packs, ammunition, guns, radios and precious equipment were doomed to drown in thrashing waters before any effective rescue teams could be thrown into use!

Salvo after salvo of self-propelled rockets fired into positions! With savage authority anti-aircraft guns from assorted naval ships, gun crews tense and daring expelled bristling torrid streams of missiles into the cliffs, and when an almost non-existent enemy aircraft appeared a heavy barrage of swift multi-colored tracer shells literally lit the greying dawn! Had more planes appeared their effectiveness would hardly be likely against the circling ships to which was attached great barrage balloons, forming a tremendous "umbrella" protection. In the course of events some lighter craft received direct hits or struck concealed underwater mines and some settled fast to the bottom, carrying with it many of the crew.

Zebra-like broad black and white stripes painted under the wings of all American planes easily distinguished them from the enemy and they were flown only during daylight.

Commanding all German operations were Feldmarschal Karl Gerd von Rundstedt, Commander-in-Chief OB West, which included all troops in France, Belgium and the Netherlands. von Rundstedt reported directly to Generalfedlmarshal Wilhelm Keitel, Chief of Staff of all German Army (Wermacht) ground troops. Feldmarshal Erwin Rommel, the famed "Desert Fox" commanded Army Group B (7th and 15th Armies and 138th Corps) and reported to OB West (theoretically von Rundstedt).

The German 7th Army for months had been accentuating field maneuvers in this northern neck of France and had long sensed an Allied invasion somewhere along the coast of that country. Despite months of short-wave monitoring, radar searching, code deciphering, logistics, spying and even second-guessing the exact location of this probable invasion thrust . . . and when . . . obviously was insufficiently determined by them! And yet, as a precautionary measure great concentrations of heavy artillery and shore batteries were prepared near the most vulnerable landing areas susceptible to any seaborne invader . . . stretching from the northernmost section of Holland for some five hundred miles along the English Channel over the northern tip of Normandy all the way down to Brest on the Brittany peninsular facing the Atlantic Ocean.

It was reasonable to assume, and history would bear it out that enemy logic concluded Normandy to be especially sensitive to Allied attack. As a consequence this entire territory was saturated with obstacles of pernicious destruction that included underwater mines, reinforced barbed wire, hundreds of trip land mines, underwater tank traps made up of crisscrossed steel girders, teller mines planted in abundance on the beaches, and assorted deviously arranged similar obstructures that would prove extremely costly should any invader make the attempt. Machine guns and mortar fire and heavier shore guns "pinpointed" on these uncleared obstacle-laden areas would produce sudden death for many of the infantry storming ashore in the first attacking waves.

One of this operation's most serious prime factors with which to be reckoned was the element of weather; a vexing problem that meterologists had studied, evaluated and pondered for nerve-wracking weeks. Because local knowledge and all weather reports deemed it the most advantageous period the first week in June was viewed as a most desired time to strike. This channel coast down through the years claimed a notoriety of transposing a calm atmosphere almost suddenly and with less than adequate warning into a raging storm. On the eve of the selected sailing date *that is exactly* what took place; a storm with such rising velocity that the original release required a strong re-evaluation!

June 5th was picked for the invasion but the storm's mounting force during the approaching hours . . . one of the most severe in recent years, much consultation was sought and many moments of agonizing deliberation was shared by General Eisenhower and his staff . . . for they now were faced with the crucial decision of unleashing this mighty machine early morning of the 5th and face the questionable consequences . . . or gamble that the weather would several hours hence be more permissive.

SHAEF headquarters at Portsmouth, England was a brisk scene of much soul-searching! With expert and almost feverish thoroughness opinions were exchanged, maps were scanned over and over again, weather estimates revised and although professional evaluation was asserted by each subordinate; history would subsequently reveal that this ultimate and monumental decision rested entirely on the shoulders of the Supreme Commander, Allied Expeditionary Forces. Brevity of time made the decision imperative. It was reached and confirmed . . . and the invasion was rescheduled for the following morning . . . Tuesday, June 6!

Years later commenting with the author at Valley Forge, Pennsylvania, General Eisenhower recalled:

"We weren't as openly excited as one would think, though inwardly nerves were jingling a little; and although everyone moved at a faster pace an unusual business-like atmosphere existed. I kept wishing for time. Time to do this, time to do that . . . just time! But we knew there was no more time available. What we were to do we *had* to do now!"

"I kept telling myself, 'If we could only halt that storm for just 12 hours!" Concluding with a slight grin of nostalgia, he remembered:

"You were the boys that we had to depend on, and I recall thinking momentarily about how nice it would be out there with you fellows!"

Though somewhat tempered at the time of scheduled release the storm was still in progress and could yet conceivably imperil the success of this great task. There was imminent danger of prolonged hesitation for *indeed* too much was at stake already, and of paramount importance a mounting security risk became too great a threat to wait another day!

The tides along the Normandy coast was another important feature given careful advance consideration. So treacherous are these waters in the central sector of the proposed landing areas that in the very early morning in a one-hour period the tide rises an estimated eight feet to cover virtually the entire beach. Without careful planning such an almost untenable disadvantage could well-bring disaster to the entire operation. This is where the northern coast of France paralleling the Bay of Seine and the English Channel suddenly forms a sort of arc and the coast line swings straight out for about sixty miles into the Channel forming the east coast of the Cotentin peninsular. As a consequence the normal flow of tides is violently interrupted and reverberations are felt all along the peninsular shoreline.

Everything was planned to the minute . . . each individual relegated his specific responsibility. Yet, in spite of the many preparatory rehearsals, voluminous hours of intense briefing and long-range technical planning, preliminary operations did not by any means go according to carefully detailed schedules.

Under direction of the combined American-British 21ST ARMY GROUP commanded by General Sir Bernard L. Montgomery, who, wearing "two hats" also maintained responsibility as deputy invasion commander, the entire invasion planning; code named "OPERATION OVERLORD," called for five synchronized Allied landings to be made simultaneously on the northern coast of France . . . stretching some fifty miles from the Cotentin peninsular *east* to just beyond the Orne River. "OPERATION NEPTUNE" represented the code name for the actual assault landings.

Lt. Gen. Omar Nelson Bradley's United States FIRST ARMY, answering to the code name of "Master," comprised of the VII and V CORPS, struck at beaches in the American sector. Near the once-undisturbed villages of St. Martin de Varreville and St. Germain de-Varreville on the central coast of the peninsular, Maj. Gen. Raymond O. Barton's 4TH INFANTRY DIVISION under jurisdiction of VII CORPS made the initial landings on "Utah Beach." Under V CORPS supervision some eighteen miles further southeast . . . Maj. Gen. Clarence R. Huebner's veteran IST INFANTRY DIVISION backed up by the 29th INFANTRY DIVISION, commanded by Maj. Gen. Charles Gerhardt, along with attached highly-trained combat teams, among them elements of the 2ND and 5TH RANGERS; struck furiously against rugged "Omaha Beach" near Vierville-sur-Mer and St. Laurent-sur-Mer. Once ashore 29TH DIVISION's ultimate task was to turn west and link up with VII CORPS while IST DIVISION swings in the opposite direction to eventually link up with British troops landing further east.

Lt. Gen. Miles Dempsey's British 2ND ARMY was given assignment to attack simultaneously three beaches still farther east of the American sector. The all-British 50TH DIVISION of XXX CORPS thundered ashore at "Gold Beach" near the channel town of Arromanches. The Canadian 3RD DIVISION and the English 3RD DIVISION both under direction of IST CORPS, struck in strength at "Juno" and "Sword" beaches, respectively. In the darkness hours before, the British 6TH AIRBORNE DIVISION had jumped inland within the vicinity of the Orne River estuary near Caen.

Success or failure of the "Omaha Beach" operation was the responsibility of V CORPS. In England since the summer of 1942 it had earned a reputation of being the oldest U. S. tactical force in that country. Commanded by Maj. Gen. Leonard T. Gerow, a former commander of the 29TH DIVISION, having accompanied it to England in October, 1942; was himself experiencing his first assault command. "Omaha" proved to be the more rugged of the landings what with steep precipitious cliffs overlooking the Bay of The Seine confronting the assault troops immediately ashore. German gunners maneuvering among these jutting cliffs tenaciously employed a brutal stream of death down on the half-foundering, half-bewildered American attackers. Still the GI's roared on! In the meantime Navy DUKWs' shuttled back and forth with uneasy stubborness discharging heavy quantitites of supplies and equipment. Considerable cargo, due to quick disbursement was gobbled up in the violent surf; but still the greatest quantity was getting ashore . . . sufficient enough to get this operation going! Not too many minutes could elapse from this timetable! It must get moving . . . and *moving* it did!

Fifty-six-year old Maj. Gen. Clarence R. Huebner, an aggressive disciplinarian and long-time soldier who began his military career as a private, now commanded not only the IST INFANTRY DIVISION but the entire beach assault. He recalled:

"I was ordered to take "Omaha" and we set about doing just that. I knew we had the boys that could do it too. We were at first getting a lot more fire than had been anticipated and couldn't understand it. Later, we learned the Germans had an additional Division that was not supposed to be there and we had not counted on it. Once, when the fighting grew intense one of my subordinates . . . in exasperation, came to me and said: 'General, we're losing a lot of stuff out there; those 88's are killing us! I don't know if we're going to get up there or not!' I told him we had orders to take "Omaha" and that's what we're going to do!"

"Not until we captured Caumont a few days later," said he, "could we really be sure of success. When the Germans lost that town some 20 miles straight in from the beach it hurt them badly and caused them to disperse deeper inland. It was a strategic road junction and was served by a railroad to bring in supplies. Had we not taken it when we did, we could have been cut off and probably it would have been hell to pay!"

Troops seeking refuge from murderous enemy fire in nature-eroded rocky coves and gaps became quickly organized and in the face of direct enemy fire mortar-propelled grappling hooks were fired upwards to catapult scaling ropes over the cliffs. Newly-devised steel extension ladders were quickly pressed into use and the highly-trained Rangers began the ardous labor of scaling the cliffs. Entrances to the interior of Normandy were hastily blown into the rocky cliffs by combat engineer demolition forces. Still under heavy fire, grinding bulldozers with steel bullet-shield guards erected to protect the operator began the tenacious burden of removing heavy rock and grading of useable roads and passageways. Mine experts and bomb disposal squads resumed the suicidal task of locating and destroying the many explosive mines planted and concealed in and about the beachhead complex. Signal Corps experts labored feverishly establishing temporary communications between ship and shore while infantry combat teams groped throughout established positions, silencing vicious enemy gunfire still threatening and harrassing the beach. All of this under withering fire!

The full flower of daylight found frustrated Germans still employing heavy firepower, but giving ground . . . and in the

"Omaha Beach" sector the beach villages of Vierville-sur-Mer, St. Laurent-sur-Mer and the larger coast town of Colleville-sur-Mer soon were in Allied hands.

Against a stubborn enemy on "Gold," "Juno," and "Sword" beachheads British and Canadian troops were having their hands immeasurably full! While initial landings were successful enough the Germans were unleashing such a perpetual counter-fire from the hills that only pure grit and determination of United Kingdom forces enabled them to maintain the precarious foothold that they had so laboriously won.

In the American landing zone further northwest on the peninsular troops of the United States VII CORPS while faring far better, were nevertheless finding "Utah Beach" no easy task to dismiss! Commanded since February by 48-year old Maj. Gen. J. Lawton Collins, an aggressive well-seasoned veteran of the Solomon Islands, VII CORPS after much map consultation already knew that unlike "Omaha", "Utah" possessed a terrain more suitable for landing forces, in that there were no rocky cliffs to encounter, few non-detectable gun emplacement positions and no real natural fortifications. These assets would produce far fewer casualties. A reinforced concrete sea wall approximately three feet thick built steadfastly into natural sand dunes partly covered with grass, constructed primarily to keep high tides from inundating this low region and stretching for miles along the beach did afford the enemy some protection. Further; with acres and acres of dense marshes and bog that lay between the beaches and solid terrain of the interior . . . far less than a mile inland, the Germans could employ no favorable escape routes from the beach.

Despite heavy pre-invasion bombing from Allied planes . . . Marauders . . . Mitchells . . . Flying Fortresses . . . Liberators . . . Havocs, all devastatingly saturating the proposed inland invasion routes prior to the airborne landings, the beaches were still well-fortified; and though the Allied attack from the sea struck with resounding fury our invading forces suffered voluminous losses.

Now while this seaborne invasion was progressing at top speed it must in the meantime be remembered that some five hours prior to this great thrust Allied airborne troops had already swooped in in gliders and were in spotty combat with the enemy! In the early hours prior to the glider attack thousands of paratroopers were dropped to set up markers and establish drop zones for closer coordination that would better facilitate landings of the incoming gliders. These were the "pathfinders" and thousands of American lives depended on their success. Maj. Gen. Maxwell Taylor's 101ST AIRBORNE DIVISION had parachuted into areas north of Carentan just behind the approaches of "Utah Beach," chief purpose to seize bridgeheads over the marshes that separated the beaches from the interior and to prevent closing of the beach exits thereby allowing the seaborne forces access to the interior. Further; they were to disrupt all communications utilized between the enemy beach defenders and troops to the rear. At the same time part of this force was to move south of Carentan for an eventual link-up with American forces breaking out of "Omaha Beach."

General Taylor years later would command the EIGHTH U. S. ARMY in Korea, and even later would distinguish himself as Chairman of the Joint Chiefs of Staff; recalled the pre-dawn flight:

> "When we left the airfield in England it seemed no time before we were out over the Channel. Though it was dark the Channel looked brightly spread below us and even at 10 to 12,000 feet the water's turbulence could be detected although to us it appeared to be little more than small ripples. Moving over the French coastline we ran into a few clouds and it began to get bumpy. Moving in closer enemy flak started exploding around us. My thoughts then were just like all the rest of the men, and that was to get out of that plane and get on the ground!"

Maj. Gen. (General) Matthew B. Ridgway's 82ND AIRBORNE DIVISION had descended west and around St. Mere Eglise and even farther inland astride the vital Merderet River in an effort to seize and control the important crossroads in that area and guard against a counterattack from enemy forces in the northwest. This accomplished it would greatly facilitate the advance of oncoming landing forces. Fleeting hours of dogged desperate fighting raged between American paratroopers and the enemy; casualties reaching alarming figures and extremely so with the airborne troops. Suffering from thirty to fifty percent casualties both killed and wounded and losing almost sixty percent of equipment, many small companies were gravely affected! The *so* unfortunate troops in many of the invading gliders never got a chance to feel ground under their feet . . . for most of these gliders, brought in by fliers of the IX U. S. AAF Troop Carrier Command and having been detached from towing connections of the DC-3 cargo planes were on their own to land blindly in the darkness. As a consequence many of these lightly constructed gliders dashed to pieces against trees, hedgerow embankments and hilly terrain . . . fatally trapping numerous troops ensnared therein.

General Ridgway easily recalls:

"One of the most vivid aspects in my memory regarding this operation was the constant humming of the aircraft while soaring out over the English Channel. The unusual brightness of the channel waters thousands of feet below suddenly disappeared once the French mainland appeared; then it became dark . . . very dark. The aircraft began its descent and in a moment or two, enemy "ack ack" batteries were in action. We could see the small bright puffs of fire down there throwing projectiles at us. We came in so low that at times the fog obscured the wing tips and then I *really* became alarmed that we might be too low for an effective jump! The green light came on and out we went! It was rough . . . and I mean rough, but it was *damn* good to be on the ground again!"

Deputy commander of the 82ND AIRBORNE, 36-year-old Brig. Gen. James M. Gavin, who in August would be placed in command of the DIVISION . . . to become the youngest DIVISION commander in the Theater, (He would be promoted to Lt. Gen. by the war's end. Moreover, he was appointed many many years later in 1961 U. S. Ambassador to France) recalled moments of anxiety prior to jumping:

"It was quite different from Sicily and Salerno for when we jumped considerable opposition arose but nothing in comparison. Over Normandy the air was thick with flak, some of it splitting through the sides of the aircraft. You could see the small orange flashes of anti-aircraft guns thousands of feet below and in no time the air was cracking with flak! We wanted to get out of the craft and get down there quick as we could! *Afraid*? . . . no, you couldn't say that we were afraid . . . in the general sense, because we were highly trained and had been through this before. Tense, anxious, unquestionably; but every trooper knows the danger of his mission and rarely is the trooper who is not ready."

The morning rolled on and as day began to break on Normandy's beaches most obstacles having confronted the Allies had been cleared to the extent that an increased percentage of supplies were being landed with greater expediency and less loss. Tented aid stations were hastily set up, feverishly employing all available medics to care for the wounded. More tanks and artillery sloughed through the roaring surf to join the infantry pushing inland! The frantic German fight to retain positions and reverse this assault had been hard and relentless but efforts were appearing vain, and by the time complete daylight cloaked the Normandy area some 125,000 American, British and Canadian air and seaborne troops, supported by special French and Polish forces had set foot on the continent of Europe! But . . . "D-Day" in the American sector had cost upwards of 5,000 casualties; killed, wounded and missing.

Despite adversities; some anticipated, others never dreamed of... General Bradley's highly competent FIRST ARMY had achieved a successful landing on the supposedly impenetrable fortress of Europe! Lt. Gen. Dempsey's British 2ND ARMY had a strong toehold as well! The Germans were now cognizant of the fact that they no longer could throw the Allies back into the sea . . . Hitler's mythical "Westwall" . . . his "Festung Europa," had been cracked wide open and a sea of American, British and Canadian fighting men were pouring in!

"What would have happened had the assault on "Omaha Beach" faltered? the author asked General Bradley many years later. "What if the Germans had been successful in throwing the assault back into the sea?"

With emphatic sincerity the General replied:

"There was never any doubt in my mind that the invasion would not succeed. We knew of course that "Omaha" would be the toughest. But if, however, the operation at that point appeared to go badly and we stood in jeopardy of losing the beachhead we had an alternate plan to withdraw and move the entire assault to "Utah" . . . and could have done so under cover of the mighty Naval guns off shore."

He again implied:

"But still again, we were unanimous in our conviction that this was not going to happen."

***

Back in England the next couple days were consumed in preparation of our inevitable shipment and all equipment was given a thorough "going over."

Three men, hospitalized for several weeks stood the danger of missing the evacuation. T/4 Wilbur McClymont was part of the kitchen personnel but because of a severe leg injury had been in the hospital for a month. Ray Setter, an industrious T/4 from Automotive was convalescing slowly from a recent appendix operation. Lester Howlett, a dark-eyed slight of build Pfc. whose quiet unobtrusive manner made him inconspicuous except at assemblies remained in a bad way following a freak mishap near Cheltenham, a jeep accident in which S/Sgt. John Morris and Pfc. Art Fealk also were involved . . . the latter two coming through unscathed.

Earlier apprised of the company's four-man understrength, Lieutenant Orsenigo, now settled in his new capacity as C.O., questioned Botting:

"What about it Sergeant; can we get two of these men? I understand we've just received two men from the replacement depot and I'd rather not go there again if we can help it."

One of the newer officers, feeling that time would not permit, interjected his thoughts and suggested that those hospitalized remain and proceed with acquisition of new replacements.

"You don't know those men in the hospital, do you Lieutenant?" came a quick retort from Botting. "Well, take it from me, they're valuable to us and they started with this company and I'm sure they wouldn't appreciate your thoughts."

Without waiting for a reply that he felt was sure to come, he turned to the new C.O.:

"If you say so, there'll be no new replacements if we can help it. The two new radiomen, Border (Norman) and Gerstner (Ed) will stay and they'll be an asset. Howlett, I'm afraid is out of the question and last reports indicate Setter is not ready. McClymont is way up north somewhere and has been for a long time." He added with an air of confidence:

"With your permission, we'll get him anyway."

Dispatched to a military hospital at Whitechurch in County Shropshire at a location approximately 40 miles south of Liverpool and almost 200 miles north of our camp a driver and an aide carried implicit orders:

"Don't come back unless you bring McClymont with you!"

Now it was Saturday morning, June 10. Each was packed and ready and a little after nine o'clock we rolled out of Lopcombe's Camp. Light rain began to fall and clusters of fog fast began hampering visibility over the broad plains. Ten miles west across the plains we moved into Salisbury and from here a southwestern course was mapped. Twenty-two miles beyond Salisbury the smaller city of Blandford was entered. One hour later after executing several stops along extremely narrow roads the busy and well-camouflaged marshalling area just beyond, though still within sight of Dorchester in County Dorset was found. However brief the entire distance . . . only 45 miles, some two and a half hours from point of origin to destination was required!

We were placed under six-hour alert almost immediately but in less than an hour the status changed and it became "immediate alert." Joviality existed while the entire day of the 11th passed on. Early afternoon of the 12th the C. O. was advised:

"The 126th Ordnance will proceed in three sections and will reassemble at a specified point upon arrival destination."

All Recovery section personnel proceeded with evacuation preparations . . . after receiving confirmed sectional forwarding instructions. Packing in a hurry they underwent a thorough inspection and as a tightly-knit group . . . quickly moved out.

"We're off! So long you guys!" Someone shouted confidently, "See you on the other side!"

"Man!", we thought, "*how* we would like to be moving out with you!" Everyone originally assumed without question that this *really would* be the case, but latest evacuation instructions would prohibit.

"Boy, that sounds strange!" commented one; "On the other side?"

"Good Lord!" thought another, "Can this be true already?"

But of course it was true . . . and as one thought about it the realization became sobering, though in reality *we knew* we could not have been more ready.

Remainder of the day saw all vehicles and weapons again checked and reviewed by a camp equipment inspector . . . with particular emphasis placed on sound waterproofing of *all* equipment.

The major was not a big man but he had a booming resonant voice, almost as if he were using a megaphone. He was the chief inspector and because his voice was one of strong vibrance and clear one's attention was not easily diverted when he was around.

"I don't give a damn what else you do, but by *all means* keep those points and plugs dry!" he emphasized; "Otherwise you've had it!" Continuing, he added: "You'll be no better and no worse than your waterproofing application. But don't let it frighten you, because it *can* happen . . . several vehicles have already been pulled out of the surf just for that very reason. Some have just had to be abandoned for awhile."

Vitally important was this waterproofing compound in that it covered and kept dry all essential parts of a motor vehicle while in operation. Though effective for only a brief period there was no better substitute in the event of vehicle immersion and odds gave smaller vehicles a fifty-percent chance of becoming no less than half-immersed. It served further as a rust preventive for the heavier weapons that may become soaked when rolling from ship to shore. Should this element be improperly administered a vehicle stood in jeopardy of stalling before reaching shore and under these and other unforeseen circumstances might well end in disaster for both vehicle and driver and imperil those following.

This same night of the 12th the rest of the company were sleeping . . . or in some fashion trying to . . . and by the time midnight rolled around a summons to organize and prepare to evacuate was served. *Here it was! Immediate alert!*"

Facetious as it would appear . . . and though at the time it was no laughing matter, someone suggested that perhaps FIRST ARMY was "fattening us up for the kill" . . . for here was enjoyed far and away the most nutritious and palatable food since the days of the United States some four months previous; surpassing even, that in Camp Kilmer. Everyone was given the privilege of eating all he wanted, an option that was well-challenged. The big mustachioed mess-sergeant allowed with a grin:

"Eat heartily boys, 'cause you won't see none of this for a long time!"

"Some morale booster that character is," commented one.

To be able to eat heartily, however . . . and enjoy it, was an attractive thought, probably not likely to be forgotten and at the time appeared worth the unlimited "hustle and bustle" of this highly active marshalling area.

Amidst continuous clanking and creaking of heavy tanks and weaponry and crawling war machines the balance of the 126th crept out in the very black of night, employing no detectable vehicle lights whatsoever and in snail-like fashion convoyed fifteen miles down to the beach area of the once-peaceful summer resort of Weymouth on the English Channel. Under a large open canvas tent . . . its' roof noisely and strongly buffeted by unruly winds blowing in from the channel, the Red Cross canteen service had in haste, prepared a final steak dinner on the beach's damp almost obscure sands. Extremely dark, so impenetrable in fact that even from a brief distance the faces of those serving were not fully recognizable. The crashing of the breakers against the surf, and sharp winds whipping across the sands did little to help the setting . . . for already cold, digestion of the steak was not easy.

Tuesday morning of June 13 was no more than two hours old when we began steering vehicles for proper placement into the ship. Because vehicles of a necessity had to be backed up the ramp into the LST, considerable time was consumed in shackling and shifting them on top deck and below. We would learn, *long* before reaching the other side the tremendous value derived from this chaining and shackling. By 6:30, yet before daylight, the job was completed. Another hour and a half and it was close to eight o'clock, and departure orders had not yet been dispatched. Suddenly and abruptly the ship's sirens screamed an impromptu alert! For a moment a disquieted feeling hung over the area.

"For God's sake . . . what is this?" thought an already anxious Botting.

"What is happening?" said Jim Black, the young Lieutenant who with misgivings thought we should have left long ago. Catching his breath, he thought; "What are we supposed to do? Do we run? Do we hide? Do we jump in the water? Just what in the hell *do we do?*"

He remembers answering his own question in a split second.

"You don't do a *damn thing*, Jim, 'cause there ain't a damn thing *you can do!*" His fears were disquieted.

We waited . . . but nothing happened. What was going on? Necks craned upward scanning the skies for signs of danger. Anti-aircraft gun crews in readiness, jumped to their posts . . . waiting. In a short time an authoritative voice came over the loudspeaker:

"Back to your posts. Continue with loading procedures!"

The alarm was of no consequence. What *did* happen? No one offered a clear explanation. Did some crewman press the button accidently, or did some GI hit it out of curiosity? Normally used as a distress signal or warning of approaching enemy aircraft it did, however briefly; throw a sober feeling of almost frantic helplessness into many . . . and in short; literally "scared the 'pure devil' out of everyone!"

Mid-morning of the 13th was partially shrouded in fog as the LST motors started their powerful throb. The craft shuddered briefly and began to glide from the harbor, and almost before anyone was aware a good bit of water separated the ship from shore. So here . . . standing on deck and watching the green hills and shore of England disappear in the slowly lifting mist, illusions of the many good times and old friends left behind in that brave and proud kingdom dominated our vision . . . and like thousands of others we could scarcely believe it as we wondered what was waiting for us on the other side. A form of solidarity seemed to move among the men as General Eisenhower's brief "D-Day" message continued to ring in our ears:

" . . . Soldiers, sailors and airmen of the Allied Expeditionary Forces:

"You are about to embark upon the great crusade toward which we have strived these many months. The eyes of the world are upon you. The hopes and prayers of liberty-loving peoples everywhere march with you.

"You will bring about the destruction of the German war machine, the elimination of Nazi tyranny over the oppressed peoples of Europe and security for ourselves in a free world.

"Your task will not be an easy one. Your enemy is well-trained, well-equipped and battle-hardened. He will fight, fight savagely.

"But this is the year 1944. Much has happened since the Nazi triump of 1940-41.

"The United Nations have inflicted upon the Germans great defeat in open battle man to man. Our air offensive has seriously reduced their capacity to wage war on the ground.

"Our home fronts have given us superiority in weapons and munitions of war and placed at our disposal great reserves of trained fighting men.

"The tide has turned.

"The free men of the world are marching together to victory. I have full confidence in your courage, devotion to duty and skill in battle.

"We will accept nothing less than full victory.

"Good luck, and let us all beseech the blessing of Almighty God upon this great and noble undertaking."

Thus the words of the Supreme Commander-Allied Expeditionary Forces; words of confidence and encouragement that were ours to ponder, accept and abide by.

Our ship now plowing very slow against swells that strongly began to resist made footing on deck more precarious to maintain. It was now late afternoon and noticeably the wind began to pick up with tenacity. There had been no sun since morning and threatening clouds began to roll in from the east. As far as one could see in either direction there was nothing but grey-green water that along with great rolling waves had become unstable. Conspicuously noticeable by their absence was the lack of escort ships. Only occasionally did a ship appear bobbing way in the distance and even then it looked similar to the one we were on. They were, in fact . . . LSTs loaded with troops geared to land either before or after us (depending on the landing schedule).

"Where are the escorting ships?" one asked in a tone that reflected expectation of several Naval vessels for protection.

"What escorting ships?" came the vibrant reply from one who had earlier learned better. "Buddy, we're on our own now!"

Apprehension circulated and the reality of this thing "struck home!" Fears began to mount and trouble was sensed at any moment!

"What about those U-Boats . . . think we'll be spotted?" asked one.

"You suppose the minesweepers have taken care of the mines?"

soberly asked another.

"Suppose we hit one!"

"How about German long-range artillery . . . think they can reach us?"

Until the boat landed we would be hard to placate.

By 9:00 PM a blanket of complete darkness lay over the entire region and the channel was gripped in the throes of fierce winds and a great rainstorm was attacking with increasing violence! Twisting and pitching in the angered waters and with white-capped ununiformed swells lashing capriciously against the craft's steel bulkhead . . . sweeping the decks and everything on it with heavy back wash; all vehicles had to be chained and securely supported thoroughly lest they tear loose! Each man was issued an inflated rubber life-preserver and instructed the use of it . . . hoping its use would not become necessary. Sailing all day and night of the 13th, (slowing to a crawl at intervals so as not to precede the schedule) and through the dubious dark early morning hours of the 14th, little sleep of any consequence was enjoyed by the men below decks, and *none* for those on top deck . . . for the latter was keeping an unbroken alert! This was no easy chore as the raging storm exhibited its furious turbulence throughout these hours!

With temporary security of England far behind and the grave uncertainty of what may lay ahead in a short matter of time; or the possibility of what could happen to the ship at any second began to work psychologically on many. Outside the wind kept up its angry howling and inside the men kept up their cursing as they were repeatedly bounced from their unstable positions!

"God!" thought many, "how can we stand it!"

Exclaimed one, "This is murder . . . man, am I ever sick! Whatever is waiting for us over there *sure as hell* couldn't be this bad!"

"Why in the world are we taking so long?" questioned another in complete exasperation; "We must be anchored out here somewhere!"

Years later, Ted Jankowski, a former Detroiter now living in Philadelphia, said:

"*Sick*? I can't today even imagine how sick I *really* was! I couldn't even throw up, I felt so bad . . . yet I knew I had to do it!"

"I thought I was gonna' die; I *really mean it*! I was so nauseated it didn't make any difference whether I did or not!" said Bill Hunkins of Flint, Michigan.

"You know how I felt," commented Bob McNulty to the author, "because you were right there with me a good bit of the time." The now successful Detroit contractor recalled: "We were not only half-scared to death, but so sick I don't believe any medicine in the world would have cured me!"

The cool Orsenigo, now retired in New York but still reflecting his immutable expression, added:

"I was no different and I was feeding the fish at one time or another just like the rest of you fellows."

The circumstances were excruciating of course but one could suggest that part of this effect was psychological. But it was in no wise suggested that anyone was under such mental strain that a "breakdown" would follow . . . for it is boastfully known that the men of the 126th were a sturdy lot. Yet, now depressingly grimy, dirty, tense, lacking sufficient sleep, many unmanageable instances of seasickness that seemed almost impossible to endure; and to worsen matters the chemically-processed impregnated clothing producing such an unorthodox and breathtaking odor . . . carrying many beyond the point of nausea, all were constantly kept on edge. Equipped with GI "puke bags" some did not and could not wait to utilize them! No one will question the agony of this ordeal and when measuring the depth of its turbulence will easily rank it alongside any waterborne maneuver that one could ever hope to experience.

On the other hand . . . those able to consume it innoculated themselves with Navy coffee, and to go with it . . . though difficult to keep down, much praise was heaped on the ship's galley team for their tireless and unique preparation of "chicken a la king," mashed potatoes, rolls and a small portion of fruit cocktail.

THE 126TH ORDNANCE IN BRITAIN

VII

BATTLE FOR NORMANDY

It was about 6:30. Morning had come and though the rain had stopped the restless breakers had not ceased thrashing against the craft's grey bobbing bulkhead. A brisk wind continued to blow and its whining echoed through the steel rails and across the decks. As though a great curtain was slowly pulling it away darkness was fading faintly and in a matter of minutes those on deck somberly watched in anxiety as daylight began to appear. Squinting hard, we could see it . . . perhaps two to three miles in the distance . . . the greyish outline of the French coast!

"Good Lord . . . we're here!" commented one.

What were our first thoughts? Who could tell . . . there were so many!

"Would we see action immediately?"

"How much fighting is still going on around the beaches?"

"What do the Germans look like?"

"Have we gotta' dig foxholes right there on the beach?"

Most everyone kept thoughts to himself but certainly uppermost in each mind were those of his particular individual responsibility once ashore. Admittedly, foremost in the thoughts of all officers and section leaders was; "When we roll off into the water . . . what happens if the waterproofing doesn't hold out?" There was more to it than that for further thoughts were; "Who will be on hand to bail us out . . . if anybody?" The words of the camp inspector kept throbbing in many thoughts:

"Keep those points and plugs dry . . . or else you've had it!"

How did one *really* feel? We perhaps felt what realist Charles Ryan Kennedy summed up in one statement years ago: "A peculiar kind of fear they call courage."

So it was; in the early morning of Wednesday, June 14 . . . D plus 8, the 126th through bleary but eager eyes drank in its first glimpse of the battered coast of France. "Utah Beach" in all its glory loomed before us where in the early hours of June 10 . . . D plus 4, our DIVISION (9TH) had landed, and where only in late evening of yesterday the last German shells ceased their sparodic harrassment.

Barrage balloons evenly spaced were dominant over a wide perimeter of the beach and with their powerful steel supporting cables, some operated by a winch apparatus and others attached to wrecked or disabled heavy equipment and some water craft, extended several hundred feet above the ground. Extremely vital to the beachhead these balloons represented a primary defense against possible low attacks by enemy planes and apparently were not as easy to deflate as would be presumed. Tremendous in size, these inflated objects were shaped somewhat like a sausage and filled with a type of light gas (helium). On one occasion as we were preparing to debark, one of them . . . its cable violently straining at its mooring, suddenly became detached and bolted rapidly up into space, the long cable trailing! Drifting and rising so rapidly and to such lofty heights, despite the undimmed morning atmosphere it soon became impossible to follow with the naked eye . . . or for that matter; binoculars. It leaves one to wonder just exactly whatever became of that balloon.

Moving closer to the beach several yards to our left in deeper waters we viewed with awe as swells rippled against the superstructure and masts protruding from a sunken Naval vessel. The morning was sunny and a lively wind was blowing white lacy clouds along at a rapid rate under a blue sky as the vehicles rolled off the LST onto the uncertainty of a beachhead that was only five miles wide in either direction and a front that now had penetrated eight to ten miles in depth.

"Keep moving! Keep moving!" came the order from the Beach Commander, and since deramping from the LST in two sections communications became confused. The first section followed a track leading up Red Beach to the north and the second group, unaware or ignoring the lead section began pursuing a course in the opposite direction. A beach MP, racing in a jeep halted the first jeep for correction.

"You're not the first group to have this problem" said he; "but step it up! Step it up!"

Though the busy beach was humming with activity . . . still no one could help but divert his attention to the disabled but imposing German '88mm gun jutting from one of the concrete beach emplacements and pointing direct to the region from which we had come. The mouth of the once-deadly monster split and peeled back for about six inches like a potato it appeared as if an incoming projectile had been carefully aimed, fired and miraculously "bullseyed" into the barrel. Representing but one of several revolving gun turrets set in concrete bases to deter any invader we would soon learn that this gun like many others later seen had been purposely destroyed when abandoned by a retreating enemy.

Small landing craft and wrecked equipment were disseminated in the surf and about the beach; hundreds of land mines, their charges now detonated by combat engineers and bomb disposal squads lay in several distinct piles. Hundreds of rifles discarded by both enemy and American troops alike bedecked all parts of the area as were numerous belts of ammo. Steel helmets and gas masks lost in great numbers by each side were scattered and strewn.

Many German prisoners, some wounded . . . others much more fortunate, were clustered in groups on the beach under close guard awaiting transportation back to PW camps in England as were many wounded Americans seeking similar evacuation back across the English Channel to military hospitals. At frequent intervals the wind brought to our ears echoes of artillery blasts together with exchanges of machine gun and small arms fire from the distance, for it was in the extreme early hours of this morning that the last enemy resistance on the ten-mile beachhead supposedly was silenced.

Tidal experts had already told us to expect the water to be at a precarious height and fearing improper timing we envisioned some vehicles stalling and possible bogging in the sandy bottom prior to landing. The 126th reaped the harvests of good fortune as the tide was in a receding process during this period and waters ascended no higher than the floor of most vehicles and all equipment moved ashore unobstructed. Fortunate indeed; for by time the last vehicle rolled down the ramp the tide had dropped to such a depth that no more than six inches of water and surf-lashed sands were ours to cope with.

Dale Thatcher watched the ramp slowly descend and then splash broadside in the water. He was first in line and moving down the ramp did not know what to expect when his halftrack weapons carrier entered the water.

"Water came halfway up the hood and covered the front wheels" he recalled; "But it wasn't near as bad as I expected." The stocky dark-haired S/Sgt. from Erie, Michigan *really* knew how to "wheel" a vehicle, and his co-driver, Gerald DeBacker, a lanky T/4 from Detroit and an expert motor "troubleshooter" was ready to put it back together should anything go wrong! The two would be the first to reach shore.

Rolling up a small narrow-gauge road that emerged from Beach Exit No. 2 the company . . . now split into at least four small groups, began to view with awe the war's aftermath.

Long subjected to a tremendous over-capacity of tonnage during the past few days this roadbed of reinforced sand and gravel was in bad state of repair, and with almost daily reappearances of great holes torn by vicious shellfire, extremely soft shoulders and countless jagged pieces of shrapnel still embedded along the route didn't help it at all. Because of these elements the march inland was extremely slow and precarious. Disabled tanks, light artillery and rifles and smaller vehicular equipment littered the roadside.

Enemy landmines . . . their detonators removed, gas masks, layer after layer of unfired machine gun and small arms ammunition and a tremendous number of the new type cleverly-designed rubber lifebelts previously issued by the Navy lay scattered along this entire route. The narrow roadway surrounded on either side by shallow marshes and swamps contained patches of muck and in some spots, quicksand. Several bodies of Americans as well Germans . . . not yet retrieved, their grey-green uniforms easily distinguished from the GI olive-drab, lay partially hidden in shallow pools and sparse undergrowth. Further beyond the marshes some dead, though already identified by Graves Registration specialists, awaited removal from ditches and fields; resembling something that is seen somewhere in motion pictures. It was incredible!

With bulldozers and roadgrader equipment the Ist. Engineer Special Brigade was given assignment of clearing up the beach. This would result in removal of demolished and stalled equipment and would eventually find beach exits and feeder roads restored to a more serviceable stability. This unit also inherited an unenviable task of burying the dead . . . and on a level area of terrain several yards inland from the beach with reluctant aid of a selected few captured Germans; some of the first GIs to fall in France had been collected and were in a crude fashion being buried as we passed.

A few minutes had elapsed since our scattered remnants again formed two groups and both sections pulled separately up from the beach. No more than ten minutes later the sandy passageway had been breached. Utilizing a more suitable two-lane macadam road approximately two miles carried us into St. Marie du Mont . . . the largest of the beach villages to fall into Allied hands in the "Utah Beach" sector.

Though relatively brief the battle for St. Marie du Mont had been furious, and though some street-fighting and hand-to-hand combat had prevailed within the village itself destruction of dwellings was limited primarily to the approaches. As our convoy rolled through narrow cobblestoned streets . . . some chunks dislodged and the rubble now bulldozed to one side, the few French civilians who had returned to the village registered only mild enthusiasm; obviously still reeling from shock of the recent horrendous bombardment.

Representing the first French civilians thus far encountered we could, after viewing the shattered condition of the community only shake our heads and well-understand their nonchalance. No one could help but note appreciatively the small hand-made American and French flags pridefully displayed at many conspicuous points.

The marshes now behind we advanced further inland and rapidly approached the *real* hedgerow country. An occasional "Achtung Minen" sign prominently displayed along the roadside was further substantiated by lines of white tape staked by Engineer mine-sweepers marking off forbidden areas. Damage inflicted on the spotty farmhouses and dwellings was widespread . . . only a few remaining intact and even less escaping unscathed, for this locality prior to serving as a battleground for ground troops had even before suffered a catastrophic pounding from big Allied Naval guns and saturating bombardment from U. S. and Royal Air Forces. Mammoth shell holes and bomb craters dotted the fields and some roads and at intervals it was not uncommon to view livestock and horses, many with cavernous mortal wounds lying in meadows or ditches . . . innocent casualties of war. The broiling sun now administering its' torturous temperatures was adding not only to discomfort of the heavily-laden foot soldier but played havoc with the dead animals. In far greater number were cattle, now bloated *far* beyond normalcy, rotting and emitting an odious stench that so filled the air so as to bring agonizing gasps from all that had the displeasure of being nearby.

Predominantly rural, the inhabitants of Normandy were saddled two major vocations. Production of butter cheese and breeding of cattle. Though not necessarily a backward people by nature; a wide cultural gap did appear to exist between this region and the more populated industrial and educational centers of France. As a consequence cultural, social and economic views . . . and most definite political expressions by those of this region differed habitually with other provinces. Perhaps for this reason the German occupation of Normandy presented no *real* burden to these people. Moreover; to a degree it had actually stimulated their economy. No doubt; occupancy of Americans in lieu of Germans was preferential; but having learned for four years to live with it . . . herein posed a question of some magnitude as to whether a perditious destructive war *was worth* the price of changing occupation forces. Was it any great satisfaction to see homes destroyed and their personal treasures maimed and displaced? What gratification was there to see farms and grazing lands ripped apart and animals lying dead and rotting in the fields? Obviously little analysis was needed to see why many Norman villagers and peasants were in no great receptive mood!

Though difficult for us to understand at the time, we should have understood that with the presence of German occupation authorities for some four years much propaganda describing the Americans as "uncouth," "vicious" and "stupid" became embedded in the minds of many of these people who had no other way of knowing. Many had approached, and self-admittedly; the point where they really didn't know fully just what to believe. The war had hit these Frenchmen hard and it was difficult for them to become convinced of the *real* necessity of it!!

Just short of the western approaches of St. Marie du Mont an MP roadblock that left passage uncoordinated caused the two units to again become separated. Two-and-a-half miles west beyond this point the lead group left the road and turned off into a designated de-waterproofing area partially concealed by surrounding thick hedgerows . . . within the confines of a small intersection named Les Forges. As many of the engines had become dangerously overheated; their intake and airflow having been purposely sealed, immediate removal of all waterproofing compound and tape from the machines' vital parts became the first order of the day. Some thirty minutes later the other section appeared . . . thereby allowing for a more cohesive command.

Now much past noon and as many hours had elapsed since any of us had eaten the announcement of "chow" would certainly have to soon fit into the course of plans. Yet, though it was *indeed* long past the normal period many somehow had little stomach for eating. Perhaps in light of the excitement during the brief march up from the channel, or possibly the incessant pounding of the heavy guns to which we were so definitely unaccustomed caused many appetites to diminish. Most would say the sight of long-bloated livestock lying dead on adjoining property did it . . . and the stench of fallen GIs that FIRST ARMY Graves Registration was removing in quite an immodest way from around this and other nearby areas did not help.

"Chow" finally was announced though . . . *without* a "menu" and each man "selected" the same thing . . . "K-Rations!"

"Here," section leaders were told; "Pass these out . . . and have one yourself in the meantime!"

Familiarization of the packaged contents would become imperative in that beginning this day we would learn full well what role the K-Ration was to play in the way of sustenance for many days hence. Closely resembling the proverbial "cracker jack" box they were packed in three waterproofed paraffin-coated boxes . . . each clearly marked "Breakfast, Dinner and Supper," each box packaged separately and all three weighing less than two pounds. One could, for good measure wash the whole mess down with a dissolved bullion cube or packaged ("ugh!") coffee also found in one of the boxes. No one had to take second thoughts to compare these rations to the highly exquisite food "gobbled up" during that brief encampment at the marshalling yards in England.

"Who can eat this damn stuff!?" was the first cry of many.

"You'll eat it or starve," was the factual response.

Many suffered from stomach cramps in the beginning . . . but representing some 3,500 calories it did in the end fulfill the purpose for which it was designed. Some time later we would be issued "C-Rations," which consisting of canned meat products combined with vegetables, potatoes and rice was far more palatable.

***

In England on the last day of March the 126th. was assigned to the 6th. Ordnance Battalion, which unit commanded by Lt. Col. Martin F. Shaughnessy, an astute well-disciplined officer whose prominent Massachusetts accent easily identified his presence, maintained headquarters some five miles west of Salisbury located in what was generally known as the "Grimm's Ditch" community. Now in France we were still under jurisdiction of the 6th. and the next major step then, was to contact the Battalion from which the company would receive its' first assignment. Despite some preliminary entanglement this contact was in an amazingly short time made secure.

Now located approximately two miles north of Carentan . . . a vital road junction that only until yesterday, the 13th., the enemy had splashed with artillery; and slightly less than two miles south of the village of St. Mere Eglise where in the early days of fighting the 4TH INFANTRY DIVISION had relieved an embattled 82ND AIRBORNE DIVISION, we awaited orders. Somewhere around 2:00 PM Battalion instructed us to move forward, secure "as best you can" a well-concealed area and prepare for service operations.

To "size up" a suitable location a "recon" party was dispatched, and with little or no real training they were instructed to "free it of all objects detrimental to safety." The fear of explosive mines was instilled in the hearts of everybody long ago and before the team entered an area that was deemed appropriate, two FIRST ARMY GIs from an Engineer bomb disposal squad was summoned to probe the field for us. Two mines were unearthed, defused and detonation triggers pulled out.

On one of the briefest trips to be made on the continent . . . slightly more than a mile, we advanced to a location interspersed with stooped willow trees that overshadowed much of the area and surrounded completely by hedges so thick that the view from inside was all but impenetrable. Just off the main supply route leading northwest to Cherbourg this was no more than a mile east of Chef-du-Pont, a little railroad stop where less than twenty-four hours before was cleared by U. S. forces.

Defensively the enemy enjoyed a tremendous advantage in this hedgerow country. There was no question that whoever controls the hedgerows (the French called it "Bocage") pretty well controls the scene . . . that is until either his ammo expires; forcing surrender, or a direct hit by artillery or an equivalent high explosive silences him. Not only was he to a great extent well-concealed and well-entrenched but cognizant that this was his maneuver ground several months prior to the invasion he had become well-conversant geographically with a general outline of the Normandy region and by this time was nonetheless adept in making his moves. This meant no less that while the Germans were securely "dug-in" the painful task of dislodgement fell to American and British forces. Success or failure of this task depended on "recon" teams when evaluating enemy strength. Once such positions were located they were bathed with such withering fire that oftimes positions had to be abandoned. Allied forces quickly moved in . . . routing them out into open ground to literally "pour the heat on!!" Many violent skirmishes resulted . . . each bearing obvious evidence that casualties were to increase tremendously in the days to follow.

The 82ND AIRBORNE had slashed hard at Chef-du-Pont and even here bitter scars of war remained as evidenced by a vast amount of spent shell casings, used and unused ammo, strewn grenades and rifles, a number of explosive mines that were hastily abandoned by the retreating "Boche" and an ever-increasing occurrence of finding a body of both friend or foe. Throughout the surrounding vicinity . . . in the fields . . . in ditches and streams . . . caught in the hedgerows and swamps were those who had become heroes early. In the very early days it was not uncommon to find bodies of the airborne who had jumped on "D-Day," but never felt the ground. Here and there a discarded soiled battle jacket displaying the "Screaming Eagle" insignia of the 101ST AIRBORNE or the "Double A" of the "All-America" DIVISION that the 82ND preferred to be called, further substantiated this. The grey-green jacket with swastika emblem emblazoned on the left hand side told a story too, of tragic German misfortunes.

Wrecked gliders adorned this vicinity . . . some only slightly damaged, some upended and shattered when smashing into hedges. Many, many of these troop-laden machines, as they swooped in seeking a landing in the early morning semi-darkness were destroyed by the enemy's sturdily-erected obstacles. Parts of these gliders were salvaged by those industrious enough to salvage them and before the MPs moved in became immediate "property" of the first to reach the demolished craft. Many drivers of smaller vehicles took similar advantage, dismantling the gliders' plexiglass windows and reshaped them so as to later act as auxillary windshields for their own respective vehicles.

That a zealous alert existed the first night in this yet unfamiliar location cannot be questioned! Especially was this true at each guard post . . . for no one could intelligently perceive the outcome of our first night in France. The reverberating roar of any artillery gave cause for each man to swear it could be none other than German! For a time it was almost a constant thing! Each time the chattering of machine guns or sharp incessant throb of the enemy "burp gun" echoed throughout swamps and woods new doubts and fears arose unabashedly within each of us . . . and thus setting off a chain of rumors!

"The Germans have broken through! . . . I *know* they have!" "Let's get the hell out of here!" Everybody was ready to "haul tail" it out of here . . . but nobody considered "where to!"

The truth was obvious and confirmed . . . from the beginning no troops were greener or untried or in any way less novice, particularly at this moment than those of the 126th . . . be it infantry, quartermaster, signal . . . or any within the region!

Earlier notification that 9TH DIVISION's G-2 operations would periodically funnel information to us with regard to the enemy's capacity, his locations or immediate plans gave some encouragement and credence to our status. As yet however, nothing had been received. To our credit though no one allowed much time to elapse before gaining clear identification of the low thud and quick "boom-boom" of the German '88mm, the ear-splitting "W-H-A-M" of FIRST ARMY'S 25-foot barrel high velocity 155mm mobile gun that made one's stomach quiver, and the hollow thunder that identified the shorter 155mm howitzer and the reliable 105mm howitzer, both capable of a range of more than 14,000 yards. Despite lack of briefing of 9TH's G-2 we gained full respect for them all early!

On occasion many wandered inadvertently into forbidden or questionable territory and through lack of identification often wound up on a wrong road. Because so many of these roads, narrow gauged and closely banked with high mounted hedges bore such a close resemblance to each other it became a common error in the beginning. Especially was this true at night and until one immediately gained confident recognition of assigned code names that identified individual units he suddenly became conscious that he had wandered into territory where he should not be and it was time to beat a hasty retreat . . . now! . . . and do it quick!

We were earlier warned to familiarize ourselves with code names and signs, especially those bearing association to us. There is little question that had it not been for these innumerable military codes displayed on markers attached to trees, posts, wrecked equipment, etc., marking unit locations, and the many precautionary danger symbols of mines, blown bridges, areas under enemy fire, etc., warning one to beware, at several intervals along the roads these mistakes could have in most cases resulted in fatal ones. To be alert one only had to heed well-posted warnings . . . "Danger Mines!" . . . "Danger – Road Under Encmy Fire" . . . Warning – This Bridge Under Enemy Observation."

Those having deployed reasonable enough time on the road soon learned unit locations by the many code signs placed at conspicuous spots. We had already identified "Jayhawk" with VII CORPS and whenever "Notorious" signs appeared it was obvious that some part of 9TH DIVISION was near, and from that we knew our location couldn't be too far away. Moreover, we made it a point early to note that whenever "Metric 16" appeared, which by no means was spread over as wide a scope as CORPS or DIVISION we knew we were "home!" Due partly to inexperience and an excessive amount of curiosity, there is little argument that during the early days of Normandy on several occasions some of us though not cognizant of the full danger stood just one jump ahead of becoming a war casualty that *could* result in one's insurance collected and a "gold star" replacing the white one now hanging in the window back home!

As this campaign grew with intensity and despite numerous endeavors and personal misgivings the time element became relatively brief before one would really "wise up" to the stark fact that danger lurked most everywhere . . . and that we were right in the middle of a zone where a heated game called "war" was being played . . . and each side playing "for keeps!"

With strong respect for the unknown each of us "dug in" here and the depth of each foxhole would well-express obvious anxiety as to what may or may not take place. Spasmodic showers fell the very first night. The following afternoon brought more rain and before darkness descended there existed a drenching downpour. By morning of the third day all exposed foxholes had undergone a transformation into a quagmire of mud, adding to already existing discomforture and frustration of its occupants. Comfort or no comfort, complete justification was felt to spend the entire night in these hollow dwellings, for time will not easily erase the bleak uncertainty of the first twenty-four hours for the newly-arrived 126th . . . what with the dark sky turning crimson with incessant flashes from thunderous blasts of field artillery and highly-sensitive anti-aircraft batteries raging with authority against the few German planes daring to venture over Allied territory! Even the repeated clanking and rumbling of increasing M-4 Sherman tanks moving round the bend that swings northwest just in front of our area on the way to the front; their 350 h.p. Continental and Ford engines emitting a monotonous roar from 34-ton dark grey hulks did very little to ease our subtle fears of insecurity . . . even though we knew they were ours.

So dense and so heavily concentrated were AA-gun batteries that when taunted in the slightest by enemy planes their multiple-mounted 40mm and 50mm guns sent up a barrage of red hot projectiles unmatched in consistency by any other group of weapons on the continent! Lt. Col. C. O. Burns, commander of the 376th. AAA Battalion (attached to 9TH) had warned his men to "eat up" anything that flew at night! Heeding his instructions to the letter, this Battalion obviously *kept* an enormous "appetite." Their brisk red and white tracers brightly outlining a barrage in multi-patterned streams toward the objective, these missiles ejecting so thick and so close from automatic weapons in practically every field, one felt in an imaginary sense that he could *almost* reach out and grab a handful.

There existed for a time unloading irregularities on the beach. Somewhere along the line supervision had become lax and additional manpower was needed. Hasty and indiscriminate unloading of ships and the inability to identify and report huge stocks dumped on the beaches would affect supplies, weapons, vehicles and spare parts. Correct identification and disbursement of ammunition became a problem of main concern. Therefore before beginning our own operations it was not surprising and we were not perturbed when called upon to perform supplemental duties that oftimes bordered on the hazardous. "Rest" was a forgotten word and when aroused almost any hour during the night many were dispatched to the beach to assist in unloading equipment.

Maj. Gen. Henry Sayler, the Chief Ordnance officer in the European Theater was vehement in his order:

"Get it off the beach without delay!"

Equipment . . . mobile and immobile; weapons . . . light and heavy, vital supplies and ammunition were feverishly classified and moved to other less conspicuous areas with greater haste. Other personnel kept communications transmitted between company, battalion and DIVISION Ordnance while still others maintained innumerable functions that at the time may have seemed insignificant but were nevertheless essentially solicitous to the broad drive now under way.

We experienced during the second morning a jolting alert . . . the company's first! Sometime in midmorning Lt. Jim Black and Private Harry Regester, dispatched to reconnoiter the woods some one hundred fifty yards to the west for a sizeable cache of German ammunition that someone earlier had reported seeing suddenly stopped short when hearing inaudible voices. Spotting two armed figures haltingly approaching in the distance suspicions skyrocketed! Almost simultaneously each pair spotted the other, and startled; both took immediate cover! "Germans!" thought the young Lieutenant; "They've gotta be!" Still alarmed, though quickly regaining his composure and drawing upon what bit of German phrasing he thought appropriate the Lieutenant in his raspy voice called out to the "intruders" in a commanding tone that sounded to them like:

"Kommen sie hierer mit hande hoch!"

Not easily discouraged an immediate answer of pistol and rifle shots returned the challenge! Motivated by this answer it was followed by carbine fire! More pistol shots! Thinking again . . . and not wanting to get into a real "fire fight" Black and Regester moved with unusual agility and initiated a hasty exit from the woods . . . back through the high grass and into the company area!

"Afraid?" Black later commented, "No, not really . . . we just weren't ready to get into it, that's all!"

The sharp alarming exchanges of gunfire found nearly everyone in the complement quickly grabbing his rifle and awaiting the next move.

Dashing into the CP in a heavy pant, Lt. Black blurted; "Captain . . . the woods are full of Germans!"

Looking up from his chair in the cramped camouflaged CP trailer, Orsenigo, now a captain, questioned in a collected voice, but one that revealed traces of amusement. "Germans huh? You're sure of this?"

"No question about it!" came the confirmation. "Saw them with my own eyes!" Black was sincere though a slight tinge of exaggeration seemed to have crept into his tone of reply.

"I'm not kidding, Captain;" he added . . . "Who do you think I was firing at!?"

Lowering his coffee cup, his usual expression of equanamity changing to slight alarm and his voice rising a bit, the Captain retorted;

"You were firing at Germans? . . . The *hell* you were?"

"The *hell* I wasn't! Now if you don't believe it, you just go out there and take a look for yourself!"

"All right, Lieutenant, don't get excited, just hang on!"

Frank Linzinmeir, a beefy bespectacled Master Sergeant from Marysville, Ohio and one who never failed to answer an early "chow" call, was ordered to investigate.

"Get a detail out there Sergeant and see what the hell is going on," instructed the Captain; "and don't dare pull those triggers unless you *really know* what you're shooting at!"

Halfway through the field of high grass that separated the woods from our area Linzinmeir and party halted abruptly . . . astonished to note two uniformed figures, who not yet in an identifiable position were holding aloft a white cloth and with some hesitancy, approaching from the opposite side.

"Uh-oh!" whispering to his companions, "Watch it and hold on now."

A sign of surrender? Surprise melted into a little embarrassment when the "enemy" turned out to be two GIs from the 9TH Signal Corps, who after checking some communication wires strung along the road were simply looking for a short-cut through the woods to their own campsite! Though a little shaken, the GIs; both seasoned veterans of North African and Sicilian campaigns were no less perturbed with this confrontation.

When asked, "Why did you fire on us?" the logical reply was easy. "The same reason you did," spoke a burly Sergeant; "Because when you called out in German, we thought you were 'Krauts' too!"

Reverting to his usual low-key approach the Captain shook his head slightly and only grunted for he knew that at this early stage such an experience could happen to anybody. A trifle embarrassed and shaken a bit too were our participants and it cannot go unsaid that they were for a time, warmly reminded of this miscalculation.

To this period both elements of the 126th., having departed the marshalling area in England several hours prior to that of the third section still were unaccounted for. It then came natural for many speculative views to be aired as to what could have happened during this time. One advanced the possibility of having been integrated into some other unit whose personnel may have been lost in the invasion. Another suggested that maybe their craft "might have met with disaster" and destroyed while crossing the channel. Even further; "Could they have encountered some red tape difficulty and perhaps not yet even left England?" Frequent visits to the beach checkpoint brought the same answer . . . "the 126th. landed on the 14th!" Beyond that, we continued to wait.

"Red tape" was the answer . . . and these two groups had become entangled into an endless footage of it! A 'foul-up' in forwarding orders caused their reluctant detention on the channel beach in England for almost two days . . . frustratingly watching ship after ship leave the port. One unit under command of Lt. Jim Prendergast, following a rocky trip across the channel rolled onto "Utah Beach" a little past midnight June 16 and encountered a troublesome adventure getting ashore. Though the first of the company's units to leave the marshalling area in England it was the second group to arrive on the continent. Minutes after the last vehicle moved up onto the beach what was thought to be several planes roared out of nowhere, and somehow dodging the protective barrage balloons proceeded to "work the sands over" . . . strafing the north end of the beach. Said Prendergast:

"You couldn't see 'em but it seemed like their grinding throbbing engines were right on top of you!"

The many "ack-ack" guns strategically-spaced over the beachhead immediately took action and suddenly the air was torn apart and the sky aflame with blinding flashes and rushing flak! Witnesses recall a couple of the planes shot out of the sky; one exploding into the channel . . . the other crashing inland while a more fortunate one made a break southward and survived to fight another time.

The action was brief and intense but the boys involuntarily had come dangerously close to receiving their first "baptism of fire."

Recalls Prendergast:

"Rattled . . . and by now somewhat mindful of what may lie ahead we pulled ourselves together and attempted to coordinate efforts whereby we might locate the company's main body."

As had been the case of the first landing party two days earlier, so it was with this section . . . to find itself a little questionable of its' actual whereabouts . . . to say the least; probably lost! With flashlight in hand Sgt. Mike Scott, the Recovery Section leader, called to Lt. Prendergast:

"Where to now, Lieutenant?"

Now in a state of irritation and semi-exhaustion, the curly-haired Lieutenant yelled back in words that rang with sarcasm:

"That's what I'm trying to find out! You got any suggestions, Sergeant? Bring that flashlight over here!"

Still on the beach and poring over maps draped across the hood of a jeep they were caught in a dilemma as to which way to go. Two MPs in a jeep clearly marked "Beach Police" rolled up and commanded:

"Douse that light . . . on the double!"

Pointing to a beach exit which no one could see in the distance, though obviously there; probably Exit No. 3 at the north end of the beach, a further command followed:

"Get moving Lieutenant, take these vehicles off the beach!"

"Where to from here?" asked the befuddled Lieutenant, perhaps a little stung from the rolling commands of an enlisted man.

"Keep rolling forward and watch the signs till you see something better to go on!" came a dramatic answer. "What a stupid sonofabitch he is," thought Prendergast; "What does he expect me to do, roll back aboard ship? Go forward is the *only* thing I can do."

Only a brief span elapsed in this answer-searching and in spite of continued darkness this group seeming to travel many more miles than they actually did, followed markings and made their way to the same de-waterproofing area used by the first section.

As the greying strains of dawn gradually began replacing the shadowy forms of night and while the task of getting the machines back in shape was well-under way this group again dashed for cover as an adjoining vicinity was savagely though briefly strafed by a single plane in two ferocious swoops. They came in at treetop high and were gone before any effective ack-ack could be brought into play. Later in full daylight with all machines, motors and parts restored to normal working order extensive consultation began with Military Police checkpoints.

"Metric 16? Nobody checked in at this point."

Field telephones began to jingle! Maps were spread out! Much individual unit consultation! One MP finally suggested:

"Let's check with 'Jayhawk Ordnance."

"Jayhawk?" replied Prendergast. "You mean VII CORPS? Hell, I doubt if they even know we exist."

A little conversation on the phone and the MP reports:

"Sir, 'Jayhawk' Ordnance reports 126th Ordnance arrived on the 14th and should be assembled in Les Forges area."

"Well, the roadsign out there says this is Les Forges and they could be in any of these apple orchards. Let's start looking for 'Metric 16' signs!"

"Sir, you want we should call FIRST ARMY Ordnance?" suggested the MP.

"N-a-a-h, you say they're around here? We'll find them."

The main complement was found when a scouting team recognized by accident a company vehicle on the road.

Under command of Lt. Lineberger the third section arrived afternoon of the 16th., and enjoying an uneventful but slightly bumpy voyage across the channel landed with no difficulty. He was extremely proud that everything had gone as planned. The Lieutenant did in fact take great pride in most everything he did.

Reid Lineberger, a quick-witted North Carolinian who had earned his commission through the rigors of OCS entered the army at an age that many would prefer not to. One to weigh all factors with realism before making a decision, stuck to it when that decision was reached . . . and when it was reached, he was hard to sway. Looking after his troops as would a "mother hen" gradually he earned the respect of all. Whenever a problem of indecision arose he always presented the same recourse: "Now let's get the facts! Now, let's get the facts! It ain't worth a damn unless you've got the facts!"

By four in the afternoon all three sections were together and we became a single company again.

By the time complete unification was again established the company had become plagued with a diminishing food supply. Wholesome ingredients had for a time been secured and prepared by the field kitchen but during the last few meals were alarmingly skimpy at each serving. Unjustly accused by some of holding back on us . . . and even admonished for having been lax in sufficient preparation the cooks could not have done better for it was simply a case of running out of food! Having gone through what they considered a period of frustration in trying to locate the company's main complement and headquarters the last unit had upon arrival, visions of a warm meal waiting . . . but hopes were quickly dashed when offered only a couple of large chocolate bars. A GI issue, the Army called it a "D-Bar" and strongly resembling a thick Hershey bar was rich with specially seasoned ingredients. Supposedly equaling a full meal it was bitter . . . but surprisingly did the job. Too; it was the only nutrition enjoyed by each of us for the past twelve hours.

"What the hell is this?" inquired one of the new arrivals in alarm.

"It's your supper," retorted Sgt. Fleming sternly.

"My supper? What'dya mean my supper? A candy bar?"

"I mean damn well what I said . . . your supper! You'll eat what the rest of us eat!" the Mess Sergeant replied, his eyes bulging and his breath coming in short spurts; "I've got enough problems without you guys coming in here bitching!"

"Is this all you guys have . . . really?"

"That's it!" was the reply, " All day long!"

In the early days the few food supply depots, or "dumps" as GI language commanded found it necessary to shift locations at least once daily for obvious camouflage reasons. This policy in effect, sufficient contacts with these depots were exceedingly difficult to maintain by all units . . . nonetheless our personnel. Ammunition, gasoline and supply "dumps" all had the same problem; shift from time to time, or face the possibility of liquidation by a venturesome enemy aircraft.

Quartermaster depots later moved on an average of four days to catch up with Army troops. But as one moved . . . one group remained behind at the original location to service companies until a new location was established. This became sort of "leapfrogging" and was a process that did not always suffice for some supplies, parts, etc., even food needed immediately may not be left at the original site but enroute or possibly already at the new depot site.

Exceptionally firm and allowing no "horseplay" in his field kitchen . . . nor in his feeding routine, Herb Fleming had carried the rank of Staff/Sergeant for quite some time and was the type of Mess Sergeant who prided himself to see that his men ate good, and whenever procurement was possible he always seemed to wind up with good rations.

Losing directions was not a new thing for many troops in Normandy during this period because when daylight subsided everything was done in blackout . . . absolutely no lights of any description to be utilized in the open. Other than the tiny almost insignificant-appearing slits of light beaming from covered and painted headlights; jeep and truck drivers, ambulance drivers and even tank-men relied entirely on the natural clearness of the night, and full clearness was experienced only when the moon was in position to illumine the dark. These absurdly small slits of light . . . "cat's eyes" we called them; none supposed to exceed more than an inch in length and half an inch in depth, proved to be of greater benefit to approaching drivers than its' own.

In most cases, especially on smaller roads in an area nearest the active front those innumerable lines of illuminous tape markers detecting concealed mines and to warn of bomb or shell craters so hastily and roughly, yet effectively strung and posted by combat engineers vastly aided all drivers. For self-preservation one very quickly learned to adapt himself to the darkness and thereto acclimating himself with the situation. Rain at night compounded problems and brought on particularly distressing driving conditions as the moon became obliterated. Consequently, no natural light was penetrable through the dark infinity, and a drivers' duties with all of his additional hazards commanded the envy of no one. It took coordination and application and he drove mostly by instinct. Moreover; especially on bad nights . . . if never before having traveled a particular route one had to grope his way along the roads and be braced at all times to counter the possible shock of running off that road, hitting an unfilled crater or perhaps smashing into someone . . . as was the misfortune of many.

We viewed with sober apprehension as file after file of doughboys, their hollow eyes and weary bearded faces bearing expression of the horror and despair of battle plodded past our area enroute to rest areas. It quickly gave alarm for some to express:

"Boy! Look at those guys . . . they're beat! Is that the way we're gonna look in a few days?"

"You'd look like that now," came a reply, "if you had been through what they have!"

As truckload after truckload of bedraggled German war prisoners shuttled back through this location on their way to PW compounds clear impressions were assumed that the battle for this sector was hastening to a profound conclusion.

With all towns and communities immediately north and west of this region now under allied control orders came directing us to move in a northwest direction . . . for in order to establish a more cohesive Division-Battalion-Company communication it became imperative to move closer within the region of DIVISION activity.

In early morning of June 19 M/Sgt. Frank Linzinmeir, heading a scouting party of three; lanky small arms specialist Al Rapin and T/5 Henry Boudreau of Fitchburg, Masschusetts . . . the company's only *genuine* French interpreter, set out to locate a suitable operational area that would put us within the zone of DIVISIONAL operations. They would roll northwest for almost 20 miles to within the vicinity of Briquebec, a strategic intersection of some 1,500 that sits astride the principal north-south St. Sauveur-Cherbourg artery . . . just 16 miles south of the besieged city of Cherbourg.

Reporting on his return late the same evening that a suitable location had been found Linzinmeir nevertheless warned; "there is still a hell of a lot of firing going on around there somewhere!" He made special reference to an abrupt thunderous blast from a well-camouflaged 105mm howitzer behind a hedgerow. Listeners could hardly contain smothered laughter as he smashed his big fist into an open palm and blurted:

"I didn't know it was there . . . none of us did! It damn near knocked us off our feet, and I don't mind admitting . . . it just scared the living hell out of me!"

The abundance of personal equipment strewn around that location, sparodic machine gun fire in the distance and bodies of those that had fallen in battle gave evidence that something had indeed been going on . . . and not too far was *still* going on!

What Linzinmeir and his party *did not* know at the time was that in the vicinity of the diminutive village of St. Jacques de-Nehou a fierce enemy counterattack had been launched in the early dark hours of yesterday (18th) morning! No small scale attack this thrust involved a good portion of a regiment from the German 77th Division desperately seeking escape from gradual entrapment in the upper peninsular.

Bearing full brunt of this attack was the Ist Battalion of 9TH DIVISION's 39th Infantry Regiment. Though caught somewhat off-balance in the beginning the Battalion quickly pulled itself together, and summoning the power of all its' mortars wrecked plans of the enemy; beating them back across the River Seye north of the village. Heavy casualties were inflicted and so badly damaging the attackers that the effort was abandoned and initiative was crushed. Striking deeper demoralization the German 77th Division commander; Generalmajor Rudolf Stegmann was mortally wounded in this action.

This Battalion earned for itself a distinguished unit citation for this action . . . and rightly so; especially when a Battalion can play havoc with a regiment! But the 39th. *was like that*! They were proud of their slogan . . . "Anything, Anytime, Anywhere – Bar Nothing!" Ever since Colonel Harry Flint took over as Regimental commander in Sicily in July, 1943 and introduced this slogan, the regiment carried it with pride through the remainder of that island conflict and the five successive bitter campaigns that would follow on the continent. Soon becoming prominent on helmets, eventually emblazoned on trucks, every jeep and even each artillery piece . . . the motto, enhancing an imaginary prestige became a sort of "battle cry" that each man through regimental spirit would back up!

Through previous military operations the wispy wiry Colonel had instilled a formidable "esprit de Corps" within ranks of the "Falcons" that never seemed to falter. A month following this last smashing success however, "Paddy" Flint would no longer be with them. A sniper's bullet would see to that.

***

Following an almost five-day occupancy the 126th. in early afternoon of the 20th moved forward.

Grinding across the River Merderet at Chef-du-Pont we continued through ancient and now heavily-devastated Pont l'Abbe, where, on a grassy knoll immediately east of the village stands solemnly and picturesquely and oppressively burdened with encroaching vines the oldest monastery in the Cotentin section of Normandy. Along this route we consistently viewed with dismay the death and destruction littering roads and fields . . . hundreds of bloated livestock dotting pastures that had encountered death during the holocaust of war . . . great quantities of demolished equipment rendered useless by both Allied and enemy guns . . . and somberly the hushed silence of a few heroes that lay scattered where death had met them. The company crossed the River Douve at the battered and heavily-mined town of St. Sauveur l' Vicomte where elements of the 9TH DIVISION's 47th Regiment two days earlier moved from a position two miles north on that river to strengthen and pass through an embattled 82ND AIRBORNE DIVISION, who weary from a series of blistering enemy counter-attacks doggedly had held their own.

General "Slim Jim" Gavin, the 82ND's assistant commander, recalls:

"A great mass of Germans far outnumbering our troops

were bottled up west of St. Sauveur between the Douve and an attacking force from our 508th Regiment pressing in from the west. A railroad line running north-south was behind them and they were loading everything they could on flat cars for an apparent desperate evacuation. I had not yet seen so many Germans assembled and it appeared that they were as anxious to get out as we were to get in! They were tough but they soon learned of our persistence."

Continuing northwest in a scorching afternoon sun we reached our destination some four hundred yards west of St. Jacques de Nehou.

As FIRST ARMY Ordnance Officer, Colonel John B. Medaris (later Maj. Gen.) naturally assumed the ultimate responsibility for all Ordnance activities in that Army. This would embrace Ordnance administration, liaison and coordination within four active CORPS, thirteen combat divisions, (this would soon change) a number of Ordnance Groups, innumerable Battalions, companies and many other related units.

Colonel Medaris and his staff were "hard put" to constantly seek and explore new avenues of efficiency that would keep weapons and machinery operational. Various approaches must be sought to keep in check the proper distribution of equipment and greater expediency must be applied to allow for faster release of an ever-increasing demand of parts supply which now was numbered in the thousands. Malfunction of guns and heavy weapons and tanks became a serious problem and would have to be alleviated. All ideas and suggested theories would bear evaluation and once adopted would come under heavy scrutiny, thence funneled to research labs and proving grounds . . . in hope of ultimately developing into increased firepower and mobility at the front. Everything from more devastating high explosives . . . sharper contact for spark plugs . . . wider track for tanks to greater expediency in gun tube replacement for the mighty 8-inch or 240mm howitzers underwent careful study. Multiple problems arose and minds were strained to find answers for perpetual improvement in every item. General Medaris later recalled:

"We in FIRST ARMY wanted to keep intact the reputation for efficiency that we had earned during our first few weeks in the field. But more important than that, we didn't want anybody years later to point a finger at Ordnance and say . . . 'we let our boys down.' We knew the combat boys had a hell of a job to do and we were going to do everything possible on our end to see that they kept up that good job."

At the same time organizational efficiency became a prime responsibility. Reliable units with proved records were sought out. No easy task; officers and men excelling in proficient leadership were constantly screened, selected and placed in strategic units that would lend unflinching support and coordination to CORPS and FIRST ARMY Ordnance. Selections and actions that followed allowed us to feel that we would soon belong to just such a unit.

The day following arrival in St. Jacques the 126th was ordered relieved from attachment to the 6th. Battalion and in the same order assigned to the 184th. Ordnance Battalion. An air of confidence settled amongst our staff for now they were certain of stable leadership when it was learned that General Collins had handpicked this Battalion for his forward operations. Commanding the 184th. was a much-talked about former executive officer of the 6th Battalion . . . Major Robert Hudson, a lanky thirty-one year old Georgia textile engineer who sometime later would receive the silver leaves of a Lt. Col. A real task-master, and recognized for his consistent competence he would be heavily depended on . . . and by the same token he would heavily depend on us. Beginning early in the Normandy fighting this spirited organization became one of VII CORPS' Ordnance Battalions through which orders for supply, repair and technical work were funneled to the six, eight and sometimes ten companies revolving under its' jurisdiction. One would find it hard not to believe that the VII CORPS Ordnance officer; Colonel Arthur Luse, exuded unequaled confidence in this particular unit as this Battalion represented VII CORPS' . . . as well as FIRST ARMY's *most forward* Ordnance Battalion throughout most of the entire European conflict.

Asked why 184th. Battalion was selected to maintain this position, Colonel Luse recalls:

In the first place the 184th. was placed in command of a greater number of supporting companies than is ordinarily allocated a Battalion; and being a relatively new Battalion was made up of a nucleus of well-trained personnel from several units to supplement its' staff. Major Hudson had already established for himself a reputation of unusual efficiency and with the tremendous responsibilities in the coming weeks that we knew lay before us we felt that of our attached Ordnance units the 184th. was best equipped to handle the forward maintenance that would be required."

By June 20 the 126th Ordnance, in addition to assignment to the 9TH INFANTRY DIVISION and attached to the United States FIRST ARMY, also operated under the authority of VII CORPS through the 184th Ordnance Battalion. The channels seemed endless. How far did it extend? We soon learned that extension would go just as far as one would let it! A change would come on July 1, when all VII CORPS Ordnance troops now functioning under command of the 224th Ordnance Base Group, would report to 52nd Ordnance Group.

St. Jacques de Nehou, a community registering a population of something like one hundred people sits back almost a quarter of a mile west of an intersection of the main St. Sauver-Bricquebec highway and six miles south of the latter town. Twenty-two miles north lay the prize port of Cherbourg. Unlike some Norman villagers the people of St. Jacques expressed great satisfaction that the "Boche were kaput" . . . and seemed just as pleased that the Americans had moved in.

The Germans had many references but there was no changing the French term . . . "Boche." Its use was exercised all over the country, and not at all unlike the English reference of "Jerry" reflected a strong uncomplimentary flavor. In times past they were known as the "Hun." During the American Revolution some were called "Hessians" and in the first World War with a degree of sarcasm they were called "Heinies;" but we just couldn't seem to find any other term to use except . . . "Kraut."

We were never at a loss to make friends, and among the local people only a brief time passed before French youngsters beaming with enthusiasm and curiosity were gifting us with eggs and other appreciative favors. These gifts were not without their rewards however, for we doled out candy (which they inventively called "Bon-Bon") and other treats from our K-Ration kit that we could easily do without. The youngsters got a big kick out of watching us develop our first French phrase of personal importance . . . "Avez Vous des Ouefs" . . . which meant simply . . . "Have You any eggs?" Not spectacular by any standards and to the average person perhaps silly, but it was a phrase that contained a good deal of humor and created many wholesome laughs; and when stenciled on the front of the convoy's lead jeep one can only imagine the tremendous depth of curiosity emanating from the French wherever we went. It was all in fun and the results of this scintillating question in predominantly rural Normandy proved not only to be amusing but became nutritiously profitable.

Those desiring to get closer to God either joined townspeople and peasants at the age-old village Catholic church, sought solace and comfort by a visiting Rabbi . . . or participated in frequent Protestant services held by greying Chaplain Edward Lorenz of the 184th Battalion, who when periodically making his rounds never failed to bring along his own portable field organ.

Although set off topographically in squares by mounds thick with hedgerows the spacious fields possessed very few trees and basically we were denied any real or natural camouflage. Even with our handmade camouflage nets concealment from the air was virtually impossible. German "recons" visited this vicinity with regularity, often swooping so low over the fields that at times the pilot's profile was easily distinguished. With no apparent intent to cause any particular disturbance for a time Allied anti-aircraft often mercifully held their fire in some instances . . . despite their bold daylight provocative tree-top skimming. That the planes would not use their weapons cannot go unsaid for whenever a handsome target presented itself it was subjected to a quick stream of missiles! An exposed ammo dump, a loosely-guarded truck convoy or possibly a careless or confused Allied troop concentration became a "golden opportunity" for "Jerry" to release a bomb or expend his ammunition. But regardless of their intentions . . . we *still* "ran like hell" for cover!

As our convoy moved in two Frenchmen in great haste were helping our advanced group bury two German soldiers found in a field. Together with other questionable incidents gave us cause to be reasonably certain that somewhere in this vicinity more of the enemy *could* be roaming or hiding. This unwelcomed thought became a reality quicker than expected when headquarters received a dispatch of alert advising that a German patrol of undetermined size had slipped through the lines and could quite possibly be close by.

"In this vicinity! *IN THIS VICINITY!!*" the stark reality quickly seeped in! "Come on!" shouted an alarmed Botting, "Let's get our 'fannies' in high gear!"

Immediate alacrity arose in the breast of each man and a feverish responsibility became the general feeling as the hours ticked by. Captain Orsenigo passed the word down . . . "Keep your rifles close at hand . . . and," he added, "don't panic!" Gradual tension mounted to such a pitch that ironically most were soon wishing the "Jerries" *would* show up, for by now we were ready to pull triggers irrespective of our security! During the night no less than three of the guards, succumbing to an assumption that the enemy was "creeping up" on his post fired "nervous" shots at "positive but unidentified" targets!

"Good God! What's that?"

"Who fired that shot!?"

"Did they get 'em!?"

"For God's sake, will you be quiet?" were some of the impulsive queries coming from an aroused and shocked group.

One can only imagine what this did to the already frayed nerves of the balance who were spread all along the hedges and back in the pasture. Shortly before noon the following day three young frightened Germans were captured in an abandoned garage some thirty yards east of the main entrance guard post. Six more were picked up nearby.

In the dead of night when enemy shells crashed in the distance far to the north and our own artillery whistled overhead from positions south of us, sometimes spiraling a little off target . . . most foxholes felt the brunt of shovels digging a little deeper! While no one failed to count his blessings that none made a direct hit in our location, there were other companies operating within our region that did not share that luck!

The sound of enemy artillery was nothing new to us, but in late June a new sound appeared . . . an eerie sound piercing the soft summer evenings that gave us much alarm. Because of the screeching sound reflecting from its' projectiles we called them "screaming meemies." Though a mean weapon of destruction it was designed partially to penetrate a soldier's emotions. When fired in multiples their ghoulish screams and subsequent explosions, as one GI put it . . . "will bring out beads of perspiration on a guy as big as ice cubes!" The German term was Nebelwerfer, and basically a newer weapon it would be used to some degree throughout Normandy but usually to supplement depleted artillery. A multiple-barrel, 150mm mortar mounted on wheels and fired electrically it was much equivalent to the U. S. 4.5-inch rocket launcher. Its' destructive power was deadly, its' accuracy questionable, but its' psychological use effective. The Nebelwerfer would become far more active during the fall and winter months.

Late the first night of the 20th., against a gloomy cloudy backdrop heavy rains accompanied by gusty winds lashed across the fields scattering tree limbs and even ripping some tents from their stakes. A heavy overcast accompanied with intermittent rains and brisk winds made life dismal for the first two and three days and left patrol duty a lot to be desired. If we thought we were having problems it was like a

"Sunday School picnic" compared to the beach operations. Equipment and floating unloading ramps were being swamped and demolished as thunderous waves and breakers pushed by fierce channel winds lashed mercilessly all along the coast!

Still the main objective of FIRST ARMY at this time was the Naval Base-seaport of Cherbourg, a city of some 38,000 situated on the peninsular's broad northern tip on the English Channel. With this port in Allied hands and possessing the well-established harbor that it does, the number of men and amount of materiel now coming ashore at the two main beachheads of "Omaha" and "Utah" could be landed ten-fold with greater expediency and increased efficiency. This in itself would eliminate not only many landing hazards but a considerably shorter waterway route would be effected between the British Isles and the continent.

9TH DIVISION's 47th. and 60th. Infantry Regiments, together with elements of the 82ND AIRBORNE and 90TH INFANTRY DIVISIONS had already met with unscheduled success in cutting the Cotentin peninsular in half and reaching the city of Barneville on the Atlantic Ocean. This action thereby virtually sealed all escape routes to and from Cherbourg. At the same time other units of the 9TH were vigorously mapping plans and putting them into operation in laying siege to the city of Cherbourg to the north.

Readers of the Monday afternoon June 19 edition of the Chicago Daily Times viewed headlines that read:

"CHERBOURG UNDER SIEGE!"
"25,000 Nazis Face Death Or Surrender"

An article followed:

"The spearhead of Lt. Gen. Omar N. Bradley's spectacular drive to capture this big port, developed by Napoleon, was the U.S. 9TH DIVISION. Capture of a French Naval Base would be an old story for this Division for the 9TH ... under command of Maj. Gen. Manton S. Eddy broke through German defenses to take Bizerte, Tunisia 13 months ago."

The 9TH in a dynamic all-out offensive toward capture of this port city would lose several tanks and other heavy equipment and our Recovery section crew was hardpressed in its diligence all day and into the night. Retrievable bulky equipment including halftracks, jeeps, trucks, ambulances, etc., were brought in and diagnosed as to the extent of repairs possibly to be administered. Unless totally demolished, ninety-five percent were either put into use again or parts were used to repair other machines. If thought not repairable they were left in the field. The hazards accompanying such retrievement resulted in the company's first casualty by direct enemy fire.

On one of the many tributary roads feeding into the main Cherbourg north-south artery just north of Briquebec . . . a town some fifteen miles north of our area, in search of such salvageable equipment, Lt. Jim Prendergast and Mike Scott, the red-haired chief of Recovery from New Jersey were near victims of the unexpected. Rounding an almost blind curve they were met suddenly with a cracking fusilade from an enemy light automatic weapon!

"Blam! . . . Blam! . . . Blam! . . . Blam! . . ."

"My God! I'm hit! . . . Lieutenant . . . I'm hit!"

Losing control of the machine and veering into a ditch, both heaped themselves into the ditch and instinctively began exchanging fire with the gunners. As Prendergast said later;

"There wasn't a second to think . . . we just blindly rolled out of the jeep into a ditch and without even thinking began firing our weapons. We didn't see the Germans but knew they were across the road! Then, they fired at us again, and almost immediately an engineer patrol moving along the same road came upon the scene and went into action, apparently catching the Germans in a crossfire.

"It was funny," he continued; "when the Engineers showed up the 'Krauts' didn't even put up a fight and all were taken prisoner. I believe there were four."

Blood seeping from gaping wounds in the upper left arm and left thigh Scott was rushed to an aid station . . . and subsequently evacuated to a base hospital in England, he never returned to the company. Sgt. Elmer Wagner, a twenty-six-year old tall broad-shouldered Texan with ruggedly handsome features and answering naturally to the name of "Tex" and one with whom no one in the company wished to "tangle" physically, moved up to the Staff Sergeant slot and immediately assumed command of the Recovery section.

On Tuesday, June 20 Supreme Headquarters, AEF announced:

"Cherbourg Four Miles Away!"

The BBC radio in London confirmed this on the same day . . . adding further;

> "The veteran 9TH DIVISION spearheaded the deepest drive directly south of Cherbourg — death pocket for perhaps up to 50,000 Nazis — advancing to St. Martin Le Grand only four miles away."

and still the same day the Rennes, France (German controlled) radio, obviously hard-pressed, reported;

> "Heavy Allied Naval guns have been shelling Cherbourg all day — and Allied planes have been showering bombs on the Fortress installations with fresh U. S. Infantry and tank troops now also taking part in the assault on Cherbourg."

Long minutes following the invasion had turned into hours and the hours into days and nights; endless days and nights with every moment a new raw, bitter experience with the immediate future being prognosticated only by the Allied High Command. So, up to this period sixteen days had passed and the calendar showed June 22. In this period of time the large key towns of Valognes and Montebourg had fallen into Allied hands. Only Cherbourg remained the ultimate prize that would allow for complete Allied control of the peninsular. But Cherbourg was a natural fortified stronghold and within and around its' environs were heavily garrisoned an estimated 30,000 to 40,000 troops. Though some newspapers claimed 50,000 FIRST ARMY G-2 reported less than that. Further; the Defense Area Commander . . . General Karl von Schlieben, was not accustomed to the term, "capitulation."

With the passing of morning this day was entering into the threshold of a beautiful sunny afternoon bathing these fields with an unusual warmth. Though untrue, all fighting seemed momentarily to have subsided . . . as if waiting for a signal to commence or conclude the conflict for a time. Artillery thunder had ceased and no machine gun or "burp gun" echoes were heard to break the prolonged silence. One could in fact gain an illusion that the stillness and tranquility of this summer afternoon could almost give evidence that the war *really* ceased to exist. Someone was heard to say . . . "Who could be mad enough with anyone to fight on such a beautiful day?"

This serenity was shortlived when suddenly from the west the unmistakeable drone of many airplane motors reverberated faintly in the distance! The monotonous deep humming sound grew with intensity; louder and louder, making it obvious that many aircraft were involved! Then high, very high in the sky . . . small silhouettes of planes came streaking into view . . . perhaps some 10,000 to 12,000 feet . . . approaching our direction in great formation!

"What was this?" came questions, "Is this the enemy . . . could this possibly be disaster??" The big question swelled; "Whose are they. . . and where are they going?"

The world had long sensed the power of the German aerial forces and over the past three and four years Europe itself had long known its' ferocity and the viciousness with which it had so ignominously displayed. Memories were not dimmed of the early days when the dreaded death-carrying JU-88's and Heinkels exhibited their ruthlessness over lightly defended heavily populated centers in Holland, Belgium, Poland and France. Not easily forgotten were the lightning-like Stukas that terrorized defenseless retreating columns (many horse-drawn) who had been no match for the "blitzing" well-organized German Army. To many . . . the German Luftwaffe was all but invincible, predicated on the fact that such swift European victories were attained with little aerial opposition of any consequence. Up to this point however, these once-powerful forces had produced no *real* threat to Allied operations though many commanders were prone to wonder just when and where they would strike in great strength. Previous statements widely circulated rumored that Hitler had promised his armies the Allied forces would not last more than a month after the invasion . . . that they would be "swept off the continent with a bloodbath such as never would be forgotten!" Now for a few frantic moments speculation began to swell amongst us that perhaps this *was* coming to pass; perhaps Hitler's threat was taking effect . . . this *could* be the so-called conquering Luftwaffe springing to life!! All of this was reflecting uneasily in our swift reeling thoughts!

Somebody brought out a pair of field glasses.

"They sure as hell are not our planes," someone offered, "They're not German either!" Squinting hard through the glasses one shouted, "Hey, wait . . . they look like 'Limey' planes!" Raising his voice, "They *are* 'Limeys'!" A closer look and attitudes changed . . . there was little question now! In well-formed clusters they kept on coming until completely passing over. By time the third or fourth squadron reached overhead the first planes . . . now far beyond us, had already committed their bombs over targets less than twenty miles to the north! Nor was this the end of it; for from the same direction roared another squadron of planes . . . well-spaced and carrying a heavier drone and appearing to be in even greater numbers!

"Let's have those binoculars!" came the cry! Field glasses easily recognized this group! There . . . insignia blazoned plainly on the lower side of the wings . . . a white encircled star . . . United States Air Force! Relief unmatched by any yet experienced enfolded for at the time we were in no way aware of the significance behind this impressive and awesome display of air power.

1:00 PM was only a few minutes old as the planes approached specific targets and bombs began their irretrievable descent! Fighters first . . . and the mediums followed! Placidity of the sunny afternoon was turning into chaos for the enemy caught in and around the fortress city as Allied planes committed destruction from the skies! Great puffs from enemy ack-ack batteries frantically defending the city filled the sky . . . thickly infesting the air with flak! Ground fire found targets too, and a number of planes burst into flames! While it was thrilling to see parachutes open for many fortunate crew members there were others that perished. Immediately determined from our distant point of observation the airmen suffered only light comparable losses. But on the ground it was yet another story. The enemy suffered tremendously, yes; but released prematurely some explosives and fragments caught segments of the 9TH DIVISION forward elements; and many ground troops became casualties.

What *was* happening up there? What was this all about? The action followed a surrender ultimatum offered the enemy and General Collins had made the choice clear on June 21st.

"Cease all hostile actions or Allied operations will proceed with all weapons at its' command!"

This was Thursday, the 22nd of June and the Germans had been given until nine o'clock AM with which to comply. As American forces were displaying no restraint in laying siege to the city's approaches this ultimatum rapidly dwindled. The hours had now passed and no word from von Schlieben. It was now obvious that the Germans had elected to fight on. General Collins and his field commanders were aware that capitulation was not far off and doubtless the enemy was in accord though not prepared to concede. Shortly before noon the stocky light-haired VII CORPS commander flashed word back across the channel to England where on several bristling airfields an air armada with bomb-bays loaded awaited only the command to ascend skyward and prepare to engage in an unprecedented mission. At 12:40 PM ten squadrons of Mustangs and rocket-firing Typhoons from the RAF led the way! Almost 1,000 planes from the U. S. IX Bomber Command followed . . . involving fighter bombers and mediums, to thrust their tons and tons of explosives on enemy positions!

The planes now streaking overhead on their way back to England gave evidence that the Allied Bomber Command had fulfilled its' promised threat as enemy positions, access approaches and parts of the city was left a shattered debris-strewn smoking wreck. A precedent had been established for this was the first large Allied air strike of any consequence directly supporting ground troops since the pre-invasion bombing of D-Day; and there was no question that this was the most spectacular foray that we had thus far observed in this campaign!

Immediately following this eighty-minute bombardment American troops resumed their offensive and the ground war moved again into full swing! Nothwithstanding the terrific aerial pounding just encountered the Germans continued to exhibit an incredible show of obstinacy against the attackers. This was short-lived and the great onslaught picked up momentum and cracks began to appear in enemy defenses all along the line!

Capturing enemy pillboxes now against weaker opposition; moving forward with every deft blow that at times brought on house-to-house fighting; the battle stubbornly continued throughout the next three days and by late afternoon of the 25th the Germans painfully resolved themselves to the fact that Cherbourg was lost. The prisoner count was swelling and many were actually waiting in groups to be taken.

By noon of June 26 elements of the 4TH, 9TH and 79TH INFANTRY DIVISIONS had the city firmly secured and Gen. "Lightning Joe" Collins' VII CORPS wasted no time in confidently proclaiming victory. Cherbourg thus became not only the first major port to fall into Allied hands but also the largest city on the continent captured to date.

General Eisenhower, years later in conversation with the author admitted that the fall of Cherbourg; "brought my first real sigh of relief since the successful landings." In further summation, the General said:

> "This really was one of our most outstanding achievements and while the assault moved with precision it was by no means an easy task. Trying to dislodge an enemy locked in natural fortifications like Cherbourg requires much planning, patience and daring."
>
> "But we had three fine Divisions working on this assignment, and of course I always had the utmost faith in Joe Collins and there never was a doubt in my mind that he couldn't control any objective assigned him."

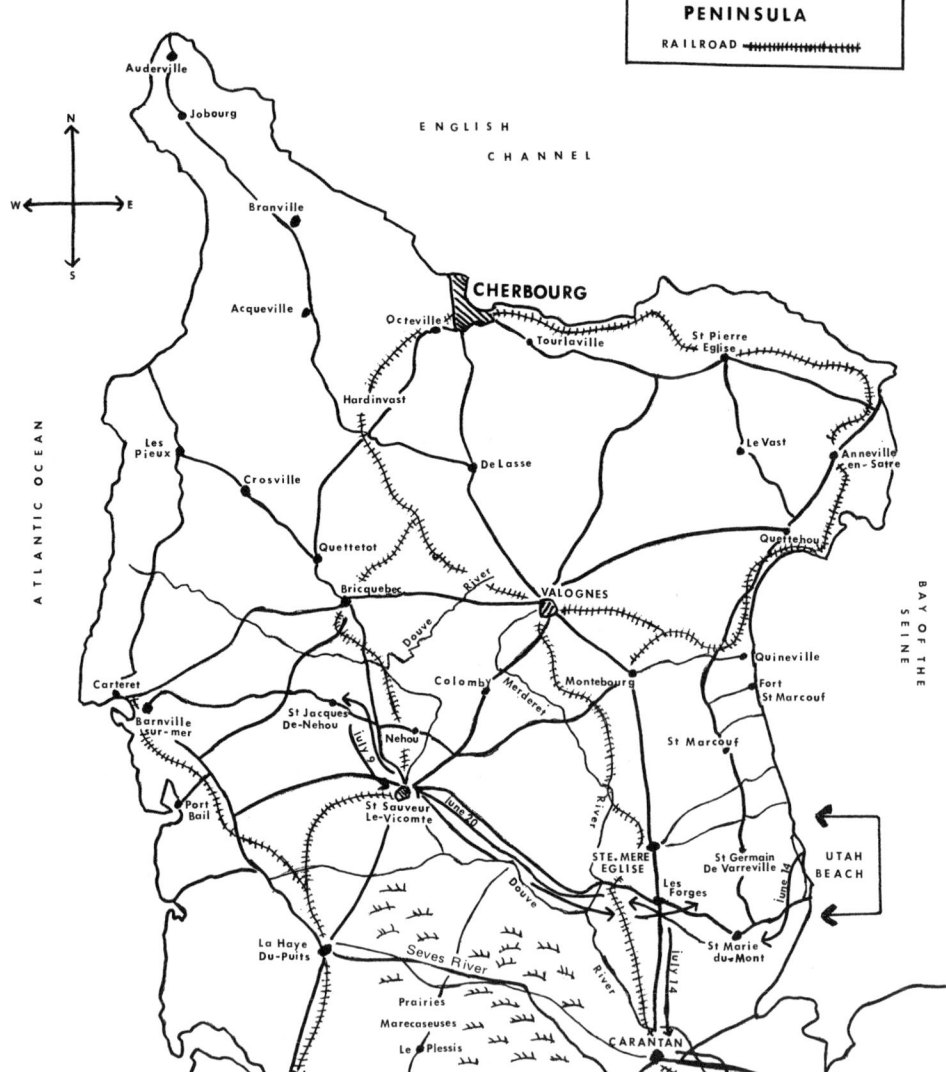

VIII

DRIVING FOR SAINT LO

The very first days of July found Allied forces deployed on a solid front some seventy miles long. Following completion of the Cherbourg campaign FIRST ARMY began initiating with great haste preparations designed to throw a broad offensive from the base of the Cotentin peninsula that would eventually pierce into central France. To approximate the identity of the Cotentin area one would find it bounded by Cherbourg on the north, Avranches on the south, the Vire River on the east and the English Channel on the west. The projected offensive would in effect, subsequently clear Normandy and the French west coast of the Germans.

Liquidation and control of the vital highway complex of St. Lo became FIRST ARMY's prime objective.

The U. S. VIII CORPS, under Maj. Gen. Troy H. Middleton, a former commander of the 45TH INFANTRY DIVISION in Sicily; operating straight down the west coast corridor in the direction of the Brest peninsula and armed with full power of the 82ND

AIRBORNE and 79TH and 90TH INFANTRY DIVISIONS . . . with the 8TH INFANTRY DIVISION in reserve, opened the offensive early July 3rd., aimed at the highway junction of La Haye du Puits directly south; embracing a front that extended broadly through the Mont Castre Forest to just beyond the sprawling marshes of the River Seves (Prairies Marecageuses).

General Collins' VII CORPS started its' attack in the early morning hours of July 4th., long before the sun began to break through; and to guide the "celebration" of that traditional holiday into motion General Collins set off the first artillery fusilade personally; displaying a foray of "fireworks" such as never before had been exhibited! General Bradley added to the fireworks at noon of the same day as he pulled the lanyard string of a 155mm "Long Tom" that became the signal for every artillery piece in FIRST ARMY to fire almost simultaneously! Two outstanding features relative to this exhibition would solemnly be remembered. First; these "fireworks" were of a most deadly caliber . . . and most emphatically, *this was no holiday*!!

We were awakened long before daybreak by the tremendous thundering of artillery that seemed to come from all around. The ground quivered and the atmosphere seemed to be coming apart! Some messkits hanging from tent ropes rattled musically.

"My God! How close are they?" someone questioned.

The horizon was lighted with perpetual blinding flashes and the stillness of the early morning was split with a continuous resounding roar of FIRST ARMY's mightly guns! As one GI put it; "It sounded and seemed as if *all hell* had broken loose!" . . . and for the Germans . . . it actually had!! This unrelenting concentration of 105's, 155's, 240's, heavy 8-inch guns . . . and every type of artillery possessed by FIRST ARMY lasted for about two and a half hours; unquestionably the war's heaviest barrage yet!

Initially relying on the 4TH and 83RD INFANTRY DIVISIONS and beginning north of Carentan straight down a corridor that extended some four to five miles wide from the River Taut bottomlands west to the outer marshes of the River Seves (Prairies Marecageuses) the CORPS virtually straddled the Carentan-Periers road. 9TH INFANTRY DIVISION, regrouping following the Cotentin peninsula action would join the offensive in a short time.

Early morning of July 7 found the XIX CORPS, commanded by Maj. Gen. Charles H. Corlett, a former commander of the 7TH INFANTRY DIVISION in the Pacific and having become operational on the 14th of June to assume an important role in breaking out of the "Utah" beachhead; opening its drive. The 29TH and 30TH INFANTRY DIVISIONS, supported by the 113th Cavalry Group on the eastern flank of VII CORPS concentrated its main effort astride the River Vire. The 3RD ARMORED DIVISION was in reserve near Isigny . . . ready to support either/or both of the latter CORPS.

Still commanded by Maj. Gen. Leonard Gerow and now comprised of the 1ST and 2ND INFANTRY and 2ND ARMORED DIVISIONS, V CORPS maintained an action of stability farther east . . . sandwiched on the west flank by XIX CORPS and the east by the British SECOND ARMY. Its' main objective was to drive deeply southeast below St. Lo, thereby allowing the other three CORPS to establish a pincer movement around the city and at the same time engulfing the exposed eastern flank of the German 7th Army.

On July 9 we moved back twenty-nine miles south toward the beach region to camp and await further disposition at the intersection of Les Forges located on the main north-south St. Mere Eglise-Carentan artery. Company casualties to this point included S/Sgt. Mike Scott, wounded near Cherbourg; T/4 Ed Klabough, a tall redhead "eager beaver" from Detroit who sustained injuries during the beach landing . . . resulting in later evacuation back to England; and S/Sgt. Russell Van Vactor, a former artilleryman turned cook from Seeleyville, Indiana, injured aboard the LST . . . though having since rejoined the unit.

As one expressed it; "without apple orchards we'd be up the creek" and this brief settlement offered no exception. The trees made good natural camouflage though our nets were utilized extensively to make doubly sure concealment from enemy aircraft was reasonable. With an unusual show of air hostility, primarily directed at knocking out American beach assemblies and particularly disrupting heavy traffic on the road to Carentan and south, we were in this location subjected heavily to falling shrapnel and flak.

Most of this superseded firing of anti-aircraft guns located in adjoining fields. With voluminous concentration of such anti-aircraft batteries strategically spaced, Luftwaffe adventures were short-lived and became more of a nuisance than a real threat.

It is when firing subsides that the greatest danger of falling shrapnel exists . . . and that is the time to run for cover! There is no question about the authenticity of an oft-repeated anxiom . . . "What goes up — must come down!" When this jagged metal is first detected whizzing straight down within our vicinity . . . within earshot of any of us, slicing the trees and slashing through the bushes all around, those who had not done so frantically sought cover . . . for it is deadly no matter whose flak it is! In Normandy as the casualty toll climbed many deaths were attributed to this hazard.

At the intersection of Les Forges in a corner field diagonally south across from our location, French civilians under supervision of American soldiers were busy swinging picks and pushing shovels as many new graves were being dug for the many GI bodies already collected and deposited, and one of the first American military cemeteries was in the making.

One morning late in June . . . near this intersection the Captain's driver-aide . . . with a messenger, forced to pull to the side of the battered Carentan road lest they block two "VIP" jeeps coming up close, was startled to note one containing Generals Eisenhower, Bradley and Air Marshal Tedder on a beach inspection. The driver was moreso moved when he came practically "eyeball to eyeball" with the Supreme Commander in his jeep now moving almost to a crawl, who exchanged salutes with a slight grin and an affirmative nod.

The principal towns of Carentan, Isigny and several adjacent communities had been taken, lost and re-taken and at this point were secure in American hands. There are some twelve square miles of marshes around Carentan and the swamps were nothing less than treacherous to the foot soldier. The land is soft and moist, a vast network of canals and ditches . . . at sea level in many instances replete with shallow ponds and slime. Only via the causeways making up the roadways is it possible for a vehicle to navigate. Battles in and around these deceptive marshes had been fierce and all through swamps surrounding that battered town lay bodies that had not yet been found; both Germans who had lost and Americans that had helped make it a victory. One could venture almost anywhere throughout this entire section and find it not at all uncommon to locate bodies, and at this point indications were obvious that the Germans were falling back slowly . . . doggedly . . . almost systematically . . . but making the offensive pay *dearly* for every foot of ground taken!

Now below Carentan our advances were beginning to show signs of increased acceleration! Ground advances now annexed in terms of miles previously were calculated in the measure of yards. Often as much as two hundred yards had constituted a good day's gain.

Even as these new advances were made; so were rumors . . . rumors to an extent that the end of August could very well see the end of the war. Though actions had been going well these rumors were without true foundation and were not viewed with favor by many. Some prisoners were even expressing their optimism that the German Armies were near collapse. But the war's end? It couldn't be that easy! Not yet! Yet it was always amazing how with great speed, rumors circulated among troops; amazing still, when the *same* rumor persists in other units though they may be miles apart. Yet, on the other hand . . . to see operations escalating with strong consistency did much for morale. A tremendous number of enemy prisoners continued to fall into our hands and the American casualty rate had leveled off with moderation. In the closing days of the Cherbourg campaign we had seen truckload after truckload of prisoners in almost convoy procession barrelling toward the beach zone . . . eventually to P.O.W. camps in England. VII CORPS already was reported to have captured some 40,000 since D-Day.

Pincer movements successfully applied by FIRST ARMY'S gigantic offensive was playing havoc with the enemy and gaining momentum with each advance. For a time it appeared a sure rout but the formidable well-protected cathedral city of St. Lo stood directly and defiantly in the allied path and *here* the enemy refused to yield!

St. Lo is one of those names, like Verdun, Gettysburg, Stalingrad and Thermopolae that will retain its' place in history so long as men, not missiles, fight battles. Embracing a peacetime population of approximately 11,000 St. Lo unobtrusively, though distinctly centered as an important gateway to inner France. Little heard of outside France prior to the war, fate would play a violent hand . . . making certain that soon its' emergence from obscurity would painfully earn for it a place in military history as one of the most strategic and difficult objectives encountered in the second World War. Situated primarily on low ground and located near a prominent bend of the deep and swift River Vire, the city is ringed by hills in sort of an arc. Representing a hub of main arteries that lead in all directions St. Lo was a prime obstacle; a "cinder in the eye" . . . and one that *had to be removed* before successful operations could continue. Allied military planners were unanimously cognizant of the existing reality that a mighty thrust must be concentrated on this stubborn bastion and liquidation of the enemy from this stumbling block was inevitable.

Already outdistanced by our DIVISION by two or three days we awaited only the word from DIVISION Ordnance to move forward . . . and we waited eagerly. The "go" signal came late afternoon of July 14 to move south. It was noted that we had been on the peninsula exactly one month. Next morning with no great rush; it was in fact almost noon before rolling out of the Les Forges. On through the small community of Blosville where VII CORPS had recently headquartered and further down through St. Come du-Mont we crossed the tiny River Groult. In less than a mile we came into Carentan and picked our way slowly through that shattered town.

Here was the scene of utter destruction . . . clumps of crumbled masonry, much shattered glass . . . dwellings blackened and reduced to rubble . . . debris once choking the streets now bulldozed in heaps out of the way . . . war machines burned out and abandoned. Dead from both opposing forces distinctly segregated lay grouped in clusters off the main thoroughfare awaiting identification by VII CORPS or FIRST ARMY Graves Registration. Through this ruined town the stench of decaying flesh was not easily avoided and lingered unyieldingly with us for quite some distance.

A brief distance out of Carentan the convoy turned from the

Carentan-Isigny road at the petite and rubble-strewn village of La Fourchette to move south onto a key St. Lo road. A strategic canal where the River Taute flows into the Vire was crossed . . . though not before taking alarming cognizance of the battered sign at the canal's approaches erected by FIRST ARMY engineers that blared dramatically:

"THIS BRIDGE UNDER ENEMY OBSERVATION"

It was a small and narrow bridge but had been an artillery target for a long time and with consistent accuracy was knocked out and rebuilt several times.

Some six miles further we reached St. Jean de Daye; an unimpressive town that had been fought for and subdued by the 30TH INFANTRY DIVISION operating on the east flank of the 9TH INFANTRY, and whose obstinance was evidenced by clear signs of a furious tank battle recently staged in its' streets. Heavy casualties were inflicted by both victor and vanquished. In a later furious armored assault by counter-attacking German panzers Lt. Col. Maxwell Tincher's hard-hitting 899th. Tank Destroyers earned for themselves a Distinguished Unit Citation, in that against heavy odds they had with their mounted powerful 76mm cannon packing a 3-inch high velocity shell that could pierce the heaviest armor, dueled point blank with Germany's famed Panzer Lehr Armored Division and prevented the enemy from severing and controlling the Carentan-St. Lo road.

Our "recon" team swiftly scouting through here a day earlier had reported seeing "many dead German and American GIs sprawled all over the place with all types of personal gear scattered everywhere." Said one, "Boy! . . . it looked like Custer's last stand!" When the initial convoy rolled through the dead were gone but the streets were still cluttered with heavy rubble and disabled armor.

Moving due west of St. Jean broken choppy war-ravaged roads continued to be encountered . . . strewn with tons and tons of devastated enemy equipment. Shortly after passing through little Goucherie, our advance was halted when occupying three small fields in an apple orchard a few yards south beyond a drab abandoned village of closely-knit dwellings whose bullet-splintered roadsign identified it as Haut Vernay.

Situated almost a mile north of the more vital Tribehou, Haut Vernay two days earlier had been annexed by elements of the 3RD ARMORED DIVISION and 113th Cavalry Group but only after a murderous clash with the enemy. Lifeless "Krauts" . . . their shattered bodies and personal items viewed earlier littering the vicinity had been proof positive. When the "recon" group came in they reported with much alacrity the dissemination of helmets, gas masks, boots, mess kits, belts of ammo, panzerfausts, hand grenades, broken Mauser rifles and bazookas and lesser types of equipment scattered all over. Graves Registration troops had done their job by time the company's main complement arrived. Trip mines were still in abundance and though in most cases marked areas identified their presence, every step taken was viewed with extreme caution.

In the holocaust of war it is expected that a good number of individuals will of a necessity become subjected to close calls . . . many less memorable than others. Each man, though having his own experiences would not always feel deposed to talk about it . . . and though spectacular or less . . . some far more harrowing than others, could produce such a sustained lingering effect that many cared never to discuss it. He would simply be content to live alone with it . . . hoping eventually to erase the incident from memory.

With another member of the "recon" team, Mike Springer crept into Haut Vernay in early morning a day ahead of the company. Only the day before, following a bitter fight did the town fall to U. S. troops; and now, not long abandoned and cleared of some dead lay open. The husky active T/4, his short trim moustache ever-prominent, suggested giving the town the "once over." Some would later suggest "looting" was uppermost in their minds.

"Ridiculous," says Springer, "What the hell was there to loot; and besides, who needs to?" He strongly added, "I got enough 'crap' to carry around as it is!"

That term was not to be taken literally for every GI on the continent agreed there was a broad difference between "souvenir hunting" and "looting."

"Even at that," replied the agile Detroiter; "we weren't even looking for souvenirs . . . just simply looking around."

The place was small; deserted . . . except for the echo of barking burp guns, coughing mortars and the reply of 50-caliber machine guns across the swamp and the Taute River flats far to the southwest no sign of life stirred anywhere. Entering a doorway of a brick dwelling curiosity turned to alarm when a single shot rings out shattering an upstairs window!

"God!" grunted Springer in a startled expression, "Where did that come from?"

Throwing themselves to the floor . . . and slowly looking up and through an adjoining half-darkened bedroom doorway they shuddered to see in that very room bodies of three German soldiers sprawled in unique positions . . . having obviously met their deaths a short while ago!

"Good God! Look at that!" whispered one heavily. "Just *look* at those Krauts!"

"You look," replied Springer; "I'm *looking* for a way to get the hell out of here!"

On the bed lay one with out-stretched hand who doubtless had sought futilely to administer sulphur powder to stem the blood flow from the massive wound on the left side of his lower abdomen. Congealed blood from an ugly chest wound covered the jacket of one as he lay half-in and half-out of an over-sized wicker rocking-chair. Still another was propped up against one corner of a wall, his hands and legs bathed with blood and sulphur powder sifted all over . . . an apparent attempt to stop the flow. Only a few feet in front of them in the semi-darkness of the same room Springer spotted a fourth German lying on his back. He too had tried to administer the powder.

Another shot rings out and splinters into the doorway through which they had entered!

A frantic whisper! "It's a sniper . . . it's gotta be! Get back! Get back!"

Both were seized with the same thought;

"Get the heck out of here . . . now!"

Curiousity replaced reasoning and somehow sufficient courage was mustered to determine the origin of the shots. When upon pumping two, three or four shots across the street through open windows and shattering others from whence it was thought the shots came, and receiving no return fire . . . it was concluded the apparent sniper had elected to depart . . . doubtless making his way out through a growth-choked portion of the swamp. As he reported later;

"We were both damn glad of it!"

Concluding that this is only one brief incident superseded by many . . . Mike Springer, though hesitant to ramble on about it, would for a long time remember the "one who got away" at Haut Vernay! He will remember too, the six SS troopers whose bodies were torn and filled with slugs and scattered in death between the hedges and the ditch behind the house as those who *didn't get away."*

Pocketed in a rather unique situation we viewed with some concern **FIRST ARMY** heavy artillery firing from positions behind and over our heads and the infantry moving with caution against bypassed and trapped enemy clusters across the swamp just west of this location. Too close for comfort we cringed each time the great 155mm 'Long Toms' ripped the air apart with their message of destruction that caused the ground to rumble with such vibration that loose dirt from sides of most foxholes caked off and trickled back into the holes! Across the barren swamp toward Tribihou Island to the west small puffs of smoke from bursting shells were visibly detected as they searched for targets! Though quite some distance beyond the familiar and incessant bark of the feared and respected "burp gun" continually reverberated its' authority to our ears day and night.

The German "burp gun" has been mentioned on numerous occasions and the justification of its' identity is without challenge for its' action is quite like the real gastric sound . . . a staccato of several sharp repiticious "burps." Unique in operation actually it was strangely akin to the American 50-caliber machine gun though somewhat smaller and had to be fired with these short bursts lest the bore or barrel become dangerously overheated. Moreover; the barrel was interchangeable and at times when intensity of battle neccessitated the weapon to be in continuous use, firing of this gun subsided very briefly . . . only long enough in fact for the barrel to be replaced. This operation took just a matter of seconds and the firing immediately resumed.

Sgt. Botting looked out from the CP one morning toward guard post No. One which policed the main entrance, to see the sentry on duty engaging in an apparent verbal struggle with two middle-aged Frenchmen, who with hands gesticulating excitedly appeared much disturbed.

"No compre! No compre!" came the sentry's repiticious answer. The Frenchmen were persistent and by the time the sentry had exhausted all patience, having repeated "No compre!" perhaps a dozen times his voice had crescendoed to almost a shout.

Tall tossel-haired Vic Sienko was one not easily rattled but at the moment his lack of French comprehension had pushed him to the point of frustration. "I said, *NO COMPRE*, dammit . . . and that's final!"

"What's the trouble out there?" called Botting.

"I don't know Sergeant, but these 'Frogs' are mad as hell about something!"

"Bring 'em in here." was the order; "and somebody go find Boudreau and tell him to come up here . . . *on the double*!"

Henry Boudreau, the not so tall stocky French-Canadian from Massachusetts, perhaps the youngest man in the unit and who was always called on whenever we got into trouble with the French, calmly set the visitors at ease and let them spill their complaint. Obviously amazed and amused at the rapidity of his comprehension smiles slowly replaced frowns of dismay. Boudreau summed it up and turning to Botting, said:

"Sergeant, they are upset because some of our men have swiped some personal items from their homes."

Botting flushed.

"What kind of items . . . don't they know there's a war going on? Where the hell have *they* been?"

A brief interrogation followed.

"Personal items, they say; and they also say they are *well* aware of the war . . . probably better than we are."

"Sounds like a lot of 'bull s--t' to me," came the reply.

"How do they know our men took them? How do they know it wasn't some other outfit? How do they know it wasn't the Germans that did it?"

A few words from Boudreau and the visitors again replied, simultaneously pointing to the back of the orchard.

"They say they saw a couple of our men bring the stuff into this area through the back road."

"They did, huh?" . . . Okay Boudreau, tell 'em not to worry about it. We'll check it out and if the stuff is in the company area" assured Botting; "it will be returned today." His voice trailing; "Now, get them the hell out of here."

Satisfied and thanking all present, the Frenchmen exited and headed back toward Haut Vernay.

Captain Orsenigo, seated calmly near the doorway of the CP, had observed it all without saying a word. Now he spoke;

"Sergeant," he ordered, "I want that stuff returned and I want it to be known right away that there will be no looting in this outfit!"

Field-stripping a cigarette in his habitual nervousness, he repeated; "I mean . . . *no looting*!"

The "word" became law at a noon formation and before darkness settled the Recovery section was minus one large wall mirror, a large fancy antique clock, one thick bed comforter and a multicolored well-worn carpet that graciously had lined the inside of a puptent-covered foxhole.

Nothing was said however, a day or so later when a cow was killed, strung up on an "A-frame" and professionally drawn and quartered so as to provide a thick handsome steak to every member of the company. Nothing should have been said . . . for the owner was well-paid for it.

Southeast, perhaps five hundred yards below us in the Hommet Woods elements of 9TH DIVISION's 899th. Tank Destroyers, along with combat teams of the 9TH's 47th and 60th Infantry Regiments had three days earlier repelled a fierce enemy counterattack . . . an attack bent on splitting FIRST ARMY forces that would gain control of the vital St. Lo-Isigny road. Praise was administered these DIVISION units for this action along with the 899th's dramatic display of tenacity at St. Jean de Daye, some three miles due east did much to break the back of Germany's famed Panzer Lehr Division!

In the meanwhile; aside from irregular appearances by enemy

planes during the day, nightly "recon" missions usually constituting a single plane and seldom hostile operated on an almost fixed pattern. So prompt and consistent in fact were these aircraft . . . not missing the evening hour of 10:30 five minutes either way throughout the entire Normandy campaign . . . that subsequently they were dubbed by Allied troops as "Bedcheck Charlie" . . . a name that would well-identify them throughout the following weeks. So accustomed did we become to it that when approaching there was little cause for alarm. One would shrug his shoulders and say;

"Hell, don't worry about it, that's just a "recon" job."

Because of the British time standard which they called "double-summer time" which set the clocks ahead two hours, darkness came late in Normandy . . . most often not falling until after ten o'clock.

On or about the third day we received in tornadic fashion a turbulent rumor, one that had already become widespread throughout this entire section. Without checking it out someone had started it by strongly suggesting that the Germans, in their desperate determination to stem the tide of the American onslaught had resorted to the use of the one dubious weapon that had long been feared and not yet completely discounted! This was the ultimate instrument . . . *poison gas*! Now, when this "sure thing" started intangible evidence to give it a sound basis was parlayed from the fact that no less than the "higher brass" appeared gravely concerned! The manipulation of and the overt testing of masks by troops hurriedly passing through the thoroughfare further substantiated its' veracity!

We dared not believe it . . . it *just could not be true*! Yet, when one closely observed actions of other GIs who appeared equally as concerned it appeared to produce conclusive evidence that this "gas" rumor was for real!

"Have the Germans gone crazy?" thought many. For . . . not since Italy's abominal invasion of Ethiopia in 1935-36 had poison gas been used in warfare! The League of Nations had many years before adopted an historic ban against its use in warfare!

Now we were *greatly* alarmed!

"Shall we call Battalion, Captain?" asked Botting.

"Call 'em later, just see how many masks are around," was the calm reply.

"My God!" some reasoned, "If this is the real thing . . . what will we do? How will we protect ourselves? What kind of gas is it? Nerve gas? . . . Chlorine? . . . Mustard gas? . . . Phosgene? . . . Would it result in slow asphyxiation? Would it affect our heart action and take us away quick? Would we notice signs of skin burning first?" Recalling well, that our training in prevention of gas had been exceedingly limited. How limited, we became quickly aware!

"My God!" though those statistically minded, "How many were aware that a good percentage of Americans died as a result of poison gas attacks in World War I?" Many, as kids, had heard their fathers talk about it . . . especially those having served in France in the first great war. Thoughts of desperation raced through our minds!

"Can't we get out of here? How is this gas delivered?" Explosive shell cases? Dropped in bombs? . . . From tanks of some low-flying plane . . . as one would spray crops at home? Was anyone's color shield (located on the shoulder of each jacket) changing color?"

As a matter of fact, what had happened to all the color shields??

Some became almost frantic! We remained this way too, until the later hours . . . still not really believing, but waiting . . . waiting . . . until gradually piecemeal revelations would unfold to tell us that this had been a gross misinterpretation of the real thing!

What had happened? What had *really* happened?

Though several schools of interpretations were distributed, someone in authority summed up the rumor's foundation . . .

On the main supply route leading south into Tribehou . . . a distance perhaps of half a mile beyond our area; a small but vital bridge had been "zeroed in" by enemy artillery for quite some time and in the process of several shellings its' destruction was imminent. One of the incoming shells hit and demolished a high-caliber ammunition truck camouflaged nearby, setting off a series of tremendous blasts! A light but penetrable wind blowing with consistency from the west carried with it unidentifiable chemical fumes into the nostrils of already suspicious Allied troops. As fumes spread . . . thus did rumors! Proportionate confusion would well express the actions that followed . . . and nothing at the moment could keep it from becoming widespread! Within our own company few gas masks could immediately be located . . . and in sheer disgust many were quickly remorse to recall that the impregnated clothing having been patterned as a preventive against possible body attacking gases or chemicals had long before been discarded!

When official confirmation came in late evening, verifying that this matter was no more than a frantic and loose assumption grown quickly out of proportion, relief such as had not been known for many days engulfed the company!

From this, a very serious fact was revealed . . . and there was little question as to its' authenticity. Maybe it was true . . . perhaps the enemy, bitter or frightened over a badly faltering war effort, had at some point shown some inclination to possible use of this weapon, and had such plans been put into action undoubtedly an unparalleled chaotic situation amongst American and British troops would have existed. An equally disordered situation would have been rampant among whatever French civilians were located in the region. It was generally known, however; that the German High Command had been made aware of the tremendous supply of poison gases cached away in England under Allied control. Should the enemy decide to unleash this weapon there was little room for doubt that an earlier doom would be spelled not only for their armies in the field but for the 'Fatherland' of Germany itself! Moreover; the Allies, with controlled air strength were in a position to drench every German city in that nation.

***

Probably the most hard-pressed of all fighting men in Normandy at this point were soldiers of the armored units. Troops usually assigned the task of paving the way or supporting the infantry were well-equipped, well-trained, armed with tremendous firepower, and ordinarily when the front lines began to sag represented strong pillars of salvation. Yet, confronted with a natural immoveable obstacle of endless hedgerows these "armored powerhouses" often found themselves helpless to pursue the enemy to any great advantage and even while initiating the slow ardous and almost impossible task of plowing through, or even rolling over these hedgerows, became themselves a profitable target.

The true mission of cavalry (or armor) is to provide a light highly mobile force of great fire-power capable of performing reconnaissance, counter-reconnaissance, security, screening and offensive and defensive missions. Tanks were not to operate singly as this method normally proved disastrous. For proper effect, employment in mass was the only means of attaining results. Throughout the entire campaign, the principal of tank employment in mass proved sound. The big M-10 tank destroyers did not necessarily share this problem in that because of less thickness of armor plate ordinarily reverted to a "hide-hit-and-run" operation.

But high priorities exercised by both American and British alike, would be placed on armor. The Germans too, had long known of its' significance and placed strategic importance on its' deployment. In his book, "Tank Warfare," armored expert Kenneth Macksey observes:

"Both (General) Montgomery and his opponents, Field-Marshals von Rundstedt and Rommel, were in accidental but mutual agreement that the final outcome would be decided by tanks, no matter how crowded with artillery or infantry the battlefield would become or how intense the intervention by aircraft."

Generals Eisenhower, Bradley, Patton and Hodges were in full accord.

The primary mission of the tank destroyer is to destroy hostile armor. Inasmuch as it did not have sufficient armor plate to protect itself as did the combat tank, especially from anti-tank weapons and enemy tanks as well, its' initial superiority for such missions lay in its' superior gun power. Field strategists were becoming greatly concerned, for losses due to slow advance were increasing alarmingly and time was too valuable for this condition to continue.

Ideas, methods and theories were exchanged in an effort to

afford tankmen a better break in this struggle against not only the common enemy but these nature-supported barriers as well. A simple solution, advanced by a single GI was welcomed and accepted by those in high authority that reached all the way to the Supreme Commander. A sharp pronged cutting device, some eight to ten inches long, would be attached to the front of all attacking tanks, three and four thick steel blades mounted on a steel bar or welded to the machine itself . . . jutting out in the forefront of the vehicle, performing like a scoop. Unique in its performance; much in fact, like that of a bulldozer, a Sherman tank, called in this instance, the "Rhinoceros" . . . with its armored beef of 34 tons would ram a hedgerow at a good rate of speed, all the while keeping on an even keel, its purpose to plow through almost impervious roots and earth . . . virtually penetrating the mound! This would clear an entrance through which infantrymen could dash for a more maneuverable position.

The Ordnance Department was ordered to make available immediately such instruments and equip all tanks possible. On the continent this department went to work and the 126th became one of the first units in VII CORPS to so execute this order. Under cover of tarpaulin canopies generators hummed, acetylene torches burned, and mallets banged against metal as men sweated through the night to get this project moving. When put into action this instrument made the difference and was used with great efficiency throughout the balance of the "hedgerow campaign."

Bob Hudson, then a major and 184th Ordnance Battalion commander, and now a textile engineer in Greenviile, S. C., recalls the action of the 126th in tackling this problem.

"The telephone jingled shortly after lunch in my CP and it was Colonel Sams of 52nd Ordnance Group calling a meeting of all battalion commanders. He said General Bradley had ordered all Ordnance units available to start putting things together immediately. The 126th was the first company that I called on for this and your men went to work immediately and by next morning several tanks were ready." He added; "We both know now what this really meant . . . not only to the tankmen but to general morale of the entire FIRST ARMY."

Colonel Sams, in later evaluation said:

"There is no doubt but that the design, development and manufacture of this device (hedgerow cutter) furnished a major contribution to the success of the operation which resulted in our forces breaking through the German lines and the subsequent race across France."

He further concluded:

"In addition to its contribution to the tactical success of our forces, the hedgerow cutter was directly responsible for preventing the loss of many lives and of many critically needed tanks."

To sum up the tremendous disadvantage facing the allied advance one would almost have to see or be confronted at first hand with these hedgerows to actually fathom the obstacle presented. Great mounds of earth rising a good four to six feet from ground level and averaging a thickness of five to seven feet across. In most cases a drainage ditch approximately one foot wide ran its' entire length. Moreover, across the top of these earthen mounds thick hedges grew unendingly, their identity could in no way be related to the flimsy hedges that normally are found in one's front yard at home. The stalks at the base measured offtimes from eight to ten inches in diameter. Brambles, vines and foliage interwoven around bushes and briars, often with wire entangled within the growth jutted an additional three to four feet above the mounds to make visibility on either side completely negligible from the ground.

Almost every field in Normandy (most averaging approximately 200 ft. x 400 ft.) was separated and completely surrounded by these obstacles except for individual small entrance passageways normally measuring no more than five to six feet wide.

For centuries Norman farmers had utilized these hedges to enclose orchards, fields and the like and basically were designed to protect crops and cattle from the ocean winds. In some instances fields were separated by small alley-like sunken roads five to seven feet wide and utilized by farmers that preferred them to main thoroughfares when walking livestock to and from pasture. Hedgerows flanked these small roads on either side to follow them the entire distance. Due to many explosives planted by a retreating enemy this played havoc with advancing troops, and faced with hedgerows that lined each side these small roads for a time became something of a death trap for many GIs.

Although fighting continued in every degree to be bitter and costly, since consummation of the Cherbourg campaign countless hazards of a necessity still remained to be overcome. But now, FIRST ARMY appeared to be ahead of its' timetable. Noncombatants had tirelessly contributed their efforts, strongly reflected in reconstruction of bridges, stringing and relaying communication wires over and under roads, through trees, across swamps and virtually everywhere. Removing obstacles and making extensive and complexing repairs to roads was incessant. Because most main arteries were in a constant state of repair not only from shelling and bombing, but an over-capacity of traffic. Engineer road repair units held high priority and rarely was there found any let-up in this back-breaking task.

Secondary roads required constant attention too, and had to be hastily engineered if kept open. Detours were effected at best vantage points to keep in fluid motion over-worked supply trucks hauling ammo, troops, rations, medical supplies, vehicle parts and the like from beaches to the front. Considering all of this . . . along with obstructions of many variances, it would appear that American ingenuity was concerting an impossible task.

In the face of these perpetual accomplishments there now was in the making one of the greatest tasks of military strategy that called for brains, brawn and sheer power.

Even though at many points the rail-highway hub of St. Lo could have been by-passed it still remained a "thorn in the side" of the now over-zealous Allied drive. There could be no brushing aside the stark facts . . . St. Lo had to fall . . . and that was proving no easy task! The 29TH INFANTRY DIVISION had long been hacking at it; the 2ND had exerted their efforts; so had the 30TH, 35TH, 3RD ARMORED and numerous combat striking elements.

Already proved . . . this vital bastion afforded the enemy great natural defenses and they were "dug in" in and around it as compact as a "tick on a dog's back!"

The city was long-suffering, having been heavily bombed with regularity some two months before its' siege, and by D-Day some 800 of its' citizens already lay dead beneath its' rubble. This was perhaps the enemy's last great defense area before falling back into the spacious depths of France and *he* would let *his* obstinance be felt and his endurance be tested at all costs!

By mid-July General Corlett said; "too much time, effort and manpower have been consumed by ground forces toward capture of this vital city," and XIX CORPS now placed heavy emphasis on its' capture.

Following three days of continuous ground and aerial bombardment, and heavily flanked by United States forces on the north, east and west, enemy resistance from the city began to show signs of weakening.

Early July 18th XIX CORPS dispatched a Task Force from the 29TH INFANTRY DIVISION to move on the city. Backed by the 113th. Cavalry Group this Task Force entered St. Lo . . . engaging in some house-to-house fighting and subjected to sparodic sniper fire. By late afternoon the city was firmly secured. The 35TH INFANTRY DIVISION quickly moved in to establish a complete defense of the entire CORPS sector. Within the next two days FIRST ARMY would claim complete control over the city. The grueling day-by-day, step-by-step agony of the ground forces would however, be temporarily overshadowed by the dramatic touches of OPERATION COBRA!

A carefully devised plan was laid out by FIRST ARMY and the combined air forces . . . a plan in brief terms that would initiate a mass bombing just southwest of the city; to be followed with an immediate dynamic thrust of armor and infantry.

The sunny mid-morning of July 25th brought the unmistakable vibrations of mighty airpower concentrations that startled everyone into dropping his immediate task. Roaring distantly from north, northeast and west . . . the drone with every fleeting minute increasing into a great gradual crescendo! Ten o'clock had barely passed before they were streaking directly above, becoming in a matter of minutes the main attraction of every soldier in this corridor of Normandy. This superlatively planned operation was designed to break, demoralize and destroy masses of enemy troop concentrations now controlling the many highway arteries that lead in every direction. Now cognizant of this deadly assignment everyone viewed with great respect the tremendous display of Allied airpower which by now completely engulfed the sky in a web-like fashion.

This operation was planned and partially became functional on the 24th., though called off when several formations found it impossible to identify specific targets . . . though not before some bombs had been released.

To the east . . . to the west . . . to the north, as far as the human eye could see an endless procession of aircraft with their mighty monotonous drone as steady as that of a thousand electric fans continued to move southward! On they came!! As one put it; "reminding one of a great mass of giant birds in slow motion flying south for the winter."

Coming in at 8,000 to 10,000 feet flights of twelve . . . forty eight at a time! Another fifty at another angle came thundering across the blue horizon! Some 350 fighters first . . . followed by 400 mediums; then more than 1,500 B-17's, B-24's and B-25's of the 8TH and 9TH TAC AIR FORCES, until numbering nearly 2,500 . . . a foray of air power such as never before had been exhibited in aviation history!

Already the first planes were dropping their smoke signals a considerable distance ahead of the poised but firmly "dug in" American infantry; these signals acting as a distinct zone of division between enemy and Allied lines with bombs to be dropped several hundred yards forward *beyond* the signals.

Then . . . without warning, a great disaster was about to strike! Many officers and GIs looked up to observe that *"Something is wrong . . . drastically wrong!"* A shifting wind caught the falling smoke signals previously released by the planes and subsequently sent them drifting back toward the region presently occupied by American troops . . . north of the Periers-St. Lo highway! Before the next wave of planes were aware of this gross error their own deadly bombs were released and now inextricably pummelling earthward in sickening screeches! Direct into our own territory!

"My God! What is happening?!!!" was the cry of ground commanders!

Confusion and chaos ran among the troops for a brief but hectic time as American ground positions and observers were hit . . . and hit bad! Among other divisional casualties, including several in the 30TH and 4TH INFANTRY DIVISIONS, scores of 9TH DIVISION troops were subsequently killed and wounded in this horrifying miscalculated action! In a short space of minutes this agonizing error was swiftly relayed and corrected and this regrettable action was quickly compensated by the 8TH and 9TH TAC as they rained death and destruction on their original targets!

From our location to the northeast this great drama was viewed with awe and much speculation. Nothing yet had equaled this magnificent display of power! We were . . . in no uncertain terms, eternally grateful that these bombs were falling from our planes and *not* those of the enemy!

Explosions rocked the region with such continuity that the very earth remained in a continuous rumble; even our clothes and helmets were set to a trembling motion! As countless columns of greyish smoke blending into one huge pillar climbed into the blue sky, showering flak bursts from enemy anti-aircraft guns reached out and claimed a bomber and it became heartrending to see that plane explode or catch fire and start its' downward dive. We helplessly watched the more fortunate crew members bail out . . . hoping that they might alight and find refuge in Allied territory. We stared anxiously.

"See any parachutes?" asked one.

"No, . . . yes, . . . there's one!" and then everybody would take up the count; "Two, three, four" - then somebody said with relief; "They're alright!" From our observation point we noted only five or six planes to go down. With no letup the bombing continued for approximately two hours and even after subsidence of this action bombers continued to pass over.

Some 6,000 tons of bombs had fallen with a bomb landing an estimated average of fifteen yards apart. German positions were blasted beyond complete recognition over a radius of approximately three miles. Tons and tons of equipment were demolished and transfigured, or rendered useless when covered by dirt and debris. All enemy communications were ripped and definitely destroyed; many tanks overturned and out of action, and hundreds killed and wounded. By their own count the Germans suggested that over 1,000 perished in the holocaust. In this fashion no army in the field had ever taken such a widely-scoped trouncing as those receiving this devastating saturation. The 8TH and 9TH AIR FORCES working in close coordination with ground units had unleashed a spectacle that the German Luftwaffe even in its' *best days* could not have claimed! It was a great victory, yes; but in some sectors of American positions there was no elation . . . and frantic calls for blood donors came piercing from the front as FIRST ARMY GIs began digging out their own victims of the bombing. Prominent among them; Lt. Gen. Lesley McNair, Chief of United States Army Ground Forces; . . . killed while observing the action from a forward foxhole.

The next morning, July 26th. headlines of the Richmond (Va.) Times Dispatch gave a boost to those questioning the foothold of Allied forces in Normandy:

"NORMANDY STALEMATE ENDS IN MIGHTY ALLIED DRIVE"

"Record Air Armada Aids Land Armies"

Additional emphasis was reported in an adjoining column:

"So great was the aerial destruction to the German communications lines that Allied headquarters had reason to believe the Germans were confused over where the land blow was being struck and the locale of the offensive was kept secret for almost twelve hours in order to capitalize on the German's plight."

Years later when asked by the author why American troops were allowed so close to assigned bomb lines, and "wasn't it an extremely dangerous risk?" General Bradley replied:

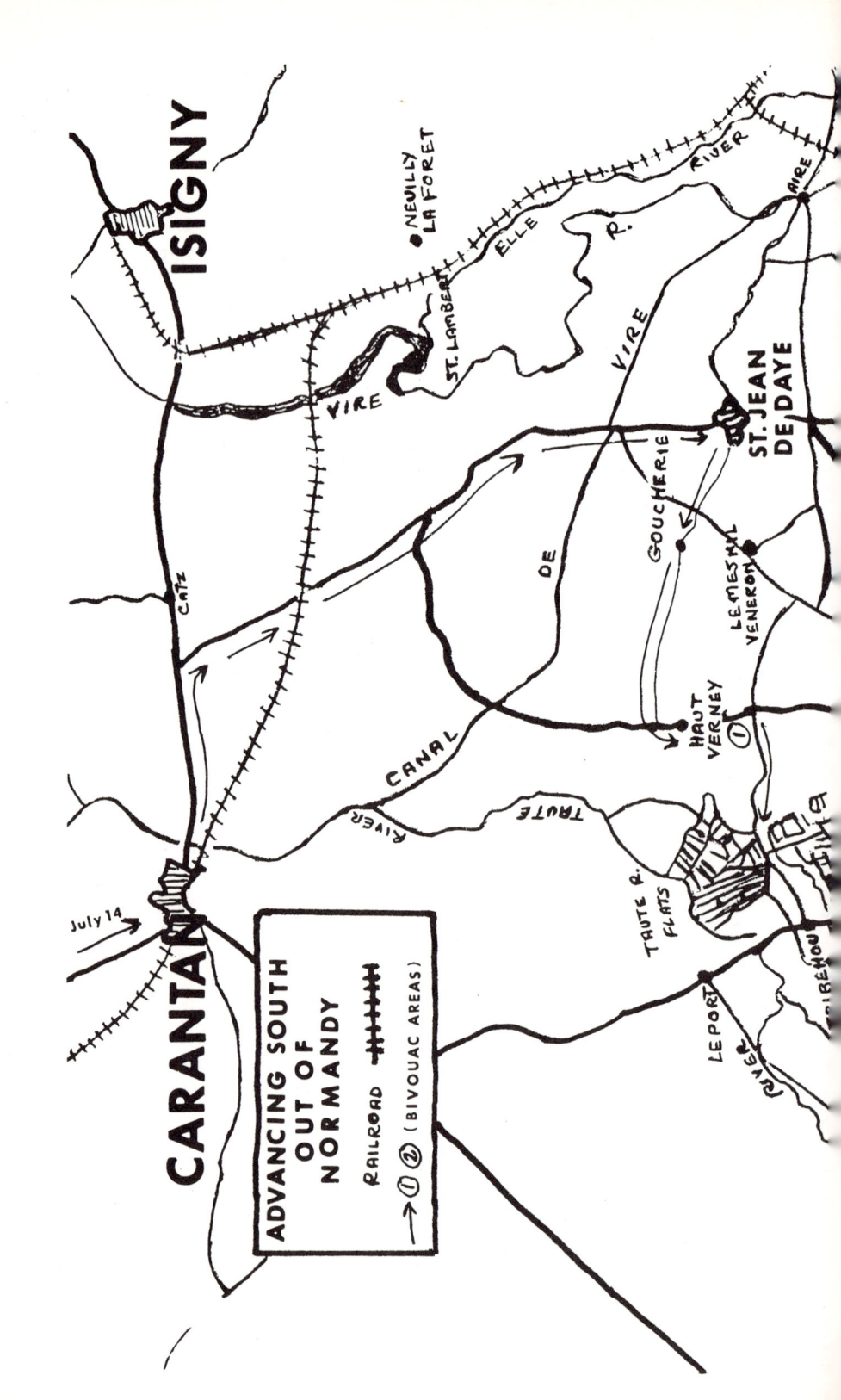

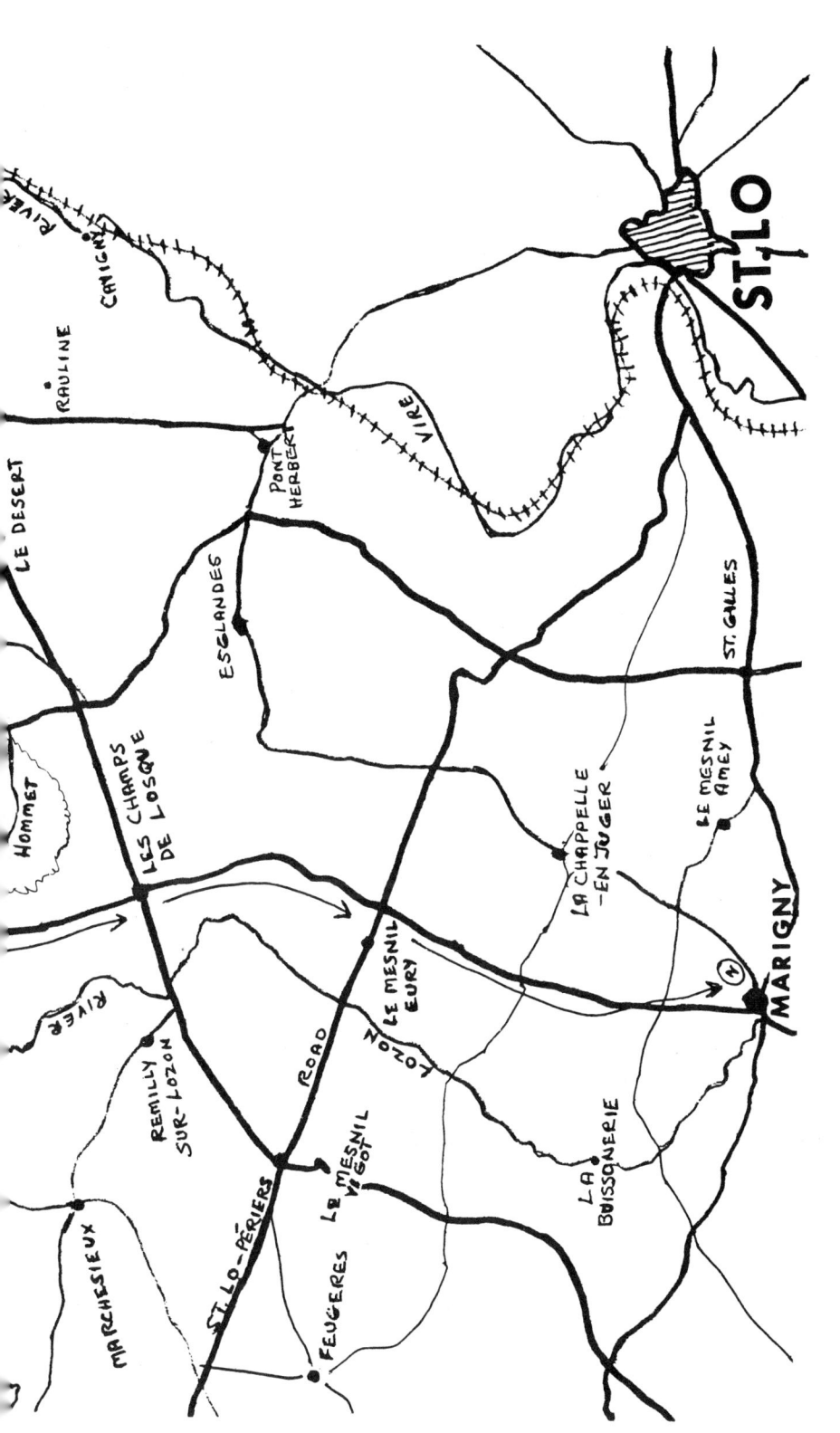

"It had been a question of deciding whether you would lose more from the bombs than from the Germans, for if the troops had been pulled back far enough from the bombs the Germans quite possibly would have had time to recover their own fire power."

The battle for St. Lo and its' subsequent fall opened the door for the breakout of Normandy and history would record it as one of the most decisive battles in the European Theater. General Bradley's immediate evaluation of this strategic importance would a few years hence ring true as to its' real value when later in his book, "A Soldier's Story" and still later in an interview with the author he stated:

"It instantly banished any lingering doubt on the outcome of the war. If the enemy could have contained our beachhead he might still have hoped to negotiate a peace. But once we had broken out of the beachhead to race across France to the German frontier, the enemy could no longer hope for a German victory or even the prospect of a prolonged stalemate."

Supported by 155mm 'Long Toms' and swarms of dive bombers, troops on top of Shermans were sparking the greatest tank charge in the history of American warfare as immediately following this violent aerial bombardment the ground forces now poised and ready, aggressively went to work! In truculent fashion the Periers-St. Lo road was taken . . . initiating the drive beyond St. Lo. VII CORPS was spearheading a drive aimed south through Marigny, and with this achievement FIRST ARMY was finally blasting its' way into the inner depths of France!

IX

CHASE ACROSS FRANCE

The first of August brought about a change in operations of FIRST ARMY. Now over-ladened with many more combat divisions than any army ordinarily would carry, this mammoth fighting machine by due process . . . would formulate its' combat units into two armies. The FIRST ARMY would receive a new commander. Tall, erect and impressive fifty-seven year old Lt. Gen. Courtney H. Hodges, a former commander of THIRD ARMY and lately Deputy FIRST ARMY commander and though a non-West Pointer was a meticulous, cool soft-spoken soldier bearing much prudence and military science and who rose to generalship through the ranks . . . a feat that always commands respect of all subordinates. He was revered too, as one who took a genuine and sympathetic interest in soldier's problems.

The highly-strengthened United States THIRD ARMY operating under the code name of "Lucky" would be commanded by the much-celebrated field strategist and armored expert; Lt. Gen. George Smith Patton, Jr. Now fifty-nine years old and well-recognized for his exploits in the North African and Mediterranean theaters, and though a trifle flamboyant but nonetheless temperamentally dramatic when the situation called for it, General Patton had for some time become admirably known to the military world as "Old Blood and Guts."

Both armies would be under direction of 12TH ARMY GROUP now commanded by Lt. Gen. Omar Bradley, the highly-skilled tactition of successive accomplishments as II CORPS commander in Tunisia and Sicily . . . and moreso credited with the complete buildup and recent successful FIRST ARMY operations in Normandy. The fifty-one year old Bradley, moving up from FIRST ARMY would soon bear a distinction of commanding the greatest number of troops of any Allied field commander.

Though continuing to direct operations of 21ST ARMY GROUP, British General Bernard L. Montgomery, at fifty-seven would be elevated to rank of Field Marshal in the latter days of August.

The FIRST Canadian Army, commanded by Lt. Gen. Sir Henry Crerar had already become active on July 23 and now was operational in the Caen area.

The FIRST Allied Airborne Army, under command of Lt. Gen. Lewis H. Brereton was created and became functional on August 2nd. Both armies under command of Field Marshal Montgomery's 21ST ARMY GROUP.

The Germans too, were making drastic changes in the field when in early July Generalfeldmarschall Guenther von Kluge, bristling with a string of successes on the eastern front replaced Field Marschal Karl von Rundstedt as Commander OB West. He already had and would continue to have the opportunity to lay his record on the line against growing Allied forces breaking out from Normandy.

From Haut Vernay on the 29th we quickly moved across the River Terrette into Tribehou and rolling through the town with great haste swiftly passed through the little highway junction of Les Champs de Losque. Continuing, the convoy crossed a much-shelled Periers-St. Lo road near Le Mesnil-Eury and constituting a distance of fifteen miles we found ourselves moving in from the west looking down from lofty slopes into the demolished little town of Marigny. The 9TH DIVISION had battled to keep the west road open to allow "recon" teams of the 1ST INFANTRY and 3RD ARMORED DIVISIONS to clear the town. Few communities had we entered to compare with the savagery of Marigny. The town was decimated . . . devastated . . . almost in some locations, reduced to dust . . . and many, many dead Germans lay scattered in its' wreckage.

An apple orchard's natural camouflage was utilized just a few yards beyond the town's southern approaches.

No time was wasted "digging in" and extensive use was made of these holes long before the convoy completely disassembled. We scattered when a venturesome enemy plane suddenly swooped over to interrupt our unloading and all surrounding ack-ack went to work with rhythmic ear-splitting fury and jagged metal started falling all over the place! This prompted many, as the campaign moved forward, to cover foxholes with logs, plywood and in some instances when possible . . . doors.

It was something like eleven o'clock and a broiling sun showered its' rays in unmerciful proportions. The flak then stopped! The ack-ack batteries became silent . . . for out of nowhere arose a U.S. fighter plane to challenge the foe! Then another joined the attack! For the next eight to ten minutes we gazed in wonder at the skillful uncanny acrobatics some 8,000 to 10,000 feet above!

"Boy! *Look! Look! Look!*"

"Man . . . he'll never shake that 'Mustang'!" commented one; "Man . . . *he's had it!*"

"That's not a 'Mustang' . . . that's a P-47!" corrected another; "Look at that nose!" And so it went . . . though actually it was hard to tell at that height and it really made little difference . . . for "Jerry" was doomed. He was soon plummeting to earth in the distance trailing a plume of dark smoke.

It was with great admiration to behold the death-dealing contests by U. S. and German fighter pilots as they maneuvered in and out of position in the skies. They called the American P-51 with its' narrow nose, a 'Mustang' and the P-47, its nose more oval, a 'Thunderbolt' . . . and to see them, with capable speeds of almost 450 m.p.h., though considerably less in this maneuver, shake itself loose from the deadly barking twin 13mm cannon of a German

'ME-109' or offtimes a 'Focke-Wulf 190' with its' bristling 20mm guns . . . and both capable of the same air speeds as the U. S. planes, in reverse; to watch them roll . . . to see them bank and twist . . . to see one or the other either go down in smoke or break loose to fight another day was a thrill of thrills! Without question; to us on the ground it was something of an aerial show . . . but we were well-aware it was a bloody business that certainly commanded the respect of all ground troops from top echelon to bottom.

On another occasion three enemy fighters caught in a crossfire from surrounding American "ack-ack" batteries were in serious jeopardy! A torrid scene developed as thousands of tracers coming from every field went up to meet them! The noise was deafening and the planes elected to duel with the ground batteries! It was a mistake as one plane caught fire and crashed immediately. Making a hasty departure the other two, for the moment, were more fortunate! Dangerous as we knew this action to be, it was incredible as we just stood out in the open . . . neglecting to take cover, and with necks craned upward became momentarily hypnotized by the unique but deadly transaction! We didn't stand there long though . . . and dashing pell-mell for safety familiar shouts filled the air!

"Here it comes!"

"Hot stuff!"

"Get the hell out of here . . . but quick!"

And then it came! . . . "Z-I-N-G! Z-I-N-G! Z-I-N-G! S-W-I-S-H!" . . . jagged metal raking the vicinity!

A small fragment of this sharp shrapnel found its' mark early, but by sheer fate . . . death was cheated! Pfc. Rufus Strickland was in the immediate act of jumping into his foxhole when a piece of flak, piercing the air probably from one of the 90mm guns firing from an adjacent field . . . "KLUNK!" . . . a direct hit on his helmet . . . injecting a respectable dent in it! Luck was with him as he in only that split-instant put the helmet on! "Strick" in a later event, would find "Lady Luck" passing him by.

Two shattered German tanks, their tracks ripped and turrets scorched and blackened from obvious internal explosions . . . one with two splintered gaping holes the size of a grapefruit torn through its' armor squatted in one corner of the orchard. Warrant Officer Rueth wasted no time identifying them as Mark IVs. Someone, questioning the German-born officer's correct tank identity, very quickly became the recipient of Sgt. Botting's stinging rebuttal!

"Listen, if the 'Kraut' says it's a Mark IV . . . it's a Mark IV, you can bet your tail on that!" . . . adding, "he knows these tanks better than the guys that built them!"

Because of Mr. Rueth's German background Botting unwittingly tied the inference of 'Kraut' to him . . . though with caution and never openly. It was a reference that the Germans were not particularly fond of and a sharp quick glance from the Old Warrant Officer one morning upon overhearing his comment was message enough to the First Sergeant that it was not appreciated, and that he too, stood the danger of a "bite in the tail!" The Mark IV, a 23-ton vehicle bearing a 75mm gun was employed in large numbers in Normandy, and while this particular tank was more heavily armed and carried thicker armor it was less mobile and less dependable mechanically.

The same number of broken-track U. S. Shermans perhaps fifty yards across the field gave mute evidence that the action had been quick and a "one-two punch" was delivered by each gunner.

Two weeks before leaving England a ruptured appendix had hospitalized Ray Setter, a chunky quiet heavy-set T/4 from Detroit . . . and ineligible for immediate discharge the company had journeyed to France during the invasion days without him. Soon released from a military hospital in northern England he somehow wound up in an infantry replacement depot in France some three weeks following our departure. His desire to contact the 126th was insatiable; for after all it was with this company and with these boys that his military obligations began. By means of hitch-hiking, grasping bits of information at every opportunity (questioning MPs seemed no avail) and at all times keeping a sharp roving watch for familiar vehicle markings, he had moved over a good portion of the VII CORPS region in an unceasing personal effort to locate the company. His almost futile attempts began to bear fruit when one day on the dusty broken traffic-laden Marigny-St. Lo road leading south into Marigny, amidst a group of replacements alighting from a truck for a brief stretch who were already enroute for possible infantry assignment, he spotted one of our company jeeps caught in a bumper-to-bumper traffic jam. Immediately recognizing the driver and Lt. Black; he grabbed his bags, bolted from the group, yelling in a quick turn of the head . . .

"I'll see you guys later!"

Tossing his bags into the jeep, the dust-covered T/4; still clad in Class-A "OD" uniform pleaded:

"I'm Setter, Lt. Black; remember me? I've been looking for you guys for a month!" Redfaced and panting, he continued; "Can I go back to the company Lieutenant?"

Momentarily stunned, the Lieutenant asked;

"What do you mean? Go where? What'r you talking about?" The Lieutenant was *not really* aware that Setter had even left the company.

"Back to the company Lieutenant, back with you guys! Don't you remember me? I've been in the hospital and have searched everywhere for you guys!" Again he identified himself; "I'm Setter of automotive!"

"Yeah, yeah, sure . . . sure, Setter."

"How about it, Lieutenant?"

"Hell, I don't know," he replied . . . still startled. "Hold on a minute, I don't know." Then in a flash he said; "Okay, dammit . . . hop in! Hop in! We'll just see what happens!"

But Setter was way ahead of him, sitting in the back of the jeep before the Lieutenant finished.

It was *highly* unusual and even Black admitted great surprise; but only a matter of time and shuffling of a few papers found him back on the company roster. It was easy . . . for he had his own papers with him! If those misty eyes held any significance they were plainly tears of relief and security . . . and his repetitious expression held a strong meaning:

"You guys just don't know! You guys just don't know!" . . . he meant every word of it!

On July 28 General Collins ordered the 9TH DIVISION into reserve and a brief rest. Now almost a week later with the DIVISION back in action orders came to move. Early morning of August 3rd we left Marigny and some 12 miles beyond bounded over another branch of the River Terrette at a demolished little railway junction at Carantilly where shattered tracks sprawled listlessly down from a wrecked railroad overpass. Shifting to low gear the convoy vehicles began a long slow climb up the steep incline that led to the much larger town of Cerisy-la-Salle nestling high on the hill. Within the next fifteen miles several streams leading into the River Soulles were crossed before reaching Notre Damede-Cenilly, a shell-gutted highway junction that fell earlier to elements of the 2ND ARMORED DIVISION. Southeast through Le Guislain we crossed a key east-west highway and a few miles beyond decided to set up bivouac within sight of a diminutive village called Maupertuis.

No eye could escape the ring of German 47mm anti-tank guns once boldly guarding the town's northwest approaches, abandoned but otherwise in good condition . . . and although aimed at everything coming down this route they would soon become another statistic to swell FIRST ARMY's compound of captured enemy equipment.

One vast field dotted only here and there with trees was commandeered; this space to contain almost the entire complement. On the second morning we were reluctant to lose one of our "favorite sons" to the 3424th Ordnance (MAM) Company. Months later we were deeply sorrowed to learn of Bill Schuch's untimely tragedy.

. . . Private William Francis Schuch from Chicago, was killed May 6, 1945 only two days before the war ended in Europe. While on detached service with another GI their three-quarter ton weapons carrier, leaving the approaches of a bridge near the Rhine River and rolling immediately onto the span a well-concealed explosive mine was detonated, destroying and blowing the vehicle and occupants overboard. The explosion was savage and both perished in the Rhine!

. . . Bill Schuch was a loud lovable guy just turned twenty-two years old. He excelled in softball and boxing, was quite musically inclined . . . always singing; always a great fan of popular songs . . . a great clown . . . he was the self-styled company barber and although losing his teeth at an early age was outstandingly physically fit. Never lost for a "wise crack" . . . slow to real anger and never subjected to "brooding," Bill accepted the army life as it came . . . and in a sort of respectful way held great contempt for Army "brass." All in the original 126th loved him and there is no question that his personality will always be indelible in our memory.

The war became more and more fluid as the days passed and although our moves were more frequent the company yet had a considerable amount of work to accomplish. There was still two or three tank motors to maintain, an abundance of jeeps with multiple problems and more than enough 6 x 6 trucks to service. Artillery pieces and rifles were high on the priority list but moving so often and so rapid little time was assessed to do any *real* maintenance work. Parts and accessories became a problem for frequency of supply depot relocation required extra hours for "parts chasers" to complete their mission.

When a depot moved, either for camouflage necessity or for reasons of expediency it required much consultation with Military Police check points and often a good part of a day could be expended to find it again. Without the proper parts and equipment work could of a necessity be held up to a serious degree. Ed Roenicke and Dave Howey, two energetic T/5's from Michigan kept an exhausting pace in their search for vital parts, and again the *biggest job* was locating the parts depot. Whether rain or shine . . . day or night, they kept moving . . . bringing in badly-needed items and going back for more.

The kitchen personnel, working always under something of a strain in the field, but diligent in their quest for top rations were at times instrumental in securing the new type provision now appearing on the scene. Classified as "Ten-in-One" . . . it was to prove highly successful in that the quality of food henceforth was looked upon with greater favor. Packed in cardboard containers, ten to a box "Ten-in-One" was simply a single packaged meal made up of dehydrated ingredients, that included canned meat, breakfast bacon, vegetables, canned fruit, pudding, crackers, coffee, etc. The real secret, however, lay in the fact that one now had a little more time for its' preparation. In spite of this newly acquired ration other means of getting food was learned. Late one evening, for example; the delicacy of a steak was for a second time enjoyed. How? In many units an unfortunate cow strayed a little too close to a guard post at night and "would not halt when challenged!" Russ VanVactor, a prototype butcher from Indiana turned in his second professional job . . . when a hefty carcass of beef was strung up under the trees and pleasing steaks were carved from it. Though this practice was not widespread it was short of unusual for in other units it was reported that this same kind of "cow trouble" existed . . . and although the French "raised hell" often . . . they were well-reimbursed.

Much bartering transacted between French peasants and each of us. Town residents got in the act too. We were happy to trade candy, tobacco and other items which were almost non-existent to them in exchange for fresh eggs, vegetables and occasionally poultry. Some, less discreet and ignoring the goodwill of trading, found it nutritiously lucrative to simply dig up a supply of potatoes and other lighter vegetables while the convoy was in progress.

Almost four days had passed. The CO was satisfied that the area was well-policed and Maupertuis was left to another unit as the convoy resumed and rolled through the crossroads village of Maupert. A stretch of seven to ten miles carried us down into Percy. Once a proud town of well-kept homes and impressively-stocked shops along narrow streets dotted with evenly-patterned cedars . . . but now gutted buildings with blackened windows and crumpled masonry. Army communications wire covered in web-like patterns virtually every tree and post. Percy had paid a terrible price when caught in the midst of a fierce brief struggle, changing hands several times before falling to elements of the 9TH and 28TH INFANTRY DIVISIONS. Just inside the approaches lay scattered many enemy helmets and the now-familiar black oval gas mask canisters. Collected in a small field awaiting Graves Registration processing lay several dead . . . carefully watched over by a small MP detachment.

We kept moving to follow the now dusty crumbling south road for about ten miles all the way into Villedieu-les-Poeles. Hundreds of destroyed vehicles and wagons, innumerable dead horses, a number of wrecked German armored vehicles and enemy tanks and much miscellaneous wreckage scattered all along the hills that bank either side of the road and much of the countryside drew mumbled and open comments. FIRST ARMY artillery and 9TH TAC fighter bombers had wreaked havoc on retreating German columns.

Via a treadway bridge engineered by the 4TH INFANTRY DIVISION we crossed the River Seinne (not to be confused with France's largest river . . . the Seine) flowing through the town's battered center, and once cleared began a steep winding ascent east where looking back down from the high ground surrounding Villedieu where dust from grinding convoys swirled to heavily pollute the air one could get a "bird's eye" view of the limited destruction wrought on the town. On through the small village of St. Cecile we quickened our pace to continue west for some four miles where leaving the highway we turned east to twist down a narrow deep lane that led to an area situated on the southeast approaches of a little community called Fontenermont.

With ample room to spread out bivouac was confined to open pastures and an abandoned farmyard. Digging foxholes presented no problem and toward evening two enemy planes swooping low on two occasions gave us an opportunity to use them! The natural camouflage of well-spaced trees was an important one in this region as directly across the road from our CP was established a temporary PW enclosure. Much captured enemy materiel, rolling stock and weapons in separate groups were compounded in a field, surprisingly unguarded. On the other side in a hedge-enclosed shaded area lay perhaps 150 dead, where in neat rows and segregated by uniform we viewed with respect. Already identified by dog tags and personal papers they awaited removal to an American cemetary and an area reserved for burial of German soldiers.

Aaron Katz, a Brooklynite who gave up OCS to remain a Private was shifted to 2nd Ordnance (MM) Company . . . vehemently against his will. Putting up a stiff argument he soon learned there was nobody around to "hear him." Bill Henninger, a stocky T/5 from Detroit and often subjected to a touch of "hard luck" . . . this time lacking familiarity of a German Luger pistol, went into shock when . . . "B-L-A-M!" a bullet accidently penetrated his hand. Minutes later he was evacuated to an aid station. He too, would fail to find his way back to the company roster.

The closing days of July found General Patton's THIRD ARMY driving hard down the west coast toward the Brittany peninsular while FIRST ARMY was "hell bent" on spreading out toward the middle of France with Paris a particular objective.

On August 7 a blight suddenly dimmed the picture! With sudden fury in the wee morning hours the German Seventh Army, utilizing three crack armored divisions amassed its almost exhausted strength and in a fierce counterattack charged headlong into VII CORPS positions! With no aerial and little artillery support and attacking on both sides on the strategic highway junction of Mortain with nearly 200 tanks the primary order pointed to capture of Coutances and push to Avranches on the sea, some thirty miles to the west. Should this breakthrough meet with complete success communication lines between the FIRST and THIRD ARMIES would be imperiled, possibly divided . . . and by regaining Avranches a continuous defensive line would be re-established in Normandy and the Germans would eventually gain an operational initiative.

Smashing directly into elements of 3RD ARMORED and 30TH INFANTRY DIVISION defense a desperate situation quickly enveloped both units. Another fierce assault struck the 1ST DIVISION sector south of Mortain, and later in the morning broke through areas maintained by the 113th. Cavalry Recon. Squadron and strongly threatened 9TH DIVISION's 39th. Regiment near the River See.

By daybreak American artillery in savage and voluminous barrages located the attacking columns and kept the Germans immobile all day of the 7th. Though the coordinated attack threatened the entire VII CORPS bridgehead south of the River Selune and could well have destroyed supply installations and communications, the CORPS "called the Germans' hand" and within twenty-four hours mustered a strength of seven combat divisions to blunt the attack. The 2ND ARMORED sped into position to support the 9TH INFANTRY and the 35TH INFANTRY joined in the assault. The 3RD ARMORED shot spearheads directly into the Germans from the south and the 1ST, 30TH, and 4TH were already heavily engaged.

Although another feeble thrust was made by German spearheads toward Avranches on the 11th., the crucial five-day battle that could have been extremely critical was all over by late afternoon of the 12th. Beaten back by armored superiority and determined

GIs; strongly supported by 9TH TAC pursuit fighters and RAF rocket-firing Hurricanes and Typhoons the desperate attack lost its' strength and the enemy became badly disorganized, suffered appalling losses (almost 100 tanks) and were subsequently routed. The enemy force was shattered but it had not been an easy task . . . for this action had caused the 9TH DIVISION alone to suffer over 1,000 casualties.

What were the chances of the counterattack's ultimate success? Many years later General Collins told the author:

"With the successive good showing of our field forces thus far in Normandy and the impetus with which we were now moving, plus the fact that reinforcements were rushing in daily there never was any room for doubt in my mind that VII CORPS would hold at Mortain." He added; "We had too much going for us. Fortunately endowed with sound leadership, an abundance of materiel and weaponry they could not cope with our airpower."

and when suggesting hypothetically . . . "suppose they just momentarily could not have been stopped," the stocky General replied:

"Oh, they blitzed through alright! Sure, they surprised us. But, look; we only had seven divisions to close the gap, and they were not in fixed positions. But we *knew* after sizing up the situation that they could do the job. Should we have pulled another three divisions from the line and put them into full action there wouldn't have been a German left in the pocket!"

General Montgomery's forces were busy too. The FIRST CANADIAN ARMY during this same period launched a massive attack southeast from Caen toward Falaise (some 12 miles east of Mortain) and the entire German 7th Army was faced with the threat of a double encirclement.

FIRST ARMY did not let up and fanatically pressed its initiative . . . tearing the entire enemy structure in Normandy apart! With armored columns leading the way and aircraft acting as eyes we were bounding into the newer regions of France. By the middle of August the Normandy "hedgerow-hell" was far behind and the Allies most decidedly had complete control of the northwestern territory of France!

Yes . . . the "hedgerow-hell of Normandy was far behind, but far from forgotten. Veterans of the 9TH had left many buddies back there . . . buddies that had fought side by side in North Africa and Sicily; sharing in the long rest in England and harboring every hope of riding with the DIVISION to victory in Germany and eventually . . . home. But in death . . . what has been done cannot be undone; for in victory the good has to be taken with the bad; the sorrows with the joys and hopes with the disappointments. As the French express it . . . "C'est le fortune de Guerre."

As for the 126th., our own experience of these past two months had become invaluable and with swift movements that lay ahead it meant "so long" for an occasional steak and fresh eggs, and more than likely heavy falling flak . . . to say nothing of the indomitable calvados.

***

With an abnormal flow of heavy traffic that increased with each day the brittle roads had long buckled under exceptional wear and tear of machines for which they were not built. Holes of many dimensions were torn, tremendous cracks and huge chunks of asphalt savagely ripped out of place . . . always in a bad state of repair and often keeping road engineers a jump behind. Yet, these dogged engineers, working round the clock . . . exerting super-human effort filling craters in the roads, constructing by-passes and removing wrecked vehicles accomplished the impossible and all key roads were kept in full capacity almost continuously.

Possessing top priority on the roads because they were needed drastically; tanks, ammunition trucks, guns . . . heavy and light jammed all routes . . . racing to bolster an offense that at this advanced stage kept a confused enemy perpetually off balance. The Germans had left the gap wide open and full advantage was being pursued as more and more allied divisions were pouring onto the continent!

Since "Operation Cobra" VII CORPS had gotten off to a good start. Fast-moving FIRST ARMY reportedly had captured some 28,000 prisoners in July, and what the ground troops failed to crush Allied air support finished. United States fighter-bombers left nothing to chance attacking horse-drawn wagons, trains, gun positions, warehouses, railroad and highway bridges, road junctions, ammo dumps and troop concentrations. Morale of FIRST ARMY accellerated fast. General Bradley had already attested to that in a July 28 message to General Eisenhower;

"To say that we are riding high tonight is putting it mildly. Things on our front really look good."

At this date things continued to look good, and that it contributed greatly to *our* morale was without question; and it did in fact, soar even higher when it was learned the company's next move would constitute the most extensive of the campaign thus far!

An unusually colorful daybreak came up on August 14th as the convoy crawled out and moved approximately three miles due west. We then crossed the River Baign to roll into St. Sever-Calvados, a shattered community that the 28TH DIVISION had swept clean ten days before. Continuing, and turning off at this point we moved directly south through two-and-a-half miles of thickly wooded area identified as the Foret de St. Sever.

Out of this continuous umbrella of trees we crossed the River Barbot and moved into St. Pois. Miles of surrounding hilly terrain and steep valleys lay before us . . . and then behind us. On through burned-out Cherence-le-Roussel, Bellefontaine and the still smoking rubble of St. Barthelemy our convoy hurdled the River Cance and moved through battered outer ridges of partially-destroyed Mortain; the shattered cathedral town that, caught in the throes of the recent vicious though unsuccessful German counter-attack had changed hands a score of times. A key road was mapped, and moving back slightly southeast a little more than ten miles . . . and crossing the River Selune at the approaches of St.

Hilaire du-Harcouet, we moved into that battle-torn town.

St. Hilaire du-Harcouet, fifteen miles east of Avranches . . . with all its' melodramatic beauty sits on an extremely elevated plateau commanding for miles and miles a view of rolling countryside and deep ravines. Two days earlier when the company's "recon" squad entered the town they were amazed to observe at first hand, though at some distance to the east a full active skirmish several hundred yards down in the wooded valley. American tanks with their flash and boom! . . . and low flying P-47's coordinating support of combat infantry teams of the 90TH INFANTRY DIVISION, were methodically engaged in decimating a pocket of resisting Germans.

They watched in awe as highly maneuverable piper cubs acting as forward observers darted deftly in and out of the zone . . . pointing to and relaying by radio enemy positions to American ground troops below. Often referred to as "Grasshoppers" (LV-4) these light craft as observation planes were the eyes and ears of the field artillery and tanks. Throughout the war they also were invaluable for use in courier or liason service. Widely used too, for photographic scrutiny, they rushed emergency supplies and immediate evacuation of wounded.

The convoy continued. Slightly southwest of St. Hilaire, on through St. Symphorien we skirted the road junctions of Buais, Fougerolles and Desertines . . . each approximately five miles apart and each fortunately escaping the *real* viciousness of war.

Several streams branching into the River Ourd were breached . . . their bridges still intact, and when in late afternoon reaching the small village of Colombiers, three open fields were commandeered to set up camp immediately beyond the village.

Representing the first American soldiers ever seen we were with great enthusiasm accorded an unusual welcome! From many dwellings and windows in some fashion was draped small hand-made flags bearing American and French national colors. On one occasion just before entering the village approaches a long fence ran alongside the road for perhaps a hundred yards. On each post was attached the stars and stripes and French tri-color flags, or a reasonable facsimilie closely resembling it. Townspeople eagerly expressed their cordiality as we were presented with bouquets of wild flowers and roses. They brought tomatoes, fresh eggs and other attractive items within their means. It made us begin to think that this was *just too much*! Too, with these gratuitous gestures of friendship it was becoming increasingly evident that the French would more and more express openly their great appreciation and would no longer hide feelings for the sacrificial gallantry of American boys toward the liberation of their country. It is true perhaps, that to them this appreciation came a little easier inasmuch as they were spared the destruction inflicted in upper Normandy.

Geographically this part of the country is open. It is spacious and fairly flat and is the very type of terrain for which the tankers had long been hoping, and from our present Colombiers location no more than ten miles lay between this position and one of the key east-west Paris arteries. The weather for several days was balmy and had neared perfection in every way. Enemy opposition throughout this particular sector was unbelievably sparse and when a challenge arose it was quickly dispelled. Important at the moment was the central east-west Paris highway . . . and now pretty much under FIRST ARMY control to a point some forty miles west, there was little to stop us from going directly to that capital city of two million captive and apprehensive people!

We remained in Colombiers two full nights. The second morning found us moving through the community's narrow streets where many had already gathered to bid us "bon voyage." Some tossed flowers and others uttered warm cheers and blew kisses. East up through Gorron we rolled and eased across two streams branching into the River Piscine where on an extended knoll to the north a newly established FIRST ARMY GI cemetary was nearing completion. Nearby, a cemetary for German soldiers also under control of FIRST ARMY was in operation. Picking our way along shattered roads that led through hilly and partially-devastated Ambrieres, we rolled onto narrow treadway bridges that led across the Rivers Varenne and Mayenne. Even secondary roads were heavily pitted and the going was slow through the small village of Chantrigne. Picking up a highway at the somewhat larger town of Lassay we again began to move with dispatch. On through Charchigne, breaching the tiny River Aisne at a vital highway intersection of Javron and feeling we had had enough for the day moved into an apple orchard situated equally between Les Chappelles and St. Aignan, two small towns of little signigicance.

During these swift encampments (and when compared to the slow tedious efforts in upper Normandy they were swift *indeed*) the almost natural concealment afforded by innumerable apple orchards disallowed use of the camouflage nets that were so feverishly and meticulously prepared in England . . . and they rarely were unpacked.

Three nights passed quickly, and breaking camp we moved on through the busy town of Couptrain further east. Crossing the River Angleine at Mehoudin we rolled something like eight miles due north . . . and shortly afternoon moved into a lovely little town called La Ferte Mace.

Built on and around natural elevated acreage that overlooks the River Courbe the general surroundings of La Ferte Mace are well-noted in peacetime for its' popular camping and fishing areas. Having escaped the ravages of war, as one viewed this panoramic scene of stucco-finished houses with bright tiled roofs intermittent with lacy cedar trees; with rock-crested walls criss-crossing down the slopes, the town looked as though it had never ceased to be open to those prewar luxuries.

The Captain and his staff selected two vast fields . . . or pastures as it were; separated by a single-lane unpaved road . . . hardly more than a path perhaps three-tenths of a mile in length and bordered on either side by tall evenly-spaced stout cedars. This constituted the only entrance to or from the main road.

The battles north of Argentan . . . and particularly the general region in and around the key city of Falaise had been raging for several days. With support of British and Canadian forces pushing down from the north, doggedly and systematically a gigantic noose was being employed by V, VII and XIX CORPS from the south and west that slowly would result in entrapment and bisecting of General Paul Hausser's German 7th. Army, and damaging severely the entire structure of Fieldmarschal Gunther von Kluge's ARMY GROUP EAST.

Pocketed between the ancient cities of Argentan to the south and Falaise to the north in a stretch of terrain less than 25 miles wide the German Seventh and Fifth Panzer Armies faced gradual decimation. A tight vise systematically applied by the Canadian FIRST ARMY on the north and American FIRST ARMY on the south doubly insured this. Sensing the gravity of the situation von Kluge had earlier warned his deputy commanders:

"We shall hold fast, and if no help arrives in time to improve our position fundamentally, then we shall die an honorable death on the field of battle."

The Allied front resembled an irregular horseshoe virtually encircling the major segment of German forces in Normandy. Frantically racing pell-mell from the trap toward the east the situation of enemy forces was more than desperate; it was grave . . . and hourly became untenable!

Emphasizing the gravity of the now threatened enemy, TIME MAGAZINE on August 15 carried a dramatic article:

"Now the Germans were running as their fellow sufferers had learned on the Eastern front, that retreat for an army without air cover is an inferno, that no devils in hell could be worse than the pursuer's ground-hugging planes . . . stabbing and jabbing with cannon, rockets, fragmentation bombs and machine guns!"

A critical shortage of tanks, gasoline and ammunition and the constant threat of Allied planes all over the battlefront diminished prospects for an orderly escape. Units became intermingled and all movements were constantly under threat of American artillery. Tanks became immobile for lack of fuel, many guns useless because of erratic deliveries of ammunition . . . and with communications almost non-existent the Falaise pocket was reduced to a 15-mile wide gap. Desperately trying to escape complete encirclement the Germans were caught in an inferno of destruction. Germans surrendered in droves as the roads became clogged with vehicle wreckage and armaments of every kind. Artillery pieces, vehicles, radios, supplies and tanks were lost. Roads and fields were littered with dead and wounded; carts overturned and dead horses and cattle lay everywhere as artillery from two allied armies and massed air forces pounded the shrinking pocket mercilessly.

The front page of the Atlanta Constitution's August 17 issue was alive with the action:

"BRADLEY CRUSHING ELEVEN TRAPPED DIVISIONS AS CANADIANS FIGHT WAY INTO FALAISE!"

VII CORPS alone took 3,000 prisoners in a five-day period. U.S. forces took some 25,000 prisoners while the British and Canadian forces captured another 25,000. Fieldmarschal Walther Model on August 17 replaced Fieldmarschal Guenther von Kluge as Commander-in-Chief of all German forces in the west (OB West) and became Army Group B Commander as well. When the battle ended three days later an estimated 40,000 to 50,000 Germans had escaped, but some 10,000 enemy dead were left on the battlefield. Nonetheleast of enemy dead would be von Kluge himself . . . for a few days hence he would take his own life.

General Eisenhower, referring to a passage in his book "Crusade in Europe" describes the scene:

"The battlefield at Falaise was unquestionably one of the greatest "killing grounds" of any of the war areas. Roads, highways, and fields were so choked with destroyed equipment and with dead men and animals that passage through the area was extremely difficult. Forty-eight hours after the closing of the gap I was conducted through it on foot, to encounter scenes that could be described only by Dante. It was literally possible to walk for hundreds of yards at a time, stepping on nothing but dead and decaying flesh."

This dynamic, brilliant and successful execution by allied forces in closing the Falaise Gap virtually would erase all major German operations west of the River Seine.

With General Patton's THIRD U. S. ARMY moving at will all over the Brittany peninsular and FIRST ARMY having closed the Falaise Gap, hence pushing on to Paris a consistent front practically ceased to exist in this battle-weary corridor of northwest

France. Sparodic fighting did continue on a far lesser scale as enemy elements haphazardly attempted a mass withdrawal; a withdrawal that presumably would terminate somewhere within the depths of the Belgo-German border. An obvious completed allied victory, the battle of Normandy rapidly developed into the battle for western France. Now it was "*Roll . . . and don't spare the horses!*"

***

Within the confines of this picturesque location at La Ferte Mace a series of inter-company events added a little drama that otherwise could have wound up as another link in the chain of unspectacular encampments.

The crack of a carbine late one afternoon turned all eyes toward the Automotive section. A muffled moan directed all attention to the puptent of Bob Covie, a big boisterous private from Detroit. Someone came running toward the CP and met Botting a few yards away.

"Sergeant, you'd better come . . . that damn Covie has shot the hell out of himself!"

"Covie!?" muttered a not-too-astonished Botting to himself. "That damn Covie . . . ! What in the hell has he done now!"

He quickened his pace, and panting slightly was at the tent in no time.

Cognac had gotten the best of several GIs for a time but calvados was worse. Too much of it could and would easily separate a man from his senses, and in such an apparent condition Covie had slithered into his tent. The bullet, tearing through his shoe and ripping a nasty hole in the flesh put him in shock. He could not even speak. No time was lost in evacuation to an aid station . . . thence to a rear field hospital. Nonetheless, nothing was again heard from this colorful character during the entire course of the European campaign.

Questions circulated.

"Was he really intoxicated?"

"Did he know what he was doing?"

"Was this an impulse?"

"Was it planned or was it really an accident?"

Covie was not too far from being the largest man in the company, and near thirty he often expressed his intent dislike for the army. Those close to him attested to his extreme displeasure to go overseas and when sailing for Normandy he appeared at times almost frantic. Everyone has a right to be afraid and perhaps Covie headed the list . . . as more than once he stated that he expected to be home before the war was ended. Now he probably would get his wish.

"Therein lies a paradox," one expressed it; "so afraid of being shot by the enemy . . . he shot himself!"

What *really* happened? Only Bob Covie could supply that answer.

Along a northwest corner near the cedar-lined road where the Supply section was spread, Olen Hilditch, a slim sandy-haired good natured and quick-witted T/Sgt. from Columbus, Ohio was digging a trench. An impulse told him to shift his body to one side . . . but in so doing he could not have known the miracle in that act. Had he not made the shift at that split moment a bullet from Tom Roberts' newly-acquired P-38 pistol without question would have erased him from the company roster, for the missile entered the trench bank behind about thirty-six inches above Hilditch's very tracks!

"Roberts! You damn fool!" blurted the startled sergeant; "You simple-minded moron! What are you doing! What's the matter with you?"

Shocked perhaps more than Hilditch; Roberts, a young tall muscular T/5 could only answer feebly;

"Gosh, I'm sorry, Sarge . . . I missed you, didn't I?"

"Missed me? Damn right you missed me! It's not so much what you did, it's what you could have done!"

"Sarge . . . wait a minute, I . . . "

"Oh for Christ sake, Roberts!" Hilditch, now ashen and badly wanting to really "chew him out" but now lacking both the heart and strength could only mutter faintly;

"Will you please throw that damn thing away?"

The German P-38 and Luger weapons were extremely hair-triggered and were not the toys that many painfully learned in the weeks that followed.

Since the invasion, by due process many changes in personnel had been consequential in the 9TH DIVISION . . . changes ranging from top regimental commander all the way down to buck private. Death and wounds constituted the preponderance of changeovers but many of these alterations were also attributed to transfers, hospitalizations and special assignments. In other instances, some . . . due to diminished leadership qualities that somehow had transformed them into misfits were justifiably relieved of that respective command. The greatest overall change came on August 10th; that is as far as the entire complement was concerned; when General Eddy's command of the DIVISION came to an end.

Big, tall and easy-going Manton Sprague Eddy had led the DIVISION in the North African and Sicilian campaigns. He likewise enjoyed the temporary sojurn in England and painstakingly had steered it throughout the Normandy operation. As a consequence, with this personal and long-lived association his ties with all in the 9TH had grown ever so strong . . . and they likewise with him. General Bradley; measuring the depth of Division leadership since the North African theater, would later say of him:

"Of all the commanders, none was better balanced nor more cooperative than Matt Eddy. Manton liked to count his steps carefully before he took them."

General Eisenhower said:

"Matt Eddy was one of my long time friends and at no time did it ever waver. You could always count on him, and when making a list of all field commanders . . . you could place him at the top anytime."

General Collins was in high praise:

"Matt was nothing but the best and he gave his maximum to every problem assigned him. His evaluation of the probable defenses of Cherbourg and suggestions as to how to approach the fortified city was one of incalculable value, and far less casualties than ordinarily would have been resulted."

General Mark W. Clark recalls:

"He was a long time friend of mine, a real personal friend. He did a tremendous job in North Africa and Sicily and I was sorry indeed to lose him when the 9TH moved to England. A great commander!"

General Matthew Ridgway recounted:

"My association with Matt Eddy goes back a long time. Over the years we remained friends and during that time he never engaged in inter-military pettiness. His feet were on the ground at all times and he was with no exception one of the best field commanders during World War II."

Yet . . . when "top brass" recognize military prowess and the summons is there the call must be answered. Thus General Eddy was elevated to a higher authority and went on to gain even greater laurels in commanding THIRD ARMY's XII CORPS . . . and later, a third star.

Maj. Gen. Louis A. Craig, a former commander of the 97TH INFANTRY DIVISION and later the XXIII CORPS was picked to command the 9TH. A participant of several campaigns during World War I this country was not new to him. A stocky "two-fisted" leader marked with efficiency, he too would weigh a situation carefully before issuing an order. General Craig brought with him stability and experience . . . proved many times in the days that followed. Years later during a visit with the General the author was told:

"I loved the 9TH and under my command we went through a lot of battles together during the time I had it. But while I always had the utmost pride and confidence in the DIVISION it was really Matt Eddy's DIVISION and I give him all the credit for building the fierce "esprit de

Corps" that stayed with it until the end of the war."

Noon of August 22 under a cloudy sky found us moving east from La Ferte Mace and in less than ten minutes we had crossed the River Courbe. On through Joue we rolled and soon after jumping the River Odon and grinding up a high winding rise we marveled at the imposing walled fortress-like cathedral while entering the quiet city of Carrouges . . . where on August 11th the French 2ND ARMORED DIVISION encountered and subdued a surprised and confused German armored column. Several miles due east carried us through the northern fringes of the Foret d'Ecouves, a two-and-a-half mile span of woods where five days earlier remnants of the German 9th. Panzer Division were again cut up and captured by the same French armored division. On into Sees, a junction city strung along the banks of the River Orne, where dominating the entire rolling region for miles stands a thirteenth-century cathedral of heavy gothic design. Its' elegant delicately designed high towers spiraling skyward reflects a striking pose of strength that cannot be avoided. Further through the immaculate streets of Courtomer we became aware at this point of a dangerously receeding supply of gasoline.

Decisions! *Decisions*! "Can't we continue further?" came a request from one of the junior officers. A quick "no" solved the problem, and proceeding to camp in another beckoning apple orchard within sight of the farm community of Prepotin that sits just beyond the eastern banks of the River Sarthe, we called a halt.

Now located an equal distance between Moulins la-Marche to the west and Tourouve to the east no one could help but immediately note the six hollow Mark IV tanks almost neatly parked . . . each scorched and burned inside, each shortly before blasted into submission as our troops thrust their way through. Almost blocking the single entrance to the only advantageous area that could be found in which to set up camp one would from a distance gain the impression that the tanks were acting as some sort of bulwark protecting this location.

"Shall we move 'em, Captain?" asked Botting.

"No, leave 'em where they are, they just might be booby-trapped."

"Listen, Cap'n., Recovery can hook one of their wreckers onto them and have 'em out in no time."

The Captain *was not* the easiest person to be moved after he had given an order. "Leave 'em alone . . . and make damn sure our guys don't climb all over them. Somebody will get hurt just as sure as hell."

Botting was insistent. "We can have better access into and out of the area."

"*Leave them!*"

Hardly had we settled when ununiformed visitors came and offered their services, and for the first time since the early days of Normandy most experienced the luxury of having their clothes thoroughly washed. There was nothing to it! The local peasants simply took them down to a nearby stream, soaked them awhile and virtually "beat" cleanliness into them! For the most part they were releasing an air of gratitude and would have performed this task for almost nothing. They were however, always rewarded with the indomitable chocolate bars, excess packaged rations and occasionally . . . money.

Pending transactions with a forward fuel dump and parts depot our rest became one of merely marking time and very little work was performed.

Another German set-back was struck and became of historical importance August 15th., when the Armed Forces Radio announced that "Operation Dragoon" was launched and the United States SEVENTH ARMY had, under command of Lt. Gen. Alexander Patch, stormed in from the Mediterranean and successfully landed on the shores of southern France down near the Marseilles sector. Tuesday morning headlines of the August 15 edition of the Cleveland (Ohio) Plain Dealer was more dramatic:

"ALLIED MEDITERRANEAN FORCES INVADE SOUTH COAST OF FRANCE!"

"Landings are Reported Along Coast Between Marseille and Italy"

Further substantiating this dynamic thrust, a smaller column continued;

"Great fleets of ships and planes take part; Initial Objectives are gained in the first hour against light resistance!"

Without question . . . the Germans were *in for it now*!

The litter of enemy wreckage again came into prominence and appeared more profuse with our more distant moves. While one didn't have to look for it the evidence was there. Discarded and disabled machines were found not only on main roads but on side roads as well. One could look into fields . . . even in narrow almost obscure uncharted paths and note shattered vehicles, flak guns and light artillery . . . many partially hidden and abandoned in an obvious frantic effort for concealment by some means of camouflage. In a desperate attempt to escape marauding American and British fighter planes there was hardly anything else to do. Tanks of all dimensions, motorcycles, halftracks, armored and staff cars were noted, all obliterated by combined teamwork of planes and ground troops . . . some, noted by our "recon" team, still containing crews sprawled grotesquely where immediate death had been met.

The enemy too, had means of exacting a toll of GI lives and this was exemplified by the one weapon feared by every foot soldier. Most reverently respected and profusely hated was the explosive land mine; a deadly device, ever treacherous . . . some plastic, some metal, hiding in the deep grass or buried just enough to be covered with a paper-thin layer of earth and often concealed so as to blend into the natural texture of surrounding grass, foliage or debris.

Antipersonnel mines, about the size and shape of an ordinary tin can were much in abundance. Loaded with approximately two pounds of TNT and a sensitive fuse that could be set off by the weight of even a small man its power could tear a man's leg off! Another antipersonnel mine called the "Bouncing Betty" could be set off by trip wire, and when done so an inner cylinder immediately hops into the air three or four feet and explodes. Small steel balls shoot out with tremendous power in all directions for about two hundred yards, severely maiming or bringing death to all in the immediate proximity. The German anti-tank mine about the size of an average phonograph record, three to six inches thick and carrying ten to thirteen pounds of explosives and buried from six to eight inches in the ground requires a heavy vehicle to set it off. Many "booby traps" wired with explosives were found in many inconspicuous places . . . many too late.

One was always skeptical of these instruments of death, no matter where he traveled . . . for the obvious fact long was revealed that too many were planted for minesweeping engineers or individual mine probers to completely remove and at the same time keep an exhausting pace set by forward elements.

Ever since setting foot on the continent many had experienced at least a moment of extreme anxiety and of a necessity became involved in actions never fully revealed. Some of the Instrument section, for instance; at times worked up and down the line with infantry units repairing mortar sights and other small delicate instruments. Some in the Artillery section can relate an endless number of anxious moments while working with DIVISION field artillery and Tank Destroyer units. Moreover; the several other sections that supported front line troops will rarely if ever, be awarded recognition . . . nor do they seek it. For a project well-done, yes; but a contribution toward the enemy's destruction in line of combat; no. A Legion of Merit perhaps, or possibly a Bronze Star more than likely would be awarded.

In the normal course of operations Ordnancemen do not act in the capacity of front line troops but *it is true* that while servicing these units at their respective battle stations; be it two weeks or two days . . . the often overlooked fact remains that in so doing they become equally subject to the same conditions as front line men, though fortunately in a brief status. If glory is the "word" then it should never in any sense be extracted from the combat soldier, for his merits speak loud and clear . . . and no one until he has served in that capacity could know the apprehension with which he lives from day to day. Famed army war artist, Bill Mauldin summed it up well:

"Look at an infantryman's eyes and you can tell how much he has seen."

On the other hand while the Ordnanceman does not seek to thrive on glory his satisfaction is derived with the realization that his task in supporting the combat soldier has met with success. Adding credence to this fact General Bradley emphasizes in part, his view:

"It can be properly stated that no combat unit could be wholly efficient unless it was supported by a well-trained Ordnance unit."

Lt. Gen. Clarence R. Huebner, CG of the 1ST INFANTRY DIVISION, and later FIFTH CORPS states:

"An army cannot operate in combat without good Ordnance troops and the commander who neglects them does so at the risk of being defeated on the battlefield."

Though FIRST ARMY's fierce and swift drives were met with much elation, tremendous problems regarding transportation and supply suddenly became compounded. Great distances now lay between Base depots and truckheads, and initial stocks were hardly moving into a new depot site before "recon" was being conducted for an area further forward. A huge QM supply depot had opened at Vire August 12 and another at St. Sever de Calvados on the same day. Both carried Class I, II, III and IV items which took care of all basic necessities; clothing, food, gasoline and parts but even now they were too far behind . . . more than 150 miles from the fast-moving first, second and third echelon troops. Even the great Ordnance Base Depot opening on August 29 at Cherbourg was just too far away for effectiveness. Truck transport strained at the breaking point!

By the end of August the ration stockpile was dwindling and not only was there but little reserve of gasoline but other supplies were far below required consumption. FIRST ARMY during August would receive only sixteen percent of all requisitioned supplies, and badly needed now were replacements for medium tank engines, tank tracks and tires.

Though Advanced Section Communications Zone (COM Z) controlled all depots since first of August, thereby relieving FIRST and THIRD ARMIES of such responsibility it did little to correct the gnawing need for speeding up supplies. By the middle of August the entire army reserve was depleted and questionable maintenance from day to day caused this to be the most critical supply situation experienced on the continent.

When T/5's Stan Paczas and Ed Roenicke, along with Dave Howey were running supply allocations at all hours of the night and day in Normandy . . . searching for a particular depot or a particular base in an effort to secure vital parts, it goes without saying that at times it could be a dangerous and precarious business. T/5 Frank Szabla too, knew the hazards of continuous road usage, for commandeering the big 6 x 6 truck hauling larger parts he could pass *only* when someone would let him. Blinding rains, broken highways, confused map interpretation, unfamiliar routes . . . often on roads that were virtually impassable. At times, unable to pass and caught behind a tank convoy whose asphyxiating fumes made one sick to his stomach and whose tracks grinding deep against loose road pebbles and torn asphalt chunks peppered those following close behind . . . a driver did not find this task an enviable one. Johnny Morris, an efficient T/Sgt., but nonetheless a typical "wise guy" from Newark, New Jersey who knew all the answers, came within a "hair's breadth" of losing his life during an extremely bad night on just such a mission as this. With the campaign's well-paced drive and thunderous onslaught however, this task by now had become alleviated considerably.

SHEAF headquarters and 12TH ARMY GROUP coordinating with top field commanders were putting into action plans for the liberation of Paris. Somewhere around August 22-24 General Craig and his DIVISION staff were laying plans to follow VII CORPS orders to set a course due southeast within a close proximity of Paris . . . though a course that would not encompass the city itself. The 126th. Ordnance made preparations to follow.

Late morning of the 23rd. saw messkits washed, bedrolls packed and parts stacked to indicate another hurried move that would carry us through Tourouvre, thence sharply northeast to St. Maurice. Twelve kilometers straight east put us into the lovely town of La Ferte Vindame, a vital junction with a complex of roads jutting out unevenly in all directions. Because plans were not prearranged to locate a site, the Captain and his staff decided on a bivouac spot enroute. This appeared a likely region. Approximately three kilometers east of La Ferte Vindame on the edge of la Puisaye the vehicles now so heavily caked with dust so as to conceal our unit identification bounced and rolled in single file into a harvested wheatfield, formed a sort of "wagon train" circle and called a halt in the center of the field. Sensing little need for it, camouflage security was eliminated. Convoy mileage for the day approximated a dramatic *thirty miles*!

Sid Olivier did not have an enemy in the world that he was aware of and for the most part bubbled with personality, and because of his adept prowess with the accordion . . . he was dubbed the "Italian Troubadour." Admittedly, Olivier was no virtuoso . . . nor did he profess to be but he knew almost every "tune in the book" and had it not been for his instrumental implementation the evening may have found many tempers growing short what with the heat, grime, dust and growing impatience of the hot grueling convoys. Yet, the evening moved in a different direction as many were caught up in extensive singing . . . harmoniously unpolished though it was. All the strain and anxiety pent up during the twisting, bouncing convoy was released to allow for one of the most pleasant evenings enjoyed for a good length of time.

T/4 Chet Harris, along with T/5's Henry Boudreau and Ed Tarasiewicz were singled out to join Lt. Lineberger for an "advanced team" to move ahead and secure another suitable location that within the next 24 hours we would hope to occupy. An adjustment could be made to practically any spot at this stage in light of the fact that extensive maintenance plans were practically set aside and prospects of remaining in one spot for any length of time was questionable. Advance scouting parties were easy to find too; especially as we drew closer to Paris. So enthusiastic did it become that soon rumors were heard "rank was pulled" to get this coveted assignment!

It was after dark late the same evening when two of this group returned and declared the mission accomplished. The other two remained at the forward site.

"We'd better get on the road soon as possible" declared Lineberger, "because every damn unit in FIRST ARMY is moving down that road to the east!" Continuing, he said . . . "No kidding! You just won't believe it! Convoy after convoy is rolling toward Paris! We didn't have much of a problem getting down there but it was 'hell' coming back. Talk about traffic! Man . . . ! Vehicles weaving in and out of convoys! We could'a had a head-on collision a dozen times!"

Orsenigo, replying cooly, said: "We'll hit the trail first thing in the morning."

"Uh-uh," shot back an anxious Lineberger; "We'd be better off if we were on the road right now! *Right now!*"

"Calm down Lieutenant," mumbled the Captain softly; and with no intent of sarcasm . . . added with a sly grin; "Why don't you go over and join the boys in singing."

The bespeckled Lieutenant, a smile of exasperation across his face and recognizing the futility of his suggestion . . . turned around and headed for his tent, saying nothing. Short bursts of laughter interspersed with uncoordinated strains of "Roll Me Over In The Clover" and "Beer Barrel Polka" wafted across the field from the center of the main bivouac. But at the moment the Lieutenant wanted none of it. It had been a big day for him and he was dead tired.

In the morning the move would be continued. A route was charted that would take us within close range of Paris . . . and yet, around it.

The sun was up fully on the 24th as we broke camp. The road was clear and within a few miles Senonches was entered and cleared. A main supply route was selected southeast of the larger town of Chateauneuf and we began to encounter sparodic traffic. The road was battered and chunky all the way to Maintenon and it was a relief to call a halt before crossing the River Eure east of that city. Certainly no less than two hundred yards wide at this point this body of water with several marshy islands of saplings jutting out of its' broad expanse and spanned by a multi-supported weaving treadway represented the widest crossed in France up to this time. Much in evidence on both sides of the river was enemy wreckage . . . for Allied artillery had wreaked carnage and destruction on

German forces jammed at river crossings . . . desperately trying to cross.

The road beyond carried us across the River Voise and prior to entering Epernon we hurdled the River Droutte. Twisting crazily but paralleling this river for several miles one wondered aloud . . . "Who could have engineered so outrageously a main thoroughfare?" We did however, make ourselves content to simply take in the pictorial countryside with its' many small canals occasionally spotted with small barges and overshadowed with well-spaced poplar trees. We moved into Rochefort-en-Yvel and crossed the River Remarde to follow that particular flow for several miles . . . in fact almost all the way into Ollainville, a community as impeccable and well-kept as any we would encounter. Here we would rendevous with an advanced group, who arriving the day before remained near the edge of the city waiting for us.

A distance of seventy miles was engrossed and all agreed beyond a doubt that it was the most extensive thus far. Though starting very early in the morning and soon accompanied by a glaring sun it would not go down in the record books as one of our most comfortable days, for who would have dreamed that some five hours would be required to reach this location; and further, who would have dreamed that such traffic would be encountered?

Just as Lineberger had said, truckload after truckload of infantry and supplies streaked continuously down the main supply route that through necessity saw our convoy several times pull over and let pass. Yet, with our many stops . . . each lengthy in scope; the lack of road priority denied us the non-stop that we would have liked. We saw little cause to worry about it though, for on the surface this would appear to have been little more than an exciting though broad "sight seeing" trip when compared to the fast and reckless convoys of troops passing. We knew what "luck" was while moving through many towns of historic interest and took the opportunity to note at first hand the *real* vineyards that made up the Calvados sector of France.

As an air of uncertainty prevailed in relation to 9TH DIVISION's actual participation in FIRST ARMY's concentrated drive on Paris, our plans called for locating within the vicinity of Ollainville that lay some twenty miles or so west of that capital city. Securing this location had been the responsibility of the "recon" team and they did not let us down. We moved through Ollainville and rolled to the town's eastern approaches into an extended heavy growth of trees, heavily entwined with foliage and underbrush that resembled anything but an operational area.

Though now well into the afternoon Captain Orsenigo had already issued dutiful warning *not* to roam beyond the fringes of this area. This warning was predicated on a report from an engineer mine-probing unit that was still in the process of performing this unenviable task. This too, was contrary to our usual course of action. Some twenty yards north on one of the access roads twisted and mangled were remains of a jeep, blown apart . . . having made contact with an apparent well-concealed mine! With this grim reminder skepticism abounded . . . for until the mine-probers completed their job no one could yet tell if and where others may be planted around this location!

Now the great metropolis of Paris lay a scant thirty-two kilometers (twenty miles) east. During the past three and four years thousands of Parisians sought residence in several outlying towns from that capital city because of the enormous pressure and irritations that began to be imposed from the moment the German Army occupied the city in June, 1940.

With much reluctance those fortunate enough to make an exodus did so. Every little suburban town harbored some or many members of a Parisian family. The small town of Ollainville was no exception, as were other nearby communities; . . . Arpajon, Longjumeau, St. Michel, la Ville du Bois, St. Germain, Linas, Ballainvilliers . . . everywhere!

In these amiable people we were finding a comparatively different personality than those met in preceeding sectors. Perhaps their mode of dress made the difference for it was indeed a bright change to note colorful patterned women's dresses as compared with the drab homespun garb worn in Normandy. Everything appeared more fashionable . . . beauty more pronounced. Homes, streets, gardens were neat, tidy and suggested orderliness. Quite an upgraded philosophy of life appeared presented and this was personified in many ways. One would not have to converse too long before becoming infected with their natural extroverted attitude, and though it mattered little, certainly no one was concerned with matching the sophisticated climate of the great city with the vast less progressive rural areas of Normandy. Each had its place and each, during the occupation, contributed or suffered accordingly. One must, however; consider the obvious and note that the flourishing of styles should have been no big surprise . . . for only a stone's throw away lay the fashion capital of the world.

Especially prominent were expressions on faces of the older people, who having grown more adamant and hard through years of deprivation due to enemy occupational restrictions; gave way to radiant cheers and jubilance as their dreams of a liberated France seemed to be coming true.

Moving deeper into France our welcomes became more profuse, hurrahs resounded stronger and crowds exuded greater interest when lining the streets in towns that had escaped the ravages of war. For, no longer were we making our way slowly through rubble-choked and debris-cluttered streets but rather skirting at a slightly accelerated pace. The enthusiasm and unrestrained clamor could well be likened to that of a climatic spectacle at some great event! The applauding and ecstatic crowds, aware that they could not always reach out with consistency and present us with flower bouquets, literally threw them . . . many often falling wide or short of their intended recipients. Flowers were not the only token they wished to extend. Vegetables of many variances, particularly tomatoes were part of their expression and they well knew that we could put them to substantial advantage. In anxiety and emotional exhuberance they were hurled along with the flowers . . . in some instances falling short to sometimes smash harmlessly against sides of the vehicles! Often we returned the compliment and tossed rationed cigarettes, chocolate or crackers into the crowd to set off a mad scramble that was something to behold.

One afternoon a small group from our company dispatched two 3/4-ton trucks to transport those desiring . . . some ten miles southeast beyond our location . . . direct through Arpajon to a secluded branch of the River Orge that long had served as a semi-remote swimming locale. Wanting to share this rustic spot with American GIs, some of the youngsters showed us the way, hoping this would give us a welcomed relief from not only the grinding pace but from a unusually sultry August sun as well.

It was the return trip back into the city that produced the flavor of the afternoon's rollicking events!

Rolling back through the town at about the time most people were returning from work . . . (life went on despite the war) we again were warmly subjected to affections of the crowds. At one point we noted a group of younger children assembled with flower bouquets and batches of fruits and vegetables . . . hopeful of stopping or at least slowing the first American vehicle passing that way. With eager thoughts of exchanging their wares for the oddities or souveniers sometimes offered by soldiers, these youngsters spotted the two small trucks making their return trip through the town. Both vehicles were well-crowded with two or three standing upright on the open tailgate . . . beaming immacuately from a refreshing swim. Drinking in the warm exciting ovation of the crowds there was, though tempting, little intent given to stopping . . . despite ominous pleading gestures of the children.

"Les Americain! Les Americain!" shouted the children; "Arret! Arret! S'il vous plait!" But there would be no stopping! Then once again with the highly excitable French youngsters, bargaining gave way to excitement and they began tossing everything in the baskets at the elated grinning truck-laden GIs!

Dick Jaffee, a lanky Jewish sergeant from Chicago, standing on the flat open tailgate . . . highly pleased . . . gesticulating to the crowd a fixed smile of acknowledgement while absorbing this flattering adulation, remarked:

"Boy! How about this! Isn't this great? Man, we've got it made! I mean, have we *ever* got it made! Too bad the papers can't get a picture of this!" He was almost ecstatic. "Just *look* at those excited kids, will you!" Suddenly . . . "S-P-L-A-T!!" An apparent overripened tomato, thrown indiscriminately in the direction of the fast-moving GIs found its mark abruptly and squarely on the side of the head!

The compliments quickly vanished! With more shock than anger, and with little restraint Jaffee blurted: "What in the . . . ? . . . Why — you little 'Frog' . . . I'll!" . . . The broad beaming countenance would be seen no more during the afternoon!

The middle of August found Allied patrols reaching in and clearing practically all of the western suburbs leading into Paris, and the revered capital city; now faced with an encroaching famine of food, coal, gas and electricity stood on the brink of allied entry. The French underground collaborating with the fast-growing Maquis had operated secretly for months and by now stood well-prepared to rise and strike at the uneasy Nazis within the city. This action, following detailed planning by underground and military forces would be coordinated with that of the confident advancing allied liberating troops.

A ticklish and fearful question existed too; one that pointed to a monumental decision from the German garrison commander; General Dietrich von Cholitz. Would he order the city's destruction rather than submit to capture? Would Paris become a battleground rather than fall to the allies intact? From the Fuehrer his orders were explicit . . . for part of Hitler's decree specifically stated:

"Within the city every sign of incipient revolt must be countered by the sharpest means, including public execution of ring leaders.

"The Seine bridges will be prepared for demolition. Paris must not fall into the hands of the enemy except as a field of ruins."

The Paris liberation began August 23 when the city was entered at three points as the United States V CORPS released Maj. Gen. Jacques Phillipe Leclerc's French 2ND ARMORED DIVISION and the American 4TH INFANTRY DIVISION under direction of FIRST ARMY's V CORPS. Sharp skirmishes at points around Quai D'Orsay, Place Vendome, Palais Bourbon, Ecole Militaire and spots along Rue de Rivoli raged near the heart of the city. By noon of August 25 Paris was declared officially in Allied hands.

Monday morning's edition of the Chicago Daily Times August 26 carried big bold type headlines:

"PARISIANS GO WILD AS YANKS LIBERATE CITY!"
"ARMY SEES WAR END BY OCTOBER 1!"

This jubilant victory followed by just one month the smashing American breakthrough at St. Lo.

An official liberation annunciation on August 26 by French General Charles de Gaulle, who as Chief of the Free French movement said, in part;

"France will take her place among the great nations which will organize the peace. We will not rest until we move, as we must . . . into enemy territory as conquerors."

At the same time he proclaimed the National Committee of Liberation the provisional government of the French Republic. Two days later the Allies presented a parade of military might that moved through the heart of Paris.

Frenchmen say that not even during the time of Napoleon . . . not even the German capitulation in World War I had such a mighty victory spectacle as this ever before been seen. It would in the end add a glorious climax to the return of prestige and much honor to the broad-avenued two-thousand year old city! Followed by tanks and armored vehicles hundreds and hundreds of soldiers ceremoniously marched proudly and triumphantly straight down the great Champs Elys'ees . . . one of the widest streets in the world.

Past the Arc de Triomphe . . . down through Place de la Concorde they strutted with bands blasting their loudest, flags flying their brightest, and since the American 28TH INFANTRY DIVISION, now regrouping at Versailles west of Paris was selected for this tumultous display of emotions, their fresh immaculate uniforms (hastily cleaned) represented the American Army at its' finest! The city was bursting with excitement . . . every window filled with shouting, waving, applauding people exhibiting almost fanatical ardor as part of this long-awaited demonstration! Lampposts, trees, rooftops and every conceivable vantagepoint was occupied! Flags descriptive of every major Allied nation were attached to every object attachable; French, British, American, Russian, Belgian, Dutch and that of Luxembourg were especially prominent!

The thousands upon thousands of Paris citizenry were completely wild with joy, shouting and gesticulating with roaring exhiliration; and before the parade reached its' climax these swirling masses had swelled to a pitch of near hysteria to become absolutely out of hand; actually mobbing the already deeply moved and thrilled parading soldiers . . . many of whom by now were finding it difficult to maintain *their own* self-control! The uproarious and unrestrained crowds now uncontrollably intermingling surged into ranks of the soldiers, virtually "swallowing them up," as it were; to create such a high-spirited riotous stampede that they for a time became irretrievably "lost!" This was an experience beyond their wildest dreams!

Turn the clock back four years and some two months to the summer of 1940 and survey a marked contrast of the victorious German forces sternly and solemnly marching in cadence down this same broad avenue to occupy the city; who with their slow drab rolling and beating of drums struck sorrow, fear and dejection into the hearts of every patriotic Frenchman!

There have been so many individual tales relative to and revolving around Paris' liberation that it would become a researcher's nightmare to confirm and contain them. Many GIs laid claim to having been among the first to enter . . . and perhaps justifiably so, but those fortunate enough to have been on hand or even visit the city during the first hours and even the subsequent days following could certainly bear testimony that it was the most *spectacular* celebration that could ever come his way!

As unscheduled successes of FIRST ARMY gradually mushroomed into an almost hysterical race for the German frontier the way was led for CORPS, DIVISION and supporting units to follow. Various elements of 9TH DIVISION had for sometime been outdistancing each other; and in so doing of a necessity greatly accellerated the frequency of moves by maintenance, medical and supply troops. It remained then, that in vigorously attempting to maintain a contact of any stability with our DIVISION in the following few days would prove exhaustive for the 126th. Moreover; as the gap between DIVISIONAL structure and our company appeared to be widening by the hour a decision was adopted to keep rolling when possible, forget about road clearances and simply . . . "let the chips fall where they may" until a more coherent contact with DIVISION Ordnance became less problematical.

Everybody seemed to be in a hurry; every vehicle seemed to be moving at great speed! Fresh American tanks making their long journey from rear echelon distribution depots moved at a rapid pace (a contrast indeed to their slow lumbering efforts in the early days in Normandy) toward a piecemeal front that at this time was congealing at various spots somewhere up in northern France . . . far beyond the eastern banks of the River Seine. We were long delayed at a crossroads point late one morning as an extensive English artillery convoy . . . part of the British XXX CORPS; apparently far out of route moved past our convoy and we viewed with amusement their truck-towed medium guns bouncing "like rubber balls" over the dusty and deteriorated roads.

Increasingly amusing too, were the numbers of French bicyclists appearing on the scene at intervals on the streets and from out of side roads, and even on the highways . . . all pedaling at breakneck speed . . . to *where*, it seemed inconsequential!

To effectively pursue the enemy, now in headlong retreat it became necessary to move the infantry as expeditiously as possible and all available trucks were utilized to transport them for miles and miles. Infantry combat teams, who for so long had stalked and second-guessed the hedgerows and marshes would be spared the ordeal of walking and wasted no time climbing aboard tanks and trucks when the opportunity presented itself.

The war was accelerating fast and facilities for handling prisoners became acute as the trend of captured Germans began to rise to voluminous figures. From D-Day through August 25 FIRST ARMY had bagged more than 100,000 prisoners. Further, some 30,000 Germans had been wounded and FIRST ARMY had buried more than 15,000. As a result of swift advances many were bypassed in villages or wooded areas leaving to troops following, whether combat, service or supply, the somewhat precarious task of effecting either capture or liquidation. Aided by the now fast gathering French Maquis; or for a better name, the Free French of the Interior (FFI) who unobtrusively began showing up at almost every town and hamlet, this task became easier.

Many non-combat units inadvertently became involved or in some way participated in the capture of a prisoner or prisoners, and so great were their numbers one wondered just how many more could be left. Moreover, this situation, coupled with a mass enemy retreat on all sectors presented the newspapers, war correspondents and broadcasters with opportunities for great morale-building stories and feature articles . . . articles that offtimes carried synthetic hopes. This media hastened to create magnified impressions that resounded over much of the world . . . in substance, that the European conflict was hastening to a quick end.

Doubtless because of excessive transmission of daily news accounts that strongly grew optimistic, the same peace rumors were circulated early in July. Even Prime Minister Winston Churchill, speaking to the House of Commons on August 1st. surmised:

"The war approaches perhaps its' closing stage;" adding, "I no longer feel bound to deny that victory may come perhaps soon."

On August 31st. General Eisenhower voiced anew his confidence that "victory over Germany was possible in 1944 - for the Nazis were running out of manpower." Newspaper columnist Walter Lippman, in an article dated August 28th. in the Washington Post noted that "Lt. Gen. Kurt Dittmar, speaking for the German Army has told the Germans that they are on the verge of a complete military catastrophe."

All of this sounded good to us and our hopes were as strong as others that its' credence would bear a strong application toward ending the war soon. But unfortunately all of the newspapers, all the war correspondents, each of the broadcasters and most of the world grossly underestimated the discipline and ability . . . the capacity and stamina of a well-trained and astute fighting machine such as was the German Army.

***

Early morning of August 28th was set for leaving Ollainville and in a few minutes we would pass on through Arpajon, a major city straddling the main Paris-Orleans highway, and situated an equal distance between both of these cities. Instead of reaping the good fortune of moving north through Paris, Battalion orders directed us to drop just a little further south and work around the city. One of the more adventuresome Lieutenants suggested we try a little detour and "work our way through Paris" anyway . . . despite orders from both DIVISION and Battalion.

"Why not, Captain . . . it wouldn't be much out of the way," adding, "don't you think we are entitled to a good look at it?"

"Are you crazy?" suggested one of the more reserved officers. "You wouldn't get through that city in a week."

Sgt. John Morris of Supply spoke up. "Listen Lieutenant, that city is crawling with MPs. They've got road blocks and check points all over the place . . . and boy, you'd better have certified orders signed by Roosevelt himself to get through!"

"How the hell do you know, Morris?" mused Botting; "sounds like you've been there."

"Sergeant, how you *do* talk!" shot back the adventuresome supply sergeant.

The Captain, displaying little interest in the conversation, handed one end of the map to Botting, saying;

"This is the route we are taking," and running his finger along a highway encircling Paris south, gave little indication that he had even heard the suggestion.

"Paris is out?" questioned the Lieutenant.

"Forget it."

"Forget it?"

"Yes, dammit . . . forget it!"

Some Ordnance units felt sufficient to sort of settle down; some in open areas and some in tents, not with apathy but almost a feeling of permanence. Colonel Medaris, FIRST ARMY Ordnance Officer, sensed this and issued orders to keep units moving in an effort to produce flexibility. All the way to the German frontier most of the company's time would be spent on the road, passing unmolested through numerous towns and communities, most due to the rapid advance of Allied armies would escape the wrath of war. We would continue rolling along roads that increasingly far better conditioned did on the other hand appear to become narrower with no shoulders, close up against tall poplar trees with which they were lined. Many rivers would be crossed, some so narrow that by the time a larger vehicle's rear wheels reached the bridge's center the front wheels were already on the other side. In effect, straddling the bridge's entire length.

Farms and meadows passed into view. We swept over the small River Juine and reached the town of Le Ferte Alais. Two more rivers; the Essone and Ecole in quick succession were hurdled, bringing us onto the approaches of the lovely city of Melun at the River Seine. A hard glance at the map made it evident that we had moved south, then east . . . and so doing had engulfed the outer ridges of Paris in an obvious half-arc from Arpajon to Melun.

Two days of fierce fighting had raged in and around Melun before the city fell to the 7TH ARMORED DIVISION. Hard-pressed small artillery and tank assaults pushed the Germans out early on August 25.

Twenty-five miles southeast of Paris Melun is divided by the Seine into three sections. With the main highway bridge destroyed we crossed the river in mid-morning on a treadway bridge in the center of the city where the river is stretched the widest; some 350 feet. The city's east wing was heavily damaged and several disabled tanks and light artillery pieces added credence to the heavy assaults that were concluded three days previous.

In less than fifteen minutes Melun was cleared and some four miles northeast beyond the main highway we moved due east. On a secondary road that splits cultivated fields and one that, soon deprived of its' hard-surface gradually narrowed to little more than a wide path on which one vehicle could not pass another, we slowly crept into a woodstudded thicket.

Having logged sufficient distance the day's motorized march was deemed adequate. The order was passed;

"We'll bivouac here and nobody unloads except the kitchen."

By five o'clock all procedures were completed. The field kitchen was set up and chow was waiting.

A single unkempt lane with long rows of trees . . . varying in prominence with maple, oak and poplar running its' length, surrounded by unevenly-spaced thickets of bushes and scrub-trees would well-describe the location. This area, less than a mile east of a community called Moisenay-le-Grand and approximately forty miles southeast of Paris was, no less than closely akin to an "oasis of green wooded growth" situated in the middle of acres and acres of farmland.

Within close radius of Paris and its' surrounding communities this type of wooded "oasis" was not uncommon and there were in addition several private well-cared-for forests utilized for hunting of fowl and other light game. These forests served Allied troops well ... not only as a camouflage media but as a relaxing "rest stop." Even though we didn't consider it necessary this sparse natural camouflage would serve a surprisingly notable purpose.

At the extreme end of this lane an asphalt road lay horizontal east to west and fed into a main artery a few miles east. Fifty yards or so on the other side of the road amidst well-groomed cultivated gardens loomed majestically a seventeenth-century chateau known as Vaux le Vicomte. Therefore, something like one hundred yards separated this chateau from our company space. Within the next few hours our association and relationship with this handsome structure would become *ever* so close; to be remembered for several years to come . . . perhaps to many, *never* to be forgotten.

Many attractive chateaux, multi-spired cathedrals and monastaries reeking with medieval flavor were observed with interest as we moved through some of France's cultured regions but with the brisk pace of the past several days closer inspection was out of the question. Now finally, we were face to face with a magnificent work of architecture and here was a great opportunity for a more desired examination.

All of the surroundings and most especially the beauty of its' spacious and meticuously groomed courtyards with countless deliberately placed boxwoods trimmed in minute order, thousands of multi-colored flowers of many variations well-spaced around carefully trimmed lacy hedges made the setting absolutely enchanting. Viewing the prominently embanked moat that completely surrounds the castle . . . separating the building from its' gardens, did in an imaginary sense bring to reality that which had been known only in story books of long ago. Caretakers revealed this building to have been occupied some one hundred years previous by Louis XIV of France and prior to our arrival had served as headquarters for a German Army Regional Command.

Faced at home with a rapidly dwindling supply of badly needed raw materials the Germans during occupation of the building stripped it of all copper, brass and precious metals. The structure otherwise, was left in good state both externally and internally.

Though the 126th. sojourned here only a single night events were fast shaping that for many would seem to triple that length of time.

The evening developed into one as peaceful as any the summer had yet produced and midnight was fast approaching. The front . . . could it be placed in that category at this period continued to lack depth as the enemy continued his wholesale retreat. The war as far as we were concerned was quite some distance beyond and momentarily forgotten; and with exception of the already posted guards most of the company had dismissed their inner tensions, rolled up in their blankets and called it a night. With no apparent danger of falling flak or artillery bursts existing anywhere near the accepted chore of digging foxholes would for this reason serve no useful purpose and this task was abandoned.

Peace existed in its' rarest form. *But not for long*! For suddenly and without warning sharp rifle shots from the rear cracked the darkened silence! A slight pause . . . then more repeated shots!! Quickly this August evening transformed from one of tranquility to an ominous air of uncertainty!

No order needed . . . men bounded from their respective resting places immediately alerting themselves for a ground attack . . . taking refuge behind trees, bushes and vehicles . . . falling prostrate to the ground . . . wasting not a moment in this transaction! Then . . . silence . . . long moments of waiting . . . and with no more shots coming forth . . . imminent thoughts widely throbbed that perhaps this was only a momentary skirmish. "The guards are now in complete control of the situation" reasoned many. This thought became a reality when most eyes shifted back to the direction of the commotion to strain through the veiled darkness and note a German soldier, hands over his head . . . flanked by two of our guards coming down the path leading into the central area.

What happened?

The three guards assigned that post; T/3 Werner Lasch, T/5

Leon Musielak and Private Tony Hizon (an impulsive young Filipino lad who long had yearned for such as this) were startled to look up and suddenly see coming out of nowhere two figures aided by the evening's brilliance steathily and probably unaware of their direction approaching the post. Their manner of approach suggested suspicion and a sharp challenge was issued! All of this was done in seconds! Obviously too shocked to immediately heed the abrupt command, both instinctively opened fire and rushed for a break in opposite directions!

"CRACK! CRACK! CRACK!" came the sound of carbine fire from the guardpost!

Surely wounded one managed to elude the guards to disappear in the darkness. The other after a few steps . . . threw up his hands, yelling . . . "Kamerad!"

"CRACK!" came another shot from the guards into the darkness!

"*Kamerad*! *Kamerad*!" shouted the German, his hands straight up.

"You bastard, you better yell 'Kamerad! . . . and you better yell it loud!" replied one of the clearly excited guards.

Interrogation was brief and the lone prisoner revealed that so swift had been the American advance that they were cut off from their unit, and though knowing well the dangerous odds . . . were attempting to locate their lines. Amazingly cooperative and perhaps still finding his predicament a little hard to believe the German was ordered into a jeep and plans were made to transport him to a PW stockade believed somewhere northeast of Melun. However dramatic this episode the evening's festivities had only begun . . . for suddenly two German night-fighters swept in from nowhere and swooped just above the treetops! Two more joined them and the shooting started! It was near midnight and the silence was gone!

Banking and diving at will and with "murder in their eye" the planes fired short staccato-like bursts into field, road and forest. Someone in the Recovery section wanted to pull the wraps off one of the truck-mounted 50-calibers and "have a go at it," but another; reasoning better . . . pulled him down.

"Maybe they're not after us!" said someone at the CP.

"Maybe not," replied Captain Orsenigo; "but just lay low . . .

and for God's sake, no shooting! Maybe they'll just take off if nobody shoots back!"

Maybe they *would* have . . . but too late now for it was time for the "ack-ack" to go to work! All surrounding anti-aircraft batteries raked the sky in an attempt to bring down a plane. The "ack-ack" boys became our salvation . . . and prior to this we didn't even know they were here! Never to be underestimated those guns made the air literally ring with flying steel, and tracer missiles whizzed in all directions to give us the first firing experienced in several days! Though greatly alleviating the overall predicament, we felt helpless . . . absolutely helpless!

Before ignition of the prisoner-laden jeep was even turned on glowering enemy flares had started their almost silent drop from several hundred feet . . . fast creating a sort of greenish unnatural lighted appearance that gradually enveloped this entire area and would expose much of this equipment. Down . . . down . . . down drifted the flares! Producing a sort of hissing sound the closer they descended the brighter the picture! When the flares were dropped instructions that sounded frantic were shouted by Captain Orsenigo to take cover . . . but he was wasting his breath for the men were already scrounging for cover wherever it could be found! Cognizant of our immediate lack of preparation our plight grew more acute with each fleeting second! (Later, one could question . . . "Who was *ever* prepared?")

Despite the backdrop of trees and foliage trucks and all vehicular equipment gradually formed outlined silhouettes against the flare-brightened region and gave the planes an opportune target. The 376th AntiAircraft Battalion now with serious thoughts *very definitely* had its' hands full . . . throwing 30's, 40's, 50's and even 90mm shells at the violently maneuvering planes and still had not brought one down! Not even a falling flare had been liquidated! Bushes and foliage all around and even the road across the entrance caught the sharp thudding impact of jagged shrapnel from expired "ack-ack" shells! "W-H-A—N–G! . . . Z-I-N-G-G! . . . Z-I-N-G-G! . . . W-H-O-O-S-H!" Then . . . the inevitable came! The bombs started their earthward plunge!

Those that have experienced the screeching crescendo of a descending bomb and the long moments required to reach its' target will certainly forever view it with fearful respect! This is especially true if you think that you will become its' recipient! You can't get close enough to the ground and no matter the depth of the trench or foxhole it is *never* deep enough! Feverishly, almost hysterically you try digging deeper with your bare hands, and one even imagines his helmet will be a salvation! It has been said that a piece of past history looms within the inner conscience as you swear and promise the Almighty that you "will serve him and follow the straight and narrow the rest of my days if allowed to come out of this in one piece!" Many of us can attest to that!

Not many fell but each time a bomb started its' scream each man *swore* his name was on it . . . and before that, as projectiles raked the bushes, they too . . . belonged to each individual; and those very few that *had* dug holes were quickly joined by those that *had not*! The explosives landed in surrounding fields and across the road . . . "WHUMP! WHUMP! WHUMP!" The terrific impact of explosions felt no less than right in our lap! "WHOOM! WHOOM! WHOOM!" Phosphorous, anti-personnel, light and medium bombs fell at random . . . many no more than fifteen or so yards away. There is no question that ever-skeptical Sgt. Johnny Morris and T/4 Tony Puchala are ever likely to forget the one that came so close to their truck that contained many highly inflammables . . . which included more than one case of dynamite! Someone in panic shouted:

"Move that truck! Move that truck!"

Stung and angered Puchala shot back:

"Where the hell you gonna move it to?"

He was right! "Where *could* you move it at this stage?"

In the meantime prior to this action occupants of the chateau had inadvertently, carelessly or otherwise left many of the lights burning and for a brief period flashed them off and on. Consequently, as approaching planes drew near it obviously was assumed that this prominent and well-lighted building housed some type of headquarters for Allied forces. Conclusive thoughts however, suggest that the mammoth FIRST ARMY supply and ammunition dump at nearby Melun was the *real* prime target and this multi-lighted chateau only presented an "accidental" but opportune target.

A group dispatched to investigate and curb this conspicuous flashing of lights; Lt. Lineberger, T/5's Tom Endean, Harold Knowles, James Locke and Ted Jankowski were caught within the chateau grounds as the bombs fell. Terrified and no less confused as to what course to take . . . that is; whether to remain within the building or not; each looked to the other for the answer!

The Lieutenant shouted:

"I'm staying right here . . . and suggest you do the same!"

Lineberger did just that but everybody else bounded through the nearest exit.

"What's the matter with you guys . . . didn't you hear what the Lieutenant said?" shouted one endowed with obedience; "He said to stay here!"

"I don't give a damn *what* he said . . . *I'm gone*!" and Jim Locke bounded down the concrete steps and desperately made for a nearby wooded area as fast as his short frame would carry him! Ted Jankowski threw himself to the ground, and waiting for the worst . . . groveled frantically with his hands into the courtyard! Tom Endean; who as company mail clerk had handled his duties methodically and one never known to succumb to excitement, dropped his helmet and jumped into the frontal moat, not knowing or caring the water's depth, but weighing his chances there as against stopping a piece of shrapnel or suffering possibly concussion! In fast order, Harold Knowles, now out of breath . . . joined him!

"Ack-ack" continued its' saturation of the air . . . searching and pouring heat into the raiders! Enemy activity began to wilt and they suddenly subsided. Now their motors trailed off and they were gone. The strafing and bombing ended almost as abruptly as it started! Though many prayers and countless vows were passed in a short period the "Gods of Fortune" apparently had hovered over the 126th for it emerged from this action without a single casualty!

As an unbounded queasy relief and a strange silence began settling over the area our strong uneasiness continued to abound, for even as the raid ended lights within the chateau continued their spasmodic flashing. On and off! On and off! Someone suggested that the occupants "are bound to be close to a state of shock!"

The Captain was almost furious!

"Shock or no shock . . . I can't help that! Somebody is still playing with those damn lights!" He directed Botting to "get a detail over there pronto!"

Botting got a detail all right . . . but after this past transaction he was in no mood to be diplomatic.

"We've had enough of this crap! I mean *enough*!" Bellowing with little restraint, he called:

"Hilditch, Felt, Linzinmeir, McNulty, Morris . . . Let's go!"

They knew what he meant. Lt. Black joined them. They advanced a few yards to the road and stopped. Raising carbines to their shoulders, Botting commanded:

"Aim for the windows!"

Shots echoed across the courtyard . . . "CRACK! CRACK! CRACK! KA-POW!" It was too far away to hear the tinkling of glass, but it was there!

A few more shots and the message was conclusive! The lights flashed no more! The occupants kept them off.

Attention now turned to the prisoner taken during the evening's early hours. Throughout the entire attack he elected to remain frozen in a sitting position in the jeep's rear seat . . . daring not to move. Physically he had kept almost motionless but mentally he had been "going through hell!" *He* knew . . . and *we* knew that had he made a wrong move it most certainly would have been one of his last. Yet, despite what his fate might have been one could not help but inwardly admire his immense outward show of stoicism during this alarming ordeal.

"Take that 'Kr aut' the hell out of here!" ordered the Captain.

S/Sgt. Henry Hunt motioned for Jim Tyrrell and Walt Perliskey to join him in that task. The two T/4's, both still trying to catch their breath and still smarting from the evening's excitement quickly climbed into the backseat. Fingers triggering their carbines, the German remained in the passenger seat just in front of them . . . his arms arched and hands clasped in surrender fashion on his head. Hunt moved out fast and little time as possible was anticipated in search of the nearest POW Collecting Point. It did not turn out as easy as expectations would warrant, and as each later related; "The search developed into almost a real first class wild goose chase!"

"First, and to begin with we weren't even sure we were starting in the right direction," recalled Tyrrell. "There were encounters with civilians, some wearing the French army tunic with no other sign of military dress and some had FFI armbands that looked anything but authoritative. And there were others, but everyone of them appeared to be indifferent. We went up side roads, back roads and even turned back on FIRST ARMY's main supply route a couple times," related the 33-year old Brooklynite; "and soon it began to get a little ridiculous as it appeared we were getting exactly nowhere!"

Little or no light could be shed as to the location or even *existence* of a POW stockade. Still shaken by the recent bombing within this locale many were wary of anything military and doubtless found it difficult to muster up a cooperative spirit of enthusiasm. True, it was understandable but it was beginning to cut tempers short. Several GIs were queried and *not one of them* seemed to know anything about the location of a POW compound. Moreover; most encountered that evening could not with any coherence tell where they were going or even the location of their own unit. Some could not, in fact, properly identify the town in which they were now in!

"Hell," said Tyrrell, now a banker in Manhatten; "I got so tired of this 'mumbo-jumbo' that I even thought of asking the 'Kraut' prisoner if *he* knew of a stockade!"

Along the way one motley group of Frenchmen strongly suggested thoughts of their own as to how the prisoner could be eliminated and appeared ready to take him. Walt Perliskey, a slight Polish lad who did a lot of thinking but rarely had *anything* to say about *anything* until it was carefully thought out was ready to agree with the Frenchmen's suggestion:

"Why not just drop him off and forget it, Sarge?"

"Now wouldn't that be stupid," replied Hunt; "Those 'Frogs' would shoot him in a minute!"

"So what?" mumbled an exasperated Perliskey.

The young German by this time having sensed that *same* thought, appeared *more* than eager to move on.

Picking their way through a partially burning community at the outer ridges of Melun the trio came up close to a Frenchman slowly pedaling a bicycle who obviously did not want to stop. A couple shouts to him proved futile. Speeding up a litte so as to cut in front of him, Hunt . . . his patience now gone, yelled:

"If that damn 'Frog' don't stop, pull him off the bicycle and *make* him talk!"

A few gestures of the hands, a few shrugs of the shoulders and it was quickly known that he would be of no help.

Shortly afterward on the edge of the community . . . almost by accident they came upon a large roadsign that read clearly, almost as if in mockery:

JAYHAWK POW COLLECTING POINT AHEAD

An arrow pointed to a VII CORPS compound far less than a mile away. Considerable persuasion was necessary before the prisoner was accepted.

"We already got 'Krauts' coming out our ears!" came a staunch announcement from an MP guard.

"What are we supposed to do with him?" shot back the burly Hunt.

"Take him back with you - turn him loose - give him to the 'Frogs' " came a sarcastic reply . . . "We don't give a damn!"

"The hell with that! We've brought him a long way," insisted Hunt; "and we've had him too long already! *He's yours!*"

Verbal exchanges became warmer, finally drifting into nothing more than small talk and the German was put out. There remained no choice other than to be accepted and he was left to join his fellow comrades in the already overcrowded and bulging enclosure.

Back at the encampment each man a few hours later . . . no less than at daybreak, was ready to pull out at a moment's notice, awaiting *only* the word. Captain Orsenigo wanted to move out right after "chow" . . . with or without sanction of DIVISION Ordnance. Botting was against it, and muttering under his breath for a moment could no longer contain his displeasure.

"What in the good Christ is wrong with you Captain," he blurted; "We've just set up and you want to move *out*? Let's take another day rest! Hell, the 'Krauts' aren't coming back!"

"Sergeant," replied the Captain in his steady but monotonous voice; "I appreciate your concern but I can't hear you. I'm *still* responsible for this company and I say we're moving the hell out of here . . . *and fast!*"

"What is there to be afraid of anyway?" continued the Sergeant; "The other section leaders don't want to leave."

With a slight pause and forcing a slow grin so as to collect himself, the Captain looked Botting straight in the eye and spoke softly:

"Tell them to get ready."

It may have been a coincidence . . . but the other staff officers were either neutral or conveniently busy. They would have none of this controversy.

The tall New Yorker was a restless individual and he expressed himself further;

"Do you know how lucky we are? Do you know that? Suppose those bombs had *really* hit us . . . and it was just a miracle they didn't; we'd be in one hell of a fix!" He continued; "Why should we deliberately get involved in something that might just cause casualties . . . something that just might neutralize our efficiency? We've got work to do . . . we haven't got time for that kind of crap." Emphasizing his point, he added; "No sir! We've been lucky so far and have done all right . . . let's keep it up!" Concluding, he said; "We're moving out, Sergeant."

Climbing into his jeep . . . always the Number One vehicle in each company convoy, and easily identified by the "Chiappa Quel Vien" slogan brightly stenciled on its' side, he and his driver sped the five or six miles to St. Germain-Laxis northeast of this location to consult with Lt. Col. J. D. Childs, the folksy pipe-smoking slow-talking DIVISION Ordnance officer.

Lest anyone form an impression that this former West Pointer's slow deliberate talk meant that he also was a slow thinker, they would soon find out that he was a soldier who well-knew his business and one who held responsibility for all 9TH DIVISION Ordnance activities and its' related units.

General William C. Westmoreland, Chief of Staff, United States Army, then a Colonel Commanding 9TH DIVISION artillery and two months later DIVISION Chief of Staff, in an interview with the author at the Pentagon, was high in his evaluation of the conservative Childs and saw him as an efficient and exacting field officer:

"The wellspring of ordnance support to the 9TH DIVISION during the entire European Theater operations was the DIVISION's extraordinarily effective Ordnance Officer, Lt. Col. Jefferson D. Childs, who displayed outstanding qualities of leadership and initiative in maintaining constant contact with tactical commanders and taking a personal interest in following up to see that their needs were met."

Because they too were moving out, the Colonel, raising his eyebrows slightly and lighting his pipe with little expression offered no objections . . . saying:
"Okay, but clear with your Battalion."
We were on the road long before noon and as speed was of essence it was expedient that we again select a key highway for travel. That the roads were busy was an understatement and though our priority was not the highest we needed them *too*! Though even at this moment thickly infested with supply-laden trucks and a steady stream of combat replacement troops forcing us to work into the traffic pattern there was no denying that the main supply routes still represented the most expeditious for convoy movements. Less than an hour was required to reach the rushing River Aoon . . . thence on through the lovely town of Chaumes.

With increased frequency from this point mute evidence of brief but savage skirmishes began to appear. Here and there a figure clad in the American olive-drab uniform, though not as many as those in greyish-green of the Wehrmacht, lay sprawled and crumpled by the side of the road or in the midst of wreckage. This had been an enemy on the run . . . but unfortunately could not run fast enough. Noted too, was a tremendous amount of cluttered horse-drawn equipment out of action that seemed to belong to another era, though because of depletion of machines had of a necessity borne small artillery, ammunition in wagons and weapons. Sprawled alongside wreckage too, were carcasses of horses well into process of bloating and decaying in the hot August sun.

Straight east we moved; across the Rivers Yerres and Aubetin and within two hours entered busy Coulommiers. It was getting late . . . evening was not too far away. Directing the convoy to the side of the road, the Captain instructed Lt. Lineberger and his driver to move forward and find a spot suitable for evening bivouac.

"We'll remain here," he said; "but be back at this spot in an hour."

Dark clouds began to emit slight precipitation as evening fast approached, and in far less than an hour we were pulling into two small orchards on the eastern fringes of an attractive little village called Boissy le Chatel.

Our advances far exceeding prognosticated schedules we had for some time experienced frustrations in an attempt to keep messages fluent between battalion, company, CORPS and DIVISION headquarters. Now closer contact with each segment became more cohesive despite the stepped-up progress of combat units now facing sparodic opposition. The light rain continued off and on during the three-day encampment but did little to dissuade the townspeople from visiting with us. Trading much-welcomed potatoes and fresh eggs we also took advantage of sampling genuine French wine and champagne, assured that it came "straight from the celebrated vats of Rheims and Epernay." From their many visits to see that we were supplied it was reasoned that these delicacies were in great abundance. There was of course, another reason. They were simply curious, for Americans obviously were something of a novelty to them, and as they expressed it, we were among the very first they had ever seen. From this, we had little to complain about!

Along with wine a new and refreshing beverage was appearing with increased frequency . . . "apple jack."

Under a greyish cloudy backdrop of annoying precipitation it was almost noon when we moved out on the 31st., and less than thirty minutes were rolling northeast through Rebais. Several miles beyond . . . coming upon Nogent, a community hugging close along the steep banks of the River Marne . . . we crossed this famed river at that point. The heavy mist had turned into a light rain and never let up as the Marne was followed all the way into the great battle center of Chateau Thierry. Though it was late afternoon few people were scurrying about. A busy gendarme stood in the townsquare, and as if wanting to be some kind of an official involved in this convoy he saluted and made some affirmative gesture to each vehicle as it passed. Two shattered enemy tanks with heavy guns drooping and tracks blasted, together with three or four splintered anti-tank guns strewn around the square had long ceased to be an obstacle and the convoy cleared the town with dispatch. Other than shrapnel-pocked scars chipped into a few buildings, several shattered windows and some rubble now bulldozed aside in the streets the town experienced no real damage.

What a contrast to just twenty-six years previous!

The brief skirmish staged two days ago could not in reality be written in the same book as that destructive conflict which reduced this very town to rubble in the first World War. The great battle that had roared and lingered for many days inflicting carnage and thousands of casualties on either side . . . a murderous battle that had long filled the pages of history and had passed on to glory remains indelible as one of the most decisive and costly in human lives throughout French history!

Frenchmen tell us that named for one of the medieval French provincial kings, Thierry; who erected a castle at this point and named it for himself, this town in World War I experienced perdition in the most truculent manner, changing hands many times between the defending French and invading Germans. A climatic "high water mark" was reached when a massive enemy drive threatened the French with a rout that could end nowhere short of Paris . . . a retreat that would have engrossed some one hundred miles! The newly arrived American troops, part of the Allied Expeditionary Forces headed by General John J. Pershing were brought into action at this point, and with support of "crack" troops from the 2ND and 3RD DIVISIONS . . . backed by Marines itching to fight; the enemy drive was sustained! The German invaders began to wither and were pushed back through eastern France and eventually across their own border.

How different the approach now! This very town two days ago was captured intact by the 3RD ARMORED DIVISION, with combat teams of both 9TH and 5TH INFANTRY DIVISIONS following close behind.

Now in low gear our convoy wound steathily up the hill rising east of the town and obvious notation was made of a handful of German prisoners now in process of burying their own dead on the hillside. Just above at the summit impressively overlooking the entire region stood a massive monument erected by a grateful French Government commemorating the dead of the participating American units in the heroic stand in 1918 around this location. Carved in gigantic letters on this broad grey-white granite monument is an expressed tribute to those lost in that struggle . . . reading:

"THE GLORY OF THEIR DEEDS WILL LIVE FOREVER"

Having reached the hill's northeastern summit; one of many forming a backdrop about Chateau Thierry, the Marne countryside lay outstretched below us and with that famous river winding distantly through the valley . . . visions of the fierce battles of 1918 staged by French, German and American doughboys on this historic battleground were recreated vicariously in many of our imaginations.

Continuing northward and moving swiftly through three small quiet towns of Verilly, Epiedes and Beuvardes we reached in a short time the more active and much larger town of Le Ferte en Tardenois. A brief encounter with a "rag-tag" cluster of excited civilians herding a group of frightened young Germans in the center of the main street appeared more amusing than serious as they flagged down the convoy and noisily crowded around. Amid much jumbled confusion they pleaded not only for weapons with which to rout the enemy from the forests but wanted some physical assistance as well.

"Tell them to get the hell out of the way Sergeant," said the Captain as if presupposing the next step.

"Wait a minute, Captain; it won't take a minute. Let's see what's up."

"Le Boche! Le Boche!" . . . a Frenchman pointed frantically to surrounding forests.

"Les bois sont pluns d'Allemands!"

"Donnez-nous des armes!"

"Aidez-nous a les dispenser!"

"We knew what this meant! Isolated groups of Germans! But we weren't about to give them weapons or go with them," recalled Captain Orsenigo; "for at that particular time and excited as they were, there's no telling what might have happened."

All of us knew that they weren't kidding; but at this point we really didn't care . . . for further up the road in those woods an overnight campsite had already been selected. The French wanted weapons bad . . . they wanted vehicles . . . but most of all, they wanted some Americans along for reassurance!

"Nothing doing!" ordered the Captain. "Keep going! Let the 'Krauts' stay in the woods. They'll come out when they get hungry. Let the 'frogs' figure this one out by themselves."

He meant it!

Sympathizing with their plight though not heeding their alarms and pleas we rolled less than half a mile north beyond the town, turned into a break in the forest . . . Foret de Nesles . . . and broadening a wide path through underbrush halted after penetration had seemed sufficient. It had been a twisting, rather dismal trip with several stops involved and since noon we had moved *only* forty eight miles.

Thinly dispersed, one learned it a "ticklish" task because of extreme density of foliage and underbrush to move from one spot to another after dark and for this reason, together with gathered skepticism that others too, inhabited this forest we hardly dared venture more than a few feet from personally selected sites.

The First Sergeant, at a late evening formation echoed the C.O.'s orders:

"Stay alert but steer clear of firing your guns!"

This order needed more clarification and prompted Sgt. Hilditch to question in a somewhat frustrated but subdued tone:

"What are we supposed to do, Sergeant; just let the 'Krauts' advance on us and do nothing?"

Botting was waiting for him, and with a slight grin reeking of sarcasm, replied:

"Don't worry Hilditch; the guards at each post will have that responsibility . . . and if that happens and you hear shooting you'll *then* know what to do!"

"Like hell I will!" the lanky supply section leader replied; "I'll be so damned scared by that time that I'll be too busy filling up the latrine and won't be able to fire a gun!"

The sharp sound of rifle shots and occasional burp gun fire splitting the otherwise silence of the night meant no less than someone had made hostile contact or had cornered an enemy group lurking somewhere within this tightly-knit forest for it was full of German stragglers. This impelled all guards to adopt an unusual alert position in the event some of these "lost" Germans might inadvertently or accidentally "stumble" through our encampment. We definitely didn't want any more of that! These skirmishes predominantly were confined amongst the enemy and the vigorous "Kraut-hunting" Free French of the Interior and we were content to keep it that way. Something *could*, we reasoned, go wrong and we *could* find ourselves right in the middle of it.

This French national organization obviously but understandably not under the best management appeared endowed *more* with an insatiable desire for action, adventure and revenge rather than real patriotism dramatically became known as the FFI. They were however, a determined group and their effectiveness in putting out of action and diligent sweeping "round-up" of bypassed Germans alleviated considerably the task of U. S. forces whose time could be spent in other duties. The FFI quickly became the greatest morale force in France in unifying resistance movements during these days and not only was this action carried out with efficiency in this Marne sector as well as the entire northern region but during the previous hard-pressed months of fighting in all parts of France.

Late in the afternoon of the second day we would experience an interesting session with the French.

Two civilians with black armbands, indicating association with the liberation movement dashed breathlessly into our CP jabbering in voices that crescendoed into an unintelligible pitch and gesticulating wildly as if the world were coming to an end!

"Somebody get Boudreau!" yelled the First Sergeant.

"Hey Boudreau!" one shouted. "Up here, Boudreau . . . on the double!" the cry passed on down to Small Arms Section. "Come on up here and see what these 'Frogs' want!"

A translation revealed that nine German SS troops were at this moment held at bay by a group of FFI in a shack less than a mile away. Against his better judgement Captain Orsenigo nevertheless relented and a halftrack was dispatched which almost immediately became filled with *our own* volunteers. By the time it moved a few yards to the main road several Frenchmen who suddenly came out of nowhere climbed in . . . each well-armed for the skirmish presumably to follow!

"Everybody out!" called Botting. "Come on, let's go! . . . everybody out but four men. Let these 'Frogs' do this job!"

The shack was found and with dramatic cautionary maneuvering a position was established before the dwelling in a sort of "C"-shaped arc. Each Frenchman looked to the other for leadership. A signal was given and everyone simultaneously opened fire! An ultimatum followed; one that challenged the Germans to surrender! No response! Another fusilade! . . . Again no response! "Something must be wrong!" someone figured. "No white flag? Maybe they have all been hit!" A skeptical Frenchman, streaks of sweat running down his face and sporting a not-too-clean beret, mustered enough courage to creep close enough to investigate . . . and was startled to learn nobody was inside! The "besieged" enemy had fled before the eager and tenacious "would-be" captors arrived. Their flight was short-lived for capture awaited them further back in the woods by another group of alert FFI.

September was here, and the forest having served its purpose we moved out on the 2nd following an early breakfast. Winding northeast nothing of importance was encountered while moving on up and through the village of Chery-Chartreuve.

***

"Boy! These 'Frogs' must eat a lot of apples!" someone remarked.

True; this was predominantly orchard country rather than farmland and one could view acres and acres of apples . . . drooping from trees much in abundance but not yet large enough for consumption. The soil, crustier and darker than seen in other areas of France lacked development that some say, *without* confirmation, is a result of the many great battles moving across its terrain. Another theory, perhaps truer, is the fact that not too distant east begins long ranges of deposits of coal and ore. This region, with prevailing bareness, many open wheatfields, here and there an apple orchard, sparse population and little industry proved to be a little monotonous until forward elements rolled into the old town of Fismes.

A startling spectacle witnessed at Fismes was strongly commensurate with similar events now progressing in many towns and villages throughout liberated areas all over northern France, to become increasingly personified following the liberation of Paris. As will happen in most any enemy-occupied country; there will be some, exempting neither man nor woman, who will almost without exception find it expedient to put national pride asunder and temporarily "forget" whatever hollow patriotism existing . . . either for monetary purposes or simply to gain favor of the enemy. Black marketeering and prostitution strongly stands out as heading a long list of normal bargaining favors . . . often, as the situation warrants, transactions of this nature though on a so-called "business" level could well be categorized as weakness of the individual. Yet, on the other hand, and conveying no excuses; for want of survival it sometimes may be found *necessary*. It is too, sound reasoning to say that *no one* is qualified to judge another's actions until he or she is confronted with a similar problem and thereby forced to make a decision accordingly.

Even at this early date men were swiftly being brought to trial over much of the nation. But here in Fismes in this particular instance it was the women that unfortunately faced the accusers. From the looks of things the "finger of guilt" was steady. Normally prostitution has few scruples and while no basic intention was intended to wrong the country these women were accused of willfully "collaborating" by sharing their person to make life considerably more comfortable for Germans during the occupation. "Collaboration," Webster says; is "the act of working together" and a "collaborationist" is "a person who cooperates with or traitorously aids an enemy nation or an occupier of his country." Did they violate the nation's trust? By many standards this action could be more explicitly defined as fraternization rather than collaboration. Nevertheless, as far as the highly sensitive French were concerned the slightest comforting favor allowed the Germans was viewed as an ignominious and unpardonable act. Not quite . . . but dangerously bordering on treason.

In Fismes this small frightened and repentent group of women were ushered into the town square and as the town populace jeered approvingly, each woman's head was roughly shorn of its' locks . . . the hair clipped to the scalp. Often when the crowd became unruly clothes were snatched and torn, in some instances almost ripped off! Almost ceremoniously (the French loved ceremonies) denunciation by a spokesman followed and the accused were pushed from the square, slowly chased down the street and often out of town with harsh insulting words of condemnation ringing in their ears! Offering no resistance they felt fortunate . . . fortunate *indeed* to be escaping with their lives!

In almost innocent anxiety some of the children . . . caught up in the atmosphere of disorder and not fully realizing the full significance of what had happened picked up rocks, sticks or whatever was available, tossed them . . . and taking a cue from their elders added jeers of their own, increasing further humiliation on the fast-departing accused.

Sitting alongside the townsquare in a jeep one of our group remarked; "Wasn't this a bit pagan according to our standards?" Most were unanimous in the answer.

"If the townspeople think this was justification for their actions, then who were we to question?"

Another agreed similarly, and added:

"Let's just see what *our* boys do when *they* get into Germany. We'll just watch the patriotism then."

The rest of the convoy soon caught up and followed the small lead group onto a narrow secondary brittle road . . . long suffering for lack of maintenance and continued north. Across the River Vesle at Breuil-sur-Vesle . . . on through adjoining towns of Romain, Ventelay and Rouey and a few miles further crossed the historical River Aisne near a dimunitive village called Pontavert.

Corbeny is a lovely intersection town situated on the main east-west Rheims-Laon highway and is about equal distance between those two cities. The swift-flowing River Miette was crossed here and we moved in great haste northeast through Berrieux, Goudelancourt, Sissone, Lappion, Dizy-le-Gros and into Montcornet. We crossed the Rivers Hurtaut and Serre and several miles were clocked before the wide rushing River Brune was checked. Some twenty miles beyond a halt was called and three small adjoining fields were commandeered within sight of the little hamlet of Jeantes.

Soissons had long fallen to the 3RD ARMORED DIVISION. The 4TH INFANTRY DIVISION and a combat team of French armored forces had likewise taken St. Quentin while the 1ST INFANTRY DIVISION was pushing well up to the Belgian border. The British had encircled Le Havre north on the channel . . . and the important city of Lille was well in hand. Canadian forces were mopping up the coast in and around Dieppe and Calais, putting out of action flying bomb sites that for three months had harrassed England. Hedgerow-to-hedgerow war had given way to speed, precision and choice targets as the Allies moved about at will and though savage skirmishes did occur it was virtually certain that the Germans would be the heavy loser for a good many reasons . . . chief among them:

1. They now were decisively outnumbered.
2. Overwhelming Allied air superiority would not let them rest.
3. Much of their rolling equipment in this sector was reduced to secondary or outdated models; in many cases horse-drawn vehicles.
4. Fighting a desperate retreating action kept them continually off balance.

Insofar as the western front was concerned Germany stood alone. Her opponents, showing no mercy were many. Time was in nowise on her side. The aerial bombardment of this nation would increase and would soon strangle her economy and obliterate all communications. The last great battles were yet to come . . . and they would not be, according to the onrushing Allies, long delayed.

By the first week of September the watching world was fully

aware that the war was drawing closer and closer to "Jerry's" own home soil!

Contact with DIVISION units increased with greater frequency by time the 126th arrived in Jeantes and with many DIVISION groups scattered in strategic spots over a wide vicinity, G-2 had confirmed that even now some armored troops were not too far from the Belgian border.

Several days had elapsed since any of the men had felt the comfort of cleanliness. It had in fact been several weeks though for most of them they didn't care. *They* had a theory! Men like Ernie Koudelka for example . . . the stubby tough "rough and ready" T/4 from Chicago and one who lost little sleep over the bath issue, summed it up thusly;

"Gritty and dirty . . . so what? The hell with it! That's war and war is dirty! We'll take a bath when the war's over!"

Many miles on dusty roads had been clocked and though accompanied by rain when entering this present location the prospective notification of an Army shower unit located near this area was quickly confirmed. Compliance with the necessary shower requests were immediate and group after group sought after that mobile facility with eager dispatch.

In the past few weeks reports of extreme Nazi brutality reached our ears. We had with much antipathy read of these renegade acts from time to time and though comments were exchanged in this regard the stories were coming too frequent to dismiss as mere exaggerated "tall tales." In fact, the closer the German frontier loomed the more frequent and appalling became these accounts. Reports of despicable, unwarranted crimes against humanity really had not affected any of us too alarmingly earlier since it had not actually involved any one of us personally. These reports did not include the "death camps" located deep in Germany as their true identity had not as yet been revealed to the outside world. Concentration camps for political and war prisoners yes; but "death camps" as we were to later know them . . . no.

Most of the free world had read of Nazi confiscation of private property. Alleged mistreatment of the aged and infirm, imprisonment of political factions, unmitigated brutality and in general personal persecutions were also known. Many who were fortunate enough to escape the country had known the experience. They knew what it was and appalling as it sounded did not hesitate to confirm it. "Had not the Nazis perpetrated the war?" they asked. "Had they not broken every rule of the Geneva Convention?" Then as a further summary; "Then . . . if allowed to do all of this, were they not capable of performing any act they wished . . . no matter how wicked?" Earlier, in appeasement it was easier to turn one's head though and pretend it wasn't happening rather than take a firm stand and initiate some action in this regard! It perhaps was easier to say "It's none of our business!" This form of apathy had existed in the late thirties . . . and as the free world finally admitted, that was far *too long*!

We were in Jeantes only a few minutes before first hand evidence of just such crimes were laid before our eyes.

The small hamlets of Jeantes, Bancigny and Plomion were ringed close together, each separated by less than half a mile; forming a very closely knit community. Ascending nearer this region with great dispatch 9TH DIVISION troops planned to plough right through this energetic community. The Germans in great haste were making preparations to evacuate, probably without incident. Cognizant of this and relying on the salvation of approaching Americans the French populace . . . insatiated with revenge and fight and sparked by unrestrained youth suddenly became fired-up and seized upon the opportunity to openly heckle the retreating Germans. Their patience unchecked, though they should have known better; it was a bad approach for already humiliated by imminent defeat this "needling" became more than the infuriated and embarrassed enemy could endure. This as a major excuse, the Germans set off a diabolical last minute destruction of the area.

Perhaps because of its' extreme northeastern location from the other two villages and with the enemy moving out with great speed by the time Jeantes was reached it was spared this experience. Little Bancigny was burned to the ground with hardly a building left untouched! It was Plomion however, that really felt the brunt! Not only were many homes ravaged but every French male found on the streets or within sight of the Germans regardless of age was rounded up, hands bound behind with crude barbed wire, brutally manhandled . . . then shot to death before the eyes of onlooking friends or relatives! Here were the shocking facts right before our eyes, and many viewed the bodies of these fifteen Frenchmen as they lay side by side on a bed of straw in a barn.

Following two days of mourning . . . a few of us joined the community in their sadness and grief to attend a highly emotional mass funeral for the unfortunate victims.

Germany had in late June unveiled what they had greatly purported to be a new "secret weapon;" its' purpose not particularly to deter the invading armies but rather to throw a wave of terror into civilian ranks in England. This weapon, named the V-I (meaning simply Revenge Weapon) measured twenty-five feet in length, maintained a forward wing-span of roughly fifteen feet and a rear wing-span of ten feet. One ton of explosives was carried in its' warhead . . . and equipped with a 130-gallon gas tank was powered by a jet-propulsion engine. The V-I has an approximate range of 150 miles and moved at about 360 miles per hour. and because of its' relatively slow speed many were shot down by Allied aircraft.

This machine produced a terrifying noise which actually preceeded its' arrival. Imagine, if you will; a ten-ton truck with a straight exhaust, running at full speed through a narrow echoing valley and a fairly vivid description can be visualized! The English and Americans called it the "Buzzbomb" and by the war's end it had brought death to thousands of people.

Two nights prior to leaving Jeantes we were awakened and startled as this weapon was heard approaching from the east and though we were not yet familiar with the "Buzzbomb" could not immediately grasp the identity of its' unusual noise . . . but it definitely was different from any that had been heard before. Then . . . suddenly the noise was reduced to a loud rattle. Then . . . no noise, only a whistling screech closely akin to that of a falling bomb. Then . . . crash! But no explosion! Next morning accompanied by several mystified Frenchmen in a nearby wheatfield the weapon though badly crumpled, was viewed practically intact and we thanked our stars that somehow it had refused to explode.

Now approaching the geographical region in northern France and southern Belgium which would constitute one of the routes over which these weapons would pass, we would in the coming months become far more familiar with them . . . a familiarity that at times would give us many anxious moments!

Considerable work was heaped on us here and much light maintenance was in evidence. Repairs to engines, artillery, half-tracks, machine guns, gun sights, precision instruments and even delicate adjustment to watches. "Where are they all coming from?" one was prompted to ask. A reply sufficed . . . "That is not the question, it's where they're going that matters!" It became a time to catch up on much-needed repairs and sharpen the "gear mesh" of the DIVISION for battles that inevitably were to come.

The month of August had *indeed* been a busy one for the entire FIRST ARMY. Over 10,000 work orders had been processed, particularly on mobile vehicular equipment. Excessive maintenance was administered on every class truck, especially the ¼-ton, 3/4, 1½, and 2½ ton. The M-29 weapons carrier and many combat vehicles passed through shops and 1,275 work orders *alone* were recorded for tanks, both medium and light.

Many new friends were found and much unauthorized promiscuous "cruising" was done by all that took the opportunity. It became a pleasure to roam the countryside, particularly to visit a handsome old chateau . . . who with its high stone walls and huge iron gates and ancient framework presented an etching of antiquity in a setting of architectural designs from the eighteenth and nineteenth centuries. People were friendly everywhere and apparently were in earnest to exude hospitality in sincere fashion.

The "recon" team returned and after three nights and two full days an order was given to break camp and prepare for an *extremely* long move. Promising to be interesting and unusually scenic, it would in fact take us out of France.

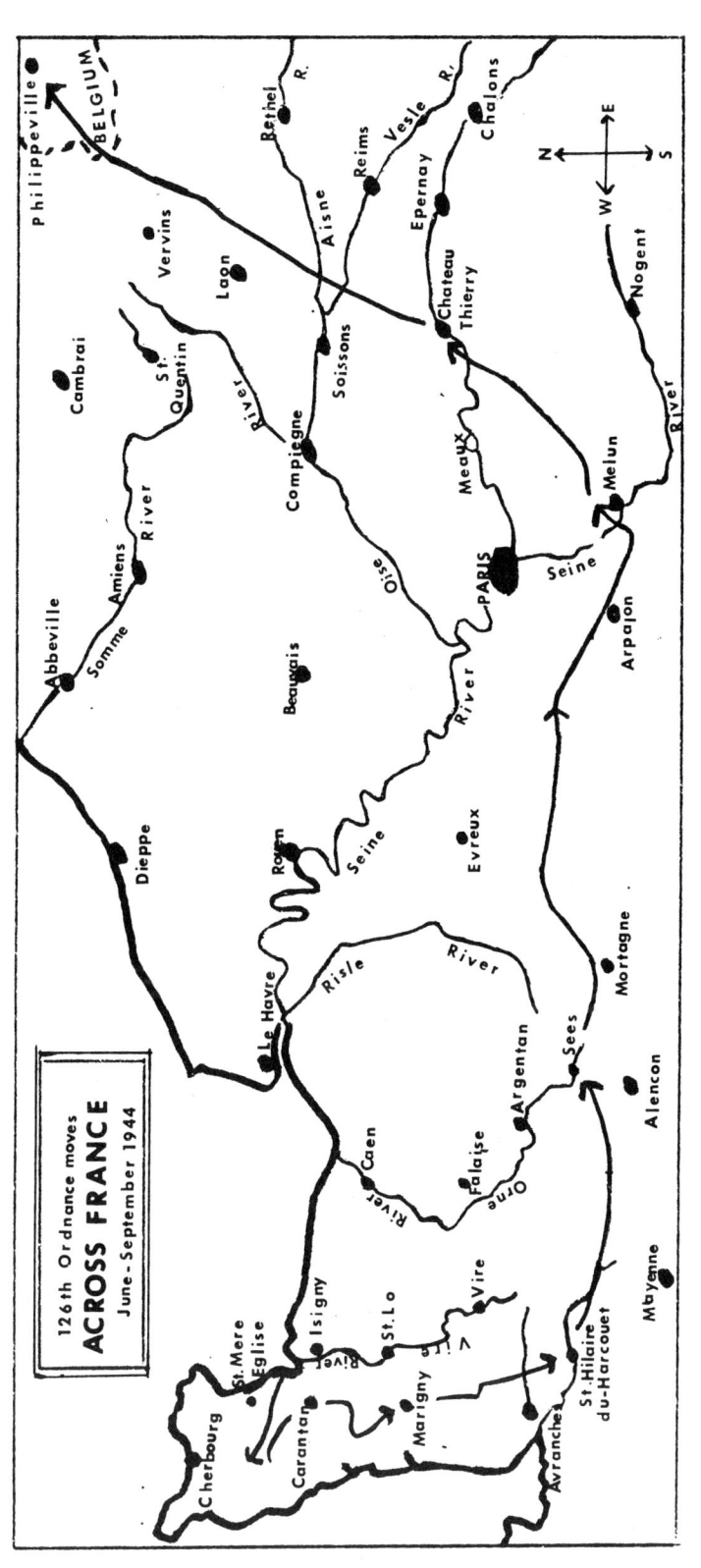

X

BELGIUM – LAND OF ENCHANTMENT

The liberation of Belgium commenced as armored units of the 9TH INFANTRY DIVISION began crossing the border in the early hours of September 2nd. This was near the town of Monignies . . . chief objective to push on to the city of Charleroi. Just inside Belgium the 3RD ARMORED DIVISION was chasing the Germans out of Mons while the 1ST INFANTRY DIVISION ripping through Avesnes had encountered the completely befuddled German 7th. Army rushing "pell mell" away from the British sector east of Brussels desperately trying to escape entrapment. Harrassed from the air, ambushed by Resistance forces, attacked by Allied spearheads, low on ammunition, little fuel and ineffective communications the Germans were easy prey and Allied planes and artillery used every advantage and showed no mercy in leaving hundreds of motorized and armored vehicles destroyed and on the battlefield thousands of dead. Conclusively . . . some 30,000 Germans were made prisoner.

On September 5th, showing much enthusiasm and exercising as little procrastination as possible Jeantes was left very early in the morning . . . and soon crossing the River Huteau we continued to chart a course on overly-used roads that were badly in need of repair. Rolling through many small bright and jubilant communities and hamlets of little significance, the lovely town of Aubenton was reached perhaps less than an hour from departure. Across the River Thon we rolled and several miles further the River Sormmone. A small group of children standing by the road just inside Rocroi cheered every vehicle in the convoy as it passed. Perhaps it was meaningful as this was the last French town of any consequence; statistically less than two miles from the Belgian border.

That it was a late Tuesday morning when we entered the little village of Le Bruly meant nothing special until it was learned that we were actually crossing into Belgium. In little more than an hour we would be further elated to know that we were twenty-five miles inside that country's border.

A close comparison of notes revealed that during our two months and twenty-two days running across France, seventeen encampments were completed; and as a unit convoy . . . had traveled a distance of six hundred and five miles! Many individual company vehicles had racked up a great many miles beyond that what with various assignments but as a company unit *six hundred and five miles* had been accounted for since rolling onto Normandy's beaches.

Moving up through this beautiful corridor of Belgium, through the heavily wooded forest . . . Bois de Couvin; we came upon a small stream in this unfamiliar kingdom . . . the River Noire; and crossed a single-lane bridge so narrow that it became necessary to slow to a crawl for fear of scraping against the rails. Now moving almost due north we continued on through the closely-knit communities of Couvin, Marienbourg and Neuville . . . and rolling across two twin canals, the Blanche and Brouffe rounded a bend to suddenly find ourselves entering the outer limits of Phillipville . . . the largest town in lower Belgium thus far. Shifting in a westerly direction we added fourteen miles before halting in a sparsely-planted apple orchard at the village of Rosee.

Service elements of the 60th. Infantry Regiment still occupied one section but as we prepared for "chow" the following morning they quietly waved while moving out.

We must have been ahead of our timetable too, for prior to arrival of American troops only a brief period had elapsed since the enemy departure. In a secluded space adjacent to the orchard almost obscured by trees and surrounded by a six-foot stone wall was centered an attractive stately old mansion that gave this location its' real significance.

Though somewhat smaller than the average French chateau, this building recently serving as a group headquarters for German forces revealed its' prominence by an unusually heavy abundance of records, files and an assortment of swastika-stamped papers that lay scattered in unpatterned disarray. Moving out in obvious haste the enemy left behind smashed office furniture, slashed curtains and light fixtures ripped from walls and ceilings. Moreover, in perhaps a last fling or perhaps recklessly sections of the interior had been put to the torch. Noted especially were partially-burned papers or documents that though not completely consumed were nevertheless too far gone to provide any potential clue as to their importance.

Directly behind but in the same courtyard two weatherboard frame buildings, though poorly constructed but erected to house additional troops were part of this headquarters complex. In much the same condition scattered debris within added credence to a disorderly retreat.

Though only a shell of its' former strength, a battered old upright piano, bordering on antiquity had been left behind in what no doubt had been a recreation room. Still stalwart enough to exude a few more melodies the much-scarred instrument doubtless had "rung out" with many Germany rhapsodies and harmonious voices had accompanied with songs of victory for the Fatherland. Now we would take a turn at it and the tenor of our songs and music would be altered considerably to fit the reckless mood of those talented enough to wring from it melodies and victory songs of another kind!

With FIRST ARMY'S swift advance it was necessary to again cut through and around the enemy in many cases . . . thereby isolating them in small groups. The wooded area surrounding Rosee at this point contained many such groups as this and it became something less than a novelty for combat and non-combatant units alike to come upon stragglers and take them in. Occasionally a unit received notification that surrounding areas contained unknown numbers of the enemy and an organized armed team would in a short time flush them out of hiding. In many instances most were "lost" and voluntarily surrendered themselves to the nearest American unit. When on occasion we became involved in this "roundup" it was questionable as to *who* was the most beweildered; we . . . or the Germans!

Belgian de Resistance Forces functioning quite like that of the FFI played an exacting role in the decimation of these stragglers.

Because of a fast-growing gasoline shortage Privates Dave Leichner and Art Fealk became inadvertently involved in the apprehension of just such a group.

Dispatched to a FIRST ARMY gasoline dump just north of Phillipville and roughly twelve miles south of our present location Leichner and Fealk were under orders to secure a six-by-six truckload of fuel. Loaded in five-gallon "Jerrycans" this would represent roughly seven hundred gallons of much-needed gasoline. A few miles south on secondary roads winding through a forest they yielded to an arm-flailing small group of highly-excited BFR gathered almost in the center of the road. With all wildly gesticulating at once it became so unintelligible that hardly anyone less than an accomplished linguist could decipher the problem.

Fealk recalled with a chuckle the gist of the conversation exchange as from the beginning, (because of the excitement) it was difficult to interpret:

"Aw right! Aw right! What the hell's the matter with you 'Frogs' anyway!" He was not one to mince words and always bluntly came to the point. "Some of you keep your mouth shut and let's get together . . . and don't all of you talk at once!"

The jabbering surprisingly subsided and one stepped forward to speak. Thickly accented but with excellent English he spoke:

"We wish your assistance," he said; "to help capture some Germans resisting nearby. Will you help us?"

"Where is nearby?" Fealk inquired.

The spokesman pointed wildly beyond the woods . . . "Over

there! Over there! la maison," quickly translating he added, "house . . . in a house!"

The BFR doubtless could have handled it for they had sufficient weapons but with a couple of experienced American GIs as part of the team a more intrepid feeling existed. The American uniform was well-respected and in the long run, self-admittedly increased the feeling of security.

The chubby Detroiter turned to Leichner and questioned;

"How about it, Dave . . . you game?"

Not one known to stick his neck out, Leichner replied:

"The hell with that idea . . . might get shot . . . for what?"

"Ah-h-h, c'mon . . . might have some fun" . . . and with a sly grin added; "might even get a medal!"

"A medal? Who the hell wants a medal?" Though he knew Fealk to be kidding, added; "You serious? You really want to go? Okay, hell, okay with me. Let's go!"

Through an unfamiliar forest crawling with foliage and wondering all the while "for what are we doing this?" . . . they dubiously followed the Belgians and came upon a very small farmhouse nestled alone among the trees with a single path leading to it. From a safe and unobtrusive position in the brush . . . obviously skeptical of everything that moved one Belgian kept an uneasy watch on the quiet dwelling.

Tempered warning was given the enemy to come out and surrender . . . but in reply surprisingly only one emerged and even as he did one of the Belgians in great anxiety opened fire and the lone German fled back inside.

"You stupid s.o.b.!" called Fealk. "What the hell did you do that for? Now we got to start all over again!" With an exasperated shake of the head he concluded: "Damn, that was dumb! I ought to throw your tail in there with them!"

Leichner, not a serious bone in his body . . . and almost doubling up, was trying hard to contain himself from open laughter.

Fealk recalled:

"Electing then to make a battle of it the Germans returned the fire, immediately bringing eager retaliation of the BFR. Following some twenty minutes exchanges of intermittent machine gun and rifle fire in which Leichner and I did our share, wisps of blue-black smoke suddenly began to drift from the dwelling and the next thing we knew the place was on fire." Continuing he said: "We assumed it came as a result of an accident inside."

Realizing the certain futility of resistance shots from inside dropped off to a trickle . . . then silence. A large white cloth appeared from a door slowly opening with caution . . . signaling conclusion of this high-spirited fire fight. Dubiously waving a white flag of surrender the 'Krauts' shuffled out one at a time; the personnel including one Captain, one Lieutenant and fifteen enlisted men. Offering no resistance they climbed up into the still empty truck and were taken back to the company area at Rosee. The Belgians were delighted! They wanted to climb into the truck too, but Fealk "shooshed" them off.

"Get the hell off here, we've had enough trouble with you guys! Go find yourself some Germans of your own!"

Coming out of the CP as the truck rolled in T/4 Bob McNulty, a company clerk; was startled and stopped in his tracks.

"Good Lord . . . Look at the 'Krauts'! Just *look* at those 'Krauts!'" he spoke alarmingly to himself. "Sarge!" he called, "Come out here! You won't believe it!"

Leichner stepped down from the passenger side of the truck as Botting came out.

"What the hell are you guys doing, Leichner; where'd you get all those 'Krauts'?" Hesitating before speaking again Botting showed signs of agitation . . . "and what're you going to do with them?"

Never one to be serious Leichner just laughed and said: "Watch this, Sarge!"

"*HANDE HOCHE!*" he called in German.

At this command all hands in the truck were quickly raised with elbows extended and placed on the back of each head. The rumpled unshaven Leichner slapping his thighs with both hands, cackled with laughter!

Now a bit rattled, the First Sergeant became intense.

"Cut the crap, Leichner! You trying to be funny?"

"What'dya mean funny . . . just showing you some discipline, Sarge; that's all!" His laugh trailing off and appearing a little disappointed; "Man, look at that discipline!" With that he commanded in German the equivalent of . . . *"AT EASE!"*

The Captain came out and walking up close to the men, spoke softly but sternly:

"Take the 'Krauts' out of here and get 'em to a stockade."

"*What stockade*, Captain?" questioned Fealk.

A quizzical look fell across the Captain's face and he replied:

"*What stockade*? Who gives a damn *what* stockade? Just ask the first MP you see; he'll direct you!" Concluding with an order, he said:

"Do it now!"

Consummated in a short time the Germans were deposited at a 9TH DIVISION PW Collecting point. It had been a busy day and results of the assignment totaled seventeen prisoners . . . and no gasoline!

***

A few miles northwest of Rosee the 9TH DIVISION had encountered unexpected trouble in attempting to seize the bridge over the Meuse River at Dinant. The 9TH did not wait and the 60th Infantry Regiment led the attack. Steep precipitous cliffs rise from the opposite bank and from that site stiff fanatical enemy resistance imperviously pinned the Americans down. Tossing hand grenades down from the lofty heights. leveling bazookas, pinpointing direct fire on GIs rushing the embankment prevented an immediate successful crossing of the river. Again and again several attempts were made by assault groups in rubber rafts but in each instance the craft was destroyed or upon reaching the opposite shore were killed or captured. One entire luckless platoon without complete clarification of orders sought a crossing and reportedly were never heard from. Air and artillery support was called but the "Jerries" would not turn loose!

The 60th "Go-Devils" . . . living up to their reputation, were not to be denied . . . doggedly and relentlessly continuing the pressure! This condition existed for a little more than two days when with aid of the 3RD ARMORED DIVISION who had forced a crossing further north . . . the Germans under cover of darkness, bearing the strain no longer, went into retreat. On September 7 the full DIVISION bridged the vital Meuse at this point.

A city of boundless beauty, Dinant during pre-war times was the focal point for vacationers from all over Europe. Famed for the magnificent 'Citadel' cathedral, its' great cascade parks and attractive fishing and canoeing areas further along its' high banks . . . a surrounding forest, well-cared for, is a paradise for hunters of light game. The ancient fortress built into the rocky cliffs overlooking the Meuse, commanding a view of the entire valley . . . breathtaking in scope, has become almost a shrine for sightseers.

Mid-morning of the 11th, crossing a treadway bridge at Dinant . . . supported at each end by a crumbling remains of the original structure where the span surely could not have been less than 250 to 300 feet wide we wound slowly up the steep incline, past the ancient fortress and resumed a pattern that charted our course eastward on the key and soon-to-be familiar highway . . . N36. Almost everyone operating a vehicle in VII CORPS with regularity would in time lend some association with this particular stretch, for it would tie in with a main supply route from the fast-growing supply center at Soissons to the mammoth FIRST ARMY Class I and II Supply Depot soon to be established at Liege, thence to the several smaller truckhead dumps near the active front.

Now in the midst of some of Europe's most beautiful scenery the convoy rolled through bright and well-kept communities of Sorrines, Achene, Ciney . . . each lively with gaily waving children; to cross the small River Bocq at Hubine and moved several miles northeast through Havelange to finally make our way over the rock-studded River Hoyaux at Pailhe. Our destination still a good distance beyond we pulled to the side of the road and engaged in a brief halt, and in spite of the bicyclists weaving by . . . together with several slowly-gathering curious onlookers we continued to enjoy the relief that nature deemed necessary while we could.

A resumption of travel carried us through Pont-de-Bonne, to barely skirt Limet and St. Severin where we turned off the main highway just a few miles southeast of the key city of Liege.

Liege, one of Belgium's largest and most active is a cultural city of 150,000 and bristled to receive us inasmuch as we would represent some of the first United States troops in that region. Noted for its' many iron and steel plants, zinc smelters, and glass factories that work closely with several nearby mines, it was a "prize" that the Germans did not want to relinquish. The 3RD ARMORED DIVISION had moved into the city surprisingly against light opposition only to find the many magnificent bridges spanning the Meuse that runs through the center of the city, shattered and blown. We had hoped to move through the city but ordered to follow 9TH DIVISION's active eastern course were denied that honor. We would, a few days hence make up for that disappointment.

Now on roads that were in no-wise as wide as those in the United States and no match for the heavy lumbering giant American vehicles, we wound through Rotheux and came upon Esneux, a lovely community resort divided in the center by the well-groomed Ourthe Canal; a work of beauty as the early afternoon sunlight gaily played its' rays against each ripple. Receiving greetings from many, including several bathers who exuded little concern for the war's existence, we rolled past the colorful brightly pastel-trimmed houses and into the scenic hills . . . to a broad spot near the small community of Hautgne, where from our lofty position it was possible to look down and give unlimited observation over the entire restful town.

Three slightly sloping fields, one leading to a walled archaic monastary almost hidden by rangy foliage; no established pattern of dispersion was implemented for orders were standing to be prepared to vacate "at a moment's notice."

Surpassing far beyond a "moment's notice" this extension carried us through the remainder of that day and the entire night. Though there was no guarantee that trouble would not come we viewed this encampment with complete confidence that it *would not*, and a relaxed atmosphere settled over the company for the entire period. It was a night of unusual warmth and clarity, and embracing these natural elements the sky became a sort of stage that would present us with a "drama" that was simply ours for the watching.

In the not-too-distant city of Liege, roughly eight miles to the north and now in American hands, enemy night fighter-bombers slipping out of Germany continued to present in small measure a constant threat to Allied supply depots and smaller "dumps."

While always a threat, they did on the other hand present "juicy" moveable targets this night for FIRST ARMY's many hungry "ack-ack" guns which for miles around were interspersed. "WHOOM! . . . WHOOM! . . . WHOOM!" . . . like a thunderclap the groundbased 90mm monsters reverberated throughout the mountainous region! Hits were scored and as each plane exploded successively, from our somewhat towering position under the brilliance of the lucid sky one gained an imaginative impression of huge matches striking in the sky. Though enjoying a temporary respite we nevertheless were dependent on guards at the three assigned posts who while enjoying an air of remission had not for a moment forgotten that many of the enemy . . . mobile or otherwise remained well-concealed and probably desperate in the surrounding hilly forests.

Privates Robert DePrey and Ed Zielinski, who no matter what the task or no matter the effort . . . their labors somehow winding up in the "hard luck" column, were some eight days previous dispatched to an active Ordnance Supply Depot in Arpajon to deliver a supply of repaired M-1 rifles for distribution.

Since their departure no word had been received and inasmuch as more than sufficient time had been allowed for unit location it was reasonable to assume that the two could have been enticed to risk a tempting visit to Paris, almost in line of route. That spirited city at this point was still a bit wild and the air to a great degree had not completely been cleared of "liberation fever."

Late the ninth morning a jeep whose unit identification was foreign to ours rolled past guard post No. One and up to the CP bearing three passengers. DePrey and Zielinski stepped out and the jeep rolled away. Looking much like two little boys that had just messed their pants, their facial expressions while walking up to the CP bore clear indication that there would be a lot of explaining to do, for from what hardly would have necessitated more than a two-day assignment had been stretched to eight days. What was the result? As a matter of fact . . . where was the truck?

Botting wasted no time and went at it immediately.

"Well, you've finally decided to join the war! Okay, let's have the story."

"Look, Sergeant . . ."

DePrey did the talking.

"It took a whole day to locate the depot and since it was near supper time we decided to locate a transient mess-hall further in the city and come back later to deliver the rifles. We got into a hassle at the messhall with a group and wound up spending the night there. Back at the Ordnance Depot next morning we made our delivery and then figuring there was a little time to consume we decided to just take a quick run into Paris since we had not as yet been there."

With short, quick gestures of the hands, DePrey continued. "After stopping briefly at a restaurant we continued on into the city and parked the vehicle and then decided to take a stroll and see the sights." His characteristic squint now more prominent because of the bright showers of sunshine, he went on . . . , "Sergeant, we couldn't have been gone more than an hour and *you can imagine* our shock to find the truck gone when we returned!"

"I can imagine." interjected the amused First Sergeant.

Zielinski, perspiring and displaying obvious fatigue, spoke up; "The first MP we saw wasn't much help. He just wanted to know, *'What else was new*? He did tell us where we could make a formal report . . . and we did." Continuing, "we were directed to an Ordnance unit located in a hotel in Paris and the Colonel in charge told us not to worry and assigned us to a room."

Leaving a vehicle on the streets of most any town in France, unguarded; fast became an almost unpardonable act of negligence. Vehicles had disappeared by the dozens in Communications Zone territory alone in recent weeks . . . literally stolen. Though inadvertently, both fell prey to this error, and of all the most susceptible places; Paris . . . where pilferage and growing theft of military supplies and equipment abounded in great magnitude!

"Did it occur to you to have the MP's or the Ordnance communicate with us?" asked Botting.

"No. Sergeant, we just decided to search the city till we found the truck."

"You mean to say it took you guys eight days to make up your minds to come back?"

Perhaps this was so! Eight days and nights in Paris? One could have a good time in Paris during those days! But alas; . . . there is an imminent quote that stands strong and true, "He who dances *must* pay the fiddler!"

"Sometimes I think both of you guys are stupid. Well, its' your tail . . . there's no choice but to have you sign a statement of charges and pay for the truck, and whatever else the "Old Man" wants to hang you with will be his business," grunted Botting.

Both were charged with the vehicle's responsibility and made to forfeit some fifteen dollars in pay. That's about as far as it went, and perhaps were the army claims books opened today it is probable that DePrey and Zielinski *are still* charged up with this article!

Late morning of the 12th found the company in hot pursuit of the German border . . . *straight east*! Confronted with small winding narrow shouldered gravel roads we found every hamlet a friendly delight. Louveigne was entered. Continuing to twist very slowly through the hilly countryside, now bathed in brilliant sunshine this entire route presented a perpetual rhythmic wave of green rolling hills. Finely cultivated farms and evenly-spaced trees nestling against well-patterned fences made one marvel at the almost breathtaking and delightful beauty that was southeast Belgium, for hardly had such well-tended landscape been noted since arriving in Scotland seven months before.

We hurdled the narrow twisting River Hoegne at Theux, and a brief distance due north found us fast-grinding into the industrial junction of Pepinster. Spanning the Vesdre Canal we continued straight east. At this point all attention was diverted to small clusters of civilians enthusiastically milling and gathering on each side of the road. Beaming, waving, and sparodically breaking into cheers, they began with a slight halt tossing flowers at our slowly proceeding convoy.

Moving through the adjoining town of Ensival and onto the approaches of Verviers the gatherings began to increase proportionately and cheers grew more intense! We began suddenly to get the feeling that this must be a planned greeting of no small dimension and apparently was intended for the first convoy of the day! This was it . . . and in a few moments we would be on the threshold of receiving our most exhilarating welcome of the war!

The fast-moving 3RD ARMORED DIVISION had little more

than cleared the entire city twenty-four hours earlier when our convoy began entering the streets of Verviers. From the city's approaches everyone . . . seething with excitement, assembling restlessly or rambling gregariously in and out of their own groups waved and applauded as if participating in a long-planned festival! Everybody seemed to want a part of it! Flags representing Britain, Canada, United States, France and the ever-present attractive red, yellow and black tri-color of Belgium were heavy in prominence in every window, on every available pole, on fenceposts, gates or anything to which it could be anchored.

Continuing through this festive industrious city of some 39,000 happy people; past the mammoth railroad station, around the Place de la Victoire, and taking a sharp turn to the right just inside the city . . . one that would seem almost to reverse our course, we began the ascent up a steep cobblestoned incline that runs through the heart of the city's apparent best residential area where nestled comfortably close to the wide sidewalks was row upon row of magnificent homes. One could not help but note the obvious and meticulous care in which the apartment buildings and private homes along this stretch were kept, and a closer look revealed an astonishing similarity to dwellings found in the central and eastern regions of the United States.

Ostensibly dressed in their best apparel these people with growing jubilance continued to openly exhibit great joy and exhuberance all the way up the hill. Openly brazen now, many charged up to the slow-moving vehicles to more closely present us with flowers! As a further act of appreciation . . . a small few of the younger ones, particularly the girls; made an attempt to climb in and with little reluctance on the part of some, were assisted into our jeeps and open trucks and most every type of transportation making up the convoy. A scornful signal from the C. O. in the lead jeep ended that!

"Bienvenue les Americains et Anglais!" . . . "Allemagne Kaput!" . . . "Belgique et Amerique toujours!" Many such "Huzzahs" rang from the crowds! Though it would appear that days had been spent for welcoming preparations, the ecstatic display of the many stately and homemade banners majestically beaming enthusiastic and flattering salutations all doubts of a 'Royal welcome' of sincerity were dispelled! With increasing ebullience these people were exuding their maximum warmth and appreciation, though at the same time this served as a great opportunity to exhibit emotions that long had been seeking release. Evidence too, pointed to the fact that we were the first Americans that many of these people had ever seen.

Hands outstretched, pleading faces and jockeying for position eager children as in other countries importuned for the bars of precious American "chocolate," while others in obvious prominence presented the "V-for Victory" gesture that prevailed along this entire route. It was amazing to note how the "chocolate" and "Victory" expressions carried such far-reaching continuity, for this had been experienced all the way from Scotland.

Reaching the city's southeastern approaches we turned from the main thoroughfare into a lane bordered by giant hedges. Halting some fifty yards beyond we commandeered three vast open fields that in better times was used as a public park . . . where situated on a high but sloping incline overlooked the surrounding countryside and the now liberated textile city of Verviers.

Lt. Jim Prendergast, heading a small advance team selected this attractive spot the day before, because . . . as he recollected; "Representing probably the last encampment before going into Germany it would with the ample space give us a good opportunity to stretch out." Assisted by Walter Makos, a quiet slight T/5 from Chicago whose eyes bulged in great anxiety when wanting to make a serious point; and T/5 Moses Gianoplos, an adventuresome twenty-year old sloe-eyed Greek lad from Detroit, who with such a yen for dress perfection somehow arranged to have his uniforms . . . even work fatigues, appear as if they were "custom made," could not have realized at the time the real morale significance this location would have.

By the time vehicles were brought to a halt and a bivouac pattern established much of the enthusiastic crowds who by bicycle and on foot had surprisingly maintained an almost exhausting pace behind the slow lumbering convoy were not too far away. Having worked themselves into an almost exhilarated frenzy over our response these people obviously were not yet about to descend from the clouds of this highly-excitable atmosphere. Before anyone had *completely* unloaded they were there . . . all over the place; wandering promiscuously throughout . . . talking, laughing and finding nobody a stranger.

The Captain, always wary and trying hard not to implicate the company in anything obligatory he thought unnecessary, turned to company clerk Howard Thompson, a jumpy but lively and efficient twenty-two year old crew-cut T/4 from Ludington, Michigan and ordered him to "get these people out of here!"

Ordinarily this was the First Sergeant's chore but at the moment he was not around.

Discarding some paper work, Thompson; always answering to the name of "Buck" glanced up and was astonished to look straight into the eyes of two lovely lasses standing astride the open CP door . . . warmly beaming greetings that would be hard for any weary soldier to ignore. Exasperated; he gave comment to the Captain's order;

"Captain, under these conditions, how can I run these girls off?"

Orsenigo, quickly cognizant of the situation, chose his words carefully . . . and probably hoping the visitors could not understand English, replied:

"You handle it! That will be your problem! Tell them 'Off Limits' . . . anything . . . but keep them the hell out of here!" Trying hard to keep from chuckling openly, he added;

"*Walk* them home if you have to!"

Thompson acceded to the Captain's suggestion and was last seen for the day walking the two maidens, arm in arm . . . across the green and through the entrance. Stopped for a moment by Lt. Black, Officer of the Guard, he was asked;

"What's *this* all about? Where the hell are *you* going?"

Thompson told him. The Lieutenant wanted to comment . . . but could only say:

"Well, I'll be damned!"

Their spirit of enthusiasm was too much, and subjected to unusual persuasiveness one just could not . . . short of insults or bodily ejection . . . keep them out! The Captain realized this in short order and issued no more orders for the evening. Completely obsessed with a desire to see and talk with us and to exchange souveniers, friendliness seemed to reflect no bounds. Inquisitiveness became an understatement for they could and *did* fire questions which answers were repeated over and over. Deluged with personal invitations to visit into their homes down in the city was a courtesy eagerly taken advantage of . . . whether authorized or not. This was the beginning of a binding friendship among many that together with later contacts developed into a lasting affection for the city. In the dark months that followed when the city became the recipient of several "buzz-bomb" attacks we felt it a personal grief. Without question, Verviers could come close to equalizing Blagdon, England as one of our most venerated European encampments. Almost . . . but not quite.

Interesting indeed it was to note the different dialects spoken by people of so small a country. In central, south and southeastern Belgium the inhabitants speak basically the same language as the French. Those in the north and northwestern areas speak a mixture of French and Dutch which constitutes the Flemish language; and on the Belgo-German frontier both French and German tongues are prevalent. Though both France and Belgium border the personal characteristics of the two countries is an interesting study in contrast.

Bearing a population of some 8,500,000 (1940) and although approximately one-tenth the size of France, Belgium appeared to maintain an atmosphere of strength, patriotism and strong affection that was obvious in every aspect of contact. Personal salutations appeared extended with greater warmth, the girls were viewed as possessing a more pronounced natural beauty and arguments could be heard that their dress rivaled that of those living around Paris. (Here one's own personal viewpoint is challenged . . . for after a few months on the continent they were all beautiful)! There was no mistake however, that at the moment from any viewpoint one was shown such personal attention it would appear almost as "though one had returned home a conquering hero."

Long after departure from Verviers to enter Germany one would revel in a rare opportunity to return and visit the city . . . always to find a renewal of courtesy and affection from friends. Truly . . . in Belgium, during this period at least; it was a proud time to be a GI for the uniform and intentions of the American soldier was viewed with great respect.

In the meanwhile 9TH DIVISION's main task force having cleared Spa, a resort town slightly to the south, and dashing boldly up through the beer-producing town of Malmedy . . . occupied earlier by the 4TH CAVALRY GROUP, now was cautiously pushing onto the German border.

How often has been quoted the old adage . . . "All good things must come to an end!" When orders came necessitating the evacuation of this location and directing us to move east, this proverbial phrase was found to be exceedingly true. *True* most especially because of the obvious realization that this illustrious welcome *would be the last*! No longer were we to share in the lively enthusiasm, cheers and laughter of a liberated people. No more "Vive l'Amerique!" No longer would we be showered with flowers and favors as was experienced these past few months; and no longer would we be welcomed with open hearts of sincerety that had been heavy for so many years. For . . . *now* we were going into Nazi Germany!

In some way obtaining prescience as to our departure date and knowing distinctly that only Germany could be the ultimate destination, several women, children and men alike made it a point to arise early enough to be on hand as we left. It was Saturday, the 16th., and rolling through the city's eastern area early amidst scores of cheering flag-waving townspeople our already warm feelings for them ascended even higher as they amplified best wishes and good luck salvos until the very last vehicle cleared the outskirts!

"The 'natives' are restless this morning," remarked the Captain, casually acknowledging applause from the crowd.

"Yeah," replied the First Sergeant; "go ahead Cap'n, it won't hurt to wave back."

Turning to the crew-cut brown-eyed Sergeant in the jeep's back seat and replying with a chuckle, the C.O. commented further:

"I gotta say one thing though; somebody has done some damn good public relations work to get these 'Frogs' up this early. If it was me I'd be sleeping right now and leave the cheering to somebody else."

"It ain't you though, so let 'em have their fun. Keep smiling and enjoy it because you sure as hell won't see anymore of it for awhile."

But both knew perfectly well the great honor extended us and they knew also that undeserving as it was . . . they were in full accord and like the rest of the company, were "eating it up!"

Hurriedly through Dolhain and Limbourg, we rolled five more miles to enter the key Belgo-German frontier town of Eupen . . . a community in question but taken earlier without incident by the fast-rolling 3RD ARMORED DIVISION.

Situated just inside Belgium a short distance from the German border Eupen was included in that strip of territory extracted from Germany and ceded to Belgium emanating from the Treaty of Versailles immediately following World War I. Habitually German and speaking that tongue, it was well-understood why American troops were cooly received with a distinct air of animosity while rumbling through the cobblestone streets. No smiles, no cheers, no victory slogans . . . only the fixed stares born of perplexity and confusion. Yet, despite the natural suspicion of its' inhabitants Eupen reeked with antiquity and remained quaint and attractive. Much of the town is built on a low level until reaching the extreme eastern section, where suddenly the road extends to a gradual elevated incline. Traversing up this lightly winding stretch we reached a point where a study of terrain contrasts is unavoidable. To the west was viewed Belgium's beautiful rolling countryside . . . still partially enshrouded in the morning mist, and to the east the dark misty and forbidding forests leading into Germany through which in a few minutes we would enter.

As the war progressed Eupen would later serve its' purpose well for the FIRST U. S. ARMY, not only as a rest center for troops but harboring a mammoth ammunition and supply dump, an Ordnance heavy maintenance repair shop, an airstrip for observational light cub planes, and a much-needed and much-used base hospital.

XI

GERMANY – THE THIRD REICH

In late afternoon September 11 in the V CORPS sector, patrolling deep in southeast Belgium a team from the 5TH ARMORED DIVISION crossed into Germany to the west bank of the Our River near the village of Stalzemburg just north of Luxembourg. At about the same time a patrol from the 4TH INFANTRY DIVISION crossed the same river near the village of Hemmeres just southeast of St. Vith, Belgium. These troops became the first Allied soldiers to cross the German border in this campaign and historically representing the first to *invade* Germany since Napoleon. Less than two hours later a reinforced infantry company from the 28TH INFANTRY DIVISION crossed near Weiswampach.

It didn't take long for word of this long-awaited accomplishment to flash back to the States for next morning's edition of the Milwaukee (Wisc.) Journal blared headlines:

"YANKS ARE INSIDE GERMANY AT TWO POINTS!"

"Smash Across Reich Border, Drive Deeper!"

On the 12th, in Tuesday morning's early hours in the VII CORPS sector a patrol of FIRST ARMY's 3RD ARMORED DIVISION began crossing the German border slightly east of Walheim and just south of Aachen and a few hours later slightly southwest but even nearer Aachen the 1ST INFANTRY DIVISION occupied the little village of Gemmenich. Following close behind, the 30TH INFANTRY DIVISION was battling for Maastrict . . . a large frontier town in Holland. The 9TH moved in quickly and after immediate penetration of the first "dragon teeth" defenses, was credited with becoming the *first* Infantry Division to *completely* breach the Siegfried Line.

The very next day, the 13th., the same prominent newspaper carried an Associated Press article to further substantiate FIRST ARMY's progress and would relate additionally to action of the VII CORPS:

"American doughboys invading Germany have captured Rotgen, 9 miles southeast of Aachen and 6 miles east of Eupen, and quickly penetrated 'primary enemy defenses' in the area, an AP dispatch from Rotgen said Wednesday."

FIRST ARMY'S progress was indeed phenomenal for reports now showed a total of 169,706 enemy prisoners bagged since beginning in Normandy; 15,000 of these during the past week. In less than a month General Hodges' fighting machine had advanced from St. Lo, moved through and around Paris, rolled up into western Belgium to clear stragglers of the enemy's 7th. Army, thence onto the German frontier. A distance of some 750 miles.

Now disposed with units in five countries . . . France, Belgium, Luxembourg, Holland and Germany, and commanding a broad front beginning a few miles north of Aachen, stretching some one hundred fifty miles south to a point about fifteen miles below Luxembourg City; FIRST ARMY now embracing 3 CORPS, (the V, VII and XIX) 8 combat Divisions (5 Infantry, 3 Armored), 3 mechanized Cavalry Groups, 9 seperate tank battalions (7 medium and 2 light) 12 Tank Destroyers, 31 Anti-aircraft, 3 Field Artillery and 3 Chemical (mortar) Battalions, approximately 1,000 tanks and a number of Engineer, Signal, Ordnance, Quartermaster and other service units to total a strength of 256,351 men; prepared to throw its' might against the West Wall and begin the invasion of Germany.

***

Trudging east from Eupen a narrow mud-churned road leading through the dismal, swampy and eerie Forest of Eupen was followed . . . a road that in no-wise was constructed for armored vehicles. Moving with caution around three U. S. combat vehicles that at three separate points were hopelessly abandoned in mired "chuck holes" too deep for immediate retrievement, our gain was not too extensive before it appeared that we too . . . with our heavy equipment might become a victim of this almost hub-deep mud that once had been a roadbed.

A small branch leading into the Iter River was crossed, and emerging from the dark dank forest into full daylight again a small settlement identified as Petergensfeld was immediately entered to constitute the last outpost before reaching the German border. In fact, less than one quarter of a mile further . . . cresting a hill the company through a slowly lifting mist suddenly looked down in the distance on the quiet little railroad town of Rotgen, the first town in Germany to fall . . . and in a matter of minutes proceeded to cross the border at that point. Located on a key north-south road this town was but seven miles south of an ancient metropolis already quivering under trained sights of FIRST ARMY's boisterous guns . . . the vital German industrial city of Aachen.

This was the 16th and though the company's entire complement was now in Germany and would even at this date represent some of the very first Ordnance troops to establish bivouac in this country, Captain Orsenigo and his aide for "recon" purposes had entered the country morning of the 14th. There followed amongst troops boasts with reference to "who was first to enter Germany and some had cut it so close as to suggest beating the actual scouting troops by "at least two days." While there existed no particular honor, no medal or citation . . . not even a substantial acknowledgement alluding to first entry these boasts became only superficial. It did however, provide an additional subject with which to talk and argue.

So far as we were concerned, official entry into Germany was substantiated when the Captain and his driver-aide moved in on the 14th. First in many places, they could continue in the future to see quite a lot together.

Settling down in three open fields hemmed in on all sides by thick fir trees and evergreens, we became aware that this provided the only protection we could expect. With immediate dispersement of vehicles and equipment into a natural camouflage of beckoning trees and bushes that overlooked and in some instances separated the fields, orders were firm to "take special precaution to see that nothing is left openly exposed." Situated on a high rolling hill that descended into the Rotgen valley below, it was a spot that commanded a colorful view of dense forests for miles and miles. Now cognizant of being one of the first Ordnance companies on German soil we began a survey of the operational tasks that lay before us.

The convoy lumbered into this space under low and dark swift gathering clouds that would not allow the sun to break through a single time and long before complete darkness an acute awareness of extremely sensitive terrain would make our acitivities infinitely more dismal as each day dawned. Softened by heavy rains that for several days and nights saturated this region preceeding our entry we would in a couple of days become poignantly aware that the heavy tonnage would in no way be a match for the quagmire of mud gradually enveloping the entire area. Rains had subsided briefly but again began their relentless domination on the night of the 16th! In spite of unfavorable elements, foxholes were ordered dug for the first time in many days. Though the order to dig was issued the attempt became one of feeble proportions and this task was useless. By morning each hole would contain its' own level of water and implementation was impractical.

Prior to evening "chow" a formation was called and Sergeant Botting gingerly reflected orders of the C.O.

"Men . . . you are in Germany now and no longer among

friends. There will be *no* fires or lights after dark and you *will* keep your rifle with you at all times. No vehicles will leave the area without special permission." Continuing, he warned; "Be wary of all civilians. There will be no looting and there definitely will be no fraternization! Repeat;" and he was emphatic, "No fraternization! I don't have to tell you the penalty for that!"

The bulletin board in front of the CP where these orders would be posted in the morning would spell it out in detail.

Yes, we were now in Germany . . . but one found it hard to be jubilant for velocity of rain the first night was unparalleled by any experienced previously! Even those supposedly camping advantageously adjacent to and beneath the semi-shelter of thick fir trees whose bedding, reinforced by heavy underbrush and further supported by three or four blankets on top of that found themselves saturated and soggy long before dawn as water running in small rivulets literally became something like two inches deep on ground level. Nowhere was there anything resembling a dry place and as mud began its' inevitable formation guards who already elected to be on wide-eyed alert in line of duty found this task to be inconceivably rough! Ill-prepared and somewhat spoiled by an excessive indulgence of past crowd adulation, unanimously we began to ponder long and hard as to "what had we done to deserve this!"

Perhaps the most discomforted group during the night were those assigned guard post No. 2, who through necessity remained in semi-crouched positions in a roadside gully until relieved by other sentrys that had little to look forward to except to share the same wretched misery. Night guard hours began at 6 PM and ended at 6 AM in the morning. Three shifts were involved requiring two guards each, with each standing duty two hours and off four hours. More advantageous observation could be achieved from this particular spot for from this rather repugnant position a wide perimeter would be scanned and at the same time some protection was afforded the sentries. Long before midnight the water level rose to half the capacity of the gully and a rapid flow downhill was consistent . . . made so not only by the incessant downpour but by water draining and descending from top of the hill. Tense and anxious and employing no shelter whatsoever the men, ammunition, rifles and gas masks were soaked far beyond easy drying and though shifting from one position to another it was found that additional mud was produced with each shift. There were two choices. Remain in that position and endure the disagreeable elements in the inky blackness . . . or abandon the post! The *latter* could not be done! Attempts at erecting a 'lean-to' came to no avail . . . ending in collapse with each blast of heavy rain. As one of the guards said when relieved by others at midnight:

"You can't see nothing and you can't keep dry, so you might as well try to enjoy it . . . 'cause there's not a damn thing you can do but sit here!"

A battery of 155mm's from 9TH DIVISION's 26th. Field Artillery were solidly positioned in an adjoining field and for two days had lobbed shells far beyond the forests. Tonight was no exception, for all night long despite the storm these powerful "Long Toms" gave the Germans no rest! Consequently, their thunderous earth-shuddering blasts and blinding flashes together with the hideous streaks of lightning and sharp rolling bolts of thunder splitting the infinity of darkness; moreover, the low whine of incoming enemy shells expending in muffled explosions not too far away, found the 126th. viewing its' first night in Hitler's "invincible" Germany as absolutely miserable!

Some slept in truck cabs, some in shop trucks and others in the backs of trailers partially protected by canvas. Dry places came at a premium . . . they hardly existed. Luckless Sid Olivier had earlier spotted a trailer with a built-in top of plywood covered by tarpaulin, and taking special note of this several times before nightfall made up his mind that unless someone beat him to it this is where he would spend the night. Muddy boots and damp clothes notwithstanding he crawled up in it after dark without even questioning the dry blankets neatly spread, in obvious preparation for someone's use. Well on his way to what he hoped to be a fairly comfortable night's rest he was awakened by a pair of hands slightly less than violently shaking his feet!

"Wassa' matter? Wassa' matter?" as only he could mumble; "Get the hell away and let a guy sleep!"

"Out, Olivier! . . . Out now!" commanded a sturdy accented voice; "This my place!"

The slightly balding Olivier, never one for pretense and hardly one for finesse; returned, "That's what you think . . . I got here first! Now get lost out in the rain somewhere!"

"Olivier, how you like to be permanent latrine orderly?" came the broken-accented voice with a twinge of German. A ring of recognition suddenly dawned on him, and he then knew that voice belonged to Warrant Officer Rueth . . . who in no-wise was kidding.

It was still pouring down as Sid Olivier stalked off into the darkness mumbling remarks that were overlooked, though highly uncomplimentary to an officer.

When FIRST ARMY arrived at the German border, Ordnance had in hand only the minimum supplies it had been able to move forward . . . and it was at the end of a supply line over 350 miles in length. Moreover, it was feeling uncomfortably the shortage of Class II and Class IV supplies . . . parts for artillery and smaller weapons, tank engine parts, truck engines, tires, etc., and there followed a mad scramble at forward Depots for procurement. FIRST ARMY would in fact, during September receive only ten percent of all parts requisitioned. Due mainly to long-distance deliveries that resulted in an acute shortage of transportation gasoline allocation became a critical problem. Even the pipeline being established from Cherbourg to near the Paris region had not yet alleviated this problem. An average consumption of 571,000 gallons was felt daily in FIRST ARMY and when vehicles traveled to gasoline dumps for this item, often a great line of trucks would be encountered awaiting similar allocations, each asking the same question: "When will the gasoline arrive?"

We too, began feeling the "pinch" and it appeared likely as the days passed we would remain within this vicinity for a prolonged period. It also became evident that the procurement of fuel, vehicle and weapons parts, clothing, and most especially food rations of reputable quality would continue to be met with alarming difficulty. Hot or even warm meals were gradually reduced. A hot meal now simply meant warmed-over canned rations of the "Ten-in-one" caliber.

In an abandoned store someone located a great quantity of packaged German pancake flour, and though it was old and not the best of flavor it did provide us a temporary respite in the form of a morning meal. Some five miles to the north in a sort of "no man's land" at the south approaches of Aachen, now under siege, despite spasmodic chatter of distant machine gun fire, some four hundred grey and itchy woolen blankets were confiscated from an unattended German supply house. Further; from one of the captured but unguarded veneer factories near Lammersdorf an attractive supply of plywood sheets was brought in and utilized as "lean-to's" against the open wind and rains. Some trimmed these sheets down and made them into weathershields to enclose vehicle cabs that would afford ample protection against the raw winter winds that lay ahead for those whose jobs called for continuous use of the roads.

Lammersdorf is a small drab town thirteen miles southeast of Roetgen. Ringed by hills and high forested ridges that are dotted with pillboxes, militarily it marked an important link to the vital highway leading northeast to Huertgen. In essence, it stood as an important gateway to the Siegfried and to the Huertgen Forest itself.

Recently cleared by 9TH DIVISION's 39th Regiment there came persistent reports of several scavengers roaming about the town. Col. Hudson of 184th Battalion directed our company to dispatch an adequate detachment (usually three or four men) to patrol until further notice the damaged though still useful Otto Junkers Metals Industries plant to prevent possible looters from removing anything of near value. Looting, pillaging and even vandalism was not necessarily restricted to soldiers, for returning civilians who risked trickling back into a captured town were hardpressed to seek and scramble for anything that could be useful.

Enemy shells fell at intervals in and around Lammersdorf even as infantry rear guards were leaving. As our special detachment rolled into town and took up positions the shelling had tapered off considerably, but still considered alarming. Toward evening the tempo of enemy mortar shells began increasing . . . crashing in the streets, bursting into buildings and exploding violently against walls that showered the area with a spray of shrapnel that was aptly described as "sounding like nails plinking against concrete!"

With this hostile action an unusual course of maneuvering was quickly facilitated. Concrete guardposts were utilized immediately. Three posts, each approximately six feet high and strangely shaped much like an inverted cone whose round concrete reinforced walls some six inches thick and distanced about fifty feet apart originally were constructed for plant watchmen and designed to accommodate two persons tightly squeezed in. Said one of the guards;

"A direct hit by artillery fire would have chipped it into several hunks of concrete . . . and it was pure hell to hear pieces of shrapnel 'plink' against it while we were on the inside! Another thought came to our minds though, and that was . . . suppose we were on the outside at this moment!"

Early the next morning the inevitable happened! Before proper cover could be effected a piece of shrapnel from one of the bursts found its' mark and left a gaping blood-spurting slit in Teofil Skiba's upper left arm! So shocked was he that he never uttered a sound! He was quickly dispatched to a rear aid station and quite paradoxically *while there* . . . "WHUMP!" . . . another shell crashed in the vicinity and a tiny fragment ripped higher into the same shoulder!

Recently receiving the stripes of a T/5, Ted Skiba was a quiet portly Polish lad of twenty-one from Detroit's neighboring Hamtramck and because of his listless and unconcerned nature would appear least likely to receive a wound. Subsequently evacuated from a FIRST ARMY hospital and from the continent to England he would never return to the company roster.

Several counter-attacks had been registered northeast of the town but sometime around nine in the evening of the 21st confirmed reports reached our CP that "Jerry" was mustering forces in a main effort to break through to the Rotgen area. Sitting astride the main east-west highway it would meet with almost exacting logic that Lammersdorf would feel the assault!

Unaware of this report the three remaining men at Lammersdorf would be "sitting ducks" in the face of such a thrust! Hiding his true feelings the Captain maintained his usual calm manner and called to Botting:

"Round up a detail now Sergeant. Don't alarm the company but get those men at Lammersdorf!"

The Sergeant, at the moment not comprehending the urgency replied:

"Most of the drivers are out now, Captain; I'll grab one when he comes in and send a detail."

"Maybe I didn't make myself clear, Sergeant," came a quick retort from the lanky C. O. "I don't give a damn *who* you round up, but do it now! Now if you can't do it, I will!"

Botting quickly comprehended.

Who was available to go? It was dark and none of the regular drivers with assigned vehicles could at the moment be located. Compelled to immediate action the First Sergeant felt he didn't have time, or didn't want to take the time to dispatch a messenger. The 28-year-old Botting was in no way slow-witted. He was in fact, one to move fast.

"The hell with that 'wait until tomorrow' bit," he reasoned; "You can't afford to wait . . . especially during those days, 'cause tomorrow there's another problem waiting for you. As far as the Captain's order for a rescue team, I don't believe I really grabbed the exact substance of his command. He often spoke in a sort of monotone, you know."

In an arm-beckoning gesture he commandeered the first person he saw.

"Come on Connors! Come on Felt! . . . Let's go!"

"Go where, Sergeant?" Dick Felt and Phil Connors through natural instinct, questioned the action and destination.

"Get in the truck, dammit . . . and let's go!" thundered Botting. Arrogance was not intended, but still it was a direct order and there was no question that his tone *meant business*! Though the enemy thrust did not begin until early morning the action of Botting and his team might have saved three men, for by early afternoon of the 22nd word was received that the northeast area of Lammersdorf was again in receivership . . . in the hands of the Germans!

"We jammed ourselves into the cab of the three-quarter ton and Botting drove like 'hell' all the way," recalls Felt; "saying very little but running off the road several times and onto what little shoulders there were. I could see nothing and don't see how he could, for the rain was blinding and it was extremely difficult to see through the downpour dashing against the windshield . . . and though those tiny slits for headlights meant little he toyed with the 'bright-dim' foot switch so much I thought I'd go out of my mind! Neither of us were completely sure of the way and once when we rounded a sudden curve and abruptly came upon a narrow bridge, I thought . . . 'Man' . . . *this is it!*" Continuing, he said, "Connors sat there and other than grumbling a couple times, never said a word. But we made it, and somehow found the guys with little trouble and came on back."

Though under the circumstances initiating camouflage as best we could, the narrow breadth of endless fir and spruce trees gave us little choice but to draw up as close to them as possible.

Try as we may, exposure to aircraft could not be completely avoided. An almost tragic reminder of this weakness came on the second day when lining up to wash messkits following a late noon chow.

"*Krauts*! *Krauts*! *Krauts*!" came a shout as someone, pointing his finger skyward at a 45-degree angle indicated immediate danger!

"*Look out*! *Look out*!" came another cry! "Here they come!" Two enemy fighters (some quickly identified them as ME-109's) spotted our location and looking up we were horrified to see them coming in from the east, leveling off in the distance and zooming straight for this location for what would appear to be "easy pickings!" No time to think! No time to take cover! Mess kits flew . . . rattling briefly in the air and ending with a tinkling thud as they hit the mushy earth. Everyone fell flat and braced for the worst!

"Tac-a-tac-a-tac! Tac-a-tac-a-tac!" The air was split with a staccato of blasts! "God help us!" someone muttered.

Now . . . what seemed to be the inevitable *never* took place! Another factor entered the picture! *Fate*! Yes . . . fate, but one that was ready! The planes did not change course but they unquestionably changed targets for immediately hungry anti-aircraft guns in adjacent fields welcomed the two-plane target and ack-ack spewed fire with a deafening roar! The battle was on! It seemed surely that every piece of artillery in this region was trained on these twisting targets and with thousands of explosions of dense almost impervious flak bursting overhead, the inexhaustible streams of tracer bullets searching for their mark and the excitement emanating therefrom . . . any "4th of July" fireworks celebration anywhere in the states would have had plenty of competition!

With regained composure we quickly realized what was next to come and with great speed picked ourselves up and dashed for cover as shrapnel from the skies began to fall all over the place! Painfully aware by this time of the grevious consequences that have come to many a GI when struck by this metal that carried almost the impact of a bullet, it took no direct command to disperse!

Picking himself up out of the mud, looking skyward and slowly wiping his fatigues, Botting could only say:

"*Damn* that was close!"

As for the planes; to fight it out with the ground-based "ack-ack" proved a futile effort because they were caught . . . and we watched them . . . smoking as they fell seperately behind the distant ridge of trees!

***

Time continued . . . and the days clicked by.

The enemy in the field was doing an excellent job in keeping FIRST ARMY at bay but with the prevailing elements in late September becoming increasingly unfavorable it was evident that we were going to have "Old Man Weather" to contend with as well. During autumn and winter this region historically is noted for long periods of light rain and snow. The fall and winter of 1944 would, however; experience weather of near record severity as rainfall exceeded far above average and snow and freezing temperatures came early and remained for long periods. It was a tough time *indeed* to fight a motorized and mechanized war. The continuous rains caused minor floods. The elements necessitated incessant road repairs, and restoring downed communication lines became a monotonous task for the signal corps and special forces.

Infantry and tankmen found it sorely difficult to cross swollen creeks. This then, increased the responsibility of the engineers, for without prior preparation by construction battalions these obstacles could not be bridged with dispatch. Air ceilings often reached incompetent proportions and heavy artillery after being positioned for a few days in pastures of sensitive terrain found themselves lacking true coordination in fields of mud.

General William C. Westmoreland, then DIVISION Chief of Staff recalled that;

> "finding suitable artillery positions because of the fickle terrain was perhaps the most difficult of all problems to overcome as far as the big guns were concerned. Often true firing coordination could not effectively be maintained because of the shifting weight of heavy weapons. Braces were applied every day to correct this when necessary."

Truckhead operations, because of inclement weather encountered considerable difficulty. Many installations becoming completely bogged down in mud found it imperative to change locations frequently in order to continue operations. Many instances saw loading and unloading of vehicles executed from the roadside only, with commodities moved by hand-to-hand into and out of the dump areas.

We too, were not without troubles. The entire area, its' viability seriously questioned, had turned into a mass of almost gelatin-like sloshy mud that in many spots, if one was not careful he could mire halfway to his knees. All transports bogging down with regularity became helpless until pulled out by means of a cable and winch attached to heavier vehicles. Despite utilization of broken twigs and limbs, scraps of underbrush and trimmed logs for which purpose it was to create some type of base, or mat; the interior of many puptents was not spared the omnipresence of mud and water. It always seemed to find a way to ooze through!

In the face of this rapidly worsening situation there was no justification to remain in this space. There was no point . . . we must move out! Automotive was all but trapped and could no longer operate effectively. Mud had compounded the maintenance problem. One could not work under vehicles . . . jacks sunk under vehicular weight and parts were lost in the elements. Our artillery section could no longer pull those big burly howitzers from position to position in such a small area that daily became minimized because of increasing depth of some several inches of mud! Shop trucks and two-and-a-half ton 6 x 6's had filled their own tracks with broken logs and stones several times and even the kitchen had shifted from several different positions. The desire to move was further enhanced by an ever-increasing boldness of the Luftwaffe, who having become aware of this now conspicuous location was also doubtless cognizant that our "ack-ack" security had vacated the adjoining fields. In intrepid fashion on two successive occasions, though withholding their fire, they made low sweeps and passes . . . one at noon that saw messkits clatter helter-skelter as we broke frantically from "chow" lines!

It no longer would be feasible to operate as was done in Normandy and northern France where work could be performed in wooded areas or in tented bivouac locations. In those days no billits or shop space was required and movement became virtually simplified. Now it was different, moves would be far less frequent and we *had* to get inside. Movements were in fact, during this period practically negligible. Short distance moves became necessary, especially when the muddy fields began to hamper operations. The cold weather was coming fast and FIRST ARMY instructed units "to establish installations . . . wherever possible, in the proximity of houses which could be used as billits for troops." Billits *would be* nice, but for the time being we would not be that fortunate. They just weren't available! But we had reached and passed our "peak" insofar as this area was concerned, and *move we must*! *Imperative*! Through Colonel Childs, General Craig, the DIVISION C.O. had issued orders for all Ordnance units to "utilize every part, conserve every tire, and put all mobile and functional equipment back in operation with the utmost dispatch." Our move was pondered. But where? . . .

for not too far distant along the north-south battle zone the war was in full swing and practically every available or near suitable location was already taken by other combat headquarters or supporting service troops or well-positioned artillery batteries. The search ended as the second week of October approached. The day was much like the rest, dismal and dreary with a grey gloomy pallor stretching over the entire region . . . but we rolled out of this highly despicable area, long devoid of its' usefulness.

We moved north, less than a mile . . . straight up the Aachen-Roetgen highway. When the European conflict was to end some eight months later our records would reflect this to represent the shortest of our mobile marches.

Situated alongside the west shoulder of the north-south Aachen-Roetgen highway, a highly important main supply route for **VII CORPS**, this spot . . . perhaps the most suitable thus far, not only was spaciously sufficient to conduct operations but possessed a natural camouflage as a deterrent against possible enemy air activity. Vehicles normally could come and go with daily operations unmolested under protection of a natural "umbrella" of spruce, fir and pine trees making up the eastern fringes of the Foret d'Eupen. Though trees were well-spaced, some averaging perhaps six to eight feet apart in this particular segment of the forest, it was nevertheless almost impossible to dig foxholes with any adequacy because of shallow interlocking roots.

The weather in no way grew better. It did, in fact grow worse! Yet, we were not to experience the deterioration of the previous area's terrain. Because of falling leaves, twigs, branches, pine needles, etc., ostensibly the top soil had grown hardened through the years to create a natural "cushion" whereas the last area . . . with its' absolute open exposure left the terrain at the mercy of the elements. From the beginning the weather at this new encampment appeared to remain in a stagnated dim state. Rain clouds dominated this region continuously and by actual count rain fell daily for fifteen consecutive days. The sun's appearance, even when it did break through was brief and to experience as much as two full hours of sunshine was a rarity.

Chiefly for lack of civilian offers as had previously been experienced in less hostile locales, we did our own laundering, though to little avail for hardly was there ever enough sun to dry clothes after they were washed. Quartermaster mobile field laundry units gradually increasing operations in this area soon came to the rescue and that problem was alleviated.

The Captain was up early. He was in fact *always* up early. It was cold and misty but that did not deter him from his daily ritual of shaving with a helmet full of cold water. All of the other officers though shaving in a like manner heated their water on the mobile kitchen stoves which were lit at five-thirty each morning.

"Damn, you're a brave soul, Captain;" remarked the 1st. Sergeant one morning when passing his tent on the way to chow. "But boy, what a glutton for punishment."

"You're just not the rugged type, sergeant," replied Orsenigo in his good natured tone. "You guys have got to get with it. Cold water's good for you; get's the lead out in a hurry! Gives you a good start!"

"Yeah, but starting the day with a raw face sure as hell won't make me a hero. Not in this kind of weather. I'll be more like an ogre . . . and the men won't like that!"

Orsenigo, throwing his head back and laughing, his face still covered with lather, muttered in barely audible tones; "Some crap, sergeant, some crap!"

Some of the men heated their water in helmets by open fires which each section was authorized. This privilege, with stipulation that fires would burn *only* during the day sometimes was abused. On occasion in certain areas they were seen burning after dark. This responsibility lay with the section chiefs who simply had let it pass.

It was cold one early evening and darkness had come early when the 1st. Sergeant dropped down into the Service section area. Three glowing fires, though contained in open empty barrel drums warmed the evening air and the scintillating aroma of burning logs reminded him of camp fires during the early days of bivouac.

"How long you gonna let 'em burn?" questioned the sergeant in a soft tone. "The Old Man is raising hell because they're still going."

"They're just little fires, Botting;" spoke up Sam Parrinello, the short energetic section leader. "You can't see 'em but so far. Hell, it gets cold around here."

"The Old Man can see 'em, and that's enough. And it don't make much difference whether they're little or big. The 'Krauts' can spot 'em and that's what they're looking for."

"Krauts? *What* Krauts?" retorted Parrinello who delighted in the pursuance of an argument. "How many times has an enemy plane been over? It's been a week since we've heard one."

"It only takes one, Sam . . . just one. All he's gotta do is drop just one of his 'eggs' and that's it. What'd'ya want? You feed these fires all day! You guys keep this up and there won't be any woods around here . . . you'll chop 'em all down!"

"Suppose we just cut it to one . . . and dim it down?"

"Talk to my 'fanny', Parrinello; 'cause my face is tired! Don't give me a hard time. No deal."

Taking a long sip from his well-stained coffee cup, Botting turned around, and haltingly looked back at his not-easily persuaded friend:

"Remember; no fires."

In Roetgen, a little more than a mile south, a huge tent was erected at the 709th Ordnance facility and arrangements were made with army Special Services to show movies once a week. Though the Hollywood-made films were current and did much to give us a badly needed lift it became a hardened chore to attend. Confronted with nights that could get no darker and devoid of all lights for driving the one-mile trip never ceased to be hazardous, for forced to move at a snail-like pace vehicles because of complete darkness stood the danger of running off the road. This did, in fact become frequent and many was the vehicle that wound up in a ditch . . . often resulting in damage and injuries to its occupants.

One remembers sliding into a ditch with a weapons carrier.

Grinding deeper into the mud with each attempt at extrication proved exhaustive. The vehicle was abandoned and all ten men sloughed the full mile in blind rainy darkness to the camp site. Another driver, making an approach to the main highway from the muddy passageway that once had been a road, turned sharp to the north and unaware . . . missed the highway completely! "KA-RUMP!!" A heavy jarring thud shocked the occupants as the vehicle pancaked into a three-foot wide open culvert . . . unseen by the driver! In another instance, the Captain's driver-aide, turning onto the highway in a dark heavy downpour had only exchanged gears when he and the First Sergeant along with the C.O. crashed blindly into the rear of a stalled 2½ ton GI-laden truck! More prominent than the collected bruises resulting from injuries was the shock that came from the sudden unexpected jolt of a blind crash.

The persistence of rain, moreover almost every evening made it miserable from the beginning, and returning to our campsite under these conditions there was little choice except to grope one's way through to his specific location. This meant occasional tripping over tent ropes, stumbling into an uncovered hole, bumping headlong or scraping against wet low-hanging branches. To say the least, many arguments against leaving our campsite at night could be advanced.

Besides becoming the first town in Germany to fall Roetgen would hold additional significance, in that on September 20 Archbishop (Cardinal) Francis Spellman conducted his very first religious service for American troops on German soil. Those from our unit able to attend this communion were accorded that privilege.

Slightly northwest of the camp within 200 yards lay a portion of the highly-publicized Siegfried Line, which long had borne an obvious reference as "dragon teeth." So named because of its' almost paradoxical resemblance of the real thing these supposedly indomitable "teeth," though well-structured were in most instances hardly more than steel beams embedded four or five feet in the ground and encased in a cement foundation. Blocked off in reinforced concrete they were shaped up somewhat like miniature pyramids. Five rows of blocks beginning in height from two-and-a-half feet in front to rise to almost five feet in the rear. Roads leading through the blocks were obstructed by steel gates, and though these gates and obstacles could be removed by attacking forces it would not be an easy task because of the heavy fire that could come from nearby pillboxes. Rivers, lakes, railroad cuts and fills, sharp defiles and forests were natural obstacles and separated the "teeth" at intervals. They too, were not easily penetrable by an attacking force.

With construction beginning in 1938 and upgraded constantly through 1942 this barrier acted too, as a sustaining demarcation separating Germany from western bordering countries beginning from a point north of Aachen near the Netherlands border and extending some two hundred miles south to the boundary of Switzerland. Beyond these obstacles east, lay the *real* defenses of the German frontier.

Deep steel-reinforced concrete pillboxes, blockhouses and observation posts . . . more than 3,000 of them, strategically spaced, well-camouflaged and deeply implanted into earth bunkers ringed the countryside for almost the same distance as the "dragon teeth." Behind these pillboxes in staggered positions were more of the same . . . forty to fifty feet deep, twenty to thirty feet wide and twenty to twenty-five feet high with walls and roof three to eight feet thick. Additionally, reinforced by heavy wire-mesh they were in some cases supported by heavy steel beams. Beyond were still more until it appeared that even the most formidable foe could never penetrate them all.

Dug in on high ground behind our location perhaps half a mile to the west, actually at the opposite end of the forest were clusters of FIRST ARMY heavy artillery that for several days roared thunder from their 240mm monsters to spell misery for the enemy . . . and at times uncertainty for us. Most pronounced at night the firing shuddered the very earth around us and as the echo of incoming enemy artillery and sometimes that of the indomitable German "burp gun" reverberated throughout the woods and valley a tense atmosphere drifted and settled over the area not infrequently.

Enemy "recon" planes visiting with regularity, especially at night, appeared content to make a sweep, gun their motors a couple of times and leave. Only once in this location did we experience hostility when an over-zealous pilot, perhaps for want of curiousity swooped down on this stretch of trees one evening with machine guns blazing! No retaliatory action was taken and he banked off and left the scene. No injuries were inflicted . . . but as the Automotive section chief remarked at "chow" next morning:

"We didn't panic, but I don't mind saying . . . it scared the living hell out of everyone of us!"

Was anyone else alarmed? Hardly a fair question! Captain Orsenigo had long ago warned:

"Don't try to be a hero and get us all in trouble. Don't dare fire on planes . . . day or night. We are no match for them." He added; "Leave that for the ack-ack 'pros' . . . they know what they're doing."

The temptation often was strong, but obedience was personified!

Less fortunate was the ill-fated 974th Ordnance Evacuation Company, headed by our former commander . . . Captain Clyde Miller and which company having established bivouac several days following our entry was camped in an adjoining portion of the Foret d'Eupen some one hundred fifty yards south of our location.

In late evening of the 14th the same type "recon" plane swooped threateningly over their area but withheld its' fire. In thoughtless anxiety one of the GIs jumped up on a truck, threw back the bolt of a mounted 50-caliber machine gun and blindly went into action . . . firing several bursts that abruptly penetrated the darkness with streams of red tracers! Silhouetted against a very dark sky, displaying no lights whatsoever and the entire scene cloaked in infinite darkness chances of immediately hitting the plane were highly negligible. But the damage had been done! Probably damaging the pilot's ego more than anything else! Banking his plane he leveled off above the treetops and fully gunning his motors returned in a low sweep. Soft sounds of "swoosh! . . . swoosh! . . . swoosh!" filtered from above . . . falling into the midst of an unsuspecting company of 157 men! Anti-personnel bombs! Like giant firecrackers the night air was split with a series of sharp explosions!

On his way earlier to a nearby fire tower in the forest to observe incoming enemy shells exploding in the distance, Captain Miller recalled:

"I was shocked when I heard one of our own 50-calibers go off and when the plane made its' turn to come back I knew there was going to be trouble. Lt. Paris, our Executive officer was with me and before we could even think good the plane dived low and several swishing sounds filled the air." Continuing, the beefy Captain explained; "I knew *exactly* what it was and I shoved Lt. Paris full force and fell to the ground with him just as the explosions rocked the forest!"

"Paris! Paris!" cried the Captain; "They hit the CP! They hit the CP! Let's go!"

Grasping, crawling, frantically and blindly trying to run through the underbrush and maze of trees . . . terrified with thoughts of what they were sure would be found among the din of shouts and moans already filling the area they were on the scene in no time. "Though it seemed we had run a mile" says Miller, "actually we were only a few yards away!"

One of the officers, almost in shock, staggered toward Miller with a blood-soaked GI dead in his arms and literally sobbing:

"Oh God, Captain . . . What am I going to do with him! What am I going to do with him!"

That and the fate of the others would be decided before morning. Of 28 casualties taken, 6 had met immediate deaths, 8 seriously wounded, 5 of which would not live twenty-four hours and 9 others wounded but would survive.

The 974th. had an excellent record. They had moved swiftly in evacuating the "big stuff" and War Correspondent Ernie Pyle, spending two days with them in lower Normandy had written highly commendable articles on their performance.

Back in Roetgen . . . the 709th. Ordnance got a taste of erroneous strafing by two P-47's that wounded only one person. *This* . . . in broad daylight! From that incident on they became highly wary of *all* aircraft.

On the 17th Sergeant Gordon Barrett, a darkhaired "string bean" from Montpelier, Vermont and one of the company's earlier non-coms was enticed to join the 974th Ordnance. Sorely depleted in personnel as a result of that tragic bombing three days earlier Captain Miller badly needed administrative personnel. Moreover, he long had remembered Barrett's exceptional administrative competence for he had been an excellent company clerk under Miller.

"Why are you leaving us, Barrett?" asked one.

"I don't want to leave, really . . . but hell, what would you do if you were offered a First Sergeant's rating?"

Someone ventured; "Barrett always loved stripes. So stripe-happy in fact, that I'll bet he even sews them on his underwear!" Chuckling, he added; "I'll bet he can just taste those 'top-kick' hooks right now."

He could! . . . and he would soon be wearing them.

Since leaving England in June no additional personnel had been added to the 126th roster. In mid-October the first replacement would come in.

Jim Glore was a quiet Pfc. from Atlanta, Ga., and at thirty-six a little older than most of us. He was however, an experienced automotive 'front end' man and little time passed before his value was recognized. Though a little sensitive he would soon become aware that he must learn to live with the fact that he was one of the company's few southerners . . . in the midst of a preponderance of Yankees!

***

Since entering Germany on September 11, FIRST ARMY to mid-October had penetrated only twelve miles and shockingly had suffered some 20,000 casualties. Now face to face with the German 7th. Army; and with supply lines dangerously overextended and having reached its' vulnerable   point

... with fuel, ammunition and food reduced almost to a ration basis . . . the weather doing little to improve, intensifying in severity and supported by unprecedented rains . . . with many of the vital arteries and practically all secondary roads succumbed to the omnipresent mud and becoming less navagible with each day; by the second week in October it did not take the wisdom of a philosopher to recognize that FIRST ARMY's long and well-paced drive was sustained and operations were settling down to slow and bloody war. Congrous of this and much as we disliked it the 126th began to concert preparations to remain in this dismal part of the Eupen Forest, "sweat out" the chain of events . . . and make the best of it until something better could be afforded.

In the midst of Autumn the winds began to pick up its' pace and the air was becoming more brisk; the days became shorter and darkness came earlier to make the nights grow longer. It was getting colder too, which gave admonition that the season was near a change and winter would soon be reckoned with. Determined GI ingenuity was stressed and a way was usually found to combat these problems . . . though not always completely successful, but at least temporarily.

While the weather was fast coming to fore as a major source of conflict other adverse situations had to be faced. Maintenance became an agonizing factor, and because of mud repair shops had to be moved time and again to firmer ground. Because of overloading and lack of preventive maintenance a mounting strain on equipment grew that caused breakage of axels as well as defections to gears and transmissions. Further, this caused heavy depletion of tire reserves, for by now tire expiration was averaging about 12,000 miles and thousands had to be replaced weekly. Vitally-needed two-and-a-half-ton trucks, the real "workhorses;" were vulnerable and following the rapid advance across France most (particularly those of the QM) were in serious condition. Tightening nuts and bolts and occasional cleaning by driver and his assistant would hold up only temporarily. Trying to maintain exhausting schedules and rolling most of the time at reckless breakneck speeds . . .

often with improper loading, innumerable accidents resulted and this practice contributed rapidly to deterioration of roads.

Supply and how to keep it at consistent levels fast developed into a real and constant source of worry to field and depot commanders and military planners. The bulk of American supplies was coming in at two ports; Cherbourg and the Normandy beaches, and to effectively transport it from these locations to a front almost five hundred miles away was a critical issue. With tracks of most vital French railways still incapacitated; all railroad stations, roundhouses, machine shops, junctions and rolling stock still pretty much of a shambles, and despite engineers and railway construction battalions as well as French and Belgian laborers working 'round the clock to repair lines running deep into the active American and British war zones it was imperative that transportation in the meanwhile improve vastly. Trucks were now doing the job and would of a necessity continue.

Even into mid and late September supplies had to move via this media. This reckless inexhaustable fleet of military trucks, by now gingerly known as the "Red Ball Express" dominated most main highways with a constant stream of vital supplies and equipment. The "Red Ball route" was a designated route operated by the 471st. Quartermaster Group which basically extended to Soissons, France for distribution to other truck lines to forward depots and into the war zones. Hundreds of them rolled out daily from Cherbourg and the beaches to the south and east . . . four and five hundred miles, speeding equipment, spare parts, ammo, fuel and food to advanced dumps in the war zone. They moved . . . and they stopped for nothing! As one of our drivers so aptly put it; "Man, the way those 'ziggy-boos' gag those trucks, General Motors ain't never going out of business!"

In mid September however, the 12TH ARMY GROUP had required something like 13,000 tons of supplies per day; 5,400 tons of this to FIRST ARMY alone. Truckers unfortunately, could only deliver about 11,000 tons per day during this period. By October 1st. sufficient repairs to railways alleviated the situation to an extent that trucks from the beaches could transfer cargoes to trains at Paris and the trains could roll to railheads near the war zone. Soissons soon became a railhead, and then Liege. The "Red Ball Express" did continue its' magnificent performance . . . operating until November 16, and during its' eighty-one days of agonizing road torture had carried 412,913 tons of supplies.

The battles for Schevenhuette and Germeter were over and so vicious and concentrated were they that proof was abundantly clear that the enemy planned to yield no ground and the German High Command's adoption of a determined stand was evident!

On FIRST ARMY's northern sector the long-besieged industrial city of Aachen, though under heavy bombardment since mid-September became the main concentration of VII CORPS.

Aachen; historic gateway to Germany with a pre-war population of 165,710 was of paramount importance as an east-west route even during the height of the Roman Empire expansion. Named Aix-la-Chappel by its Medieval Emperor, Charlemagne; it was in fact during the Middle Ages recognized as the seat of the Holy Roman Empire. The oldest city in the Rhineland and situated just north of the Eifel Mountains and a scant few miles east of a point where boundaries of Germany, Belgium and the Netherlands meet, it is well-noted for ancient mineral baths and is an important manufacturing center; particularly of products made from iron, zinc and lead which are mined near the city. A great rail center, its' military value lies in the roads that spread out from the city in all directions. In 1944 its' significance pointedly marked it as a major key to the second most heavily fortified portion of the West Wall. Thus, to capture this vital city would greatly facilitate an Allied advance through the Siegfried Line.

The first of Hitler's large cities doomed to die, Aachen was well-fortified by its' inner walls and the prominent hills that dominate the city from the northern fringes . . . and as history will relate, proved to be one of the most difficult cities to secure by the Western Allies. For a fact, Aachen did not die easily. It wasn't until her fanatic and gallant defenders were driven back into the heart of the metropolis and either annihilated or captured that she fell. General Hodges assigned VII CORPS this task. VII CORPS sent the veteran 1ST INFANTRY DIVISION on October 8th to start the attack from the south and borrowed RCTs from XIX CORPS' 30TH INFANTRY DIVISION, already operating north of the city; to commence the attack from that direction. Two days later 1ST DIVISION began an encirclement of the city that seemed only to solidify defenses.

Fierce "see-saw" house-to-house fighting mounted . . . spreading into the intricate sewer systems and each block was defended with renewed fanaticism. Because of its' thick walled buildings and cellars American light artillery and mortar fire along with punishing blasts from 105mm's mounted on tanks had to be employed from block to block before American forces could successfully advance while heavy artillery pounded German communications to the rear! Pitched battles that included many dedicated city policemen, along with ill-trained Volksturm became so intense that it seemed the fall of Aachen would mean the fall of Germany itself! Isolated skirmishes raged . . . gradually mushrooming into big ones! Crucifix Hill, Observatory Hill, and Farwick Park . . . each involving employment of grenades, flamethrowers, tanks, bayonets and even dynamite before the defenders would be dislodged.

On October 10th the 1ST DIVISION commander, General Huebner, issued an ultimatum through leaflets that should have but did little to encourage the city's surrender:

"The city of Aachen is now completely surrounded by American forces. If the city is not promptly and completely surrendered unconditionally, the American Army ground and Air Forces will proceed ruthlessly with air and artillery bombardment to reduce it to submission!"

The ultimatum ignored, the next day and during the following two subsequent days 9th TAC sent 650 fighter-bombers at intervals to attack the city. In a coordinated attack twelve artillery battalions firing 10,000 rounds of explosives wreaked havoc on the besieged bastion! This was just the beginning, for incessant attacks of artillery and relentless assaults by fighter-bombers continued with ferocity!

During the last few nights from our wooded location six miles south of Aachen raging fires within the city could visibly be viewed glowing beyond the rolling hills and over the entire territory. Crushing blows from armored units and infantry moved ever closer to add finishing touches that ultimately would bring the city to its' knees!

How much longer could the carnage last? It would for awhile continue, for Colonel Gerhardt Wilck, a new German commander in the last days, took control of the city's waning defense . . . and on October 19th issued his Order of The Day to the almost crippled but fanatic defenders:

"The defenders of Aachen will prepare for their last battle. Constituted to the smallest space, we shall fight to the last man, the last shell, the last bullet in accordance with the Fuehrer's orders."

"In the face of the contemptible, despicable treason committed by certain individuals, I expect each and every defender of the venerable Imperial city of Aachen to do his duty to the end, in fulfillment of our Oath to the Flag. I expect courage and determination to hold out. Long live the Fuehrer and our beloved Fatherland!"

Aachen was burning furiously now!! It was a nightmare and her courageous defense was failing! The last few days found the city completely in the hands of VII CORPS . . . all opposition was broken, and by noon of the 21st, Aachen was ours!

Aachen was a wreck, and one American observer described it well:

"Burst sewers, broken gas mains and dead animals have an almost overpowering smell in many parts of the city. Streets lined with shattered glass; telephone, electric light and trolley cables are dangling and netted together everywhere, and in many places wrecked cars, trucks and armored vehicles and guns litter the streets."

The Germans lost over 100 tanks and suffered over 5,000 killed, wounded and missing. 12,000 enemy prisoners were captured during the siege. United States casualties during the siege amounted to some 3,000 killed, wounded and missing.

Years later visiting his Washington, D. C. apartment, the author sought General Huebner's evaluation of this particular siege:

General Huebner: "One of the most complex of all battles. A city, particularly a large well-structured one as this, is always tough. It is not like fighting out in the open where no fortifications exist, for in Aachen there were no shortcuts, and every inch had to be fought for. Well-fortified, the Germans felt if they could successfully defend this city, then the Americans might have second-thoughts about advancing in Germany." The General continued; "Look at St. Lo . . . not even a fraction the size of Aachen; and how long it took to rout the enemy. But they were professional soldiers in St. Lo, whereas the Aachen defenders were only a handful of that type along with scattered ill-trained troops and wary civilians . . . but dedicated and uncertain at the thought of surrender. What if they had all been professionals like at St . Lo? It would *really* have been hell!"

Mid-October also found the well-fortified but not too impregnable Siegfried Line pierced in many places. Yet, its' most vital points continued obstinate from every angle. The 9TH and its' supporting units had long since captured Camp d'Elsenborn and the hill towns of Monshau and Hofen several miles south in that age-old disputed region of Belgium near the German border; and for the one month's fighting on German soil the DIVISION's accomplishments were incredible. A number of unit citations for outstanding performances would bear this out. In this drab rain-soaked northern sector; namely within our present perimeter, the little towns of Brandt, Schmidthof and Rott had fallen. Further distant Zwiefall . . . Vicht . . . Mausbach . . . Lammersdorf had been cleared, but a great wooded barrier . . . the Huertgen Forest; an almost natural fortress looming in front of the entire VII and V CORPS, continued to block the entrance to the inner Rhineland.

To begin an inevitable drive to the Roer River and in order to probe deep into the Rhineland's heart, this almost invincible and seemingly impervious Huertgen Forest must be cleared and secured. The enormity of this undertaking would prove to be beyond anticipation of both CORPS and this monstrous task would continue throughout most of the winter months and would consume a tremendous loss of life. The Forest, unanimously recognized as a sort of "key to the door" that once secured would allow FIRST ARMY to spread all over the Rhineland. Strategic preparations to "get that key and open that door" was concerted by the 9TH DIVISION. The 9TH would be first to enter the Huertgen and by mid-December four more combat Divisions would share heavily its' torture . . . the 4TH, 8TH, 28Th and 83RD INFANTRY DIVISIONS, and an RCT of the 5TH ARMORED. Units from the VIII CORPS too, would have a part in it before it was over . . . operating on the southern flank of FIRST ARMY.

A few days after VII CORPS started its' attack on September 16 it became shockingly obvious as the casualty rate began to climb that strategy had to be revised. The attempt was called off on September 30. General Collins' original theory of the attempt on this part of the West Wall was one of simplicity, but sound:

"If we could break it, then we would be just that much to the good. If we didn't, then we would be none the worse."

Then when the first penetration into the Forest was stopped, he remarked:

"A combination of things stopped us. We ran out of gas — that is to say, we weren't completely dry, but the effect was the same. We ran out of ammunition; and we ran out of weather. The loss of our close tactical air support because of weather was a real blow."

What was so mysterious, so unwavering, so formidable about the

Huertgen Forest? Let us take a closer look at it:

From the onset this dismal forest harbors an undeniable eerie and forbidding appearance. With trunks of the tall trees beginning very close to the ground each fir interlocks its' body with another, so thick in fact so as to be almost impervious to sunlight infiltration. A solid mass of dark inpenetral green confronts a person in a standing position and only when a man is lying in a prone position on the ground or perhaps crawling low on hands and knees is visibility of any consequence certain. Fifty square miles of these fir trees with their jutting unending roots dominate the Rhineland.

The few narrow roads winding through the forest were each heavily mined and road blocks were set up at strategic and most susceptible points . . . even the mud-churned roads running through the man-made firebreaks, these extending possibly for 1,000 yards across, were only wide enough for two jeeps to pass. These roads were heavily concentrated with machine gun and murderous artillery fire which meant that until these guns were silenced or knocked out it was practically impossible to advance on these passageways. Often the Germans placed trees across these small passages and then in some fashion "boobytrap" them. In the face of that, at the sound of the trees being moved the enemy very quickly concentrated his artillery, mortar and small arms fire on them.

By the time heavy snows began to accompany the relentless rains and enjoined by freezing weather, only a great degree of intestinal fortitude kept a man going . . . and digging foxholes in the hard root-studded ground became almost an impossibility. Even those fortunate enough to dig and establish some kind of defense were never free from the harrowing danger of the omnipresent hot shrapnel splattering from vicious tree bursts as enemy shells crashed above and through the trees. Throughout the Huertgen Forest men of the **9TH DIVISION** experienced agony and an untold measure of mental anguish, and as the infantry advanced or retreated the dead were of a necessity left behind where they fell. Heavy shellfire prevailed every day during this furious campaign and probably the trees as long as they remain will forever bear the scars of war . . . these scars in time, perhaps to act as a symbol for those men who entered the cold green forest ... never to emerge again.

The cruel battle for this Forest raged throughout the Fall and into the winter months and Graves Registration of FIRST ARMY and both CORPS did a more brisk business than at any time on the continent. In the 31 days fighting following the November 16 offensive to mid-December six German Divisions would be battered and FIRST ARMY casualties would rise to some 25,000 killed, wounded and missing; and more than 8,000 additional would become victims of the weather elements.

XII

FOR BETTER OR WORSE

Since beginning of the forest battle in early September the 9TH DIVISION had set an exhaustive pace which now was beginning to show. Following four months of continuous combat since the invasion an appalling turnover in personnel, a continuous upgrading of depleted vehicles, gradual deterioration of supply and attack routes, and probably uppermost, the depressing morale of "old-timers" . . . men who had already spent weeks on the line with no let-up was becoming alarming. Weary of mind, weary of soul, weary of perpetual responsibility . . . charting courses, crucial decisions, many having turned into disaster; creating new theories . . .all of these intangible factors were weighting down the top brass as well as subordinate officers. To continue the maximum effectiveness there could hardly be any choice but to give the entire DIVISION a badly-needed rest for rehabilitation. Surely no one was more aware of that than General Courtney Hodges, FIRST ARMY Commander, who on October 25 granted that relief. Plans were made and put into effect to pull the DIVISION from its' present battle zone and shift its' entire complement to a mild but alert reserve holding position in southeastern Belgium, several miles from the front.

"Tired?" replied retired General Craig to the author's question many years later. "Yes, that was it, just tired . . . but not in the exhaustive sense for there was a lot of spunk left in the DIVISION." The General, who was fifty three years old when he took command of the 9TH in August of 1944, went on to explain.

"It 's hard to imagine an entire Division becoming tired but when you consider that the 9TH had been on line continuously since the brief rest in late August you can well imagine the sluggishness existing not only physically but on the command level as well. All this in spite of many new replacements. We knew of course it wouldn't take long to regroup because the 9TH had been through this before."

Orders were immediately consummated and the DIVISION began on October 26 its' move from the present battle zone in Huertgen Forest's Germeter-Schmidt-Vossenach area. The entire complement would shift to an assembly area some forty miles south around Camp Elsenborn where it would relieve the 4TH INFANTRY DIVISION of a mild holding position on the right flank of V CORPS . . . a broad front extending some five miles. The 28TH INFANTRY DIVISION would replace the 9TH in its' previous battle position and the 4TH would be transferred into the VII CORPS zone further north. (The 9TH would continue active in this holding position but a few days, thence move into a reserve status . . . and rest!)

Now as the DIVISION was released from the murky Forest so we were from the Foret d'Eupen and Saturday morning of the 25th found us anxiously completing preparations to leave the Rhineland and move back into Belgium. Expressing no regrets we wriggled free of this rapidly deteriorating location, rolled southwest through Roetgen and followed the exact route (this time in reverse) back across the Belgian border and into Eupen that had been utilized almost six weeks previous when first we made our original entry into the "Fatherland."

An abandoned rug factory was occupied in Eupen and we thoughtfully called it "home." Unquestionably this was welcomed with enthusiasm specifically as it represented the first actual shelter in many weeks . . . the first roof structure over our heads since England and every advantage was taken of four pleasant restful days; days which brought about good food, dry bedding and welcomed showers.

In mid-morning of Wednesday, the 29th., the reluctant company again became a convoy and found itself for the second time within five days rumbling through rain-slicked cobblestoned streets of Eupen, thence directly south on the sagging and battered road that was to bear an over-abundance of military tonnage within the next few weeks. Barren in scope, the Belgian countryside in this particular territory bore a strong resemblance to that of the Rhineland. Noticeable especially as we entered the unfamiliar Foret d'Hertogenwald where tree-studded hilly terrain gradually becomes prominent and rises and falls as one approaches the villages of Hestreux and Dressart. Yet, ironic it was to note immediately out of the latter village the lowlands began to appear to become heavily dominated with acres and acres of marshes. We crossed two rushing streams, swollen far beyond normalcy . . . making up the Helle and Warche Rivers, wound through the narrow streets of Breverce and into quaint and busy Malmedy. The significance of Malmedy can best by remembered by its' unscratched setting of dignity at the time of our entry, to later bear a terrifying destruction in the turbulent weeks to follow.

On across the twisting Warchenne River at Malmedy . . . east through the important road junction of Waimes and Butgenbach, now north and around the huge and well-hidden reservoir-lake into which flows the Warche . . . we followed a tiny road winding through this poorly cultivated area that led us into the strategic village junction of Elsenborn. Almost a mile west lay outstretched . . . quiet, drab and deserted Camp d'Elsenborn.

Contiguous with the western German boundary this hilly southwestern region of Belgium was inclusive of that strip of territory ceded to that country immediately following the boundary revision policy emanating from the Treaty of Versailles in 1919. Dually linguistic, though speaking predominantly the German tongue most inhabitants, though friendly but unable to completely conceal an unfathomed allegiance to the Fatherland, did nothing to obstruct Allied operations, and were in fact for the most part friendly.

Situated on one of the most elevated locations in southeastern Belgium the former old Belgian Army camp prior to seizure in the late days of September acted as a maintenance operations base for units of the German Army that at intervals, darted in and out of here. The main thoroughfare, a gravel road ran straight through the reservation . . . from east to west, entrance to exit. Long before falling to U. S. troops it had been subjected to fierce artillery fire and received more than one tactical bombing from Allied planes. As a result, the camp . . . particularly vital thoroughfares, was in an extremely deteriorated condition by the time we arrived.

DIVISION Special Services made lucrative use of the single rehabilitated Post theater, running current movies and occasionally importing a live stage show. Appreciative though they were, if one could withstand the gross comments and "cat calls" from restless GIs directed at the participants on the screen or stage while in progress, and if one could focus his eyes strong enough so as to penetrate an ever-increasing haze of cigarette smoke then perhaps this entertainment could be considered enjoyable.

Due to antiquated and battered plumbing outdoor latrines continued to be used grudgingly. Although GI ingenuity managed to install a shower post, a perpetual breakdown was experienced due primarily to lack of proper parts. How anguished and distressed one became when halfway through a lukewarm shower the water would suddenly cut off, leaving him dripping with water and GI lather-less soap in an unheated shower room with near zero weather abounding! How hilarious it was to be nearby and hear shouts of infuriation and cries of distress! The language wafting from the shower room was strongly indicative of the frustration and agony that followed. It was funny! Funny, that is . . . until it happened to you!

On the 10th of November in a quiet process of relieving the 9TH INFANTRY in this sector and fresh from the United States by way of the United Kingdom, GIs from a newly-arrived DIVISION . . . their bright white and blue checkered shoulder patches easily identified as the 99TH INFANTRY DIVISION; were unobtrusively, though securely pitching tents and occupying ground within the perimeter of the Monshau Forest as well as east of and surrounding Camp Elsenborn. They would for an immediate time relieve elements of the 102ND CAVALRY GROUP, 5TH ARMORED DIVISION and 9TH DIVISION, allowing the latter, now in V CORPS reserve, to go into complete rest.

Throughout most of November and the early part of December this camp saw much of the 9TH billited within her boundaries, especially service troops, Engineers, Signal and related personnel, along with DIVISION headquarters. Units of the 376th. Anti-Aircraft Battalion were spaced at strategic surrounding locations. Though this complex was utilized partially as a rest area for infantry and other combat units, these troops nevertheless underwent daily drills, brief hikes, arms inspection and routine perpetual rigid training lest they lose their fine fighting edge.

***

During October the status of spare parts reached the lowest point in the campaign. This had particular reference to engines and engine parts for trucks of the ¼-ton and 2½-ton class. Recoil gun mechanisms suddenly became critically short and 155mm gun tubes just could not be found. Small arms weapons were not being replaced fast enough, to say nothing of an acute shortage of small arms weapons parts. FIRST ARMY had in fact, only received 18.2 percent of *all* parts requisitioned!

Something *had* to be done!

Something *was* done!

Closed factories were reopened and rehabilitated, and contracts were awarded civilian manufacturers! Little time elapsed before heavy artillery carriages and small arms magazines and parts were turned out in factories in Liege. Tires were manufactured and recapped and tubes repaired in the same area. Another factory specializing in rebuilding tires was opened in Paris as was batteries and medium tank engines in locations around the same city. A firm was named in Charleroi to rebuild mortars and mortar sites, and all over Belgium factory furnaces were rekindled to produce parts for grenade launchers, rifles and gas masks. Spark plugs came off small assembly lines as did defrosters, windshield wiper blades, shock absorbers and bayonets.

Garment factories did their job too, and soon we would fare as well as combat troops and be furnished wool jackets, shoepaks, overshoes, service boots, panchos and wool gloves.

In mid-October the gigantic Ordnance Base Depot opened in Paris, and even though the largest in Europe it would have problems too. Transporting critical items to the front was chief among them.

Because of minimization of the Luftwaffe new rail depots began cropping up at several points . . . Pepinster, Trooz, Herbestahl, Mangee and Theux, none beyond thirty miles of our location. Later Spa and Bastogne would serve well as depots. Supplies began to come in faster and by mid-November the parts and critical items picture had improved greatly. Throughout November FIRST ARMY would do well and receive 75-percent of *all* items requisitioned.

The 126th got down to business immediately and conscientiously sought to repair anything the DIVISION had to offer. Ray Twiss, a rangy six-foot-two Master Sergeant in charge of Automotive and a regular army soldier who listened carefully and spoke only when he had something constructive to say; along with T/Sgt. Harry Pitman, a pudgy Ohioan who always hoped for, but never expected perfection were continuously on the job and saw that extraordinary work was performed on essential types of vehicles just about as fast as Recovery could bring them in.

The Service section remained busy for a time, working all day and at times into the night welding steel "tacks," or for a better description . . . cleats to tank tracks to give them stronger traction.

In mid-November a sort of stalemate existed all along the central and southern sector of FIRST ARMY's line and it appeared that nobody was going anywhere for a while. Though it could not last and a build-up was evident we prepared to make ourselves as comfortable as was possible under the circumstances. While we were busy with our problems with relation to the war and continuing bad weather, back home in the United States emotions of another kind was in full swing as the ballyhoo of an national election campaign was fast drawing to a close. The first Tuesday of November found the American people going to the polls and early the following morning we were not too alarmed or surprised to learn that Franklin D. Roosevelt was elected to an unprecedented fourth term as President of the United States; having defeated New York's Governor Thomas E. Dewey by a wide margin.

Through the medium of Yank Magazine and the Army publication; "Stars and Stripes," we kept abreast of action and events in other parts of the world. Even at this time on the other side of the globe the Japanese were experiencing a turn for the worse as General Douglas MacArthur, having already returned to the Philippines was directing his task force in "mopping up" operations in Leyte. V1 and V2 rockets continued to cause some rising hysteria in southeastern England. Far to the east across the European continent the Russians were striking hard through Hungary, now menacing Budapest on the Danube . . . and rolling onto Yugoslavia. U. S. Air Force bombers continued their 'round the clock bombing of vital installations on Germany and the Japanese homeland while ships of the U. S. Navy kept up its' watchful vigilance, bombarding strategic targets as the situation demanded. General Mark Clark's FIFTH ARMY doggedly continued to escalate its' mountainous operations in northern Italy, while at the same time the United States SIXTH ARMY GROUP, having become operational September 15th, and under command of Lt. Gen. Jacob L. Devers was swiftly moving into the Vosges Mountains down between the Alsace and Lorraine sectors. The 1st. French Army, now functional was moving in to join this GROUP. British forces in Holland were all but bogged down in mud and General George Patton's U. S. THIRD ARMY, having encircled the ancient fortress of Metz and boisterously knocking at its' gates, was at the same time preparing a strong thrust to the Saar . . . slightly more than a hundred miles south of us in France.

Each day added a degree of severity to the weather and the late days of November brought the long-threatening snows that at times turned into a series of blizzards. Previous shelling and air attacks on Elsenborn ripped great holes in many parts of the camp; some several feet deep. Though a haphazard and apparently poorly supervised attempt had been made to fill them, the surface was in many unsuspecting places anything but firm and caused vehicles on many occasions to become alarmingly mired . . . some so helpless that additional motive power was utilized for their retrievement. Here, trucks were *really* feeling the brunt. Unprecedented demands were prompted because of deep mud that required numerous replacements to brake linings, brake hoses and especially tires. Much shrapnel lay scattered and embedded in the narrow roads causing innumerous flats to jeeps and trucks, all of which meant that somebody was working all the time during daylight hours, especially, even if it meant nothing but repairing tires!

Of a certainty similar elements and logistical problems plagued the newly-arrived NINTH U. S. ARMY who on October 22 moved into a zone in the northernmost part of the 12TH ARMY GROUP, just north of Aachen; between the FIRST ARMY to the south and the British 21ST ARMY GROUP on the north.

Commanding the NINTH ARMY, General William H. Simpson, now retired in San Antonio, Texas, well remembers some of those problems:

"We were still receiving additional Divisions to build up the NINTH ARMY to full or near full strength. We finally wound up with 3 CORPS and 12 Divisions (3 armored and 9 infantry). We sought elbow room in which to operate which necessitated an early attack on our first objective; Geilenkirchen, a railroad town on the Wurm River, to widen the Army sector. This was preparatory to the big attack that was planned for mid-November.

"Ammunition, particularly artillery was low and came at a premium, and so critical did it become that it became necessary to set up a program of rationed allocations in order to build up a reserve for the heavy battles that were to come. This system worked well and by the time winter was over the ammunition was no longer a problem. But, two of the major *immediate* problems was the unfavorable weather and ever-present mud."

Despite countless inconveniences we proceeded with great effort to make our billits as "homey" as possible. Hastily constructed, most of these single-story multi-roomed structures were equipped with a much-repaired pot-bellied stove, and replenished with a great quantity of charcoal bricks found in storerooms we enjoyed, indoors at least, an extended warmth that was not expected. Many dwellings too, were equipped with built-in bunks with covered straw mattresses. The former German occupants would never know of our full appreciation of these luxuries.

Darkness found all guards dutifully tending assigned locations. At times in the vast unlimited sky-obscured darkness . . . with all lights restricted, and without proper voice identification recognition could never be certain even while standing face to face! One could on the other hand on a clear night, marvel at the unique streaming white vapor trails etched high in the brilliant sky by formations of Allied bombers. How tragic it seemed that from this unusual beauty death would in a matter of thirty minutes or so, rain from those bombers on German cities! The R.A.F. dominated skies at night while daylight found the U. S. Air Force maintaining that position.

In France during the latter days of August our first introduction to the V-I self-propelled rocket came to fore. We were not in Elsenborn long before that introduction would develop into a close association and we would be subjected to Hitler's infamous "secret weapon" for the next several weeks! The V-2, a faster, deadlier and almost soundless rocket would not bother us in this area. It would however, hasten the death toll in England and the Germans were employing it at every opportunity. Prime Minister Winston Churchill spoke of their plight and gave a well-defined appraisal on November 11:

"The use of this weapon (V-2) is another attempt by the enemy to attack the morale of our civilian population in the vain hope that he may, somehow, by this means stave off the defeat which faces him in the field."

Released from several firing pads some seventy-five to one hundred miles inside the German border, some launching sites established west of the Rhine and others on the east bank, these rockets (V-I) at this point were primarily directed to fall into the Belgian cities of Liege, Brussels and Antwerp in an effort to disrupt Allied communications, destroy supply dumps and particularly damage and harrass port operations at Antwerp. While some believed them to be timed for release in the Verviers-Liege area where large formations of Allied might was concentrated, long range stability was never known to be among its better qualities and more than fifty-percent never reached intended targets. Crashing into open fields and meadows, exploding into mountains and lofty peaks and plummeting crazily into forests many tragically and unintentionally often terminated and exploded in populated segments of smaller towns . . . often in streets or private dwellings. The destruction, death and perdition following such an explosion is horrible to recall! Several locations surrounding Elsenborn suffered heavily the destructive consequences as did some U. S. military units.

The afternoon was late as we were making preparations for "chow." A dull roar came distantly from the east, gradually then quickly crescendoing to fill the air with ear-splitting vibrations. Hearts raced faster for everyone knew what it was! Because however, of its unusually low approach and moving with apparent great speed it obviously was different from the others.

"I knew when I first heard it that the thing wasn't going to make it," said Dick Felt, the wiry hollow-eyed staff sergeant from Flint, Michigan. "Don't ask me how I knew, but it wasn't just a guess," he remembered shortly after; "something told me; Felt, old buddy, you better start saying your prayers 'cause this is it! But I quickly thought; Good Lord, this just *can't* be! . . . Not yet! *It just can't be!*"

Someone shouted: "There it is!"

It was a cold day. It was cloudy and grey but visibility was not so bad that one couldn't clearly make out what it was.

"*Look! Look! Look!* came shouts.

We had seen them before. We had watched in almost trembling anxiety as they roared on over to continue their westward flight . . . to carry their two thousand pounds of destruction somewhere else.

The roar continued. But not for long! Then, with almost unanimous expectations . . . the sputtering began! The motor was quitting!

"God! Oh my God!" shouted one. "We're gonna' get it! We're gonna' get it sure as hell! *We're gonna' get it for sure! Man . . . this is it!*"

Suddenly it fell, spiraling in unpatterned zig-zags . . . much like a kite helpless without a wind, falling crazily to the ground. A frantic scramble followed; to where it would have made little difference for the devilish device was no respector of target areas! In a second it was down! Then a million to one chance came! Luck hovered over us again . . . as its final spiral swooped it out, like a paper glider . . . beyond the trees west of the camp.

The explosion was earth-shattering!

"KA-W-H-O-O-M!!" . . . a black pillow of smoke arose in the distance and we shuddered to realize that to somebody somewhere nearby the horrors of hell had been inflicted! It hit in the midst of the bivouac area of a service company of the 9TH DIVISION's 15th Engineer Battalion. Damage was tremendous! Vehicles torn apart and overturned and personnel quarters shattered and demolished! Injuries came to several. Tragic, yes; tragic indeed . . . but remarkable too that only three perished in the violent explosion.

One soon got accustomed to the jarring passing of the flying bomb, but the violent roar . . . suddenly giving way to staggered sputterings, denoting depletion of fuel . . . *this* became a terrifying signal that the machine was about to begin its' zig-zagging plunge, and then completely out of control could crash anywhere in the vicinity! This truly, then . . . became a signal to make a chaotic dash for anywhere . . . or nowhere! This too, if one had not already done so . . . was a commanding signal to say his prayers!

Though none fell directly in our midst we nevertheless throughout the full encampment watched some pass and watched some fall, and by this action there was little wonder why Camp d'Elsenborn bore the nickname . . . "Buzzbomb Alley."

Heavy snows long engulfing this camp had with their wind-swept drifts, covered several bomb craters to an extent that only if a person stepped in one would its' location be known. Sometimes, especially after dark and in complete blackout through a misguided step, a person could find himself up to his waist in snow.

To this end, a trench running the length of our company area lay alongside the road where all early morning formations were held. Some five feet in depth and perhaps two feet across, it too at times was concealed by a blanket of snow. Because of the short days a formation scheduled at six AM would find the company reporting in darkness.

"T-e-n-n-n-hut!" . . . Platoon roll call! Platoon report!

"First platoon all present and accounted for, Sir!"

"Second platoon all present and accounted for, Sir!"

"Third platoon all present and accounted for, Sir!" . . . and so it went. Announcements. Orders of the day from the C. O., etc.

"T-e-n-n-n-hut!" . . . a brief silence . . . then, "Dismissed!"

There then followed a frantic dash of disorder for the "chow" line! Neglecting to follow prescribed footpaths at the end of the trench or failing to locate it in the darkness . . . or in fact, simply forgetting the existence of the trench a scrambling melee developed as men stopped short and toppled on top of each other in snow-concealed ditches! Several mornings this reckless ritual was repeated, and with messkits and helmets clanging against another . . . some briefly lost in the snow . . . it became something short of bedlam! It was nevertheless, one of great fun!

As the last week in November began, rumors of discouraging proportions fell on our ears.

"Captain Orsenigo is leaving us?"

"Did you hear the rumor that Orsenigo is transferring?"

"Hey, is there anything to the Captain leaving the company?"

"Orsenigo leaving? The *hell* you say?"

These were but part of the "scuttle butt" whispers a few days before it actually happened. On November 26 it became a reality for through transfer we lost not only the Captain but 1st. Lt . John Wallace as well. Because he was a man not easy to get close to . . . either conversation-wise or socially, Lt. Wallace's performance was difficult to evaluate. We were however, unanimous in our reluctance to lose the Captain. No goodbyes, no fanfare, no speeches. He was one that did not require that. He slipped away early one morning in his jeep and that was it. It was not at all easy to see him go for somewhere along the line in the back of several minds it was felt that he had been let down. Why this feeling, one could not be sure. He was without question, fair. He was friendly and he was understanding, and he respected the GI as he would want himself respected. One could come up with any number of intangible comments, but one of the non-coms expressed it well. "He was," he said, "just a helluva good Joe." But when he went away we never saw him again.

Many years later in his Mount Vernon, New York home Orsenigo recalled:

"Hated to leave? Damn right I hated to leave," he said with some amusement; "and although I moved up to a higher command, that is; a larger company, I felt just like you guys would about leaving a group that you had been associated with for so long. After all, the 126th had a lot of spirit and remember, we had served a lot of time together and went through some pretty doggone anxious moments in those several months. We did have a lot going for us."

Folding his arms across his chest he concluded:

"Yes, I hated to leave all right, but a soldier quickly learns to adjust."

Botting stepped back in the Orderly room, remarking;

"Well, the 'Old Man' is gone."

"Yeah," came a reply from Thompson, the company clerk, a reply that seemed devoid of enthusiasm; "wonder who we'll get next?"

"Well, whoever it is he's gotta go some to measure up to the 'Old Man'." Stopping short for a moment he theorized: "But what the hell . . . it really don't make a lot of difference when it comes right down to it. We're still gonna' have to break him in anyway."

Just before noon two days later a jeep pulled up in front of the CP and out clambered a not-too short stocky officer neatly attired, except for a well-worn helmet, in field-dress OD's. Ostentatiously sporting shiny silver bars of a First Lieutenant; his jeep crammed with duffle bag, foot locker and bedroll he issued brief instructions to his driver and stepped inside.

"Hot damn!" muttered the First Sergeant peering from the front Orderly room window; "Looks like our problems are going to be over."

"Yeah," replied Thompson, glancing at his watch; "just in time for chow too."

Boldly walking into the Orderly room the new officer announced:

"I'm Lieutenant Weinberg."

And just like he had always been around, followed with a gentle but imposing command:

"Have somebody get my stuff out there, will you?"

Somebody did and we would be leaderless no longer.

1st. Lt . Bennie Weinberg, an alert ruddy "spit and polish" 33-year old Texan with short-cropped hair, recently from 4TH INFANTRY DIVISION Ordnance took command immediately. Already recommended for Captaincy he was an exacting and proficient officer, though nevertheless we would find him greatly lacking in patience. He was too, one that if prompted could reach a boiling point almost instantly.

"A good soldier? Unquestionably. But he was," as one of the officers suggested; "a sort of miniature George Patton . . . without the pearl handles."

Scholarly, balding 1st. Lt. Robert Howe from Independence, Missouri, bearing a perpetual smile smacking of a tinge of mischievery, and one who corresponded regularly with a hometown friend . . . Mrs. Harry S. Truman, assumed the position of Supply officer.

Lieutenant Weinberg, looking smart in his combat jacket and .45-cal. pistol strapped at a fashionable angle on his hip made his mark early as far as we were concerned when following a personal inspection of the company quarters the first night of his command, followed it with his summation during a special assembly late the next morning. Hands on his hips, his squinty eyes shifting from one end of the column to the other, and addressing the company in his Texas drawl, said; (in effect)

"Your records show you're from North Carolina. Well, lemme' tell you something. You're a hell of a long way from Carolina now and you sure as hell show it! How you've got by this long beats me!" He began to let it run full measure now. "I wanna tell you from the beginnin' that you're about the saddest looking bunch of sacks I've seen in a long time. Some of you are out of uniform . . . some of you are here at formation without your helmet . . . some without leggings . . . a couple of you don't even have your gun with you! What kind of soldiering do you call that? Some of you have only your knit cap on; and you *don't* make formations with a knit cap!"

His dramatic "dressing down" did not let up.

"Sergeant Botting and I made an outside inspection of the grounds and quarters last night and I noticed several of your 'winders' were leakin' (meaning inside light penetration). I want that corrected and corrected now! A couple of you when leavin' your quarters had your doors wide open without even dousing your inside lights. The Germans *would love* to see that! There will *not* be any more of that! You know what I mean? From now on all formations will be made with proper attire of the day and I've given Sgt. Botting orders to see that this is carried out or your tails will be ridden unmercifully until you do!"

With some hesitancy, he concluded:

"That's all!"

The Lieutenant, for a moment shifting his head at an angle as if expecting someone to answer him, turned on his heels and walked off. Botting, almost bursting with a desire to comment . . . but, like the soldier he was; reasoned better. He simply rolled his eyes in an "Oh Brother!" gesture, set his jaw firm and in an authoritative voice spoke loud and brief.

"All right . . . you heard the C. O.! *Dismissed*!"

"Boy!", we thought, "we hadn't caught so much hell since early basic days!"

Breaking ranks, a lot of grumbling took place and it would continue . . . though not openly.

"Was this 'Toughie' out of line," we wondered, "or could we *really* be deserving?" Further thought would have us asking ourselves;

"Maybe we actually had become a little lackadaisical, and maybe we *were* 'sad-looking sacks' . . . but it sure didn't sound good to hear someone else say it!"

Whether we liked it or not everybody now knew where the new C. O. stood and though liking it or not . . . we would as a unit . . . "smarten up," or stand the danger of a transfer!

Private William Muzbeck, a congenial but discontented cook from the Wolverine State, who through habit "bitched about everything that came down the pike" and whose physical ineptitude unfortunately presented an older appearance than his forty years, was, through exhaustion lost to the hospital . . . never to return to the company. Stephen Wickes and Robert Jones, two taciturn Privates but compatible young New Yorkers; Poughkeepsie and Endicott, respectively; became new replacements. We received additionally from FIRST ARMY's active replacment depot Corporal Willard Riley, a somewhat disgruntled Scotchman from Santa Paula, California; *short* on hair but *long* on dry wit; *disgruntled* rightly so, for at thirty-six years of age he already had endured eighteen months in Iceland before our company arrived in Europe.

***

On November 16, supported by the largest air attack in direct support of ground troops in history, the FIRST and NINTH Armies began their long-delayed Fall offensive on a gigantic scale. OPERATION "Q" (QUEEN) saw 5,000 mediums and fighter bombers from the 8TH and 9TH TAC and R.A.F. drop 10,000 tons of bombs along the front in areas from the northern Roer plains to a point below Dueren at the northern base of the Huertgen Forest. Selected target areas were established in the Eschweiler-Weisweiler industrial complex and the Dueren-Juelich-Heinsberg region and these specific targets included communications centers, roads and intersections, personnel and field installations, enemy command posts and generally direct support of ground missions. An hour-long barrage from FIRST ARMY artillery; almost 700 heavy guns, hundreds of tank guns, mortars and rocket projectiles that expended some 90,000 rounds of ammunition! At the same time NINTH ARMY fired over 500 artillery pieces. It was "hell to pay" for the Germans as only one can imagine, and because ragged clouds dominated the skies we could not see the great air armada, though for a long time a thunderous ground barrage could be heard rumbling far in the distance. Morning headlines of the Philadelphia Inquirer on November 17th furnished the American people a glimpse of the action:

"SIX ALLIED ARMIES SMASH AT GERMANY! 1,500,000 ATTACK ON 400-MILE FRONT!"

and to all its' readers, further elaboration followed:

"General Dwight D. Eisenhower opened the grand winter offensive against Germany Thursday, sending 6 Armies of about 1,500,000 men over the top on a 400-mile front behind the greatest aerial support bombardment of all time. More than 3000 planes, including 2,400 heavy bombers, and thousands of guns, each firing a round every 15 seconds scouraged the enemy lines ahead of the FIRST and NINTH ARMIES just before they attacked at 12:45 PM."

From Germany several weeks previous our exodus into a zone of closer Divisional coordination had of a necessity allowed for a temporary serverance from the 184th Battalion in VII CORPS. Though still under regional jurisdiction of 52nd. Ordnance Group we immediately became attached to Major Lester W. Schuler's 177th. Ordnance Battalion and on October 26th passed into the V CORPS zone. Activities would be coordinated with this Battalion until the 10th of December when assignment would put us back in VII CORPS to again work with the 184th Battalion.

The massive and important dams, embracing some 200,000 acres and controlling floodgates of the Roer River recently were under heavy siege by FIRST ARMY, though capture was yet denied. 9TH TAC dive-bombers sought to crack its' thick concrete shell, inflicting massive indentions and small craters but consequential damage was yet to no avail. An artillery forward observer, bringing a mortar-sight in for repairs, swore to us that through binoculars he had seen bombs actually "bounce off" the thick reinforced dam structure! This was later substantiated by official reports.

Now a strong military concept was fast-shaping that favored a broad front to press for an undaunted drive that would carry the Allied armies beyond the Roer. "OPERATION Q" was fulfilling that concept! By the first week in December the "Old Reliables" (one of 9TH's many references) was on the move again . . . ordered into VII CORPS zone several miles northeast in the Rhineland's Merode-Schlich area located some three miles west of Dueren on the northern ridges of the Huertgen Forest. It would take over from the 1ST INFANTRY DIVISION a position that in conjunction with the 3RD ARMORED DIVISION would attempt a spearhead thrust toward the Roer River. This relief changeover was completed by December 7 and in the face of this . . . the 126th. again prepared to roll.

It was very cold early on Saturday morning, the 9th., when our convoys rolled out of the muddy camp through the western entrance exactly opposite from which had been entered over a month previous. There was little choice but to move along a single twisting road that through freezing and thawing time and again became unevenly rutted and warped. Into and through a drab village called Sourbrodt we lumbered across a low dangerously eroded causeway that cuts through the windy frozen marshy wastes so prevalent at the base of an extremely lofty portion of southeastern Belgium, to finally come upon a key and familiar highway extending north to Eupen. Heavy flakes of snow having started so early and so swiftly in the morning was in a short period accompanied by hard-driving combinations of rain and hail . . . greatly reducing travel efficiency and considerably hampering speed.

"Boy!" . . . muttered many; "Is it *ever* cold!" It was for a fact so cold that in open vehicles the elements on some windshields froze. With icy gusts of wind searing intermittently few miles were encompassed before every single one of us were chilled to the bone!

Up through Eupen and on to the most important Eupen-Aachen artery moved the convoy, turning off on crater-filled back roads at Eyenatten. We again crossed into Germany at the village intersection of Lichtenbusch and in a short time picked our way into two small hamlets; Obr-Forstbach and Kornelimunster where thousands of feet of web-like communications wire draped helter-skelter amidst shell-pocketed structures told a story of American impatience. Though still very cold, the snow had stopped and only a thin blanket of white lay over the rolling hills. The roads, though hard-surfaced were in a crumbling condition and made the going very slow as we moved up an extensive hill to carry us a brief distance just short of Aachen. A heavily damaged concrete bridge structure spanning the tiny Inde River was crossed and we moved on into Brandt, a small town much less than a mile southeast of Aachen.

Some six miles southeast from debris-strewn Brandt over half-frozen muddy rolling terrain we moved into the battered old city of Stolberg . . . one of the Rhineland's chief industrial cities.

The rubble and shattered masonry was tremendous although most had been bulldozed in heaps to the side and we continued forward in search of a bivouac location. At the extreme eastern end of the city a cluster of several abandoned buildings was selected . . . most choked with crumbled brick, splintered frames and shattered walls although amazingly allowing almost unlimited space for operations. What once had been a proud corner beer parlor would now house the Command Post (CP) . . . and within a radius of two blocks all sections found suitable billits and work areas. Directly across the street east from the CP . . . in what appeared the only dwelling to escape serious damage, the kitchen and mess hall set up operations.

Following a long slashing siege and having suffered through unlimited artillery and mortar attacks, much light bombing and house-to-house combat, Stolberg fell to the newly-committed **104TH INFANTRY** and a RCT of the **3RD ARMORED DIVISION**. Straddling a key Aachen-Cologne highway, this highly productive city proved effective as an artillery observation post for OB units of the VII CORPS. Spurred on by ever-present mud and scattered debris and broken glass at every turn we laboriously toiled together and in time transformed these shattered quarters into a fairly liveable state. Discovering two firmly-constructed air-raid shelters almost hidden in the midst of this maze of disfigured buildings we would not know at the time the great security they would lend . . . not only from hostile aerial operations but from stray incoming artillery.

One of these shelters, located just within reach of the kitchen would prove its' worth on several occasions during "chow." While sufficiently strengthened with concrete and reinforced steel this shelter was designed to contain but a few people . . . perhaps a comfortable capacity of twenty at the most. We were forced on several occasions to seek refuge in that bunker . . . capacity limitations notwithstanding.

Midnight was perhaps an hour away and except for a few prolific card players, most had turned in for the night. Only the guards maintained a constant vigil, and vigil it was for it was a time of uncertainty. Hostile activitiy was fast looming as enemy planes suddenly roared in over the city . . . two at first, then joined by others that made it five. Sleep would become a forgotten word as those within range charged down steps, across streets and through doorways in a frantic dash for the shelters!

Diving, rolling, banking, fiercely strafing indiscriminately and bombing installations in a wide perimeter in and around the city the planes followed by dropping luminous flares that briefly lighted the entire area as if all city street lights had been turned on! Anti-personnel bombs fell and were scattered at will and multi-colored tracer missels spewed recklessly, hungrily searching for targets on the ground as the enemy apparently hoped to disrupt communications and destroy supply concentrations commensurate with FIRST ARMY's Roer River offensive!

A stream of missels tore into the messhall roof and into the adjoining structure! Plinking was heard when some ricocheted off the streets . . . and a tremendous repetition of hollow "KA-RUMP!" thundered a few yards away. Stomachs became as hollow as the explosions!

"Good Lord! What was that?" came a startled cry. "What the hell *was that*?!"

Trying to get under the flak, struggling in near suicidal efforts to zig-zag through the maze of fire the Germans displayed a fierce tenacity to wreak all havoc possible!

"Boy!!" marveled one excitedly, "Have those 'Krauts' got guts! This is wild! This is fantastic!"

"Yeah," replied another; "but what a bunch of unsociable bastards!"

Far up to the east a plane exploded in a flash that for an instant sent flaming particles down! Another looked as if it spurted flame and in the complete blackness, disappeared! With reckless abandon time and again a plane swooped down to surely as low as 300 feet . . . seeming to taunt ack-ack positions! Sweeping low as would be dared one could almost hear every piston violently throbbing in hollow pounding engines as FIRST ARMY's teeth-clenched, wildeyed ground-based anti-aircraft men, feverishly on the job countered with a hail of steel that one could almost walk on!

"*GET 'EM! GET 'EM! GET 'EM!*" came the cry!

30's, 40's, 50's and even 90mm guns that could reach up to almost two miles threw more shells than had ever been seen before as the sky was honeycombed with orange, white and glowing red tracers that literally turned the darkness into a fireworks of ear-shattering explosions! The din of noise was unbelievable! The flashes tremendous!

In the midst of this turbulence those in the shelter, while wincing at the great thunder outside endeavored to bolster their wavering composure to a great degree by singing Christmas carols! Armed with this fixed much-wanted confidence all in the bunker claimed the morale *never really* faltered. The other shelter, situated much further out of reach was not used. Strains of "O Little Town of Bethlehem, how still we see Thee lie" and "Silent Night, Holy Night" circulated inside the tight compartment. But outside, as far as these words were concerned, they had little meaning . . . for nothing could have been further from the truth! Maybe it was a "holy night" but it was hardly anything but "silent!" Spirits descended to an all-time low with those billited too far away to enjoy the asylum offered by this bunker. They had to endure the consequences . . . and they . . . had . . . a rough night! These spirited actions continued at intervals for over two hours, for no less than three occasions the men left the shelter, confident that the action was over . . . only to rush back when the planes returned for another trip.

Wee morning hours found the tempestous festivities reduced to one of tranquility and long before dawn "Jerry" must have recognized the failure of his ambitions. No one can say that "he" didn't try though; and perhaps some damage was done, but little did "he" know that each time "he" came around . . . we left our resting places and made a "bee-line" for the shelters! "Jerry" could not have been much more exhausted than we, as at near daybreak we began clambering out of the damp shelter for the last time, and though individual expressions were sober and subdued . . . they were many.

"Man . . . somebody really pulled the 'Krauts' chain last night!"

"Boy, I'm beat!"

"I'm sure gonna write my congressman about this crap!" . . . and more than one was heard to say:

"Man! I'm hungry . . . let's eat!"

Though in Stolberg this particular night overshadowed others we would not be deprived of these nightly interruptions and eventually this became nearly a matter of routine. Daylight harrassment was no exception and we learned to be alert from morning to night.

Several hundred yards west of this location a battery of U. S. 240mm guns were solidly dug in and at given intervals of the day and night roared thunderously at the enemy in the Eschweiler-Weisweiler area some 10 or 12 miles to the northeast. These were but part of the mighty guns backing up FIRST ARMY's thrust across the Roer plains. So powerful their velocity that even from the distance between their position and ours one's clothing shuddered in trembling patterns at each firing. As the night air was torn apart by each blast it was easier to maintain a positive degree of courage *knowing* that these great long-barrelled 28-ton destructive weapons, boasting a maximum range of some 25,000 yards and when in position projecting a 360-pound shell, was on our side.

Less encouraging though, was the stark realization that the enemy *too* possessed the equal of these weapons, and some several miles east of Eschweiler these guns were also in action, both for efficiency and in retaliation for FIRST ARMY's death-dealing "240's!" With a gigantic 280mm retractable gun mounted on a railway flat car with uncanny power to deliver a missel over 60,000 yards the Germans appeared to be engaged in a "hide and seek" game. With its' fearsome power this monstrous weapon upon firing recoiled and disappeared into obvious protection of camouflage. From this . . . with return of the enemy's hostile fire we found ourselves at times almost in the path of their artillery as it crashed periodically (not directly) but in and around this vicinity! We winced repeatedly as the hollow thunder of the enemy railroad gun indicated a projectile was on its' way and only seconds later shells were whistling overhead or on either side of us (though distantly) and we were greatly sobered to see explosions rising in puffs some distance to our north! Shouts of "incoming mail!" were loud and frequent . . . as on two occasions hits were scored on the glass factory several yards to the south . . . sending up a shower of shattered bricks and powdered masonry! Some exploded short of our area . . . too close for comfort, and deep in the battered city itself. There appeared to be no set pattern either day or night, for whizzing and screaming in dangerously close vibrations easily rattled our occupied buildings and we viewed with intense alarm . . . skeptical lest the next one "was it!"

"My God! We're caught in the middle!" came frantic reasoning. "That's what it is! We're boxed in!" Increasing in intensity for a time each looked to the other for a sign of solace or even a word that would dispel growing individual fears.

"Aw, what you guys worried about?" someone quipped; "it's just routine, it'll be over in a minute; we're not gonna' get hit!" That the validity of this comment was true one could not be sure, but psychologically it produced strong merits in suppressing anxieties. When someone broke the tight air of uncertainty and spoke in reassuring tones that smacked of just a thread of confidence . . . there followed a general feeling of relief.

Though the full emotional impact never reached a full crest the balanced composure maintained by the men of the 126th was commendable as all assigned tasks continued to be executed efficiently despite the unusually boisterous and intensive aerial interference and the perpetual exchanges of heavy artillery . . . even though we *were not* necessarily the intended recipients.

As Allied air power continued its' heavy bombing concentrations against the great metro city of Cologne . . . some fifty-five kilometers (35 miles) due east of Stolberg, we could on a clear night observe powerful beams from enemy searchlights streaking up from the city . . . frantically seeking to pinpoint a bomber, now tormenting the great Rhine city with destruction. In size percentage, Cologne then represented perhaps Germany's most heavily bombed city west of Berlin. Though we could not have been aware of it at the time, Allied ground troops were still some two and a half months away from that metropolis and it was almost inconceivable that we were so close . . . yet so far away. Moreover, crucial events were now in the making that would put us still farther away.

XIII

SURPRISE IN THE ARDENNES

The war on FIRST ARMY's northern and THIRD ARMY's central fronts was in full progress during the second week of December, but that dubious strip of snow-blanketed winding mountains and valleys making up the central and southern sectors of FIRST ARMY's domain was disturbingly quiet and had remained in something of a status quo for some time. Aside from an occasional flareup; mail call, chow call and guard duty were the chief proponents of a day's activity.

Some 75,000 or so American troops were maintaining a thinly spread line extending from the northern boundary of Luxembourg in a swaying line for approximately eighty-five miles north to just beyond the enchanting community of Monshau, a town just inside Belgium along the border that separates this country from Germany. Here, little more than a holding action was in progress at this time, save of course routine patrolling. Maj. Gen. Troy H. Middleton's VIII CORPS comprising two veteran but weary infantry Divisions; the 4TH and 28TH; and two relatively inexperienced Divisions, hardly having received their "baptism of fire" . . . the 106TH INFANTRY and 9TH ARMORED, held positions extending from Echternach (just inside the Luxembourg border) north. Making up the balance of that eighty-five mile front running in a "snake-like" course to and just beyond Monshau; two infantry divisions . . . the veteran 2ND and the little experienced 99TH INFANTRY, along with the 14TH MECHANIZED CALVARY GROUP were under command of Maj. Gen. Leonard Gerow's V CORPS. A wide unmanned gap, sticking out like a "sore thumb" existed between the exposed flanks that separated both CORPS. Things were quiet . . . but would not be for long.

Inactivity ended abruptly as this entire front exploded in violent fury in the bleak misty morning of Saturday, December 16! Unusually heavy enemy long range artillery barrages were reported very early in the morning near Roetgen, Monshau, Eupen, Malmedy, Verviers, and St. Vith; and suddenly from out of the forests, down from the hills steeped with snow and across snow-drifted fields German troops in white-sheeted camouflage came storming . . . armed with an arsenal of weapons that no one dared dream could have been assembled! "Operation Grief" was unleashed! The Germans, under direction of Field Marshal Karl Rudolph Gerd von Rundstedt, the former old Prussian German Army Chief of Staff who had commanded all western field forces when the allies stormed ashore in Normandy in early June, and again attaining command the first of September; launched in complete surprise a heavy counteroffensive against front line positions, artillery emplacements, command posts and communication areas at five vulnerable spots that began just north of Luxembourg City and extending almost to the Belgian city of Malmedy to the north. Though von Rundstedt now commanded all German forces in the west as well as the entire overall operation, actual direction of the offensive lay in the hands of Field Marshal Walther von Model, a wiry veteran who had experienced successes on the Russian front and who had masterminded the ill-fated German retreat from the Falaise gap in August. Comprising some 200,000 combat troops assembled three miles in depth on an assault front stretching for 60 miles, von Model in command of Army Group B based success on a simple pre-attack order:

"Quick exploitation of the successes of the first day of the attack is decisive. The first objective is to achieve liberty of movement for the mobile units."

Preceeded by well-trained parachutists from the 6th SS Panzer Army and backed by regulars of the 7th and 15th Armies and the highly elite 5th and 6th SS Panzer Armies, comprising twenty divisions making the initial assault, with ten more on alert and six in reserve . . . von Rundstedt gambled heavily on surprise, speed and unlimited firepower. To insure a complete sweeping success he insisted in fact, on nothing less than the total maximum that could be mustered by the Wehrmacht. As a result, in the first few hours appalling losses were suffered by American troops in this region! Forward units along General Middleton's VIII CORPS front; namely, the 9TH ARMORED and 106TH INFANTRY DIVISIONS, neither yet committed to battle of full scale dimensions caught the solid brunt of the blow! Their positions were encircled and enemy artillery literally hacked them to pieces! Caught completely unawares the veteran 28TH and 4TH INFANTRY DIVISIONS, stalwart as their records could boast were struck with so much force that they were quickly disorganized physically, mentally and materially and forced to withdraw! Further north in General Gerow's V CORPS sector the 99TH INFANTRY, in action less than two weeks, and battled-hardened 2ND INFANTRY were overwhelmed and quickly mushroomed into confusion! Lines were penetrated, troops were routed and many units disintegrated into almost annihilation before becoming cognizant of what was happening!

An existing low air ceiling offered the enemy a tremendous advantage! There was in fact, no ceiling; for an impenetrable fog hung listlessly below treetop levels and completely dominated the scene for perhaps some thirty square miles. Belgian-based American fighter pilots, exasperated and hungry to do battle could take no consistent action for days; and for each day . . . moreover, for each hour deprived of action, constituted a gauge by which enemy ground successes would be measured. Could our fighters have been fully deployed . . . could the ceiling have lifted twenty-four hours it is doubtful the German penetration would have gone into its' fourth day! Von Rundstedt doubtlessly calculated this risk, for lacking the necessary strategic reserves to doubly insure this thrust the weather factor appeared to have been systematically timed to the apparent plan.

"Hit when Allied ground and air forces can take no immediate retaliatory action," he reasoned. "Hit when obvious air superiority is contained and ground troops are suffering grossly from imbalance and confusion!"

The validity of his diagnosis would for a time prove correct!

Somewhere FIRST ARMY G-2 had slipped up, for the enemy's early success could also be measured by FIRST ARMY's complete lack of preparation in this sector. Under normal conditions even the most capable G-2 from any organization would not have suspected; for this mountainous region of the Ardennes with its' murderous dogged terrain was anything but susceptible to any major offensive by either side. There are no large cities in the Ardennes. Dotted with small villages whose winding streets restrict all major traffic to single lanes, troop movement as well as vehicular passage were certain to become easily blocked in villages at points of ascent and descent. Moreover, it is an expansive region where heavy rains abound . . . raw harsh winds sweep across the plateaus and lingering freezing weather is not uncommon. The ferocious snows already banked in some spots five to eight feet deep . . . brittle narrow single lane roads running up and down the valleys, hardly capable of supporting sixty and seventy-ton war machines and already dangerously impassable because of ice and snow . . . and thousands of acres of pine and fir trees so spaced as to present an almost impossible task for any opposed mechanized force to successfully break through. On the basis of this, expediency to troop movement . . . particularly on a large scale would appear to be exceedingly limited even in *good* weather. Only a completely dedicated or completely desperate field strategist would undertake to forego these elements and gamble for victory. Von Rundstedt fitted at this moment in both of these categories . . . and he was *willing* to gamble!

FIRST ARMY slipped up? Perhaps that was the understatement

of the war! General Hodges and his staff were simply unaware, certainly of its magnitude, as was 12TH ARMY GROUP whose Intelligence section had earlier reported:

"It is certain that attrition is sapping the German strength on the western front."

Field Marshal Montgomery's 21ST ARMY GROUP had blatantly stated:

". . . the enemy is at present fighting a defensive campaign on all fronts; his situation is such that he cannot stage major offensive operations."

Further; from SHAEF, General Eisenhower's G-2 had stated:

". . . the Germans are all but finished!"

Indeed, it had appeared that way! The best assessed estimates had reported some 4,000,000 Germans killed since the war started. They had suffered 1,200,000 casualties during the last three months and *better than one-half* of these in the west! Now with something like a quarter of a million enemy troops engaged in this offensive, Allied commanders were prone to ask . . . "Where the hell are they all coming from?"

The United States, Britain, and in fact the entire free world wondered anxiously what was happening, for complete reports trickling via wire services could not yet know the enormity of the attack. On December 18 the Durham (N. C.) Morning Herald blared bold headlines:

"GERMANS OPEN ALL OUT SMASH IN BELGIUM"
"Yanks Forced Back Five Miles"

This pretty-well reflected the message of all the nation's newspapers on that date.

Supported in strength by almost a thousand tanks . . . Tigers, Panthers, Mark IV's and Mark V's, most equipped with high-velocity self-propelled guns, and many with circled white stars painted on its' side; camouflaged so as to resemble U. S. Pershing's and manned by personnel in American uniforms. Hundreds of halftracks and armored vehicles roared into action, 1,900 pieces of heavy artillery . . . some motorized, a few horsedrawn; countless assault guns, assorted weapons and thousands of revitalized white-sheeted camouflaged highly-trained infantry, and in fact every last man, gun and tank that could be stripped from the German war establishment that may be pressed into the attack . . . all of which had been assembled amazingly in secrecy for this dynamic thrust. The attack in the first few days gained monumental progress . . . advancing far beyond anticipated dreams of this task force! Tons and tons of American equipment went up in smoke, hundreds of vehicles destroyed . . . hopelessly abandoned or ultimately captured and advances continued! There seemed no stopping the onslaught! Town after town was falling; Stavelot . . . LaRoche . . . Rochefort . . . Houfallize, each in time, to be reduced almost to rubble! Civilians caught in thunderous crossfires could not get out! *Here* the casualty list was mounting in sickening numbers!

Pointed straight for the Belgian city of Liege where lay FIRST ARMY's greatest supply dump the systematic thrust was part of a "blitz" strategy designed to stretch across the full breadth of Belgium to eventually engulf the vital port of Antwerp . . . through which American supplies were pouring. This accomplished, FIRST ARMY inter-communications would be completely incoherent and already overstrained supply lines could become severed. FIRST ARMY would fight desperately and see that this did not happen . . . and ultimately the drive would reach no closer than twenty-two miles southeast of Liege.

When asked by the author his first thoughts when positions were overrun, General Middleton replied:

"At VIII CORPS headquarters we registered no shock at all. We had been putting on a 'rubber duck show' . . . so to speak; trying to draw the enemy to the front. Because of our thinly spread line General Bradley had warned against it, saying that inasmuch as this area was not new to the Germans and there were many key points open to exploitation, we were only courting danger. One high ranking British general, reviewing the area, said we were absolutely crazy in our pretentions! They hit with 16 divisions while we were maintaining an 88-mile front with 3½ divisions, and although anticipating some kind of enemy 'push' we did not expect it to be that big. 12TH ARMY GROUP had feebly reported that a possible enemy breakthrough might be attempted along the NINTH ARMY front, but did not feel with the prevailing elements and impossible terrain that it would be true along the lower FIRST ARMY line. We really didn't know on the 16th. just what the Germans were doing because you couldn't even get a cub plane in the air due to the clinging fog."

The General was asked;
"Looking back on that bleak December morning, how would you now evaluate that same position?"
His reply required little thought:

"Of course I would make some changes. When one looks back on it, it was a blessing in disguise because it did shorten the war considerably inasmuch as the enemy threw his last best punch at us. That the drive would *really* succeed was doubted by practically all the German generals, even von Rundstedt himself. Only Hitler had faith . . . and that was blind."

At the snow blanketed resort of Spa some nineteen kilometers west of Malmedy and about an equal distance south of Verviers in the huge ballroom of the Hotel Brittainique, FIRST ARMY headquarters communications center, though far from suffering confusion was however bristling with excitement and vigorous activity! Hardly anything less would be expected for reportedly the enemy had hit massively at five places! General Hodges and his staff in constant touch with General Bradley's 12TH ARMY GROUP were feverishly trying to establish some line of defense in as many places. The fact that General Eisenhower had been elevated to an unprecedented fifth star on the 17th held little significance at the moment as battlefield responsibilities mounted. Strategic redeployment of thousands of troops now dubiously swirling in full battle would not be easy! Moreover, Spa would not remain FIRST ARMY headquarters for long as the Germans had reached to near the Ambleve River just below Spa, and enemy shells reaching to within close proximity called for a fast but orderly evacuation. New headquarters would be established some twenty miles northwest at Huy.

"How was the evacuation carried out?" Lt. Gen. William B. Kean (then Maj. Gen. and FIRST ARMY Chief of Staff) was asked. "Knowing the enemy to be so close and the possibility of a further penetration at any time, was there any sort of panic?"

"Not in any sense," relates the General. "We were concerned, yes; and we had cause for alarm, but so far as I could determine it did not show. General Hodges *was not* an alarmist, even during periods of deep concern, and his entire staff sought to emulate his example." General Kean continued; "In this instance no one exhibited a big rush and it was orderly . . . almost the same as an ordinary move. Our personnel were quartered in billits in several of the rambling cottages and former guest houses spread out in this popular health resort and I watched them pack trucks and jeeps in careful haste. At a given signal we moved in two convoys and my driver and administrative assistant and I waited until the last jeep pulled out and we fell in behind them. We were the last vehicle to leave."

Up at Stolberg several miles to the northeast and quite some distance away from the fury of the breakthrough, though minor in comparison we were having our own problems!

***

Winter's frigidity was everywhere. Snowdrifts piled high in spots; every bush . . . branches of fir and evergreen trees heavy with snow bowed helplessly to the ground. Each branch coated with translucent ice sparkled like diamonds when the sun dared break through intermittently. Roads were caked with ice and one either trudged almost knee deep in snow or walked very precariously in paths that were dangerously slippery with hard-crusted snow . . . and lacking the sun's penetrable rays, fast turned to ice.

Treacherous indeed were the icy roads and the sun did not always shine. One day in early December the Captain and his driver-aide were rounding an extended blind curve on a cobblestone street in Stolberg where from the opposite direction the view was completely obscured by a corner building. It was late afternoon. Clouds rolling low, were dark and dismal and it was cold, bitter cold. Streets were not only icy but a cold steady drizzle beating down made them even more so. At a speed of about 35 miles per hour the driver suddenly realized a possible danger looming should another vehicle suddenly approach from the opposite direction. The Captain had the same thought. Feeling the jeep suddenly slide a little the driver edged slightly over into the left lane for better balance and to avoid spinning. It took only fractions of seconds for the two to reach the same thoughts simultaneously:

"What if an approaching vehicle has the same problem!"

Suddenly the "problem" became a reality! There bearing down on them headon were three U. S. Sherman tanks partially straddling the middle of the narrow street!

"Good God, Corporal!" shouted Weinberg; "Hit the brake! Hit the brake!"

No order could have been so hopelessly inappropriate! Swerving to the right, then to the left and putting full pressure on the brake, the jeep, though speed subdued slid headlong into the lead tank . . . the giant 34-ton steel hulk skidding slightly with its' brake application against the icy street! The jeep crunched up almost like someone wadding a piece of paper! His steel helmet smashing violently up against the glass windshield, the Captain spun out on the icy ground! The Corporal, still hunched up against the steering wheel . . . more embarrassed than hurt . . . thinking, "Boy, *will I ever get* a tail chewing for this!" could not believe what had happened.

"My God, Corporal!" muttered the captain as he looked up, almost in slow motion, from the ground, "What in the hell . . ."

Disfiguring smaller vehicles obviously was nothing new to the tank driver as when slowly poking his head up from the open turret he appeared anything but non-plussed; saying, "Boy! these roads around here are slick, aren't they!"

On this day they were.

Though destruction was prominent in the crushed remnants of smaller towns in this region along the Belgo-German frontier, the inescapable traces of the Christmas season could not be shut out. Though in many instances a shambles, individual dwellings were restored quickly as possible to a liveable stage. Well-worn decorations were feverishly displayed inside while families solemnly made preparations to continue in the somewhat subdued spirit of the season. In Stolberg during the several nights prior to Christmas eve at times strains of Christmas carols in German drifted faintly through the cold and crisp air and during a night of quiet stillness more than once penetrated the ears of a GI sentry on duty. Children in innocence, oblivious of the war's seriousness waging distantly; gaily and enthusiastically awaited the coming in a few days of "Kris Kringle" . . . while those in the surviving villages just across the Belgian border awaited the *sure* arrival of "Pere Noel."

Because elements of the 9TH DIVISION was called upon to contribute its' experience and firepower in this fast and furious effort to halt and drive back the enemy it became necessary for the 126th to follow extremely close and lend its' ablest support. From DIVISION Ordnance Colonel Childs passed the "word" down and and the cold clear morning of December 24 found a shivering and discontented company preparing to move again . . . but this time *back* into Belgium to become a participant in the Ardennes Salient, which by now was well-known to all as the "Battle of The Bulge."

West from Stolberg we again crossed the rock-studded Inde River . . . rolling through the village of Eilendorf, thence directly over warped and broken roads into the ruined city of Aachen. The familiar Aachen-Eupen highway was utilized and the Belgian border was recrossed a few kilometers southwest of Aachen. One group of the convoy, already frustrated by treacherous frozen roads whose brittleness increased with each vehicle, experienced provocative "buzzing" by swooping aircraft that somehow managed to elude the alert "ack-ack". Several instances found this group dangerously halting, abandoning vehicles and dashing for cover in the nearest cove of safety!

The slippery spotty ice-encrusted roads at this point were jammed with vehicles now in the throes of redeployment . . . some moving to rear positions and some to the front. Long ignored was the order for seventy-foot space interval between vehicles. Shifting convoys often became separated . . . much precious time was consumed . . . parts of convoys inadvertently found themselves mixed in with other units . . . and at times, though rare; the traffic situation on these narrow low-shouldered roads found itself just short of chaotic proportions!

FIRST ARMY quickly authorized and put into effect a priority system that allowed strategic units to enjoy their road prerogatives, and when such units approached with vehicles properly identified it strongly suggested that convoys of a less vital nature pull off the road allowing free passage for those so marked. This movement was handled recklessly and at times violently . . . and rightly so for time was of essence! Many a stubborn or slow moving vehicle with less priority found itself smashed and disfigured by a priority-laden tank or heavy piece of equipment who in desperation did not have time to argue and used his road prerogative to the fullest!

ARMY, CORPS and DIVISION Military Police were everywhere and they had themselves a field day! Had traffic-oriented MPs known, they would have braced themselves for the worst . . . for between the 17th and 26th of December when the enemy counter-offensive maintained its' most critical period, forcing troop redeployment to reach its' highest activity, FIRST ARMY traffic headquarters reported clearance of 196 convoys, involving 48,711 vehicles and approximately 248,000 personnel. During that ten-day period it would appear that every single unit in FIRST ARMY was involved in movement!

Five miles west of Eupen we rolled through connecting towns of Dolhain and Limbourg, took a turn south from the latter and halted one mile from that point. A spacious two-story garage-auto assembly building . . . long abandoned, located on the swift-flowing Vesdre River was selected for our quarters . . . this location seven miles southeast of Verviers and within the confines of a sleepy little hamlet named Goe. This may not have been the proper time to ponder over it and perhaps it was purely mental; but it was *damn good* to be back in Belgium!

Christmas came and was well-celebrated with a highly welcomed dinner of turkey, apple pie and all the trimmings! It was a little reminiscent of home and though some of us griped orally, we were well-aware of the good fortune to be spared the ominous hardships endured by so many of our buddies who even at this moment were enduring the open cold and chilling discomfort of a foxhole. Some of us shared part of Christmas day in dwellings of Belgian family friends . . . and in so doing found a little bit of "home."

A week later with great enthusiasm we ushered in the New Year of 1945 with wine, cognac, music and *much* singing!

New Year's Day of 1945 was greeted hopefully by our seven officers and one hundred and fifty one enlisted men . . . unanimous in a view that a few months hence would see the end of the war with Germany.

But this day also registered the largest Luftwaffe air strike over Allied territory of the entire European campaign, a strike that destroyed over 100 Allied planes on airbases in Belgium.

Alertness very quickly became the watchword of every single one of us as soon as two factors detrimental to our security was revealed. First; and most important at the moment was an awareness of an ever-increasing infiltration of English-speaking German soldiers into the ranks of several FIRST ARMY units. Many having parachuted into Allied territory under cover of darkness had worked their way through unsuspecting lines. Properly dressed in uniforms from captured or dead Americans, bearing "dog tags" together with papers of identification, and boldly utilizing captured American jeeps bearing individual unit markings and displaying the well-learned GI slang with emphatic daring that in normal use was not easily detected, part of the plan called for one or two of them to slip in unostentatiously as a replacement in some depleted unit. High on the enemy priority list were communications centers, where they would learn vital information relative to position, unit strength, immediate plans, location of badly-needed supply depots and an overall general picture.

The success of the entire operation depended upon the enemy's ability to maintain the impetus of the offensive. It was imperative that he reach his objectives, particularly the Meuse bridgeheads, before Allied reserves could be brought into action. Furthermore, he had to strike with great rapidity in order to seize gasoline dumps and other supply installations before they could be destroyed or evacuated. American food, fuel and ammunition were highly important for without an abundance of these critical items the offensive could not succeed. Von Rundstedt had in fact declared that, "devoid of their capture, success of our thrust cannot be sure and accurately measured." This then, became a primary responsibility of infiltrationists.

Faced with this prospect that could *well* spell disaster, FIRST ARMY worked fast; too fast for the enemy, for millions of gallons of gasoline were feverishly evacuated by 10-ton semi-trailers and hundreds of railway cars. In the first forty-eight hours the well-planned work of the sabotouers did show some promise. A fraction of success was theirs for a brief period and this daring game gradually and surreptitiously ended. Most were apprehended . . . not however, before some appreciable damage had been inflicted. Occasionally a gasoline dump mysteriously exploded . . . vital roadsigns were changed, causing misdirection; an ammunition dump was blown up and to a small degree communications were entangled or severed to cause temporary disruption.

Army Intelligence presented several plans for apprehension and some were quickly adopted for counteraction. Relatively simple in its' form, the "roadside quiz" particularly proved effective. Roadblocks at strategic intersections, and at less conspicuous points by heavily armed guards underwent stringent supervision. Rigid attention was applied to each occupant of each moving vehicle. Irrespective of rank every driver and individual passenger was halted at this point and methodically interrogated by Military Police with such unassuming tricky and informal questions as:

"Who is Betty Grable's new husband?"

"Who is Lil' Abner's girl friend?"

"What cigarette is Two to One?"

"What does Eleanor's husband do for a living?"

"Who wants you to 'Come up and see her' sometime?"

The slightest touch of suspicion brought further questions . . .

simple but conflicting:

"Who is Number One quarterback for the New York Yankees?"

"In what part of Chicago would you find Brooklyn?"

"What would you do in the event an aircraft carrier flew overhead?"

"To whom did heavyweight champion Joe Louis lose the title?"

These were but a few of the many other catchy questions that were fired in rapid succession at the person or persons halted, and quick stable answers were expected! Rank was no exception; credentials did not matter and no one was excluded from 'on the spot' quizzes. No general officer, regardless of ARMY, CORPS or DIVISION rank, not even a top commander; in fact not even Field Marshal Montgomery or General Bradley himself was immune. This became almost a sure-fire method for eliminating imposters and one by one they began to fall! A soldier, American or British did not act "cute" at such questions; for deliberate failure would in a short moment find him looking into the barrel of a Thompson sub-machine, an army 45-cal. pistol or the deadly carbine, and into the firm face of an MP who demanded with authoritative expression:

"Soldier, answer the damn question!"

These interrogators had no time for foolishness for this was now a deadly business!

Another bleak factor with which we had to contend was a reappearance of the dreaded "Buzz-bomb." Last annoyed by this weapon over Camp Elsenborn skies, we would find this area no less attractive by its' presence. Though several air miles west of Elsenborn, Goe lay directly in a geographical line for these monsters to pass . . . enroute to Liege and Antwerp. Consequently, when passing over Elsenborn they would in a fast matter of minutes be thundering over Goe in quest of intended targets! Spaced at intervals of fifteen minutes early in the evening, their appearance as the evening wore on increased and the space interval decreased considerably . . . often to an average of one every five minutes for a given time. After midnight noticeably the firing halted.

"Terrifying! Terrifying!" recalls Bob DePrey, the skeptical "Hoosier" GI who in no way enjoyed the romance of war. "To look up at the orange-red flame spewing from the tail of those damn things against the backdrop of a black sky and endure that vibrating thunder, sent chills up and down my spine every time! And any man who says it didn't do the same for him has either got to be a liar or just ain't human!"

As was true in Elsenborn; many fell short of their target in this region. The beloved city of Verviers, seven miles west, was an unfortunate recipient on several occasions as these deadly robot bombs; bearing 2,240 pounds of high explosives, exhausted in flight plunged into the city to leave death and destruction in its' wake!

Tony Spaich, a dark-haired blue-eyed shop supply assistant, who stayed on the road a good bit of the time in quest of badly-needed parts; recalled a harrowing experience and noticeably his blood pressure rose as he first related it:

"Two of us in a jeep had just entered the city from the west one chilly afternoon around four o'clock at about the same time a "Buzz-bomb" roared in from the east. Already at a low altitude and suddenly losing power its' jet-propulsion engine quickly started sputtering and then quit altogether. Pummelling down in unpatterned spiraling and obvious indirection we stopped, realizing with swift horror that this very street . . . this very spot could in a matter of seconds conceivably receive the impact! I said to my friend, "My God, Butts! Here it comes!" The very thought was so great we almost fainted! There was no need to run, for with irregular zig-zagging it could hit any place! As we watched with hearts in our throats, down it came . . . into a group of buildings just two streets behind us! A thundering blast shattered windows around us as people, fearing the worst, cowered in prone and stooped positions!"

Spaich was careful to point out:

"One additional twist could easily have put it right in our lap! We picked ourselves up in a second, jumped back into the jeep and raced around the corner to the stunned scene.

A great cloud of smoke and dust had begun its' billowing ascent while a shower of bricks, mortar, powdered masonry and particles was descending over a wide area! For a moment, nothing seemed to move . . . almost like a photograph! People appeared to be in the same animated position as when the blast occurred! Shocked and bleeding faces projected the swiftness with which it had occurred . . . and screams were already in the air! A prominent textile factory in this mixed residential-industrial area was the direct recipient and within it's demolished hulk flames were licking hungrily to consume its' shattered remains. Frantic screams from survivors trapped inside sent passing soldiers (a truckload of American Negro GIs just happening through from a mobile shower unit) tearing frantically into the debris! Several perished in the immediate explosion and others trapped in its' aftermath, succumbed before rescue could be effected."

Horrible! . . . *God*! *It was horrible*! . . . but there would be many such scenes in the coming months!

The lofty heights of the hill several hundred feet west beyond our quarters late one evening became an unevasive target as a "flying bomb" failed to clear the top! This earthshaking explosion shattered some windows, trembled buildings and injected a sickening feeling into already diminished spirits!

The Sergeant-of-the-Guard reported that Herman Shaffer, an even-tempered GI from Indiana . . . maintaining his duties at Guard Post No. Two was no longer in a position to challenge anyone. The violent explosion had left him glassy-eyed and speechless.

Ray Setter, the usually spunky Automotive kid from Detroit *really* let it all go the same evening, when voicing his frantic displeasure before turning his stomach:

"Damn these bombs! . . . Damn the Krauts! Damn Hitler! . . . Damn the French! . . . Damn the Belgians! . . . Damn the whole business!" His vehemence spoke for all of us. At times it could almost rock one out of his senses!

The chill of that memorable winter of 1944-45 will rank with the most vicious when for a period blinding blizzards showed southeastern Belgium no mercy. Temperatures dropped far below any we had yet endured but particularly noted were the three grueling days and nights of January 19, 20 and 21st. For those assigned guard duty at night . . . "walking the post" even with a couple pairs of extra socks or extra shirts and often one or two additional suits of underwear failed to dispel the frigidity that simply had to be endured. Though thick combat boots, buckled at the side, had replaced the antiquated laced leggings the penetrable cold would not be denied. In the wee morning hours amidst numbing howling winds Lt. Prendergast, when making his rounds as Officer of the Guard received a very poignant reply, one that would express collectively the near zero elements, when in general conversation casually questioning a guard who was in the midst of his two-hour duty:

"Cold, soldier?"

"*Cold?*" replied the hunched-up shivering sentry; "Lieutenant, it'll freeze your tail off in a minute if you don't keep moving!"

Without the proper clothing . . . it *would*!

With the prevailing ferocity of heavy snows that turned off and on and continued severity of cold weather leaving the roads a sheet of ice, S/Sgt. Dick Felt, a former automotive parts specialist from Flint, Michigan had his hands full all the time keeping company vehicles maintained and in running order. Tire chains for wheel traction . . . towing chains for heavy equipment . . . replacing snapped fan belts . . . supplying Prestone anti-freeze for each machine . . . dispatching of each vehicle . . . all fell the burden of the 31-year old Felt and his able assistant, Art Fealk.

While the German counteroffensive on December 16 forced the Army to take up temporarily new defensive positions, relocation of most Ordnance units was speedily accomplished. Ordnance lost practically no supplies by being overrun and was able to render service and support at all times. Battle losses were heavy but Ordnance continued unbroken service. Favorable working areas in most instances allowed us to maintain great efficiency even during the worst of weather.

Detached service (DS) became vitally necessary for many throughout these crucial days and a few found themselves almost on perpetual leave from the company. Theirs fell the task of lending assistance to and evaluation and supervising repairs and adjustment of small arms, artillery, vehicles, guns and virtually every instrument used to punish the enemy. Here, experience paid its' way! But while performing these tasks with expediency these men were subjected to the same elements and same dangers confronting combat troops whom they were assisting.

Once, when on DS assignment with a segment of the 47th. Infantry Regiment, T/4 Ernie Koudelka and Pvt. Harry Regester found themselves boxed in an area of much enemy mortar fire and more than once cringed from countless tree bursts that showered their area with shrapnel. Little choice was theirs but to wait it out before budging from the spot! A chunky Chicagoan, obstreperous when he wanted to be . . . the 22-year old Koudelka could go for days without shaving or combing his hair and he was as tough as anyone around, but was quick to say:

"If you think them damn tree bursts don't make you say your prayers you just try it. Regester and me and some other guy just laid there under the wrecker and damn near cried as mortar shells cracked all through the trees! A nearby tank company was the target but we were caught in between and you could hear the metal plinking against the truck several times! I knew what Regester was thinking and he knew what I was thinking and all the time we were having the hell scared out of us!"

Though dead serious, a half-smile drew across Koudelka's face and he finished:

"When it was over Regester never said a word. I don't know what happened to the other guy. We just threw that truck in gear and got the hell out of there!"

Big Virgil Bishop, the happy-go-lucky character from Kentucky, who openly declared from time to time that he would "rather be hunting rabbits than 'Krauts' " . . . and always sporting a slight limp and ominously proud of those bright sergeant's stripes; with

Joe Buday, a short personable T/4 from Detroit . . . perhaps ten years older than most of the personnel, and who would before the winter was over lose the end of his right forefinger, while retrieving two incapacitated tanks near Elsenborn on orders from the 746th Tank Battalion, found themselves "boxed in" and unable to move for a time as enemy shells suddenly began pounding areas several yards west and around them. It was brief and no one was able to establish a purpose for only wooded acreage existed for miles. The sudden presence of a lone ME-109 swooping low at treetop level just above them added further mystery to the episode and when it banked and returned for another low-level sweep, mystery turned quickly to desperation!

Joe France, a three-striper more than once, and though one with a heart as "big as all outdoors" could when caught in a subdued mood get mean to the point of great concern. The 30-year old Kentuckian *could* get rough . . . and liked it that way, until . . . as he expressed it . . . "it *really* gets rough," endured considerable hours supervising and handling service repairs with personnel of the 899th Tank Destroyers. Bill Workman, a good-natured, long-legged T/5 who long had been identified with the kitchen personnel . . . though having recently joined the Recovery section, did because of a slight defect answer to the name of "Badeye," along with Ed Chrusiel, a slender almost frail T/4 who did his very best to endure the army's torturous field regimentation, and who surely would have at times chewed his fingernails to the skin had he not, in a moment of disgust, tossed his GI teeth into the swirling Atlantic enroute to England, seemed to age momentarily when experiencing what they considered several sharp "close ones" while working up close with the embattled 899th.

Able artillery men like T/3's bold-eyed Rocky Mico, the quiet Italian lad from Youngstown, Ohio; chunky Chet Harris, his short blond curly hair always unruly and easily distinguished by his crisp Massachusetts accent; and Lawrence Bonnell . . . older, wiser and endowed with unusual diplomacy and a knack for getting along with everybody; and Carl Ross, a clean-cut alert and bright-eyed youngster who possessed a rare ability for always sticking to the brighter side of a problem, "dug in" with several units of DIVISION field artillery for days to make sure the great weapons continued to fire . . . and in so doing prepared to share the same fate as these forward units. The 20-year-old Ross, a fine saxaphonist in lighter moments, looked at DS philosophically:

"We were just as apprehensive as the positioned artillerymen but we figured what was good for them was good for us. Look; if trouble came, and there *were* many anxious moments, we were no better than they and would stay right there and stick it out with them. Maybe it sounds a little bold, but if they "got it" then we would too."

Jim Burke and Ted Jankowski, two industrious T/4's, along with Instrument specialists T/3 Harold Johnston, T/4 Sidney Veal and T/5 Buster York Runyon will not forget the thin line between life and death that dangerously confronted DIVISION artillery and infantry units daily. They know . . . for they worked under the same conditions with these units for several days! Al White and Martin Underhill, both T/3's and inseperable buddies, who with unusual sunny dispositions . . . tackled with ease any problem assigned them. Bill Scott, a brawny but ever-doubting T/5 worked harmoniously with these two in the Service section and the three were quite prolific in creating a winch-type device, that when attached to tanks would become priceless in supporting forced crossings of treacherous rivers yet to be encountered.

There was plenty of work to do in the company workshops too, particularly in Small Arms. Lights in the shop trucks burned late into the evening as some teams worked in shifts. Rifles, their front sights bent, some firing pins defective, stocks split or broken came into Small Arms section by the dozens. The heavy .30-caliber M-I, the heavier BAR and the lighter carbine were most prominent.

"With all these defective weapons, FIRST ARMY must be taking a break!" mused big Fred Hult, a fatherly T/4 who had learned his trade well some sixteen months ago at Aberdeen Proving Ground. George Frey, a slight personable Pennsylvanian who too had schooled at Aberdeen and who recently had earned his T/5 stripes, reminded Hult that FIRST ARMY would not suffer long for "we have plenty brand new rifles that have yet to be uncrated and cleaned."

"We really ran into the big brass today," reported Olen Hilditch, returning from a parts supply search. Near St. Vith, some 15 miles south of Goe where roads were shattered . . . it would seem . . . "beyond repair," where mud had replaced what was once asphalt surface. Where mud and grime having dried, saturated with rain and churned by multiple-ton vehicles so as to be turned into mud again; where "chuck holes" were created, filled and unearthed time and again Hilditch and the Captain's driver-aide were detoured because of heavy repairs being administered the main highway. "Two jeeps together pulled onto this perhaps half-a-mile battered road. Three bright stars set in a red background was attached to the bumper. We pulled to the side, almost sliding into the ditch and as they churned slowly past all hands went up simultaneously in exchange of salutes."

The slender sergeant recalled; "I said, 'Good God' Butts! . . . that's Ike himself!" A second glance and, "Hey, that's gotta be Bradley, too!" Sure enough, bundled in trenchcoats in the backseat . . . sporting three stars on their helmets sat the two great military commanders . . . Courtney Hodges and Omar Bradley.

Reaching Goe on December 24 we were assigned immediately to the 177th Ordnance Battalion. Under jurisdiction of 52nd Ordnance Group since September 1st we would continue in that capacity though now would be in V CORPS zone. Since December 20th the FIRST and NINTH U. S. ARMIES, for want of improved communications had after some misgivings been placed under command of Field Marshal Sir Bernard L. Montgomery's 21ST ARMY GROUP on the north. We as a small unit didn't feel much different in that now our fate for a time would lay in the hands of a British field commander. This status would remain in effect until January 17 when FIRST ARMY was reassigned to General Bradley's U. S. 12TH ARMY GROUP.

Never did there appear a time of idleness during this period, or better yet it could be said that we would not allow idleness to infiltrate. Though not always exciting offtimes some type of entertainment was created.

After hours two or three poker games always abounded and in many instances the dice were allowed but little rest throughout the complex. While proving interesting for many these prolific pasttimes remained unprofitable for others, especially those who having been "taken to the cleaners" suffered the inconvenience of remaining "broke" until the first of the month when payday rolled around. Stan Sieminkiewicz, the big blonde husky cigar-chomping T/4 from Saginaw was extremely adept at cards and everytime he got into a poker game good fortune seemed never to pass him by. He was loud, but by and large good-natured and big-hearted. "I'm not always that lucky," said he; "but when you tangle with this big "Polock" in a card game there'll be no mercy. The rich are gonna' get richer and the poor are gonna' get poorer!" He was often not far from wrong.

Ping pong games, a little boxing and self-imposed calisthentics kept many physically active, though when not on the alert most were content to pass the evenings listening to the Armed Forces Radio Network . . . now beamed in from Paris. No one ever tired of listening to the priceless humor of Bob Hope and dry wit of Fred Allen or Jack Benny. The great bands of Harry James, Tommy and Jimmy Dorsey . . . Les Brown . . . Tony Pastor . . . Glen Gray . . . Kay Kyser . . . Gene Krupa . . . Woody Herman as well as Glenn Miller's own Armed Forces band then headed by Sergeant Ray McKinley easily dispelled the drudgery of a hard day and the "Saturday Night Hit Parade" kept us abreast of the latest song hits. The lovable voices of Ginny Simms, Frances Langford, Jo Stafford, Frank Sinatra and Bing Crosby kept a sometimes sagging morale in high order, reminding all that better things were in store when the war was over.

It was a delight too, whenever a Red Cross Canteen servicemobile stopped in our location to serve a potion of doughnuts and hot coffee. The thrill was not so much the doughnuts and coffee as it was to exchange glances, quips and conversation with the uniformed American girls.

"Where you from?"

"New Jersey . . . Detroit . . . Houston . . . Atlanta . . . California . . . Charlotte . . . Kansas City . . . Brooklyn . . ." All the home names were the same and it really didn't matter where they were from; it just sounded good to hear them say it!

"You look a lot like my girl friend back home . . . your eyes, or something," was a stock statement.

"Yeah! Yeah! . . . sure," came indiscriminate replies. Maybe they did, but smiles and acknowledgement met with approval . . .

for it had all been heard many times before!

Evening was a time to catch up on conversation, to argue politics, adjust "pin-ups," and even do a bit of clothes washing. One could, for that matter do a little mending or sewing. It was especially a time to catch up on overdue letter writing. In the essence of brevity the popular V-mail forms were available, but as the evenings lengthened many yearned to pour out their hearts in lengthy pages to girl friends, wives and loved ones . . . despite the strong measures of censorship, and each letter before leaving the company compound would be thoroughly scrutinized. Be that as it may . . . FIRST ARMY's APO No. 230 continued to do a brisk business.

Armed with a few packs of cigarettes, a sufficient number of chocolate bars, a borrowed jeep and an interpreter some of the more "jazz-minded" sped to Verviers and did a little "horse-trading" . . . winding up with enough proper musical instruments to form a small band. From this transaction the company's own combo came into being, and henceforth called themselves . . . the "MUSIC MAKERS."

Recently promoted to First Lieutenant, Jim Black received on the second day of January jolting news of an impending transfer to another unit. On January 4 that order became a reality. The slight-of-build 24-year-old Lieutenant had been with us for exactly one year and yet we had sort of counted him as one of our original members, and though he had tried hard in his own novice way to be strictly "GI" his efforts were accepted goodnaturedly. Early morning of the 4th . . . sporting a fur-lined dark charcoal leatherette jacket he briefly shook a few hands in front of the CP, then climbed into a jeep and was on his way.

Replacements began to trickle in and on the afternoon of the same day, Harold Lovette; a slightly over-weight but quiet and immaculate Second Lieutenant from New Jersey joined our ranks. John Durham, a T/5 carbuerator specialist moved in from a 60th Infantry service company. From the 26th Ordnance, to whom was lost Lieutenant Black; and which company often incorrectly identified with our own came two different personalities . . . but both soldiers in their own right. Albert Maschek, preferably answering to the name of "Mickey," a former Clevelander and an old hand at supply administration . . . already carrying a T/3 rating, who no matter how vexing the problem or prolonged and grimy the encampment never failed to appear immaculate, quite like in fact one ready for a fashion show. "Had he been killed," jested one; "he probably would have been the neatest corpse in FIRST ARMY!"

In the same transfer order, Raymond Wright . . . a lanky T/5 mechanic from Iowa, was the extreme opposite. Short, busy George Diehl, a quiet taciturn T/5 fresh from 709th Ordnance . . . never seen when on duty without his carbine securely strapped to his shoulder, or having it always within reach when eating or sleeping . . . was, as he put it; "just happy to be alive."

Johnny Morris, the stocky 28-year old Tech/Sgt. from Jersey, who long had shown an inclination to display his imagined "ruggedness" and often openly expressing a desire to be identified with activities near the front, fulfilled one of his insatiable ambitions when on the last of January he was appointed chief of the Recovery Section. Now he could "legally" roam nearer the front! S/Sgt. Tony Puchala, an exacting inventorist . . . and one bent on keeping the Section on an even keel, took over as chief of company supply.

On roll briefly was 2nd Lt. Gerald Hall from the overstaffed 544th Ordnance Heavy Maintenance Field Artillery Company. So brief was his tenure (two days) that most of the company never knew he was ever in the area.

Monday, January 29 was sunny but cold and started as a day no different from any other. Only to Lt. Weinberg would it bear some personal significance, for before morning ended he would be elevated to full company commander rank. When emerging from headquarters shortly before noon he was no longer a Lieutenant for it was noted that firmly attached to his tunic and field jacket shoulders were the shiny silver double bars of a Captain.

A rash of accidents came at intervals. Sprained ankles, a broken arm, a light skull fracture were suffered . . . and more serious the loss of forefingers came to two different personnel.

Just outside the CP where several men were working the chilled morning atmosphere was broken with a tremendous "W-H-O-O-M!" Lineberger quickly joined Botting at the window to see several men rushing to the attention of one outstretched on the side of the icy passageway.

"What's going on out there? What the heck was that?" became a dual thought. Botting stepped quickly out the door and immediately recognized an air of urgency.

"Strickland just got his face blown in!" someone offered excitedly.

"Oh, my God!" thought the "topkick" as he hurried over to the stricken GI.

Unconscious, and a small emission of blood from the nostrils and along the side of his mouth could in no way tell the full extent of injuries. Rufus Strickland was an easy-going, good-looking kid from South Carolina and having just been promoted to T/5 weighed it goodnaturedly. With a welding torch he was in the process of cutting the top from a large empty gasoline drum whose fumes had not yet been fully released. The explosion knocked him back some ten feet and he fell in a heap when it blew up in his face! He was rushed to a V CORPS aid station and quickly evacuated to a field hospital. A very serious injury was diagnosed though the full extent was not known for a time, as he never returned to the company. We deemed it a tragedy for "Strick." Extremely amiable and personable, one would find it hard to forget his helmet-cooked "southern-brewed stews" in Normandy when chickens were more available, a stew so pleasing that as he expressed it . . . "just won't quit!"

We said goodbye to good-natured Louis Wolak, who with heavy misgivings was shifted to another Ordnance company that was short on experienced Recovery personnel.

(. . . Strong, robust and conscientious twenty four year-old Louis Wolak from Cicero, Illinois was killed at Huckswagen, Germany April 19, 1945. Louis can well-be remembered for his terrific appetite. That guy could eat anything, anytime, anywhere. He was an excellent sportsman . . . loved to sing, though unfortunately plagued with the knowledge that he "couldn't carry a tune in a box." Often when singing along with a voice on the radio he would stop short and say: "Boy! I wish I could sing like that!" The reply was too tempting to conceal; "So do we, Wolak, so do we!"

Most remembered of his traits . . . when the daylight details were finished and dark had long settled in, Louis could be seen roaming from section to section . . . visiting, conversing and just being a pal to everyone.)

***

Explosively the days passed . . . and the weeks . . . and long before the end of January the tenacious "bulge" that had put such a dent in southeastern Belgium . . . to say the least in FIRST ARMY's line; was by combined might of American, British and Canadian ground and air power beaten back across Germany's border and again the war was whirling on the enemy's own home soil. This concentrated Allied victory notwithstanding, a terrible scar had been left within a wide perimeter of southeastern Belgium frightfully exemplified by the almost inestimable damage inflicted on personal property and the hundreds and hundreds of civilians, who in the course of the holocaust perished or now lay maimed. Many fighting units had carved heroic names for themselves through the blood of fellow comrades . . . many of whom lay in FIRST ARMY's Henri Chappell cemetary, or still remained unaccounted for in some snow-covered areas.

Losing little time the FIRST ARMY commander, General Hodges, had placed Lt. Gen. Gerow's V CORPS along the northern shoulder of the penetration, who with four Divisions protected for 20 miles the vulnerable ridges and possible gateways along the Elsenborn-Monshau corridor. Lt. Gen. Matthew Ridgway moved his XVIII AIRBORNE CORPS into position on December 21 and went into action on the left of V CORPS . . . an immediate objective to check the enemy thrust along the Ambleve River. On the same day the VII CORPS . . . with it's back almost to the Meuse, directed a frontal attack stretching from slightly north of Marche some twenty-five miles all the way down to share an interlocking boundary with that of Maj. Gen. Middleton's VIII CORPS to the southwest. Units of the British XXX CORPS assembled in strategic areas not too far east of the Meuse on the west flank of VII and XVIII CORPS with assignment to protect that river and thwart possible crossings. Other British troops engaged the enemy wherever they were found and where further thrusts appeared conceivable. General Patton dispatched from THIRD ARMY the III CORPS with three Divisions to check a dangerous expansion of the German salient to the south while THIRD ARMY's XII CORPS, commanded by Lt. Gen. Manton Eddy, deep under the thrust of the Bulge . . . maneuvered with swiftness to protect the southern shoulder against possible collapse along the outer ridges and northern boundary of Luxembourg. Methodically and machine-like the United States forces set out with dedication and firmness to smash the counteroffensive and vowed ultimately to destroy all German forces in the field.

By the eighth day von Rundstedt recognized the imminent danger that lay before his troops and the counteroffensive was stopped dead in its' tracks! The enemy's greatest penetration in depth of sixty miles and a width of forty seven miles, both measured in terms of airline miles came on the tenth day of attack, and on January 2, seventeen days after the initial assault he had been fought to a standstill! By the time the Allies launched the main counterattack, the following day . . . January 3, the Germans had utilized 8 Armored and 20 Infantry Divisions, plus 2 Mechanized Brigades in the ill-fated gamble. The U. S. forces had in the field 8 Armored, 16 Infantry and 2 Airborne Divisions, and despite the slippery mud and icy roads . . . maintained a fixed purpose to reduce the Bulge.

Moving with determination and dispatch all U. S. and British units had performed well. "Crush the Krauts!" became the battlecry. Every battle was vital and each individual performance important. Service troops, Signal, Engineer, Transportation, Ordnance and even cooks in some instances were caught up in part of the battle. When all guns were silenced and the clatter of battle far removed, evaluation of strategic unit action came to fore . . . and when recorded many stood high! Among the more notable performances one could not forget the 7TH ARMORED DIVISION's gallant effort at the vital rail-highway town of St. Vith that could fill pages with individual acts of heroism. The determination of the 1ST, 9TH, 30TH and 99TH holding the northern shoulder along Elsenborn ridge stood out as a monumental highlight; and the 82ND AIRBORNE and 84TH IN-FANTRY DIVISIONS fighting see-saw skirmishes in the

Manhay-Marche-Hotton region was surpassed by none. Embattled, under heavy bombardment and encircled by three German Divisions at Bastogne . . . and faced with possible annihilation the 101ST AIRBORNE DIVISION exemplified magnificent courage to the highest degree when standing strong for several days and refusing to capitulate. The 4TH ARMORED DIVISION's slashing breakthrough out of THIRD ARMY from the south through enemy lines to relieve the beleaguered 101ST in Bastogne will long stand as a tribute to the armored forces. As battles are seen in perspective, military historians will not omit the dramatic three-day struggle ending on Christmas Day pitting Maj. Gen. Ernie Harmon's U. S. 2ND ARMORED DIVISION against the crack German 2nd. Panzer Division, which crucial battle halted the enemy's last great thrust and its' deepest penetration to carry the Bulge to Celles . . . a community seventeen miles east of Dinant on the Meuse. When this fight ended 2ND ARMORED had destroyed 81 Panzer tanks, bagged 1,200 prisoners and counted some 2,500 killed and wounded.

Unquestionably, the thirty-day campaign had been costly to the Allied forces. Approximately 59,000 casualties; 6,700 killed, 33,400 wounded and 18,900 missing. FIRST ARMY *alone* suffered 40,151 . . . and the U. S. reportedly lost enough equipment . . . food, clothing, rations, gasoline, and vehicles to equip two full divisions! But the Germans; *how they suffered*! Pursuing U. S. and British artillery and harassing fighter-bombers wreaked havoc, carnage and wholesale destruction on retreating columns! Whole convoys, jammed bumper to bumper were ripped to pieces and virtually destroyed as they streamed down muddy and cratered narrow roads desperately trying to get back across and beyond their own border! In only fair condition when the enemy smashed through on December 16, the narrow winding roads now having suffered an extreme over-capacity of tonnage for which they were not constructed; experiencing merciless bombardment from artillery and air, constant churning of thousands of tank treads and other armored vehicles . . . to say nothing of a natural deterioration brought on by weather elements, one would only have to imagine the horrible conditions with which the enemy had to contend while in near-chaotic retreat.

FIRST ARMY Report of Operations on January 22 accorded a harsh summary:

"The enemy was withdrawing rapidly. Reports from the air indicated most of his movement of trucks and armor was toward the east, with a great deal of the movement taking place during daylight. Convoy movements as large as 500 to 1,000 vehicles were observed. Below St. Vith this movement was especially pronounced, commencing as far forward as just in rear of his front lines from Crombach all the way down to the vicinity of Ourthe. Planes of the U. S. IX and XXIX TAC and British TAF reported the best day's activity since the invasion, destroying well over a thousand vehicles, fifty-plus tanks and almost four hundred military cars."

When it was over we were particularly appalled to view the plight of Malmedy, once a hospitable lovely community, who because of U. S. aircraft negligence suffered near complete destruction. With an established railhead at Zuelpich, Belgium the German 7th. Army concentrated heavy supplies and fixed communications. Zuelpich was an intended target for the 8TH AIR FORCE IX BOMBARDMENT DIVISION, but on December 23 through miscalculation six B-26's strayed off-target by several miles and hit instead the center of Malmedy to the north with tons of bombs! On December 25, tons of bombs from four B-26's of the same BOMBARDMENT DIVISION again through misidentification strayed from an original target and smashed the town a second time! It was a time of horror and though deeply regretted little restitution could be made to survivors and the many civilians that perished! To us who earlier had made friends in cafes and homes in the town, it marked a *personal* tragedy!

Malmedy would be remembered for another tragedy too, for earlier on Dec. 17 at an intersection just south of this town between the tiny communities of Modersheid and Ligneuville some one hundred twenty captured and disarmed American GIs were "massacred" by a forward Panzer Group from one of the first enemy penetrations. Strong in memory especially for this particular intersection was no stranger to many and had from time to time been used by several in our company whose primary function called for extensive road travel. With improper timing, on the wrong road . . . or even in this instance on the *right* road at the *wrong* time this dismal and dispicable misadventure *could* conceivably have included any one of us!

Conclusively, as the smoke of battle cleared away; though at the beginning brows of the Allied High Command having become somewhat furrowed . . . there was little question but the Germans had found "Operation Grief" a painful and most unprofitable venture. Years later in his post-war summation, von Rundstedt reviewed this operation as one of poor calculation:

> "It was a non sensical operation, and the most stupid part of it was the setting of Antwerp as the target. If we had reached the Meuse we should have got down on our knees and thanked God . . . let alone try to reach Antwerp."

It was a bitter failure and the failure was abysmal! Moreover; with decimation of some 200,000 soldiers . . . killed, wounded, missing and out of action from this operation alone, and the best of their legions on the western front shattered, shivering and demoralized . . . the heaviest fighting of Europe appeared to be diminishing.

XIV

DESTRUCTION IN THE RHINELAND

"Le Boche Kaput!"

"Le Boche Finis!"

That was the exhuberant cry heard from most every Belgian in the eastern part of that country! Having suffered through horrifying carnage and destruction during the past two months it was *more* than an expression . . . more than a plea . . . it was a prayer! Still, there was a good bit of truth in that expression. The "Boche" was somewhat "kaput"; he was booted out of Belgium all right . . . but . . . he was *not* yet finished! There were many rivers to cross, many foxholes to dig, many bombs to fall, millions of rounds of ammunition to expend yet, acres of real estate to be demolished . . . and thousands upon thousands to die before he would be finished.

For every practical purpose all of the air had been completely deleted from the "Bulge" and von Rundstedt and his shattered armies had taken refuge throughout the hills and bulwalks of the Rhineland. The highly-touted Nazi dream of rolling back the might of the Allied armies in western Europe had disintegrated.

The Wehrmacht was to be given no rest . . . no moment of respite . . . no real chance for regrouping! The very late days of January found Allied plans in the making for the beginning of a great frontal assault across the Eifel hills and Roer plains. This action would commence on the 28th. The late days of January also saw the creation of another American Army on the western front whose function at the moment would place it in reserve until full coordination could be effected. Leaving the V CORPS, Lt. Gen. Gerow, later to receive a fourth star, was given command of the new FIFTEENTH UNITED STATES ARMY.

This gigantic thrust would mean involvement of all combat troops in the American FIRST and NINTH ARMY regions as well as the British 2nd Army, most of whom prided themselves now as seasoned veterans. "Veteran" could easily be an overly-used inference, but in this instance its' application could not have been more adaptive for now looking back through the campaigns of Normandy, Northern France and the recent ill-fated Ardennes Salient, or the Battle of The Bulge no better description could be applied to participating troops than . . . "veteran." The 1ST and 9TH DIVISIONS, which according to General Eisenhower were his "two top combat DIVISIONS in the European Theater," could reach further than that . . . to the broad battlefields of North Africa and Sicily where the "Big Red One" and "Old Reliables" first came to establish a mutual respect for the other. There were many, many of those arriving from the States either with established units or as replacements, just in time to get caught up in the "Bulge." But by and large those who participated in this recent action . . . and survived . . . were more than prepared to accept any of the consequences that lay ahead in the battle for the Rhineland.

The 9TH's main objective now lay in the seizure of the highly important dams that controlled flood waters of the Roer River. Four major dams, representing a water capacity of 148,650,000 cubic meters stood as a prominent threat for FIRST ARMY's entire active front, as complete release of these waters could flood the whole central region of the Rhineland . . . without doubt *seriously* stalling advance of the Allied armies. The same four dams were attacked by air in early December but the effort was abandoned when the enemy attack hit on December 16. The very last day of January signaled the "jump off" for the 9TH . . . together with the 2ND and rehabilitated 99TH INFANTRY DIVISIONS. All three continued to operate in V CORPS zone, which command only recently passed into the hands of Maj. Gen. Clarence Huebner, now having relinquished command of the 1ST INFANTRY DIVISION. Selected to spearhead the drive in this sector this assignment would carry them into the Rhineland's rugged mountains and thick woods. Swift rivers and still lingering banks of snow would have to be encountered as well as the unenviable entanglement of the forbidding Monshau Forest.

The ever-informative STARS and STRIPES, endowed with an uncanny "nose for news" was aware of the drive also, and though datelined January 31 reported in part the following day:

"Three more FIRST ARMY divisions, the 9TH, 2ND and 99TH jumped into the assault on the Siegfried Line today and made advances up to four miles in bitter cold and deep drifted snows. By nightfall the fixed Siegfried fortifications were only about three miles away."

Though a tremendous undertaking for these Divisions who had within the space of the last six weeks experienced more than a share of warfare, a regrouping had been called for, and they were ready. When the 9TH on February 17 moved from V CORPS into the III CORPS zone of operations, General Huebner, now having acquired a third star, acknowledging fully the long combat relationship between the DIVISION and V CORPS; dispatched a letter of commendation to General Craig for the 9TH, which, in part expressed his feeling of pride and respect . . .

"By long experience in combat you have learned to beat the enemy at his own game. Recently you have defeated him on his own ground. The men of your command function with an ease of efficiency that mark them as Masters in the art of warfare. It is with regret that I accept the loss of the 9TH INFANTRY DIVISION to another command."

C. R. Huebner, Lt. Gen.
Commanding, V CORPS

***

This enormous concentration would mean the pulling up of stakes for hundreds of units; many of whom had been encamped in a single spot for as much as two months . . . not unlike that of a circus in fact, who having performed in the same location so long, pulls up its' equipment to perform in another town.

Early evening of March 1, following chow, Captain Weinberg in a brief assembly passed the "word" to us and made it explicit;

"Men, the party is over. We've had it pretty well made the past few weeks, but in the morning we're going back into Germany."

Lowering his voice a little and exhibiting that familiar uninviting flashing of eyes, he continued:

"Be prepared to move out around noon tomorrow, and see that *nothing* is left behind!"

Sounds of scuffling feet, barking orders and clanking of hammers and wrenches reverberated much of the night and the roar of motors became a monotony throughout the building as preparations to move out got under way. The next day found all trucks packed . . . sufficient rations drawn and dispersed . . . and quick goodbyes extended the many friends within the vicinity.

Whatever lingering forebodings one might have had with regard to going back into Germany were nothing that a warm nutritious lunch couldn't cure, and as soon as messkits were washed and the kitchen facilities assembled into the lone truck assigned that group we rolled out of the drafty garage complex. Across the adjoining sturdy concrete ramp that bridged the narrow ice-coated Vesdre River wheels of the convoy started its' crunch against the snow-crusted icy roads that would take us eastward. *Again* eastward into Germany . . . this time to slug to the finish!

From Goe the twisting Vesdre was followed for some six miles over a different route; one that approached Eupen from the southwest. A hard turn southeast of that town put us on the Eupen-Monshau highway that for a given number of miles was a stranger to no one . . . our convoy twice before having traversed it. South beyond Eupen some twenty miles we by-passed but moved almost within sight of Monshau, a town steeped with many legends and long-cloaked in mystery and one that somehow had been spared the *real* destruction of battle. Near the village intersection of Mutzenich our vehicles with an air of monotony again lumbered across the German border. We would from this point chart a course slightly northeast and would with dismal impressions, behold some of the most ravaged shellpocked landscape and battered dwellings since the Normandy campaign. Shattered bridges lay in twisted heaps and great jagged bomb craters dotted the fields! Several tiny communities were entered . . . each torn and bearing the scars of heavy battle. Every home demolished and contiguous property disrupted and greatly damaged. Rollesbroich, gutted and broken was but a sample of that noted along the next several miles.

Less than ten minutes after crossing the narrow rushing Kall River we were trudging through devastated Richelskeul.

On through the once-dreaded Huertgen Forest we moved . . . an eerie picture of death, desolation and violence and presenting a somber impression that hardly would be forgotten. Barely a tree, great or small was left standing in its' entirety . . . some blasted at the top . . . many reduced to shattered stumps . . . others suffering shell marks deeply implanted in the trunk. German and American motorized equipment and tanks, wrecked and helplessly incapacitated, their great hulks and broken tracks sprawling uselessly in grotesque patterns. An endless number of root-studded foxholes and splintered log bunkers were everywhere. Broken and discarded rifles . . . shell casings, entrenching tools, greatcoats, blankets, belts of ammunition had not yet been picked up. Boots, helmets, panzerfausts, unfired enemy grenades, (GIs *respectfully* called them "potato mashers") gas masks and much personal equipment was strewn helter-skelter by those locked in mortal combat during this stalemated slaughter that see-sawed back and forth for several weeks! This mute evidence was but a *minor* picture of the truculent struggle that had been the Huertgen Forest. If one wished to paint a picture of the perfect battleground he would have to look no further than the Huertgen Forest . . . for surely it could provide the setting.

Only patches of snow appearing now, the roads leading from this point became almost impassable for what had once been a solid earthen roadbed was now transformed into a pudding-like spread of mud. It was near four in the afternoon and the strong icy winds prevailing over this elevated region soon gave way to freakish hail; strongly resembling in fact, something short of a sleet storm, and lashing about us with unrelenting fury . . . seeming almost to punish us for passing this way. If *we* weren't being punished our vehicles surely were for mud was in many instances engulfing the wheels up to the axels! A sheet of ice beginning to form on the windshields of the lead vehicles prompted the First Sergeant to exclaim . . .

"MY GOD! *What next!*"

The vehicles' four-wheel drive gearmesh became the salvation for many. More than once a vehicle slid helplessly into a ditch . . . and became the very devil to pull out! Wheels spun! Mud flew! Men cursed! Tempers flared and frustrations exploded! Because of the tremendous bombardment widely saturating this entire perimeter many shell fragments littered the roads causing some flat tires and seriously impeding our advance, adding further frustrations that had already engulfed every driver.

"OPERATION Q" had helped tear this region apart in November, and weeks of consistent shelling, aerial attacks, heavy rains, partial melting of snows (only to freeze again) and suffering a hundred times its capacity of military traffic and tonnage had reduced the roadways to a state of utter perdition. This was; without exception, the worst route ever traversed by our company . . . and several anxious moments produced serious doubts that we would immediately get through! Reaching for his map case and after carefully tracing the route of march the Captain seemed a bit perturbed when remarking:

"I know one damn thing, this is one hell of a way to get to where we're going!"

It did indeed appear to be a wholly circuitous route, but a closer study of the map and a closer look of the battered and torn terrain would confirm that there was no other way.

Despite multiplicity of adversities . . . continually enhanced by harsh weather elements, we labored at our murderous grind through the Huertgen ridges and by time the gutted town of Germeter was reached we considered ourselves victorious in that only two or three flats were suffered and though experiencing several close calls not a single vehicle was abandoned to the mud. A brief distance beyond lay the town of Huertgen itself; splintered . . . hardly a shell of its' former being . . . completely annihilated! A church, gutted to ugly proportions; torn dwellings punctured with innumerable shell holes; horses and livestock . . . long decayed and decomposed would serve only as a starter to bear description. It seemed incredible a town could be so utterly disfigured! Yet, to scan back over the continuous unprecedented shelling, saturation bombing and armored skirmishes during the almost four months of battle in and around the Forest obvious answers were found for the wide-spread destruction.

Rolling through what remained of Klienhau where from a junction roads jut out in four directions . . . and pondering again if we would really get through this sea of mud we turned hard south and three miles beyond over bumps and gravel-filled shell craters now sunken and muddy, slowly plodded into a small community whose missile-scarred sign identified it as Brandenberg. Road shoulders were dangerous and the going was treacherous while maneuvering to carefully avoid a great number of mines that originally planted in the snow now were strewn about . . . lying ugly and exposed in ditches and on either side of the road. "Were they all detonated?" we wondered. Maybe they were and maybe not. There was no one around to confirm or deny and no one felt so inquisitive as to investigate! Four miles farther we were in Bergstein, a hamlet smaller yet . . . but little more than a heap of broken rubble.

A battered terrain in no way suitable for traveling, causing many delays and much inconvenience one only had to turn the clock back to the early days of December and picture the great battles that had raged in and around here. Only experience or wild imagination could visualize the harrowing days and nights suffered by GIs of the 8TH INFANTRY and 5TH ARMORED DIVISIONS who, emerging from tormenting days and nights of hell in and beyond the Huertgen Forest, and joined in the last days by a Regimental Combat Team from the 2ND RANGER BATTALION found no respite from the Germans in battling for these hills and ridges. Though roads already being infested with mines they encountered additional minefields intricately implanted and so

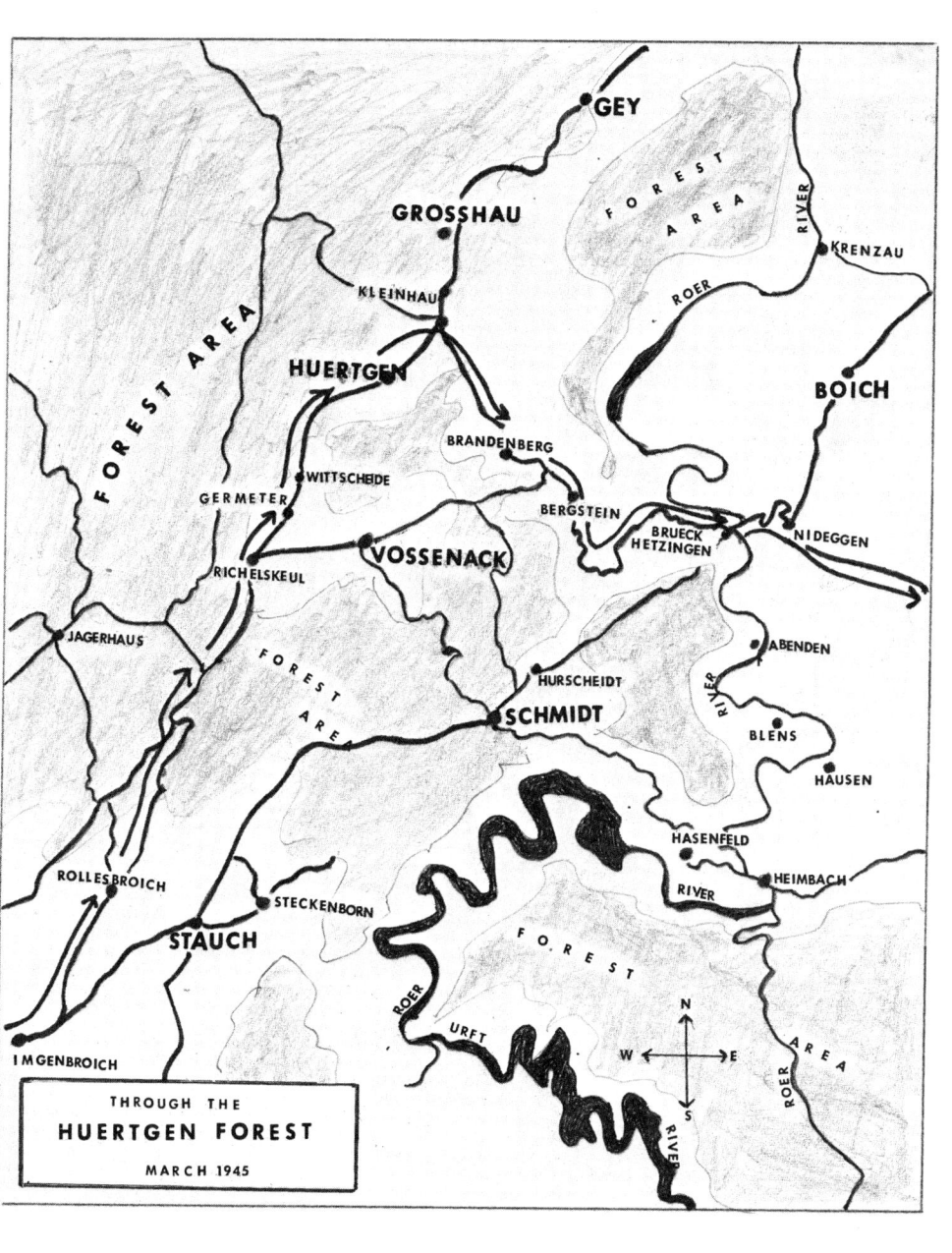

effectively blocking passage several American tanks met destruction when attempting to maneuver. Forward troops . . . suffering staggering casualties had to employ heavy fire to destroy barbed wire and log emplacements that concealed automatic weapons . . . only to find that immediately around the next bend was more of the same! The route, a former highway running southeast from Klienhau to Bergstein and loping along the spine of a ridge formed a narrow corridor between two woods. The fight for it was mean and deadly! Each advance was heavily paid for in blood and by the second week in December when Brandenberg was reached it took vicious hand-to-hand combat with tommy guns, grenades and rifles to flush the stubborn enemy from its' cellars! Bergstein was a repetition of the same!

Down broken eroded roads winding around precipitous hilly slopes and rounding a bend, we noted with respect a monster of a tank menacingly sitting astride a lofty ditchbank with its prominent 88mm muzzel looking right down the road at us.

"Boy! Just look at that bastard, will you!" exclaimed a wide-eyed Botting. "That's *gotta* be a King Tiger!"

"Wha'dya mean King Tiger? How the hell do you know?" retorted the Captain with a twist of tease in his voice.

"How do you know its *not*?" shot back the First Sergeant . . . a little indignant that he questioned. "Captain, I know a *little* something. Look at that damn '88 sitting up there! Those little tanks don't carry that around!"

Not as fast and maneuverable as the 47-ton Panther, the "Tiger" (PKW VI Tiger II) was the biggest and heaviest of them; weighing 67 tons and though slower in speed than the U. S. Sherman, possessed side armor plate 180mm thick and 40mm top surface . . . making penetration extremely difficult. Carrying one '88mm gun protruding from the turret and two 7.29 machine guns in front, a shell from a 90mm mounted on a U. S. Pershing had been known to ricochet off the seven-inch front armor plate of this steel monster at 3,000 yards. It would take the big U. S. TD, the new M-36 . . . with its long barrelled 90mm moving in close and attacking the enemy's vulnerable sides to get the job done.

Botting continued:

"You see all these damn holes around here, don't you? That

bastard did it! Man, he'd knock out anything we could put up!"

"Yeah?" questioned the spirited Texan; "All except one. Somebody got to him . . . and looks like they did a right fair job. He looks *dead* to me!"

The Sergeant mumbled something inaudible. Nerves *were* frayed a bit but the C. O., caring not to continue the issue, only chuckled and muttered softly, almost to himself:

"Aw, Sergeant, for Christ's sake!"

The banter was getting a little out of hand and both knew it. A few seconds later, Botting; leaning hard against the back of the jeep seat remarked . . . half under his breath:

"Boy, that must have been one hell of a sweet target."

Several yards beyond around another bend that descends so suddenly the employment of foot brakes was necessary, we came upon the almost hidden community of Brueck Hetzingen in the flat bottom of the Roer valley where the diminutive Kall flows into the Roer River. Commandeering several battered but liveable dwellings on the extreme western approaches we would remain in the community for a brief period before attempting to cross the Roer; that swollen body of water now some two hundred yards up ahead to the east.

Completely deserted . . . a vivid picture of war's devastation was portrayed throughout. No single dwelling . . . no barn . . . not even a commercial edifice had escaped the tremendous pounding of artillery, the slashing of armor and bursts of small arms fire throughout this entire region. Cratered shell holes spotted the hillsides . . . many trees decapitated; their trunks churned and chipped by incessant and indiscriminate firepower. On an angled slope to the extreme southwest several wooden markers of apparent German construction mutely told of hasty burial of enemy soldiers and officers. Moreover, so desperate and furious had been bombardment and fighting, resulting in ultimate withdrawal that even at this time an occasional body was found that had not been recovered by Graves Registration troops.

Carefully placed signs warned of possible scattered undetonated explosive trip mines in several spots and until accuracy of FIRST ARMY engineer mine detectors completing a clean sweep, these questionable areas were carefully marked off with illuminous tape.

This would guide one to and from places that required only absolute necessity . . . and this was carefully adhered to. One wrong step could end in nothing less than agony . . . moreover, a ninety-percent chance of fatality.

Light rain fell almost every day . . . increasing by evening to a heavy downpour. There was in fact little relief from at least a continuous drizzle almost all the time. A cloudy nebulous curtain hung over this region and hardly was the sun ever seen during the entire encampment. Visibility much of the time was hindered and the fast-growing presence of mud was greatly enhanced that increased the misery of already chilly existing conditions. Treacherous yet was the rising waters of a small tributary stream of the Roer leading through this property whose overflow was bringing vehicular traffic dangerously close to a standstill into and out of the company area.

Why then, did we remain here. *Why*? Simply because there was no other place to go!

The slashing two-pronged drive following the broad Roer crossing kept all FIRST ARMY combat and service units on the move! New objective . . . *the Rhine*!

Dug in several yards on either side of this location and behind us highly active batteries of powerful 155mm guns ripped the dark night apart . . . roaring a constant message of authority to the enemy far beyond the eastern banks of the Roer! These positions were vacated and the artillery moved forward on the second day . . . so far distant beyond the river that only muffled rumblings were heard and faint flickering of flashes, much like heat-lightning on the horizon danced far up ahead. Though far away this was still indicative of the enormity of U. S. firepower! The progression of such advances strongly supported a signal for the 126th to move beyond the Roer, and though here but two full days we had *long* been ready to pull out.

The continuous swirling pace on the roads, most broken, gutted, warped, clogged with traffic, began to exact its' toll on drivers. Ever at the wheel . . . not only in convoys but on other assignments, two of them . . . T/3 Steve Koziol and T/5 Jay Stone, both suffering physical exhaustion were admitted to the infirmary, thence to a field hospital. Though far from stretcher cases they were nevertheless ordered hospitalized for several days and the company would be far beyond the Roer before they returned.

Shirley Patrick from Port Huron, Michigan was a cherubic good-natured but fidgity individual, who beginning his military service as a mechanic turned early to the kitchen simply because a T/5 rating was readily available in that capacity. During the months following the dark-haired dark-eyed 23-year old Patrick found it to his liking and his proficiency soon positioned him to one of the company's better cooks. In late February he was selected by FIRST ARMY headquarters to serve on its' galley staff and he would join that facility immediately. His departure was fast; so fast in fact that few goodbyes were extended.

The morning of March 5 found a heavy mist still hanging under an extremely overcast sky. We rolled, and some one hundred fifty yards farther found us in the center of this community's gutted remains that hugs closely the shoreline of the Roer. The panorama of shattered surroundings made one wonder just how furious had been the river crossing several days ago. How many casualties were taken? How great was the firepower? To what degree had been the tenacity of the attack, and in what way had if differed from other crossings?

***

Forcing a river crossing is never an easy task. Forcing the fast flowing Roer dominated at this location by strong defenses on the hills which rise sharply from the east bank would be one of the meanest. Aerial observation and III CORPS G-2 reports bore clear indications of enemy artillery and mortar positions on the high ground that "looked right down our throats" and all assembled troops on the low west bank. Flanked on the north by VII CORPS and on the south by VIII CORPS, all observers of III CORPS . . . now spread out on a seven mile front conceeded that to employ a crossing at Brueck Hetzingen would increase the casualty list tremendously.

The FIRST ARMY commander, following additional study and consultation with CORPS and DIVISION commanders ordered the attack shifted to the north where VII CORPS operated on a more suitable terrain . . . broad flat plains extending from Aachen east to Cologne, and where waters of the Roer flowed freely though with a little supression, and where crossing obviously would be less problematical. On February 23 the 1ST INFANTRY DIVISION was ordered to move north along the west bank into VII CORPS zone and bridge the river in that area. Having made the crossing this force proceeded to attack the enemy's northern flank . . . moving south along the east bank to an area where a bridge was thrown across the Roer allowing the 9TH INFANTRY to cross at that point. The 9TH in turn followed the same pattern; attacking and clearing the enemy south along the east bank to a point where another bridge site was established at Brueck Hetzingen, allowing the 78TH INFANTRY DIVISION to cross. It had not been easy, but that was several days ago.

Noting with some apprehension the precarious sway of the treadway bridge, caused by the river's strong current, Captain Weinberg muttered casually but with some misgivings:

"I don't know if we want to cross this bridge or not."

Botting egged him on, with a reminder that a "Purple Heart" might be in the offing if we didn't make it.

Dead serious now, the Captain turned and retorted quickly;

"Who the hell wants a "Purple Heart?" Now a little perturbed, "Is that all you guys think about . . . a damn "Purple Heart?" . . . I swear, you'd slice your own throat if you thought you'd get a medal for it!"

"Boy! Are *we* touchy this morning!"

"You damn right I'm touchy! Here we're confronted with a bridge that might fall in and you're talking about a medal!"

"Captain; just for the hell of it, I'm not interested in a medal any more than you are. Just in a kidding mood this morning, that's all. Now let's get on across before that MP over there gets on our tail!"

The MP *was* anxiously beckoning and we rolled over the span where the river looked to stretch some one hundred feet from bank to bank and in a spot where obviously shelling had been intense.

A tremble and definite vibration was felt as the tremendous turbulence of the swift current tugged at the bridge and swollen waters all but overflowing its' banks was greatly exemplified by the mighty cables attached and running taut from the bridge to two powerful trees supporting it against the ominous strain of the river's force. Rushing along at an estimated twenty miles per hour at this spot it was feared too, that one snap of the cables would mean disaster for the bridge and everything on it! It was unlikely of course that this would happen.

Grinding slowly and a bit tenaciously up winding steep slopes on almost insurmountable mired trails that once had been a road, though long torn up by tank treads one could readily visualize the extremely precarious undertaking this had been for infantry and armor preceeding us! Looking over and down the bluffs an angled drop of perhaps one hundred feet awaited the unfortunate; and at the bottom of these eroded treacherous slopes wreckage of some Allied vehicles and machines together with German equipment, including horses, were sighted . . . all having met swift and grisly disaster apparently from either slipping or careening from these lofty heights.

From the top we soon touched the southeast approaches to Nideggen where from our mobile position shattered dwellings could be viewed in the distance and which strategic town fell to the 9TH DIVISION a few days earlier.

There did appear beyond the western heights of Nideggen a vast difference in topography. Though not really cognizant at the time and doubtless cared less we were entering the *real* heartland of the Rhineland. Here a more densely cultivated plain would be noted and rolling hills all but disappeared allowing flowing rivers to be kept in check. There was however, no escaping the mud!

Nothing new was encountered that had not been encountered before. Rains came and went, perpetual mud and sunken roads became commonplace and littered wreckage told of retreating armies. The aftermath of war was everywhere . . . demolished homes and farmhouses . . . destruction of vehicles, tanks and artillery . . . their shattered hulks blackened and drooping. Fields and roads unearthened by mammoth bomb and shell craters was in wide evidence and a great number of splintered and discarded enemy rifles and ammunition lay in heaps. Noted too, were six American Shermans evenly spaced and blocking the left lane of the road whose 34-ton hulks now out of action and whose long-barrelled 76mm guns would fire no more.

Decaying livestock and horses littered pastures and roadsides. Still further, sprawled in death was a small number of German and American soldiers. One German soldier, seemingly with his back braced against the side of a ditch, his greatcoat turned up around his neck and his arms stretched straight upward seemed to be gesturing . . . "Kamerad!" Doubtless his surrender had not been shouted fast enough and rigormortis had set in . . . for he had been in that position for no less than two days!

Some roads appeared to be totally lacking in planned engineering and many so hurriedly laid that they were yet uncharted and several portions here and there were obviously marked off with the familiar white illuminous tape indicative of land mines that were yet to be expended. Across asphalt roads of increased stability . . . but so acutely in need of maintenance that many were in a treacherous sagging and cracked condition. We encounted several small destroyed bridges, necessitating time-consuming detours through muddy shallow riverbeds and open fields. The 126th. rolled through Berg, a strategic farm town and at this point crossed the narrow and swollen Neffel River. The heavily-pounded almost impassable villages of Wollersheim and Langersdorf were skirted to reach the bomb-wracked vital highway intersection of Zuelpich.

A chill wind was blowing across the plains now and though the distance had been short we were weary.

"How far have we been? How soon will we find a bivouac area?" Questions began to crop up and though we had only been rolling for a couple hours the creaking, slow grinding motorized march appeared to have taken all day. Map consultation put us for the moment just within the western approaches of Zuelpich. A halt was called to survey our position. It was however, an opportunity for a much-needed stretch, a brief cold "chow" of C-rations and later with trench shovels in hand many headed for the woods and gutted buildings for nature's private physical reliefs that had long been in the making.

Up ahead far in the distance could be seen a steeple still intact and part of the superstructure of archaic old St. Peter's Church, an edifice completed in the 13th century and long revered in western

Germany. Further north on the same hill distantly was noted an aged castle, remaining defiant and whose history dated back to the middle ages.

Almost a mile beyond Zuelpich a tiny river junction was crossed where the Roth flows into the Blet. Durscheven and Euenheim were entered and cleared without incident and early afternoon found us rolling into smashed Euskirchen, a former town of much prominence located on the Erft Canal. Along the battered streets it was a bit startling to note several German soldiers, apparently unguarded, clearing rubble. We looked . . . and they looked back.

An important rail junction; Euskirchen had been subjected to terrific bombardment by air and artillery until not one building was left intact! Where obviously stately and prominent homes once stood immaculately along the banks of the Erft, great shell craters of rugged ugly emptiness; strewn debris of plaster, chunks of stone, brick, shingles and splintered frames grimly and mutely told a story of transition. Several yards upstream drooped and twisted rails reached out in grotesque patterns from a shattered double track bridge spanning the Erft that in better times served transportation between Euskirchen and Cologne.

A treadway bridge span provided access over the canal, rumbling uneasily with the approach of each vehicle and some one hundred yards beyond shattered structures we were on the Cologne highway. A full turn to the north and two miles further we reached Derkum to occupy that road junction community. Though not the most suitable, our bivouac choices became slim indeed and a complex of private dwellings was selected for a temporary encampment.

Situated some 300 yards east of the Erft Canal and but seventeen miles south of Cologne . . . a great Rhine city now under heavy siege, Derkum was but one of many small towns and communities that having been ill-informed of the well-paced Allied advance labored much in ignorance as to its' rapid onslaught. Most townspeople felt it their duty to defend respective communities and basically unaware of disastrous consequences by failing to evacuate many sought fanatically to pursue this defense to the end. Ill-equipped with outdated rifles and faulty pistols and inexperienced panzerfaust teams who truly had little stomach for it;

absolutely devoid of any real effective advanced planning and embodying little or no natural defenses this resistance proved of no consequence and in most instances, tragic. Following the first or second blast from one of the '76mm guns mounted on the creaky U. S. M-4 Sherman the peoples homeguard, or "Volksturm" threw down their arms and surrendered. Despite its' distasteful use much enemy material was uncovered from time to time. In many towns, Derkum proving no exception . . . was found piles of rifles, shotguns, bayonets, knives, ammunition, demolition charges, grenades and more prominently, the one-shot anti-tank weapon known as the panzerfaust . . . that when used effectively could pierce seven to eight inches of armor plate. These weapons were turned over to the town's Burgomeister for subsequent delivery to the American Military Government.

Civilians who had in the past affiliated themselves with or assumed positions within the Nazi party, or those that bore sympathetic party leanings . . . or even those that had directed or assisted in slowing the Allied advance through this and other towns were very quickly singled out. This required temporary detention in a selected building where well-guarded and under wary eyes of the Military Police, personal interrogation was thorough by special forces of the now present AMG. If careful and meticulous screening found further usefulness to the Nazi "cause" no real threat they were released to their respective homes. If on the other hand any threat *was* noted it meant shifting back to a higher echelon of tribunal where further action would be meted accordingly.

On the other hand, the AMG also called together the "leading people," that is; the most responsible citizens and entrusted them with administrative duties. They in turn would seek out those with specific skills, especially in counseling so as to put the town on a new footing of stability.

Deep in the heart of this Rhineland territory the German people dared to dream of anything *less* than victory. Admittedly, never could one have conceived of the swift advance of American forces! Never would they have dreamed of the enormity of Allied power, capable as it were . . . of penetration so deep into this country . . . and the adamant and puzzled expressions registered on their faces could not belie their feelings!

No natural camouflage existing, the company dispersed into several groups and sought occupancy in abandoned individual homes and buildings, finding it necessary in some cases to move into dwellings presently occupied by civilians. Though an obvious air of discontent and animosity naturally existed these people never openly complained or expressed dissatisfaction in any way. They did in fact quietly and methodically resume daily chores and with a faint smile of uncertainty did at times manage an occasional nod of formality. A gradual willingness to extend services unfolded but only after our own exhibition of friendship was accepted. This was one of welcome for it meant cleaning of quarters and washing of clothes. Our rations appeared far more attractive than did actual money though most preferred cigarettes or chocolate or coffee, but for the most part we repaid them for these tasks with invasion currency. Though many took second looks at the new type German marks issued recently by the U. S. Military Government this form of American exchange soon became as receptive as had been in more friendly countries in the European theater.

From a forward FIRST ARMY Depot near Euskirchen Class II (food) rations were procured and warm meals would again bolster our morale against the chilling damp weather. Walls were knocked out and rooms widened to establish a make-shift kitchen in the waiting room of a battered and long-abandoned two-story railroad station, and dining facilities were arranged so as to easily accommodate the entire company at one feeding.

For two days VII and III CORPS heavy artillery batteries leveled barrages from locations around our encampment. By the 9th of March they had established new positions several miles forward so as to facilitate more direct fire into enemy positions on either side of the Rhine.

For the moment one could divert attention from the war's action and contemplate the plight of civilians. A devastating effect on pride and morale was without question, but one could not help but ponder the depth of their *real* feelings. Like the world coming to an end perhaps? For them . . . could this be true? How kindly were they looking upon this sweeping occupation of their country? What kind of inner reaction was registered with regard to the "barbarious Americans" wantonly digging holes in their fields, needlessly moving into field-stocked farmhouses, to say nothing of re-charting and ripping their roads to pieces? To what extent could one stand the swelling pain of standing helplessly by and watch reckless GIs from a "corrupt" foreign land severing and tampering with communications and in general destroying private property? A horrible nightmare! That's what it was! But, on the other hand . . . "*This just couldn't be*!! Invasion of the Fatherland? . . . Impossible!!" Did not the inimitable "Fuhrer" stress the impregnability of the "West Wall?" Did not Propaganda Minister Joseph Goebbels publicly and vehemently promise that no foreign invader could ever set foot on the sacred soil of the Fatherland? Did not Reichsmarshal Hermann Goering announce with all confidence and unequivocally that no enemy plane could ever penetrate the impenetrable German air defenses! But by the same token, was not the Rhineland remilitarized (though in direct violation of the Treaty of Versailles) . . . and wasn't defenses of the Siegfried Line strengthened beyond reproach! Then to add a seal to these highly plausible statements . . . each designed obviously to conceal uncertainties, one recalls reading or hearing of the synthetic boasts of Adolph Hitler at the beginning of his beastial reign, stating something like . . . "If given ten years no one would recognize the old Germany?" The reality of it was but a wild dream . . . yet there was irony in it for this earlier proclamation by the Reichsfuhrer was coming true only too fast! One only had to step back and survey its' ruins and say; "Yes, *Just look at it*!!"

Steel-rolled window shutters were shut tight on every shop, and increasing in prominence in every region of the Allied advance a white sheet or cloth of some description was clearly displayed on most buildings and practically every private home, a somber symbol fully emphasizing neutrality or surrender. What a striking significance of comparison! This drab signal of defeat against the bright tricolors of French, Belgian and Dutch flags now flying so triumphantly in western Europe, proudly representing liberation and freedom! It was *indeed* a contrast of extremes, for to the western Allies this country was providing an exception to the rule . . . this one had to be conquered!

Defeat is bitter and victory so sweet! Involuntarily the French and Belgians had tasted both. The Germans earlier had reveled in synthetic victories but would for a long time learn to live with this crushing defeat! Without question resentment resounded in the depths of every heart, and while this indignation fermented primarily because of deep national pride and deflated honor . . . in a great sense they too were being liberated! Liberated from a yoke of overwhelming pressure . . . from national disunity . . . from political oppression and terrorism . . . and from a disgraceful horrible war that never should have been. Seldom was this resentment expressed openly and very few would dare verbally admit their real feelings. In the obvious grim facial expressions it was easily detected as they watched in apalling unavailing disbelief and often solemnly stared through cold weary eyes of adversity.

Whether by choice or otherwise they were caught up in the monstrous wave that supported and carried Hitler to the crest of unprecedented totalitarian rule. As the wave descended it became their plight to follow him on his mighty plummet into the absymal pit of destruction and chaos . . . many in the meanwhile feasting blindly on propaganda that "all is well." When the *real* truth came to light it was too much to digest. Now that it was about over there would be those who would say . . . "I had no part in it!" Others would swear that their household "did not agree with Hitler . . . but what could we do?" Many were quick to say . . . "I had sympathy for the Jews . . . the Poles . . . the Russians and all," concluding; "But I had to turn my back." Moreover; "We did not know . . . we were not told the truth!" Much of this may have been true . . . but it was too late! It was a study of humiliation, a shattering of national pride, and summarily; it was a complete and horrible shock to an industrious obedient people whose armies less than two years ago basked in the conquest of many nations, occupying no less than three-fourths of the European Continent!

Even long after Germany had been flayed into submission; moreover, long after the war's ending many were inclined to allude to the obstinate though somewhat rational theory;

"We (Germany) didn't lose the war . . . we just didn't win it!"

The Nazi system was easy to denounce now. Oh yes! . . . and how many times did one stand up and repudiate it! How many stood long to announce vehemently that "I could never give any sympathy or encouragement to the Nazis nor exact any delight from those early victories!" Only from a fanatic would there be an admission of such a feeling! Not a bit unlike, for instance, Simon Peter who time and again announced undying devotion for his Master, and later wound up three times shouting . . . when the chips were down;

"I KNOW HIM NOT!"

"Who was a Nazi and who wasn't?" The whole countryside was probably crawling with them but advancing troops did not have the time or facilities to worry about it. As far as we were concerned it was inconsequential . . . for this still remained the job and responsibility of the AMG and they would in time determine who would or could make trouble. They did it methodically and effectively.

On the other hand, as events heightened and time hastened and as hordes of American soldiers poured along the narrow roads and broad fields deeper into the Rhineland and further regions of the "Fatherland" civilians began to view with lightened astonishment the carefree friendly gestures and the easy-going disposition that was characteristic of the American GI. They would soon learn that the years of propaganda pointing out the stupidity, the lack of discipline and henious nature of the American soldier was but propaganda indeed. Enlivened by an unexpected show of GI friendliness little time passed before a reverse in hostility was displayed and many cold stares began to thaw . . . to give way to much-needed expressions of warmth. In many instances, especially between civilians and German-speaking GIs a mutual feeling of confidence began to spark and with the passing of that crisis, particularly amongst rear echelon troops . . . the job of the GI became somewhat mitigated.

Pressing deeper into the Rhineland a revelation was noted to give evidence that we *too* for a time had labored under misapprehensions. There were some among us and many back in the United States, who reasoning unrealistically had harbored skeptical notions that within the Nazi doctrine little room was reserved for recognition of the Diety of God . . . and as a consequence church worship in Germany was experiencing a serious decline. Diminishing all over the country to such an extent that the mention of God rarely passed the lips of those formerly concerned. Had early Nazi victories reduced the German people to a state of apathy, and in so doing closed their hearts to the need of God? What about the individual home . . . what was the thinking here? Had family worship, long traditional in the greatest institution in the world, diminished? On the other hand; were many Germans fearful of open worship lest they be criticized by those with party leanings? "Germany," some of us had heard, "no longer worships God."

These unfounded assumptions, though repeated often, were never seriously accepted by us and during a discussion on the subject a reasonable conclusion was expressed by beefy Frank Linzinmeir, the philosophical Master Sergeant.

"Just think of all the massive churches we've passed as well as the smaller ones. Since we crossed beyond the Siegfried Line you see them everywhere you go. Of course many are pretty-well damaged and some destroyed, but my thinking is that somebody is bound to be attending these churches that are still available. We have, in fact seen this on several occasions. So, nobody is going to make me believe that these people are going to turn off religion that quick, especially with all the hell they're going through."

One would only have to note the great religious background of Germany to dispel any such doubts. Theologians, architects, composers, scholars, poets and writers of the intellect deep in the annals of Germany's history long had left firm and intelligent contributions that helped undergird that nation's strong religious heritage, each in time drawing heavily and humbly on that unfathomable source for inspiration and guidance.

What *was* true, however; was that while individual worship continued . . . freedom of religion *was not* allowed after the National Socialists came into power in 1933. The Nazis had promised to promote what they called *positive Christianity*. But this turned out to be a persecution of the Jews and forcing all established Protestant churches to unite under direct government control. A movement designed to establish a kind of nature worship, to be known as the *German* religion. This only accellerated the persecution of Jews and resulted in confiscation of property. Many later were driven from the country or killed. Many Protestant ministers and Roman Catholic priests were thrown into jail or concentration camps when they protested the anti-religious activities of the Government.

Along the continued eastward move we soon learned that the Rhineland region, though heavily Catholic was predominantly and historically Lutheran. Our thoughts changed from doubt to satisfaction as attention became focused more than once on the well-kept and impressive wayside crucifix shrines conspicuously erected at many rural road intersections. Moreover, on the walls of most homes was found meticulously framed some familiar Biblical inspiration . . . a symbol of strong family religious ties. In some instances too, was noted a reproduction or painting of Christ or the Virgin Mary . . . *proof* that individual worship continued in strength. Proof too, remained positive that individual feelings are basically the same the world over.

***

Cologne, the great Rhine industrial and cathedral city was toppling as VII CORPS gave priority to its' capture. General Collins sent elements of the 104TH and 8TH INFANTRY DIVISIONS with support from 3RD ARMORED to secure the city and GIs from those units were doggedly moving in to fulfill that order. At the same time further south along the Rhine in III CORPS northern zone the 1ST, 9TH and RCTs of the 87TH INFANTRY DIVISION were mopping up in and around the culture-shrouded city of Bonn.

Unless a physical connection linking the east and west banks of the Rhine was captured or abandoned (intact) top Allied military planners and observers skeptically envisioned forcing this vital river, this last great natural barrier protecting the heartland of Germany, as developing into perhaps one of the most violent efforts of the European campaign. Enemy possession of the high ground on the eastern bank was a paramount factor with which to deal. Advantaged with shorter supply lines and with fixed positions he could release everything musterable at advancing troops attempting to cross the river.

Embedded deep in the hearts and minds of the German High Command too was an appalling and undeniable fact that faced with piecemeal reversals during the last several days against the

Allied onslaught, this "sacred" body of water *could* very well be crossed by invading forces! While *indeed* "enemy forces could be slowed and discouraged in their quest for bridging," reasoned German commanders, irreversible evidence was all too prominent that in the end the swift advancing western Allies would *not be* denied that crossing. Even now there appeared little or no chance of the enemy holding the Rhine. It was an opportune time for presentation of some type of negotiable peace . . . remote as chances appeared. The High Command obviously was not prepared to do that . . . and the Germans would fight on. To hold at the Rhine then, represented their last hope; for . . . to lose this formidable body of water could conceivably mean to lose the war! Historically and geographically to the Germans the Rhine River means what the Don means to the Russian; what the Thames means to the English; the Seine to the French . . . or for that matter what the Mississippi means to the Americans.

As enemy and Allied field commanders, straining with binoculars in the fast brief decisive hours, looking across the river . . . studying positions and pondering immediate moves, surely an air of uncertainty swirled in the minds and hearts of hungry, beweildered and exhausted German defenders. Though most were cognizant at this point that no barrier, river or anything else could stop the Allied armies from spanning this wide busy body of water, they would nevertheless fight on! Uncertainty would have existed *indeed* had they been fully aware of the strong preparations for this great hurdle . . . ready by FIRST ARMY to be put in action.

Anticipating destruction of all bridges by a retreating enemy FIRST ARMY assembled in vital places some 100,000 tons of equipment that included great sections of treadway, ponton and the heavier Bailey bridges, 4,600 boats and 2,500 outboard motors had been drawn up. Some 215,000 feet of structural steel, 8,000 feet of chain, 315,000 feet of wire rope, 6,000 ponton bridge floats and 5,000,000 board feet of lumber was ready in waiting! Many heavy, medium and smaller cranes along with hundreds of assault craft to include LCVPs, LCMs and DUKWs were brought to the scene! Unusual indeed was it to see uniforms of United States Naval personnel so deep inland in the heart of an active Army war zone; but they were there . . . almost nine hundred, well-prepared to operate the 124 naval craft assembled along the region of the Rhine. All possibilities had been weighed and for the moment nothing was overlooked that would jeopardize the success of a single broad thrust across the river!

Instructions had been issued by General Hodges to the Commanding General of III CORPS that advancing units were to take advantage of any favorable opportunity which might arise for seizing a bridge across the Rhine. The infantry and armor operating under the 9TH ARMORED DIVISION were planning just that. Now an unexpected development was about to take place, a development deeply appalling to the Germans but one that would border on a miracle . . . certainly so far as the western allies were concerned!

The mobility of Maj. Gen. John W. Leonard's 9TH ARMORED DIVISION . . . in its' fierce drive to the Rhine in order to trap all Germans possible was one of reckless daring. Within the Kothen Forest on March 7th elements of that DIVISION were encircling a disorganized pocket of enemy in hard retreat several miles south of Bonn . . . almost within sight of the Rhine. On either side of this pocket armored infantry was fast reaching Remagen, an immediate objective . . . though its' future significance unaware. An ancient town of approximately 6,000 perched on the west bank of the river and located about twenty five miles north of Coblenz, Remagen is an equal distance south of Bonn. 9TH ARMORED patrols, gleaning through heavy mist from a lofty height looking down toward the river were shocked in almost disbelief to behold some distance beyond . . . the outline of a combination foot and railway bridge that spanned the entire width of the Rhine!

Swiftly transmittal of this unexpected prize flashed to 9TH ARMORED headquarters, thence immediately to III CORPS. FIRST ARMY received the message quickly, then on to 12TH ARMY GROUP where General Bradley pondered briefly a decision.

When asked his first thoughts when receiving the message of the bridge find, General Bradley said:

"A sudden shock. When Courtney Hodges called on the phone from his headquarters in Spa I had just returned to my CP. It took a few seconds for the impact to settle because it was a funny thing that I had been hoping secretly all day that a bridge would be found undamaged across the Rhine. You see, I was just like most of the rest . . . and Ike had the same thoughts, I really didn't think when we drew up plans for the Rhine crossing that we would get a bridge. We were in fact, prepared to make the full assault . . . though I never believed it would be quite as brutal as many thought, especially in view of the tremendous equipment preparations and the seemingly general collapse of the German following the "Bulge."

The General continued:

"Suddenly the real impact hit me and I advised Hodges over the phone to survey everything carefully and shove everything he could across. We would see to it that the bridgehead got plenty of air cover.

Another thing; not everybody was content with the bridge capture . . . skepticism prevailed in some areas. But I was so elated at the moment that I wanted to get down and cross it that very moment. Of course that was impossible and it was several days before I even saw it."

Remembering his first reaction to this now historic seizure, General Eisenhower recalled:

"I was at dinner in my Reims headquarters with the CORPS and DIVISION commanders of the American airborne forces when Bradley's call came through. When he reported that we had a permanent bridge across the Rhine I could scarcely believe my ears. He and I had frequently discussed such a development as a remote possibility but never as a well-founded hope."

In the few anxious hours that followed, combat teams of the 9TH ARMORED rushed orderly though cautiously into this area to establish a solid bridgehead. In a few hours the world would know this structure, spanning the Rhine for 1,069 feet, as the Ludendorf

Bridge; a single span double track impressive old framework of skeletal steel girders blackened with age and supported by stone-block foundations rising out of the water to gradually wind into 150-foot high towers, and looking out over the Rhine commanded a broad view in all directions for miles.

Quick decisions were registered and despite prospects of an enemy demolition blast, that coming at any moment surely would destroy the structure and anyone on it, replaced caution and the 9TH ARMORED gambling precious time against a precious opportunity decided to "go for broke!" This determined fighting force seized the initiative and against almost fanatic opposition smashed onto and across the bridge! A combat team from 9TH INFANTRY's 47th. Regiment at the moment in harmony with the 1ST INFANTRY DIVISION vigorously clearing Bonn some twenty-five miles to the north, was ordered to the bridgehead. Over rugged terrain in the dark this unit dramatically proceeded to engage in a nine-hour forced march to reach the embattled area. Temporarily attached to 9TH ARMORED this Regiment entered the attack and battled in force across the bridge in early morning of the 8th. Only then did Colonel (Maj. Gen.) George Smythe's 47th. "Raiders" realize the distinction of becoming the first troops of an infantry Division to cross! Two RCTs of the 78TH INFANTRY DIVISION were quick to follow!

The Germans in shocking disbelief surely *could* not and *would* not believe it had happened and for several dramatic hours vehemently used all means at hand to suppress the tide! But it was too late! The dynamic thrust of American forces and the enemy's failure to reverse it left little question that long before noon of the 8th this vital portion of the Rhine was now all but ours!

The news quickly spread to all units and our general reaction was simply:

"Crossed it so fast? . . . The hell you say? . . . Man, that is hard to believe!"

Electrified too, were the people back home when bold news headlines such as the New York Times' March 9 issue blared:

"U. S. FIRST ARMY ACROSS RHINE SOUTH OF COLOGNE"
  "Bridgehead is Firm; Most Of Bonn Seized!"

This represented similar headlines all over America!

In this fast and furious attack time very definitely became a principal element and with close support of 9TH TAC air units FIRST ARMY ordered as many troops as could be forced across the bridge. The gigantic assault plans previously arranged were sidetracked although some of the equipment would be used, but concentration now centered almost exclusively on this coveted span. In the few days following the initial crossing, division after division thrust its' might across the bridge as tanks, mobile vehicles, men and equipment jammed night and day in a bumper to bumper procession . . . in almost endless convoys to get to the other side. 9TH INFANTRY personnel performed magnificently in keeping all communications open from east to west and back across and Lt. Col. George E. Pickett's G-4 section maintained amazing control in constantly shifting transportation, materiel and supplies across the span. Commenting on problems and logistics encountered Colonel Pickett recalls:

"Of course the biggest problem from the beginning was consistency of enemy artillery fire directed against the bridgehead, and until these positions were located we would have to live with this problem. By the third morning these positions were identified, and almost by accident. The bridge was situated near a bend in the river and we could at times see muzzle flashes from light artillery dug in southeast on the high banks around this bend. Though silenced from time to time this fire cropped up again and again until our ground and air persistence forced evacuation of positions."

The Colonel continued:

"Despite erection of a pontoon bridge several yards upstream traffic never let up and both spans flowed to capacity. I still recall the orderliness of the operation both day and night, and this was amazing . . . for we felt that nowhere in the world does it get any darker than at that point on the Rhine! The road networks immediately on the east bank became a problem at times. Everything went uphill and with its' quick turns and elevated grades and forking out in many directions traffic could not move with complete simplicity. We were fortunate however, that no towed artillery moved over either span during the ten-day period prior to collapse of the Ludendorf bridge, for it would unquestionably have slowed operations."

Though the Germans in hasty retreat had exuded laxity in not destroying the bridge they had become awakened to this miscalculated blunder and by no means were asleep now! Commenting on this action, the German Home Service (DNB) in a radio broadcast said:

"The enemy in a major surprise thrust which by a lucky chance, succeeded in capturing an undestroyed railroad bridge. Successful German counterattacks have been immediately opened against the bridgehead and reportedly other Allied attempts are imminent." Of a certainty "heads would roll" as a result and in frantic desperation heavy attention was focused on the "lost prize!" Artillery fire in tremendous quantities pounded that vital link and the vicinity, several with astounding accuracy . . . striking the bridge. Fighter-bombers with fixed daring and in strength swooped in close and released bombs! Once at noon an impressive squadron of German aircraft appeared and in furious and savage maneuver dive-bombed, strafed and employed maximum tactics to knock out the bridgehead and its' defenses! Again, highly maneuverable ME-109's and FW-190's struck with suicidal fury! The efforts were breathtaking but futile! It was however, the largest formation of enemy air-power exhibited over Allied territory since New Year's Day! The increasing vigilance and accuracy of FIRST ARMY anti-aircraft guns, particularly those mounted on mobile half-tracks brought enemy losses in this bold display of hostility to staggering figures . . . contributing immensely to the already obvious waning of Luftwaffe power. Moreover; *never* again on the western front did an enemy air formation of this size appear.

Without question security of the bridgehead was immense! Large concentrations of "ack-ack" took a heavy toll of enemy planes each time they dared attack. Density of anti-aircraft fire surpassed by nearly fifty-percent that maintained for the protection of the Normandy beaches. Heavy clusters of "ack-ack" used for defense of high priority targets rather than dispersal throughout zone of action had proved highly remunerative in each instance since Normandy. Crossing of the Roer in February was a good example, and protection of the Rhine bridgehead was no exception. Concentrated firepower around vital targets resulted in greater attrition of Luftwaffe and when attacking areas heavily defended by "ack-ack" the cost of enemy planes ran high.

Barrage balloons further substantiated protection. In addition; 155mm howitzers, tanks, tank destroyers, assault guns and numerous automatic assault weapons covered the river from the west bank. Protective measures from underwater activity, small submarines and floating mines were thwarted by depth charges detonated at intervals. Nets were strung at strategic spots to deter possible demolition swimmers and suspected underwater mines. Even radio monitoring air waves in use by civilian or enemy military personnel were screened. Fighter-bombers at intervals gave strong air cover.

John Morris; the restless, sometimes impulsive Sergeant charged with responsibility of Recovery, returned from a trip to the bridgehead and reported with much excitement:

"You just wouldn't believe it . . . the traffic moving across that span is tremendous! There wasn't a foot of space between vehicles and equipment for hours, and man, you *talk* about "ack-ack" . . . that place is just busting wide open with it! A couple planes came over while we were there and there must have been a million guns shooting at once! *Damn*, what noise!"

Botting, unimpressed . . . asked:

"You sound like you went across the bridge . . . and I wouldn't be a damn bit surprised if you didn't." With a quick double-take he added softly; "You did, didn't you?"

Clad in a much-used slightly stained brown leather jacket, the self-styled adventurer . . . believing himself to possess much "savoir-faire" cocked his head back and with a facial expression contorted in his familiar "Who me?" manner, neither confirmed nor denied the inference . . . merely replying with an expression so as to indicate slight pain that there was any doubt.

"Why, Sergeant;" not particularly sarcastically, "how you *do* talk!"

"Let me tell you something, Morris," replied the Sergeant. "Now look; I've had it up to here!" With the flat of his hand extended across his throat he continued. "I mean . . . *right up to here* I'm through protecting you guys, 'cause one of these days the "Old Man" is gonna' get tough and he's gonna' throw the book right at you . . . and when he does . . . you're not gonna' have a leg to stand on! And," he added soberly, "I'll tell you one more thing; you better not come crying to me!"

A little stunned; Morris looked, disbelievingly.

The stocky "top-kick" was not finished, and pointing a stern finger at the bushy-haired adventurer he leveled his statement squarely:

"You think that's Tennessee maneuvers out there? You think you're out on the rifle range in Butner or someplace? I'm not going to make an issue of it, Morris; but I can tell you one damn thing . . . you keep it up and one of these days a 'Kraut' is gonna' pop up somewhere and you're either gonna' get your tail shot off or wind up in the middle of a fracas where you'll wish you'd never been!"

Sometime later Botting was candid in his summation of Johnny Morris:

"He was not lazy by a long shot and could when he wanted to, really be an effective guy. When he set his mind to it he could get the job done. No problem! But on the other hand, with his restless nature . . . when it came to 'goofing off' . . . that is, insofar as wanting to see what was going on out there . . . that guy had no equal!"

With most 9TH DIVISION combat units now across the river and other backup and service troops in staging areas awaiting crossing it became necessary for the 126th to follow. Now about two days behind we prepared to move down into the Remagen area for a more harmonious contact with the DIVISION.

Against a grey drizzly backdrop pushed by a chilled wind Derkum was vacated in mid-morning of the 11th as our convoys segregated into three sections and began the move southeast along the same highway route traversed up from Euskirchen five days before. Skirting around the gutted portion of that bombed-out rail center we followed the sagging asphalt road . . . now with chunks displaced here and there that pointed distantly to Remagen. At Cuchenheim the Muhlen River was crossed and from this point for a stretch of some five miles several detours were employed because of the main road's fragmentary condition. Multiple bomb craters, once deep and precarious . . . haphazardly filled with crushed stone began again, because of unprecedented traffic to show ominous signs of deterioration. Moreover, the abnormal flow of heavy tonnage that at this stage saw no end kept construction engineers jumping to keep all bridge spans to maximum strength. A road repair task force was on alert at all times.

The Scheiss and the Jung, two small rivers of little significance were hurdled. The enemy had left a tremendous amount of discarded equipment and smashed wreckage scattered along the route, and shortly after winding through Drees . . . a community all but leveled, we crossed the Stiefels River and rolled into shattered Rheinbach. Looking as though caught in a gigantic web, what with thousands of feet of Army Signal Corps communications wire entwined and entangled in and around every object useable, Rheinbach represented a vital crossroads center.

Less than two miles east of Rheinbach lay the even smaller junction of Meckenheim. Now in rubble; the roofless and skeletal walls with hollow blackened windows reflected a mute story of horror. Rather than retreat, an enemy troop concentration elected to make a fight of it here. Forced to remain or otherwise, civilians had not made an evacuation. Had a realistic report been evaluated of the crushing power of the Allied momentum perhaps this gesture of defiance would not have materialized. American artillery literally saturated the town and 9TH TAC was called upon for an air strike. The defenders of Meckenheim, by refusing to evacuate virtually committed suicide as bombs fell beyond, wide and "on target" to leave it a smoking ruins! Many, including a number of children perished in its' destruction. While returning to headquarters at Derkum from a "recon" assignment that because of detours made passing through Meckenheim imperative, two of our men related a crushing story of tragedy as they saw some of the children still being dug and retrieved from the debris.

Roads were better up ahead and flat country began to give way to a more hilly terrain. Womersdorf, Ersdorf, Gelsdorf and Ringen were put in the distance without incident. The Altendorfer and Swist Rivers were crossed, their swift waters and high banks twisting eastward to the Rhine, and by late afternoon descending from the western heights, the three-sectioned convoy, now close together looked down on its' immediate destination . . . the prewar resort town of Bad Neuenahr on the Ahr River.

Situated but five miles short of Remagen Bad Neuenahr rated high amongst vacation-oriented towns in the Rhineland, and its' many cottages and guest hotels of alpine decor was "made to order" for hundreds of American troops awaiting orders to cross the Ludendorf bridge. Captured by the 9TH ARMORED DIVISION March 7 convoy after convoy halted here; some camping openly and others finding brief comfort in fully utilizing individual dwellings.

Almost overnight winter's last gasps were fading and noticeably warm winds started to hint that Spring was only days away. To some in fact, Spring did come sooner than expected, for displaying a premature enthusiasm several GIs on a warm day couldn't resist the beckoning waters in the narrow Ahr River that flowed lazily through the town to empty into the Rhine. To look down on this lovely resort from the surrounding heights would represent a painter's dream. Situated in a shallow valley of near-green and endowed with meticulously patterned well-spaced trees, a natural camouflage advantage was upheld that obviously less imperiled chances of air attack. Enemy "recon" planes, though never failing in nightly visits did little more than swoop over and race their motors. Once, however, a fighter ventured in and doubtless through indecision and without a specific target . . . dropped one bomb at the far western end of the community. Little or no damage was inflicted and not one injury was reported. With the opportune concentrations of U. S. troops and materiel one questioned the Luftwaffe's hesitancy to saturate this region with at least one major attack. Suffice it to say the aircraft could not be spared and were badly needed to bolster defending troops on the other side of the Rhine.

A complex of rambling old buildings identified as "Apollinaris

Mineral Distillery" would serve for a time as company quarters. Located on the east end of Bad Neuenahr this British-owned distillery of varying degrees of mineral water was abandoned intact by the owners and throughout its' vast productive and storage sheds sufficient space for indoor quarters, shop and service facilities for artillery and vehicle repair would be arranged. In a brick three-story administration building facing the main east-west road the 126th, would on the first floor establish headquarters . . . leaving the two upper floors, accessible only by a narrow stairway, for personnel housing quarters. The entire complex was connected by a wide underground passageway tunneled under the main road, designed for shuttling this product from building to building. The 709th Ordnance quartered in buildings adjoining us and spread their shops in areas in the southern half of this location.

Truckloads of infantry . . . mortar squads . . . heavy artillery . . . tanks, and assorted heavy battle machinery claimed priority on the roads and tirelessly these units maintained an around-the-clock domination of the single main artery that skirted our area. Despite nauseating exhaust fumes emitting from powerful 470 hp Ford V engines our confidence soared as with pride we marveled at the new 43-ton M-26 Pershing tanks lumbering through. Their new wide-tracks creaking and clanking on the asphalt became a monotony, but their long-barrelled flash-muzzled 90mm guns protruding from steel turrets of double thickness struck an authoritative pose and was now a somber answer to anything the German Panzers could muster. Heavy artillery booming from positions west of this resort were pulling out and joining the "push;" a "push" that long graduated from a stage of excitement now bordered almost on the point of hysteria! Signal communications were shortened. Supply depots moved as forward as would be dared and aid stations were moving their units as close as possible to maintain the flow of wounded. Moreover, a great number of Ordnance specialists went forward to join line troops in a joint effort to keep weapons operational.

Breakfast was less than an hour past and the twangy aroma of coffee still in the air as the section leaders began assembling in the CP.

"What's up?" questioned one . . . for the hour was a little

unusual for staff meetings.

"Beats me," replied another, "Botting just said to get down here on the double."

"Maybe we're going across."

"I doubt it yet, we've still got a hell of a lot of work to do here."

Botting came in with the Captain following.

"Come on in," the First Sergeant beckoned; "and close the door." He then put the Cadre "at ease."

The Captain, dropping a batch of papers on his desk, shuffled his feet slightly and slouched back in his chair. Hesitating slightly, he spoke:

"I'm going to come right to the point, men. Rather than call a general formation this morning I figured it best to talk to you section leaders and *you* pass it on directly to your respective groups."

He stood up and continued:

"I have heard two or three reports from the 709th that some of your men are not cooperating with them. Col. Childs himself told me late yesterday afternoon that some of your automotive men refused to send a team over to 'pull a drive shaft' that was needed right then."

Ray Twiss, the bold-eyed Master Sergeant in charge of Automotive broke in immediately.

"Beg pardon, sir; but at that time all of our men were busy and we couldn't spare anybody."

"The Colonel said his man was told that we didn't intend to send anybody and to get his own men to do it," replied the Captain. "That right?"

"Well, I tell you, Captain; the Lieutenant from 709th was kinda demanding. I didn't think his attitude was quite becoming an officer and when he asked the second time he was practically shouting. You see Captain, that crowd over there gives you the idea that we are their subordinates and everytime they speak we're supposed to hop to it. Well, maybe we are, but it hurts like hell to be looked down on and be treated like dirt . . . especially when we know our men are just as good as any of them, maybe better when it comes down to the mechanics of the thing."

The Sergeant concluded; "When I suggested he get his *own* men to fix that drive shaft, he really got huffy!"

The Captain shifted to another incident.

"The 709th Artillery officer wanted an inspection team to give them a hand with two or three minor repairs on guns and he says we sloughed them off. That right?"

Al Marshall, the slim light-haired Sergeant in charge of artillery; taking the defensive, answered quickly:

"Captain, that's the biggest bunch of 'goof-offs' I've ever seen. I'm not kidding! They wouldn't think of pulling a man off one of their jobs and sending him. And how often do they go to other companies and ask them to do something?"

Captain Weinberg paused, and then as if he wanted to say it all in one word, spoke:

"Okay, I'm going to give it to you straight. First, I'll tell you something that you obviously don't know. The 709th happens to be very fond of the 126th and I've heard it from the 'horse's mouth.' Not only from the officer's but also from 'non-coms.' Colonel Hudson up at Battalion knows this and even Colonel Childs and his assistant, Major Waikart . . . have passed their sentiments as well; saying that the 126th can always be depended on. Colonel Childs as DIVISION Ordnance Officer is responsible for all Ordnance functions in the 9TH DIVISION and attached units and we're *not about* to let him down. Maybe the 709th does get a little huffy now and then, but what the hell; everybody does once in a while." Sitting back down and making a great effort to remain collected, he continued; "Now the 709th has a job to do. They're going to be riding our tails pretty close from here on out 'cause when we cross that river no telling what's going to happen. I want that spirit of cooperation to continue, and you can tell the men just that. If it don't somebody is going to be missing around here. Those combat units up there need replacements every day! That's more than just a warning . . . that's a damn fact!" A pause, then "Dismissed!"

From this point few misunderstandings would occur, and when they did it went no further than it began. The 709th continued to share buildings next to ours and the "close cooperation" continued. It was a neat and simple function. When an item was received requiring heavier maintenance than 709th was set up to handle it was funneled over to the 126th. When it was too heavy for us it was referred to a heavier Ordnance company better equipped to handle that particular work. This process appeared to have allegations of "passing the buck" and though our cooperative association was close we learned early that the 709th, though a highly skilled unit was quite adept at "passing the buck." We soon became a bit adept too, in playing that same game.

There is no substitute for sunny skies and the whole countryside reveled in it during our entire encampment.

Beef stew was served for the "umphteenth" time and the evening meal was attended casually as the men lingered indifferently over the broad awkwardly erected tables. The din of noise from boisterous voices was unusual . . . much like an echo chamber, and perhaps justly so because of wide hollow halls that lead into the large bare storage room of the distillery shed now utilized as a kitchen-dining hall. A casual glance up from the table toward the ceiling brought a shout of "Good Lord! Look at that!" Another took up the cry; "Hey! You guys . . . Look!"

In a second most eyes were looking up at flames shooting out through a narrow metal chimney attached to an oil-fired messkit washer igniting the dry tarpaper roofing. Before most were aware the blaze spread and the fire moved outside onto the roof of the messhall. The aged framed structure and fragile tender sunbaked tarpaper was no match for the fast-moving flames and it quickly spread through the brittle rafters. Only a few minutes elapsed before the entire messhall was threatened . . . as was the headquarters building to which it adjoined.

As flames spread, so did indecision. Rushing up the narrow stairway in headquarters building evacuation became uppermost in most thoughts. Dropped from windows gentle at first, duffle bags, helmets, shoes and personal belongings hit the ground. The minutes flicked by and a couple glances out the window at the fast rising billowing smoke caused personal belongings to be literally *thrown* from the windows! Suddenly; almost as if a whistle had blown the thought occurred that perhaps attempting to *halt* the blaze *might* be the sensible thing to do. The flames by now had become a roaring fire! The shocking reality of darkness descending rapidly and the prospect of not bringing it under control before that time brought a sobering thought. It could very well light up the entire area . . . and make for an excellent target for enemy planes! Despite plenty of "ack-ack" protection it very well could bring on a messy situation should the enemy desire to strike at the heavy concentrations of supplies and equipment at Bad Neuenahr.

Botting moved fast and took charge quickly!

"Come on you guys, get your tails moving! On the double!" he thundered. "*Run, dammit, run!*"

Organization quickly came to fore and we did with great haste get a "move on!" Bucket brigades were relayed until someone located some firefighting equipment within the building. Axes, hoses and first class equipment were parlayed into action. Elements from several nearby units joined us and though long after darkness had settled, the fire was brought under control. In its' entirety several moments of excitement was experienced, but had the Luftwaffe been "up to par" it would have been exciting *indeed*!

John Pastovich lay on his back on his cot. Sweating, flushed and breathing heavily he wondered what was happening to him. He had exerted much energy in helping fight the fire and perhaps "got a little carried away" in the several anxious moments. He had a slight shoulder pain too, and the excessive perspiration began to cloud his glasses. Mr. Rueth and Botting came in and after talking a moment or two decided it best to release him to an aid station for observation.

"Sergeant, I wanna' cross the Rhine with you guys," he said.

"You just go on up and let the 'Doc' take a look at you and he'll probably release you in no time. You know, and I'll be brutally frank, this could be symptoms of a heart attack. I doubt it though on account of your age."

"A heart attack? Me?" He was twenty-two. "Damn, Sergeant ... how encouraging can you get?" Thinking it over he muttered softly; "Cheez, I hope not." Shaking his head slightly, "A heart attack? Man!"

It was diagnosed as a heart irregularity and the husky Pennsylvanian never got his wish. We would cross the Rhine without him and he never returned to the company.

***

FIRST ARMY's position on the east bank strengthened hourly and it was driving hard to expand the bridgehead, and while enemy defenses were basically weak . . . now bogged down facing the British in 21ST ARMY GROUP on the north and the THIRD and SEVENTH ARMIES in the south they began to show definite signs of strengthened reaction . . . demonstrated in piecemeal counterattacks. Though rugged wooded terrain made rapid advances difficult it did on the other hand offer topographical advantages for protection of the bridgehead. By March 12 FIRST ARMY had operating across the Rhine other than the captured railway bridge, a pontoon bridge several hundred yards upstream at Remagen, a treadway bridge just below Bonn and three ferries. Later the river was bridged just south of Cologne and by the 15th several crossings were made north of the Ruhr area. The III CORPS commander had given the 9TH INFANTRY DIVISION orders to attack eastward . . . spearheading through the center and the 78TH INFANTRY would be responsible for penetrating the northern arc of the bridgehead. While the 9TH ARMORED remained in reserve at the bridgehead the 99TH INFANTRY moved to the right and attacked south along the river. The high commanding ground was secured and III CORPS now penetrated deep into the hilly terrain that dominated for miles the eastern bank of the Rhine. By the 18th so deep had become the penetration that heavy artillery began crossing the Rhine and General Hodges divided the bridgehead between the III and VII CORPS. The 12TH ARMY GROUP commander, General Bradley; ordered FIRST ARMY to expand operations east of the Rhine. On March 25 with three CORPS, FIRST ARMY launched the coordinated attack to break out of the Remagen bridgehead extended to the east while in the meantime constantly widening and reinforcing the bridgehead to gain maneuver room. Each CORPS was assigned an armored DIVISION to give it a powerful striking force capable of sustained power deep in enemy territory. These armored units could move rapidly over suitable terrain . . . disrupting and disorganizing enemy lines of communication in rear areas. From positions on the west bank of the Rhine the heavy guns of the

32nd Field Artillery Brigade gave tremendous support in reinforcing fires of the three attacking CORPS.

So intensive was pursuit of FIRST ARMY that by late March the supply problem again cropped up. To combat this the U. S. Military Railway Service went to work laying cross ties, spreading ballast, and making repairs to yards that allowed rail lines to open and again be extended and used *west* of the Rhine! Lack of trucks suitable for carrying vital supplies reached a critical stage. Supply depots, in addition to the one heavily drawn on at Euskirchen was established at Bonn and Remagen and later at Coblenz on the east bank of the Rhine. It was late in March and time was growing short for the 126th to remain on the west bank. What we had to do must be done quick and after almost two weeks of intensified work interwoven within an air of relaxation the company's schedule to cross the Rhine was at hand. This could put us in a far better position to render stronger active support to DIVISION.

That a small "recon" team from our company had already crossed the river, having done so early morning of the 25th., was not intended as a secret but there were those that wanted to consider it as such. The Captain had simply sought to "keep it as quiet as possible lest the men get restless," and he had the First Sergeant select two available men . . . plus a driver to scout for an operational location. Representing the first troops of the 126th to cross the Rhine, Warrant Officer Rueth, T/4 Phil Connors and T/3 Cal Maidment, along with the Captain didn't feel any different about it but they were successful in selecting a spot in the hills approximately fifteen miles beyond the river.

Maidment, the slim blond 21-year-old small arms technician recalled:

"The pontoon bridge stretched for so long it seemed that by time we reached midstream we were riding right on the water level. Hardly a ripple was seen and then only slightly when the weight of our jeep approached, but because of its unusual length the bridge wavered from time to time and gave us an uneasy feeling."

Capt. Glenn H. Collins

1st/Lt. Clyde L. Miller

Capt. Alfred Orsenigo

Capt. Bennie Weinberg

1st/Lt. O. R. Lineberger

1st/Lt. James Prendergast

W/O Anton Rueth

1st/Lt. James Black
1st/Lt. Jack Palmer (rear)

1st/Sgt. Manley Botting

H.M.S. Queen Mary

Company headquarters (Blagdon Court), Blagdon, England.

Main gate entrance to Camp Butner, North Carolina, 1943.

Bracing vehicles and equipment aboard LST for the Channel crossing.

Coming in at low tide on busy Utah Beach.

General Eisenhower and Gen. Sir Bernard Montgomery discuss vital invasion plans. Spring, 1944.

General Bradley pulls lanyard of 155MM "Long Tom" commemorating 4th of July and signaling First Army drive into lower Normandy.

U. S. M-4 Sherman tank blasts through Norman village.

American armor put out of action in France. August, 1944.

Roadsign in lower Normandy.

Gen. Dwight D. Eisenhower
Supreme Commander
Allied Expeditionary Forces

Gen. Omar Bradley
CG — 12th Army Group

Gen. Courtney H. Hodges
CG — First U. S. ARMY.

Lt. Gen. (Gen.) J. Lawton Collins
CG — U. S. VII CORPS.

Lt. Gen. (Gen.) Leonard T. Gerow
CG — U. S. V CORPS, 1943-1944.

Lt. Gen. Clarence R. Huebner
CG — V CORPS, 1945.

Maj. Gen. (Lt. Gen.) Manton S. Eddy
CG — 9th Infantry Division, 1942-1944.

Maj. Gen. Louis A. Craig
CG — 9th Infantry Division, 1944-1945.

Lt. Col. Robert A. Hudson
C. O., 184th Ordnance Battalion

The "dragon teeth" approaches to the Siegfried Line along Germany's western frontier.

Mud and destruction in Huertgen, Germany, March, 1945.

First Army GIs move into the Ardennes to halt the Bulge, December, 1944.

Fierce blizzards strike southeast Belgium, December-January, 1944-45.

MEETING IN BELGIUM WITH THE SUPREME COMMANDER

Front row: Lt. Gen. George S. Patton, Lt. Gen. Omar N. Bradley, Gen. Dwight D. Eisenhower, Lt. Gen. Courtney H. Hodges, Lt. Gen. William H. Simpson. Second row: Maj. Gen. William B. Kean, Maj. Gen. Charles H. Corlett, Maj. Gen. J. Lawton Collins, Maj. Gen. Leonard T. Gerow, Maj. Gen. Elwood Quesada. Third row: Maj. Gen. Leven G. Allen, Brig. Gen. Charles C. Hart, Brig. Gen. Truman C. Thorson. (MP's unidentified).

Erroneous 8TH Air Force bombing left Malmedy, Belgium a shambles.

Germany's V-I "Buzzbomb" struck terror in the hearts of all GIs.

The 126th. waits to bridge the Rhine River, March, 1945.

The Roer valley was shattered and gloomy.

Cologne cathedral overlooking the Rhine. Shattered and shaken but not destroyed, March, 1945.

L. to R.: T/4 Robert McNulty, T/4 Howard Thompson and the author. Camp d'Elsenborn, Belgium, November, 1944.

Company headquarters, Bad Neuenahr, Germany (The Apollinaris Building), March, 1945.

Sergeants Tony Spaich, Sam Parrinello, Sol Kaufman and Frank Linzinmeir. Goe, Belgium, January, 1945.

Henry Boudreau congratulates newly-commissioned 2nd/Lt. Harold Johnson.

T/4 Louis Wolak

Kassel's magnificent buildings were in ruins.

Dick Felt and Art Fealk kept the motor pool running.

German prisoners file to the rear as American units move forward in central Germany, 1945.

L. to R.: Sgt. Carl Ross, Sgt. Al Rapin, T/5 Ed Tarasiewicz and T/5 Mose Gianoplos pause in Verviers, Belgium.

Homeward-bound aboard the "Boshfontaine," December, 1945.

Sergeant Olen Hilditch

"The battle for the Huertgen Forest was hard and bitter and one of the most costly."

"With a sickening screech and scrape of bolts ripping from metal beams the 30-year old Ludendorf span trembled, swayed and collapsed into the Rhine!"

XV

COLLAPSE IN THE EAST

The formidable Ludendorf Bridge so miraculously found unimpaired on the 7th was through German indecision and reluctance, playing a mighty role in what appeared to be the last major campaign. Indisputably the span had added zest to the pursuing western Allies and unquestionably this stroke of luck had reduced FIRST ARMY's timetable. Above all, it had for both sides reduced the casualty list which in nowise was light. But on March 17, after suffering heavy enemy harrassment and artillery bombardment, and weakened after supporting a continuous flow of heavy traffic far beyond normalcy jamming across day and night, the bridge vibrated and gave a mighty shudder! With a sickening screech and scrape of bolts ripping from metal beams the thirty-year old span trembled, swayed and collapsed into the Rhine! A great heap of twisted steel! With it, some to their deaths went several men who with round-the-clock laborious hustling kept repairs to a minimum in keeping it operative during its ten-day function.

The "early" spring was brief and a chilly low hanging mist persisted as the 126th Ordnance in early morning of the 26th reached the Rhine at Remagen. A broad lettered sign erected at the base of a treadway bridge invited the attention of everyone.

THIS BRIDGE CONSTRUCTED BY THE
148TH ENGINEER CONSTRUCTION BATTALION

A lower sign boastfully read:

"ASSISTED BY THE U. S. NAVY"

Uneasily onto the span we rolled where some two hundred yards downstream through drifting fog could be viewed the wreckage of the ill-fated Ludendorf Bridge. Small signs along the way reminded us to keep at 50-yard intervals and in a matter of minutes and something like 1,000 yards the much-battered waterfront town of Erpel was reached on the west bank. Winding through the rugged but scenic hills that at given points one could look down on the Rhine and on across fields that bristled uncomfortably with chilled March winds wreckage of incapacitated enemy equipment was noted, littering many roadsides and fields. Tanks, half-tracks and military vehicles of all types clustered in groups and streaked with brownish-greenish camouflage were either destroyed or abandoned . . . and from this burned-out wreckage one could only imagine the diminishing morale existing within German ranks after having failed miserably in an abortive attempt to check the Allied crossing of the Rhine.

An approximate fifteen mile roll into the hills found us moving into Kalenborn, a shattered town where scowling D-Day veteran, Lt. Col. Clarence Hupfer's ("Back up to Nobody") 746th Tank Battalion teaming with a RCT of the 899th Tank Destroyers only days before had encircled and viciously destroyed a foundering Panzer unit, knocking out armor and clusters of supporting infantry. The powerful new 45-ton M-36 TD's of the 899th supported with heavier armor plate and higher velocity 90mm guns and rocket launchers that had in February replaced the old and slower M-10's, and though not quite as maneuverable as the "King

Tiger" did give the enemy much consternation with this ferocious increased firepower.

The Kalenborn community was a picture of complete desolation, most dwellings devastated and reduced practically to splinters. We considered ourselves fortunate *indeed* to find quarters in an abandoned estate where the large stone mansion, obviously of former prominence suffered little damage. We wondered however, as incoming enemy artillery at intervals pounded uneasily some distance to the west desperately attempting to fend off slashing columns of infantry and armor threatening the heartland of central Germany, perhaps if our arrival had not been too soon. Warning signs were explicit . . . reminding all personnel that all mines had not been removed and the conspicuous "Achtung Minen" sign planted just off the narrow entrance-exit, though carefully marked off kept skepticism at a high pitch. In the high grass to the rear of the area two shattered GI bodies found by the "recon" team on the first day . . . and removed the same day, bore an obvious indication of misinterpretation of warnings.

Three enemy tanks; tracks smashed and broken, its hull scorched and burned were silhouetted in a one-two-three position on the lofty heights to the east. A gaping hole ripped in each exposed side indicated no less that its' armor had been pierced with a direct hit. One U. S. Sherman, blackened and burned lay on its' side.

The fragrance of fresh brewed coffee in early morning is always tantalizing to the nostrils of GIs in the field. It had a special effect on a chilly crisp March morning for the six unknown GIs being sheperded up to the front of the chow line. Shivering, disheveled and dirty we wondered how they rated such apparent first-class attention.

"Who the hell are those guys?" asked one in astonishment.

"What's the big idea?" questioned another; "who's that bunch of line-buckers?"

Mumbling was toned down respectfully when it was learned they were 9TH DIVISION infantrymen just escaped through enemy lines, having been captured a few days earlier. By chance, the driver of the small weapons carrier transporting them to the rear felt compelled to stop here for chow.

Rains came. They stopped. They came again . . . and they

continued to be a real problem. Extremely sensitive terrain so prevalent in the Kalenborn area proved a formidable opponent for the four and six-ton wreckers, and the agile manner in which these and other bulky vehicles twisted and turned through and around mired spots became one of unusual maneuvering. *This could not go on for long*! It had in fact become acute . . . most especially around the only entrance-exit location accessible to this compound where each day wheels churned a little deeper.

It was mid-morning and the rain though still threatening through murky clouds had turned to a fine drizzle. Puddles of water stood in every low spot throughout the yard as the Captain, during a routine morning inspection approached the automotive area. The small cramped building used for vehicle repair was still being utilized though much of the work still had to be done outdoors where several vehicles awaited attention. Present unfavorable weather had reduced operations to almost a standstill.

Sergeant Twiss, standing at the wide sagging doorway of the make-shift shop quickly wiped his oily hands and greeted the Captain with a snappy salute.

"Morning, Captain."

"Morning, Sergeant."

Without pausing, Weinberg through his alert beady blue eyes looked around and spoke quickly.

"What are all these men doing just hanging around? How come they're not busy? We got a lot of work to do Sergeant, and we're behind now." Without waiting for an answer he continued. "You know that, don't you Sergeant?"

"Yes, Captain . . . I know that."

"Okay, then, how come?"

Non-plussed for a moment, this suddenly seemed all the owl-eyed Sergeant needed.

"Sir; something's got to give around here . . . and I mean, it's got to give pretty quick 'cause if we don't get out of this damn place soon we're going to have to cease operations. Cap'n., we've just about had it and we can't accomplish anything just sitting here." Seeming almost wanting to apologize for saying it, Twiss continued; "Now, you asked me Cap'n., and I'm telling you how it is."

The Captain, already exasperated and painfully aware of the existing fast-deteriorating automotive work area pushed his helmet back with the back of his hand, and true to his reflexes when vexed . . . arched his hands on his hips and retorted:

"You think I don't know we've got a problem? You think I don't know it's been raining every day?"

"Uh-Oh!" thought Twiss; "Here it comes! He's going to go into one of those fits just as sure as hell!"

"Listen, Sergeant;" continued the Captain, "I'm the one that's catching hell from DIVISION because we're not delivering any thing! *I'm* the one they want the answers from! *I'm* the one that's got to do the worrying! It's *my* tail that gets the chewing, not yours!"

Looking up at Twiss he pointed a gloved finger and followed with a toned-down challenge:

"Tell you what, Sergeant; if you want to go out and find us another area, go ahead. If not, just stop bitching and sweat it out like the rest of us until I can find one . . . okay?"

The words were sharp and not very pretty though both knew the logic in them. That Twiss was displeased with them was obvious . . . particularly so when noting several automotive men working within earshot. The tall spare sergeant was a good soldier and a proud one, and because of these two qualities he swallowed the rebuff unflinching. That was part of the army game and he had been chewed out before. Fixing himself erect, setting a firm jaw and taking one step backward the 30-year-old sergeant looked the C. O. straight in the eye and executed a sharp salute . . . at the same time through pursed lips striking a crisp curt reply:

"*Yes sir*, Captain!"

There was much truth in the fact that we couldn't go any place until there was some place else to go. Furthermore, until clearance was obtained from Battalion or DIVISION Ordnance we still would not roll.

***

Unable to maintain a cohesive defense against the slashing thrusts of American armor, by the 27th of March FIRST ARMY had advanced 35 miles east of the Rhine. Except in isolated cases where delaying action was employed, resistance grew weaker. III CORPS continued the attack across open country, while the VII CORPS on the northern flank was subjected to heavy counterattacks that held up seriously crossing the Sieg River. American artillery was heavily concentrated and deployment of fighter-bombers were brought into action. The monstrous 240mm and 8-inch guns pressed the attack and several days of fighting saw the German defense crumbling. These next few weeks were the decisive weeks . . . decisive that is, for the German High Command. For, with the Allies . . . their work was already cut out and enemy capitulation could be expected within these few weeks. With the Russian armies hacking unmercifully on the eastern front and driving with grim determination; the western allies doing likewise all along the western front and though dangerous and astute as they had proved to be, the German armies ultimately could only hope for a miracle . . . which prospects at this stage seemed relatively remote.

On the east bank of the Rhine one of FIRST ARMY's greatest assets lay in control of Germany's broad expansive Cologne-Frankfurt superhighway . . . or as the Germans called it; the *autobahn*. The great majority of roads on the east side far outstripped those traveled on the opposite shore. Superiority in highway planning and engineering was obvious and due largely to less Allied artillery and aerial bombardment as was applied to roads in the Rhineland, they were by the time of our approach in a far better condition.

Surpassing any type of road or highway found in the European Theater the meticulously-constructed and well-paved autobahn proved to be a convoy's delight. Representing but part of one of many such coordinated superhighways making up a vast network over much of Germany this section was first to fall into Allied hands, and despite destruction of bridge approaches and bridge spans . . . either by the retreating enemy or our own forces the many forced marches and time-consuming convoys became far more orderly and movement was greatly accellerated.

This four and sometime six-lane system of expressways and freeways was designed to link each major city with the next, and

377

despite distances . . . eliminating city traffic through by-passing. The thriving industrial Ruhr, for example was linked to Frankfurt by some 155 kilometers and one could travel an additional 275 kilometers and reach Munich . . . deep in Bavaria. Northeast from Munich almost 400 kilometers would carry one to Chemnitz, with a visit to Nuremberg along the way. 230 kilometers to the north lay Berlin, with Dresden in between. From Berlin straight across the northeast plains almost 500 kilometers would be required to reach the industrial Ruhr, encompassing Magdeburg, Hannover and Dortmund along the way, and completing a sort of cycle of highways without real interruption. Other notable cities throughout the country; Hamburg, Leipzig, Brunswick, Kassel, Bremen, etc., are inter-connected in the same process.

In the days following buildup of the aggressive war machine Adolph Hitler ordered construction of the superb highways primarily for military use and by the outbreak of World War II some 1,260 miles of these long range autobahns had been completed within the country. This however, was meant for use by German military only! With this great overland advantage his armies could move with great expediency and maneuver more freely to all fronts once his insatiable campaign to conquer Europe was launched. Hitler prided himself with these great roads and expressways, sensing the full benefits his victorious legions would reap therefrom; and agreed . . . for an astounding number of years, *reap* they did! But . . . and most of the world surely will agree; that at the time of construction and even during his early lightly opposed campaigns, *never* did he *dare dream* that someday these same highly effective superhighways would aid advancing Allied armies in the crushing and disastrous defeat of his own!

Slashing across the great autobahn FIRST ARMY by the end of March was prepared and only awaited orders from 12TH ARMY GROUP to attack east through Giessen and up toward Kassel.

The Kalenborn encampment lasted only four days, and as the 709th Ordnance with whom we had again shared an area cooperatively, packed late on the second day and would leave early morning of the 30th, we would prepare to follow close. Much scurrying was in order before close contact with the DIVISION could again be made. This movement would complete the longest single convoy yet undertaken by the 126th. It would cover eighty eight miles! Two hours more than anticipated was required, for as we followed along the great superhighway traffic became tremendous, and because of destruction of many concrete bridges spanning railroads, lower roads and waterways . . . many more detours were confronted than had been seen in quite some time. Despite the dismal rainy weather that at times multiplied growing adversities, the trek was in itself an "eye opener" and much comment centered on the obviously superior quality of German cultivation and construction as compared to that in the Rhineland.

Now off the autobahn we rolled east on through deserted and slightly damaged Freilingen and Langenhahn to reach the highway junction of Rennerod. Not a roadsign was noted . . . but long dependent on maps we gauged our mileage and halted in a little hamlet that in this extensive rural district appeared to be in the middle of nowhere.

"The sign says this is Niederwalgern," somebody said when dismounting.

"Nieder . . . *what*? What sign you talking about?"

"Niederwalgern, dammit! Can't you read?" came another blast.

"So . . . where the hell is Niederwalgern?" came a quick retort. "What's its claim to fame? They all look alike to me."

"Niederwalgern is where you will be staying for a couple days," commented one of the Lieutenants, "and it don't make no difference how you spell it. And just for the hell of it don't just stand there bitching, start unpacking and let's get this stuff out of the rain."

A small drab unimpressive almost isolated rail community, much in fact like many others that we had already encountered Niederwalgern was as least an attractive community as we would ever enter. It was difficult to identify on any except minutely detailed maps, the nearest city of consequence being Marburg . . . some fifty kilometers to the northeast. Hundreds of acres of well-cultivated land partitioned in obvious individual farms gave a clue to the predominant livelihood of those living for miles around. The local sawmill and railroad station would suggest that only a scant few escaped the rigors of farming. Light operations commenced even before most of the complement had been quartered as small arms weapons were almost a week behind in repair.

The two-story railroad station, battered partially by age and partially by overuse from less than careful GIs, housed much of the company personnel while others sought quarters in abandoned individual dwellings. Guards were quickly dispersed to strategic locations and suspicions of possible sabotage earlier reported by a number of other units prompted suggestions to immediately establish machine gun posts. Order of the day to all guardposts read:

"Observe maximum discretion before taking action"

Contacts with DIVISION Ordnance was hastily established . . . now several miles east of this location. It was good to be out of the rain and better quarters would continue to be in our favor from now on. Tented bivouac was a thing of the past for obviously there seemed to be an abundance of factories, breweries and abandoned enemy barracks to serve as shelter. This not only would account for some comfort but allow for setting up shops and would prohibit interruption of service to combat forces. The main problem seemed to be keeping up with the fast-moving combat troops now deployed along a 200-mile front. Supply trucks were making excellent time on the Rhine plains compared to the slow dragging efforts in the lower Eifel and upper Rhineland.

Late morning of the 5th found us rolling into the highway junction of Herborn, some fifteen miles northwest of Niederwalgern. Guesswork was out for without maps one could have his choice and take any one of the many roads jutting out from this town like spokes in a wheel. In less than two minutes however, there was no question when a sign was spotted . . . "Marburg, 21 kilometers."

In this predominantly rural region in the heart of the Province of Hesse the twisting road, sagging at intervals carried us through thousands of acres of farmland, intensely impressive in the wake of obvious meticulous cultivation. In less than an hour we began to note clusters of civilians, most on foot, pulling small wagons of personal belongings and others with horse-drawn carts shuttling to and from the prominent city of Marburg . . . which in a few minutes we would enter from the south.

Situated on the Lahn River and famed for its' coveted four-hundred year old university and library, Marburg's transportation facilities had felt the brunt of a brief smashing bombardment, though the city itself spared the ravaging and complete destruction of war. The 9TH TAC air forces had done its' work well and left in shambles the great railroad station, blocks of surrounding edifices and the mammoth rail yards whose disfigured tracks in many places now curled skyward several feet. Against light resistance that brought limited destruction to its' western suburbs the 3RD ARMORED DIVISION entered Marburg on March 28 and by noon hostilities ceased in the city. Three days following our entry FIRST ARMY would establish headquarters in the city.

Crossing the Lahn the main road to the east, as a result of enemy-seeking rocket-firing fighter bombers now was in such condition to greatly discourage passage. Stop and go! Stop and go! Stop and go! Twisting and winding slowly along this route, dodging at intervals army engineers and road grading machinery, we passed slowly trucks loaded with crushed stone that were followed by several enemy prisoners relegated to put the road in Class A condition. Munchausen was but a small community . . . so small in fact that the convoy's lead vehicle exited before the last vehicle, well-spaced, entered. The main road beyond reached the point of impassability and some eight kilometers along a secondary route carried us into the larger road junction of Allendorf.

Quarters were quickly secured for all sections and operations began immediately. Cleared without incident on March 29 by the fast-moving 9TH ARMORED DIVISION, Allendorf, to be our camp for a considerable time, was spared the war's tragedy insofar as destruction was concerned. Most inhabitants . . . surely no more than 1,500 electing to remain even during the rapid Allied advance never displayed a single act of animosity. Absent too, were the usual cold stares that one had learned to expect . . . a trait during this period generally characterizing the German people. When entering the town we soon were aware in fact that perhaps we were in the midst of an atmosphere that would be far more amiable than had been seen in sometime. Hardly had we settled when diplomatic action on the part of the local citizenry gave supporting evidence that our presence was actually welcomed.

We soon learned why!

Many Russians, some with entire families . . . released recently from prison compounds had taken refuge in this village. Much to the dismay of the local townspeople the American Military Government Authority placed some in homes with smaller German families, especially those inhabiting larger dwellings. Many of the Russians, along with other Croatian mixtures, family groups . . . quartered in dwellings directly behind and alongside our camp and this would give us our actual first contact with these unfortunates. Extremely crowded conditions, improper sanitation and endowed with a sensitive nature . . . patience and tempers ran short. An unusually rough and hard-looking people; their standard of living had descended to zero, hardly above in fact, that experienced by animals. Discipline had all but disintegrated within these groups and morals were shattered, so strongly evidenced by nightly parties heavy with boisterous singing, wild shouts of laughter and yells. Fierce threats and spontaneous fights occured with regularity. The years of pent-up emotions and agitation had to be released!

Surveying the situation early Captain Weinberg let his wishes be known. Sergeant Botting, during a morning formation passed along these orders early.

"You all know the situation across the alley. I know most of you do because a couple of you were seen coming back from there last night. The Captain *does not* want to see anymore of that. There's nothing but trouble waiting for you over there." He scanned the line up and continued. "I know some of you can pretty well speak the language and you're probably gonna' feel sorry for them, but you can't do a damn thing for them. The Army is feeding them so the orders are to stay away." Again leveling his voice, he concluded; "If you don't want a sweet case of V. D. then that's the place to stay away from."

Though the Red Army was having its' problems on the eastern front, collapse of the Nazi Government was imminent and cracking of the German armies was evident on all fronts in the west even in the early days of April. There existed however, a great pocket of enemy in the mountainous region known as the Ruhr area. Within this area lived in peacetime some 5,000,000 people. Its many industrious iron and steel mills are built within reach of rich coal and ore mines and this was Germany's greatest war materials producing area.

As the western allies continued the fierce drive east General Bradley instructed General Hodges to "clear the pocket and advance to the Elbe." General Simpson's NINTH ARMY would lend assistance to the north. General Hodges assigned this task to III CORPS and the XVIII AIRBORNE CORPS, the latter having again become functional in FIRST ARMY April 2. VII and V CORPS would continue to direct the attack eastward toward the Elbe. Liquidation of this dangerous pocket commenced on April 6 and suddenly FIRST ARMY found itself fighting on *two* fronts . . .to the west to reduce the Ruhr pocket and to the east to reach the Elbe. Employing eight Divisions in conjunction with NINTH ARMY units coordinating in rugged hilly terrain found "ack-ack" gun fire and anti-tank guns providing the major opposition from enemy firepower. The enemy was fast being squeezed into a giant enveloping maneuver. The Birmingham (Ala.) Age-Herald announced in two-inch headlines on Monday, April 2:

"ALLIES WELD RING AROUND RUHR"
U. S. 9TH and 1ST ARMY JOINED"

Decimation of this enemy mass, at first estimated at 150,000 troops would mean the shattering of Army Group B and a substantial portion of Army Group H . . . under direct command of German Feldmarschal Walther Model. This would also mean the capitulation of the highly industrial cities of Dusseldorf, Essen, Wuppertal, Dortmund and several important mining and factory towns . . . each at one time mighty war producing centers.

The enemy employed every groud tactic available in frantically attempting a breakout. If successful such a bold move would enable them to attack FIRST ARMY's rear positions . . . unquestionably delaying the eastward Allied dash for the Elbe. Heavy concentrations of air and ground power began to take its' toll and on the 14th the pocket was split in two. The situation became obviously hopeless and enemy units began surrendering en masse. On the 16th all organized resistance in the *eastern* sector of the pocket ended and endless streams of prisoners filled compounds. Complete resistance ended on the 18th and the battle of the Ruhr pocket was over. Army Group B, consisting of a major portion of the Fifth Panzer Army and elements of the First Parachute and Fifteenth Armies was destroyed. A great portion of Army Group H was also lost. Almost 325,000 Germans, including twenty four generals and one admiral, more than double the original estimate were put out of action. Many tanks and guns were destroyed or taken and personnel killed and wounded ran high. At the moment this would represent almost one-third of the enemy's available soldiers. The enemy would *never* recover from the "Ruhr pocket" debacle. All leadership of any stability had gone and a wave of demoralization swept over the enemy forces in the west. Moreover; with the suicide of the brilliant field strategist; Fieldmarschal Walther von Model on April 18 . . . morale would reach a new low amongst enemy troops.

Years later, General Matthew B. Ridgway, commanding general of the XVIII AIRBORNE CORPS and at the time heavily engaged in the Ruhr operation, was asked by the author the possible existing chances for the enemy to break out of the pocket.

"There was little or no chance," replied the stalwart General. "He (the enemy) was covered deep on all sides and to initiate and complete a breakthrough would have required a maximum effort of unusual strength with which at this time he was not equipped."

General Ridgway, whom a few years later would command the EIGHTH U. S. ARMY in Korea and shortly thereafter succeed General Douglas McArthur as Supreme Commander for the Allied Powers in the Far East, continued:

"On the 14th I sent Fieldmarschal Model a note, apprising him of the hopelessness of his plight and the folly of its continuation. He was also reminded in the note of a similar decision facing an honorable and distinguished field commander some 80 years ago; General Robert E. Lee, who rather than continue an impossible struggle that needlessly would sacrifice the lives of many soldiers, made a major decision that not only would save countless casualties but preserve his honor as well. I pointed out that General Lee's fame in the hearts of his countrymen and in the annals of warfare has ever since remained a bright page in our history. The Fieldmarschal elected to fight on and four days later his forces were destroyed or captured. Model took his own life on the same day."

Operating out of headquarters at Winterberg General Craig, the cool but hard-hitting 9TH commander recalled the fantastic bagging of enemy troops.

"It was all but over. Everyone was aware of that. Yet, we did not anticipate the hard fighting that lay ahead in the Harz Mountains. But hard-fighting it was . . . though in a few days the bottom dropped out of the whole German army and that was that!"

With the closing of the Ruhr pocket the FIRST and NINTH ARMIES linked west of Paderborn to continue the eastward drive.

Faced with mounting reverses in the west and east the Germans ordered every male in the Reich between the ages of sixteen and sixty two to register with military authorities. The official German Radio (DNB) added, "for active defense of the Nation . . . under penalty of being punished as deserters." The Germans were literally scraping the manpower barrel . . . rounding up deserters or those lost from their units. Newspapers had earlier recorded General Eisenhower's message to the German army, advising them of the futility of continued destruction and urging them to forsake the Fuehrer:

"Surrender call comes as Yanks sever Reich Ruhr basin and drive within 170 miles of Berlin and 135 miles of Munich."

On March 30 for strategic reasons 9TH DIVISION had shifted from III to VII CORPS but the evening of April 4 found the DIVISION moving back into III CORPS zone, with CORPS now commanded by Maj. Gen. James A. Van Fleet had spread over much of the western region beyond the Rhine. 9TH DIVISION had during the last several days aided III CORPS in closing the

Ruhr pocket, clearing enemy stragglers and isolated groups around the Winterberg area high in the rugged terrain and wooded mountainous area in the Harz Mountains. Encountering stiff resistance around the Winterberg area from small arms, bazookas, automatic weapons, mortar and artillery fire advances became more hazardous when the DIVISION ran into numerous road blocks and heavy armor. After eleven days of heavy fighting against a stubborn enemy over difficult terrain all enemy resistance ceased in the Harz Mountains on April 20 as the 9TH and 1ST DIVISIONS mopped up pockets of isolated resistance. The DIVISION assembled within the perimeter of Winterberg for regrouping and refitting in preparation for the great drive that lay ahead. On the 13th, the 9TH and the 126th again became part of VII CORPS.

During the past several days many of the company drew on-the-spot repair assignments with combat units of the DIVISION; to aid as the case may be. Others drew specialty assignments with the undermanned 709th Ordnance some fifty kilometers north in the mountain convalescent resort of Winterberg nestled high in the 3,000-foot heights of the Harz Mountains.

Throughout this refitting all Ordnance units now with better access to parts and supplies worked long and hard. The 126th, personally congratulated by Colonel Childs, engaged in some of its finest work. In almost assembly line fashion entire jeep engines were replaced again and again under supervision of Russ Spanninga and Jim Huddleston; two of Automotive's most conservative T/3's. Each day was highly active down in Automotive as combined efforts of varied ranked technicians like Jim Hansen, Charles Switzgable, Wayne Engles, Lee Shaw, Bill Atherton, Herman Shaffer, John Johnson, Robert Turvy, Glenn Hall, John Natoli, Dale Thatcher and many others was scored with a touch of professionalism. An exhausting pace was maintained repairing and installing radiators, setting piston rings . . . cleaning and replacing carburetors . . . head gaskets . . . broken fan belts . . . welding . . . repairing transmissions . . . replacing wheel bearings . . . assembling rebuilt GMC engines in exhausted trucks, and numerous minor and major adjustments. Men in other repair sections, exuding tireless diligence, openly utilized personal unique skill for which they were trained in handling tasks that would lend unlimited support in this last assault.

Jake Cohen's Small Arms section was deluged with broken M-1's and carbines, defective firing pins of automatic Brownings and the 45 cal. Thompson. Mortar sites and even watches came pouring into Chet Percy's Instrument section . . . and none were turned away. Over in Sergeant Olen Hilditch's Supply section highly capable Sam Kaufman and Ed Peszko, along with Technicians Walt Perlisky, Ted Potok and Martin Davidson became "work horses" . . . never derelict in their duty. Keeping the shop functioning, identifying and completing job orders and handling endless enormous paper work was a great reponsibility to Sergeant Tony Spaich and T/4 Jim Tyrrell, and though inseparable buddies, took great delight in constantly needling each other. Gripes and complaints were uttered, yes; but work was not neglected!

Busy! Busy! Busy! The area bristled with activity! Everywhere men hustled! But most were not so preoccupied one mid-morning that particular attention was not given the two "V. I. P." jeeps passing alongside our quarters heading east with five large bright silver stars formed in a circle set in heavy red background mounted on the bumper of the lead vehicle. In this vehicle besides its' driver, sat Generals Eisenhower, Bradley and Hodges; Bradley sporting four bright stars on his shoulder . . . having been promoted to that rank the last day of March. Following close, the other jeep bore lesser "brass."

***

It was late afternoon. The Captain looked up from his desk in the Orderly Room and drawing a puzzled and slightly annoyed expression remarked to Sergeant Botting:

"There's a hell of a lot of noise going on upstairs there, Sergeant. What's happening up there anyway? They got a party or something going on?"

"Don't know, Captain," replied the Sergeant, at the same time motioning to one of the office staff to investigate. He returned in a short time with a wide grin.

"You ought to see it, Sarge; some of the men are using a bathtub. They've got it full of water and they're all trying to use it."

"All at one time? Using it are they? Sounds like they're trying to throw the damn thing down the steps!"

"They're having a big time, Sarge; taking turns singing and sloshing water all over the place! It s' hilarious!"

The Captain looked up again.

"Sergeant, tell them to hold it down. If they want to continue the bath, okay. But tell them to remember what I said, that this is still somebody else's property, and I don't want any more damage done than is necessary."

"Will do, sir."

It was the first tub bath for most since England . . . and for many, the first since leaving the States. Showers did suffice for most, but many considered this a luxury. This tub would be in use daily and the noise was kept to a minimum. No one seemed to care that there was no warm water, for as Lt. Jack Palmer expressed it:

"What the heck. It's springtime and everybody needs a laugh anyway. What's a better way to get it?"

In almost inaudible tones the ever-skeptical First Sergeant added more to it:

"Knowing those guys, they need both; a *laugh* and a *bath*!"

Selection of food rations continued high but as food supply depots had been greatly outdistanced, we would for a brief period enjoy the quality, though the quantity left much to be desired. Some, however, found a simple solution to correct this. After hours many continued to treat themselves to varied degrees of fried chicken . . . quietly and *reluctantly* furnished by several local individual private poultry houses. The idea was to spot a good sized chicken coop during the day and make plans to execute a quiet raid in the evening, the raiders to share the bounty. Some were reminded that this was not in keeping with the ethics of the American GI, but a quick response sounded something like; "Yes, you're probably right about the ethics, and we're going to think about that while the chicken is cooking."

Unquestionably the civilians needed all the food they could get, but sometimes the GI can become a restless demanding individual and as long as no complaint was registered from headquarters this practice would at times continue. The Germans didn't like it a bit but only on rare occasion would they risk intervention.

On April 11 much to his dislike, Private Charlie Culver, a quiet shifty-eyed loner from Minnesota was transferred to 83rd Ordnance Battalion headquarters. New replacements came in quickly. A three-quarter ton truck rolled up at headquarters at noon of the same day and four men climbed out. Helmeted and bundled in overcoats and perspiring profusely, duffle bags slumped to the ground and the men stood with rifles still strapped over their shoulders, wearily scanning this new location. One muttered; "Where are we now and wonder how long we're gonna' be with this outfit?"

The First Sergeant brought them to attention and Lt. Howe called for names.

"Corporal Hill reporting for duty, sir!"

"T/5 Miller reporting for duty, sir!"

"Private First Class Davis reporting for duty, sir!"

"Private First Class Jones reporting for duty, sir!"

"Private Harrell reporting for duty, sir!"

An almost beweilered group of GIs snatched from several different units we would know them as John, Lloyd, Jim, Henry and Bill, respectively. Shuffled from company to company within the past few months they had never really enjoyed an opportunity of initmate association with a unit that could be called their own. They *would* now, and just in time to participate in the final run of the war.

Reassigned to the 83rd Ordnance Battalion in mid-February we had since that time been under jurisdiction of that Battalion and the 184th no less than three times each. On April 12 the 52nd Ordnance Group commander, Colonel William C. Bliss issued an order placing us under command of the 184th Ordnance Battalion again; this time for the war's duration.

The Army began to initiate steps to heighten morale, and soon announcement was made that vacation passes to the French Riviera would be issued.

Exceedingly limited, much time would pass before our company would receive its' pass quota. When received, our quota amounted to exactly *one* pass! Looked upon now as something of a "grand prize" the single pass was allotted immediately and each section through a unique drawing had to vie competitively for it. The "lucky" recipient was Richard Strong, a T/5 from the Instrument section . . . strong in his opinions and one inclined to hold doubts until a fact was proved. Displaying no particular enthusiasm Dick Strong was a married man with small children and claimed to care less about the pleasures of the Riviera at this time.

"Hell," he said; "I wouldn't trade my little home town of Westfield (Mass.) for the whole French Mediterranean coast!"

Quickly someone commented significantly:

"Well . . . who else would, stupid? The point is that you're not in Westfield now! So if you don't want to take advantage of the pass, give it to somebody else!" There were dozens who would take it, but quick! Strong did not talk *too* loud and full advantage was taken of the special trip. Returning from a week's vacation from one of the world's choice resort areas quite an enlightened attitude was exuded. There would however, be more passes issued soon.

We were at breakfast early morning of the 13th when somebody blurted out shocking news. Comments reverberated over much of the messhall.

"President Roosevelt is dead!"

"My God! What did he say?"

"The President is dead?"

"He's dead! We just heard it!"

"Dead? I just can't believe it!"

We were dismayed, shocked and sorrowed *indeed* to learn of President Franklin D. Roosevelt's death, who had in late afternoon of the day before succumbed to a massive cerebral hemorrhage while vacationing at Warm Springs, Georgia.

Enemy resistance on FIRST ARMY's front virtually crumbled. The enemy seemed incapable of any hostile action beyond localized resistance at widely seperated spots. The few reinforcements he had thrown in had been overwhelmed by our strength and power and outmatched by superior mobility. By middle of April FIRST ARMY was spread out in so many places that complete depth of the front lines became difficult to coordinate.

Far back since penetration of the Siegfried Line and its' security established the western Allies had gathered momentum with each vanquished strongpoint, and all enemy resistance along the line anywhere was completely liquidated. The American and British armies had long swept the Rhineland clean, smashed across the Rhine River and were now knifing deep into the works of inner Germany. All phases had been executed and forces were moving so rapidly that often enemy patrols were captured . . . many without the knowledge even that the Rhine had been crossed! The FIFTEENTH UNITED STATES ARMY, still in reserve and equipped with one CORPS took over defense of the west bank of the Rhine between Bonn and Neuss on April 1, so as to release completely the FIRST ARMY for its' drive eastward beyond the Rhine.

CORPS boundaries and DIVISION objectives were changing faster than had been anticipated and complete identification and location of units were reported with some vagueness. Signal men encountered difficulty stringing wires effectively, prohibiting consistent communications; infantry and armored units in great haste often crossed streams and cleared obstacles long before the engineers had an opportunity to build supports simply because equipment needed for construction could not be brought up fast enough. Ordnance maintenance personnel again became hampered in repairing vehicles and weapons due principally to great distances from parts depots. Infrequent delays of parts deliveries added to the woes. Ammunition suppliers could barely keep up with the heavy artillery. These problems became somewhat alleviated as rail lines were soon established from the big new supply depot at Marburg to ammo supply points, and though by mid-April rail bridges were in operation over the Rhine the eastern front of FIRST ARMY was more than 250 miles beyond that river . . . some truckheads required excess of 600 miles on round trips. Transportation was badly needed and all available trucks were secured, including artillery and "ack-ack" cargo trucks.

Despite these shortcomings, however; somewhat effective contacts seemed always to be made with food ration depots and Quartermaster dumps. Time! Time! Time! That was the predominate factor! Hit the enemy and push him back! . . . and while he is reeling from that shock, hit him again until he loses all chance to become elusive! There was no room for any procrastination and we were all trying desperately to avoid it!

It was, in retrospect, reminiscent more and more of events following the breakout from the Normandy peninsular and the well-paced "rat-race" forged across France in the previous summer of 1944! Yet . . . it was well-understood that consequences resulting from this particular "race" would be quite different from the past summer, for all across France there was nothing but jubilation at the thoughts of being liberated, whereas *now* . . . repeatedly . . . perhaps for many it *meant* liberation; but for the majority it was concisely the opposite . . . the word was conquest!!

The VII CORPS thrust to the Elbe was already in progress. The 1ST, 9TH and 104TH DIVISIONS made up a part of the CORPS and General Collins, who on April 16 was presented his third star added two more units; the 3RD ARMORED DIVISION and the 4TH CAVALRY GROUP. Veteran Maj. Gen. Terry Allen had done wonders with the 104TH DIVISION, for having gone into action only the previous fall the "Timberwolves" had proven themselves in every engagement . . . taking a "backseat" to no one! Following completion of a thorough regrouping the 9TH INFANTRY was also to play a major role and prepared to smash east from the Harz Mountains. The 1ST and 9TH particularly had a lot in common. Together they helped sweep the Nazis from Algeria, Bizerte and Tunisia. They were a subsequent team in much of the Normandy action and it would be an honor maneuvering again with the "Big Red One."

It was chilly but clear and the morning of the 16th began as one perfect for traveling. By mid-morning our convoy was ordered eastward. Again employing the "shuttle" pattern we moved not as an entire group but rather in small units . . . three or four vehicles together. Many other units employing the same effective method did much to eliminate incessant "clogging" of traffic on roads that were now classified as expedient. Moreover, moving at 50-foot intervals this presented a far less opportunity for possible enemy aerial targets.

Less than ten minutes east of Allendorf the lower branch of the Eder River was crossed near the approaches of the ancient partially-walled city of Frankenberg. For miles and miles dense pine and fir thickets set in wave-like patterns over hillsides became a contrast of marked beauty as a more picturesque landscape began to unfold. Less evident were signs of battle though now and then an occasional disabled tank . . . or a crushed and burned weapons carrier and even a shattered artillery piece with broken wheel or barrel hanging listlessly lay in silent review off the roads and in gulleys.

On through Bad Wildungen, a quiet and quaint hamlet, twenty three miles carried us to the approaches of Fritzlar, a strategic city with a unique network of highways jutting out in all directions. The 9TH ARMORED DIVISION, following brief resistance on the banks of the Eder River, broke through and disarmed the city a few days before.

South of the city one was amazed to note the huge sprawling airfield with fighter planes still parked in concrete berths just off the runways. Incredible! Stukas . . . Messerschmitts . . . Fockwulfs . . . Heinkels . . . sitting there waiting for the word to take off! But the *word* would not come . . . for that opportunity was lost days ago! A close look at this deserted array of aerial machinery and one knew the enemy was in a bad way indeed! Though some damage was inflicted to most planes this represented the first airfield of its' kind to be captured *completely intact* by FIRST ARMY; that is to say . . . complete with planes; light bombers, fighters, etc., hangars with some undamaged repair shops and storage sheds. In these late days the opportunity to even warm its' motors was never granted most of this once-proud segment of the Luftwaffe primarily because of a serious fuel shortage that long had engulfed the Nazi war machine. So depleted was high octane gasoline and heavy motor oil that at this late stage of the war only Wermacht ground forces were allocated its use.

On through almost deserted Fritzlar we moved, noting only slight damage to industrial areas and at the same time marveling at its quaint closely-knit "gingerbread" houses where draped from many upper windows a white sheet or pillow slips or a white cloth of some description denoted capitulation. Only a few communities of little significance lay between Fritzlar and the ghostly remains of a crushed city that had once been Kassel.

Situated on the Fulda River in the central province of Hesse,

Kassel with a pre-war population of more than 200,000 fell on the 2nd of April to elements of the 80TH INFANTRY and 6TH ARMORED DIVISIONS. Boundaries of the FIRST and THIRD ARMIES paralleled briefly at the south approaches of the city, allowing for more advantageous positions of these two THIRD ARMY Divisions to move with authority against the city. Noted for the manufacture of German artillery, Junker fighter planes and particularly the highly mobile Tiger Royal tank, Kassel had been well-equipped in preparation for the air raids that inevitably were to come. 88mm gun batteries ringed the city and were placed at the most strategic spots around the suburbs, and air raid shelters were dug at many points.

Once a proud and prosperous industrial city the people of Kassel for a long time had lived well, especially during the peak of the rearmament program when no man was found without a job. The early victories of Hitler had brought approximately 20,000 slave laborers to the city and at one time this thriving metropolis possessed a reputation as one of the most industrious cities of inner Germany.

But Kassel suffered . . . and most tragically. Twenty nine major air raids had blasted her almost into oblivion in nearly five years of the war. Nearly 1,500 missions were flown on the city alone and of the 3,500 high explosive bombs and 400,000 incendiaries that fell on her, the city officials soon lost count of the dead. In October, 1943; 800 Allied heavy bombers attacked the city from two directions and dropped 1,100 high explosive bombs and 190,000 incendiaries in one hour, resulting in complete annihilation of the center of the city! In this one raid alone an estimated 20,000 persons were killed, wounded, or missing; chiefly because the alarm system had failed to sound. This was the night that Kassel really died!

When the 126th Ordnance entered the city in the bright crisp morning of April 16 Kassel was nothing but a pile of rubble. Other than alert MP's at assigned locations keeping fluid the vital traffic lanes, and a small few returning civilians groping through the ruins few signs of life were noted. Only a nominal number of skeletal frames of once great factory buildings were left standing. Unofficial records reveal that under all the rock and debris that took in most of the city were approximately 14,000 of its' former inhabitants while others rested in 1,000-person mass graves on the outside of the city. Out of its' 16,000 buildings, nearly 700 were left undamaged. The city truly resembled a tremendous graveyard; and upon entering . . . the smell of death was breathtaking and appalling. Every reason was ours to call Kassel . . . the "City of Death."

Slowly and cautiously moving through streets scattered with rubble while some passages were still being cleared by FIRST ARMY road engineers, no eye could escape without expression the hulking gutted skeletal remains of a once-great city hall sitting amidst other shattered public buildings that in more prosperous times stood prominently over the vast public parks that was part of its' setting. Beyond the city's eastern outskirts we crossed the Fulda River.

Several hundred yards beyond, the bouncing convoy reached another steel-structured bridge, obviously overburdened, spanning the wide Weser River. Reeking with antiquity and already tilted to some degree its' stability was questioned as it shook and rattled with each shift of the gears. We immediately passed into the junction of Munden on the other side of the Weser.

Witzenhausen, Arenhausen and Heiligenstadt were names we had never heard of, and only those taking notes would remember them as we picked up speed and finally reached the highway intersection of Worbis to pause, despite the few scurrying townspeople, for a roadside staff meeting of officers and section leaders.

At this period the advance of oncoming Russian troops from the east was heightened, while at the same time the western allies were pressing the gasping German armies in a vice-like grip and only the iron will of the Nazi Party and German High Command prevented a general collapse. With weapons becoming immobilized and critical shortages of fuel and ammunition a reality, reports of large-scale surrender were reaching our ears . . . some *entire* units deserting. Prisoners told of disorganization and defeat. Many enemy soldiers were discarding their uniforms to become "lost" into civilian ranks. Discord and strife was running rampart amongst field commanders as high-ranking officers were being replaced one after the other. Suspicion, jealousy, fright, disobedience and doubts of integrity were running their course amongst troops that formerly were dependable! The seeds of distrust sown, wholesale surrender became a reality . . . many surrendering to the western allies rather than face the uncertainty and wrath of reckless advancing Red armies.

Once, while detouring on a mud-churned road we slowed to a crawl to allow hundreds of dejected, ragged, tired, shivering and obviously hungry German prisoners, huddled under their grey-green greatcoats in an effort to stave off as much as possible the chilly rain . . . to pass alongside and through the only apparent passable stretch of terra firma that had not succumbed to mud. The prisoner lines seemed almost endless as they kept streaming from over the hill. Guarded by but a scant few armed GIs it seemed incredible that they could remain orderly in so great numbers. Yet, orderly they were, for certainly they were relieved that it was all over, especially with the knowledge that food and rest were waiting for them within a short period. Many were cognizant that food and rest was a great substitute for death and destruction that otherwise surely would have been waiting for them.

"Look at them poor devils," came a comment. "Boy, are they ever a sorry-looking lot."

"Yeah, but just remember, it could have been the other way around. We could very well have been one of them and *we* could be heading for the prison camps."

Another commented; "You can bet one thing, we would never have had it so good as they will."

We were all unanimous in that broad statement.

In earlier days in Normandy, or even in northern Fr ance one might have looked with scorn as groups of prisoners passed by. But no longer would this feeling be harbored. There would be no more wisecrack shouts of "Kraut Bastards!" or "Phony Hitler lovers!" or "How about it now, superman!" . . . or anything like that. No fist-shaking, no nose-thumbing or mockery for now that they were down and out most of us exuded compassion for them. Some looked up and occasional glances of common recognition were exchanged, but they were glances devoid of insults. The Germans had *had* it! They *knew* it and they knew that we were well-aware of it! No longer was it necessary to "rub it in."

Two great Russian forces were driving hard from the east; Marshal Georgi Zhukov leading the First Belorussian Army Group from the east toward Berlin and Marshal Ivan Koniev, commanding the First Ukranian Army Group approaching from southeast of the city. Both were encountering stiff opposition bridging the Oder River almost a hundred miles east of the Elbe. The British 2nd and Canadian First Armies under Field Marshal Montgomery's 21ST ARMY GROUP had advanced beyond Bremen and Hamburg and were scurrying north along the Baltic coast and in control of all northern territory along the upper approaches of the Elbe River.

General William H. Simpson's NINTH ARMY, a spearhead having reached the Elbe River on April 12, but having since pulled back, now engaged in a mopping up campaign, encountering spotty resistance north of the Harz Mountains. Having cleared Hannover and Brunswick the Army now directed a fanning out operation over the northern plains. In retrospect, General Simpson advised the author:

"Between March 24 and April 15, 1945 the NINTH ARMY made one assault crossing of the wide lower Rhine River and, in conjunction with the U. S. FIRST ARMY encircled and reduced the Ruhr, Germany's greatest industrial area. We drove 230 miles into Germany in 19 days. NINTH ARMY was the first Allied army to reach and cross the Elbe River, and its' bridgehead was being developed to continue the attack to Berlin when orders were received to stand fast. We then occupied some 30,000 square miles of Germany, from the Rhineland to the Elbe."

Commenting on his reaction when ordered to hold established bridgeheads over the Elbe, "but *not* to advance to Berlin," General Simpson still recalled, with apparent painful misgivings:

"*That* one *will always* stay with me," he declared. "When I was called to 12TH ARMY GROUP headquarters in Weisbaden, I wondered what was up."

Simpson was so stunned that he could not even remember half

of the things Bradley said from then on.

"All I remember is that I was so heartbroken that I left in a kind of a daze. All I could think of was, 'How am I going to tell my staff, the CORPS commanders and my troops. Above all, how am I going to tell my troops?"

General George Patton's THIRD ARMY, still a part of Bradley's 12TH ARMY GROUP . . . as was the NINTH ARMY, was driving hard, crushing and liquidating remnants of the German armies in the south and probing dramatically into Czechoslovakia. General Jacob L. Devers' 6TH ARMY GROUP, embracing General Patch's SEVENTH U. S. ARMY and the First French Army skirted beyond the Swiss border and shot spearheads into lower Germany. Striking east beyond Nuremburg they were reaching for Munich and would speed toward the banks of the Danube in Bavaria in a race to reach the Austrian border.

Far south . . . in Italy, General Mark W. Clark, commanding all forces in 15TH ARMY GROUP, was only days away from proclaiming a full allied victory in that battered and torn country.

Now rapidly seeping into worldwide attention was the shocking and horrifying publicity of several slave labor camps, some at this moment being overrun by U. S. troops. We began to run into a trickle of those that had already been liberated and as our advances progressed more and more of these refugees began to appear.

Roving over the countryside in small groups; traveling on foot, often three or four together, sometimes larger bands . . . men, women and children in small knots displaying no set pattern and depending on whatever nourishment that could be found. Wary of everything at first, their faces reflected the telling effects of weariness as many had wandered for miles. Seeking shelter and rest under roadside trees . . . many obviously pushing themselves beyond the point of endurance, some appearing as if they could drag themselves no further.

The smashing Allied thrust continued to capture prison labor camps and as the gates were opened thousands of exhausted souls were set free. The liberators had come! It was fantastic; but suddenly a great problem began to arise . . . one that became heavily detrimental to the advancing armies.

A point had now developed where the well-paced drive of the western allies, particularly the FIRST ARMY, was threatened with the loss of its' real effectiveness!

Soon, thousands of refugees were appearing from everywhere . . . cluttering the roads, especially the main supply routes . . . swarming across bridges that decrepit with age were almost too small to accommodate bulky U. S. equipment with any degree of safety. Horsedrawn wagons heavily-laden with refugees and personal belongings were strewn in unpatterned convoys all across roads in a state of quasi-confusion . . . their rickety equipment often breaking down, creating traffic hazards that bordered on the critical. Our contact with these stragglers increased! Wagons loaded with aged women in peasant dress . . . shouting greetings in their native tongue, men still clad in striped uniform trousers and denim coats and black peaked caps were among the great mixture of eastern European nationalities. Some were sick, some hobbling, but all smiling. Rumpled, dirty and ill-fitting garments were prominent, the striped uniform itself representing a symbol of long years of terror and depravity. Many, heavily bent with haversacks strapped to their shoulders plodded along aimlessly, and almost everyone on foot carried some pitiful bundle of personal belongings. To them, perhaps this was synonymous of what had managed to be salvaged from these past nightmarish years. Always on the move . . . to where seemed to be inconsequential as long as it was away from the war zone; as long as it was away from confinement; and as long as it promised a prospect of freedom! They were going west in their first step toward eventual repatriation to native Russia, Poland or some of the Balkan countries. There were at times, though in separate groups; Dutch, French, Belgian and sometimes Italian . . . not as heavily burdened, but pursuing the same goal. We did on occasion de-accellerate our pace to reach out and extend a portion of whatever personal food rations were on hand. Their weak and weary smiles were compensation enough.

The released prisoner slowly posed a serious threat in other ways. *His* liberation became *his* signal for revenge and in the beginning these roving bands with their unaccustomed freedom created trouble just short of chaos in towns . . . irregardless of established military control. The years of pent-up suppression, humiliation and hatred of Nazi masters would now be released . . . and this began to erupt at spots over much of the country . . . especially within a fifty to seventy-five mile radius of a liberated camp. Plundering . . . pillaging . . . looting . . . burning . . . rape . . . even murder was administered recklessly; conducted so alarmingly now that every German civilian living within operational distance of a former slave labor camp feared for his life! A wave of sympathy surely went out to the former prisoners, but severe measures would have to be taken immediately to halt this present wild display of disorder and complete disciplinary breakdown. The American Military Government was in fact moving fast with deliberate restraint to deal with this situation.

Displaced Persons (DP) camps were hastily established at strategic locations by the AMG and a tremendous task of feeding, sheltering, delousing, classifying and clothing these unfortunates was in a feverish way commenced. This alleviated greatly the task of forward troops.

Designed to move the company all the way into Nordhausen this motorized march would prove to be one of the most extensive and beyond question the most interesting since crossing the German border in September of 1944. Geographically in the Province of Anhalt this entire territory with its spacious green fields, tall pines and mirrored lakes; its' broad highways and rolling hills could reach deep into the pages of history and reveal that the American GI was *only one* of many foreign soldiers to storm across its' broad expanse!

Julius Caesar, before Christ, led his armies against German tribes along the Rhine. The Roman emperor, Augustus, in the year A.D. 9, tried to conquer all of Germany. Charlemagne, ruler of the northern region of the Holy Roman Empire, which today is France, Germany, The Netherlands, Belgium, Austria, northern Italy, Switzerland and a small part of Spain, directed his armies over much of Germany during the years A.D. 770-843, surpressing rebellions. One could point to the legions of Napoleon who carried the French wars deep into Germany; and moreover, the religious wars that became an internal struggle to develop into the Thirty

Years War, leaving much of Germany a waste, saw troops of many nations intervening and taking sides and engaging in battle within its' borders.

From our mobile position on the highways a distant and enchanting panorama unfolded . . . revealing for miles natural beauty that cannot easily be described. From its' lofty position a castle dating back to medieval times would on occasion loom in the distance, displaying a striking countenance in a setting of thinly veiled forests; forests through which Teutonic tribes wandered for hundreds of years before their history was written. Elements of history throughout this central region of Germany dated far back beyond the days of princesses, knights and even the mythical dragons and when it became our opportunity to visit one of these drafty abodes it was something of a personal thrill to associate the atmosphere with fairy tales which we remembered from long ago.

Rolling almost parallel alongside the flow of the Weser River, crossing it many times on a snake-like route and sweeping through numerous refugee-laden communities, it was noted that this particular river extended almost to the crushed and burning city of Nordhausen itself. By late afternoon of the 16th the entire company had come upon that insufferable partially destroyed city.

Nordhausen fell on the 11th to the 3RD ARMORED and 104TH INFANTRY DIVISIONS, and after its' capture troops were startled to find it a former center of activity for the preparation of the notorious V-2 rocket bombs and assembly stations constructed in mammoth underground factories. Slave laborers forcefully employed in assembling of these dreaded weapons had worked underground for months, even years . . . having rarely seen the light of day during that time. FIRST ARMY ran into something far more appalling when it uncovered one of the most active and brutal forced labor prison camps in the whole of Germany . . . this facility housing some ten thousand slave laborers.

Like the horrible death camps of Dachau, Buchenwald, Treblinka and Belsen, Nordhausen was marked for its' share of brutality . . . greatly exemplified by hangings, malnutrition, sex crimes and unscrupulous beatings that tended to bring out the sadistic character encased in the minds of heartless Nazi brutes and their associates. "Recon" members of the 126th took the liberty of inspecting parts of the camp and viewed with disbelief hundreds and hundreds of withered and decomposing bodies of former slave laborers sprawled grotesquely throughout! Hundreds of dead had already been stacked in piles as one would stack cordwood . . . and the expressions on their faces and broken withered frames made it almost unbelievable! Nothing encountered thus far in the war could so compare to the withering stench and offensive atmosphere hanging gloomily over this place and its' surroundings! Those that had not died were too weak hardly to move, their eyes fixed in a "lost"glow; the skin and flesh actually sagging lifelessly from wasted frames that revealed little more than bones. With bodies so badly emaciated and in such an acute stage of malnutrition death irrevocably claimed many. Vehemently against their will, though proceeding with a restrained degree of cooperation selected German community leaders and prominent residents of the city were forced to view the camp's horrors, and some in a complete state of remorseful dejection were ordered to bury the unfortunates in mass graves.

By the time the 126th entered the rubbish-littered streets of Nordhausen some four days behind the 3RD ARMORED DIVISION, many of these prisoners had already been set free. True; death had claimed many but those that had managed to survive in at least a semi-physical state considered themselves fortunate and were beginning to strongly express it. In striped prison garb many were roaming the streets and had gone almost wild with thoughts of retaliation! These thoughts were transferred into acts . . . and subsequently homes were ransacked and looted, windows smashed, shrubbery disrupted, private vehicles ravaged and many beatings administered! These survivors had taken things into their own hands in a complete disorderly and violent manner! Fires were rampant in several sections of the city. Destruction of personal property reached a high peak and ostensibly a drive to exterminate every civilian in their path *appeared* to be under way . . . though this may not have been the case. Who could hardly blame them! Yes, *who could* hardly blame them? Yet, this wild reckless abandoning of reason slowly began to diminish as the AMG "cracked down" and began the arduous but firm task of establishing control over the city.

We moved southwest of the city along the winding Weser River some ten kilometers where preliminary preparations had already been made to establish bivouac in the neighboring community of Sondershausen. Sonderhausen had been spared destruction when the 9TH ARMORED DIVISION, encountering light resistance, cleared it on the 12th. Through the huge open iron-grill gate guarding the entrance archway, swung wide for the occasion, the command jeep rolled slowly along the narrow stone-lined drive. The First Sergeant, hunched in the back seat stared in wonder as he noted several feet beyond, the magnificent structure partially hidden by greenery from drooping limbs of tall close-quartered trees.

"Boy-Oh-Boy!" muttered an impressed Botting (and he didn't impress easily), "Just *look* at this place, will ya! This must have been Hitler's private quarters or some big 'Kraut'!"

It was not Hitler's private quarters of course, but it was *indeed* a mansion as strikingly impressive as we would see.

"A nice piece of real estate, huh?" quipped the Captain; "But just wait till you see the inside." Weinberg himself had headed the "recon" team that located this area the day before.

Overlooking the community and roads that twist in all directions through spacious well-cultivated fields this handsome commodious dwelling and its' environs not only spared damage by advancing troops but fortunately had not yet been touched by released prisoners. Each piece of its splendid furniture had been left in place by evacuated occupants. A winding oaken stairway, innumerable bedrooms, each luxuriously furnished with carefully hand-carved beds adorned the chateau, and in one of the mammoth carpeted studyrooms almost interminable volumes of books gave it an appearance of a small stately library. The well-cared-for shrubbery and greens in the frontal expansive courtyard had not been ravished and within these confines two rare peacock birds strutted strangely proud, though a bit uneasy. A six-foot brick wall surrounding the estate afforded ample protection to the grounds from uninvited and potential trespassers.

Most of the company personnel were assigned billits within the mansion itself while the remainder found housing in comfortable surrounding quarters. In the face of all this one can imagine the toll exacted by the souvenir-hunting 126th, to say nothing of the tremendous advantage taken of this unusual privilege . . . most especially the enormous well-equipped galley and fine featherbeds.

Massive and imposing, the countenance of this chateau, its' courtyard and surroundings had been no less a thing of splendor in past years, but at the moment this splendor was only superficial for within a radius of two to three miles the atmosphere was anything but peaceful and friendly. Many slave camp inmates, now free but not yet under full control were at this moment reacting violently . . . showing little mercy to German civilians wherever encountered. Especially was this true in Nordhausen, a city now turned into one of great fear! Rifle and pistol shots cracked sharply at any time of the night, explosions became commonplace, and many terror-stricken civilians probably were saved *only* because of the quick intervention of the AMG who expediently began restoring order. More than once civilians openly sought our protection against destructive designs of the former slaves . . . now loose but near wild with freedom.

On the second day shortly after lunch the CP reverberated with heavy discourses of displeasures loudly voiced by the Captain. The First Sergeant on the receiving end, sat with unimpressed expression but listening intently.

"Lieutenant Howe and I made an inspection of company quarters and grounds this morning and I was not happy, not happy at all with some of the things I saw."

"Such things as what, Captain?"

"Such as a couple of the men walking around with civilian top hats on. One fellow had a Kraut officer's uniform on but he went back inside and took it off. One man down in Automotive was actually working with a German helmet on until I made him take it off."

"He was probably just trying to be funny Captain, that's all;" reasoned Botting, "I'm sure he wouldn't wear it around the area."

"Funny? That's not my idea of being funny Sergeant; he has his *own* helmet to wear. We're not playing games and this is not a masquerade party and I tell you something else; if he wears it outside these walls and some "trigger happy" GI sees him he might just fill it full of holes . . . without asking questions." The Captain's tone became intense but he kept it under control. "And while I'm at it Sergeant; I've seen dishes broken unnecessarily and there's been jars of preserves broken open and smashed and looks like drawers ransacked and items strewn around. This was done after we arrived and it is highly unnecessary. What I'm getting at Sergeant, is this;" and the prominent squint of the eyes made it emphatic . . . "I don't want any looting or any unnecessary destruction of property around here or any other place. These people are going to have a hell of a time getting straight when they return anyway."

Tightlipped, and continuing to remain unimpressed, Botting replied; "All right, Captain; we'll take care of it."

***

The last few days of April brought swift dramatic changes in the European campaign and the German High Command was crumbling to bits! The Nazi Chief Executioner; Heinrich Himmler was captured by British forces near Hamburg. This capture was short-lived and he was imprisoned but a few hours. Sensing the murky obscurity of his future this henious exterminator of thousands quickly bit down on a capsule of cyanide hid on his person and in a few minutes Himmler was dead!

The German Labor Party leader, Dr. Robert Ley, was captured in Austria and later committed suicide. Dr. Paul Goebbels, Germany's Chief Propaganda Minister; rather than submit to capture put his family to death . . . and then ended his own life. Hermann Wilhelm Goering; mastermind of the once prestigious but now diminished Luftwaffe and purportedly Number Two man in Germany, was captured by U. S. forces in Bavaria. To bring down the final curtain on the tyrannical Nazi empire; Adolph Hitler himself, along with his ever-present mistress, Eva Braun; facing imminent capture, was reported to have committed suicide in his private underground bunker in Berlin . . . while Russian shells were falling on the city, and only a few hours ahead of the fast-moving Red armies.

Were one to turn to the scriptures and read Proverbs 13:20 he would hear the words of Solomon ringing true:

"He that walketh with wise men shall be wise; but a companion of fools shall be destroyed."

It was a resounding finale!

The top leaders and founders of the so-long-lived Nazi government . . . having in perverted fashion tasted glory and lavish living unprecedented in power since the days of the ancient rulers, and having been responsible for deaths now totaling in the millions were finally reaching their day of reckoning! The ancient adage; "Live by the Sword and you will die by the sword" could never have been more applicable!

The last days of April also found the company preparing for its' final convoy of the war.

Sondershausen was several miles behind now and the light precipitation had ceased. Just beyond the muddy rushing Helme River we rolled into the highway town of Berga. A mile or two further west we were approaching Rossla. Winding up somehow as the convoy's last vehicle T/4 Mike Springer looked out of his window while twisting through the muddy streets of Rossla and was not at all pleased with what he saw. Three German women, heads tightly wrapped in kerchiefs struggled hard with a released Slav prisoner to retrieve a small wagon obviously loaded with personal belongings. Displaying tremendous agitation the women would not release their grip . . . tugging and shouting as if this were their last possessions on earth! The Slav, clad in oversized clothes though still wearing the striped pants from prison, shouted back and continued to yank and pull.

"Look at those poor bastards will you!" muttered Springer.

"Yeah, I see 'em." came a reply from his close companion, Bob Smith; a small energetic wide-eyed T/5 from Michigan.

"Boy, we oughta get out-a here and help those gals . . . they've got trouble!" said Springer.

"Yeah, you do that and you've got trouble too. That sonofabitch would shoot you quick!"

"The *hell* he would?"

"The *hell* he wouldn't !"

"How do you know?"

"Look, if he'd risk his life for a little old wagon, what do you think he'd do if you attacked him? I tell you what he'd do, he'd shoot your tail off! Those guys are just that wicked. Man, those guys have been through it and they're not about to take any crap off anybody!"

"If I threw this tommy-gun on him he'd sit up and take notice, I guarantee you that . . . and he'd do it damn quick too!"

"He might, but ah-h-h, keep going, let's forget about that 'Hunkie'!"

The truck kept rolling, but not as fast as Smith would like. Springer kept looking back, and with a nefarious expression he said;

"I've got a notion to go back there and kick hell out of that guy . . . just on general principals . . . and I ain't worried about his gun either!"

"Well, you better get that notion out of your head right now, man. We're probably gonna see a lot of that from here on. What're you gonna do . . . stop everytime you see something like that? What the hell, the Krauts have it coming to them anyway. You stop now and let the convoy go on without us, Weinberg will give you more hell than that 'Hunkie' ever thought of!"

Springer kept driving . . . visibly upset, and through half-clenched teeth, muttered:

"The bastard! I'd still like to get him!"

German civilians began to appear in greater number as we approached the country's central heartland; for in actuality there was no alternative . . . nowhere else to go. They had gone about as far east as would be feasible. The choice was slim and most had elected to remain in their communities and in respective homes and suffer whatever consequences awaiting. In less populated villages we rolled noisely through and there they stood, stoic and almost expressionless . . . an occasional frightened face peeping from behind half-crossed shutters. Younger children; not fully aware of its significance, often displayed the fast-waning Nazi salute . . . and we in fun gave a like sign in return . . . though often accompanied with a mild deviation of words.

On through thinly-spread Sangerhausen . . . through several

unfamiliar hamlets; each reeking with age and each dwelling displaying closed shutters and at times white sheets hanging conspicuously from windows. By noon the old industrial city of Eisleben was entered. Some twenty-five kilometers east the great city of Halle loomed in the distance. Two miles west of the city however, all eyes were glued in amazement to the tremendous aerodrome filled with Messerschmitts, Heinkels, JU-88's . . . fighters and bombers and lighter aircraft that in these frantic suspenseful days hardly enjoyed the privilege of racing down the spacious runways. Long plagued with a depleted fuel supply the Germans had been fairly successful in attempts to render them inoperable before abandonment to oncoming troops of the VII CORPS.

When the 104TH INFANTRY DIVISION reached the Salle River on the 14th at the western edge of Halle they found all bridges blown. Throwing a pontoon bridge across the Salle the first troops were greatly surprised to encounter stiff fanatical resistance from small arms fire, artillery and self-propelled guns. Surprisingly, because the bulk of enemy troops was calculated to be in headlong retreat to the Mulde River several miles east of the city. Whether agreeable or not all members of the Volksturm were recruited and forced to fight alongside German troops. Resistance accelerated! The 104TH DIVISION commander, Maj. Gen. Terry Allen, issued an ultimatum to the German Commanding General in the city but negotiations failed. The siege resumed and fighting grew with intensity . . . developing in several instances; house-to-house combat! Encircled by American troops, punished by withering fire and overwhelmed with a fast-receeding morale, its' efforts were vain and the city's defenses crumbled, and Halle surrendered on the 19th after five days of desperate fighting.

The 126th crossed the Saale and entered the great cathedral city. Here was once a city of some 285,000 people; cloaked in culture, possessing one of the finest and oldest universities in eastern Germany; home of the great composer; George Frederick Handel, and long boasting some of the most prominent cathedrals in the nation. Before the war Halle housed proficient producers of machinery, iron and copper goods, much of which was shipped out via well-channelled water passages of the navigable Saale. Yet, an important portion of this imposing city was destroyed because enemy commanders . . . easily cognizant of a "lost cause" elected to defend against advancing forces.

Our entry from the west reflected only a small degree of destruction but our motorized march through the center of the city, thence onto the north portion saw much of the city in ruins. Local fighting had been intense, but attacks from U. S. and R. A. F. fighter-bombers had done much damage before ground troops arrived.

Due north beyond this sprawling metropolis we moved, encompassing several small communities . . . each surprisingly cleared of Germans, and after some twenty kilometers we came into the refugee-laden village of Lobejun. On the northeast approaches on the far side of the village we dispersed and occupied a complex of buildings known as the Henschelwerk, a steel fabricating factory surrounded completely, excepting two strategically erected iron gates, by a seven-foot brick wall. The 126th spread out and prepared to spend the final days of the war.

When the 126th Ordnance's "recon" team first entered the cobblestoned streets of Lobejun on the 21st they were greatly amazed to behold several full-uniformed German soldiers, though apparently weaponless roaming at will. The shock on the other hand was equally as great to the Germans because this represented perhaps the first American troops to appear since the 3RD ARMORED DIVISION swept through here unopposed on the 16th. Suspensing all imagination . . . could they yet believe the American forces had possibly advanced this far? If so, would they have dared abandon caution and appear in so conspicuous a locale as this? A few civilians scurried quickly into doorways. But suddenly the "recon" driver spotted something and his heart leaped to his throat! Angling his head slightly to the C. O. he gasped in a low key:

"Good Lord, Captain! Do you see what I see? Just look at the Krauts! . . . the place is *crawling* with 'em!" Hesitating a little, he asked; "What d'ya think?"

Obviously startled but shifting his eyes and not even moving his head, the Captain whispered through the side of his mouth:

"Damn right, I see 'em! I see 'em, I see 'em! Don't even look at 'em. I don't think they'll bother us. Just keep on going and we'll see what happens."

"Yeah, maybe they won't bother us," thought the driver to himself, "but isn't that what Custer said about the Indians!"

Unmolested, but with extreme caution the jeep continued to roll. Returning the same route some twenty minutes later not one soldier appeared. It was in fact, difficult to even locate a civilian. Wondering if the soldiers had prepared an ambush along the way it was concluded the promiscuity had ended as all had apparently dispersed into alleyways and doorways and practically into thin air . . . almost as if a contagious plague were dropped in their midst! Later it was learned that these soldiers, or most of them . . . weary and disillusioned had been actually waiting in this village for the war to end. Others had been treated for wounds at a nearby hospital and long had been out of the fight though never having discarded their uniform. By the time the entire company arrived next morning all of these soldiers had made their exodus . . . or by their own choice had become civilians. We would experience no resistance in the least from any of them.

At daybreak barrel-chested John Walls, who had wheeled Recovery's big wreckers over much of the continent looked out from guard post No. One to scarcely believe his eyes. Two small youthful figures, attentively displaying a white cloth and garbed in German uniform cautiously and slowly were making their way toward him. The big 21-year old Pfc remembered:

"At first I thought they were two of our guys . . . and when I suddenly realized they *were not*, it momentarily scared the hell out of me!"

The two young Germans . . . still in their teens; hungry and weary, wanted to surrender. They wanted in fact, more than that. They wanted food and refuge and in a short time were accorded this request. Shedding jackets some time later they were placed in the kitchen and for almost a week it was not surprising to see two young German orderlies plying back and forth from the kitchen to the messhall executing their duties in excellence, and gaining weight that they never knew was possible.

"We have not seen our unit in days," each admitted; and furthermore . . . we don't ever want to see it again!"

They not only had found refuge . . . they temporarily had found a *home*!

By April 16 FIRST ARMY began closing in from three sides on the great library and fur processing center of Leipzig and placed it under heavy artillery fire. Roaring to a swift finish V CORPS dispatched the 2ND and 69TH INFANTRY DIVISIONS to capture the city. While surprisingly encountering stubborn but relatively weak opposition the 2ND DIVISION attacked with heavy and self-propelled artillery while other elements of that DIVISION, together with the 69TH engaged in heavy fighting at the great railyards and around the massive city hall. The defense was futile and the city capitulated on the 19th. On April 20 the Stars and Stripes carried headlines heavy with confirmation:

"FIRST CAPTURES LEIPZIG!"

Leipzig became the last major German metropolis to fall on FIRST ARMY's front.

Because of growing fears of a headlong collision between the western allies and the rapidly advancing Russians in the east, the Elbe River . . . extending from the Baltic Sea south down into Czechoslovakia was established as a sort of boundary between the forces closing in. The Russians were fast moving onto the Oder River, less than one hundred miles to the east and now speculation arose that even the Elbe would not suffice as a demarcation line. General Bradley on April 24 issued a directive from 12TH ARMY GROUP:

"United States forces will not advance beyond the line of the Mulde River."

The Mulde, twisting basically along the same course as the Elbe was some twenty-five miles west of the original line. Now all units *raced* for the Mulde! Prisoners came in droves, and enemy troops, opposing the Mulde River line were concerned largely with the approach of the Red Army spearheads to their rear, and fearful of Russian imprisonment swarmed into our lines to surrender. Both V and VII CORPS reported receiving into respective PW compounds, eight to ten thousand prisoners daily! All in the meantime however, thousands of *Allied* prisoners were liberated all along the FIRST ARMY line.

While the Mulde acted as a sort of "finish line" Maj. Gen. Emil F. Reinhardt's 69TH DIVISION kept on going to the Elbe where a juncture with the Red Army would be arranged. At the city of Torgau, situated on the banks of the Elbe, this unit on April 25 met the Russian 58th Guards Division to establish history's greatest juncture of two Allied armies.

Finishing a clean sweep of the forest in the extreme eastern part of the Harz Mountains the 9TH DIVISION raced on to the Mulde and on the 27th met the Russians near Proteau. Berlin was in ruins and practically all territory east of the Elbe had been overrun by the indomitable Red armies. The first days of May saw the European war swiftly drawing to a close and except for reduction of die-hard Nazi civilians and fanatic supporters or small isolated enemy units the FIRST ARMY had all but completed its' physical task in Europe.

The War Department in Washington, D. C. on May 4 directed through Supreme Headquarters that due to imminent collapse of the German Army, FIRST ARMY return to the United States and prepare for redeployment to the Pacific Theater.

May 7 on Monday was a day to take its' place in history when General Eisenhower announced Germany's complete capitulation, and representatives of the German High Command had signed at 2:41 A.M. EST, that defeated nation's surrender in Rheims, France . . . the surrender to become effective at 12:01 A.M. May 8.

Exactly one minute after midnight on the 8th the inevitable happened! All hostilities on the Continent ceased and the war in Europe ended. The guards had heard it on the shortwave jeep radio before dawn and we were *all* aware by breakfast. But formalities would be served and we were called to assembly in the sunbathed courtyard later in the morning around ten.

From one of the shop truck radios came the prominent strains of "Racing With The Moon." The resonant voiced Vaughn Monroe had already made it one of the popular hits of the day.

"Somebody turn it off a minute," said Lt . Howe as he mounted a short row of steps preparatory to addressing the group.

A directive had been relayed from Supreme Headquarters to 12TH ARMY GROUP, thence to all armies and units under its' command. From FIRST ARMY by TTX the directive moved swiftly to VII CORPS, on to DIVISION, to 52nd Ordnance Group, over to 184th Ordnance Battalion and finally to the 126th . . . all in a matter of minutes.

We listened intently as the Lieutenant read a simple but historic message:

"TO ALL ALLIED FORCES IN EUROPE –
EFFECTIVE 01201 HOURS 8 MAY ALL MILITARY OPERATIONS IN THE EUROPEAN THEATER WILL CEASE."

DWIGHT D. EISENHOWER, COMMANDING
SUPREME HEADQUARTERS ALLIED
EXPEDITIONARY FORCES
ETOUSA

Reacting with somber and light applause this message, though expected for days was nevertheless good news! There it was! It was as simple as that . . . and then we were dismissed. Early the following day, the 9th; all ears were attentive as Prime Minister Winston Churchill broadcast via BBC to the world the significance of this date.

"Man! That's it! *That is it!*" someone gave a whoop . . . *"Home!"*

This day would enter the annals of history and henceforth be known as "V-E Day," as truly it was . . . Victory in Europe!

Victory celebrations were moderate around the camp, but lights burned late during the night of the 9th as boots were shined, clothes pressed and rifles cleaned in preparation for exciting events planned for the next day. May 10 would find the 126th engaging in its' first parade since the days of Camp Butner as all units of the 184th Ordnance Battalion were selected to join other VII CORPS troops in impressive full dress parades through the streets of Halle on this day.

A mighty parade it was! Some five thousand soldiers presenting a striking performance as flags, bands and military equipment filled the streets with colorful uniformity and close cadence. Curbs and sidewalks lined with German civilians watching in awe . . . certainly did so with mixed feelings. Others from private windows and doorways viewed this illustrious spectacle with perhaps as much inner relief as did those with bewilderment, animosity and perhaps some nostalgic envy.

It was an unusually warm day and immediately following the parade many participating units assembled in the great high-steepled Lutheran cathedral in the heart of Halle where impressive memorial services were conducted by chaplains within VII CORPS units, and from whose dias some four hundred years before was preached dynamic and startling messages of religious reformation by Martin Luther.

On May 8 the mission of the FIRST U. S. ARMY was completed. In his final report, its' commander, General Hodges, who since April 18 wore four stars, was strong in praise of the ARMY's function in the European Theater, and in part he concluded:

"It is a tribute to the men and their commanders in the FIRST ARMY that all missions assigned the ARMY were accomplished successfully from the invasion of Normandy to junction with the Soviet forces."

Courtney H. Hodges
Commanding General,
FIRST UNITED STATES ARMY
ETOUSA

Having already bade farewell to FIRST ARMY we then became an integral part of the NINTH ARMY. As the mid days of May approached the 9TH INFANTRY DIVISION . . . having completed its initial task regrouped and prepared to move more than two hundred miles southwest across the country deep into the province of Bavaria in lower Germany near the northwestern border of Austria. Selected as one of the occupation units to enforce control in the American sector the 9TH would headquarter in and around the lovely and stately resort city of Ingoldstadt on the Danube River.

One would find it difficult to believe that suddenly the 126th Ordnance had after more than a year, severed connections with the 9TH DIVISION. With 264 days of combat on the Continent this tremendously spirited organization since landing in North Africa in November, 1942 had engaged in eight victorious campaigns . . . five of them in the European theater. Here was a fighting machine that through astute leadership and dependability was a recipient of 8,116 individual and unit awards and decorations, plus 105 additional citations from French, British and Belgian governments since its' early days in Africa. Were it inclined, it could also boast of capturing some 130,000 German prisoners . . . but on the *darker* side its' combat days were closing with 22,292 men killed, wounded and missing. Is there little wonder that we could say with pride: "We served a great DIVISION!"

It was "so long" to the 184th Ordnance Battalion, and inasmuch as VII CORPS moved into operational control of the NINTH U. S. ARMY we would say goodbye too, to this superb command.

***

The war's end did not relieve one of individual responsibility though it did serve as a sort of relief valve in that we desired a closer friendship with the local German populace. This was predicated on shy but obvious actions to indicate an eagerness to establish that same relationship with us soon after we arrived. With some limitations certain company restrictions would be lifted, but complete fraternization *was not* one of them. Fraternization remained . . . strictly "VERBOTEN!" This order was met with gripes that were not unusual . . . but the general feeling was; "What the heck! . . . the war is over; we will not be moving east beyond this location and only a matter of time would see us homeward bound." In the meantime with languid spring weather splashing the countryside, what could be more conducive to mix with the young maidens of Lobejun? Yes . . . the "No Frat" order was in effect, but we would not at this point waste too much time worrying about it!

Mixing with the several *willing* Frauleins continued to remind one that direct violation of the "No Frat" order could conceivably result in a court-martial. Certainly no one at this late state desired a court-martial, but many were willing to risk it. For, if the GI with his aggressive ingenuity could find a way to beat the damnation of the Normandy hedgerows, could muster enough strategy to out maneuver the Germans on their own grounds, thus springing the Falaise trap, could rebound from shock and surprise and withstand the rigors of cold and uncertainty during the Battle of The Bulge, smash over the Ludendorf bridge against overwhelming odds of survival . . . then surely there *must* be a viable solution to this fraternization problem!

Each day stimulated interest and found cordiality of the townspeople increasing. Visiting our grounds with regularity the Burgomeister and lesser town officials set about coordinating arrangements for handling laundry on a wholesale as well as an individual basis with several industrious families. Interested civilians became eager to assume odd jobs within the company area, though the jobs were few. Those of us interested in viewing items of historic importance throughout the surrounding territory were extended invitations while guides offered their services. Much in number was found many imposing landmarks. This region contained a wealth of history, and many cathedrals . . . steeped heavy with an aura of the Renaissance period, dated back to and beyond the thirteenth century. Within driving distance of a few miles one could visit the larger cities of Koethen and Dessau to the north; and to the south, Bittefield, Halle and Leipzig . . . bearing in mind the complete absence of restaurants, theaters and the like. Sightseeing was the only attraction. But pointedly, no one was allowed to cross east beyond the Elbe River *without* express permission, and even then it was restricted only to business of a military or diplomatic nature.

The seven-foot brick wall of double thickness surrounding the Henschelwerk complex created problems for those determined to violate the "No Frat" order. Without assistance the absence of steps presented no easy chore to scale and once on top one had no choice but to jump to either side when entering or leaving. One could however, take his chances and once over the wall he could under cover of darkness make his way to the village unobserved. It was chance procedure, but with the illegality of fraternization it remained about the only way compatability could be attained. To return, to get back inside . . . thereby eluding the guard on duty meant still another gamble, for depending upon his mood, or perhaps his allegiance to duty the question remained; "Would the guard shut his eyes to this infraction?" Still a gamble; "Maybe yes . . . maybe no!"

Most guards were not particularly affected and when actually confronted with this question did not press the issue. The old German plant and grounds custodian who with meticulous care maintained a promising vegetable garden in a selected spot back against the wall really felt the brunt when less than a week since arrival of the 126th, his plants had been trampled to bits! There was little question as to who was responsible for countless numbers of footprints had an amazing similarity to those boots worn by GIs of the American army! Jumping from this wall on their way back from an *unofficial* visit to the town at a spot that in the darkness was felt relatively obscure, most had landed squarely in the old gentleman's garden!

Russian refugees; most having been imprisoned in slave labor camps and others that had been forced to do manual labor on German farms had for some time housed themselves in Lobejun and surrounding communities. Until our arrival, and we appeared to be the only American soldiers within a few miles radius; these refugees had given the local conservative communities a hard tension-filled time, particularly Lobejun; the largest of these communities. Nights of horror was experienced. Demands for food, at the moment in no-wise plenteous; intensive requests for clothing, bedding, shoes and other personal items was issued. When demands were not satisfied that particular household underwent a violent ransacking! Insults and abuses were numerous and often in the late hours suggestions for female companionship were presented. Those unfortunate enough to be faced with this request learned early the possible unpleasantries to follow should they refuse. Often, liberties would be taken anyway.

Lawlessness does not begat lawlessness and abuse does not begat abuse. On the other hand, if surveyed in terms of abuse and mistreatment suffered by these refugees and released prisoners one could say perhaps that complete justification was theirs, although rarely would small rural communities as this hardly know the *real* story of Nazism's ruthless actions. Even were they aware, what were chances of survival if one protested vehemently, and to what extent could his protests be carried? Chances are these protests, were they loud enough . . . would in the end result in his own eradication. Those were years of surpressed judgement, they were ugly times when the average German *heard* and *saw* and *did* nothing . . . for his *own* safe being. Yet, these horrors did happen and *all* must of a necessity share in the guilt. In future years when the question arises; "When does man's respect for man's dignity begin and end" . . .? It will indeed be a *good one* for researchers of human relations to kick around.

Years of depravity had extracted all dignity from these wretched survivors and to describe those in this area would be as described in previous encounters . . . just a shade above animalistic . . . almost wild! All night parties at times, noisy . . . unrealistic laughter . . . brutal fights . . . thievery . . . cursing . . . shooting and many outrageous acts of violence! On the other hand, there were times at night when group songs of their native land wafted across open fields to the ears of those of us awake and stirring in the Henschelwerk complex. These acts were mixed and never ceased, though somehow our presence was respected. We had every reason to believe that much of this respect stemmed from the fact the many GIs of Polish extraction graced our company, many speaking the Polish language fluently . . . and quite synonomous with that of the Russian made the understanding easier.

The CO relented and allowed a small few of them from time to time to help with KP chores. Exceptionally grateful, each was exhilarated in receiving a nutritious meal and cigarettes as compensation.

Occasionally a soldier or two from the Red Army strolled around outside the compound wall. Always friendly, and knowing no English, their greetings always seemed to center on state leaders:

"Americanski! Russki! Okay?" "Roosevelt! Stalin! Okay?" This was always followed with several nods of the head to make it genuinely affirmative. We replied in like manner, but when someone mentioned:

"Churchill! Stalin! Okay?" the reaction was not as amiable and followed usually with a turned up nose. For some reason the Russians were no lovers of the English.

Expressing orders of the C.O. Sergeant Botting on more than one occasion earlier warned the company as a group to be wary to these refugees.

"I know some of you are going to be slipping out of here at one time or another. If you get caught, then its your tail and don't come crying to me . . . 'cause you're going to get the "book thrown at you."

He was stronger in his further statement:

"I'm going to tell you something else though, and this comes straight from the Captain. Stay the hell away from those Russians and that crowd. I know there are plenty of them around here and you're gonna' feel sorry for them. Yeah, they've been through hell . . . we all know that; more hell than you and I ever dreamed could exist. But now they're unstable and a wicked bunch of bastards, and you won't do a damn thing but get yourselves in trouble! You'll do something else too; you'll get a nice case of V. D. quicker than you can think."

Smartly he concluded:

"You do that and you won't be seeing the States in a hell of a long time!"

A field located behind the local school near the center of town provided a backdrop for an activity that local Germans had never known. Endowed with restless talent a company softball team was organized and put to the task of competing with other units now fast moving into this area. Carl Ross, Bill Scott, Lee Shaw, Harry Kurtjian, George Leonhardt, and a jumble of enlisted athletes lifted spirits high while winning practically every game against a vast array of opponents. The visitors should have investigated first though, for every one of the above had excelled in the game while in high school. The activity however, was not without its local supporters for gradually and quietly many civilians turned out each afternoon, and somehow selecting a favorite team could not conceal the German competitive spirit; loudly at times as they watched the "crazy Americans" play the "silly" game called . . . softball.

Excepting two acts of violence Lobejun remained peaceful and congenial during our entire encampment. We were nevertheless, called upon to supress each of these acts. A fanatic Nazi follower fearing exposure threatened the life of his family . . . thence his own. Acting on a plea from several local residents three men were dispatched to the scene. Word spread and a small crowd had gathered by time the team arrived in a well-populated segment of town. Olen Hilditch surveyed the situation even before the jeep stopped. "Would they come to the rescue of one of their citizens?" he wondered. Sensing trouble he shifted his eyes out among the people and said quickly:

"Hell, let's just don't stand around, let's do what we gotta' do now!"

"What if this crowd gets a little huffy?" he was asked.

"I'm not going to stand here and worry about that. If they won't get out of the way and want to get huffy, let 'em . . . I sure as hell ain't gonna' worry about it. Let's go!"

Someone pointed the way, and double-timing up two flights of steps with weapons drawn they did not wait to knock, but rather shoved the door open and boldly stepped in! Wide-eyed and cowering against the wall the accused, a middle-aged German immediately offered his weapon with a heavily accented plea:

"Please don't hurt me."

As he was ushered out the door his wife came up to Hilditch and whispered attentively in broken English:

"Please don't hurt him, he is not well, you see."

The other incident came at about ten thirty in the evening. Two pistol shots rang out near guard post No. One at the main entrance! Mel Edwards, a member of the kitchen staff had not been on duty long, and normally the kitchen personnel were exempt from guard duty. Due to an infraction of rules the stocky T/5 was doing what he had to do. At the alarming almost shocking sound of shots he jumped quickly behind the brick wall. Lt. Lineberger, the Officer of the Day . . . hardly walking fifteen feet after routinely checking the guards, instinctively threw himself to the ground. Quickly regaining their wits they apprehended three refugees inadvertently running toward the gate. In a fit of argument a Russian refugee lay dead some fifty feet from the Post, two bullets in his chest. Those captured were taken to the CP and questioned thoroughly. *Thoroughly* was an understatement for they could speak no English and the interrogators could not quite comprehend their tongue. An interpreter tried to no avail, they were incoherent and would not comprehend. Said husky Ed Tarasiewicz, who could speak Polish well and to a great extent make himself understood with the Russians, was doing his best to interpret:

"You're fighting a loosing battle, Lieutenant. If I was you, I'd turn them loose. You're not going to get anything out of them; besides its not our problem. Probably had an argument over some liquor 'cause you can smell it all over them. You could rattle all night with these guys and still get nowhere. They're really not murderers as such, this kind of thing goes on all the time with 'em. They just don't give a damn and you can see they're not worried in the least. They're not going to bother anybody around here so you might's well turn them loose and forget it."

"What do you mean?" replied the Lieutenant. "There's been a murder committed out there! These guys have gotta be taken in!"

"Yeah, *probably* a murder, but did *you* see 'em do it? Did *anybody* see 'em do it? Lieutenant, you'll wind up in a wild goose chase and you couldn't prove a damn thing in a hundred years. The other guy probably had it coming. You'll do yourself a big favor, Lieutenant, and get rid of 'em. Let their own people take care of 'em. Hell, they'll fix 'em better than we could."

Lineberger thought about it for a minute, looked around a bit, nervously biting his lip to surpress his indecision . . . and recognizing the prominence of the language barrier as well as sensing the futility of pursuing an investigation into the incoherent jungle of refugees, he relented.

"Okay," said he; "We don't have the facts and without them you can't get to first base! I don't like it a bit, not a damn bit, mind you . . . but maybe you're right."

The Lieutenant got up, looked around some more and started for the door. Obviously not completely satisfied with his decision, he gestured with several waves of the hands that strongly told of acute frustration and blurted to the guards:

"Okay! Okay! What're you hanging around for? Get them the

hell out of here! I don't want to see 'em any longer! Just get 'em the hell out of here! *Now!*" . . .

They were immediately placed in a jeep and delivered to a nearby refugee commune. There it was assumed, justice would be best meted out by their own.

Under agreement emanating from dubious but confirmed Allied conferences held in Quebec in 1943 and more recently at Yalta in February, 1945, and finally confirmed by the European Advisory Commission in London, plans were set in motion to divide Germany . . . upon conquest, into four territories. The "Big Three" Allied powers; United States, Great Britain and the Soviet Union had now with the inclusion of France, grown to be "The Big Four" and each would occupy areas of that country so designated by the EAC. With the plan in effect this particular area which we now occupied would be annexed into the Russian occupation zone of Germany, and several days prior to evacuation the 126th represented some of the very few American forces remaining in this entire sector.

The sojurn here was rapidly coming to a close as time and again Soviet observers, their cocky unfriendly attitude becoming increasingly obvious, ventured in and around the Lobejun region . . . inspecting it for future occupation.

XVI

THE ROAD BACK

Many unhappy faces stared from the sidewalks early Wednesday morning of the 17th. A beautiful day was blossoming and though here and there a wave was extended haltingly, we were in a sense still the enemy and obviously it was a little awkward to say goodbye. But much to the consternation of these simple unpretentious villagers . . . we were leaving, and deep in their hearts saying goodbye at this time was perhaps the last thing they wanted to do. Rumbling slowly through the cobblestoned streets we were beginning the long journey west. Some weeks would pass before one would really appreciate how they must have felt at that moment and had we been fully aware at the time a wave of compassion really would be needed, for within the next few days Lobejun would be occupied by troops of the Red Army. To the villagers it was not a pleasant thought.

Could the day or weather have been more conducive for travel one might have second thoughts, for rarely were we this blessed. Nor could anyone have found road facilities more superior than this route mapped out for us. South we moved, skirting the eastern approaches around Halle, again across the Saale River, thence briefly in the direction of Leipzig . . . logging some twenty-five miles to come upon a portion of the magnificent autobahn that would stretch all the way to our destination. Cognizant that all cities would be bypassed for many miles the drivers settled down to enjoy an unusual pattern of luxury and advantage that these great superhighways offered.

Weissenfels and Eisenberg were quickly put in the distance . . . and then began a journey through the rolling province of Thuringia that would extend for almost a hundred miles.

American and British military traffic maintained priority and dominated the autobahn, though it appeared at times that little heed was paid this privilege as a strange tide of makeshift vehicles slowly began to encroach on this priority. The many different modes of transport encountered was astounding as outdated vehicles, scavenged and put in working order and manned by French, Belgian, Dutch, Polish, Russian and other Slav factions flowed off and on the autobahn . . . destined both east and west. Chugging along at a dangerous clip, black fumes emitting from exhausts . . . almost every machine was loaded to capacity with "rag-tag" happy "DPs" . . . each equipped with an apparent new lease on life! Multi-length carts drawn by farm tractors, (heaven knows from whence came the fuel . . . though mattering little for they were driven until the fuel expired; then abandoned) each dangerously straining at the seams with an over-capacity of leathery-faced men, kerchiefed women and full-faced children. Much horse-drawn equipment, several towing two and three trailers behind . . . but each tremendously packed with flag-waving, smiling, singing refugees plodded carelessly along the road.

Moreover; it was not uncommon to encounter German soldier stragglers making their way along the highway . . . some in mixed vehicles in small convoys of their choosing . . .some on bicycle. . . many on foot. Most did not seem to know where or care where they were going, but obviously everybody was going somewhere! Though exhibiting little of the warmth as did the former slaves, many waved and smiled as we passed! We waved back! "Hell, why not?" declared one; "This is a beautiful day . . . it was great to be alive . . . and a new era is about to begin for everybody!"

Sweeping through the southern approaches of Jena where the peaceful sun-bathed Saale River was bridged for the third time we moved past historic Weimar . . . one-time capital of the great German Republic of long ago, laying perhaps a mile to the north. Buchenwald was a hedious name to those who survived. Now known to all as perhaps the most frightful infamous horror camp of them all, there was little question that many years would pass before its' reputation of depressed notoriety would diminish. No more than ten kilometers slightly northwest of Weimar the now empty camp had been the scene of final repose for some quarter of a million men, women and children of Jewish blood . . . snatched from many European nations to perish at the hands of Nazi executioners. Though all bodies long removed the tortuous death-dealing apparatus remained and would for a time act as a reminder of horrendous deaths, bordering on the barbarious, of thousands whose bodies would never be recovered.

Is it any wonder why the supposedly civilized world did ask:

"How could man's inhumanity to man have sunk to these depths?"

"Could this have happened to man in other countries?"

"Could this have *really* happened in the Twentieth century?"

The whole world would like to know *why* and *how*! Some day perhaps, the answer would be analyzed and presented. But, for the present . . . of a certainty, the whole world knows only that it *did* happen!

Everything was in full bloom! The war clouds blown away and the passing landscape presenting a *so* enchanting picture one would never have believed that less than a month ago men were falling in battle over these very grounds. The autobahn wound past busy Erfurt and then almost into Gotha, where from a distance was displayed the pictured panorama of many prominent church spires and steeples. Beyond the highway junction of Eisenach a brief distance carried us over the Werra River. Hersfeld was reached and the Fulda River was crossed at that point. There was little secret the thoughts pervading one's mind here, for only too well did we remember bridging this busy waterway when racing east in mid-April . . . having just cleared the death-drowned city of Kassel a few miles to the north.

Neider Ault and Alsfeld were strategic junctions and the roads leading into and out of both towns were still very much under repair by Army construction units, and helped by German civilians. Bulldozers were busy, trucks filled with broken bricks and crushed stone . . . and heavy dust polluted the atmosphere. Though suffering a short delay for a distance of some ten miles we moved quickly some twenty five miles to exit from the broad autobahn near the approaches of Giessen. Ravished by Allied aerial incendiaries for over a year, Giessen had also presented a stumbling block for FIRST ARMY's breakout from the Rhine bridgehead until succumbing to the 7TH ARMORED DIVISION on March 28. Some six miles west of that city our convoy rolled across the twisting Lahn River, moved into partially destroyed Wetzlar and halted deep in the city where a temporary camp site was selected. Journeying all day we had in roughly eight hours clocked two hundred and forty seven miles. It would have staggered the imagination to suggest the possible time consumption had we been deprived of the autobahn.

Forty-five miles due north of Frankfurt near a river juncture where the Dill flows into the Lahn, and located for hundreds of years in the province of Hesse, Wetzlar had been a busy proud city of some 30,000 and a prime target of Allied bombing before falling to advance units of FIRST ARMY's III CORPS on April 1st. As the photography profession is aware, Wetzlar is home of the world-renown Leica camera from whose factories is produced various degrees of lens, optical instruments, binoculars and magnifying glasses. Under extensive and severe bombardment these plants were greatly damaged. Though main thoroughfares and most secondary streets had been cleared of debris, gutted and wrecked streetcars and vehicles righted and pushed out of the way and utility poles and lines cleared, much of the city remained a shambles.

The Rochling-Buderus Stahlwerk, spread out over some five acres was a steel fabricating plant much in prominence and until captured, production remained at a high peak for a great period of time. Its' physical layout included many steel sheds, several office buildings, mobile cranes and self-propelled engines and heavy machinery. The plant even possessed its' own rail facilities that stretched some two miles north to juncture with one of the main east-west trunk railroads. Somehow managing to survive the heavy aerial assaults in previous months it had suffered only relatively as compared with other parts of the city. We occupied this vast complex, taking over the three-story administrative building which housed a greater portion of our company. We immediately came under jurisdiction of the 190th Ordnance Battalion, and for a time would be a part of the XXI CORPS, THIRD UNITED STATES ARMY. An early assembly on the first morning found us listening to an unexpected and probably undeserved message which turned out to be compliments from the new Battalion commander; big hulking Lt. Col. Robert Lynn.

"Men, I don't think we're going to be together long, because we're all trying to get out of this God-forsaken country soon as we can. But I've reviewed your company record, and it is a good one. Now that it's all over, I feel that its time for less "tail-chewing" and time that someone said something complimentary to the GI. I'm saying it now. Your records also show that you were a part of the FIRST ARMY all the way from Normandy. Your campaign was a good one and we're proud to have you as part of the 190th. You're still going to have quite a bit of shuffling to do before going home, but in the meantime . . . good luck to you!"

"My aching back!" said one, "Where's he been? What's with this guy? He's running off at the mouth about things that should have been said a long time ago! That's about the only good thing anybody's *ever* said about us!"

"Yeah," replied another, "sounds good. Just a lot of crap . . . but it sounds good! I'll bet he's been wanting to make that speech for six months. They kick the hell out of the GI all during the war, and then when its all over they want to tell him how sorry it all is!"

"When are you gonna' stop bitching?" came a curt reply. "The war's over. You're on your way home. No more holes to dig. Plenty of good chow . . . so what do you want for nothing?"

Feelings would run high for the least little thing for quite some time.

Civilians returning to battered homes and disfigured property though obviously harboring a distasteful attitude, never at any time openly suggested the slightest disturbance. It was noted early, however and with some apprehension, the increased appearance of several displaced refugees seeking aid in the medium of food and temporary quarters. Settling for anything to eat and caring little where they slept they simply wanted our dependence. We did not for a time agree to satisfy their needs. From the goodness of our hearts? Duty-bound? Perhaps a little of both. But we really hoped they would just disappear. But not so, for daily increasing in numbers the burden became more than our small unit could handle. THIRD ARMY's newly established DP camp in Wetzlar soon alleviated this problem.

At the moment we were minus one officer, and the Battalion commander suggested our T/O (Table of Operations) be brought up to full strength. Harold Johnston was an exacting and personable soldier from Gagetown, Michigan and had for several months been a non-commissioned officer wearing the stripes of a T/3. Spurred on by suggestions from fellow "non-coms" he applied for, and was chosen to fill this vacancy. It was a bright May morning as the entire company beamed with pride watching Lieutenant Lineberger pin the gold bars of 2nd. Lt. on him . . . the first of our company to receive a field commission. Now it was *Lieutenant Johnston* and henceforth he would receive all the respect accorded an officer. Moreover; he reaped the good fortune when assignment allowed him to remain a company staff officer.

***

Two anxious weeks passed quickly in Wetzlar. Two weeks that produced little more than company vehicle maintenance; otherwise nothing exciting. We were ordered west . . . an order that would spell exit from this country to a destination beyond the Rhine, beyond Belgium and in fact well across the border of France. May 31st was a sunny morning that found all vehicles, weary but well-serviced, beginning a westward shuttle once more. This would reflect the company's last convoy on German soil . . . and in the face of it no one appeared to be regretting it in the least.

Through Braunfels and Weilburg, two bright attractive dimunitive villages that somehow escaped the war's wrath, again passing over the Lahn River near the eastern outskirts of Limburg we were scheduled in less than two hours to reach the north-south Cologne-Frankfurt portion of the autobahn that links the Ruhr to Bavaria. Limburg would be remembered by the great jubilation expressed nearly two and a half months previous when FIRST ARMY combat teams entered and released American soldiers and airmen from one of the largest prisoner of war compounds in this southwestern region of Germany.

Again along the broad delightful superhighway, all damage having long been repaired we followed a course almost due north . . . for, following detailed map consultation supposedly the Rhine River would be reached at Cologne somewhere around noon. At good speed . . . breezing through the countryside paralleling the Rhine, even though it lay some ten to fifteen miles to the west, noting roadsigns bypassing hamlets of Montabaun, Bevel and Siegburg . . . we spotted shortly after noon the gigantic twin spires of Cologne's majestic cathedral looming in the distance, rising high above the Rhine's rapid flow.

A backward glance that at the moment was almost unbelievable made one realize that within a period approximating ten weeks we were in actuality again crossing the Rhine via a well-constructed Bailey bridge. Now paralleling a limp remains of the once-proud Hindenburg Bridge, some one hundred yards to our right . . . who with bleak deserted towers had spanned this broad expanse for almost a mile. A Germanic symbol of bridge construction that in its' day could match most any erected in Europe . . . now lay a mass of twisted steel girders and shattered concrete ways drooping aimlessly in these rushing waters. Immediately across, we trudged into devastated Cologne.

Some say Cologne had ranked categorically as third largest city in Germany prior to the war, embracing some 850,000 people. A major target of Allied bombs since April, 1943 we had not seen any city near its' size or eminence in Germany so completely crushed! Prosperous industrial centers were smashed! The great railroad station that had interchanged hundreds of thousands to points all over Europe was left a shambles, and endless rows of once-exclusive apartment buildings were reduced to grotesque proportions! Hushed into acres of rubble was the great market place that once was a scene of entrepeneurs of boundless energy plying their goods of various commodities.

The only important structure that *really* survived these attacks was the magnificent ancient Gothic cathedral for which Cologne was known the world over. Though hit fourteen times by bombs and badly shaken by debris from nearby explosions but protected to a great degree by a surrounding ten-foot concrete retainer wall; this superbly constructed cathedral, begun in the eleventh century and towering 515 feet from the ground to the tip of its' spires was amazingly left with little damage. We moved slowly alongside and some halted only long enough to snap a picture and view in awe this tremendous work of art before resuming a course through a maze of detours around shell-gutted streets.

Out of Cologne on through the broad and now blooming countryside, we noted with enlightenment the impressive rolling green hills making up the western Cologne plains. Still imbued with the ghastly picture of the city's destruction and desolation it seemed astounding that anything would ever again grow in this region. Who could but wonder; *could* or *would* such a once-great metropolis so totally destroyed ever rebuild again to its' former state of high prominence? The months ahead would see.

War-ravaged villages and hamlets, the brutal scars of battle still prominent, now deserted and weird lay in review for the next several miles. Across the rushing Erft Canal, through Blatzheim where the Neffel River was bridged . . . and down through destroyed Golzheim we reached the Elle River. Twenty kilometers further we came upon the lifeless city that had once been a "beehive" of activity . . . Dueren.

We remembered Dueren so well!!

The death of Dueren had come as a consequence of relentless punishing attacks from the air and heavy artillery from the ground. One is not likely to ever forget the dark days during the battle for that Rhineland section as this city which contained a pre-war population of 45,441 persons was under constant seige from November through much of February. Subjected not only to aerial bombardment and long range guns the city had changed hands from German to American and back to German several times and in so doing became the recipient of attack from *both* armies. The refusal to yield in each instance multiplied the death toll and added destruction that was really shocking to behold.

One had only to recall "Operation Queen's" 5,000-plane assault on November 17 against this region, designed to support FIRST ARMY's Rhineland offensive; to comprehend the tremendous punishment administered this city. 2,500 tons of these explosives *alone* pummeled Dueren and its' congested railyards!

West across the Roer River at Dueren roads that had been black-topped several times by the Corps of Engineers still wavered with uncertainty, though in far better condition than could have been expected. Beyond the Weh River we moved into Langerwehe and then Weisweiler and crossed the narrow Inde River beyond the latter town. Ten kilometers more found us rolling directly into the destroyed road junction of Eschweiler where townspeople had returned and cooperative efforts were in process of rebuilding. As "Operation Queen" had almost obliterated Dueren, so it had Eschweiler and neighboring Weisweiler industrial areas and troop concentrations gathered therein, when from that same coordinated bombardment 4,120 tons of explosives left the two towns a shattered ruins. It *had* to be done, for capture of the Eschweiler-Weisweiler industrial area would spell access to a more open portion of the Roer plains. It would in time allow for a firm FIRST ARMY contact with the NINTH ARMY to the north and consequently set the stage for a broad sweep across the plains, the Rhine an eventual objective.

Considering the heavy fighting that had dragged on unceasingly through the winter months, and considering the thousands of tons of armored vehicles clanking, churning and maneuvering throughout this sector the roads leading from Eschweiler west were at best in remarkable condition. On across the Merz and Wurm Rivers, each creating white rapids that glittered in the afternoon sun as the rushing waters dashed against well-spaced rocks, and on through the outskirts of familiar Eilendorf we made our way finally into the shattered metropolis of Aachen. Now in the heart of where FIRST ARMY began its' great offensive against Germany, this too was the region in which *we* first entered the Rhineland in September, 1944.

On through Aachen and her western suburbs one looked with awe at the heaps of twisted reinforced steel and shattered stone that once had been almost unapproachable pillboxes and bunkers, and had so stubbornly defended the city from vicious Allied attacks. Many weeks had passed since we had seen these formidable fortresses and since that time Army demolition squads had dynamited and destroyed them. Roads were repaired and streets were completely cleared of debris, but the once prominent buildings with shattered hollow brick walls continued to present an unforgettable picture of desolation and ruin. Though grass had started growing in spots the grounds remained churned and ripped and shell-pocked from saturating explosions during the city's seige months ago.

Aachen looked relatively much the same as when we left several months before; the crumpled and crushed remains of a shameful foolish war, and one had to have a touch of pity to look at the remnants of this once-great industrous city and see at this point very little chance of resurrection even were it permitted. These were passing thoughts and we moved on and left the people of that impoverished city feverishly building what little shelters they could with what little they had.

It was almost four o'clock and no more than five miles west of Aachen found the convoy passing over the border from Germany into Belgium. Cognizant that again we were in friendlier territory most for the moment inwardly regarded the weighty and lasting experience in Germany as a closed chapter . . . and let it go at that. They were good people, the Germans. We knew that. We knew too of the suffering and humiliation that they had endured . . . but summarily could only conclude, "What a damn shame."

Tributaries leading into the Gulpe River were numerous and the many spans narrow east of Nev-Moresnet; the first town entered since passing beyond the Belgian border. We came upon Henri-Chappell; relatively obscure outside the borders of Belgium prior to the war but since the 25th of September, 1944 a site of the largest American cemetary in Belgium. The only operating cemetary in FIRST ARMY from September through February, most graves were final resting places particularly for those GIs having perished in the Battle of The Bulge six months previous.

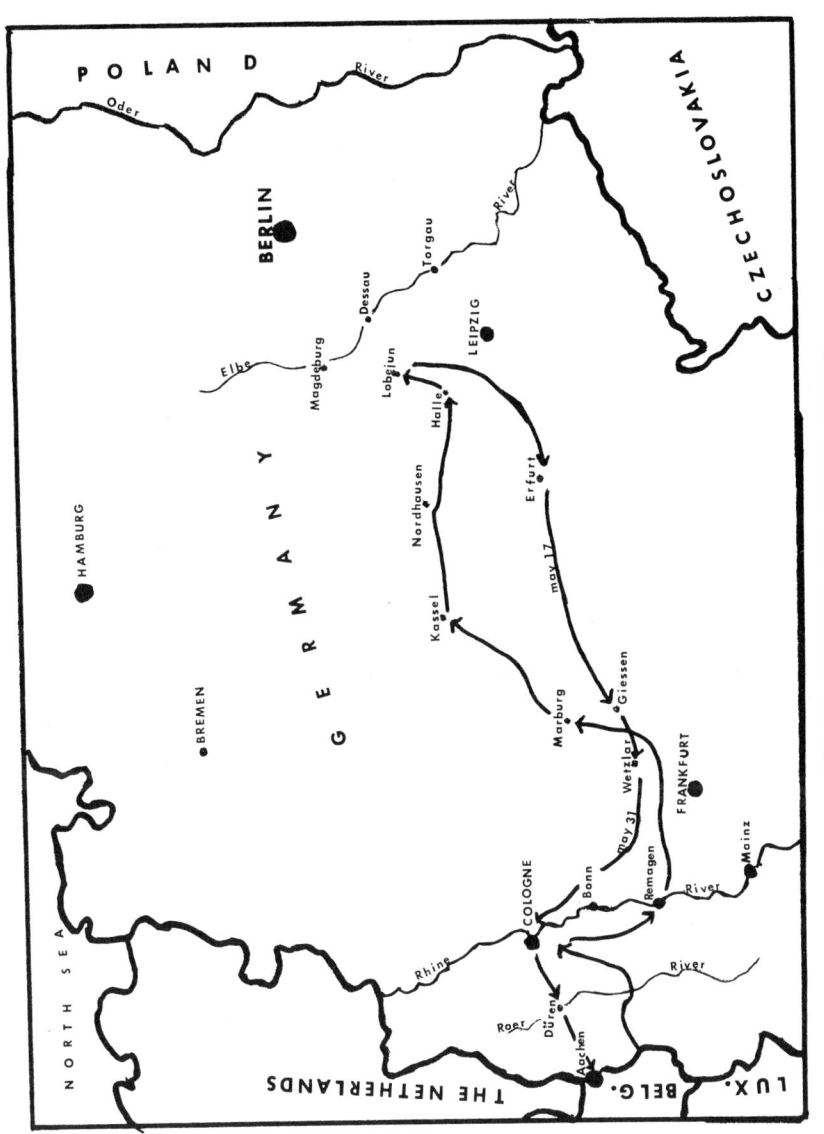

FROM THE RHINELAND INTO CENTRAL GERMANY
MARCH - MAY, 1945

Perhaps it was purely mental but it did nonetheless feel good to be back in this little Kingdom. It would however, be a little different . . . for with thousands of GIs having passed through its' boundaries since our departure several months ago we would not find it quite the same. We would for the moment not be concerned with that . . . for presented with a day that could not have been more beautiful, to drink in the placid atmosphere of a well-kept land, marveling at bright unblemished azure skies and digest the complimentary gestures of a friendly and industrious people surely would make the gloomy uncertainty of the past few months worthwhile.

Clermont, Herve, Romsee and several smaller towns were quickly put in the distance and in late afternoon we rolled into Liege, one of Belgium's chief cities and one not at all unfamiliar to us. Setting up camp in an open pasture on the city's far eastern suburbs vivid memories of Liege were rekindled even before the main complement of the 126th unpacked. Scheduling only a single night in this location would find us unpacking sparingly.

This brave city of fine buildings, a victim of relentless "buzzbomb" and V-2 attacks during the autumn, winter and early spring months saw some 1,158 of its' citizens perish and over 8,000 injured and maimed. Attacking in great numbers day and night, violently exploding into crowded apartment buildings, into private homes, in shops and theaters in busy downtown and congested areas these devilish devices sent terror into every heart as their thundering roaring vibrations gave indication of fast approach! Averaging fifty firings daily against Liege and Antwerp further west on the coast, records show that Liege was hit 1,086 times with hundreds exploding nearby. The greatest single material loss occurred when a flying bomb made a direct hit on an Allied fuel dump December 17 and 400,000 gallons of gasoline went up in flames!

Once, in late November, as Sergeant Olen Hilditch was leaving the city . . . having consummated a supply problem, a "buzzbomb" roared out from nowhere. Straight overhead he watched in stunned disbelief as it began to sputter! Gripped with fear he saw it begin a horrifying crazy spiral and pummel into the heart of downtown. The great pillar of black smoke rising in the distance told him of the results . . . all too ghastly of description!

Liege was left behind in the early morning of June 1, and while utilizing a winding well-elevated highway along the west bank of the River Meuse, the busy towns of Jemeppe, Flemalle, Engis and Huy passed in review. We crossed the Meuse at Huy and followed a course south along the western bank of that river, embracing several miles of picturesque towns and villages; most notable of them, Andrenne. Some fifteen miles further along the Meuse we moved through Marches-les-Dames, a lovely community situated in the scenic Meuse valley, and where from the great towering peaks of the rocky cliffs adorning the countryside, hugging close along the highway and over-looking the river Belgium's beloved King Albert fell tragically to his death more than eleven years previous.

No more than ten minutes found us moving into the colorful resort of Namur, a city high in industrial importance and tourism alike. The nine outdated forts surrounding the city were captured after a momentus struggle by the Germans in World War I, and though meticulously constructed and upgraded between wars these strong fortifications fell quickly to the same invader a generation later in the spring of 1940.

Again over the Meuse, and following close along the banks of the River Sambre that flows from the Meuse our convoy moved along the fertile plains of this almost flat country and passed quickly through the bright well-kept towns of Floreffe, Sart-St. Laurent, and Fosse where *finally* a portion of the River Sambre was crossed. The terrain began to show signs of a gradual rise to a higher elevation and would continue for the next several miles across rolling wheatfields and sloping green hills to present a panorama of pictorial beauty that was ours to absorb. Most of Chatelet was by-passed and some fifteen minutes later the many-spired churches of Charleroi came into sight far in the distance. Exactly thirty-nine kilometers lay between Namur and Charleroi and we moved into this prestigious city to observe a lengthy rest stop.

Two hours later through much heavier populated territory only a few kilometers separated the small communities of Fontaine-l'Eveque, Anderlues and Leval-Trabegnies; and bridging the Samme breezed through Binche, Bray, St. Chislain, St. Symphorien-Villers and by mid-morning into the beautiful cathedral city of Mons in lower southwest Belgium.

South beyond, the route was dotted with small communities and villages with bright clean-cut seventeenth century homes nestling among walled gardens and bristling commercial shops that in spite of extremely narrow sidewalks hugged up close to the streets. Many tiny water tributaries flowing into the Mons Canal were indicative of marshlands extending for many acres. Just before moving into Quievrain we crossed the narrow winding River Aurelle. Significantly Quievrain would represent another milestone, for less than three kilometers separates that Belgian community from the French town of Blanc-Misseron and at an equal distance between the two we passed over the boundary that divides Belgium from France. The 126th Ordnance, after approximately nine months was back in France!

Straight down from the French boundary a key highway carried us through Quarouble, Onnaing and St. Saulve to reach the old city of Valenciennes on the tiny Escaut Canal. At the nearby fortress of Maubeuge the weary Germans, in late October, 1918 were driven from their last stronghold on French soil.

Though the rolling green hills and yellow wind-blown wheatfields of this region exhibited a panoramic scene of beauty and tranquility, there were many of long residence who could remember . . . with much dismay when this very region, embracing many miles to the west was the scene of anything but one of tranquility. Twenty seven and twenty eight years ago when the British 3RD and 4TH Armies, supporting the hard-pressed French Army to the south faced a well-entrenched German Army on a broad front that extended some one hundred miles from north to south, engaging in frightful stalemated battles that resulted in over a million casualties. This land then was turned almost into a ravaged wilderness.

Long into the past had drifted the sharp air-splitting thunderings of artillery and shell explosions that blasted great jagged craters and created mud-infested shellholes, transforming the landscape of farms into a land of devastation. Many could remember the roar of field batteries; the din of acrid smoke from shell barrages and slow choking from mustard gas, the slime and filth of twisting waist-deep hollow trenches . . . where at a signal of synchronized shrill blowing of whistles would emerge massed hordes of steel helmets of both friend and foe moving out to attack through belts of barbed wire and a hail of machine gun bullets to engage in "see-saw" death struggles, producing on the battlefields screams of those stricken, broken and maimed . . . the heavy sighs of dying . . . and later endless lines of wounded.

Many of these people remembered it well, and almost everyone involved having lost a loved one during that period tended to shrug heads when talking about it at length. Many expressed it well:

"Both wars are over . . . and this is a new day."

So, as far as they were concerned . . . gone was the vicious thundering that brought carnage and destruction over much of this land. In bloom again were orchards that once suffered devastation by a hurricane of shells that turned it into a crimson inferno. *How this region had suffered!* But that was twenty eight years ago . . . and following the French philosophy, one would have to agree: "This *is* a new day indeed!"

Cambrai was a key town which during the first World War suffered almost obliteration in that long and now historical conflict. Notably too, Cambrai was a town wrested from the Germans by the British in November – December, 1917 . . . inaugurating the *first* large-scale major battle involving tank warfare. Cambrai this day was peaceful and pretty.

Across the well-tended Escaut Canal we moved and entered Mosnieres . . . a point where this narrow waterway empties into the St. Quentin Canal. A roadway alongside the highly navigable canal was followed and in the course of some fifteen miles we crossed this zigzagging body of water no less than five times . . . all in the meanwhile encompassing the small communities of Le Catelet, Bellicourt and Bellenglise.

At noon on the very first day of June the advance portion of the convoy rolled into the city of St. Quentin. Late in the afternoon the remainder would follow. This was our destination, and until the coming of the crisp winds in late September . . . we would call it home.

XVII

L'AFFAIR DE ST. QUENTIN

Having seen its' share of wars: first seized and occupied by the Spaniards in 1557 and almost totally destroyed in the war of 1916 – 1918, St Quentin, a city of broad avenues, closely-knit shops and multi-colored homes still manages to remain one of the most industrious communities in northern France. Established in the heart of France's sheep grazing region the city boasts a consistent population of approximately 50,000 and in prewar days was noted for production of fine embroidery and manufacturing of woolen clothing. St. Quentin also has one of the oldest cathedrals in northern Europe and though partially destroyed during the 1916 – 1918 conflict, it was reconstructed and managed again to survive this war.

The city's vital railyards suffered much damage from U. S. and RAF bombers long before Allied forces swarmed onto the European continent, and during the latter days of August, 1944 was liberated from German occupation by combined American and French forces.

Completely unpacking we laboriously began moving into an unoccupied three-story apartment building, long evacuated of its' occupants. Baggage, cots and assorted equipment was carried and some dragged into small rooms and up the narrow winding stairway until each room was filled to over-capacity with weary GIs. Supplemental quarters over an abandoned garage less than two blocks west took care of the overflow. For all the painstaking efforts to establish liveable quarters it was learned early next morning that this would be temporary indeed, for plans were already in motion for our subsequent evacuation. In less than three days this became a reality.

South beyond the River Somme, across the strikingly arched wide four-lane bridge that not only spans the river but St. Quentin's spacious railyards as well, we occupied an area perhaps a half-mile beyond this bridge in the city's southwestern suburbs.

A two-story apartment-type building . . . commodious in scope, and constructed in a U-shape arrangement overlooking a vast courtyard dominated this area. Within this complex a rambling old red brick office building . . . high ceilinged and victorian in style and a year previous housing German occupation forces, clearly noted by door markings and circular orders still taped to bulletin boards, would now house our headquarters and kitchen personnel. A fifteen-foot wide areaway led through and under these apartments into an immense area closed in by walls under skylighted roof where in times past served as an automotive garage and repair shop. In the living quarters extensive renovating began; large rooms partitioned, broken windows replaced and each department assigned space so as to reflect best operational advantage. By Thursday, the 6th of June . . . the first anniversary of D-Day, the company was set to commence whatever operations assigned.

Only one outlet existed . . . one that led immediately to the main thoroughfare. Wide enough for two vehicles to pass, it served as both entrance and exit and protected only by a large iron-grill double gate . . . which was *rarely* ever closed. This point too, represented the only guard post in the complex, and with all ammunition removed became little more than a "check in — check out" point for company personnel. The small brick building adjacent to this post just inside the area housed an old French caretaker and his family who were delighted to see this facility revived by the Americans. Food rations, long at a minimum for these people would now increase tenfold.

Under jurisdiction of 71st Ordnance Battalion, Oise Headquarters Section; the primary task assigned the 126th became one of implementing light and medium maintenance repairs on vehicles earmarked for redeployment to war zones in the Pacific Theater of Operations and within natural shop space these duties would be facilitated. Moreover, aided by a large complement of semi-skilled German PWs relegated to handle heavy duty and secondary detail work, none daring to express open dissatisfaction for fear of being relieved of this moderate ·assignment, there soon existed an atmosphere of consistent cohesion.

At an evening assembly the First Sergeant wasted no time echoing the wishes of the Captain after the Germans had completed the first day's work.

"I'll just make it short and sweet! Those 'Krauts' are here for one purpose and that is to work. Some of you are getting too friendly with 'em and I know that's not hard to do. They're not going to bother you; we don't have to worry about that. But if you get too friendly they're not going to work as hard and they'll 'goof off' at the first opportunity. Then you'll have it *all* to do! After all, they're in no mood to help our war effort. They're getting plenty to eat and have good living quarters, so to stay out of trouble hard work is what they need. Besides, they'll catch hell from their top sergeant if they don't. So, from here on let it be strictly business!"

They were disciplined well, for long before we assembled for morning chow the echo of heavy steel-tap boots were heard clomping up the street, some twenty five of them . . . in snappy cadence; and marching into the courtyard it was strict attentiveness until the stern stocky Sergeant barked dismissal.

The small group of Italian PW's, also compounded within the city . . . housed in fact in billits along the very route traversed by the Germans were not amiss to express insults of their own making each time they passed. Never losing the cadence count, never losing a step, the well-trained Germans simply ignored them.

Rue de la Fere, the main north-south thoroughfare was a busy street, and some two miles south of the city becomes Highway No. 44 . . . leading several miles beyond to communities with which we would soon become familiar; La Fere, Soissons, Laon and even further, Reims.

Early morning found this street alive with people streaming into the city on their way to work. Professional, commercial, keepers of shops and restaurants, and particularly factory workers to the scattered textile mills that now revitalized, began to show signs of new economic life. Situated on this busy thoroughfare an approximate twenty minute walk was required from our quarters into the heart of the city, though a trolley-car plying to and from the city . . . always trying to overcome an erratic schedule alleviated this problem for those desiring. Most always crowded far beyond capacity, by the time it reached our location this machine was in no way conducive to comfort. Often early Saturday evenings it seemed impossible to get on board; so crowded in fact that it was not surprising to see two to three GIs hanging out the door, supported only by a small handrail lest they fall off. One can imagine the equally frustrating attempts of the personable diminutive female toll collector working her way through the close-packed bouncing streetcar . . . trying to collect fares under unenviable conditions! At best, she was not always successful.

(So intrigued with this young lady was Howard Wells, a rather smallish T/4 from Michigan, hardly a mite larger than she, that he made her his bride and later brought her to America. She is, after 27 years still Mrs. Howard Wells.)

Passes were issued extensively. Forty eight, seventy two, weekend and practically any type of leave became available only for the asking. Outlying towns were visited and trips to Paris, ninety kilometers south were made. Some simply took advantage of this opportunity . . . at the moment never sure of a destination, but as long as one kept out of trouble and returned somewhere near schedule, it mattered little.· St. Quentin soon became known to many intimately and if one felt deposed to wander about the city gregariously he usually found a place of welcome. Friendships were extended from the more auspicious places; Hotel-Cafe Picardy . . . Mimi's . . . Hotel de la Paix . . . Rougemont . . . Hotel de la

France . . . the local Red Cross Club . . . Club Christophe and several cabarets of lesser prominence where lounging was frequented.

With only four other American units stationed within the city's confines; the 78th General Hospital utilizing and maintaining an old vacated brick hospital on the city's northside, the 924th Ordnance Company billited in the mammoth once-prominent Hotel Terminus on the banks of the Somme, a small detachment of military police and a tiny group that operated a transit mess for soldiers passing through; the 126th by early July came to regard St. Quentin as slightly less than a second home. Moreover; so long as we remained the city would do a flourishing business in *many* categories of exchange.

Taking advantage of an unusual opportune locale with which to perpetuate its talents the company orchestra, organized in December of the previous year, added two musicians, Skip Rinard and George Righter, both versatile guitarists, from among the several replacements from the overstaffed St. Quentin-based 924th Ordnance, to give it more depth and prompt a polished touch of professionalism. Billed as the "MUSIC MAKERS" this talented group fast developed into one of the most sought-after aggregations by military units in the entire Oise Headquarters Section of northeastern France. Performing for practically all of the army-sponsored dances in the city, which by and large were many, throughout the summer of 1945 engagements were filled for American GIs at Red Cross shows, officer clubs, and camps in many towns and locations within a 100-mile radius of St. Quentin.

To combat possible boredom recreation was pursued wherever it could be found. Selection of the most popular of the city's lounges and dance halls . . . insofar as we were concerned was not hard to do. Though by no means a new building, Club Christophe was first of all the largest and represented a place where one could meet with fellow GIs, sit with a full table and enjoy a rounded evening of beer without having to dance at all. Boisterous at times, yet it remained one of the few places that the non-professional girl frequented . . . this in itself a rarity. But *often* there was a "catch" to that. Their "Mamas" accompanied them! One will not easily forget the complete lack of sophistication exuded at these dances, for so turbulent became the atmosphere at times that an inference of "rat races" was applied with much justification. Perpetrated by loud outbursts of unrestrained laughter and yells, much pushing and shoving between GIs that sometimes involved clashes, and heated arguments amongst girls . . . jealous at suggestive exchange of glances, one often wondered how and why these functions generated interest. But generate, they did!

Other than a small window fan ill-designed to effectively stir the air there existed no air circulatory system, and completely devoid of sound acoustics the din of swirling noises made close conversation almost inaudible. Though most participants saturated with perspiration, some reeling from effects of excessive cognac or bloated with wine or beer, and enduring the stumbling motions of those too inebriated to dance and those that could not dance at all, these functions often continued into the early morning hours . . . despite a supposedly midnight closing hour. It was indeed, quite like a circus or perhaps a playground . . . in that once a person is inside he turns himself loose and almost irrespective of circumstances, *really* "lets his hair down!"

We did on occasion sponsor company dances of our own, each held at the Christophe. One of the evening's highlights came at intermission when refreshments were served . . . doughnuts, sandwiches, coffee and soft drinks. Mothers, grandmothers, and younger brothers and sisters who had accompanied many of the girls, sat around the hall during the period prior to intermission . . . watching in sparkling amusement the clownish actions of the Americans. While the evening was entertaining their real intentions became obvious when the refreshments appeared, for the hasty withdrawal from their seats turned into a "mad" scramble that saw them *literally* groping like starving puppies for these delicacies! Personal regard was cast aside and variant sizes of marketing bags unfolded as the chaperones and young ones exuded frantic and less than dignified efforts to fill them! A harsh expression from one in charge:

"Get the hell out of the way! Allez! Allez! Allez! Tout suite!" had little effect.

"Scram, dammit, scram!" yelled one in charge.

Viewing this scene for the first time, one GI expressed in amazement:

"My God! . . . Will you look at that! Will you look at them hungry 'Frogs'! They must be damn near starving!"

There was, sometimes enough left for the GIs! There followed, upon depletion of the food a conspicuous disappearance of parents and little folk. We were outwardly amused and quite naturally made inconsiderate comments. But when viewing this action realistically, we in no way considered it offensive . . . for viewing the plight of these people on the very first day when arriving in St. Quentin, when with little pails the young and old alike stood outside our dining hall importuning for whatever was left in our messkits, our emotions then were stirred to the point of recognition that these people had known much despair and had for years endured deprivation of material pleasantries.

Repairing and performing maintenance on military vehicles did not preclude the entire company's duties, for the summer of 1945 found additional interests for many who were assigned non-company tasks.

Jake Cohen was a regular army T/Sgt., and who with his prominent well-tended mustache and well-worn cigar stub bristled with nervous energy. He possessed too, an insatiable yen, as few others did, for show business. William Paulins, an unusually quiet T/5 and at times a bit moody, though most content when operating a movie projector, teamed with Cohen to assume responsibility of all Red Cross recreational functions in the city. Involving frustrating negotiations with army-leased theaters this responsibility proved often to be unappreciable and at times an almost untenable task. In addition, it necessitated not only the booking and supervision of all films and live shows brought into the Oise District, but proper distribution of all athletic equipment.

Probably through eloquent maneuvering Norton Binenfeld, a slim T/5 from Chicago landed a much-coveted job as assistant in the extremely popular local Red Cross Club, programming activities that functioned on a parity with the U.S.O. Genial James Burke, the big Staff Sergeant and former Golden Glover from upper Michigan . . . unusually adroit in all sports, earned a line position on the hard-hitting Oise District football squad, a team that would represent this particular district in northern France . . . competing against other like teams over much of the country.

Supply administrative assignments at Oise Headquarters in Rheims were handed Lt. Bob Howe and T/Sgt. Olen Hilditch and both would operate out of that city for a good portion of the summer. Considerable travel would be required and as a result much of the country was covered.

Sol Kaufman, the big busy T/3 with the built-in smile, who with horn-rimmed glasses bore a striking resemblance to Benny Goodman, had through watchful diligence enabled vehicle parts supply to operate in much the same industrious fashion as his variety stores in Chicago. S/Sgt. Tony Puchala, heading company supply since January, joined Kaufman in journeying on assignment to the Army War College established at Biarritz deep in southwestern France. Located on the Bay of Biscay at the foothills of the Pyrenees Mountain chain . . . roughly six miles north of the Spanish border, both would profit greatly from this handsome assignment and unexpected privilege.

Minor accidents took a sharp upturn and quickly came to prominence that saw fingers smashed and more than one head bashed. Serious *indeed* was the incident that put Bill Harrell on the sidelines and took him from the company roster. Carelessly handling his souvenir German P-38 pistol, the big easy-going Private First Class from Georgia became a victim of negligence when failing to remove the cartridges. Hardly more than touching the trigger . . . "c-r-a-c-k!!" At close range a missile tore through flesh . . . entering the center of the upper left thigh . . . to pass through the other side! Shocked, his first reaction came quick:

"Damn! What have I done!" . . . Look at that blood!"

Lengthy and uneasy confinement in the 78th General Hospital in St. Quentin presented him the opportunity to ponder the gravity of the accident, and would further remind *all* of the distinctive difference between the *real thing* and toys. Moreover, he bemoaned;

"This is a hell of a note! I can't even qualify for the 'Purple Heart'!"

He was two months too late for that!

Bastille Day is an important day to the French, and early morning of July 14 the nation would begin its' 156th year of celebration. Residents of St. Quentin had with intense emotions been making preparations the day before. Bastille Day is a great national holiday in France and is as much a part of their national heritage as is our Independence Day. Revolutionary forces of France on this date in 1789 stormed and destroyed the infamous Bastille (prison) that stood in the heart of Paris. Originally erected as a fortress, it long had served as a prison for political prisoners and for those who displeased the Kings and their courts. The capture and destruction of the Bastille therefore brought on an unprecedented elevation of nationalism and with it arose a new symbol of freedom throughout the country.

Parades started around ten in the morning and lasted much of the day. The scene was inspiring! Flags flying bright and prominent . . . homes overly-decorated with the French tri-color . . . children clutching small hand-flags, cheering, waving and displaying great jubilance as a part of the now moving celebration . . . in several instances trotting out of cadence behind the paraders! Streets, lamp posts, and business doorways were full of flowers! Gendarmes blowing whistles and issuing frantic gestures of the hands to keep traffic fluid . . . band after band in various succession blaring their finest! So many bands! Where did they all come from?! In sweltering heat the French in gleaming helmets represented much of the home guard; the regular troops in red berets and black tunics. French Moroccans, Tunisians, Algerians, French Foreign Legionaires and other related units were impressive and all displaying weapons of many variations from a supposedly antiquated French arsenal. The Women's Army Corps of France marched smartly by; and perhaps proudest of all, very snappy in full uniform of another era . . . the French veterans of World War One!

To them it was indeed a great day as they marched proudly down Rue Emile Zola . . . around the Place de Victoire and up through Rue de la Fere, finally to Place de Ville where though broad in scope, space could hardly contain them all and where later, impressive ceremonies would end the day. Some three hours later the celebration entered another phase, continuing an accelerated pace as the evening wore on. Into the wee morning hours the streets echoed with dancing, boisterous and endless singing . . . and much, much drinking! Though awed by the day's stirring, thunderous parades many of us, invited and taking the initiative, shared eagerly in the evening's festivities! The next day, July 15 came *too* early and proved to be a very slow one for the 126th.

***

As the war curtains in the Pacific seemed inevitably drawing to a close the army's recently established point system for individual discharge went into effect. This would in a short time result in redeployment of all eligible men with a great number of points.

How did this system function?

One hundred points constituted the maximum. A number of points were allowed for length of service, several for overseas time and points were allotted for a given number of family dependents. Participation in selected campaigns or battle zones ranked high for point consideration. All men forty two years and over were automatically eligible for discharge, and those with eighty-five to one hundred points were in an enviable position of returning to the States for eventual release. This point system quickly became a real hot conversation piece and during the early days of its' inception hardly anyone was found off duty without pencil or paper curiously determining his point status! This marked the first official step toward returning home, and while at the moment our overseas tenure exacted only seventeen months we nevertheless grew exuberant with the thought that not too many weeks would pass before we too would be plowing the high seas enroute to the States.

The point rotation system became effective August 1 and the 126th Ordnance Company, as we knew it; would begin undergoing a considerable change in personnel. Most of the original "non-coms" were first to go; Botting . . . Hilditch . . . Morris . . . Parrinello . . . Cohen . . . Marshall . . . Pitman . . . Wade (Jim) . . . Linzinmeir; those that had guided us since basic training and given us "hell" while doing so would be seen no more . . . certainly not, under Army jurisdiction.

Thousands of GIs were now boarding mighty military transports that included the great ships Queen Elizabeth and Queen Mary; many already on the high seas enroute to the United States. Some ships had already transported troops and entire Divisions with little combat time to the States for retraining and orientation for possible use in the great planned offensives now undergoing concerted preparations as the Allies sought to "ring the final bell" on the homeland of Japan.

T/Sgt. Chet Percy, a slight quiet-spoken Ohioan, and having headed the Instrument section since early training days moved up to fill the First Sergeant's vacancy. New section heads were chosen and changes made quickly. Well qualified, Wilbert Cranford would head Instruments as T/Sgt. Moving up in Small Arms, Al Rapin would also be promoted to the same rank . . . as would Stan Sieminkiewicz when he assumed command of Service section. Henry Hunt was reinstated as Motor Sergeant, a position that carried the rank of S/Sgt. Now promoted to T/Sgt., Ohioan Herb Fleming would continue his responsibilities as Mess Sergeant.

President Harry S. Truman, in office only four months, made a soul-searching decision that signaled release of the world's first atomic bomb on Hiroshima, Japan August 6. Three days later another was dropped on Nagasaki; virtually obliterating both cities and annihilating thousands of Japanese! The Russians meanwhile had crossed into Manchuria to dubiously enter the Pacific Theater. Allied concentration now focused completely on the Japanese homeland itself. To continue the war was futile, hopeless and foolish and collapse of the "Land of The Rising Sun" was imminent. The capitulation of Japan became a reality when on September 2nd aboard the USS Missouri in Tokyo Bay representatives of that country officially signed designated surrender terms laid down by the Allies.

This unquestionably meant everything to the world; but it meant something special *to us* too . . . for now there was no apparent danger of any of us going to the Pacific Theater of Operations!

XVIII

THE LAST CONVOY

St. Quentin had been our home for almost four fast months and in the very last days of September the 126th prepared to move again . . . this convoy to represent the last as a complete unit. A rash of rumors, integrated with hopes quickly blossomed into realistic thoughts that the next encampment would constitute a staging area, and from that point perhaps a ship for America would be boarded. We would have no such luck . . . for these hopes were dashed when on the morning of September 28 the convoy left the city and turned . . . eastward!

St. Quentin lay 21 kilometers southwest when we crossed the River Oise at La Fere. Due east several small villages, many now familiar to us . . . lay along the route. On through Fressancourt, La Bovette and Crepy-en-Laonais, no more than an hour's drive found us entering the old city of Laon.

How fascinatingly quaint was Laon! Its' homes and shops twisting their way around and up one of the loftiest peaks in northern France one did not look with envy on the task of many residents, who out of necessity had to make their way daily without transportation up and down these winding forty-five degree angled streets. With an unusual elevated spiraling pattern this "city on a hill" could with its' multi-spired cathedral be seen from a distance of many miles from any direction.

The many key arteries leading to and from Laon continued to suffer heavy damage as a result of the constant overflow of military tonnage and even at this period exhausting efforts were maintained to keep them operable. Asphalt trucks and workmen were laying a heavy black top coating at this moment in spots where they appeared warped and rumpled.

Over the Rivers . . . Miette and Aisne, through the larger towns of Festieux and Corbeny, embracing extremely low and marshy terrain along crumbling and decaying roads, we soon crossed the Canal de Aisne and entered the busy cathedral city of Reims.

Anyone who has studied an historical background of France will note the ebb and flow of that country's history has reverberated in some manner within the confines of Reims. One also is aware that this prestigious city is noted for its great champagne distilleries and particularly the magnificent medieval cathedral in which France's legendary national heroine, Jeanne d' Arc was commissioned in the fourteenth century by Charles VII to continue her insatiable crusade to crush the invading British. The old cathedral was badly damaged in World War I but managed to sustain this recent conflict . . . suffering no appreciable damage.

In May, over four months previous the German surrender was implemented in this city and even at this moment one of the largest German PW enclosures continued active within the city. Oise Section Headquarters was also centered in Reims . . . representing the base for all American military personnel within the region of northern France.

Further into western France over terrain that began to roll, villages noticeably became less frequent and forests more dense. We were moving through areas which some twenty seven years ago in the first World War was the scene of some of the most brutal fighting. Through this now predominantly rural country . . . along the ore and coal producing northeastern plateaus in the province of Lorraine, we bridged the River Suippe at St. Hilaire, and less than fifteen minutes rolled into Suippes, a colorless community where on a many-acred slope is located one of the largest and permanent military cemetaries for British soldiers lost in World War I.

Over the Rivers Tourbe and Bionne, and later at Dommartin . . . the Auve. A very few kilometers stretched ahead before we would enter St. Menehould . . . gateway to the aged battle-scarred Argonne Forest.

Darkened clouds hung low and persistent rain fell while we moved from St. Menehould, and with the unyielding precipitation a dismal conception of the now growth-studded Argonne Forest was viewed.

Though students of military history, armed with vivid imagination, nourish a strong conception of the ordeal marking the crucial struggle that transpired in this dispirited forest during the last great Allied offensive of the last war; the real agony and frustration that existed during this final phase of the Meuse-Argonne campaign can be perceived only by those that survived to tell it. Even as the campaign began shaping up in late September, 1918 . . . which in a few weeks would see the war's end; the enormity of its' viciousness could not have easily been predicted by the composed, confident, and to some degree; "cocky" Allies.

The American FIRST ARMY, commanded by Lt. Gen. Robert Bullard, which command within two weeks passed to Lt. Gen. Hunter Liggett, made up of the 1ST, 3RD and 5TH CORPS and embracing nine combat Divisions began the massive assault on September 26, 1918. Supported on the southern flank by the XVII French Corps and on the northern flank by the 4th French Army, aided by elements of three U. S. Divisions, the attack commenced just south of Montfaucon to extend several miles north in a sort of north-south sweeping arc beginning northeast above Verdun.

Operations were almost unbearable from the beginning, particularly because of the forest's unique rugged make-up. Tremendous hills, ridge after ridge of forested cliffs and unrestrained irregular terrain cloaked by a hideous mass of continuous unkempt woods offered little incentive for the 225,000 Allied troops dispatched to depose a stubborn entrenched enemy. Advantaged by years of topographical study and knowledge of this entire region the Germans literally knew every foot of this area. Systematically establishing their powerful 77mm guns on the high ground of the

Meuse River's east bank, the Germans trained deadly artillery down from the lofty heights to dominate the Meuse Valley. Moreover, enemy observation balloons maneuvering high above these positions transmitted instructions that allowed the artillery to direct its' withering fire into exposed and almost unmaneuverable American postions below.

American troops were confronted with machine gun nests crisscrossing every junction . . . thickets tangled with belts of barbed wire . . . snipers treacherously camouflaged in trees . . . hills bristling with deadly weapons . . . muddy ravines . . . and roads that because of incessant rains became impassable and almost unmanageable! Survivors say that it was some six weeks of hell that severely tested human endurance! Rainsoaked troops under continuous devastating savage shellfire, engaging in violent skirmishes . . . and faced with limited visibility because of heavy mist clinging to low areas found small streams almost unfordable. Six weeks of anguished "see-saw" battles that at times saw only yards gained, that produced tremendous casualties (some 117,000 FIRST ARMY troops killed and wounded) and left splintered forests, hillsides pocked and ravaged with deep shellholes, blasted woodlands and ruined hillvillages was a high and agonizing price to be paid in finally routing the German Army.

Rusty decaying barbed wire with uneven coils realistically penetrating the heavy brush and foliage clinging to unfilled trenches and growing over receeding ramparts, and broken remnants of the turbulent struggle involving German, American and French forces in the first World war became vividly alive for those with imagination when noting monuments, markers and occasional brush-infested shell craters. These would serve to remind one of the violence that brought the Argonne Forest to the forefront of notoriety with legends that belonged to another era.

Each mile eliminated triggered anxieties as to our destination. The unusual mileage consumed, and charting an almost continuous eastern direction gave rise to thoughts that we could well move across the German border and become an integral part of the U. S. occupation forces. Though little credence was given this thought, for we had earlier been assured that this would not be the case.

Leaning out of his jeep in the slow moving convoy, Ray Twiss;

the rangy rawboned Oregonian yelled back to Lt. Prendergast riding in the Recovery jeep:

"Hey Lieutenant; where the hell are we going?"

Pointing up ahead, the slender Lieutenant shouted back;

"Weinberg knows! Ask him!"

"Damned if *I'm* gonna' ask him!" shot back the old army "pro."

"Then sit back and relax, Sergeant; and let's just wait and see!"

Propping one of his long legs up against the flat dashboard, the impatient Sergeant slouched back in his seat.

"Hell's bells," he mumbled, "I don't think *anybody* knows where we're going."

Only the Captain was aware of the destination, and to suppress growing anxieties word soon trickled back that less than an hour would have us at destination.

Deep in the Argonne we rolled over the swift-flowing Biesme at Les Lslettes. Through Clermont, Vraincourt and into Parois the next few miles presented a disparaging view of many tiny hamlets and cluttered villages, each exposing shabby and generally inferior maintenance when compared to higher developed locales in other provinces of northeastern France. Many dwellings, several in sparsely settled rural areas with stables attached, displayed unusual unsanitary surroundings and obviously advanced very little from a standard of living that existed no less than fifty years previous.

The forest now behind, almost immediately the broad rapid blueish-grey waters of the Meuse was bridged and we entered the arched stone portals of the historic battle center of Verdun through which this river flows. A city of monuments; here in 1916 . . . drawing upon an almost depleted spirit of patriotism the desperate near-exhausted French forces bathed themselves in glory to win a punishing though costly victory in holding the Germans in check. Moreover, here in the summer of 1944 . . . on August 31, the U. S. 7TH ARMORED DIVISION in a three-pronged attack cleared the city of Germans and put them to rout!

Continuing east we loped along an improved but once-devastated countryside.

It was about five o'clock and the rains fell with intensity. It had been nearly an hour since the Captain indicated that a destination lay not too far up ahead. In the haze beyond, a drab village appeared and a roadsign identified it as Etain. Muddy, dismal and unattractive we sloughed on through . . . rolled some two hundred yards to suddenly come upon a fantastic scene. Through the mist almost as far as the eye could see lay row upon row of parked military vehicles adorning a broad plain of many acres. Moments later, when we stopped; the speedometer of the lead jeep indicated that one hundred sixty five miles had been clocked since morning.

A deteriorating airfield, long devoid of maintenance . . . embracing hundreds of acres, and formerly utilized as a U. S. fighter base, though long abandoned, would for the next few weeks be our camp. Except for a deserted spacious hangar and a small spindly combination administration building-tower no other permanent structure was noted, but over along the southeast corner of the field an assembled group of monotonous and empty squad tents awaited us. Drooped faces reflected disappointment at first inspection of the peakedroof dwellings, and the basic question arose unanimously:

"Where in the devil has Captain Weinberg taken us . . . and why?"

A sign of activity was nowhere to be seen, and other than our own noises hardly a foreign sound was heard; only the steady patter of rain and an occasional whine of the wind spending itself across the field . . . reminding us too, that the autumn season would not be denied.

Leaky tents . . . no flooring . . . no individual bath or toilet facilities . . . no stoves! *Indeed*, a far cry from "metropolitan" St. Quentin! We didn't like it, but we had to take it! Unquestionably, we had been spoiled! Would there be open grumbling and near-munitinous tactics as once there was when we were young immature recruits back in North Carolina? Hardly; for we were too far along for that sort of thing. We simply "raised a little hell" amongst ourselves momentarily, obeyed orders and set out to put this place in first class condition!

We looked too, with a jaundiced eye at the thousands of neatly parked vehicles (a reported 15,000) and wondered what this meant. Jeeps, trucks, tanks, command cars, halftracks and ambulances; to represent virtually every type of mobile personnel carrier in the European Theater. There existed at the moment a critical shortage of trucks for hauling food, fuel and building supplies to rebuild destroyed European cities and feed thousands of displaced persons. For, out of an estimated 102,000 two-and-a-half ton trucks in the ETO on V-E Day only thirty-five percent ... 36,000 vehicles, would be reconditioned for use within six months. Some of these vehicles would be added to that figure. Our immediate assignment was spelled out quickly. We were to implement the repair and inspection of these vehicles, run a thorough check on each machine, diagnose the problem, order parts if needed and restore it to operational condition. If this be the case and our company be charged to fully complete this assignment, we would plan to spend the next *two years* doing nothing but this! Sounded ridiculous! In addition ... there would be conducted a twenty-four watch for pilfering or theft by either civilian or soldier. All of this may have been necessary, but be that as it may; a lot of questions remained unanswered.

"Where are the work orders? Where are the classification papers? Are sufficient parts available? Where, in fact is a parts depot? Who was available and responsible for issuing a definite release committment once a job was completed?" Standing *high* among the important questions:

"Were the vehicles worth repairing ... really?" questioned one of the motor specialists, perplexed with the overwhelming reality; "I mean, Lieutenant, let's face it!"

"Look, I know it sounds unreasonable. Unreasonable *as hell*," answered Lt. Prendergast. "But that's our assignment ... and that's what we're gonna' do!"

"Okay, Lieutenant, ... but,"

"Look, you want me to show you the orders? You want me to put them on the bulletin board?" sounded an aggravated Prendergast.

"Okay, Lieutenant, Okay!" quickly changing it to, "I mean ... sir."

Simultaneously both produced smiles of understanding.

The more one sounded evaluation, the more it stood as almost a monstrous and empty assignment. After all ... with Germany and Japan both in rubble and the war in all theaters long diminished; who really would need this equipment? The 126th Ordnance had been overseas almost two years. We had taken our lumps and endured five campaigns and now in process of working homeward; but now ordered to maintain, service and put into working order some 15,000 rusting, abandoned and probably unuseable vehicles that nobody probably would use anyway . . . or even wanted, would have to be considered absurd! That it was beneath our dignity or capability was inconsequential, but having traveled a long way we were unanimous in our thoughts that this was a most opportune time to relax . . . and we would like nothing better than to execute that privilege.

Everyone was unanimous too in the expression that swirled within each thought:

"*To hell with it! Just, to hell with it!*"

But drawing on the discipline that we over the past several months had absorbed and *tried* to practice, we went at the task.

Almost twelve miles to the west was located Verdun where the population numbered less than 20,000 and where with exception of a single army-operated theater and a *very* temporary Red Cross service club, to a GI represented the end of nowhere!

Thirteen miles east of the airfield lay Metz, and though battered savagely nearly a year before by General Patton's **THIRD ARMY** remained a lovely city of some 86,000 busy people, where situated on the banks of the Moselle River . . . a full scale panorama unfolds to those viewing the city from the lofty western heights. A much larger community than Verdun it held a commanding popularity between the two so far as we were concerned, and though a small few hamlets lay scattered in between our attraction continued to center unanimously on activities within the two larger cities. This lack of interest in smaller communities, many observed, stemmed from "failure" of the few available girls in these hamlets to distinguish properly between GIs of the two predominant races that made up the United States Army.

Passes were issued to these places extensively. Eventually, almost for the asking trips to Paris, Reims and St. Quentin were granted. Within two weeks one had little difficulty obtaining leave to Verviers, Brussels, Luxembourg and Holland; and within reason, staying almost as long as he liked! With increasing liberality trips could soon be made to England, Switzerland and the French

Riviera; all expenses paid and transportation furnished.

By October 1, the Army's functioning rotation system had allowed thousands of soldiers to leave the continent, and the first week of the month this system dipped heavily into our ranks. Captain Weinberg, Chief Warrant Officer Rueth and Lt. Palmer were not long in receiving orders to leave.

The company remained "at ease" as the Captain stood before us, ready to address his last assembly. His personal belongings already packed in a jeep parked in front of the CP, and with little emotion he spoke:

"Men, I know you all want to go home, and so do I . . . only now I'm on my way. I'm not gonna' say a lot except that whether you believe it or not I think you've been good soldiers these past few months. Maybe a little ragged in the beginning, but I'm sure I was no exception. We've had a few knocks and we've done a lot of soldiering together. I'm proud of you . . . and maybe you feel I've been a little rough at times . . . and maybe I was. But, we've come through it all okay and now let me wish the best of luck to all of you and hope you will be seeing your families before long." Haltingly, he added:

"Now if any of you want to shake hands with me and say goodbye, okay; or if you want to step up and tell me how big an "s.o.b." I've been, you can do that too."

With that, a very informal salute . . . and;

"Dismissed!"

There was no response, no handshakers or visible compliments. The men were in no particular mood for either. Though they had become *better* soldiers under his command, they simply never understood the Captain.

With no fanfare, Lt. Prendergast assumed command of the company and 2nd. Lt. Harold Johnston moved up to Executive officer.

The second week of October again saw the point system tagging even more, this time to include all of the non-commissioned officers . . . together with many that first began with the company in its' inception . . . February, 1943. By this action . . . out of necessity, many changes in rank followed. It seemed in fact, that promotions came to almost everyone.

Bob McNulty, the neat and attentive company clerk . . . charged with responsibility of maintaining company records, was by his Irish nature a stickler for detail. When he moved up to First Sergeant he would be reminded from time to time that some of his actions might alienate some of his former friends. He could only reply:

"They're still my friends, if they want to be. If they get mad because I give an order that needs to be given that's just too damn bad. Just remember that I've got a job to do and they have one too. I'm gonna' do mine! That's for *damn* sure! In this position you don't engage in a popularity contest . . . 'cause there's no chance of winning."

For a very short period the company would be graced with two First/Sergeants, though only one would be in charge. Big Raymond Lee, the resonant-voiced ex-lawman from New Hampshire moving in from the 924th Ordnance at St. Quentin did in the very late days at Etain acquire that rank. The Table of Operations (T/O) would not be disturbed though, for McNulty would in a few days be caught up in the fast moving point system. Lee, who during the mid-thirties had played end on the highly-touted St. Anslem's College eleven in New Hampshire when that school was a force to be reckoned with . . . even against the powerful Ivy League teams . . . and would in post-war years become athletic director of his alma mater, still had some months yet to go. He was therefore a natural to assume the administrative command. Ironically his tenure would be shortlived . . . for less than a week he was transferred to another unit, and moving to Germany would carry that top rank with him.

Willfully capable, beefy heavy-jowled Ed Wysopal, Recovery's chief wrecker operator moved up to T/Sgt. to head that section. Artillery's Jim Burke and Automotive's "hillbilly" from Kentucky . . . lanky Bill Atherton, also attained the same rank, to head their respective departments. Frank Pesek, Art Fealk and Lynn Berndt became S/Sgts. which made them Mess Sergeant, Motor Sergeant and Assistant Automotive section heads, respectively. Throughout the fast-depleting company many technical ratings of fourth and fifth class were distributed . . . mostly to the remaining original personnel.

For almost a month we became well-acclimated to outdoor

living. With less emphasis placed on night life it would not be too amiss to note that daily participation in softball, horseshoes and other lighter sports, plus enduring the prevailing crisp atmosphere, we did as a group live healthy and admittedly during this period found it much to our liking. The drudgery of extra-curricular chores were over . . . for we had for some time been allocated a handful of German PWs to take care of these assignments. That they added something of a professional touch was evident when allowed a private tent to set up shop for barbering and tailoring. Further, they excelled in special kitchen duties, and though not actually on the company payroll . . . they did nonetheless maintain a price list to coincide with these duties. We paid without flinching!

The 126th Ordnance in late October was about to experience a complete personnel changeover. Its' ranks already interspersed with new faces succeeding those having been shipped home for discharge, would receive even more.

Sunday, October 28 was a busy day, but its' significance perhaps would become as indelible to us as did the day of February 1, 1943. To us, that was the day the 126th Ordnance began. Now on this day of October 28 as far as we were concerned, would represent its' end. Company activities would continue, without question . . . with little interruption, but it had belonged to us for almost three years . . . and now it was over. The duties, assignments, perplexities and complaints in the 126th would fall the burden of someone else as a new era began for this industrious unit.

It was mid-morning and the original men who began army life when the company was in its' infancy in North Carolina some thirty-two months ago; and even those that joined us in the very early days of Europe received orders to move out . . . a move that supposedly in a few weeks, or maybe days, would end at various separation centers in the States. From each other we had gleaned a broad personal and practical knowledge and had learned to care for ourselves daily, emergency or otherwise. A natural "esprit de Corps" had developed along the way and each had accummulated a vast array of interesting and intimate experiences that would eventually drift into memories. Each experience, however, could very well be long-lasting and possibly at times be beneficial during the approaching years.

***

Four open-top 2½ ton trucks moved out in mid-morning, heavily laden with anxious men and excessive baggage that along the way would become dissipated when some items were discarded. South into east-central France some one hundred and thirty miles into the rolling province of Burgandy we reached Dijon, an old city steeped in history . . . but bristling with activity. On the city's west side at the widely-scattered compound of the 442nd Ordnance Base Supply Depot we checked in. Exhibiting little enthusiasm over our arrival the administrative personnel had seen GIs come by the thousands as this expansive overstaffed depot was geared to handle statesbound replacements only. In a short time we would supposedly be categorized and assigned to units marked for continental evacuation.

Sparked by rumors, all unofficial . . . we began channelling our thoughts in a direction that presumably would see us journeying south to the port of Marseilles on the Mediterranean and thence initiate an exodus through that highly active facility. These aspirations would however, have to be readjusted for by the second morning it was learned that Marseilles was out of the question.

Unharmed during the war, Dijon was a hub of activity for some 113,000 busy people. The Rivers Ouche and Suzon meet at the eastern edge of the city to supply waterpower for factories that produce mustard, spice bread, textiles, chemicals, leather goods and paper. The three days at Dijon were exceptionally relaxing, and for a needed diversion near-fashionable night clubs and satisfactory restaurants were enjoyed in a city that exhibited a wealth of hospitality. Though moving out on the fourth morning we could not have been aware of the many disappointments in store before really leaving the continent . . . and we would hardly have believed one more month would pass before this would become a reality.

A truck convoy left Dijon at noon carrying about one hundred fifty men. Two additional trucks followed close behind loaded with baggage. Unruly winds lashed capriciously about heads protected only by overseas caps and some helmet liners as the vehicles speeded straight north through lovely landscaped areas that made up rolling hills, broad fields, spacious orchards and well-tended grape arbors. Langres, Chaumont, St. Dizier and Chalon-sur-Marne were among the more notable towns touched, each remembering with dismal impressions the terror of the first world war, and each having changed little over the years. One hundred fifty miles completed, we reached Reims in late afternoon.

There was in Reims a tremendous military deportation classification center through which most every soldier in northern France must be processed before leaving the continent. Suffering a constant turnover in administrative personnel, and programmed to interview hundreds of GIs daily complete efficiency could not be expected. "Halfway House" came by its name naturally for it was generally considered that once a soldier cleared this busy center he was . . . theoretically, halfway home. Designed to inventory all accummulated government-issue items used in warfare; weapons, cartridge belt, gas mask, helmet, etc., leaving clothing and the duffle bag as bare necessities, it presented a frustrating operation for many items had *already* been discarded or lost, or even abandoned . . . particularly among those having moved from place to place before reaching this center. Saddled with an overburdened feeding system that was sure to get worse before getting better, and a billiting problem that only time would alleviate, the situation at "Halfway House" would require several weeks yet before recognized improvement would be attained.

Two days passed, and now integrated with hundreds of unassigned troops, not until four PM of the third day did we board a troop train awaiting at the mammoth station in Reims. Three hours later Reims was disappearing from view. None could than have imagined that even though our destination lay some one hundred fifty miles west, an uneasy twenty four hours would elapse before that point would be reached! Were communications with veterans of the first World War at the moment possible they would have offered strong sympathy and at the same time marvel at such reduced transit time. Yet unfamiliar to us were the disreputable French troop trains that veterans in years past called "forty and eights;" wooden rail cars that in those days were built to carry up to forty men each, with a multi-ventilated car containing eight horses attached. Stenciled high across the car's side, still clearly legible twenty seven years later, one could read . . . "quarante homme, huit chevaux." With two glassless windows on each side of the coach and a small door at each end, a limited number of upright wooden benches facing a spot reserved for a potbellied stove at the end of the car . . . used seasonally in times past, though now removed; forty persons would about comfortably consummate capacity. For want of limited space and an acute shortage of rail equipment to cope with the present tremendous almost frantic troop movement, far more soldiers than capacity would suggest crammed into each car, and each accompanied with no less than one duffle bag.

One wondered aloud why the antiquated equipment. Querying himself and his fellow GI, he asked:

"Is this *really* the best a great victorious United States Army or the French government can do? Does this exemplify peacetime transportation?"

Should he consider at the moment; realistically, that peacetime conversion was a long way off and with thousands of GIs shuttling hundreds of miles from place to place over much of this country, he would find the existing hard-nosed fact that superior cars simply were not available.

That we would "survive" was without question, and though much discomfort was experienced . . . an all night bumpy rattling ride was endured . . . extending throughout the next day. The train moved through Laon, St. Quentin and Amiens and we would late in the day creep into the eastern limits of Rouen and halt.

This train, secondarily scheduled at best, executed orders to halt at all junctions, and particularly when a scheduled freight or passenger express, exercising main line prerogatives, approached; it became necessary for the lumbering troop transport to seek the sanctuary of a sidetrack.

At many stops several enterprising Frenchmen were on hand waving handfuls of oversize French currency, unrestrained in an eager desire to engage in exchange. GI clothing and most anything disposable was sought for bargaining. Stops were lengthy and numerous and at points where these Frenchmen obviously were not strangers. So heated with enthusiasm were they as the exchange pace quickened that some made an effort to squirm through the narrow windows! Physical restraint became necessary! Someone in disbelief quipped:

"Look at them 'Frogs' will you! Just look at 'em! They're trying to bust the damn wall down!"

Someone in authority yelled:

"Keep them the hell out of here!"

"Looks like you'll have to shoot 'em to do that!" came a reply. "They're wild!"

So furious and fast became the exchange of francs and goods it could be noted that many GIs, and not as facetious as it may sound, may just have begun their sales careers here as bargaining reached a fast pitch through the small unobstructed windows! Helmets and liners, leggings, cartridge belts and other items that should have been, but *were not* left at "Halfway House" were disposed of. Excess clothing, shoes, raincoats and accummulated rations passed into French hands, and in some instances a price was offered for the entire duffle bag and contents! Often too tempting to refuse, no questions were asked and the entire bag passed through the window and disappeared into the night!

This reckless bartering was repeated at various segments of the night, and in fact at almost every stop. Hundreds had traveled this route before us . . . and many was the GI that had engaged these Frenchmen in this same late hour activity.

***

"What have we got here? Boy! I've seen some sorry-looking ones in my time but this has got to be the worst yet! What prep school did you guys come from?"

Lined up for inspection and assignment we were unceremoniously listening to derisive comments from the big tough-looking well-dressed Lieutenant, who slowly scanning the front ranks of a disheveled exhausted group of GIs expressed his indignation, with perhaps some justification. With many articles lost, discarded or sold; belts, knit and overseas caps, helmet liners, messkits, overcoats, battle-jackets, gloves, etc., anything but a military appearance was presented. With some, only their immediate clothing remained . . . shirts, shoes, pants and socks . . . the chilled winds of November notwithstanding!

The Lieutenant wanted to get on with it.

"If the refugees in those DP camps look any worse, I don't wanna' see 'em. Who's in charge of this outfit anyway?"

From the end of one of the columns came a voice of authority and out stepped a slight of build T/Sgt. unknown to us until then.

"I am, sir."

"You don't keep a very good house, do you Sergeant?" questioned the Lieutenant. "How did you guys get in such sorry shape anyway?"

Looking straight at the Lieutenant the Sergeant flipped a thumb over his shoulder, much like one when hitch-hiking a ride, and said:

"Sir, have you ever ridden all night in one of those things?"

"No, but that's a lousy excuse."

Not a bit impressed with the officer's shiny gold bars of a 2nd. Lt., the Sergeant retorted;

"It may be lousy but it sure as hell ain't an excuse, especially with about ten times as many GIs as are supposed to ride, and no heat and no place to sleep." His voice rose a little but his composure did not change, and he continued:

"Take a ride sometime, Lieutenant; then you'll know what I mean!"

Established and scattered about France many redeployment camps were programmed to handle troop processing for those scheduled for immediate evacuation of the continent. Named especially for easy recognition and pronunciation, every GI in northern France preparatory to leaving would soon become familiar with Camps Twenty Grand, Lucky Strike, Philip Morris, Old Gold and Chesterfield. Additional camps were fast-rising and strung along central and northern France. Thousands of GIs would pass through camps with prominent names; names like Camp Boston, Oklahoma, Chicago, Philadelphia and New York, to name a few.

Camp Twenty Grand awaited us, a monotonous collection of squad tents located roughly two miles south of the highly venerated old city of Rouen on the River Seine and situated some ninety miles northwest of Paris. During our tenure that would near embrace a full two weeks many availed themselves of an opportunity to visit this vast eminent metropolitan area of some 275,000 . . . where firmly secured in the pages of history a visitor will not easily forget the strikingly prominent marker honoring Jeanne d' Arc in the public square, where in the year 1431 this great heroine of France was burned at stake.

The 89TH INFANTRY DIVISION had since October occupied the camp and we immediately dispersed into various infantry companies of that DIVISION's three regiments. With exception of guard duty we were spared camp work details as those duties were relegated to German PWs. This allowed for much camp freedom and our activities would hence center on Red Cross Service Club recreation, softball and other sports. Further; a slight case of boredom allowed us to follow an unregimented routine of extracting sweets and cigarettes from a camp PX.

Squad tents constituted living quarters with four to six persons assigned each. A good portion of November was consumed waiting for the DIVISION's inevitable order for ship assignment, presumably through the port of Le Havre . . . some thirty miles to the north where the Seine empties into the English Channel. Although a later date would see the 89TH INFANTRY DIVISION exiting through Le Havre, that we were not a part of it neither surprised nor disappointed us . . . for patience was fast becoming an integral part of our nature. The fact that within a period of three weeks two chief ports of debarkation (Marseilles and Le Havre) had evaded us did not dim our hopes, for within a day or so strong rumors were circulating that a third port would enter the picture!

***

We stood shivering with cold and impatience at an early morning assembly on November 20 as camp loudspeakers blared a welcomed message!

"The following names will step forward and be prepared to leave at 1000 hours sharp! Trucks will be waiting in front of the orderly room and boarding will commence as soon as you are prepared!"

The message was repeated and emphasis was placed on "1000 hours sharp." We did not need a magic formula to decipher that it meant ten o'clock sharp, and in those names most of the remaining 126th was included.

By noon some four hundred weary GIs tightly packed in a fleet of box cars watched the wavering rail siding at south Rouen gradually disappear in the glint of a mid-day sun. Though these were not "forty and eights" they were however, the next thing to it and no "joy ride" was envisioned. We were not at all concerned for there was ample room and we have been almost assured that this would probably be the *last* leg of our journey. There appeared simply nowhere else to go. Now it was on to the port of Antwerp . . . some one hundred eighty miles to the northeast!

The floor of the freight cars, each badly in need of upgrading, was where one stood, sat . . . and with his bedroll, slept. Again, sidetracks were utilized extensively. Slow down! . . . back up here! Pull into a sidetrack there! Wait! . . . wait! . . . Pull out with a terrific jerk! Then with cinders flying . . . chug a few miles further! Slow down . . . then stop, only to back up some more! Pull into another sidetrack! Back into a sidetrack! Sit there! Time? Time didn't matter! Schedules? There weren't any! But though it seemed the transport was sidetracked for hours, most every time one found a suitable spot out in the bushes or high grass, substituting for toilets that did not exist . . . a whistle blew and a hundred or so voices echoed down the line . . . "B-O-A-R-D!" How hilarious it was many times to see one having to run alongside perspiring and cursing, and hauled in because it wasn't always easy to immediately finish what he had set out to do!

The greying evening of the 22nd saw a heavily puffing engine dragging a line of GI-laden freight cars into Brussels, Belgium. With accummulated justification every reason was ours to now wonder if this *really would be* the "final leg."

A port battalion already slated for states-side shipment and made up almost solely of replacements, presented evidence of assurances that only sufficient ship space at Antwerp awaited their evacuation. We became part of this battalion, and in the meantime were free to move about promiscuously and enjoy the hospitality offered by a city of such magnitude.

Brussels is a lovely city . . . a great city bristling with an international flavor, a city cradled in history and an abundance of culture and tradition. Graced with an industrious metropolitan population of close to one million people, each resident appeared to have every reason to speak of it with pride. Fashionable night clubs and auspicious restaurants were visited where fancy meals delightfully were served unsparingly. Steaks were plentiful, eggs were plentiful, fowl of many variances was served and seafood no longer was a rarity. And wine, there was no end to it. Amazing in contrast to France . . . where to get a steak in a public restaurant was out of the question. Lamb, mutton and the like, perhaps, but no steak. It was wonderful!

Other pleasures were found at the many theaters, USO shows and public dances.

Passes were not essential and one could move about almost at will. Discipline became so relaxed that no man unless assigned a specific duty deemed it necessary to report to his respective quarters at any special time. In most instances roll call was optional; neither was daily inspection required. "Reporting in" was the choice of the individual. Though "KP" lists and guard rosters were posted at unit headquarters it was amazing to note that even though one did not show up for his particular responsibility, he could present almost any kind of excuse . . . and no matter how flimsy, usually no action was taken against him. Despite this apparent lack of discipline, or regimentation . . . rarely was there reported acts of unusual misbehavior on the part of the GI.

With a constant flow of army troops through this complex, thence to Antwerp for states-side shipment a tremendous turnover in executive and administrative personnel was exacting its' toll, and because of laxity in individual responsibility within this battalion, many suffered as a result.

How and to what extent did they suffer?

Allowed to do practically as he pleased, a soldier's name frequently was called for shipment and he was not present to answer. He subsequently was *scratched* from that particular sailing list and plagued with dubious channels of authority through which his name must again pass and be submitted, chances of getting on the next sailing list were quite negligible. Missing a scheduled shipment could sometimes set his actual sailing date back from two weeks to a month! He had to be reassigned and integrated into another unit which did not always have space available. Although not enforced, the great majority of our original company personnel had just enough discipline remaining to report to headquarters each day. Now skeptical, we were not going to allow too many more disappointments to pervade our plans.

Canvas covered trucks protected us from a light rain while moving out of Brussels on the 29th. Some forty miles to the northwest in late afternoon the small convoy began to twist through the chilly rain-swept streets of busy Antwerp. Still lying in much disrepair were many dwellings that had been direct recipients of repeated "flying bomb" attacks in the previous winter months.

Antwerp suffered from the terror of the V-1 "Buzzbomb" perhaps more than did any other European city, save perhaps London. 4,000 hits were recorded during the winter months of 1944-45, and attacks did not cease until the end of March. Of the more than 10,000 casualties registered some two-thirds of these were civilians and almost 3,000 of them were injured fatally.

Across the Escaut Canal west of the city . . . into Camp Top Hat, a scattered but orderly "tent city" spread along the sandy shores of the wide active waterway, we found quarters that was expected to represent our last on the continent.

It was Sunday, December 2, and a gloomy overcast had dominated the skies during our three days of occupation. Many returning from respective religious services would learn from those who had already been notified of an assembly set for one o'clock.

"What's up?" inquired one, hopefully.

"What d'ya mean, what's up?" replied another; "you know very well what's up. Haven't you heard the rumor; we're getting the hell out of here!"

"Yeah, I've heard the rumor . . . been hearing it for the last two months!"

"Well, you're hearing it for the last time. So get your tail in high gear. This is it!"

At one PM a many hash-marked Sergeant confirmed that very statement.

"Groups A and B will prepare at once for shipboarding. You will move out at 1600 hours (4 PM)."

"This, then *is* the real thing!" became the predominant thought.

A light snow flurry began to fall and as evening approached we were struggling with duffle bags up the gangplank onto the chilly windswept decks of a much-traveled Liberty ship; the converted Dutch cargo vessel . . . "Boshfontaine."

A thin blanket of snow lay across the decks early morning of the 3rd. The powerful motors of the "Boshfontaine" began to throb at daybreak, propellers churned and thrashed against the canal's blueish-grey waters and lines were cast off as a tug guided the great hulk into the mainstream. A chilled wind whipping uncomfortably in wisps about the ship soon blew the snow off. Standing on deck most were silent watching the buildings and church spires of Antwerp gradually fade in the distance as the ship slowly glided through the Escaut Canal. The great European adventure was fast coming to an end.

Well into the choppy English Channel by mid-morning we enjoyed from a great distance a marvelous panoramic view of England's celebrated chalky white cliffs of Dover. Late afternoon, far off our starboard side the rising green hills on the Isle of Wight came into view. Toward evening the force of heavy swells was noted and the ship began plowing into headwaters of the Atlantic Ocean.

Enduring a rough wave-lashing voyage across the extremely stormy Atlantic, that at times saw the ship's bow virtually leap from the raging waters . . . only to pound down violently against the next monstrous wave and jar the ship to its very superstructure, threatening it would seem, to literally tear the vessel apart! It became almost a three-times-a-day ritual, or for a better evaluation . . . a necessity, for many immediately following "chow" to make his way painfully to the main deck, lean on and grasp firmly the rails and spew copiously everything he had eaten. For a time seasickness ran rampant. Late afternoon of the twelfth day found every man assembled on deck, squinting through the dense haze for a long-awaited glimpse of the snow-coated Statue of Liberty in white-blanketed New York harbor. As the skyline of the great city suddenly came into view varied expressions of "Look! Look! Look!" reverberated along the rails.

"Sunofagun . . . Look at that! Just look at that, will you!"

One wondered just how many thousands of GIs had already expressed the *same* wonderment.

A tug pulled alongside and a man in civilian clothes climbed aboard, identifying himself as the harbor pilot.

A cheer went up!

"Welcome home, boys!" he shouted, "we've come to guide you in!"

A wave of applause began; and sweeping across the decks was picked up by some 1,800 enthralled GIs now crowded on scattered catwalks and beyond the ship's bridge and platforms, to gradually swell to a thunderous crescendo!

We were ready!

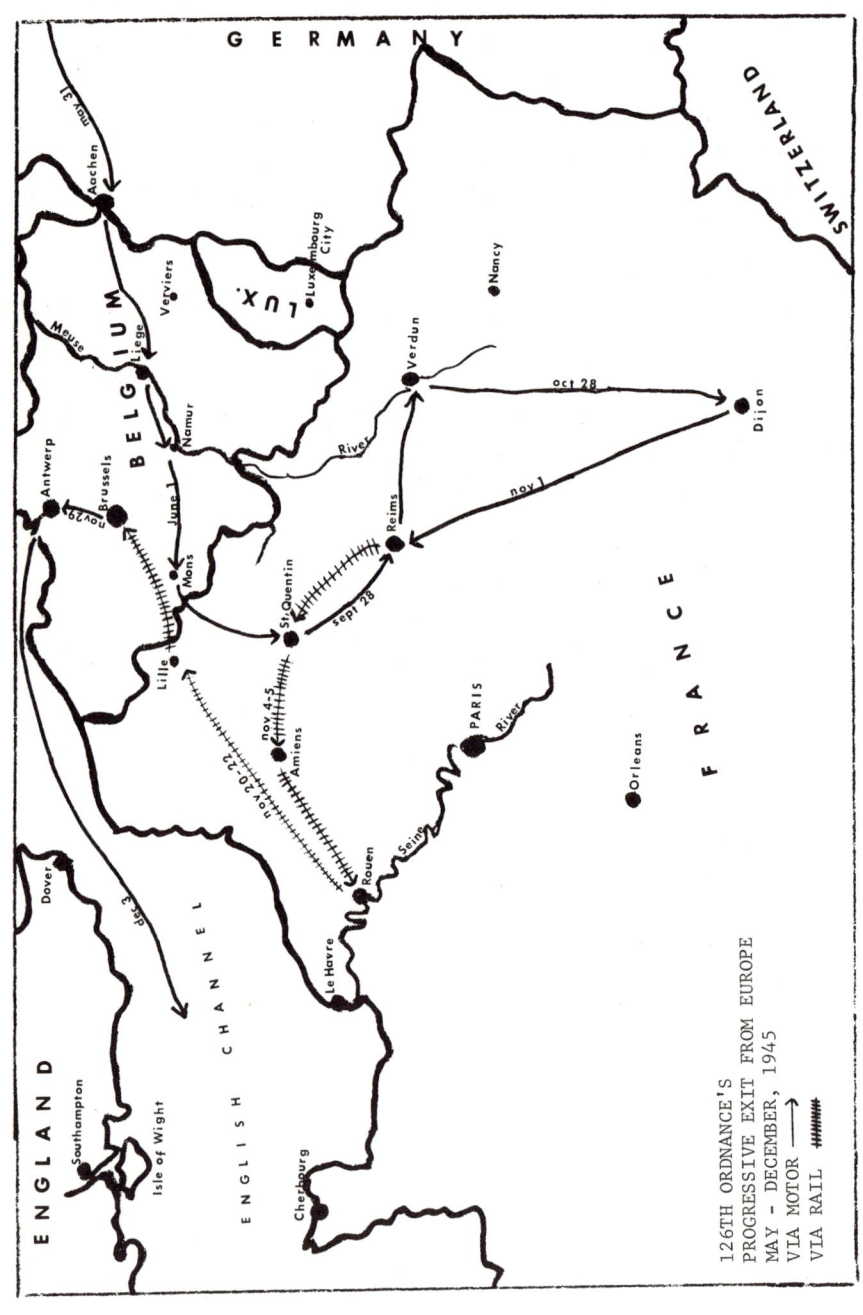

The non-professional writer has no easy task. Months, and even years of research is required; groping for the right word, re-phrasing, re-editing, correcting grammar and punctuation . . . and more time-consuming, engaging in personal interviews. Hundreds of ideas and thoughts come and go while traveling by plane, train, bus and private auto. Advantaged by the solitude of libraries, hotel rooms and of course at home helped put it all together. As time grew, so did the interest. Without, however; my original wartime scribbling in the beginning there would be no book; and I might add, this book was by no means written overnight.

"Why the book?" someone asked; "for to write a book of this magnitude is a large order." The answers are many. But the central answer is simple. Every author, when writing has a story to tell. I have always felt that we too have a story to tell. Not as glamorous perhaps or as exciting as those in constant combat, but surely . . . as the reader has noted, as important. It was too, a project that once started . . . particularly with the dearth of information at hand, simply could not be set aside.

Now gone from the scene are Generals Eisenhower, Patton, Hodges, Gerow and Eddy, as well as Colonel Childs. And too, from the scene have passed some of our company personnel.

It has been my privilege to visit several of our great World War II military leaders who served in the European Theater and whose comments are valued and are contained herein. Prominent among them; Generals of the Army Dwight D. Eisenhower and Omar N. Bradley, the latter consulted often and to whom I am indebted for writing our "Foreword." Also General J. Lawton Collins who served as Army Chief of Staff during the Korean War, and who after much research graciously submitted a personal letter of commendation. It was a pleasure too, to lunch with and visit with Generals Matthew B. Ridgway, Jacob L. Devers and U. S. Army Chief of Staff, General William C. Westmoreland. Each, a fine soldier. I am much indebted to Lt. Gen. William B. Kean who furnished invaluable material and aided me tremendously in FIRST ARMY research. General Mark W. Clark, now retired in Charleston, South Carolina and though confined to Mediterrean and Italian Theater commands during this period, did nevertheless lend considerable personal inspiration.

I likewise am appreciative of the comments and contributions given me personally by Generals William H. Simpson and Maxwell D. Taylor, Lt. Generals James M. Gavin, Clarence R. Huebner and Troy H. Middleton. Maj. Gen. Louis A. Craig and Brig. Gen. Edwin H. Randle, in whose homes I was welcomed, as well as a host of others . . . I now consider old friends. Each was proficient in his leadership; each compiled a fine record, and it is highly unlikely that the likes of such astute field commanders will again be seen in our lifetime. Moreover, it has been nothing less than a pleasure to visit with several of the original members of the 126th as well, each spurring me on to complete this story.

It is incredible to note that 27 years have elapsed since cessation of hostilities in Europe and though the allies were successful in obliterating Nazi tyranny in Europe they were not at that time programmed or prepared to check the encroachment of Communism *then* seeping into both Europe and Asia. The free world has since that time come to grips with this ideology, both diplomatically and physically. Today's dubious involvement in southeast Asia does not hold the same purpose as did the conflict in Europe and battles are waged on different terms. The allies in Europe, enjoying the full support of *all* nations *demanded* and *received* unconditional surrender from the Germans. In southeast Asia this is not the case, for to make a wrong move is to incur the possible wrath of *all* nations, *including our own,* free or otherwise. Short of total warfare, the alternative then, is to localize, contain, diffuse and phase out the present conflict while a more comprehensive solution is being initiated.

The world, because of the jet age has become much smaller and though today man's technological advances almost stagger the imagination, the basic thinking of the world seems to have changed little. Perhaps even more distrust exists among nations than did 27 years ago, but peculiarly at the same time a wider range of respect *does* exist. Perhaps this irony stems from the fact that nuclear war can be waged by all major powers, only to end in nothing less than complete disaster. Therefore, a more viable solution of co-existence must be sought perpetually. Nations have also painfully learned with much truth, that the folly of war enhances a financial burden so strenuous that stepped-up diplomacy becomes *indeed* a less expensive substitute.

***

What finally happened to the 126th and where is the unit now?

With a completely new turnover in personnel the 126th Ordnance Company on March 11, 1946, almost five months after our severance, returned to the United States and on the 22nd of that month was inactivated at Camp Kilmer, New Jersey. Thus our days with the 126th are now capsuled in memories. Of a certainty however, the crisp beauty and hospitality of Blagdon, the uncertainties of Normandy, the jubilation of a liberated Verviers, the mud and gloom of Rotgen, the cold days and nights of sheer darkness at Camp d'Elsenborn, and the swift advances and spectacular teamwork in inner Germany will in no way be considered in vain.

In the twenty fourth chapter in the book of Matthew there is a verse that reads:

"And ye shall hear of wars and rumors of wars; see that ye be not troubled; for all these things *must* come to pass, but the end is not yet."

Rare is the soldier so naive as to believe this would be the war to end all wars, but God willing . . . there would never be another of its' magnitude. The experience would remain unparalleled insofar as we were concerned . . . some of it to be applied advantageously and some of it, as the years take their toll will likely fade from memory. Whatever accomplishments attained during those days is now inconsequential, though the fact remains that our unit . . . along with all associated with the FIRST UNITED STATES ARMY played a small but vital part in concerting an Allied victory in Europe. Though we were some of the "men behind the men behind the gun," we feel our job was done well.

In order to perform well in a given assignment and attain success two particular qualities must be exercised. First; *individual* pride in one's unit becomes a tremendous asset; and a healthy abiding "esprit de corps" is essential. When on October 7, 1967 in Detroit,

Michigan after twenty two years of separation the 126th held its' first and only reunion it appeared obvious that these qualities still remained . . . and *far* from diminishing. They would however, continue to live in each heart *only* so long as we desired.

M. L. B.

BIBLIOGRAPHY

Crusade in Europe; Dwight D. Eisenhower, Doubleday, New York, N. Y. 1948

A Soldier's Story; Omar N. Bradley, Holt, Rinehart & Winston; New York, 1951

The Bridge At Remagen; Ken Hechler, Ballentine Books, New York, 1957

Battle: The Story of the Bulge; John Toland, Random House, New York, 1959

The Doughboys; Lawrance Stallings, Harper & Row, New York, 1963

The Last Act – 1918; Barrie Pitt, W. W. Norton & Co., New York, 1962

Eight Stars to Victory; Joseph B. Mittleman, Ninth Infantry Division Association, Washington, D. C., 1948

The Queen Mary; Neil Potter & Jack Frost, The John Day Company, New York, 1961

Breakout & Pursuit; Martin Blumenson, Office Chief of Military History, Department of the Army, Washington, D. C. 1961

Cross Channel Attack; Gordon A. Harrison, Office Chief of Military History, Department of the Army, Washington, D. C. 1951

The Siegfried Line Campaign; Charles B. McDonald, Office Chief of Military History, Department of the Army, Washington, D. C. 1963

The Ardennes: Battle of the Bulge; Hugh M. Cole, Office of Chief of Military History, Department of the Army, Washington, D. C. 1965

The Ordnance Department — On Beachhead & Battlefront; Lida Mayo, Office Chief of Military History, Department of the Army, Washington, D. C. 1968

The World Book Encyclopedia: Field Enterprises Inc., Chicago, Illinois

First U. S. Army Report of Operations: Volumes I, II and III

St. Lo: Historical Division, U. S. War Department, Washington, D. C. 1946

Mission Accomplished: The Story of the VII Corps, J. J. Weber Company, Leipzig, Germany, 1945

Acknowledgements

National Archives & Records Service, General Services Administration, Washington, D. C.

Michelin Maps and Guides; French and European Publications Inc., New York.

Blagdon Town Council, Bladgon, England.

U. S. Army Signal Corps Photographic Service, The Pentagon, Washington, D. C.

Newspapers:

    The Atlanta Constitution, Atlanta, Ga.
    The Birmingham Age-Herald, Birmingham, Ala.
    The Charlotte Observer, Charlotte, N. C.
    The Chicago Daily Times, Chicago, Ill.
    The Cleveland Plain-Dealer, Cleveland, Ohio
    The Durham Herald-Sun, Durham, N. C.
    The Milwaukee Journal, Milwaukee, Wisc.
    The New York Times, New York City
    The News & Observer, Raleigh, N. C.
    The Norfolk Virginian Pilot, Norfolk, Va.
    The Philadelphia Inquirer, Philadelphia, Pa.
    The Richmond Times Dispatch, Richmond, Va.
    Time Magazine
    The Stars & Stripes, War Department, Washington, D. C.
    Yank Magazine

OTHER PERSONNEL SERVING IN THE
126th ORDNANCE COMPANY
(Rank not shown)
1943-1945

Adamski, Leonard J.
Amerson, Charles F.
Armstrong, Burleigh N.
Brown, Donald J.
Burns, Mitchell J.
Butterton, Meredith L.
Buxton, Ellsworth
Card, Everett L.
Cole, James P.
Colling, Courtland K.
Dietzel, Clarence H.
Dinges, William R.
Dombrowski, John D.
Dumas, William T.
Echlin, Robert A.
Garafala, Sam
Gardner, Richard N. Jr.
Havlik, Martin J.
Krusel, William W.
LaFrazier, John A.
Lauterbach, Everett J.
Letvin, Stephen
Lyngaas, Chester W.
Mazorowicz, Richard A.
McCormick, John J.
McCormick, Sampson T.
McCutcheon, Paul J.
Mickiewicz, Joseph R.
Neil, Vernell
Ormiston, Grant C.
Owen, Russell E.
Patyna, Henry A.
Peters, Bernard L.
Radichel, Arno
Richmond, Joseph E.
Robbins, Norman F.
Rogers, Cecil L.
Rose, Herman M.
Ruess, Joseph C.
Schneider, Lawrence F.
Smith, Ernest W.
Smith, Richard F.
Sokolowski, Robert J.
Stager, Herbert T.
Stover, James E.
Travis, Bunny E.
Van Horn, Emil
Veal, Sidney H. Jr.
Vittetoe, Bobby E.
Volz, George J.
Waggoner, Denver D.
Walsh, Gerald D.
Watts, George B.
Wyzykowski, Valentine P.
Zaremba, Henry R.
Zawacki, Theodore J.

GLOSSARY OF TERMS

AAA — Antiaircraft artillery
AMG — American Military Government
APO — Army Post Office
ASTP — Army Specialized Training Program
AW — Automatic weapons
AWOL — Absent without Official Leave
Ack Ack — Antiaircraft
BFR — Belgian Resistance forces
Boche — French term for "German"
Bon Bon — candy (French)
Bouncing Betty — explosive mine (German)
CG — Commanding general
CO — Commanding officer
Com Z — Communications zone
CP — Command post
DS — Detached service
DP — Displaced person
DUKW — 2½ ton amphibious truck
EAC — European Advisory Commission
ETO — European Theater of Operations
ETOUSA — European Theater of Operations United States Army
Flak — Shrapnel (usually from AA guns)
"Frogs" — GI slang for "French"
GI — Government issue (any item but usually reference to soldiers)
Jayhawk — VII Corps code name
Jerry — English term for German soldier or airman
Jerrycans — GI army gasoline cans
KP — "Kitchen police"
Kraut — GI slang for German soldier
Limey — GI term for English soldier
LCI — Landing craft infantry
LCM — Landing craft marine
LCVP — Landing craft vehicle-personnel
LST — Landing ship, tank
Long Tom — 155mm artillery
Master — First Army code name
Metric 16 — 126th Ordnance code name
Notorious — 9TH DIVISION code name
OCS — Officer Candidate School
Panzer — German armored unit
Pokey — GI term for stockade
PTO — Pacific Theater of Operations
PW — Prisoner of War
Purple Heart — U. S. Army medal for wounds
PX — Post exchange
RAF — Royal Air Force
RCT — Regimental combat team
Recon — Reconnaissence
SHAEF — Supreme Headquarters Allied Expeditionary Forces
SS — German elite troops
TD — Tank destroyer
"The Old Man" — GI term for commanding officer
TO — Table of Operations
UK — United Kingdom
VE-Day — Victory in Europe
VIP — very important persons
1st/Sgt. — First Sergeant (top enlisted rank — administrative)
M/Sgt. — Master Sergeant (top enlisted rank — technical)
T/Sgt. — Technical Sergeant (next to top enlisted rank)
S/Sgt. — Staff Sergeant
T/3 — Technician, third grade
T/4 — Technician, fourth grade
T/5 — Technician, fifth grade
Pfc — Private first class
Pvt — Private
CWO — Warrant Officer (Chief)
WOJG — Warrant Officer (Junior Grade)
Wehrmacht — German Army (often referred to as German war machine).

INDEX

Aachen (Aix la Chappel), 248-49, 254, 261, 265, 271-74, 285, 295-96, 311, 343, 431-32
Abel, Harry G. 2Lt., 26, 40
Aberdeen, Maryland, 13, 26, 33, 321
Achene River, 236
Ahr River, 363
Aisne River (Normandy), 178
Aisne River (Picardy), 223, 449
Alexander, H. E., 22-24
Alfred The Great, 71
Algeria, 392
Allen, Fred, 323
Allen, Terry Maj. Gen., 392, 408
Allendorf, 381, 392
Allied Bomber Command, 137
Allied Expeditionary Forces, 82, 85, 98, 99, 217, 413
Allied High Command, 133, 331
Alsfeld, 426
Altendorfer River, 363
Ambleve River, 309, 327
Ambrieres, 178
American Military Gov't, 347, 351, 400, 402, 404
Amiens, 461
Amsbury, 71
Anderlues, 434
Andover, 70, 72, 73
Andrenne, 434
Andrushko, John Pvt., 39
Angleine River, 179
Antwerp, 286, 307, 315, 331, 433, 466-468
Aoon River, 215
Apollinaris (industry), 363
Appalachian Mountains, 30
Ardennes, 302, 305, 311, 333
Arenhausen, 395
Argentan, 179
Argonne Forest, 450, 452
Arkansas USS, 82
Armed Forces Radio, 73, 187, 323
Army Ground Forces, 7, 16, 22, 23, 161
Army War College, 10, 14, 444
Arpajon, 195, 196, 202, 204, 238
Arran, 55
Ashchurch, 76
Asheville (NC), 30
ASTP, 14, 26
Atherton, Bill T/3, 386, 457
Atlanta Constitution, 181

Aubenton, 230
Aubetin River, 216
Augusta USS, 82
Augustus (Caesar), 400
Aurelle River, 435
Austria, 398, 400, 415
Avon River, 59, 64, 68, 70
Avranches, 139, 173, 177
Axbridge, 64

Bad Neunenahr, 363, 364, 368
Balkan, 75, 399
Ballainvilliers, 195
Baltic Sea, 397, 411
Bancigny, 226
Banov, Robert 2Lt., 10, 12
Barbot River, 176
Barrett, Gordon Sgt., 268
Barton, Raymond O. Maj. Gen., 86
Barton, Stacey, 71
Basingstoke, 71
Bastille Day, 444, 445
Bastogne, 283, 329
Bath (England), 67
Battle of The Bulge, 311, 328, 332-33, 356, 416, 433
Bavaria, 378, 398, 405, 414, 429
Bay of Biscay, 444
Bay of The Seine, 81, 82, 86, 87
Baxter (Tenn.), 25
BBC Radio, 133, 413
Beach commander, 104
beach police, 118
"Bedcheck Charlie", 151
Belgian Resistance Forces, 229, 232, 233
Bellefontaine, 176
Bellenglise, 436
Bellicourt, 436
Belsen, 401
Belyk, Mike Pfc., 39
Benny, Jack, 323
Berg, 345
Berga, 406
Bergstein, 338, 339
Berlin, 300, 378, 397, 405, 412
Berndt, Lynn T/Sgt., 457
Berrieux, 224
Beuvardes, 218
Bevel, 429
Biarritz, 444
Biesme River, 452
Binche, 434

480

Binenfeld, Norton T/5, 443
Bionne River, 450
Birmingham Age Herald, 383
Birmingham (England), 58
Bishop, Virgil Sgt., 319
Bittefield, 416
Bizerte, 131, 392
Black, James G. 2Lt. (1Lt.), 40, 97, 115-16, 168, 211, 243, 324
Blagdon, 59, 61, 64-65, 67, 70-71 72, 244
Blanc-Misseron, 435
Blanche Canal, 230
Blandford, 94
Blatzheim, 430
Blet River, 346
Bliss, William C. Col., 389
Blosville, 144
Blue Army, 18-21
Bocage, 110
Bocq River, 236
Bois de Couvin, 230
Boissy Le Chatel, 216
Bonn, 355, 357-358, 369, 370-371
Bonnell, Lawrence, 39, 320
Border, Norman Pvt., 94
Boshfontaine, 468
Boshnakian, Hriar Pvt., 39
Botting, Manley 1St/Sgt., 5, 28, 43, 67, 78, 93, 97, 149-151, 167, 182, 187, 203, 211, 213, 219, 221, 234, 239-40, 250, 255-56, 258, 263, 292, 325, 339-40, 343, 360-61, 365, 368, 382, 403-05, 419, 446
Boudreau, Henry T/5, 122, 149-150, 192, 220
Bournemouth, 71
Bourne River, 70
Bradley, Omar N. Lt. Gen. (Gen), 86, 92-93, 131, 140, 142, 154-55, 161-62, 176, 181, 184, 190, 307-08, 315, 322, 355, 369, 383, 387, 398, 411
Bragg, Braxton Maj. Gen., 18
Brandenberg, 338-339
Brandt, 274, 296
Braun, Eva, 405
Braunfels, 428
Bray, (Belgium), 434
Bremen, 378, 397
Brereton, Lewis H. Lt. Gen., 164
Brest, 84, 139
Breuil-sur-Vesle, 223

Bridgewater Road, 59
Briquebec, 122 127, 132
Bristol, 59-60, 64, 66
British Southern Military Command, 68
Brittany peninsula, 84, 172, 181
Brouffe Canal, 230
Brown, Les, 323
Brueck-Hetzingen, 340, 343
Brune River, 224
Brunswick, (Germany), 378, 397
Brussels, 229, 286, 455, 465-467
Buais (France), 177
Buchenwald, 401, 425
Budapest, 284
Buday, Joseph T/4, 320
Bull, Harold R. Maj. Gen., 19
Bullard, Robert Lt. Gen., 450
Burke, James T/4 (S/Sgt.), 321, 443, 457
burp gun, 148
Burlington (NC), 7, 31
Burns, C. O. Lt. Col., 114
Burrington Coombe, 64
Butgenbach, 280
Butzin, Robert T/5, 39
buzzbomb (V-I), 227, 284, 286, 315-316, 467
"Buzzbomb Alley", 288

Caen, 87, 164, 174
Caesar, Julius, 400
Calais, 224
Calvados (France), 194
Cambrai, 436
Camp Breckenridge, 10, 34
Camp Boston, 463
Camp Butner, 5-7, 9, 12, 17, 26, 28, 31, 33, 37, 40-42, 361, 413
Camp Chesterfield, 463
Camp Chicago, 463
Camp d'Elsenborn, 274, 280, 282, 288, 315
Camp Forrest, 17
Camp Grant, 5
Camp Kilmer, 41, 43, 96
Camp Lucky Strike, 463
Camp New York, 463
Camp Oklahoma, 463
Camp Old Gold, 463
Camp Philadelphia, 463
Camp Philip Morris, 463
Camp Top Hat, 467

Camp Twenty Grand, 463
Canada, 241
Cance River (France), 176
Canute (King), 71
Carentan, 90, 110, 140-142, 143, 144, 145
Carentilly, 169
Carlisle, 58
Carrouges, 186
Carstairs, 58
Caumont, 88
Celles, 329
Centerline (Mich.), 13,
Cerisy-la Salle, 169
Chalons-sur-Mer, 460
Chantrigne, 178
Chapel Hill (NC), 7
Chapman, Wm. Pvt., 39
Charchiegne, 178
Charlemagne, 271, 400
Charleroi, 229, 282, 434
Charles VII, 449
Chateauneuf, 193
Chateau Thierry, 217-218
Chatelet, 434
Chaumes, 215
Chaumont, 460
Cheddar Gorge, 64
Cheek, Holman Pvt., 44
Chef du Pont, 110-111, 124
Cheltenham, 76, 93
Chemnitz, 378
Cherbourg, 110, 122, 127, 131-33, 137, 139, 141, 143, 157, 184, 190, 253, 270
Cherence le-Roussel, 176
Chery-Chartreuvre, 221
Chesapeake & Ohio Railway, 3
Chew Magna, 64
Chewton Mindip, 64
Chicago (Ill.), 5, 39, 169, 197, 225, 242
Chicago Daily Times, 131, 198
Childs, J. D. Lt. Col., 214-215, 260, 311, 365-66, 386
Chilhowie Park (Tenn.), 28
Cholitz, Dietrich von Gen., 198
Chrest, Roy Pfc., 39
Chrusiel, Edward T/4, 320
Churchill (Town of), 65
Churchill, Winston, 202, 286, 413, 419
Ciney, 236

Citadel, The (Europe), 236
Clark, Mark W. Gen., 185, 284, 398
Clermont (France), 433, 452
Cleveland Plain Dealer, 187
Clifton College, 64
Club Christophe, 440-441
Clydebank, 49
Clyde River, 58
Coblenz, 355, 370
Cohen, Jake T/Sgt., 387, 443, 446
Cole, James Pvt., 39
Colleville-sur-Mer, 89
Collins, Glenn H. Capt., 10, 11, 13, 28, 30, 33
Collins, J. Lawton Maj. Gen., 89, 126, 136, 137, 140, 168, 174, 184, 275, 392
Cologne (Germany), 296, 300, 343, 346, 353, 357, 369, 377, 429, 430
Colombiers, 177, 178
Connors, Phil T/4, 256, 257, 370
Cookeville, (Tenn.), 18, 27, 28
Corbeny, 223, 449
Corlett, Charles H. Maj. Gen., 141, 158
Cotentin peninsula, 86, 124, 131, 139, 140
Coulommiers, 216
Couptrain, 179
Courbe River, 179, 186
Courtomer, 186
Coutances, 173
Couvin, 230
Covie, Robert Pvt., 182, 183
Craig, Louis A. Maj. Gen., 185, 191, 260, 279, 334, 385
Cranford, Wilbert T/Sgt., 447
Creedmoor, (NC), 7
Crepy-en-Laonais, 448
Crerar, Sir Henry Lt. Gen., 164
Crombach (Belgium), 330
Crosby, Bing, 323
Cuchenheim, 362
Culver, Charles Pvt., 389
Cumberland County (England), 58
Cumberland River (Tenn.), 18, 22
Curacao, HMS, 54
Czechoslovakia, 398, 411

D-Day, 80, 81, 92, 137, 143, 158, 201, 438
Dachau, 401
Dale, Glenn Pvt., 39

Danube River, 284, 398, 415
Davidson, Martin T/5, 387
Davis, James Pvt., 389
DeBacker, Gerald T/4, 105
DeGaulle, Charles Gen., 199
Delaware, 41
DePrey, Robt., 39, 46, 238, 239, 240, 315
Dempsey, Miles T. Lt. Gen., 87, 92
Derby (England), 58
Derkum, 346, 347, 361-362
Desertines (France), 177
Dessau, 416
Detroit (Mich.), 4, 26, 39, 100-01, 105, 167, 172, 182, 242, 255, 317, 320, 327
Devers, Jacob L. Gen., 77, 284, 398
Dewey, Thomas E. Gov., 284
Diehl, George T/5, 325
Dieppe (France), 224
Dijon, 459
Dill River, 426
Dinant, 235, 236, 329
Displaced Persons Camp, 400
Dittmar, Kurt Lt. Gen., 202
Dizy-le-Gros (France), 224
Dolhain, 246, 312
Dommartin, 450
Donelson (Tenn.), 25
Dorchester, 94
Dortmund, 378, 383
Dorset County (England), 94
Dorsey, Jimmy, 323
Dorsey, Tommy, 323
Douve River (France), 124
Drees, 362
Dresden, 378
Dressart (Belgium), 280
Droutte River, 194
Dueren, 293, 295, 430, 431
Duke of Somerset, 65
Duke University (NC), 7
Durham, John T/5, 324
Durham Morning Herald, 306
Durham (NC), 5, 7, 31, 37
Durscheven, 346
Dusseldorf, 383
Dutch, 199, 244, 349, 399, 424, 468

East Harptree, 65
Eberle, Sidney S. Col., 12, 13
Echternach, 303

Eddy, Manton S. Lt. Gen., 77, 131, 184, 328
Eder River, 392, 393
Edwards, Melvin S. T/5, 420
Eifel Mountains, 271, 333, 380
Eilendorf, 311, 431
Eisenberg, 424
Eisenhower, Dwight D. Gen., 79, 81, 82, 98, 137, 142, 154, 176, 181, 184, 202, 294, 306, 308, 322, 333, 356, 385, 387, 412, 413
Eisenach, 425
Eisleben, 408
Elbe River, 383, 392, 397, 411, 412, 416
Elle River, 430
Elsenborn, 280, 284, 287, 315, 316, 320, 327, 328
Emerick, John Pvt., 44
Endean, Tom T/5, 210
Engles, Wayne T/3, 386
Engis, 434
English Channel, 67, 71, 76, 80-81, 84, 86, 90-1, 97, 105, 117, 131, 139, 468
Ensival, 240
Epernay, 216
Epernon, 194
Epiedes, 218
Erft Canal, 346, 430
Erfurt, 425
Erpel, 373
Escaut Canal (Belgium), 467, 468
Escaut River (France), 435, 436
Eschweiler, 293, 299, 431
Esneux, 237
Essen, 383
Etain, 453, 457
Ethiopia, 151
Euenheim, 346
Eupen, 246, 248, 249, 280, 295, 303, 312, 335,
Eure River, 193
European Advisory Commission, 422
European Theater of Operations, 42, 45, 115, 162, 333, 377, 414, 454
Euskirchen, 346, 348, 362, 370
Evans, Bruce Pvt., 39
Exmouth, 71
Eyenatten, 295

Falaise, 174, 179, 180, 181, 303, 416
Farmington, (Tenn.), 17

483

Fealk, Art (Pfc) (S/Sgt), 93, 232-35, 318, 457
Felt, Richard S/Sgt., 211, 252, 287, 318
Festiux, 449
FFI, (Maquis), 198, 201, 212, 219, 221, 232
Firth of Clyde, 55
Fismes, 222, 223
Flemalle, 434
Fleming, Herbert S/Sgt., 120, 121, 447
Flemish, 244
Flint, Harry (Paddy) Col., 123, 124
Floreffe, 434
Flying fortess, 89
Fontaine-l'eveque, 434
Fontenermont, 172
Foret d'Ecouves, 186
Foret d'Eupen, 249, 261, 266, 269, 279
Foret de Hertogenwald, 280
Foret de Nesles, 219
Foret St. Sever, 176
Fort Bragg, (NC), 39, 76
Fort Crook (Nebr.), 13, 26
Fort Custer (Mich.), 3, 5, 6
Fort Ord, (Calif.), 13
"forty & eights", 461, 465
Fossee, 434
Fougeroulles, 177
France, Joe Sgt., 320
Frankenberg, 392
Frankfurt, 377, 378, 426, 429
Fredendall, Lloyd R. Lt. Gen., 19, 22
Frelich, Newton 2Lt., 26
Frelingen, 379
French (forces), 92
French Republic, 199
French Riviera, 389, 390, 456
Fressancourt, 448
Frey, George T/5, 321
Fritzlar, 393
Fulda River, 393, 395, 425
FW-190, 166, 359, 393

Gallatin, (Tenn.), 17, 25, 26, 27
Garfield, John, 10
Gavin, James M. Maj. Gen., 91, 124
Geilenkirchen, 285
Gelsdorf, 363
Gemmenich, 248
Geneva Convention, 34, 226

Gerhardt, Charles Maj. Gen., 86
German High Command, 153, 271, 354, 377, 395, 405, 412
German Home Radio, 359, 385
Germeter (Germany), 271, 279, 338
Gerow, Leonard T. Lt. Gen., 87, 141, 303-04, 327, 333
Gerstner, Edward Pvt., 94
Gianoplos, Moses T/5, 242
Giessen, 378, 426
Glasgow (Scotland), 58
Glore, James Pfc. (S/Sgt), 268
Gloucester (England), 59
Goe, 313, 315, 322, 335
Goebbels, Joseph, 349, 405
Goering, Hermann, 349, 405
Gold Beach, 87, 89
Goodman, Benny, 444
Gorniak, John Pvt., 39
Gotha, 425
Goucherie, 145
Goudelancourt, 224
Gourock, 55
Governor's Island (NY), 66
Granville County (NC), 6
Graves, James Pvt., 39
Graves Registration, 106, 109, 144, 146, 171, 277, 341
Gray, Glenn, 323
Great Britain, 49
Great Smoky Mountains, 30
Greenock, 55, 56, 57
Greensboro (NC), 31
Grimms Ditch (England), 109
Groult River, 144
Grove, Norman 2Lt., 10
Gulpe River, 432
Gwynn, Anne, 10

Hall, Gerald 2Lt., 325
Hall, Glenn, T/4, 386
Halle (Germany), 408, 414, 416, 424
Hamburg, 378, 397, 405
Hampshire County (England), 68, 70, 71, 77
Hamtramck (Mich.), 4, 255
Handel, George Frederick, 409
Hannover, 378, 397
Hansen, Jim T/3, 386
Harmon, Ernie Maj. Gen., 329
Harrell, William Pvt., 389, 444
Harris, Chet T/3, 192, 320
Hartsville (Tenn.), 22, 24

Harz Mountains, 385, 386, 392, 397, 412
Hausser, Paul Gen., 179
Hautgne, 237
Haut Vernay, 146, 148, 150, 164
Havelange, 236
Havocs, 89
Heilingenstadt, 395
Heinkel, 134, 383, 408
Heinsberg, 293
Helle River, 280
Hemmeres, 247
Henderson (NC), 7
Henninger, William T/5, 172
Henri Chappell Cemetery, 327
Henschelwerk, 417
Herbestahl, 283
Herborn, 380
Herman, Woody, 323
Herve, 433
Hesse, 393, 426
Hestreux, 280
Hickory, (NC), 10, 30, 31
High Point (NC), 31
Hilditch, Olen T/Sgt., 183, 211, 219, 322, 420, 433, 444, 446
Hill, John Cpl., 389
Hillsboro (NC), 7
Hillsboro (Tenn), 18
Hilsea (England), 76
Himmler, Heinrich, 405
Hindinburg Bridge, 429
Hitler, Adolph, 92, 135, 198, 252, 271, 308, 317, 349, 350, 378, 394, 396, 402, 405
Hiroshima, 447
Hizon, Tony Pvt., 45, 207
Hodges, Courtney H. Gen., 154, 163, 248, 272, 278, 306, 308-09, 322, 327, 355-56, 369, 383, 387, 414
Hoegne, 240
Hofen, 274
Hogan, Richard Pvt., 39
Holland, 75, 84, 134, 248, 284, 455
Holy Roman Empire, 271, 400
Hommett Woods, 150
Hope, Bob, 323
Hot Springs, (NC), 30
Hotel Brittainique, 308
Hotel Terminus, 441
Hotton, 329
Houfallize, 307
Howey, Dave T/5, 170, 191

Howe, Elias T/5, 39
Howe, Robert 1Lt., 291, 389, 404, 412, 444
Howlett, Lester Pfc, 93, 94
Hoyaux, 236
Hubine, 236
Huckswagen, (Germany), 326, 327
Huddersfield (England), 58
Huddleston, James T/3, 386
Hudson, Robert A. Lt. Col., 126-27, 155, 254, 366
Huebner, Clarence R. Lt. Gen., 86, 87, 190, 272, 274, 334
Huertgen, 254, 338
Huertgen Forest, 254, 275-76, 279, 293, 295, 336-39
Hult, Frederick T/4, 321
Hungary, 284
Hunkins Wm. Pvt., 12, 101
Hunt, Henry S/Sgt., 211, 212, 213, 447
Huntley, Harold H. Col., 32
Hupfer, Clarence Lt. Col., 393
"Hurricane" (British), 174
Huteau, 224, 230
Huy, 309, 434

Iceland, 293
Inde River, 296, 311, 431
Ingoldstadt, 414
Isigny, 141, 142, 145
Italy, 75, 151, 187, 284, 400
Iter River, 249

Jackson, Earl E. Sgt., 35
Jaffee, Richard Sgt., 197
James, Harry, 323
Jankowski, Ted T/5, 100, 210, 321
Japanese, 284
Javron, 179
Jayhawk, 113, 119, 213
Jeanne d'arc, 449, 464
Jeantes, 224, 226, 227, 230
Jemeppe, 434
Jena, 425
Jews, 350, 352, 353, 425
Johnson, John T/3, 386
Johnston, Harold Pvt., 389
Jones, Henry Pvt., 389
Jones, Robert, Pvt., 293
Joue, 186
Juelich, 293
Juine River, 204

Jung River, 362
JU-88, 134, 394, 408
Juno, 87, 89

Kalenborn, 373, 374, 375, 378
Kall River, 336, 340
Kallet, Sumner 1Lt., 10
Kassel, 378, 393, 394, 395, 425
Katz, Aaron Pvt., 172
Kaufman, Sol T/3, 387, 444
Kean, William B. Maj. Gen., 309
Keitel, Wilhelm GenFldmshl, 83
Kennedy, Charles Ryan, 103
Kentucky, 5, 17, 320, 457
Kilgallon, Lawrence T/5, 39
Klabough, Edward T/4, 141
Kleinhau, 338, 339
Kluge, Gunther von GenFldmshl., 164, 179, 180-81
Knowles, Harold T/5, 210
Knoxville (Tenn), 27, 30, 31
Koniev, Ivan Marshl, 397
Korea, 90
Kothen, 416
Kothen Forest, 355
Koudelka, Ernie T/5, 225, 319
Kowalczeski, Richard Pvt., 14
Koziol, Steve T/3, 341
Kurtjian, Harry T/5, 419
Kyser, Kay, 323

La Bouvette, 448
Lafayette (Tenn), 25
La Fere, 440, 448
La Ferte Mace, 179, 182, 186
La Ferte Vindame, 192
Lahn River (Germany) 380, 381, 426, 429
La Haye du Puits, 140
Lammersdorf, 254, 255, 256, 274
Langenhahn, 379
Langersdorf, 345
Langerwehr, 431
Langford, Frances, 323
Langres, 460
Laon (France), 440, 448, 449, 461
Lappion, 224
La Puisaye, 192
La Roche, 307
Lasch, Wernher Pvt. (T/3), 44, 206
Lassay, 178
La ville du Bois, 195
League of Nations, 151

Lear, Ben H. Lt. Gen., 19
Lebanon (Tenn), 25
Le Bruly, 230
Le Catelet, 436
LeClerc, Jacques P. Maj. Gen., 198
Le Ferte en Tardenois, 218
Le Ferte Alais, 204
Le Guislain, 169
Lee, Gypsy Rose, 10
Lee, Ray 1st/Sgt., 457
Lee, Robert E. Gen., 384, 385
Leica (camera), 426
Leichner, Dave Pvt., 232, 233, 234
Leipzig, 378, 411, 416, 424
Le Havre, 224, 464
Lenoir Rhyne College, 31
Leonard, John W. Maj. Gen., 355
Leonhardt, George T/5, 419
Les Champs de Losque, 164
Les Chappelles, 179
Les Forges, 108, 119, 141, 142, 144
Les Lslettes, 452
Leval-Trabegnies, 434
Lewis, John L., 12
Lexington, (NC), 31
Ley, Robert Dr., 405
Leyte, 284
Liberators (B-24), 89
Lichtenbusch, 295
Liege, 236, 237, 271, 282, 286, 307, 315, 433, 434
Liggitt, Hunter Lt. Gen., 450
Ligneuville, 330
Lille, 224
Limbourg, 246, 312
Limet, 236
Linas, 195
Lineberger, Ormond R. 2Lt(1Lt), 10, 119, 192-94, 210, 216, 325, 420, 428
Linzinmier, Frank M/Sgt., 116, 122-23, 211, 352, 446
Lippman, Walter, 202
Liverpool, 94
Lobejun, 409, 415, 417, 420, 422, 423
Lopcombe, Camp, 68, 69, 73, 74, 77 94
Locke, Jim T/5, 80, 210
London Midland & Scottish Rwy., 57
Longjumeau, 195
Lorenz, Edward Chaplain, 128
Lorraine, Province of, 284, 450

Louis, Joe, 10, 315
Louisburg (NC), 7
Louisiana (maneuvers), 16, 24
Louisville & Nashville RR., 5, 20, 27
Lovette, Harold 2Lt., 324
Ludendorf (Bridge), 356, 359, 363, 372, 416
Luftwaffe, 59, 66, 69, 134-35, 142, 161, 260, 283, 313, 359, 364, 368, 393, 405
Luse, Arthur Col., 126, 127
Luther, Martin, 414
Luxembourg, 247, 248, 302, 303, 328, 455
Lynn, Robert Lt. Col., 427

Maastricht, 248
Magdeburg, 378
Maidment, Cal T/5, 370
Maintenon, 193
Makos, Walter T/5, 242
Malmedy, 245, 280, 303, 308, 330
Manchester (Tenn.), 17
Manchuria, 447
Mangee, 283
Manhay, 329
Marauder (B-26), 89
Marburg, 379, 380, 381, 391
Marienbourg, 230
Marigny, 162, 165, 167, 168
Mark IV (tank), 167, 186, 306
Marne River, 216, 218, 220
Marshall, Al T/Sgt., 366, 446
Marseilles, 187, 459, 464
Maryland, 41
Maschek, Al T/3, 324
Mauberge, Fortress, 435
Maupertuis, 169, 171
Mausbach, 274
Mayenne, 178
McArthur, Douglas A. Gen., 284, 384
McBride, Horace L. Maj. Gen., 19
McCalmont, Dee Pvt., 14
McClymont, Wilbur, 93, 94
McKinley, Ray Sgt., 323
McMinnville, (Tenn.), 18
McNair, Lesley J. Lt. Gen., 22, 23, 24, 161
McNulty, Robert T/4 (1st/Sgt.), 101, 211, 234, 456
ME-109, 166, 320, 359, 393, 408
Meckenheim, 362,
Medaris, John B. Col., 125, 126, 203

Mediterranean Theater, 164
Mehoudin, 179
Melun, 204, 209, 213
Memphis (Tenn.), 16, 19, 22
Merderet River, 90, 124
Merode, 295
Merz River, 431
"Metric 16", 113, 119
Metz, 284, 455
Meuse River, 235-37, 314, 327, 329, 331, 434, 450-52
Mico, Roco T/3, 39, 320
Middleton, Troy H. Maj. Gen., 139, 302, 304, 307-08, 327
Miette River, 224, 449
Milburn, Frank W. Maj. Gen., 19
Military Railway Service, 370
Miller, Clyde L. 1Lt. (Capt.), 33, 37, 62, 67, 72, 266-68
Miller, Glenn, 323
Miller, Lloyd Pvt., 389
Milwaukee Journal, 247
Missouri USS, 447
Mitchell (B-25), 89
Model, Walther von FldMrshl., 181, 303, 383, 384-85
Modersheid, 330
Moisenay-le-Grand, 204
Monignies, 229
Monroe, Vaughn, 413
Mons, 229, 435
Monshau, 274, 282, 302, 303, 334, 336
Mont Castre Forest, 140
Montabaum, 429
Montcornet, 224
Montebourg, 133
Montfaucon, 450
Montgomery, Sir B. L. (Fldmrshl), 86, 154, 164, 174, 306, 315, 322, 397
Moore, Joe Pvt., 39
Morris, John S/Sgt., 93, 191, 203, 209, 325, 360, 361, 446
Mortain, 173, 174, 176
Moselle River, 455
Moulins le-Marche, 186
Muhlen River, 362
Mulde River, 408, 411, 412
Munchausen, 381
Munden, 395
Munich, 378, 385, 398
"Music Makers", 324, 441
Musielak, Leon T/5, 207

487

Mustang (P-51), 165
Mutzenich, 336
Muzbeck, William Pvt., 292

Nadder River, 70
Nagasaki, 447
Namur, 434
Napoleon, 131, 199, 247, 400
Nashville, (Tenn.), 17, 25, 26
NC & STL Railway, 20
Nat'l Committee of Lib'rtn, 199
Natoli, John T/4, 386
Navy, United States, 101, 284, 355, 373
Nazi, 80, 98, 131, 198, 202, 225-26, 245, 332, 347, 351-52, 382, 392-93, 395, 400-01, 405-07, 412, 420, 425
Nebelwerfer, 130
Neffel River, 345, 430
Neider Ault, 426
Neiderwalgern, 379, 380
Nelson, Horatio Admiral, 71
Netherlands, 83, 265, 271, 400
Nev-Moresnet, 432
Neuss, 391
Neuville, 230
Nevada USS, 81
New Brunswick (N.J.), 42
Newbury, 74
Newgarden, Paul W. Maj. Gen., 19
New Jersey, 41, 42, 44, 45, 132, 191, 323, 324
New York City, 40, 42, 44, 51, 284, 469
New York Times, 23, 357
News & Observer, 11, 13
Nideggen, 344
Nogent, 216
Noir River, 230
Nordhausen, 400, 401, 402, 404
Norfolk Virginian Pilot, 81
Normandy, 80, 84, 85, 88, 92, 107, 110, 113, 121, 124, 126, 128, 130, 139, 142, 151, 153, 156, 159, 161-62, 164, 167, 173-75, 178-180, 182-84, 187, 191, 195-96, 201, 230, 248, 260, 267, 270, 303, 326, 333, 336, 360, 392, 396, 404, 416
North Africa, 19, 76, 77, 79, 117, 164, 175, 184, 185, 333, 415
North Carolina, 4, 5, 7, 8, 16, 17, 25, 30, 37, 41, 42, 291, 453, 458

"Notorious", 113
Notre dame de-Cenilly, 169
Nuremberg, 378, 398
Nye, William 1Lt., 40, 79

Obr-Forstbach, 295
Oder River, 397, 411
Odon River, 186
"Old Reliables", 294, 333
Olivier, Sirio T/5, 192, 252, 253
Ollainville, 194, 195, 202
Oise Headquarters, 439, 441, 443, 444, 449
Oise River, 448
Omaha Beach, 86, 87, 88, 89, 90, 131
Operation Cobra, 158, 176
Operation Dragoon, 187
Operation Grief, 303, 331
Operation Overlord, 86
Operation Neptune, 86
Operation Queen, 293, 294, 337, 431
Ordnance Base Section, 74
Ordnance Department, 155
Ordnance Gen. Base Depots, 17, 19, 76, 190, 238-39, 282
Orge River, 196
Orne River, 86, 87, 186
Orsenigo, Alfred Capt., 78, 94, 101, 116, 129, 150, 193, 195, 207-08, 213, 217, 221, 249, 262, 266, 289, 290
Osterman, George T/5, 39
Our River, 247
Oxford, (NC), 7
Oxman, Daniel 1Lt., 40, 79

Pacific, 48, 141
Pacific Theater of Operations, 45, 412, 447
Paczas, Stan T/5, 191
Pailhe, 236
Palmer, Jack 1Lt., 78, 388, 456
Paris, 173, 178, 181, 191-93, 195, 198-99, 202-05, 217, 222, 238-39, 244, 248, 253, 282-83, 303, 440, 445, 455, 464
Parker, Edwin Maj. Gen., 9
Parois, 452
Parrinello, Sam S/Sgt., 263, 446
Pastor, Tony, 323
Pastovich, John T/4, 368

Patch, Alexander M. Lt. Gen., 187, 398
Patton, George S. Gen., 154, 163, 172, 181, 284, 291, 322, 328, 393, 455
Patrick, S. T/5, 342
Paulins, William T/5, 443
Pennsylvania Railroad, 41, 45
Pepinster, 240, 283
Percy (France), 171
Percy, Chet T/Sgt., 387, 447
Periers, 140, 159, 162, 164
Perliskey, Walter T/4, 211, 212, 387
Pershing, John J. Gen., 217
Pershing (tank), 307, 339, 364
Pesek, Frank T/Sgt., 457
Peszko, Edward T/4, 387
Petergensfeld, 249
Philadelphia (Pa.), 26, 42, 44, 100
Philadelphia Inquirer, 293
Philippines, 284
Phillipville, 230, 232
Pickett, George E. Lt. Col., 358
Piscine River, 178
Pitman, Harry T/Sgt., 283, 446
Plomion, 226
poison gas, 151
Poland, 134, 399
Polish, 4, 212, 255, 350, 418, 421, 424
Polish (forces), 92
Pont-de-Bonne, 236
Pont l'abbe, 124
Poole, Herbert M. Col., 32
Port of Embarkation, 42, 45
Portsmouth (England), 84
Potok, Ted T/4, 387
Prairies Maregeuses, 140
Prendergast, James 2Lt. (1Lt), 40, 117-19, 132, 242, 318, 452, 454, 456
Prepotin, 186
Privoznik, James Pvt., 44
Proteau, 412
Providence, (RI), 6
Puchala, Tony T/4 (S/Sgt), 209, 325, 444
Puklus, Joe, 47
Pyrenees Mountains, 444

Quarouble, 435
Quartermaster Corps, 121, 190, 391
Quebec, 422
Queen Elizabeth (HMS), 49, 446
Queen Mary (HMS), 48, 49, 53, 54, 446
Quievrain, 435
Quincy USS, 82

Raleigh (NC), 7, 11, 37
Ramilles (HMS), 81
Rapin, Al Sgt. (T/Sgt.), 74, 122, 447
Rebais, 216
Red Army (Russian), 382, 405, 412, 418, 423
Red Army (Tennessee), 18, 19, 20, 21
Red Ball Express, 270, 271
Red Cross, 7, 46, 56, 72, 76, 97, 323, 441, 443, 455, 464
Regester, Harry Pvt., 115, 319
Reims (Rheims), 216, 223, 356, 412, 440, 444, 449, 455, 460
Reinhardt, Emil F. Maj. Gen. 412
Remagen, 355, 362, 363, 369, 370, 373
Remarde River, 194
Rennerod, 379
Rennes, 133
Rheinbach, 362
Rhineland, 271, 275-76, 279-80, 295-96, 332-34, 344, 347, 349, 351, 353, 363, 377, 379-80, 391, 397, 430, 431
Richardson, Arthur Pvt., 45
Richelskeul, 336
Richmond Times Dispatch, 161
Ridgway, Matthew B. Lt. Gen., 90, 91, 185, 327, 384
Righter, George M/Sgt., 441
Riley, Willard Cpl., 293
Rinard, Robert T/5, 441
Ringen, 363
Ritz Brothers, 10
Roberts, Thomas T/5, 183
Rochefort, 307
Rochefort-en-Yvel, 194
Rochling-Buderus Stahlwerk, 426
Rocroi, 230
Roenicke, Edward T/5, 170, 191
Roer River, 275, 294-95, 297, 340-42, 360, 431
Rollsbroich, 336
Romain, 223
Rome, 75

Rommel, Irwin Fldmrshl., 83, 154
Romsee, 433
Romsey, 71
Roosevelt, Franklin D. Pres., 203, 284, 390, 418
Rosee, 230, 231, 234, 235
Ross, Carl T/3, 320, 419
Rossla, 406
Rotgen (Roetgen), 248-50, 254-55, 263-64, 268, 279, 303
Roth River, 346
Rotheux, 237
Rott, 274
Rouen, 461, 464
Rouey, 223
Roxboro, (NC), 7
Rueth, Anton W/O, 33, 167, 253, 368, 370, 456
Ruhr, 369, 378, 382, 383, 384, 385, 397, 429
Rundstedt, Karl von Fldmrshl., 83, 154, 164, 303-05, 314, 328, 331-32
Runyon, Buster T/5, 39, 321
Russians, 199, 284, 350, 377, 382, 395, 397, 405, 411-12, 417, 421, 424, 447
Ryals, Lester 2Lt., 39, 40

Salerno, 92
Salisbury, (England), 68, 70, 72, 73, 74, 94, 109
Salisbury, (NC), 31
Salle River, 408, 409, 424, 425
Sambre River, 434
Samme River, 434
Sams, James D. Col., 155, 156
Sart-St. Laurent, 434
Sarthe River, 186
Sayler, Henry Maj. Gen., 115
Scheiss River, 362
Schfranack, Joe Pvt., 39
Schlich, 295
Schlieben, Karl von Gen., 134, 136
Schmidt, 279
Schmidthof, 274
Schuch, William F. Pvt., 169
Schuler, Lester W. Maj., 294
Scotland, 55, 58, 238, 242
Scott, Michael F. S/Sgt., 118, 132, 141
Scott, William T/5, 321, 419
Scottsville, (KY), 17

Sees, 186
Seine River, 172, 181, 198, 201, 204, 464
Seinne River, 172
Selune River, 173
Setter, Raymond T/4, 93, 167, 168, 317
Shaffer, Herman T/3, 317, 386
Shaughnessy, Martin F. Lt. Col., 109
Shaw, Lee T/3, 386, 419
Sheahan, Robert 2Lt., 10, 12
Sheffield, (England), 58
Shelbyville (Tenn), 10, 17, 25
Sherman (tank), 114, 155, 162, 167, 310, 345, 347, 374
Schevenhuette, 271
Shrewton, 71
Shropshire County (England), 94
Sicily, 76, 77, 92, 117, 123, 139, 175, 184, 185, 333
Siegfried Line, 248, 254, 264, 271, 274, 334, 349, 352, 390
Sieg River, 377
Siegburg, 429
Sieminkiewicz, Stanley S/Sgt., 323, 447
Sienko, Victor Pvt., 149
Simms, Ginny, 323
Simon, Peter, 351
Simpson, William H. Lt. Gen., 285, 383, 397
Sinatra, Frank, 323
Sissone, 224
Skiba, Teofil T/5, 255
Small, Constable (England), 61
Smith, Richard Pvt., 39
Smith, Robert T/5, 406, 407
Smythe, George Col., 357
Soissons, 224, 236, 270, 271, 440
Solomon, 406
Somerest County (England), 59, 60, 64, 67
Somme, 438, 441
Sondershausen, 402, 406
Sormmone, 230
Sorrines, 236
Soulles River, 169
Sourbrodt, 295
South Carolina, 16, 326
Southampton, (England), 71
Southern Railway, 5, 16, 41
Soviet, 422
Spa, 245, 283, 308, 309, 356

490

Spaich, Tony Sgt., 316, 387
Spanninga, Russell T/3, 386
Spellman, Francis Cardinal, 264
Springer, Michael T/4, 146, 147, 148, 406, 407
Springfield, (ILL), 13
St. Aignan, 179
St. Barthelemy, 176
St. Cecile, 172
St. Come du Mont, 144
St. Dizier, 460
St. Germain, 195
St. Germain-Lazis, 214
St. Germain de Varreville, 86
St. Hilaire, 450
St. Hilaire du-Harcouet, 177
St. Jacques de Nehou, 123, 125, 126, 127
St. Jean de Daye, 145, 150
St. Laurent sur Mer, 86, 89
St. Lo, 139, 141, 143, 144, 145, 150, 157, 158, 162, 199, 248, 274
St. Marie du Mont, 106, 108
St. Martin de Varreville, 86
St. Martin le Grand, 133
St. Maurice, 191
St. Mere Eglise, 90, 110, 141
St. Menehould, 450
St. Michel, 195
St. Peter's Church, 345
St. Pois, 176
St. Quentin, 224, 437-38, 440-41, 443-44, 448, 453, 455, 457, 461
St. Quentin Canal, 436
St. Saule, 435
St. Sauveur l'vicomte, 122, 124, 125, 126
St. Sever de Calvados, 176, 190
St. Severin, 236
St. Vith, 247, 303, 321, 328, 330
St. Symphorien (France), 177
St. Symphorien-Villiers, 434
Stafford, Jo, 323
Stalin, Joseph, 418
Stalzemburg, 247
Statesville (NC), 31
Stars and Stripes (news), 73, 284, 334, 411
Statue of Liberty, 49, 469
Stavelot, 307
Stegmann, Rudolph Gen. Maj., 123
Stewart, Tom Senator, 22, 23, 24
Stiefels River, 362

Stockbridge, 71
Stolberg, 296, 300, 309, 310, 311
Stonehenge, 68, 71
Stone, Jay T/5, 341
Stratford, (England), 59
Strickland, Rufus T/5, 44, 166, 326
Strong, Richard T/5, 390
Stuka, 134
Suippe River, 450
Suippes, 450
Supreme Commander, 79, 85, 99, 142, 155, 384
Supreme Headquarters (SHAEF), 81, 133, 191, 306, 412-13
Suzon River, 459
Swist River, 363
Switzerland, 265, 398, 400, 456
Switzgable, Charles T/3, 386
Sword Beach, 87, 89
Szabla, Frank T/5, 191

Table of Operations, 457
Tarasiewicz, Edward T/5, 192, 421
Taunton (England), 76
Taut River, 140, 145, 147
Taylor, Maxwell D. Maj. Gen., 90
Tedder, Arthur, Air Marshal, 142
Temple Meads Station, 59
Tennessee Central Railway, 20
Tennessee manuevers, 16, 24, 26, 29, 78
Tennessee Polytechnical Institute, 27
Terrette River, 164, 168
Tew, Roy Pvt., 39
Texas USS, 82
Thatcher, Dale S/Sgt., 105, 386
Theux, 240, 283
Thon River, 230
Thompson, Howard T/4, 243, 280
"Thunderbolt" (P-47), 165, 177
Thuringia, Province of, 424
Tidworth, (England), 74
Tiger, (tank), 307, 339, 374, 394
Time Magazine, 180
Tincher, Max Lt. Col., 145
Tokyo, Japan, 447
Torgau, 412
Torquay, 71
Tourbe, 450
Tourouve, 186, 191
Treaty of Versailles, 246, 280, 349
Treblinka, 401
Tribehou, 146, 152, 164

Trooz, 283
Trousdale County (Tenn), 23, 24
Truman, Harry President, 447
Truman, Harry Mrs., 291
Tullahoma, (Tenn), 17
Tunisia, 77, 131, 392
Turvy, Robert S/Sgt., 386
Tuscaloosa USS, 82
Twiss, Rav M/Sgt., 39, 283, 365, 375, 376, 451
"Typhoon" (British), 136, 174
Tyrrell, James T/4, 211, 212, 387

U-Boats, 99
Underhill, Martin T/3, 321
United Kingdom, 49, 75, 89, 281
United Nations, 98
Utah Beach, 86, 89, 103, 106, 117, 131, 141

Valenciennes, 435
Valley Forge (PA), 85
Valongnes, 133
Van Fleet, James A. Maj. Gen., 385
Van Vactor, Russell T/3, 141, 171
Varrenne River, 178
Vaux le Vicomte, 205
Veal, Sidney T/4, 321
Ventelay, 223
Verdun, 143, 450, 452, 455
Versailles, 199
Verviers, 240-42, 244, 287, 303, 312, 316, 324, 455
Vesdre Canal, 240
Vesle River, 223, 313, 335
Vicht, 274
"Victory" (HMS), 71
Vierville-sur-Mer, 86, 89
Villedieu-les-Poeles, 171
Vire, 190
Vire River, 139, 141, 144, 145
Virginia, 5, 41
Volksturm, 272, 347, 408
Vossenach, 279

Wade, Jim T/3, 446
Wagner, Elmer Sgt., 133
Waikart, William Maj., 366
Waimes, 280
Walheim, 248
Wallace, John 1Lt., 79, 289
Walls, John Pfc., 410
War Department, 22, 23, 412

Warche River, 280
Warchenne River, 280
Warm Springs, (GA), 390
Warminster, (England), 68
Warspite (HMS), 82
Washington, (DC), 16, 22, 23, 40, 41, 412
Weh, 431
Wehrmacht, 83, 215, 333
Weilburg, 428
Weimar, 425
Weinberg, Bennie 1Lt. (Capt), 291, 310, 325, 335, 343, 366, 375, 382, 403, 407, 454-53, 456
Weisenfels, 424
Weiswampach, 247
Weisweiler, 293, 299, 431
Wells, Howard L. T/4, 440
Wells (England), 64
Werra River, 425
Weser River, 395, 401, 403
West Harptree (England) 65
West Virginia, 5, 16, 24
West Point (NY),
Westmoreland, (Tenn), 17
Westmoreland, Wm. C. Col., (Gen.), 214, 259
Westmorland County (England), 58
Weston Super-Mare, 64
"Westwall", 92, 249, 271, 349
Wetzlar, 426, 428
Weymouth, 71, 97
White, Al T/3, 321
White, C. B. Pvt., 39
White, Milton 2Lt., 10, 12
Wickes, Stephen Pvt., 293
Wilck, Gerhardt Col., 273
William The Conqueror, 64, 71
Wills Player cigarettes, 60, 65
Wilton (England), 71
Wiltshire County (England), 68, 71, 77
Winchester (England), 71
Winterberg, 385, 386
Withrow, Robert Cpl., 39
Witzenhausen, 395
Wolak, Louis T/4, 326
Wollersheim, 345
Womersdorf, 363
Worbis, 395
Workman, William T/5, 320
World War I, 41, 69, 128, 152, 185, 217, 246, 434

Wright, Raymond T/5, 325
Wrington, 64
Wuppertal, 383
Wurm River, 285, 431
Wylye River, 70
Wysopal, Edward T/Sgt., 457

Yalta, 422
Yank Magazine, 73, 284
Yeo Lake, 60
Yerres River, 216
Yugoslavia, 75, 284

Zhukov, Georgie Mr'shl., 397
Zielinski, Edward Pvt., 238, 239, 240
Zinn, William Pvt., 39
Zuelpich (Belgium), 330
Zuelpich (Germany), 345, 346
Zwiefall, 274

INDEX OF INDIVIDUAL MILITARY PARTICIPANTS

U. S. Forces

First U. S. Army, 40, 64, 66, 86, 92, 96, 109-110, 112, 119, 125-27, 131, 133, 139, 140, 143-145, 148, 150, 156-158, 161-164, 169, 171-174, 176, 178, 180, 181, 190-191, 193-194, 198, 200-203, 209, 212, 228, 231-232, 236, 238, 246, 248-249, 253, 255, 258, 260, 265, 268-271, 275, 277-278, 282-283, 285, 293-294, 297-299, 302, 305-307, 309, 312-314, 321-322, 324-325, 327, 330, 333-334, 341-343, 348, 354-355, 358-359, 369, 372, 376-378, 381, 383, 385, 390-391, 393-395, 397, 399, 401, 411-414, 426-427, 429, 431-432, 450-451
Second U. S. Army, 7, 12, 16, 18, 19, 22
Third U. S. Army, 163, 172-173, 181, 185, 191, 284, 302, 328-329, 369, 394, 398, 427-428, 455
Fifth U. S. Army, 284
Seventh U. S. Army, 187, 248, 369, 398
Eighth U. S. Army, 384
Ninth U. S. Army 285, 293-295, 308, 322, 333, 383, 385, 397-398, 414, 431
Fifteenth U. S. Army, 333, 391
First Allied Airborne Army, 164
6th Army Group, 77, 284, 398
12th Army Group, 164, 191, 270, 285, 306, 308, 322, 355, 369, 378, 397-398, 411, 413
15th Army Group, 398

II Corps, 19, 164
III Corps, 19, 248, 328, 334, 353, 355, 369, 377, 383, 385, 426
V Corps, 86-87, 141, 179, 190, 198, 247-248, 275, 279, 282, 294, 303, 322, 326-328, 333-334, 369, 383, 411-412
VII Corps, 86, 89, 113, 119, 126-127, 137, 140-141, 143-144, 155, 162, 167, 173-174, 176, 179, 181, 191, 213, 236, 248, 261, 271-273, 275, 279, 284, 294-296, 327, 342-343, 348, 353, 377, 383, 385-386, 392, 408, 411-415
VIII Corps, 139, 302, 303, 307, 327, 342
XII Corps, 185, 328
XIII Corps, 7
XVIII Airborne Corps, 327, 328, 383, 384
XIX Corps, 141, 158, 179, 248, 272
XXI Corps, 427
XXIII Corps, 185
4th Military Service Command, 7

1st Infantry Division, 86-87, 141, 165, 173, 190, 224, 229, 248, 272, 295, 328, 333-334, 343, 353, 357, 386, 392
2nd Infantry Division, 141, 157, 303, 304, 334, 411
4th Infantry Division, 86, 110, 140, 160, 172-173, 198, 224, 247, 275, 279, 291, 302-303
5th Infantry Division, 217
8th Infantry Division, 140, 275, 338, 354
9th Infantry Division, 76-77, 103, 112-113, 123-124, 127, 131-133, 137, 140, 145, 150, 160, 165, 168, 171, 173-175, 184, 185, 194, 200, 214-215, 217, 226, 229, 235, 237, 245, 248, 252, 254, 274-276, 278-279, 281-282, 288, 311, 328, 333-335, 343-344, 353, 357-358, 362, 266, 369, 274, 385-386, 392, 412, 414
28th Infantry Division, 40, 171, 176, 199, 247, 275, 279, 302-303.
29th Infantry Division, 54, 86, 87, 141, 157, 158
30th Infantry Division, 141, 145, 157, 160, 173, 248, 272, 328
35th Infantry Division, 157, 158, 173
45th Infantry Division, 139
69th Infantry Division, 411, 412
78th Infantry Division, 9, 10, 343, 357, 369

494

79th Infantry Division, 137, 140
80th Infantry Division, 19, 20, 394
82nd Airborne Division, 90, 91, 110, 111, 124, 131, 139, 328
83rd Infantry Division, 19, 20, 140, 275
84th Infantry Division, 328
87th Infantry Division, 353
89th Infantry Division, 464
90th Infantry Division, 131, 140, 177
97th Infantry Division, 185
99th Infantry Division, 281, 303, 304, 328, 334, 369
101st Airborne Division, 19, 90, 111, 329
104th Infantry Division, 296, 354, 392, 401, 408
106th Infantry Division, 303, 304
2nd Armored Division, 74, 141, 169, 173, 198, 329
3rd Armored Division, 74, 141, 146, 157, 165, 173, 217, 224, 229, 235, 237, 240, 246, 248, 295-296, 354, 381, 392, 401-402, 409
5th Armored Division, 247, 275, 282, 338
6th Armored Division, 394
7th Armored Division, 204, 328, 426, 452
9th Armored Division, 303, 304, 355, 356, 363, 369, 381, 393, 403
10th Armored Division, 19, 20

974th Ordnance Evacuation Company, 78, 266, 267, 268
924th Ordnance (HAM) Company, 441, 457
26th Ordnance (MM) Company, 324
709th Ordnance (LM) Company, 78, 263, 268, 325, 364, 365, 366, 367, 378, 386
3424th Ordnance (MAM) Company, 169
2nd Ordnance (MM) Company, 172
131st Ordnance (MAM) Company, 28
778th Ordnance (LM) Company, 9
71st Ordnance Battalion, 439
190th Ordnance Battalion, 427
83rd Ordnance Battalion, 389
66th Ordnance Battalion, 33, 36, 41
86th Ordnance Battalion, 66

6th Ordnance Battalion, 109, 126
184th Ordnance Battalion, 126-128, 155, 254, 294, 389, 413-415
177th Ordnance Battalion, 294, 322
442nd Ordnance Base Supply Depot, 459
224th Ordnance Base Group, 127
52nd Ordnance Group, 66, 155, 294, 322, 413
544th Ordnance (HM) Field Artillery Co., 325
472nd Quartermaster Group, 270
113th Cavalry Group, 141, 146, 158, 173
4th Cavalry Group, 245, 392
102nd Cavalry Group, 303
14th Mechanized Cavalry Group, 303
16th Mechanized Cavalry Group, 20
7th Mechanized Cavalry Regiment, 69
32nd Field Artillery Brigade, 370
71st Field Artillery Brigade, 19
2nd Ranger Battalion, 86, 338
5th Ranger Battalion, 86
78th General Hospital, 441, 444
148th Engineer Constr. Battalion, 373
899th Tank Destroyer Battalion, 78, 145, 150, 320, 373
746th Tank Battalion, 78, 320, 373
1st Engineer Special Brigade, 106
84th Chemical Warfare Battalion, 40
376th AAA Battalion, 78, 208, 282
26th Field Artillery Battalion, 77, 252
34th Field Artillery Battalion, 77
15th Engineer Battalion, 77, 288
60th Infantry Regiment, 77, 230, 235
47th Infantry Regiment, 77, 124, 357
39th Infantry Regiment, 77, 123, 254
9th Air Force (TAC), 69, 159-161, 171, 174, 272, 293-294, 330, 358, 362, 381
8th Air Force (TAC), 159-161, 292, 330
IX Bomber Command, 137
XXIX TAC, 330
8th AF IX Bombardment Division, 330
IX U. S. AAF Troop Carrier Command, 91

495

British and Canadian Forces

1st Army (Can.), 164, 174, 397
2nd Army (Br.), 87, 92, 141, 333, 397
3rd Division (Can.), 87
3rd Division (Br.), 87
6th Airborne Division (Br.), 87
1st Corps (Br.), 87
21st Army Group, 86, 164, 285, 306, 369
50th Division (Br.) 87
XXX Corps (Br.) 87, 201, 327
Royal Air Force, 69, 107, 136, 174, 286, 293, 409, 437

French Forces

1st French Army, 284, 398
2nd Armored Division, 186

Russian Forces

58th Guards Division, 412
First Belorussian Army Group, 397
First Ukranian Army Group, 397

German Forces

Army Group B, 181, 304, 383
Army Group East, 179
Army Group H, 383
OB West (Army), 83, 164
1st Parachute Army, 384
5th Panzer Army, 180, 304, 384
6th SS Panzer Army, 304
7th Army, 83, 141, 173-174, 179-180, 229, 268, 304, 330
15th Army, 83, 304, 384
138th Corps, 83
2nd Panzer Division, 329
9th Panzer Division, 186
77th Division, 123
Panzer Lehr Division, 145, 150